JUVENILE DELINQUENCY
second edition

Clemens Bartollas
University of Northern Iowa

Frank Schmalleger
Emeritus, University of North Carolina at Pembroke

PEARSON

Boston Columbus Indianapolis New York San Francisco Hoboken
Amsterdam Cape Town Dubai London Madrid Milan Munich Paris Montreal Toronto
Delhi Mexico City Sao Paulo Sydney Hong Kong Seoul Singapore Taipei Tokyo

Editorial Director: Andrew Gilfillan
Product Manager: Gary Bauer
Program Manager: Tara Horton
Editorial Assistant: Lynda Cramer
Director of Marketing: David Gesell
Senior Marketing Manager: Mary Salzman
Senior Marketing Coordinator: Alicia Wozniak
Senior Marketing Assistant: Les Roberts
Project Management Team Lead: JoEllen Gohr
Project Manager: Jessica H. Sykes
Procurement Specialist: Deidra Skahill
Senior Art Director: Diane Ernsberger
Text and Cover Designer: Studio Montage
Cover Art: Nancy Honey/Getty Images
Media Project Manager: April Cleland
Full-Service Project Management: Andrew Jones/S4Carlisle Publishing Services
Composition: S4Carlisle Publishing Services
Printer/Binder: Courier/Kendallville
Cover Printer: Courier/Kendallville
Text Font: Minion Pro-Regular 10/12

Copyright © 2016, 2013 by Pearson Education, Inc. and its affiliates, All rights reserved. Manufactured in the United States of America. This publication is protected by Copyright, and permission should be obtained from the publisher prior to any prohibited reproduction, storage in a retrieval system, or transmission in any form or by any means, electronic, mechanical, photocopying, recording, or likewise. To obtain permission(s) to use material from this work, please submit a written request to Pearson Education, Inc., Permissions Department, 221 River Street, Hoboken, New Jersey 07030.

Many of the designations by manufacturers and sellers to distinguish their products are claimed as trademarks. Where those designations appear in this book, and the publisher was aware of a trademark claim, the designations have been printed in initial caps or all caps.

Library of Congress Cataloging-in-Publication Data
Bartollas, Clemens.
 Juvenile delinquency/Clemens Bartollas. — Second edition.
  pages cm
 Revised edition of the author's Juvenile delinquency, published in 2013.
 Includes index.
 ISBN 978-0-13-382628-9 — ISBN 0-13-382628-7
 1. Juvenile delinquency—United States. 2. Juvenile justice, Administration of—United States. I. Title.
 HV9104.B3457 2016
 364.360973—dc23
                                    2014039794

Dedication

To our beautiful children and grandchildren

10 9 8 7 6 5 4 3 2 1

ISBN 10: 0-13-382628-7
ISBN 13: 978-0-13-382628-9

Brief Contents

PART 1 — The Nature and Extent of Delinquency 1

- **CHAPTER 1** Adolescence and Delinquency 1
- **CHAPTER 2** The Measurement and Nature of Delinquency 18

PART 2 — Causes of Delinquency 36

- **CHAPTER 3** Individual Causes of Delinquency 36
- **CHAPTER 4** Social Structural and Social Process Theories of Delinquency 56
- **CHAPTER 5** Social Interactionist Theories of Delinquency 77

PART 3 — Environmental Influences on Delinquency 91

- **CHAPTER 6** Gender and Delinquency 91
- **CHAPTER 7** Families and Delinquency 108
- **CHAPTER 8** Schools and Delinquency 128
- **CHAPTER 9** Gangs and Delinquency 144
- **CHAPTER 10** Drugs and Delinquency 159

PART 4 — The Juvenile Justice System 174

- **CHAPTER 11** An Overview of Juvenile Justice in America 174
- **CHAPTER 12** Police and the Juvenile 196
- **CHAPTER 13** Juvenile Court 211
- **CHAPTER 14** Juvenile Corrections 228

Contents

PREFACE xiv

PART 1 — The Nature and Extent of Delinquency 1

CHAPTER 1 Adolescence and Delinquency 1

Defending Childhood 2
The Changing Treatment of Adolescents 3
   Youth Culture 4
Youth at Risk 5
   High-Risk Behaviors and Adolescence 6
Delinquency Defined 7
Status Offenders and Status Offenses 8
   Explanations for Status Offense Behavior 9
   Deinstitutionalization of Status Offenders (DSO) 9
   The Juvenile Court's Jurisdiction over Status Offenders 9
   Crossover Youth 10
The Contemporary Treatment of Delinquents 10
The Three Themes of This Text 12
   Delinquency Prevention 12
   Delinquency Across the Life Course 12
   Delinquency and Social Policy 13
THE CASE: The Life Course of Amy Watters, Age Five 15
Summary and Key Concepts 16

CHAPTER 2 The Measurement and Nature of Delinquency 18

Serious Juvenile Crime 19
Major Data Sources in Delinquency 19
   Uniform Crime Reports 19
   Crime by Age Groups 20
   Juvenile Court Statistics 22
   Self Report Studies 22
   Victimization Studies 24
Social Factors Related to Delinquency 26
   Gender and Delinquency 26
   Racial/Ethnic Background and Delinquency 26
   Social Class and Delinquency 28

Length and Intensity of Juvenile Offending   29
    Age of Onset   29
    Escalation of Offenses   29
    Specialization of Offenses   30
    Chronic Offending   31
    Youth Crimes and Adult Criminality   31

Prevention and Control of Delinquency   32

THE CASE: The Life Course of Amy Watters, Age Eight   34

Summary and Key Concepts   35

PART 2   Causes of Delinquency   36

CHAPTER 3   Individual Causes of Delinquency   36

Can Names Cause Delinquency?   37

The Classical School and Juvenile Delinquency   37

Rationality and Delinquency   38
    Rational Choice Theory   39
    The Routine-Activities Approach   39
    Rational Choice and Delinquency   39
    Delinquency Prevention and the Philosophy of Punishment   40

Positivism and Delinquency   40

Biological and Psychological Positivism and Delinquency   41
    Early Forms of Biological Positivism   41
    Contemporary Biological Positivism: Sociobiology and Biosocial Criminology   42
    Twin and Adoption Studies   42
    Intelligence   43
    Neuropsychological Factors   43
    Biochemical Factors   44
    The Biosocial Perspective   45
    Psychological Positivism   45

Developmental Theories of Delinquency   49
    The Dunedin Longitudinal Study   49
    Montreal Longitudinal Experimental Study   49
    Cambridge Study in Delinquent Development   49

The Importance of Theory   50

Prevention and Control of Delinquency   50

THE CASE: The Life Course of Amy Watters, Age Nine   52

Summary and Key Concepts   53

CHAPTER 4   Social Structural and Social Process Theories of Delinquency   56

Childhood Exposure to Violence   57

Social Disorganization Theory   57
- Shaw and McKay   58

Cultural Deviance Theory and Delinquency   60
- Miller's Lower-Class Culture and Delinquent Values   60

Strain and Opportunity Theories of Delinquency   61
- Merton's Theory of Anomie   62
- Institutional Anomie Theory   63
- Evaluation of Merton's Theory   63
- Strain Theory and the Individual Level of Analysis   63
- Cohen's Theory of Delinquent Subcultures   64
- Cloward and Ohlin's Opportunity Theory   65

Differential Association Theory   66
- Propositions of Differential Association Theory   66

Control Theory and Delinquent Behavior   67
- Social Control Theory   67

Integrated Theories of Delinquency   68
- Gottfredson and Hirschi's General Theory of Crime   68
- Elliott and Colleagues' Integrated Social Process Theory   68
- Thornberry's Interactional Theory   69
- Hawkins and Weis's Social Development Model   70

Delinquency Across the life Course: Structural and Social Process Theories   70
- Reduced Social Capital   71
- Cumulative Disadvantage   71

Delinquency and Social Policy: PHDCN and Lafans   71
- Early Findings from the PHDCN Study   72

THE CASE: The Life Course of Amy Watters, Age Ten   73

Summary and Key Concepts   74

CHAPTER 5   Social Interactionist Theories of Delinquency   77

Adolescent Bullying   78

Labeling Theory   78
- Frank Tannenbaum: Dramatization of Evil   79
- Edwin Lemert: Primary and Secondary Deviation   79
- Howard Becker: Deviant Careers   79
- The Juvenile Justice Process and Labeling   80
- New Developments in Labeling Theory   80
- Recent Applications of Labeling Theory   80
- Evaluation of Labeling Theory   80

Symbolic Interactionist Theory   81
- Role Taking and Delinquency   81
- Interactionist Perspectives on Gender, Race, and Delinquency   82
- Evaluation of Symbolic Interactionist Theory   82

Conflict Theory   83
- Dimensions of Conflict Criminology   83
- Evaluation of Conflict Theory   85

The Social Context of Delinquency: Restorative Justice and Peacemaking   85
- Community Conferencing and Sentencing Circles   86
- Evaluation of Restorative Justice   86

Delinquency and Social Policy: The Conflict Perspective   86
THE CASE: The Life Course of Amy Watters, Age 11   88
Summary and Key Concepts   89

PART 3 — Environmental Influences on Delinquency   91

CHAPTER 6   Gender and Delinquency   91

Child Prostitution   92
The Gender Ratio in Offending   92
Social Context of Delinquency: Gender Roles and Delinquency   94
The Female Delinquent   95
Explanations of Female Delinquency   97
- Biological and Constitutional Explanations   97
- Psychological Explanations   97
- Sociological Explanations   97
- Evaluation of Explanations of Female Delinquency   98

Feminist Theories of Delinquency   99
Gender Bias and the Processing of Female Delinquents   100
- Influence of Class   101
- Racial Discrimination   102
- The Whole Is Greater Than the Sum of Its Parts   102

Delinquency Across the Life Course: Gender and Delinquency   103
Delinquency and Social Policy: A Gender-Responsive Policy Approach   104
THE CASE: The Life Course of Amy Watters, Age 12   105
Summary and Key Concepts   106

CHAPTER 7   Families and Delinquency   108

Learning Social Roles   109
Social Context of Delinquency: Impact of Families on Delinquency   109
- Family Factors   109
- Conclusions   110
- Transitions and Delinquency   110
- The Foster Family   113

The Mass Media and Delinquent Behavior   114
    Violent TV Programs and Movies   114
    Violent Video Games   114
    Internet-Initiated Crimes   114
    Gangsta Rap   114

Neglect and Child Abuse   115
    Extent and Nature of the Problem   117
    Neglect   117
    Child Abuse   118
    Neglect, Child Abuse, and Delinquency   119

Child Abuse and the Juvenile Justice System   120
    Identification   120
    Reporting   120
    Intake and Investigation   120
    Assessment   121
    Case Planning   121
    Treatment   121
    Evaluation of Family Progress   121
    Case Closure   121
    Involvement of Juvenile or Family Court   121
    Termination of Parental Rights   121
    Prosecution of Parents   121

Delinquency Across the Life Course: Family-Related Risk Factors for Delinquency   121
Prevention of Delinquency and Social Policy: Child Maltreatment   121
THE CASE: The Life Course of Amy Watters, Age 13   124
Summary and Key Concepts   125

CHAPTER 8   Schools and Delinquency   128

School Delinquency   129
A Brief History of American Education   129
School Crime   130
    Vandalism and Violence   131
    School Bullying   131

Delinquency and School Failure   133
    Achievement   133
    Low Social Status   134
    School Failure   134

Theoretical Perspectives on School and Delinquency   134
Students' Rights   136
    Procedural Due Process   136
    Freedom of Expression   136
    Hair and Dress Codes   136
    School Searches   136
    Safety   137
    School Discipline   137

Delinquency Across the Life Course: Factors Involved in Dropping Out of School   139
Delinquency and Social Policy: Promising Interventions   139
    Improving the Quality of the School Experience   139
    Mentoring Relationships   139
    Alternative Schools   140
    Positive School–Community Relationships   140
    Reduce High School Dropouts   140
    Reduction of the Crime-Control Model in Public Schools   140
THE CASE: The Life Course of Amy Watters, Age 14   141
Summary and Key Concepts   142

CHAPTER 9   Gangs and Delinquency   144

Flash Mobs   145
Street Gangs and Organized Crime   145
Nature and Extent of Gang Activity   145
    Definitions of Gangs   146
    Profiles of Gang Members   146
    Law-Violating Behaviors and Gang Activities   149
    Gangs in Small Communities   150
    Racial and Ethnic Gangs   152
    Female Delinquent Gangs   153
Theories of Gang Formation   154
Delinquency Across the Life Course: Gang Membership   155
Delinquency and Social Policy: Prevention and Control of Youth Gangs   155
THE CASE: The Life Course of Amy Watters, Age 14   157
Summary and Key Concepts   158

CHAPTER 10   Drugs and Delinquency   159

Substance Abuse Among Adolescents   160
Drug Use Among Adolescents   160
Types of Drugs   162
    Alcohol and Tobacco   162
    Marijuana   162
    Cocaine   162
    Methamphetamine   163
    Inhalants   163
    Sedatives   163
    Amphetamines   163
    Hallucinogens   164
    Anabolic Steroids   164
    Heroin   164
Drug Use and Delinquency   165

Explanations for the Onset of Drug Abuse 166
    Cognitive-Affective Theories 166
    Addictive Personality Theory 166
    Stress Relief Theory 166
    Social Learning Theory 167
    Social Control Theories 167
    Social Disorganization Theory 167
    Integrated Theories 167

Delinquency Across the Life Course: Drug Use 167

Delinquency and Social Policy: Solutions to the Drug Problem 168
    Prevention Programs 168
    Treatment Interventions 169
    Strict Enforcement 169
    Harm Reduction 170

THE CASE: The Life Course of Amy Watters, Age 15 171

CHAPTER 10 Drugs and Delinquency 172

PART 4   The Juvenile Justice System   174

CHAPTER 11   An Overview of Juvenile Justice in America   174

Risk Assessment and Juvenile Detention 175

Development of the Juvenile Justice System 175
    Colonial Period (1636–1823) 175
    Houses of Refuge 176
    Origins of the Juvenile Court 176
    Emergence of Community-Based Corrections 177
    Development of Juvenile Institutions 178

Juvenile Prevention Programs 178
    Promising Prevention Programs 178

Diversion From the Juvenile Justice System 179
    Youth Courts 180
    Juvenile Drug-Court Movement 180

Juvenile Justice System Today 181
    Structure and Functions 181

Stages in the Juvenile Justice Process 182
    Comparison of the Juvenile and Adult Justice Systems 183

Basic Correctional Models 184
    Comparison of the Four Models 185
    Emergent Approaches to Handling Youthful Offenders 186

Treatment in Juvenile Justice 186
    Individual-Level Treatment Programs 187
    Group Programs 187

What Works for Whom and in What Context   188
　　　Graduated Sanctions in Juvenile Justice   189

Race and Juvenile Justice   189
　　　Disproportionate Minority Confinement   190

Prevention of Delinquency: Comprehensive Delinquency Prevention Strategy   190

Trends for the Future   191

THE CASE: The Life Course of Amy Watters, Age 15   192

Summary and Key Concepts   193

CHAPTER 12   Police and the Juvenile   196

Policing Children   197

Juveniles' Attitudes Toward the Police   197

Processing of Juvenile Offenders   198
　　　Factors Influencing Police Discretion   198
　　　Informal and Formal Dispositions   200

Legal Rights of Juveniles   201
　　　Search and Seizure   201
　　　Interrogation Practices   201
　　　Fingerprinting   203
　　　Pretrial Identification Practices   203

Social Context of Delinquency: The Police and the Prevention of Juvenile Offenses   204
　　　Community-Based Interventions   204
　　　School-Based Interventions   205

Delinquency Across the Life Course: Effects of Police Discretion   206

Delinquency and Social Policy: Project D.A.R.E.   206

THE CASE: The Life Course of Amy Watters, Age 16   208

Summary and Key Concepts   209

CHAPTER 13   Juvenile Court   211

The Juvenile Court Ideal   212

Juvenile Court   212

Changes in Legal Norms   213
　　　U.S. Supreme Court Decisions of Special Relevance   213

Pretrial Procedures   215
　　　Detention Hearing   215
　　　Intake Process   216

Juvenile Trial Proceedings   218
　　　Adjudicatory Hearing   218
　　　Disposition Hearing   219
　　　Judicial Alternatives   220
　　　Right to Appeal   220

    Juvenile Sentencing Structures 221

    Delinquency Across the Life Course: the Impact of Transfer on Juveniles 222

    Prevention of Delinquency and Social Policy: Excellence in Juvenile Courts 223

    THE CASE: The Life Course of Amy Watters, Age 16 224

    Summary and Key Concepts 225

CHAPTER 14   Juvenile Corrections 228

Juvenile Incarceration 229

Probation 229

Operation of Probation Services 230
- Intake 230
- Investigation 230
- Supervision 230
- Risk Control and Crime Reduction 230
- Volunteer Programs 232

Residential and Day Treatment 232
- Types of Programs 232

Types of Institutional Placement 233
- Reception and Diagnostic Centers 233
- Forestry Camps and Ranches 233
- Boot Camps 233
- Public and Private Training Schools 234

Social Context: Training School Life 235
- Training Schools for Boys 235
- Training Schools for Girls and Coeducational Institutions 236

Rights of Confined Juveniles 236
- U.S. Courts 236
- CRIPA and Juvenile Correctional Facilities 236

Juvenile Aftercare 236

Administration and Operation of Aftercare Services 237
- Risk Control and Crime Reduction 237
- Juveniles in Adult Prisons 239

Delinquency Across the Life Course: Juvenile Institutionalization 239

Delinquency and Social Policy: How to Make Juvenile Facilities Better 240

THE CASE: The Life Course of Amy Watters, Age 17 241

Summary and Key Concepts 242

GLOSSARY 245
REFERENCES 255
NAME INDEX 291
SUBJECT INDEX 295

Preface

Introducing the Justice Series

When best-selling authors and instructional designers come together focused on one goal—to improve student performance across the criminal justice (CJ) curriculum—they come away with a groundbreaking new series of print and digital content: the *Justice Series*.

Several years ago, we embarked on a journey to create affordable texts that engage students without sacrificing academic rigor. We tested this new format with Fagin's *CJ 2010* and Schmalleger's *Criminology* and received overwhelming support from students and instructors.

The Justice Series expands this format and philosophy to more core CJ and criminology courses, providing affordable, engaging instructor and student resources across the curriculum. As you flip through the pages, you'll notice that this book doesn't rely on distracting, overly used photos to add visual appeal. Every piece of art serves a purpose—to help students learn. Our authors and instructional designers worked tirelessly to build engaging infographics, flowcharts, pull-out statistics, and other visuals that flow with the body of the text, provide context and engagement, and promote recall and understanding.

We organized our content around key learning objectives for each chapter and tied everything together in a new objective-driven end-of-chapter layout. The content not only is engaging to students, but also is easy to follow and focuses students on the key learning objectives.

Although brief, affordable, and visually engaging, the Justice Series is no quick, cheap way to appeal to the lowest common denominator. It's a series of texts and support tools that are instructionally sound and student-approved.

Additional Highlights to the Author's Approach

- The lavish use of figures, charts, and line art visually attracts readers to the subject matter of criminology, making for ease of learning.
- This book moves beyond the confusing terminology found in other criminology texts to provide students with straightforward explanations of criminology's important concepts and most fascinating schools of thought. Content is readily accessible through the use of plain language and commonsense definitions of key terms.
- Cases in every chapter illustrate the principles discussed and provide true-to-life stories of criminal offenders. Thought-provoking questions within the cases provide students with the opportunity to apply what they've learned.

> **When best-selling authors and instructional designers come together focused on one goal—to improve student performance across the CJ curriculum—they come away with a groundbreaking new series of print and digital content: the *Justice Series*.**

What's New to this Edition

Chapter 1

- The chapter opening story describing the role of neurobiology in understanding behavioral development in adolescents is new.
- The section on high risk behavior is reorganized.
- The section on the promise of Positive Youth Development (PYD) is moved to a later chapter.
- The definition of delinquency is new.
- A Deinstitutionalization of Status Offender (DSO) section has been added.
- The section on Juvenile Court Jurisdiction Over Status Offenders is expanded and rewritten.
- The section on crossover youth is a new section.
- The Three Themes section has been expanded and rewritten.
- The Delinquency Prevention section now has a new discussion on resilience.
- The section on Delinquency and Social Policy is new and now includes discussion of Evidence-Based Programs.

Chapter 2

- The chapter opening story describing Texan Ethan Couch is new.
- The statistics in the Uniform Crime Reports, Juvenile Court Statistics, and Victimization Surveys are updated, and new tables have been added.
- The studies in the Social Factors Related to Delinquency section are updated.

Chapter 3

- The section on Rationality and Delinquency is expanded.
- The section on Delinquency Prevention and the Philosophy of Punishment, including General Deterrence, Specific Deterrence, and Incapacitation is new.
- The sections on Biological Positivism, both early forms and contemporary Biological Positivism, have been expanded, with several new studies added.
- Exhibit 3.1, "Functional Impairment of Delinquent Youth," is new.
- The section on Psychological Positivism has been expanded.
- There is a new discussion of Jean Piaget under the section on Cognitive Theory.

- The section on the Developmental Theories of Delinquency has been revised and reorganized.

Chapter 4
- The definition of the term "social structure" has been revised.
- The section describing strain theory and delinquency has been expanded and updated.
- The discussion of Albert K. Cohen's theory has been expanded.
- The section on Delinquency and Social Policy has been significantly expanded and updated.

Chapter 5
- There is a new introduction to the material on suicide and bullying.
- Exhibit 5.1, "Peacemaking and Criminology," is new.

Chapter 6
- There is a new "Discuss" feature at the start of the chapter.
- The discussion of gender and delinquency has been expanded.
- Exhibit 6.1, "Differences between Girls' and Boys' Delinquency," is new.
- The section on explanations of female delinquency has been expanded.
- Material was added to the section on Gender Bias and Delinquency.
- The section on new programs involving Girls, Inc. is new.

Chapter 7
- The "Transitions and Delinquency" section has been expanded.
- The section entitled "Other Expressions of Family Life" is new, and now includes discussion of the foster family and adopted children, children with lesbian, gay, bisexual, and transgender parents.
- The "Mass Media and Delinquency Behavior" section has been expanded.

Chapter 8
- The "Discuss" feature at the start of the chapter has been changed.
- The school crime section is updated.
- The section on cyberbullying section is new.
- The section on school discipline section is new, and includes a discussion of security measures, corporal punishment, and out-of-school suspensions.

Chapter 9
- The national gang data has been updated.
- The exhibit describing Father Greg Boyle, S.J., is new.

Chapter 10
- Updated drug national data.
- New Evidence Based Programs Exhibit.

Chapter 11
- A new section on "Treatment in Juvenile Justice" has been added. It includes discussion of Insight-Based Therapy, Behavioral Therapy, Cognitive-Based Therapy, Group Therapy, including Guided Group Interaction, Positive Peer Culture, and Drug and Alcohol Interventions.
- A new section, "What Works for Whom and in What Context," has been added.
- The "Graduated Sanctions" section is new.
- A new section on "Core Principles of a System of Graduated Sanctions" has been added to the chapter.
- The section discussing race and juvenile justice has been expanded.
- The material comprising the section on the "Prevention of Delinquency: Comprehensive Delinquency Prevention Strategy" is new.

Chapter 12
- The "Discuss" feature at the start of the chapter has been completely revised.
- The section on juvenile attitudes toward the police has been revised.
- Exhibit 12.1, "Building Connections between Officers and Baltimore City Youth," is new.
- The "Informal and Formal Disposition" section has been revised.
- A portion of the "Legal Rights of Juveniles" section has been revised.
- The "School-Based Intervention" section has been updated and revised.

Chapter 13
- The data on the number of cases handled in juvenile court has been updated.
- Information on the offense profile of delinquency cases has been updated.
- The results of a new study on the punishment of juveniles are now included.
- The table showing the minimum age for concurrent jurisdiction has been brought up to date.
- A discussion of the U.S. Supreme Court case of *J.D.B.* v. *North Carolina* (2011), in which the court held that a child's age must be considered in assessing whether a suspect is aware of his or her rights, has been added.

Chapter 14
- Data on the institutional placement of juveniles has been updated.
- The "Delinquency Across the Life Course" section has been revised.
- The section on "Delinquency and Social Policy" has been expanded.

Instructor Supplements

Instructor's Manual with Test Bank.
Includes content outlines for classroom discussion, teaching suggestions, and answers to selected end-of-chapter questions from the text. This also contains a Word document version of the test bank.

TestGen.
This computerized test generation system gives you maximum flexibility in creating and administering tests on paper, electronically, or online. It provides state-of-the-art features for viewing and editing test bank questions, dragging a selected question into a test you are creating, and printing sleek, formatted tests in a variety of layouts. Select test items from test banks included with TestGen for quick test creation, or write your own questions from scratch. TestGen's random generator provides the option to display different text or calculated number values each time questions are used.

PowerPoint Presentations.
Our presentations offer clear, straightforward outlines and notes to use for class lectures or study materials. Photos, illustrations, charts, and tables from the book are included in the presentations when applicable.

To access supplementary materials online, instructors need to request an instructor access code. Go to **www.pearsonhighered.com/irc,** where you can register for an instructor access code. Within 48 hours after registering, you will receive a confirming email, including an instructor access code. Once you have received your code, go to the site and log on for full instructions on downloading the materials you wish to use.

Alternate Versions

eBooks.
This text is also available in multiple eBook formats including Adobe Reader and CourseSmart. *CourseSmart* is an exciting new choice for students looking to save money. As an alternative to purchasing the printed textbook, students can purchase an electronic version of the same content. With a *CourseSmart* eTextbook, students can search the text, make notes online, print out reading assignments that incorporate lecture notes, and bookmark important passages for later review. For more information, or to purchase access to the *CourseSmart* eTextbook, visit **www.coursesmart.com.**

Acknowledgments

This book is the result of many individuals who have made invaluable contributions to this text. Foremost, we would like to thank our significant others, Linda Dippolid Bartollas and Ellen Szirandi. At the University of Northern Iowa, we would like to express our appreciation to Wayne Fauchier and Gloria Hadachek, who in various ways helped to keep the manuscript moving.

About the Authors

Clemens Bartollas, Ph.D., is professor of sociology at the University of Northern Iowa. He holds a B.A. from Davis and Elkins College, a B.D. from Princeton Theological Seminary, an S.T.M. from San Francisco Theological Seminary, and a Ph.D. in sociology, with a special emphasis in criminology, from The Ohio State University. Dr. Bartollas taught at Pembroke State University from 1973 to 1975, at Sangamon State University from 1975 to 1980, and at the University of Northern Iowa from 1981 to the present. He has received a number of honors at the University of Northern Iowa, including Distinguished Scholar, the Donald McKay Research Award, and the Regents' Award for Faculty Excellence. Dr. Bartollas, like his coauthor, is also the author of numerous articles and more than 30 books, including previous editions of *Juvenile Delinquency* (Allyn & Bacon, 2006), *Juvenile Justice in America* (with Stuart J. Miller; Prentice Hall, 2011), and *Women and the Criminal Justice System* (with Katherine Stuart van Wormer; Prentice Hall, 2011).

Frank Schmalleger, Ph.D., is Distinguished Professor Emeritus at the University of North Carolina at Pembroke. He holds an undergraduate degree from the University of Notre Dame and both master's (1970) and doctoral (1974) degrees, with special emphasis in sociology, from The Ohio State University. From 1976 to 1994, he taught criminology and criminal justice courses at the University of North Carolina at Pembroke; for the last 16 of those years, he chaired the university's Department of Sociology, Social Work, and Criminal Justice. The university named him Distinguished Professor in 1991.

Dr. Schmalleger has taught in the online graduate program of the New School for Social Research, helping to build the world's first electronic classrooms in support of distance learning through computer telecommunications. As an adjunct professor with Webster University in St. Louis, Missouri, Dr. Schmalleger helped develop the university's graduate programs in administration of justice as well as security administration and loss prevention and taught courses in those curricula for more than a decade. A strong advocate of Web-based instruction, Dr. Schmalleger is also the creator of numerous award-winning websites.

Dr. Schmalleger is the author of numerous articles and more than 30 books, including the widely used *Criminal Justice Today* (Prentice Hall, 2015), *Criminal Justice: A Brief Introduction* (Prentice Hall, 2014), *Criminology Today* (Prentice Hall, 2015), *Criminology: A Brief Introduction* (Prentice Hall, 2015), *Criminal Law Today* (Prentice Hall, 2013), and *Corrections in the Twenty-First Century* (with John Smykla; McGraw-Hill, 2014). He is also founding editor of the journal *Criminal Justice Studies* and has served as imprint adviser for Greenwood Publishing Group's criminal justice reference series. Visit the author's website at www.schmalleger.com.

"The future promise of any nation can be directly measured by the present prospects of its youth."

—*President John F. Kennedy, February 14, 1963*

1

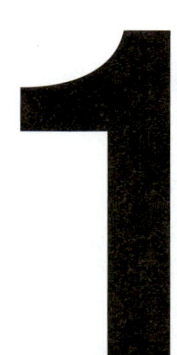

Adolescence and Delinquency

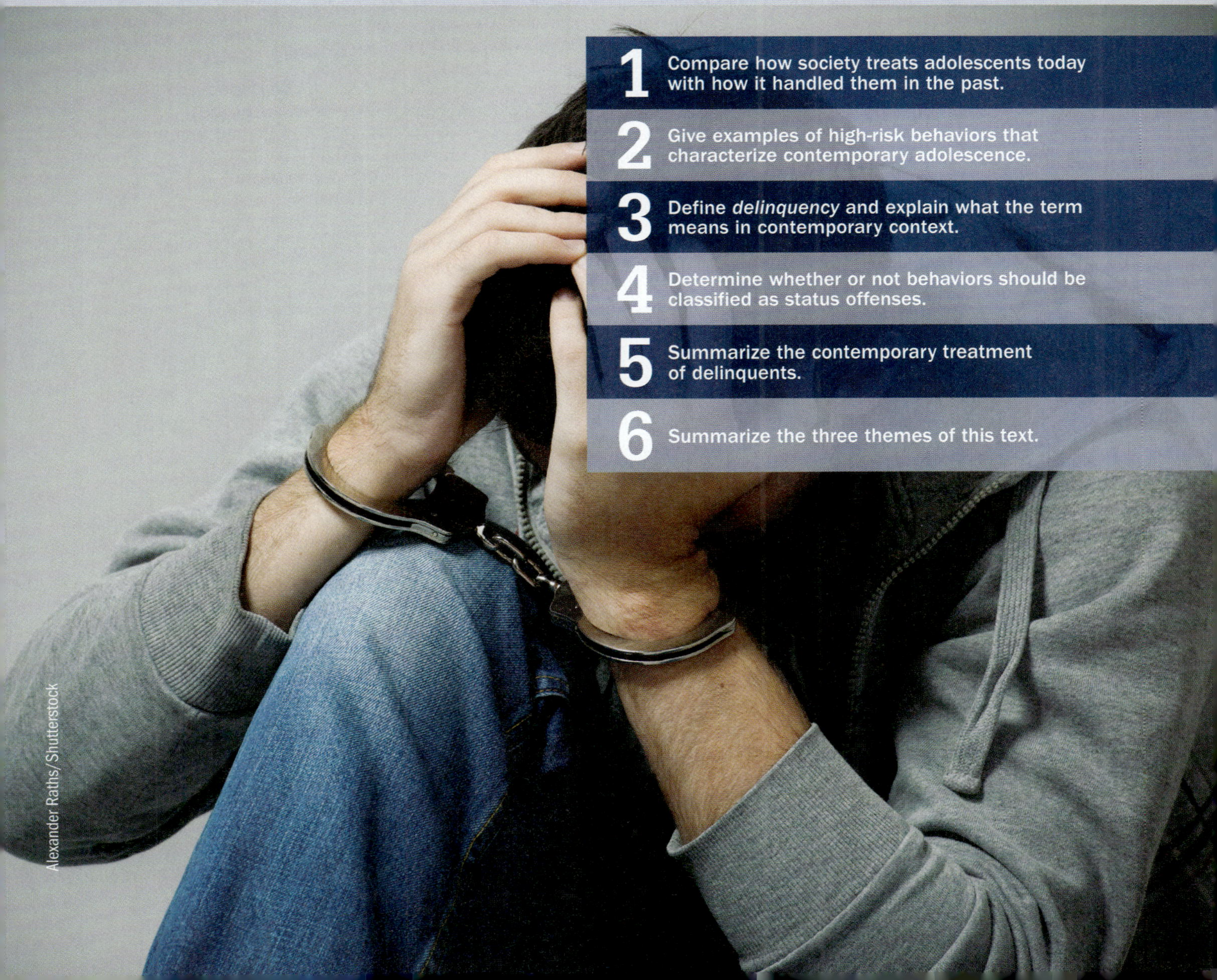

1. Compare how society treats adolescents today with how it handled them in the past.
2. Give examples of high-risk behaviors that characterize contemporary adolescence.
3. Define *delinquency* and explain what the term means in contemporary context.
4. Determine whether or not behaviors should be classified as status offenses.
5. Summarize the contemporary treatment of delinquents.
6. Summarize the three themes of this text.

Alexander Raths/Shutterstock

INTRO: DEFENDING CHILDHOOD

Sixty-five years ago, J. D. Salinger penned a book with plenty of staying power—one that's still found on the reading lists of high school students across the country. That book, *Catcher in the Rye*, was intended for an adult audience, but quickly became popular with teenagers.[1] *Catcher in the Rye* was translated into all of the world's major languages, and has sold over 65 million copies since it was first published. The book focuses on the difficulties of growing up in mid-twentieth century America, including issues of alienation, feelings of belonging, peer influences, and identity development. It's main character, 17-year-old Holden Caulfield, demonstrates many of the same traits that define today's adolescents. He's impulsive and speaks and acts seemingly without thinking of the consequences, then later regrets what he's done. His struggles with his own sexuality portray a young man with budding desires, but a lack of understanding about how to fulfill them. His lack of academic focus and a reckless tendency to get into fights with other boys results in his being suspended from school, and his frequent bouts with alcohol and minor crimes highlight his apparent immaturity.

Although Salinger's novel dramatized adolescent development in post-World War II America, it also documented seemingly timeless traits associated with teenagers everywhere. And although Salinger might not have been able to explain the emergence of those traits, recent studies in the fields of developmental psychology and neuroscience support the notion that the typical teenage brain is not mature, and that young people are routinely characterized by poor judgment and impulsivity. The latest findings on human development, which come from careful studies of human physiological development, show that the frontal cortex—the part of the brain that is responsible for self-control, effective judgment, and sensible planning—matures very slowly throughout childhood and into early adulthood. Moreover, such studies show that the development of "adult" thought patterns and self-control is perilously out of sync with the early development of the emotional brain. As a result there is a gap between early thrill-seeking and risk-taking on the one hand, and self-discipline on the other. In short, as one writer puts it, "teenagers are attracted to novel and risky activities, especially with peers, at a time when they lack judgment and the ability to weigh future consequences."[2]

Teenagers riding a roller coaster. Thrill-seeking and risk-taking are common behaviors among young people, and scientific studies of mental development show that there are fundamental differences between the brains of adults and children in their ability to assess situations and to plan effectively.

In 2010, in recognition of the fundamental differences between the brains of juveniles and adults, the U.S. Supreme Court abolished life imprisonment without the possibility of parole for persons who commit serious crimes (other than homicide) as teenagers. In that case, *Graham* v. *Florida*, the justices held that "developments in psychology and brain science continue to show fundamental differences between juvenile and adult minds. For example, parts of the brain involved in behavior control continue to mature through late adolescence. . . . Juveniles are more capable of change than are adults, and their actions are less likely to be evidence of 'irretrievably depraved character' than are the actions of adults."[3] Two years later, in 2012, the Court reinforced that view by holding, in the case of *Miller* v. *Alabama*, that "mandatory life without parole for a juvenile precludes consideration of his chronological age and its hallmark features—among them, immaturity, impetuosity, and failure to appreciate risks and consequences."[4]

DISCUSS How do the brains of children and adults differ? What implications do such differences hold for behavior?

Anyone with an interest in juveniles and juvenile misbehavior could expand their examination beyond neuroscience to include the social conditions that surround children through their developmental years. One recent study funded by the U.S. Department of Justice (DOJ),[5] for example, focused on childhood exposure to violence. It found that a majority of children in the United States have been exposed to violence, crime, or abuse in their homes, schools, and communities. The study also demonstrated that children's exposure to violence, whether as victims or witnesses, is frequently associated with long-term physical, psychological, and emotional harm. Finally, the study found that children exposed to violence are more likely to abuse drugs and alcohol; suffer from depression, anxiety, and post-traumatic disorders; fail or have difficulty in school; and become delinquent and engage in criminal behavior. According to researchers, a child's exposure to one type of violence increases the likelihood that the child will be exposed to other types of violence and exposed multiple times. Children exposed to violence are at a higher risk of engaging in criminal behavior later in life and of becoming participants in a cycle of violence.[6]

We've got to break this cycle of violence. Through enhanced prevention, intervention, and accountability efforts, I believe we can.

—Attorney General Eric H. Holder, Jr.

The Changing Treatment of Adolescents

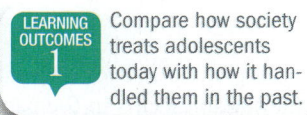

LEARNING OUTCOMES 1 Compare how society treats adolescents today with how it handled them in the past.

The primary subject matter of this text is **juvenile delinquency**. A 2014 federal government report notes that "Most people would say that a juvenile delinquent is a badly behaved teenager under age 18 who gets into trouble frequently—or, more precisely, one who gets into trouble with police frequently. The image that comes to mind is an adolescent who skips school, drinks alcohol, uses illegal drugs, steals, is often belligerent, and may be prone to violence. This popular notion of delinquency, however, is not an adequate definition for a discussion of juvenile justice practice and policy. It is far too broad."[7]

Because juvenile delinquency is the focus of this text, it is important to develop a concise definition of the term at the start of our discussion. Consequently, this text uses the following definition for the term "juvenile delinquency": An act committed by a minor that violates the penal code of the government with authority over the area in which the act occurs. Likewise, "[i]t is important to understand, however, that a "law violation by a young person is considered an act of juvenile delinquency only if the behavior meets all three of the following criteria: (1) the act involved would be a criminal offense if it were committed by an adult; (2) the young person charged with committing the act is below the age at which the criminal court traditionally assumes jurisdiction; and (3) the juvenile is charged with an offense that must be adjudicated in the juvenile court (or some other court with jurisdiction over noncriminal but illegal acts of juveniles) or the prosecution and the juvenile court judge exercise their discretion to lodge and retain jurisdiction in the juvenile court."

To bring the subject of delinquency into clearer focus, this chapter places it in the broader context of adolescence and the narrow context of those adolescents who are youths at risk. High-risk children can be further divided into delinquents and status offenders, which is what is discussed next. The chapter then examines how child delinquents have been handled from the past to the present and concludes with presenting three themes that will be examined throughout the text.

Adolescence is a term that refers to the life interval between childhood and adulthood. A 2014 publication by the National Academy of Science Press says that "[a]dolescence is a distinct, yet transient, period of development between childhood and adulthood characterized by increased experimentation and risk-taking, a tendency to discount long-term consequences, and heightened sensitivity to peers and other social influences."[8]

Prior to the 1930s, the concept of adolescence did not hold the meaning that it does today. Prior to the middle of the twentieth century, adolescents were seen as small versions of unempowered adults, lacking in social and economic status. Except for children younger than the age of seven, little consideration was given to what we now see as the special needs of children, and most children were expected to possess self-control and abide by adult standards of behavior. Since at least the 1950s, however, the term *adolescence* has come to be seen as marking an identifiable and important stage of human growth and development. Still, there is no agreed-on way to pinpoint this period chronologically or to restrict it within physiological boundaries. For purposes of discussion in this chapter, however, adolescence is considered to be the years between ages 12 and 18. Within this transitional period, youngsters experience many biological changes and develop new attitudes, values, and skills that they will carry into their young adult years.

Delinquency and other problem behaviors increase during the adolescent years for several reasons. These years bring increasing freedom from parental scrutiny, and with this freedom come more opportunities to be involved in socially unacceptable behavior. Teenagers develop new, often expensive tastes for such things as sound systems, clothing, automobiles, and alcohol, yet legitimate means for satisfying these desires are often not available. The lengthening of adolescence in U.S. culture has further expanded the crises and struggles of this life period, thereby increasing the chance of problems with the law, at school, and in the home. In addition, there is often a mismatch between adolescents' needs and the opportunities provided to them by their social environment.[9] Finally, in some cases, the unmet needs and frustrations of early childhood fester into socially unacceptable behavior in later years.

Adolescence, as a term describing a particular stage of human growth and development, evolved out of the modern notion of childhood. The concept of childhood, as reflected in today's child-centered culture, is a relatively recent phenomenon.[10] Much of recorded history reveals tales of horrific child labor, abuse, and indifference to be the fate of many children. Lloyd de Mause, an American social thinker known for his work in the field of psychohistory, described [t]he history of childhood [as] a nightmare from which we have only recently begun to awaken."[11]

The end of child labor was one of the watersheds in the development of modern adolescence. Throughout history, children have worked, but until the Industrial Revolution their work was usually done within or around the house, often outdoors. As work moved from the home to the factory, children were considered a source of cheap labor. Until the child labor laws were actually enforced, children as young as ages four and five worked in mines, mills, and factories. But with advancing technology and mechanization, children and adolescents were no longer needed in the labor market, and by 1914, every state but one had passed laws prohibiting the employment in industries of children under a certain age, generally 14.[12]

Another important stage in the development of modern adolescence was compulsory public schooling. As Chapter 8 discusses, nineteenth-century U.S. schools were violent and chaotic places in which teachers attempted to maintain control over unmotivated and unruly children, sometimes using brutal disciplinary methods. The Progressive education movement arose partly because of the dissatisfaction of some elements of society with the schools. The influence of John Dewey and other Progressive educators encouraged individualism and personal growth in the classroom. Compulsory education laws also evolved from early-twentieth-century social and religious views, which held that adolescents should be kept in school because they needed guidance and control.

A further stage in the development of modern adolescence was the development in the twentieth century of the belief that raising children had less to do with conquering their spirits than with training and socializing them. Parents in the United States, especially since the 1940s, have emphasized a helping relationship, attempting to meet their children's expanding needs in a democratic and supportive environment. An additional stage in this development took place in the 1960s and 1970s when special legal protections for juveniles were granted, highlighting the perception of adolescents as needing special attention, guidance, and support. Psychologist Erik H. Erikson has observed, "Childhood is the model of all oppression and enslavement, a kind of inner colonization, which forces grown-ups to accept inner repression and self-restriction." A chief reason for the repression of childhood, according to Erikson and others, is the lack of rights given to young people. The children's rights movement, which encompasses a spectrum of approaches, became popular in the 1970s as a means to compensate for young people's lack of rights. Consensus also increased on what components are thought necessary for an adolescent to achieve responsible adulthood.[13]

In sum, the concept of adolescence centers on a set of beliefs that emerged during the late nineteenth and early twentieth centuries. These beliefs have had the result of removing young people from the world of employment and from the mainstream of adult society. This process of lengthening childhood and delaying adult responsibilities was strongly influenced not only by humanitarian considerations but also by major economic,

Adolescence brings increasing freedom from parental scrutiny.

The end of child labor was one of the watersheds in the development of modern adolescence.

social, and political forces in society. See Table 1–1 for a visual presentation regarding the treatment of adolescents in the past and in the present.

Youth Culture

A youth culture, which has emerged in recent decades in the United States and other nations, consists of the unique beliefs, behaviors, and symbols that represent young people in society. How, when, where, and with what and whom they interact with is part of this culture. A primary feature of youth culture is the incorporation of trends or fads.[14] Youth culture has distinctive clothing styles, hairstyles, behaviors, footwear, electronic devices, and interests. Vehicles such as cars, motor scooters, motorcycles, skateboards, and surfboards—as well as personal electronic devices and video games—have played central roles in the development of today's youth culture. As will be discussed in future chapters, there are various youth cultures, and the features of youth cultures vary by class, gender, race, and ethnicity.

Body piercing—often multiple piercings for both males and females in literally every part of the body, including the tongue, eyebrows, lips, cheeks, navel, genitals, and breasts—and tattooing are widely found among some youth cultures today. Ritual scarification and 3D-art implants are popular, and so are stretching and cutting of the genitals, scrotal implants, transdermal implants, tooth art, and facial sculpture.[15]

Adolescents have always been connected to their peers, but many are now connected at all times of the day, texting in class

TABLE 1–1   THE CHANGING TREATMENT OF ADOLESCENTS OVER TIME

Historical Treatment	Present Treatment
Treated as small adults	Adolescence is seen as preparation for adulthood.
Expected to work in the home or outside the home at a young age	Employment takes place after school or on weekends and usually is seen as making extra money.
Education was seen as of minor significance and usually lasted only a few years.	Compulsory education and increased emphasis is placed on attending college.
Adolescent girls were expected to marry and raise a family.	Growing equality for female adolescents
Minimal emotional attachment to children because of high infant death rates	Emotional investment in children from birth
Children were punished like adults.	Children, especially those who commit minor crimes, are protected by the state and are placed in a separate system and are separated from adults.
Children were seen as having few rights.	Special legal protections were granted to juveniles beginning in the final decades of the late nineteenth century, continuing throughout the twentieth century and into today.

or messaging throughout the night. In addition to constant communication, adolescents are joining online groups or communities, posting numerous self-portraits (or *selfies*), and creating their own Facebook pages or InstaGram messages.

Some people use the term *Millennials* to refer to people born around the turn of the twenty-first century, and the word can be applied to teenagers and young adults today. Whatever term we use to describe today's young people, it is clear that most American youth have been strongly influenced by the media—especially social media; and that they are relatively adept at interacting with others through the use of ever-improving personal technologies. In 2014, the Pew Research Center, which notes that "generations, like people, have personalities,"[16] released a report showing that young Millennial adults are confident and open to change, but largely "detached from institutions and networked with friends."[17] Other researchers have found that today's young people are less interested in protection of the environment or developing a philosophy of life than their predecessors, and are significantly more narcissistic than earlier generations. Husband–wife author team William A. Draves and Julie Coates suggest that the behavior and values of young people today who are living in first-world nations are significantly impacted by the economic and technological implications of the Internet and personal connectivity.[18]

Think About It…

Today's youths are much more connected through the use of electronic social networking than members of any previous generation. What are the implications of such connectivity both for delinquency and delinquency prevention?

© Tsiumpa/Fotolia

One in four adolescents in the United States today is at high risk of engaging in multiple problem behaviors.

▶ Youth at Risk

The population of children in the United States is increasing and becoming more racially and ethnically diverse. There are approximately 75.6 million children, ages newborn to 17 years, in the United States. Although it may come as a surprise, there are approximately equal numbers of children in each age group: 0–5 (25 million), 6–11 (24 million), and 12–17 (25 million) years of age.[19] Children represent 25 percent of the American population, which is down from a peak of 36 percent at the end of the post-World War II baby boom in 1964.[20] The population of **juveniles**, according to a U.S. Census Bureau estimate, will increase 14 percent between 2000 and 2025; by 2050 the juvenile population will be 36 percent larger than it was in 2000.[21]

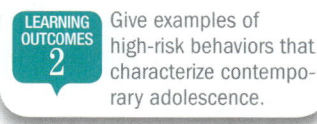

LEARNING OUTCOMES 2 — Give examples of high-risk behaviors that characterize contemporary adolescence.

As noted, diversity is increasing. In 2003, 60 percent of our nation's children were Caucasian, 16 percent were African American, and 4 percent were Asian. Since then, the proportion of Hispanic children has increased faster than those of the other racial and ethnic groups; it grew from 9 percent of all children in 1980 to 24 percent in 2013.[22]

The Federal Interagency Forum on Child and Family Statistics estimates that of the 25 million adolescents (ages 12 through 17 years) living in the United States, approximately one in four is at high risk of engaging in multiple problem behaviors. These behaviors, particularly committing delinquent acts and abusing drugs and alcohol, quickly bring adolescents to the attention of the juvenile justice system. Another 6 million youngsters, making up 25 percent, engage in risky behavior, but to a lesser degree and, consequently, are less likely to experience negative consequences.[23]

The State of America's Children 2014, a Children Defense Fund (CDF) publication, notes that "Fifty years after President Lyndon Johnson declared a War on Poverty, the United States is still not a fair playing field for millions of children afflicted by preventable poverty, hunger, homelessness, sickness, poor education, and violence in the world's richest economy with a gross domestic product (GDP) of $15.7 trillion."[24] According to the CDF, "The greatest threat to America's economic, military and national security comes from . . . our failure, unique among high income nations, to invest adequately and fairly in the health, education and sound development of all of our young."[25] CDF statistics show that every fifth child in the United States (16.1 million) is poor, and every tenth child (7.1 million) lives in extreme poverty. Moreover, children are the poorest age group in America and, on average, the younger they are the poorer they are.[26] Figure 1–1, which is indicative of the problem, shows the number of homeless children enrolled in public schools throughout the United States for the period 2006–2012.

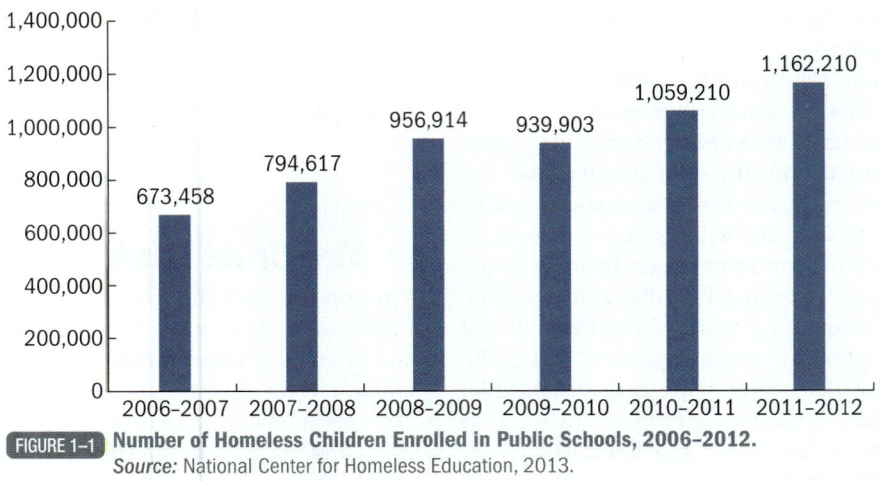

FIGURE 1-1 Number of Homeless Children Enrolled in Public Schools, 2006-2012.
Source: National Center for Homeless Education, 2013.

High-Risk Behaviors and Adolescence

Researchers have made a number of important advances in understanding adolescence and problem behaviors. Those adolescents who have the most negative or problem-oriented factors in their lives are defined as "high risk." First, high-risk youths often experience multiple difficulties: They are frequently socialized in economically stressed families and communities, more often than not have histories of physical abuse and sexual victimization, typically have educational and vocational skill deficits, and are prone to become involved in alcohol and other drug abuse and forms of delinquency.[27] The more of these problem behaviors that are present, the more likely it is that a youth will become involved in socially undesirable behaviors (see Figure 1-2).[28]

Second, adolescent problem behaviors—especially delinquent acts such as being involved in drug and alcohol abuse, failing in or dropping out of school, and having unprotected sex—are interrelated, or linked; that is, an involvement in one problem behavior is generally indicative of some participation in other socially undesirable behaviors.[29]

Third, high-risk youths tend to become involved in behaviors that contribute to unintentional injury and violence; some of these behaviors include carrying a weapon, driving when they have been drinking, riding with someone else who has been drinking, and rarely or never wearing a seat belt when driving or riding with someone else.[30]

The federally funded Program of Research on the Causes and Correlates of Delinquency (also known as the Causes and Correlates Program, which is described in more detail in Chapter 2) comprises the three coordinate longitudinal projects: Denver Youth Survey, the Pittsburgh Youth Survey and the Rochester Youth Development Study. These three projects examined the co-occurrence or overlap of delinquent behavior with drug use, problems in school, and mental health issues. Findings show that a large portion of serious delinquents are not involved in persistent drug use, nor do they have persistent school or mental health problems. However, as the problems that co-occurs most frequently with serious delinquency increase, so does the likelihood that an individual will become a serious delinquent. Study authors note that these findings mean that policymakers should focus on the importance of identifying and addressing the unique needs of individual youth, rather than proceeding under the assumption that all offenders require similar treatment.[31]

Another study analyzed the prevalence and overlap of substance abuse–related behaviors among youths. The study found that given one substance abuse-related behavior, other substance behaviors became much more likely. For example, among youths who reported drinking alcohol (23 percent of all youths ages 12–17), the level of marijuana use was 32 percent and the level of drug selling was 23 percent—much higher than in youths who did not drink.[32]

Some researchers argue that the anticipation of an early death, which gives high-risk youths a sense of fearfulness, is a contributing factor to youth crime. The contention is made that adolescents who perceive a high likelihood of an early death, which is particularly true of youths who belong to gangs, have

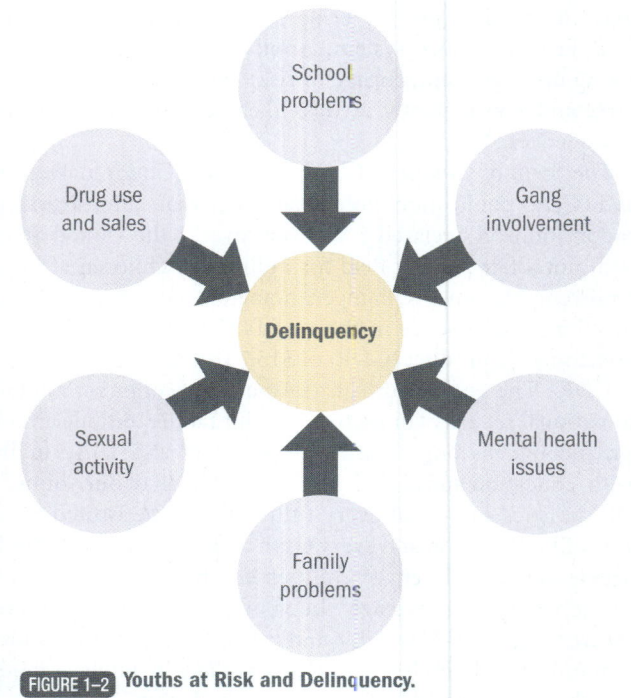

FIGURE 1-2 Youths at Risk and Delinquency.

Think About It...

The Children's Defense Fund's research publication *The State of American Children*[34] tells us that more than 6.4 million children are in families living at half the poverty level or less. For a family of four that means having an income of $11,746 or less per year. During the "great recession," the number of children living in poverty increased by 3 million. According to the CDF, "Poor children are more likely to start school behind their more affluent peers and less likely to graduate from high school. They are more likely to be poor as adults and become involved in the criminal justice system." Why is the issue of poverty so closely related to the general problem of youth crisis and the particular problem of juvenile delinquency? What do you believe society needs to do about the issue of poor children who seem to be getting poorer?

Sascha Burkard/Shutterstock

little reason to delay gratification for future benefits and, as a result, they pursue high-risk behaviors associated with immediate rewards, including crime and violence.[33]

Delinquency is one of the problem behaviors with which all but low-risk adolescents become involved from time to time (see Chapter 2). Although we use the word *delinquent* rather freely in day-to-day conversation, *delinquency* is a legal term initially used in law in 1899 when Illinois passed the first statute pertaining to delinquent behavior among juveniles. The age at which an individual is subject to the jurisdiction of juvenile court varies among states, but it is generally 16 or 17 years of age.

Some evidence indicates that delinquency in U.S. society is changing. Beginning in the late 1980s and extending throughout the 1990s, adolescents participated widely in street gangs, some of which provided a base for trafficking narcotics; had rising rates of murder; were more likely to own and use firearms than ever before; and were becoming increasingly involved in various forms of hate crimes. Many of these trends continued throughout the first decade of the twenty-first century.

Yet the average American delinquent is far more likely to shoplift, commit petty theft, use minor illegal drugs, violate liquor laws, or destroy property than to commit a violent or serious crime. In 2012, 968,534 juveniles between the ages of 10 and 17 years were arrested for 222,658 property crimes, compared with 42,378 arrests for violent crimes.[35] In other words, juveniles were arrested for committing four and one-half times more property crimes than violent crimes.

Besides committing the same crimes as adults, juveniles also are arrested for truancy, incorrigibility, curfew violations, and runaway behavior. Such offenses are called **status offenses** because they would not be defined as criminal if adults committed them. (Status offenses are defined and discussed in more detail next.) The legal separation between status offenders and delinquents is important because of the large number of arrests each year for acts such as being truant, disobeying parents, and running away from home. The Federal Bureau of Investigation (FBI) *Crime in the United States 2012 (CUS 2012)* data (see Chapter 2) reveal that three times as many youths are arrested for status offenses as for violent crimes. This ratio between status offenses and violent crimes would be even greater if truancy and incorrigibility—two of the most common status offenses—were included.

▶ Delinquency Defined

LEARNING OUTCOMES 3: Define *delinquency* and explain what the term means in contemporary context.

Juvenile court codes, which exist in every state, specify the conditions under which states can legitimately intervene in a juvenile's life. State juvenile codes, as part of the **parens patriae** philosophy of the juvenile court, were enacted to eliminate the arbitrary nature of juvenile justice beyond the rights afforded juveniles by the U.S. Constitution and to deal with youths more leniently because they were seen as not fully responsible for their behavior. The *In re Poff* (1955) decision aptly expresses the logic of this argument:

> The original Juvenile Court Act enacted in the District of Columbia was devised to afford the juvenile protections in addition to those he already possessed under the Federal Constitution. Before this legislative enactment, the juvenile was subject to the same punishment for an offense as an adult. It follows logically that in the absence of such legislation the juvenile would be entitled to the same constitutional guarantees and safeguards as an adult. If this is true, then the only possible reason for the Juvenile Court Act was to afford the juvenile safeguards in addition to those he already possessed. The legislative intent was to enlarge and not diminish those protections.[36]

Juvenile court codes usually specify that the court has jurisdiction in relation to three categories of conditions: delinquency, dependency, and neglect. First, the courts may intervene when a youth has been accused of committing an act that would be a misdemeanor or felony if committed by an adult. Second, the courts may intervene when a juvenile commits certain status offenses. Third, the courts may intervene in cases involving dependency and neglect; for example, if a court determines that a child is being deprived of needed support and supervision, it may decide to remove the child from the home for his or her own protection.

An examination of the various juvenile court codes, or statutes, shows the diverse definitions of delinquent behavior that have developed. Some statutes define a **delinquent youth** as a

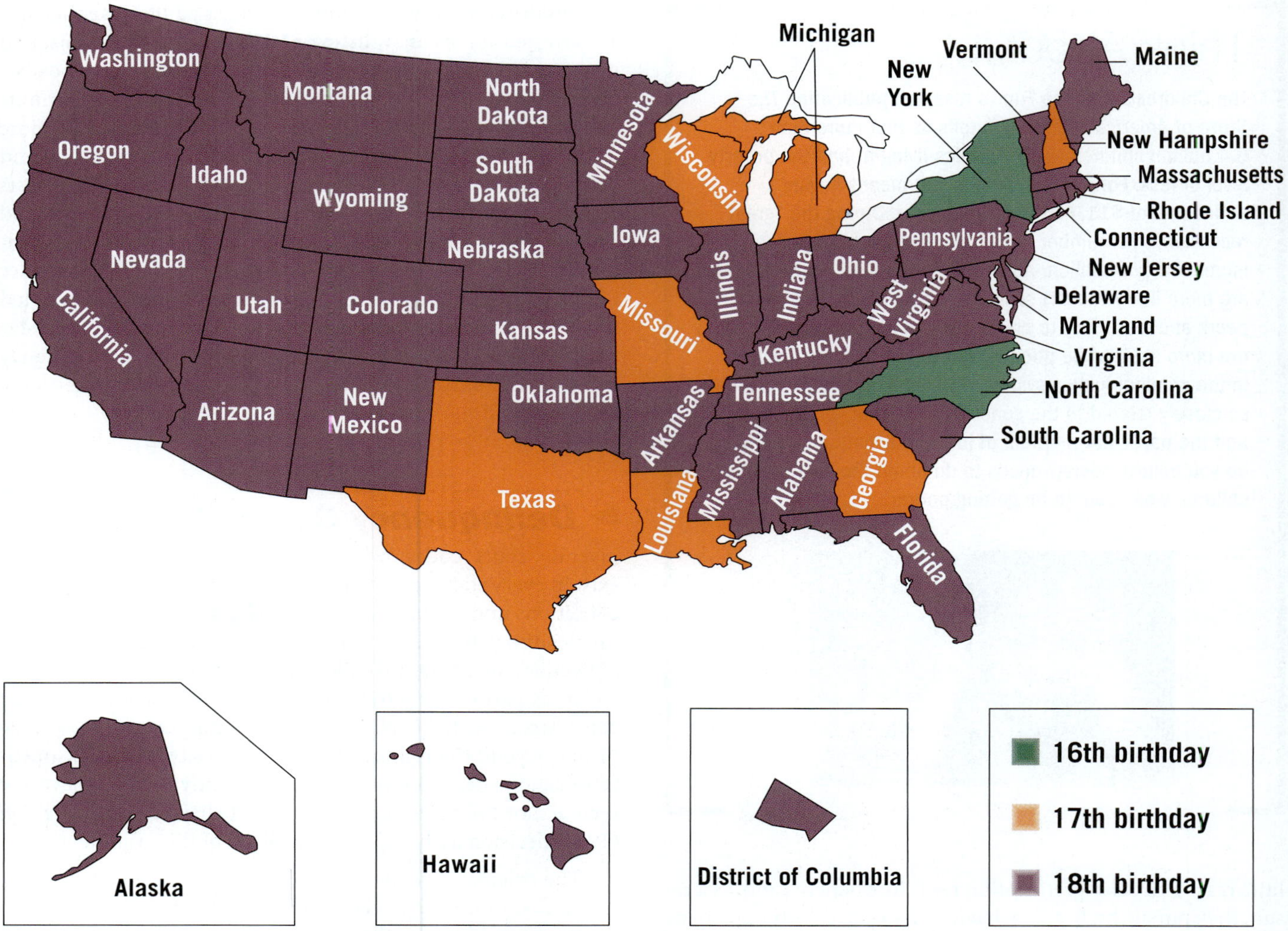

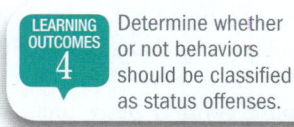

FIGURE 1–3 Limit of Juvenile Court Jurisdiction over Young Offenders by State.
Note: Wisconsin places 17-year-olds in juvenile court for misdemeanor charges, but in adult criminal courts for felony charges.
Source: Office of Juvenile Justice and Delinquency Prevention.

young person who has committed a crime or violated probation; others define a "delinquent child" in terms of such behaviors as "associating with immoral or vicious persons" (West Virginia) or "engaging in indecent or immoral conduct" (Connecticut).[37] A particular adolescent, then, could be considered a delinquent under some juvenile codes and not under others. Some controversy surrounds the issue of how long juveniles should remain under the jurisdiction of the juvenile court. The age at which a youthful offender is no longer treated as a juvenile ranges from 16 to 18 years. In 41 states and the District of Columbia, persons under 18 years of age charged with a law violation are considered juveniles. In 7 states, the upper limit of juvenile court jurisdiction is 16 years, and in 2 states, the upper limit is 15 years. (See Figure 1–3 for the upper age of juvenile court jurisdiction.).[38]

The age at which an individual is considered a minor varies among states, but it is 16 or 17 years and younger in most states.

A "delinquent youth" is a young person who has committed a crime or violated probation.

▶ Status Offenders and Status Offenses

As alluded to earlier, a status offense is behavior that is an offense only because the person involved is a juvenile. In various jurisdictions, **status offenders** are known as minors in need of supervision (MINS), children in need of supervision (CHINS), juveniles in need of supervision (JINS), children in need of assistance (CHINA), persons in need of supervision (PINS), children in need of protection and services (CHIPS), or members of families in need of supervision (FINS).

LEARNING OUTCOMES 4 Determine whether or not behaviors should be classified as status offenses.

8 Chapter 1 Adolescence and Delinquency

They also may be termed *predelinquent, incorrigible, beyond control, ungovernable,* or *wayward*. What these terms and acronyms have in common is that they view the status offender as being in need of supervision or assistance.

There are three important questions about status offenders: Why do some children become status offenders? How do status offenders differ in offense behavior from delinquents? Should the juvenile court retain control over status offenders?

Explanations for Status Offense Behavior

Generally speaking, status offenders, many of whom come from single-parent homes, place the blame for their problems on parental figures in the home and believe that fulfilling their need for a warm, accepting, and loving relationship with their parents is not possible. They become resentful and angry with their parents, who may have problems in expressing physical affection, setting reasonable and consistent limits, and showing acceptance to their children.[39]

The parents, in turn, often view status offenders as defiant, demanding, and obnoxious. Parents usually believe that they have no control over their children, who will not accept restrictions or limitations on their behavior, and a power struggle results. As a result, parents may call the police to intervene with their abusive or unmanageable children. School officials and teachers tend to view status offenders, some of whom have had conflicts with teachers since kindergarten, as resistant to authority. Besides refusing to accept the limits placed on their behavior, status offenders also tend to be disruptive, disrespectful, belligerent, emotionally withdrawn or explosive, and unfocused or unconcerned. Many are psychologically tested and are found to be hyperactive or to have attention deficit disorder. They are then prescribed varying doses of medication, typically imipramine or Ritalin™, to help them focus and control their emotional difficulties.

While acknowledging these psychological explanations, some theorists argue that society's response to status offenders, especially female status offenders, is a major contributing factor in defining who has this legal status. Society believes that young males should behave in a certain way, typically granting leniency for the right of "boys to be boys." Society's expectations for young females, however, are still based on the notion that "Sugar and spice and everything nice, that's what little girls are made of."[40] University of Hawaii women's studies professor Meda Chesney-Lind and University of Denver professor Lisa J. Pasko found during their examination of the judicial handling of female status offenders that the juvenile justice system discriminates against girls because of the fear of sexual activity.[41]

Deinstitutionalization of Status Offenders (DSO)

The **deinstitutionalization of status offenders (DSO)**, which refers to the removal of status offenders from secure detention facilities, has received considerable acceptance in the past few decades. The **Juvenile Justice and Delinquency Prevention (JJDA) Act of 1974** and its various modifications have served as the most significant impetus for the nationwide deinstitutionalization of status offenders.[42] The JJDP Act continued a DSO provision that requires status offenders to be kept separate from delinquents in secure detention facilities as a condition for states to continue receiving federal funding for their adult jail facilities.[43]

The DSO provision has been successful in encouraging states to amend laws, policies, and practices that had previously led to the confinement of juveniles who committed no criminal act. The DSO core protection of the JJDP Act is premised on the belief that juveniles who exhibit problematic behavior, but who have not violated criminal law, are more properly served by social service, mental health, and other community initiatives, and may be behaviorally damaged by placement in secure detention facilities or correctional institutions.[44] Soon after the adoption of the JJDP Act and its DSO requirement, the **Office of Juvenile Justice and Delinquency Prevention (OJJDP)** recorded approximately 171,581 violations of the federal DSO requirement. A 2013 OJJDP compliance monitoring report found that the number of annual DSO violations had recently dropped to only 6,334.[45]

The Juvenile Court's Jurisdiction over Status Offenders

Some experts have gone so far as to question the juvenile court's long-standing jurisdiction over status offenders. Critics present at least four arguments for the removal of status offenders from the jurisdiction of the juvenile court:

- The lack of clarity of many status offender statutes makes them unconstitutionally vague in their construction.
- Such laws, critics claim, are often discriminatory, especially with regard to gender.
- Although status offenders have not committed a criminal act, they are frequently confined with chronic or hard-core offenders, in defiance of the federal DSO mandate.
- The procedure of processing and confining status offenders is not in the child's best interest, and therefore violates the *parens patriae* principle that underlies the juvenile court system.
- Some claim argue that formal intervention by the juvenile court into the lives of status offenders promotes rather than inhibits unlawful behavior by identifying the child as "bad."
- It should be obvious that status offenders are a special class of youth who must be treated differently from delinquents in order to prevent them from becoming delinquents themselves.[46]

On the other hand, some juvenile court advocates have worked to maintain juvenile court jurisdiction over status offenders. They argue that status offenders will have no one to protect them if they are removed from the court's jurisdiction. They also argue that other agencies would have to take over if courts relinquished jurisdiction over status offenders, and that few alternative options are available for providing status offenders with a nurturing or positive environment.

Maine, New York, and Washington are among the states that have decriminalized status offenders, thus removing from the juvenile court's jurisdiction youthful behaviors that would not be chargeable as criminal offenses if committed by adults.[47] However, the status offense legislation initially passed in Maine and Washington was partly repealed to give juvenile courts in those states a continuing degree of jurisdiction, especially over abandoned, runaway, or endangered children.[48]

The most broad-based movement to strip the juvenile court of jurisdiction over status offenders began in New York State in 1985 with passage of the 1985 PINS Adjustment Services Act. Under that law the eligibility age for persons in need of supervision (PINS) was raised to 18 years (from what had been 16). The intent of this bill was to "prevent unnecessary and inappropriate out-of-home placements of children and youth" and to assist and support families seeking help with troubled older children.[49] In 2005, New York passed additional legislation requiring each county in the state and the city of New York to provide diversion services to youth at risk of becoming the subject of a PINS petition.[50]

It is unlikely that many more states will remove status offenders from the juvenile court's jurisdiction in the near future. Widespread resistance comes from those who feel that status offenders need the close supervision available through the juvenile court in order to prevent them from becoming involved in increasingly criminal behaviors. However, even in states that strongly support deinstitutionalization, the juvenile court frequently can still institutionalize status offenders by redefining them as delinquents. A truant, for example, may be charged with a minor delinquent offense and be brought before the court, or a court may require school attendance as a condition of probation for a previous act of delinquency, thereby bringing continued acts of truancy under its purview.[51] See Table 1–2 showing examples of status offenses.

Crossover Youth

Juveniles in the child welfare system often enter the juvenile justice system. Because these youths are known to both the child welfare system and the juvenile justice system, they are often referred to as *crossover youth*. Other terms used to describe these youths are *dual jurisdiction cases*, *dually adjudicated youth*, and *cross-system cases*.

Crossover youth commonly move back and forth between a child welfare system in which they may be seen as underprivileged youth, and a juvenile justice system that sees them as delinquents. Yet little integration exists between the two systems,

TABLE 1–2	STATUS OFFENSES
Incorrigibility at home	
Ungovernability at school	
Running away from home	
Truancy	
Smoking cigarettes and using smokeless tobacco	
Drinking alcohol	

The juvenile court can institutionalize status offenders by redefining them as delinquent or as in need of mental health services.

and little coordination takes place. In fact, in many jurisdictions, a common practice is for child welfare agencies to close the cases of children who are involved in the juvenile justice system.[52]

Many crossover youth experience co-occurring mental health and drug and alcohol abuse problems, which are left unscreened and undertreated in both systems. These youth frequently do poorly in school and end up being suspended or dropping out. Youth in the child welfare system who are placed in out-of-home settings are at greater risk of crossing over into juvenile justice jurisdiction. Child welfare placements in group-home settings, particularly, have been found to be predictive of future involvement with the juvenile justice system.

Another matter of grave concern is that the disproportionate number of crossover minority youth is closely related to the disproportionate number of minority youth in the welfare system.[53] Research sponsored by the Annie E. Casey Foundation reports that although minority children are not abused more often than other children, they are put into foster care faster, receive fewer services, stay there longer, and are reunited with their families less often than other children.[54]

Consequently, professionals in the juvenile justice system often ask "What can be done to help crossover youths and to avoid their future involvement with juvenile court?" In a report released in 2010, the Federal Advisory Committee on Juvenile Justice (FACJJ) identified promising court-related practices through which family and juvenile court programs can work together to address at least some of the difficulties posed by crossover cases.[55] Among other things, the FACJJ proposed the routine screening of youth upon intake in an effort to identify each youth's strengths and needs, as well as clear coordination of all of the different agencies involved in serving youth involved with the juvenile justice system.

▶ The Contemporary Treatment of Delinquents

The history of societal response to juvenile delinquency in the United States can be divided into eight periods: (1) colonial period, (2) houses of refuse, (3) juvenile court, (4) juvenile rights, (5) reform agenda, (6) social control and juvenile crime, (7) delinquency and the growing fear of crime, and (8) increased understanding of juvenile behavior (see Figure 1–4). This chapter examines the contemporary treatment of delinquency, but the other periods are considered in Chapter 11. By the end of the 1980s, the major thrust of crime-control policies involving juveniles was to "get tough" on serious and violent juvenile crime and to undermine the earlier reform efforts of the 1970s.[56]

LEARNING OUTCOMES 5 — Summarize the contemporary treatment of delinquents.

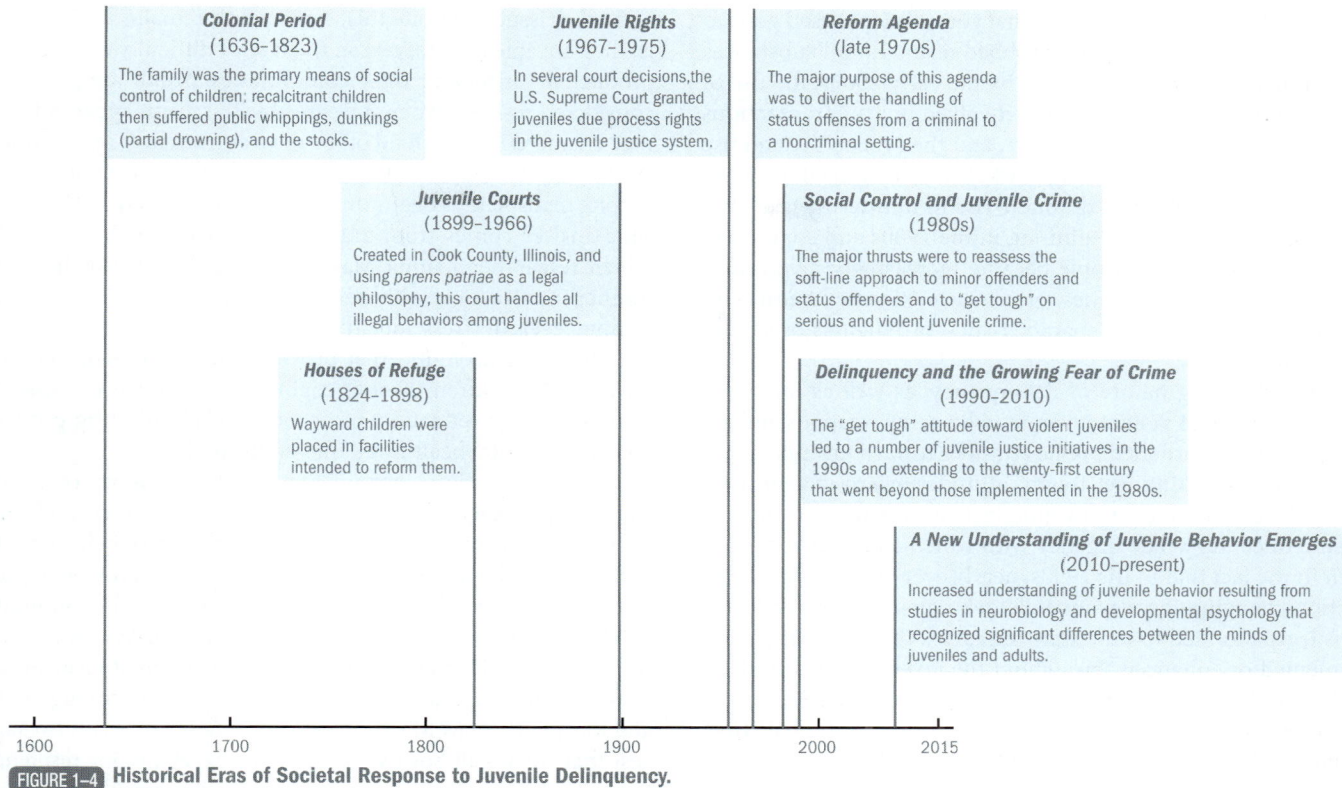

FIGURE 1-4 Historical Eras of Societal Response to Juvenile Delinquency.

Even though the federal government and the public favored a more punishment-oriented response to juvenile delinquency, the juvenile court continued throughout the 1980s to employ three approaches in handling juvenile lawbreakers (see Figure 1–5). On one end of the spectrum, the court applied the *parens patriae* doctrine to status offenders and minor offenders; as in the past, these youths were presumed to need treatment rather than punishment, because their offenses were seen as caused by internal psychological or biological conditions or by sociological factors in their environment. On the other end of the spectrum, juveniles who committed serious crimes or continued to break the law were presumed to deserve punishment rather than treatment on the grounds that such youngsters possessed free will and knew what they were doing; that is, the court viewed serious delinquents' crimes as purposeful activities resulting from rational decisions in which youths weighed the pros and cons and performed the acts that promised the greatest potential gains.[57] Their behavior was seen as being bad rather than sick and as arising from a rational decision-making process. In other words, youths in this group were to be treated by the juvenile justice system more like adults than juveniles.

Between these two groups fell youths who saw crime as a form of play and committed delinquent acts because they enjoyed the thrill of getting away with illegal behavior or because they wanted to relieve their boredom. Although criminologists usually conclude that the crimes these juveniles commit represent purposeful activity, the courts in the 1980s did not consider the youths in this middle group to be as bad as the serious delinquents, reasoning that even though these youths might be exercising free will, their behavior was mischievous rather than delinquent. The juvenile court today frequently continues to excuse such mischievous behavior.

Several interrelated social trends have recently emerged that have influenced delinquency in U.S. society in rather dramatic ways. In the mid-1980s, crack cocaine became widely available in urban areas. There was soon a large demand for this drug— some even referred to it as a crack epidemic—and this led to the recruitment of young people into the market to sell crack. By 1990, the crack epidemic had become a major impetus for the development and spread of drug-trafficking street gangs across the nation. Indeed, by the end of the twentieth century, street gangs were found in nearly every city and in many smaller communities across the United States. One of the consequences of

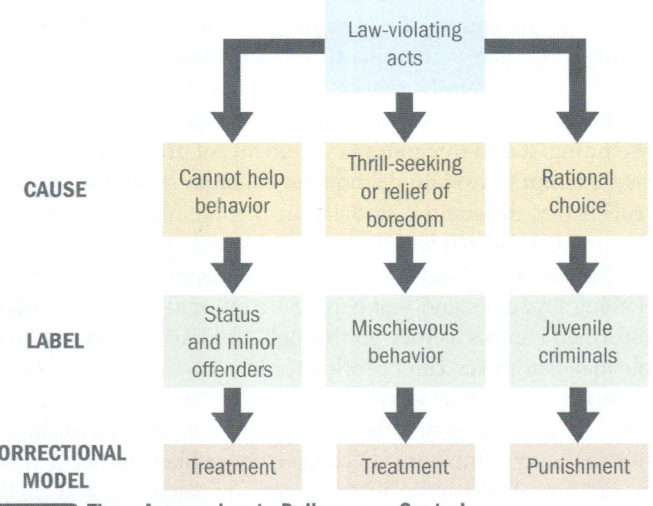

FIGURE 1-5 Three Approaches to Delinquency Control.

the illegal drug marketplace was that young people used guns to protect themselves from being robbed of the illegal substances they were carrying. Significantly, by the early 2000s, the use of guns had spread from individuals involved in drug transactions to larger numbers of young people, and the availability and use of guns, the spread of the drug market, and the growth of street gangs all contributed to a dramatic rise in murder rates among young people.[58] Finally, beginning in the 1980s and continuing through today, young people became increasingly involved in various forms of hate crimes, or crimes committed because of a victim's racial or ethnic characteristics, or religious or gender preferences.

This changing nature of delinquency, as well as increased media coverage of violent juveniles who carry weapons and are gang-involved, hardened public attitudes toward juvenile delinquents. The resulting "get-tough" attitude toward violent juveniles led to a number of juvenile justice initiatives in the late twentieth century. The urgency with which states responded is seen in the fact that in the 1990s, nearly every state enacted legislation changing the way juvenile delinquents were handled.[59] This legislation led to nine state initiatives that were either implemented or enhanced throughout the juvenile justice system, with some of them carrying over to today: (1) curfews, (2) parental responsibility laws, (3) enhanced efforts to combat street gangs, (4) a movement toward graduated sanctions (increased penalties for each new offense), (5) juvenile boot camps, (6) programs to deprive youths of guns, (7) more detailed juvenile proceedings and recordkeeping, (8) juvenile transfers to criminal court, and (9) expanded sentencing authority. All of these will be discussed in greater detail in future chapters.

and other issues. Despite this, some youth remain resilient; that is, they are able to persevere in the face of difficulty and become productive citizens of their communities. Youth are generally considered resilient when they are able to rely on apparently innate characteristics to fend off or recover from life's misfortunes.

Delinquency prevention experts ask why some youth thrive despite inauspicious beginnings while others do not.[60] One possible answer comes from a 2010 study at Duke University, in which researcher Joanna Maselko found that the quality of a mother's interaction with her young child is crucial in determining levels of stress and anxiety as the child grows older. Specifically, Maselko found that providing high levels of material affection to children through eight months of age was associated with stress reduction and produced "long-lasting positive effects on mental health well into adulthood."[61]

Some researchers contend that youth best learn resiliency when they reside in environments that (1) offer caring and supportive relationships, (2) hold high expectations for behavior and attitudes (for themselves and for others), and (3) provide opportunities for meaningful participation in family and community activities.[62] Others believe that children who survive risky environments benefit in large part from either inherent or acquired personal qualities such as strong self-confidence, coping skills, and the ability to avoid risky situations.[63] Some experts also suggest that we are all born with an innate capability for resilience through which we are able to develop social competence, problem-solving skills, critical consciousness, a sense of autonomy, and a sense of purpose and accountability.[64] Throughout this text, we attempt to identify characteristics that resilient youth possess and that enable them to realize successful life outcomes, notwithstanding the presence of other high-risk environment situations.

▶ The Three Themes of This Text

Before concluding this introductory chapter, it is important to discuss the three themes that flow through this text. The first theme focuses on *delinquency prevention*. The second theme, *delinquency across the life course*, examines risk factors that contribute to delinquent behavior and looks at how such behavior impacts subsequent life experiences. *Delinquency and social policy* forms our third theme, and it is one that asks what can be done to improve the effectiveness of treatment, to reduce recidivism rates, and to elevate the quality of young people's lives.

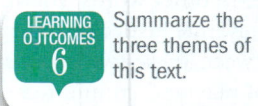

LEARNING OUTCOMES 6: Summarize the three themes of this text.

Delinquency Prevention

The first of our themes is *delinquency prevention*. The prevention of delinquency can be accomplished by effective social programs, or it may involve efforts to enhance the personal characteristics that shield young people from negative environmental influences as they are growing up. At the individual level, one of the most important concepts in the area of delinquency prevention is **resiliency**. We know that many of today's youth face a host of negative influences in their lives, including substance abuse, gang affiliation, teenage pregnancy, school violence, bullying,

Delinquency Across the Life Course

Our second theme, *delinquency across the life course*, examines risk factors that contribute to delinquent behavior and asks how such behavior affects subsequent life experiences.[65] **Developmental life-course (DLC) theory** is concerned with four main issues in the study of delinquency: (1) the development of offending and antisocial behavior, (2) protective factors, (3) the risk of offending at different ages, and (4) the effects of life events on the course of a person's social and personal development. DLC theory attempts to integrate what is known about the individual, family, school, peers, and the community with situational influences that may either encourage or discourage offending. It also integrates key elements of preexisting theories that attempt to explain delinquency, such as strain theory, control theory, differential association theory, and social learning theory (all of which will be discussed later in this text).[66]

Finally, DLC holds that human development and aging are lifelong processes and that people are rational actors who make informed choices as they go through life. The choices that people make, however, can be influenced by "turning points," or life experiences (such as getting married, finding a job, graduating from college, and so on), that strengthen social ties. According to life-course criminology: (1) crime is more likely to occur when an individual's ties to the wider society are disrupted, and (2) the trajectory of a person's life course tends to be continuous.[67]

Our second theme, *delinquency across the life course,* examines risk factors that contribute to delinquent behavior and asks how such behavior affects subsequent life experiences.

Principle 1
Crime is more likely to occur when an individual's ties to society are attenuated.

Principle 2
Delinquency and other forms of antisocial behavior in childhood are strongly related to troublesome adult behaviors including crime as well as other problem behaviors in a variety of life domains.

Principle 3
Social ties embedded in adult transitions explain variation in crime unaccounted for by childhood propensities. The adult life course matters.

Principle 4
Human agency is vitally important to understanding patterns of stability and change in criminal behavior over the life course. Individuals, whether criminal actors or not, make choices and are active participants in the construction of their lives.

Principle 5
A dual policy focus emphasizing prevention and reform should be the central feature of criminal justice practices.

FIGURE 1–6 Principles of Life-Course Delinquency.
Source: "Principles of Life-Course Delinquency" by John H. Laub, from "Searching for the Soul of Criminology Seventy Years Later" by Edwin H. Sutherland and Michele-Alder, from CRIMINOLOGY, May 2006. Copyright © 2006 by American Society of Criminology. Reprinted with permission.

Hence, it becomes important to explain why some young people experiment with acts of delinquency early on in life, but do not continue with criminal careers into adulthood.

John A. Laub identified five principles of what he, along with collaborator Robert Sampson, called *life-course criminology*. Laub asserts "that these [principles] can provide the basis of a paradigm on the causes and dynamics of crime." See Figure 1–6 for the principles of life-course delinquency, as identified by Laub in a speech given at the American Society of Criminology about ten years ago.

Delinquency and Social Policy

Delinquency and social policy forms our third theme—one that asks what can be done to improve the quality of young people's lives and provides ideas for effectively treating and controlling youth crime. In numerous publications, including the Children's Defense Fund's *State of America's Children 2014*, we are reminded of the cost to society of letting vast numbers of young people grow up without realizing their full potential. To encourage juveniles to stay on the path to successful adulthood, it is necessary to champion policies and programs that lift children out of poverty, protect them from abuse and neglect, and ensure their access to health care, quality education, and a solid moral and spiritual foundation. What this kind of success requires is healthy communities, constructive peer relationships, productive after-school and summer programs, and positive role models.[68]

When social programs are based on research evidence showing that they work, they are said to be *evidence-based*. The OJJDP offers a model programs guide (MPG) of evidence-based prevention and intervention programs, which is available on the Web at http://www.ojjdp.gov/mpg. The MPG database of over 200 evidence-based programs covers the entire gamut of youth services, from prevention, through sanctions, to reentry. The OJJDP says that the MPG "offers a database of scientifically proven programs that address a range of issues, including substance abuse, mental health, and education programs."[69] The guide can be used to assist juvenile justice practitioners, administrators, and researchers seeking to enhance accountability, ensure public safety, and reduce recidivism. See Figure 1–7 for a visual representation of the relationship between research, theory, and social policy.

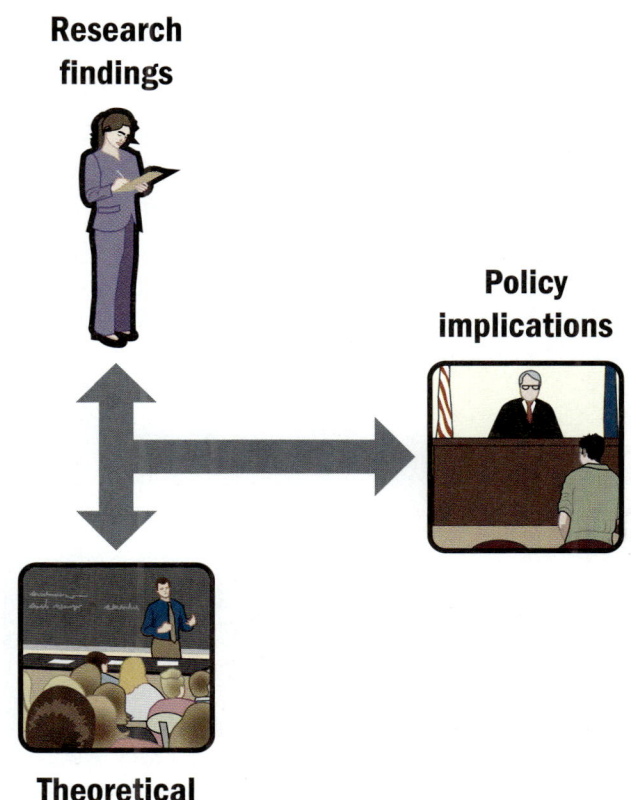

FIGURE 1–7 The Relationship Among Research, Theory, and Social Policy.

As the figure shows, the two basic tools of science are research and theory. Each helps to guide and direct the other. Research identifies appropriate methods to collect data, helps to identify concepts to be studied, tests ideas for their impact on the subject under study, analyzes-related concepts, and suggests new directions for theory. Theory points the way to new research, helps develop new concepts, builds interconnections among concepts, interprets old and new ideas, builds systems of thought, and leads the way to new social and theoretical conclusions. Research collects and theory analyzes; research discovers and theory explains; research disproves and theory reorders.[70] Policy recommendations will be taken more seriously by policymakers if they are based on research findings that are inextricably bound to sound theory.

THE CASE

The Life Course of Amy Watters, Age Five

Until she was five years old, Amy Watters didn't know that she lived a life different from most children. Shortly after she was born her mother, Kassey, was killed in a car accident. Amy was only six months old at the time, and had no recollection of her mother as she started kindergarten. She had been raised by her father, Simon—a loving, but hard-working man—and by her older sister, Jordan. On her first day in kindergarten, however, she was unsettled to see the many doting mothers who accompanied the other children to school. Amy's father had dropped Amy off at the school, leaving her in the hands of a capable teacher, before rushing off to work. Jordan, a sixth grader, had taken the bus to school.

Although Amy sensed on that first school day that something was different about her, she was unaware of recently published life-course research showing that the more mothers shower their young children with warmth and affection, the less anxious, hostile, and distressed those children will likely be as adults. Other studies, published at about the same time, revealed the important role of genetics in personality development, showing that children of parents with anxiety disorders are up to seven times more likely than other children to develop anxiety problems themselves.

There had also been another significant event in Amy's life that happened even before she was born. When her mother was eight months pregnant, a category 3 hurricane struck southern Florida where the family lived. Although no one in the family was physically injured, the experience had been stressful for Amy's parents and sister, and had resulted in quite a bit of damage to their home and to the surrounding community. Again, although Amy didn't know it, studies have demonstrated that stressful events like hurricanes can have a lasting impact on fetal development.

Discuss
1. What have been the most significant influences in Amy's young life? What things might have happened differently, causing her life to take a different direction?

Learn more on the Web:
- Learn more about the causes and correlates of girls' delinquency from the Girls Study Group via http://justicestudies.com/girls_study_group.pdf.

Follow the continuing Amy Watters saga in the next chapter.

CHAPTER 1 Adolescence and Delinquency

Compare how society treats adolescents today with how it handled them in the past.

Delinquents today are treated very differently than they have been in the past, partially because of changing understandings of adolescence. Such changes have been wrought by both cultural advances and studies of human development, including brain science and neuropsychological development.

1. How has the cultural understanding of adolescence changed over time?
2. How have such changes contributed to "the lengthening of adolescence"?

juvenile delinquency An act committed by a minor that violates the penal code of the government with authority over the area in which the act occurs.

adolescence The life interval between childhood and adulthood; usually the period between the ages of 12 and 18 years.

Give examples of high-risk behaviors that characterize contemporary adolescence.

Such behaviors include histories of physical abuse and sexual victimization, educational and vocational skill deficits, bullying, and involvement in alcohol and drug abuse.

1. Why are factors such as physical and sexual abuse, and alcohol and drug abuse, related to delinquency?
2. How are deficits in vocational and educational skills related to delinquency?

juvenile A youth at or below the upper age of juvenile court jurisdiction in a particular state.

status offense A nondelinquent/noncriminal offense; an offense that is illegal for underage persons but not for adults. Status offenses include curfew violations, incorrigibility, running away, truancy, and underage drinking.

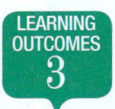
Define *delinquency* and explain what the term means in contemporary context.

Juvenile delinquency is an act committed by a minor that violates the penal code of the government with authority over the area in which the act occurs. In many jurisdictions the authority of the juvenile court extends to the 18th birthday, but some states set the 16th birthday as the limit of juvenile court jurisdiction. A few use an even younger age.

1. What definition of delinquency does this text use?
2. How do legal definitions of delinquency differ, if at all, from the popular use of the term?

parens patriae A medieval English doctrine that sanctioned the right of the Crown to intervene in natural family relations whenever a child's welfare was threatened. The philosophy of the juvenile court is based on this legal concept.

delinquent youth A young person who has committed a crime or violated probation.

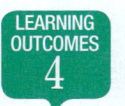
Determine whether or not behaviors should be classified as status offenses.

A status offense is behavior that is an offense only because the person involved is a juvenile. Typical status offenders exhibit incorrigibility at home, run away from home, and are truant from school. Some status offenders commit both status offenses and delinquency, and it is not always easy to separate an offending population into delinquents and status offenders.

1. What is a status offense?
2. What factors might propel a status offender into more severe kinds of offenses?

status offender A juvenile who commits a minor act that is considered illegal only because he or she is underage.

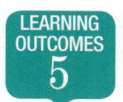

Summarize the contemporary treatment of delinquents.

Delinquents have been treated with harsher punishments in the contemporary era than they have since the beginning of juvenile justice as a separate area of offender treatment in the nineteenth century.

1. Why has a "get-tough" policy for juveniles been seen in the final years of the twentieth century and the early twenty-first century?
2. Do you think that policy will continue for long? Why or not?

deinstitutionalization of status offenders (DSO) the removal of status offenders from secure detention facilities.

Juvenile Justice and Delinquency Prevention (JJDA) Act of 1974 A federal law that established a juvenile justice office within the (now defunct) Law Enforcement Assistance Administration to provide funds for the prevention and control of youth crime.

Office of Juvenile Justice and Delinquency Prevention (OJJDP) A federal agency established with the passage of the 1994 Juvenile Justice and Delinquency Prevention Act.

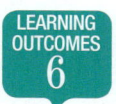

Summarize the three themes of this text.

The three themes of this text are as follows: (1) the *social context of delinquency*, which examines the environment in which youngsters grow up and by which they are influenced; (2) *delinquency across the life course*, a perspective that assesses risk factors that contribute to delinquent behavior and explores how delinquent behavior affects subsequent life experiences; and (3) *delinquency and social policy*, a theme that asks what can be done to improve the quality of young people's lives and focuses on preventing and controlling youth crime.

1. What are the three themes that flow through this text?
2. Why are those themes important to the study of delinquency?

resiliency [Def. to Come]

developmental life-course (DLC) theory A theory concerned with four main issues in the study of delinquency: (1) the development of offending and antisocial behavior, (2) protective factors, (3) the risk of offending at different ages, and (4) the effects of life events on the course of a person's social and personal development.

"Most juvenile crime does not come to the attention of the juvenile justice system."

—Juvenile Offenders and Victims: 2006 National Report

2

The Measurement and Nature of Delinquency

1. Give examples of the types of information provided by each major source of statistics on delinquency.
2. Explain how social factors such as gender, racial/ethnic background, peer pressure, and social class relate to delinquency.
3. Evaluate the factors that influence the length and intensity of juvenile offending.
4. Explain how social policies affect youth violence trends.

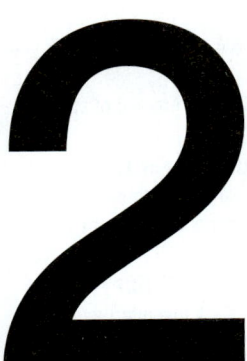

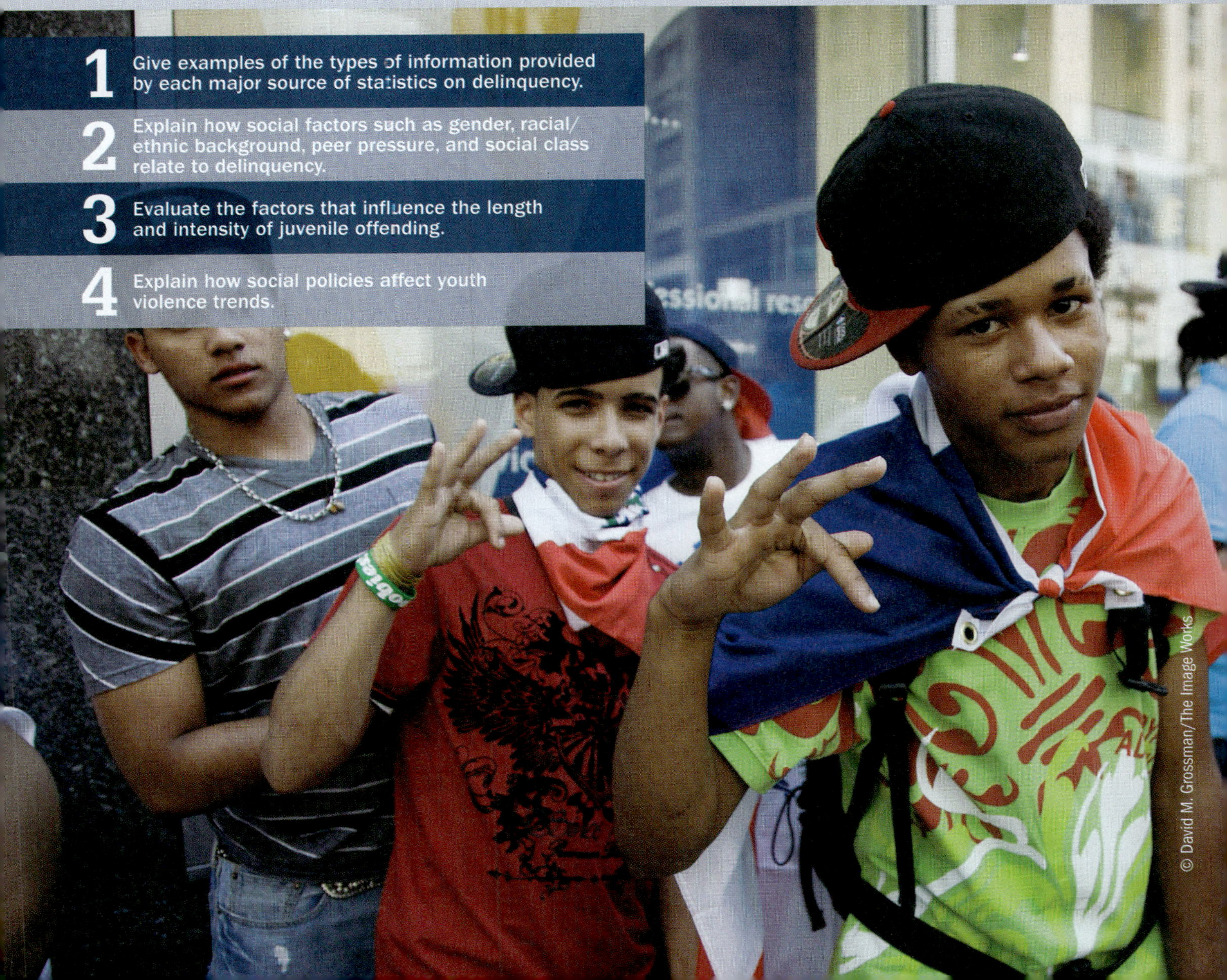

© David M. Grossman/The Image Works

INTRO: SERIOUS JUVENILE CRIME

On December 11, 2013, Ethan Couch, a 16-year-old Texas teenager, received a ten-year probationary sentence for causing four fatalities while driving his truck in an intoxicated state. He had previously pleaded guilty to intoxicated manslaughter and two counts of assault causing serious bodily injury. The crash occurred six months earlier while Couch was driving a Ford F-350 pickup truck. Couch and two of his friends had stolen beer from a nearby Wal-Mart and, while fleeing the scene at 70 miles per hour, rammed into a disabled vehicle that had parked beside the road. Couch had a 0.24 blood-alcohol content, which is triple the legal limit in Texas, and was also high on valium. The judge explained her seemingly "light" sentence by saying that Couch's wealthy parents had never taught him right from wrong. She may have been influenced by a psychologist who had interviewed Couch and cited "Affluenza" as an affliction from which he suffered. *Affluenza*, a word the psychologist coined, was meant to indicate that some people are so financially privileged while growing up that they don't acquire the fundamental values that most of the rest of us have. As of this writing, Couch remains at a juvenile detention center; his defense attorney continues to argue that he needs counseling, not hard time.[1]

Ethan Couch, the 16-year-old Texas teenager who received a probationary sentence after taking the lives of four people while driving under the influence of drugs and alcohol. Was the sentence fair? What sentence would he likely have received had he been an adult?

DISCUSS How do sensational crimes, like the multiple-fatality incident discussed here, fuel public concern over juvenile violence?

Sensational crimes committed by juveniles, like that involving Couch, have fueled public concern over juvenile crime. Even greater concern is elicited when miscarriages of justice seem to occur; the chapter-opening 2013 Texas case fueled public outrage across the nation, with many people questioning how a youth who had caused so much harm could end up with a relatively minor punishment.

In this chapter, however, we will ask some broader questions: Is juvenile crime today more serious than it was in the past? Is it increasing or decreasing? What do we know about violent and chronic delinquents? Is a major juvenile crime wave likely to engulf our society in the future? Are there more juvenile "monsters" now than there were before, or have the media merely sensationalized the violent acts of a few?

To answer these questions, it will be necessary to examine the extent of delinquent behavior, the social factors related to delinquency, the various dimensions of delinquent behavior, and the methods that are used today to measure delinquency.

▶ Major Data Sources in Delinquency

Uniform Crime Reporting (UCR) Program data, **juvenile court statistics**, **cohort studies**, self-report studies, and victimization surveys are the major sources of information that researchers use to measure the extent and nature of delinquent behavior. Knowledge of both the prevalence and the incidence of delinquency is necessary if we are to understand the extent of youth crime. The term **prevalence of delinquency** has to do with the proportion of members of a **cohort**, or specific age category, who have committed delinquent acts by a certain age;[2] **incidence of delinquency** refers to the frequency of offending or to the number of delinquent events.

As this chapter reveals, official statistics on delinquency have strengths, but also serious limitations.

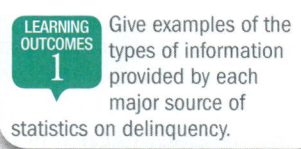

LEARNING OUTCOMES 1: Give examples of the types of information provided by each major source of statistics on delinquency.

Uniform Crime Reports

An examination of *Crime in the United States 2012* (*CUS 2012*), published by the Federal Bureau of Investigation (FBI), indicates that juveniles are arrested for the same kinds of offenses as adults, as well as for status offenses (Figure 2–1). For example, although both adults and juveniles are arrested for such serious

UCR data, juvenile court statistics, cohort studies, self-report studies, and victimization surveys are the major sources of information on the extent and nature of delinquent behavior.

Major Data Sources in Delinquency **19**

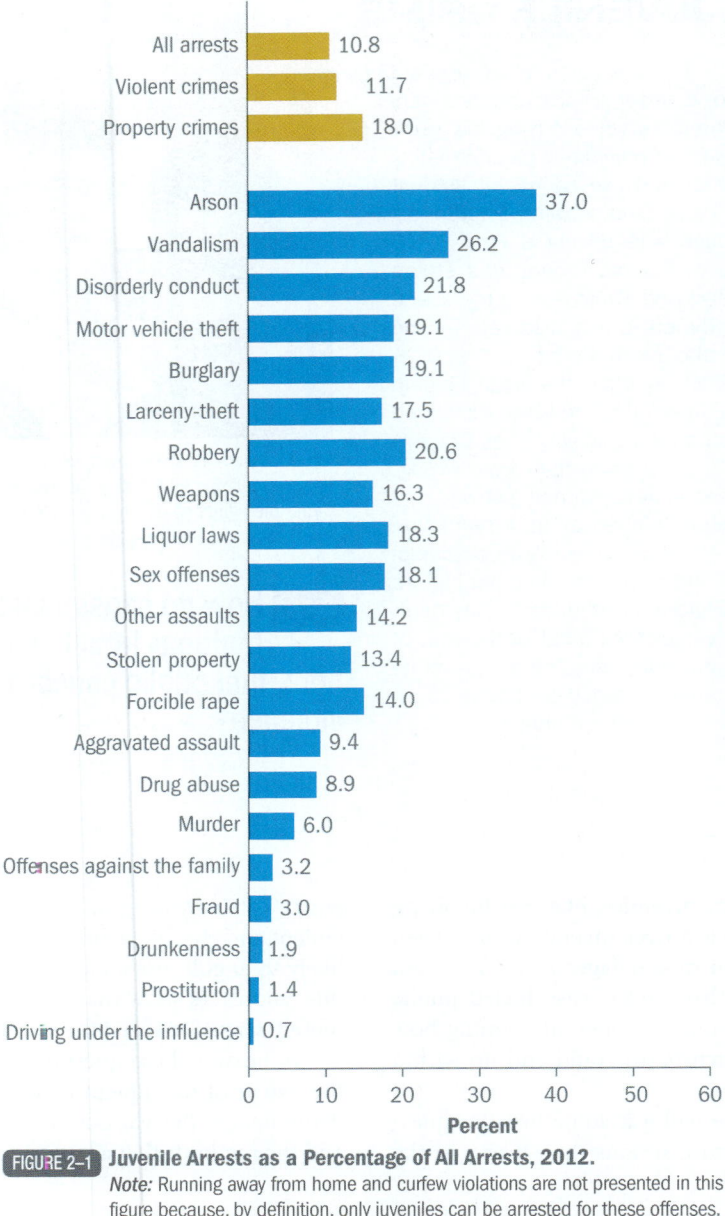

FIGURE 2-1 Juvenile Arrests as a Percentage of All Arrests, 2012.
Note: Running away from home and curfew violations are not presented in this figure because, by definition, only juveniles can be arrested for these offenses.
Source: Data from Federal Bureau of Investigation, *Crime in the United States*, http://www.fbi.gov.

offenses as aggravated assault and murder and for such less serious offenses as simple assault and carrying weapons, only juveniles can be taken into custody for running away, violating curfew, or being truant from school.

In evaluating the measurement of the extent and nature of delinquency in this chapter, one of the most important considerations is the **validity** and **reliability** of the data sources. *CUS 2010* data pose numerous problems. In terms of validity, one of the most serious complaints is that the police can report only crimes that come to their attention. Many crimes are hidden or are not reported to the police; therefore, the UCR Program vastly underestimates the actual amount of crime in the United States. Some critics also charge that because the police arrest only juveniles who commit serious property and personal crimes and ignore most of the other offenses committed by young people, these statistics tell us more about official police policy and practice than about the amount of youth crime. Moreover, youthful offenders may be easier to catch in the act of crime commission than older offenders, with a resulting inflation of the rates for youths. Finally, there is the reliability issue: Do local police departments often manipulate the statistics that are reported to the FBI? The intent may be to make the problem appear worse or better, depending on the reporting agency's agenda (Table 2-1).

Crime by Age Groups

The UCR Program examines the extent of juvenile crime; compares youth crime to adult crime; considers gender and racial

TABLE 2-1 | MAJOR SOURCES OF DATA ON DELINQUENCY

Data Source	Sponsoring Agency	Type of Information	General Findings
Uniform Crime Reporting Program	Federal Bureau of Investigation	Arrest statistics	Youth crime is widespread in U.S. society.
National Crime Victimization Survey	Bureau of Justice Statistics	Victimization data	The number of victimizations discovered is much higher than the number of offenses reported to the police.
Juvenile Court Statistics	Office of Juvenile Justice and Delinquency Prevention	Delinquency cases processed in federal courts	Most youths come into juvenile court as a result of the filing of a petition or complaint.
Self-Report Surveys	Universities/academic researchers	Individual self-reports of involvement in delinquency and crime	A large amount of hidden delinquency occurs, and is not reported in official statistics.

variations in youth crime; and presents urban, suburban, and rural differences in youth crime. Following are the chief findings of the *CUS 2012* data as they relate to juveniles:[3]

1. Youth crime is widespread in U.S. society. For example, the *CUS 2012* data revealed that 968,534 juveniles under age 18 were arrested in that year. Whereas juveniles between the ages of 10 and 17 constituted about 25 percent of the U.S. population, youths in this age group were arrested for 11.7 percent of the violent crimes and 18.0 percent of property crimes.

2. The percentages of total arrests involving juveniles are highest in curfew breaking, disorderly conduct, liquor-law violations, drug-abuse violations, vandalism, larceny-theft, and runaways.

3. Juveniles are arrested for serious property offenses as well as violent offenses. As Figure 2–1 indicates, juveniles were arrested for 19.1 percent of all burglaries, 20.6 percent of robberies, 16.3 percent of weapon offenses, 6.6 percent of murders, and 9.4 percent of aggravated assaults in 2012.

4. Juvenile murder rates increased substantially between 1987 and 1993. In the peak year of 1993, there were about 3,800 juvenile arrests for murder; between 1993 and 2003, however, juvenile arrests for murder declined, with the number of arrests in 2012 (560) averaging less than one-fifth of the 1993 figure.

5. As Figure 2–2 shows, not all types of juvenile crime are declining. Since 1980, for example, the number of juvenile arrests for minor assaults has almost tripled, and arrests

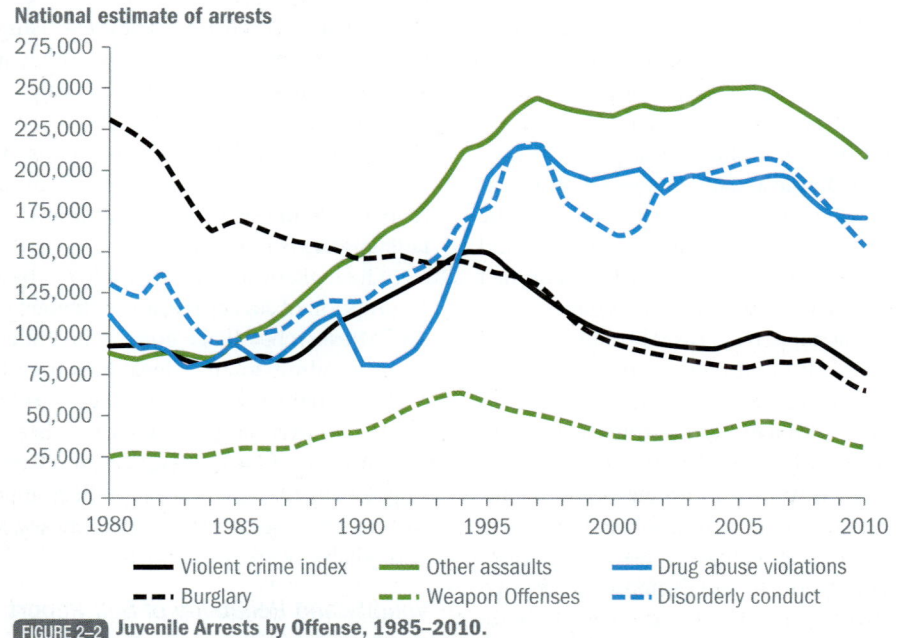

FIGURE 2-2 Juvenile Arrests by Offense, 1985–2010.
Source: National Research Council, *Reforming Juvenile Justice: A Developmental Approach* (Washington, D.C.: National Academies Press, 2014), pp. 3–34.

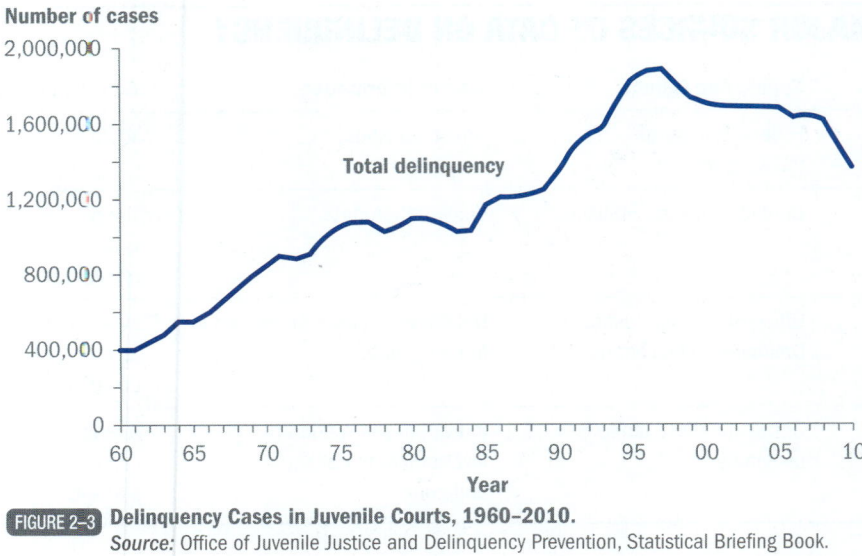

FIGURE 2-3 Delinquency Cases in Juvenile Courts, 1960–2010.
Source: Office of Juvenile Justice and Delinquency Prevention, Statistical Briefing Book.

for drug-abuse violations and disorderly conduct have more than doubled.

6. Juvenile females arrested in 2012 represented 25.5 percent of all juvenile arrests for that year.

Juvenile Court Statistics

Most information about the number of children appearing before the juvenile court each year comes from the publication *Juvenile Court Statistics*, released annually by the Office of Juvenile Justice and Delinquency Prevention (OJJDP), an arm of the U.S. Department of Justice.[4] The number of children appearing before the juvenile court significantly increased from 1960 until the early 1980s, when it began to level off. It then started to rise again and continued to rise until the late 1980s, when it began to level off again. In 2014 OJJDP released data on 2010 delinquency cases, showing that juvenile courts in the United States handled an estimated 1.4 million delinquency cases—a significant decline from 15 years earlier (Figure 2-3).[5] Thirty-seven percent of these cases were property cases, 25 percent were personal offenses, 26 percent were public-order offenses, and 12 percent were drug offenses. The largest percentage of violent offenses consisted of simple assaults, followed by aggravated assaults, and then robberies; larceny-theft made up the largest number of property offenses, followed by burglary and vandalism, and obstruction of justice and disorderly conduct comprised the largest percentages of public-order offenses.

The OJJDP describes what happens to cases brought into the system. For example, 54 percent of all delinquency cases were petitioned; that is, these youths came into the juvenile court as a result of filing a petition or complaint requesting the court to declare the youths as delinquent or dependent, or to transfer the youths to an adult court. In terms of nonpetitioned delinquency cases, 46 percent of the total were informally handled cases in which authorized court personnel screened the cases prior to the filing of a formal petition and decided not to prosecute the offenders.[6] In 2010, 1,368,200 juveniles were brought before the court. See Figure 2-4, which shows how those cases were processed.

The data found in the publication series *Juvenile Court Statistics*, like the *CUS* data, have some serious limitations. Their validity is compromised by the usual time lag between gathering and publishing these statistics and by the fact that the cases reported make up only a small percentage of the total number of juvenile offenses. Other data collected by the National Institute of Juvenile Justice and Delinquency Prevention also represent only an estimate of juvenile crimes that come to the attention of the juvenile court. Still, these national statistics, as well as statistics of local juvenile courts, provide a means by which researchers can examine the characteristics of referred juveniles and the emerging trends in juvenile justice.

Self-Report Studies

In the late 1950s and 1960s, the use of delinquency studies that relied on official statistics of incarcerated populations declined, whereas self-report surveys using community or school samples rapidly increased.[7] Like other forms of measurement, **self-report studies** have shortcomings, but criminologists generally consider them to be helpful tools in efforts to measure and understand delinquent behavior. The main justifications for self-report surveys are that large proportions of youthful offenders are never arrested and that a large amount of **hidden delinquency** is not contained in official arrest statistics.

The logic of self-report studies is based on the fundamental assumption of survey research: "If you want to know something, ask."[8] Researchers have gone to juveniles themselves and asked them to admit to any illegal acts they have committed. However, self-report studies have been criticized for three reasons: Their research designs have often been deficient, resulting in the drawing of false inferences; the varied nature of social settings in which the studies have been undertaken makes it difficult for investigators to test hypotheses; and the studies' validity and reliability are questionable.[9]

Validity and Reliability of Self-Report Studies

The most serious questions about self-report studies relate to their validity and their reliability. In terms of validity, how can

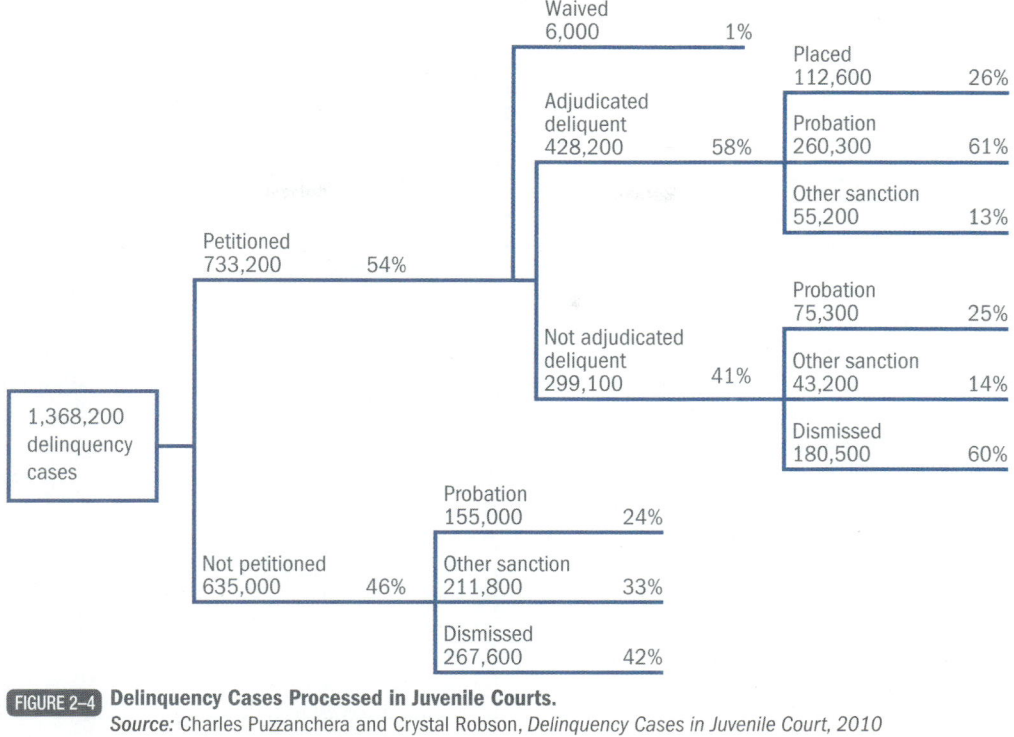

FIGURE 2–4 Delinquency Cases Processed in Juvenile Courts.
Source: Charles Puzzanchera and Crystal Robson, *Delinquency Cases in Juvenile Court, 2010* (Washington, D.C.: Office of Juvenile Justice and Delinquency Prevention, 2014).

researchers be certain that juveniles are telling the truth when they fill out self-report questionnaires? The evidence tends to suggest that self-report studies underestimate the illegal behavior of seriously delinquent youths, because any juvenile who has committed frequent offenses is less likely to answer questions truthfully than is the youth who is less delinquent.[10]

Reliability gauges the consistency of a questionnaire or an interview, that is, the degree to which administration of a questionnaire or an interview will elicit the same answers from the same juveniles when they are questioned two or more times. After analyzing the reliability of self-report studies, Hindelang and colleagues concluded that "reliability measures are impressive, and the majority of studies produce validity coefficients in the moderate to strong range."[11]

Findings of Self-Report Studies

Self-report studies also commonly agree that almost every youth commits some act of delinquency.[12] Of course, offenders who commit violent or predatory crimes are more likely than minor offenders to be arrested and referred to juvenile court; yet Franklin W. Dunford and Delbert S. Elliott found that of 242 self-reported career offenders, 207 (86 percent) had no record of arrest during a three-year period when they were involved in frequent and serious delinquent offenses.[13] (Figure 2–5 provides an example of a self-report questionnaire.)

Self-report studies conducted in the early 1990s in several locations, as part of the Program of Research on the Causes and Correlates of Delinquency, showed that a surprisingly large proportion of juveniles committed violent acts, as follows:[14]

- By the time they were 10th or 11th graders, 54 percent of the Denver (Colorado) juveniles and 58 percent of the Rochester (New York) youths reported that they had been involved in a violent crime at some time in their lives.

- Chronic violent offenders, constituting 14 percent of the sample in Denver and 15 percent in Rochester, accounted for 82 percent of the violent offenses in Denver and 75 percent of the violent offenses in Rochester.

According to these self-report studies, a large proportion of those who became involved in violent behavior at an early age later became chronic violent offenders. In Denver, chronic violent offenders reported a total of 4,134 violent crimes, an average of 33.6 per person; and in Rochester, chronic violent offenders reported 5,164 violent acts, an average of 51.7 per person.[15]

David S. Kirk, using official and self-report arrest data on a sample from the Project on Human Development in Chicago Neighborhoods, examined whether the life course of adolescent crime appears differently across self-report and official crime data and found that a sizable number of juveniles self-report being arrested without having a corresponding official arrest record, and a sizable proportion of those juveniles with an official arrest record failed to self-report that they had been arrested. Yet despite significant differences across the two arrest measures on many criminal career dimensions, parent–child conflict, effects of family supervision, and neighborhood disadvantage operated similarly across these two types.[16]

The desire to uncover the true rate of delinquency and the recognition that official statistics on juvenile delinquency have serious limitations have led to a growing reliance on the use of self-report studies. Taken together, these studies appear to reveal the following:

1. Considerable undetected delinquency takes place, and police apprehension is low—probably less than 10 percent.

Please indicate how frequently in the past 12 months you did each of the following (circle the best answer).

Stole something of little value	Never	Once	2–5 Times	6–10 Times	Over 10 Times
Stole something worth more than $100	Never	Once	2–5 Times	6–10 Times	Over 10 Times
Broke into a place to do something illegal	Never	Once	2–5 Times	6–10 Times	Over 10 Times
Beat up or hurt someone on purpose	Never	Once	2–5 Times	6–10 Times	Over 10 Times
Carried a gun or a knife	Never	Once	2–5 Times	6–10 Times	Over 10 Times
Took a car without the owner's permission	Never	Once	2–5 Times	6–10 Times	Over 10 Times
Took money by threatening someone with a weapon	Never	Once	2–5 Times	6–10 Times	Over 10 Times
Smoked marijuana	Never	Once	2–5 Times	6–10 Times	Over 10 Times
Used cocaine	Never	Once	2–5 Times	6–10 Times	Over 10 Times

FIGURE 2–5 Example of a Self-Report Questionnaire.

2. Juveniles in both the middle and lower classes are involved in considerable illegal behavior.
3. Not all hidden delinquency involves minor offenses; a significant number of serious crimes are committed each year by juveniles who elude apprehension by the police.
4. Socioeconomically lower-class youths appear to commit more frequent delinquent acts, especially in their early years, and are more likely to be chronic offenders than are youths in the socioeconomic middle class.
5. African Americans are more likely than Caucasians to be arrested, convicted, and institutionalized, even though both groups commit offenses of similar seriousness.
6. Females commit more delinquent acts than official statistics indicate, but males still appear to commit more delinquent acts and to perpetrate more serious crimes than do females.
7. Alcohol and marijuana are the most widely used drugs among adolescents, but other drug use has decreased in recent years.
8. Annual surveys of high school youths have revealed that some drug offenses have increased but others have not. Overall crime trends, especially in the population of 17- to 23-year-olds, failed to indicate any increased tendency toward criminality.[17]

Victimization Studies

Findings from the 2012 National Crime Victimization Survey (NCVS), conducted annually by the Bureau of Justice Statistics and administered by the U.S. Census Bureau, showed that persons 12 years or older suffered over 26 million criminal victimizations per year, of which almost 19.6 million were property crimes and 6.8 million were violent crimes.[18] Over 15 million crimes of theft were included in the property-crime category. Overall, the number of victimizations discovered was much higher than the number of offenses reported to the police. See Figure 2–6 for changes in crime victimization rates between 1993 and 2012, including those reported to authorities and those not reported.

NCVS data show that juveniles are highly overrepresented in comparison to other age groups in the population of those victimized. Juveniles between the ages of 16 and 19 experience the highest victimization rate of any age group for all violent crimes, and youths between the ages of 12 and 15 have the next highest rate, with rates dropping with the victim's increasing age. Data also showed that adolescents are more

Juveniles are highly overrepresented in comparison to other age groups among those victimized.

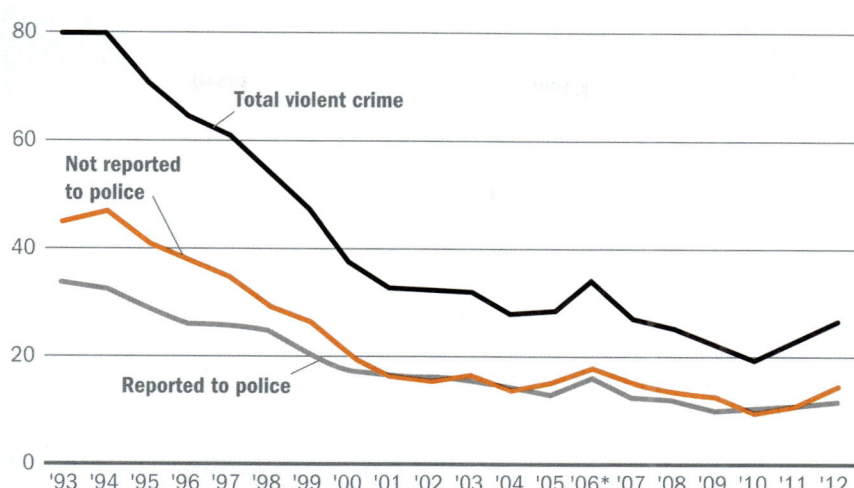

FIGURE 2-6 Violent Crime Victimization Rates, 1993–2012.
Note: Violent crimes include rape, robbery, and aggravated and simple assault. Property crimes include burglary, theft, and motor vehicle theft.
Source: Jennifer Truman, Lynn Langton, and Michael Planty, *Criminal Victimization, 2012* (Washington, D.C.: Bureau of Justice Statistics, 2013).

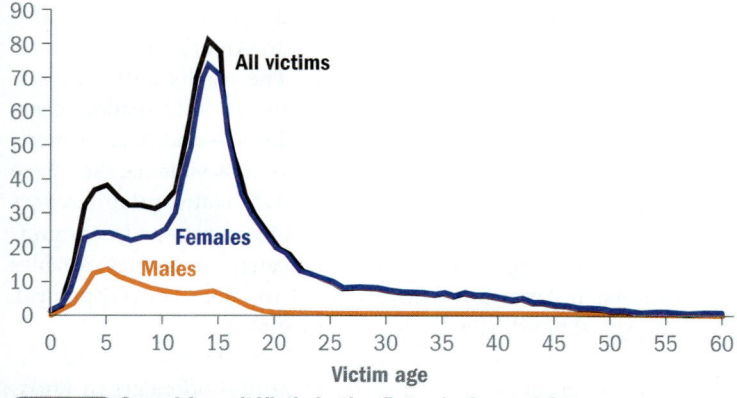

FIGURE 2-7 Sexual Assault Victimization Rates by Age and Sex.
Source: Office of Juvenile Justice and Delinquency Prevention, *Juvenile Offenders and Victims: 2006 National Report* (Washington, D.C.: Author, 2006), p. 31.

likely than adults to commit violent crimes against peers and to report knowing their assailants. Crimes against adolescents are also less likely to be reported to the police than are crimes against adults.[19]

Within the adolescent population, males are more likely than females to become victims of most violent crimes, but females are much more likely to be victims of rape and sexual assault (see Figure 2-7). The survey also revealed that African Americans are several times more likely than Caucasians to be victims of violence overall—including rape, sexual assault, aggravated assault, and robbery. Finally, the NCVS showed that persons aged 16 to 19 experienced overall violence, rape, sexual assault, and assault at rates at least slightly higher than rates for individuals in other age categories.[20]

Although victimization surveys have not been used as widely in analyzing delinquency as have the Uniform Crime Reports, *Juvenile Court Statistics*, cohort studies, and self-report studies, they add significantly to what is known about crime in the United States. Following are some of the principal findings of victimization surveys:

1. Much more crime is committed than is recorded, and the discrepancy between the number of people who say they have been victimized and the number of crimes known to the police varies with the type of offense.

2. The rank order of serious offenses reported by victims, with the exception of vehicle theft, is identical to that of the Uniform Crime Reports.

3. The probability of being victimized varies with the kind of crime and with where people live. The centers of cities are more probable sites of violent crimes.

4. Juveniles are more likely to commit crimes, especially property offenses, than any other age group; juveniles also are more likely to be victimized than any other age group.

5. African Americans are overrepresented both as perpetrators and as victims of serious personal crimes. Official arrest data indicate that a somewhat greater proportion of African-American offenders are involved in forcible rape, aggravated assault, and simple assault than the victimization data indicate.[21]

> ## Think About It...
> This chapter notes that adolescent males, generally speaking, are involved in more frequent and more serious delinquency than are adolescent females. Why does gender appear to play such a significant role in delinquency? How might gender be affected by social, cultural, and biological factors that amplify its impact on behavior?

NCVS data have similar problems with validity and reliability as the self-report studies. For example, individuals may define their victimization differently, and if they are asked more than once, they may give different answers to interviewers' questions. Another problem with the validity of NCVS data is that victimizations of people under age 12 are not included. The Uniform Crime Reports have a category of arrests for those age 10, but the NCVS does not.

▶ Social Factors Related to Delinquency

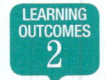

LEARNING OUTCOMES 2 — Explain how social factors such as gender, racial/ethnic background, peer pressure, and social class relate to delinquency.

The first half of this chapter has examined the extent of delinquency in the United States; the second half will focus on the nature of youth crime, another important topic in understanding delinquency. An examination of gender, racial, and ethnic relations; social class; and peer-related research reveals much about the social factors affecting delinquency in U.S. society. The importance of gender in delinquency is examined in Chapter 6, the relationship of social class and delinquency is considered in Chapter 4, and the disproportionate handling of racial and ethnic groups is a major juvenile justice concern addressed in Chapters 11 and 14. Here, we'll focus on the measurement of these important social factors.

Gender and Delinquency

Official arrest statistics show that adolescent males are involved in more frequent and more serious delinquent acts than are adolescent females. Table 2–2 details some of the findings obtained by the various data-gathering strategies. See Figure 2–8 for trends in arrest rates by gender.

Victimization data also show that adolescent females are victimized more often than adolescent males and that, generally speaking, this victimization is influenced by their gender, race, and socioeconomic status (SES). Exactly what leads to such conclusions, however, is not exactly clear. The Seattle Social Development Project's longitudinal survey of 808 youths, for example, a 2010 report, found that gender differences in rates of court referral are unlikely to be attributable to gender bias in juvenile justice processing in law enforcement activities.[22]

Adolescent males are involved in more frequent and more serious delinquent acts than are adolescent females.

Racial/Ethnic Background and Delinquency

Studies based on official statistics have reported that African Americans are overrepresented in arrest, conviction, and incarceration rates relative to their population base. In contrast, most studies using self-report measures have found that African Americans are more likely to be adjudicated delinquent but are not significantly worse than Caucasians in their prevalence or frequency of offending.[23] See Figure 2–9 for arrest rates by race.

One study, using data from the National Longitudinal Survey of Adolescent Health, compared involvement in serious violence for African Americans, Asian Americans, Hispanics, Native Americans, and Caucasians. The results indicated that African-American, Hispanic, and Native American adolescents were involved in significantly higher levels—and Asian Americans in significantly lower levels—of serious violence than were Caucasians. The researchers explained the statistical differences between whites and minority groups by variations in community disadvantage (for African Americans), situational variables (for Asian Americans), involvement in gangs (for Hispanics), and social bonds (for Native Americans).[24]

A recent study found, using both official records and self-report data on samples of serious youthful offenders in Philadelphia and Phoenix, that racial differences of the kind usually seen in the delinquency literature were not evident in their sample of serious offenders.[25]

Another recent study, using the National Longitudinal Study of Adolescent Health, found that African-American adolescents are involved in higher rates of violence, especially armed violence. This study found, however, that African Americans do not have higher rates of serious or minor property or drug crimes.[26]

A further study, this one using the Add Health data collected at the University of North Carolina and involving a national sample of adolescents, found that the combination of neighborhood context, social class, and social psychological processes can explain most of the relationship between race and violence as well as ethnicity and violence.[27]

A 2011 study found that African-American children are more often cited for delinquency infractions in school than are

TABLE 2–2 | GENDER AND DELINQUENCY—FINDINGS FROM VARIOUS SOURCES

The Uniform Crime Reports

- *Crime in the United States 2012* data show that male–female arrest ratios were five to one for drug violations, more than five to one for violent crimes, and more than three to one for property crimes.
- The gender ratios were much closer for some offenses, averaging about two to one for larceny-theft and embezzlement. The overall ratio between adolescent male and female arrests in 2012 was about three to one (females accounted for almost 30 percent of the total arrests).[i] Adolescent males are far more likely to be arrested for possession of stolen property, vandalism, weapons offenses, and assaults; in contrast, adolescent females are more likely to be arrested for running away from home and prostitution (arrests for running away from home account for nearly one-fifth of all female arrests).[ii]

Cohort Studies

- Longitudinal research adds that males are arrested for more serious charges than are females.[iii]
- Furthermore, males are more likely than females to begin their careers at an early age and to extend their delinquent careers into their adult lives.[iv]

Self-Report Studies

- Female delinquency is more prevalent and more similar to male delinquency than official arrest statistics suggest.[v] For example, Hee-Soon Juon and colleagues, following a sample of African-American children from first grade to age 32, found that females who were often punished as first graders were more likely to have later arrests for serious crimes and that males who were from mother-only families were at higher risk of having serious criminal arrests compared to those youths from two-parent families.[vi]

Victimization Data

- Victimization data reveal that adolescent females are more likely to be victims than are adolescent males and that their victimization is shaped by their gender, race, and social class.[vii]
- One study, using pooled National Crime Survey data, found that the female-to-male offending rates for aggravated assault, robbery, and simple assault have increased over time rather than narrowed, and this study—consistent with studies of adolescent girls cited later—failed to reveal an increase in violent offending by females.[viii]
- Gender differences in child abuse are particularly pronounced: Data from the federal Child Welfare Information Gateway (formerly the National Clearinghouse on Child Abuse and Neglect) showed that the rate of sexual abuse is significantly higher for girls (1.7 per 1,000) than for boys (0.4 per 1,000).[ix]

Notes: [i] FBI, *Crime in the United States, 2012* (Washington, D.C.: U.S. Department of Justice, 2013).
[ii] Charles Puzzanchera, *Juvenile Arrests 2011* (Washington, D.C.: Office of Juvenile Justice and Delinquency Prevention, 2013).
[iii] Peter E. Tracy, Marvin E. Wolfgang, and Robert M. Figlio, *Delinquency in Two Birth Cohorts: Executive Summary* (Washington, D.C.: U.S. Department of Justice, 1985).
[iv] Meda Chesney-Lind and Randall G. Shelden, *Girls, Delinquency, and Juvenile Justice*, 3rd ed. (Belmont, Calif.: Wadsworth/Thompson, 2004).
[v] For a review of these studies, see Chesney-Lind and Shelden, *Girls*, pp. 19–23.
[vi] Hee-Soon Juon, Elaine Eggleston Doherty, and Margaret E. Ensminger, "Prospective Study of African Americans," *Journal of Quantitative Criminology* 22 (2006), pp. 193–214.
[vii] Chesney-Lind and Shelden, *Girls*.
[viii] Janet L. Lauritsen, Karen Heijmer, and James P. Lynch, "Trends in the Gender Gap in Violent Offending: New Evidence from the National Crime Victimization Survey," *Criminology* 47 (May 2009), pp. 361–399.
[ix] Cited in Chesney-Lind and Shelden, *Girls*.

---

children from other racial groups.[28] Classroom factors, other school factors, and student behavior were not sufficient to account for this finding, leading these researchers to conclude that underlying social or community features, or racial bias, could explain the results.

Another recent study found that school-level characteristics (e.g., percentages of African-Americans student) were related to overall discipline levels, which is consistent with the "racial thrust" hypothesis. This hypothesis holds that larger racial minority populations cause the majority to feel more threatened by the minority, and, consequently, to prefer the use of stronger social control measures when it comes to offenses committed by minorities. This hypothesis claims to explain why minority students fare less well in school, and are more likely to disengage from school at younger ages than white students.[29] Along the same lines, a 2010 presentation at the American Society of Criminology proposed that ethno-racial inequality in neighborhood crime rates is an outgrowth of racial residential segregation.[30]

In sum, official statistics and self-reports produce conflicting data. Official statistics reported that African Americans tend to be overrepresented in rates of arrest, conviction, and incarceration, but self-report studies have found that African Americans are not significantly worse than Caucasians in their prevalence or frequency of offending. There does appear to be some evidence that African Americans and some other minorities are involved in more serious and violent forms of delinquency than are Caucasians, but this may be influenced by neighborhood context and social class.

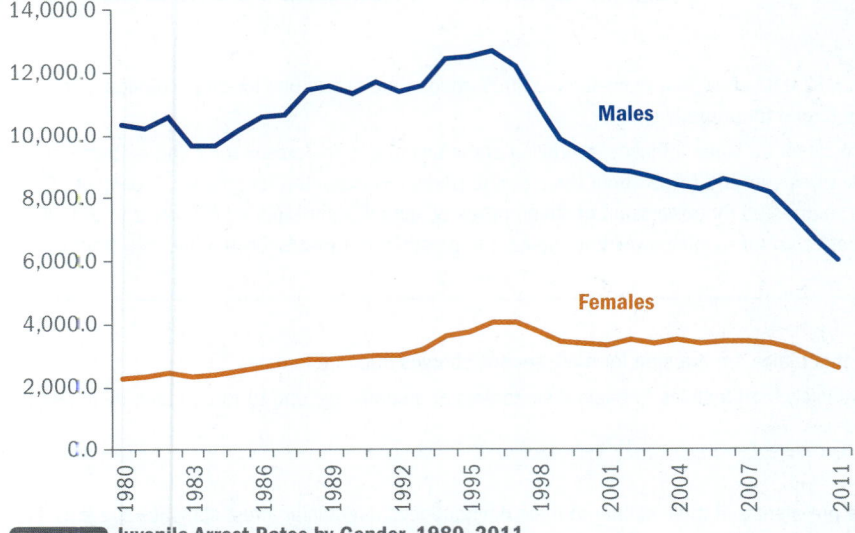

FIGURE 2-8 Juvenile Arrest Rates by Gender, 1980–2011.
Source: Office of Juvenile Justice and Delinquency Prevention, *Statistical Briefing Book*, http://www.ojjdp.gov/ojstatbb/crime/JAR_Display.asp?ID=qa05230.

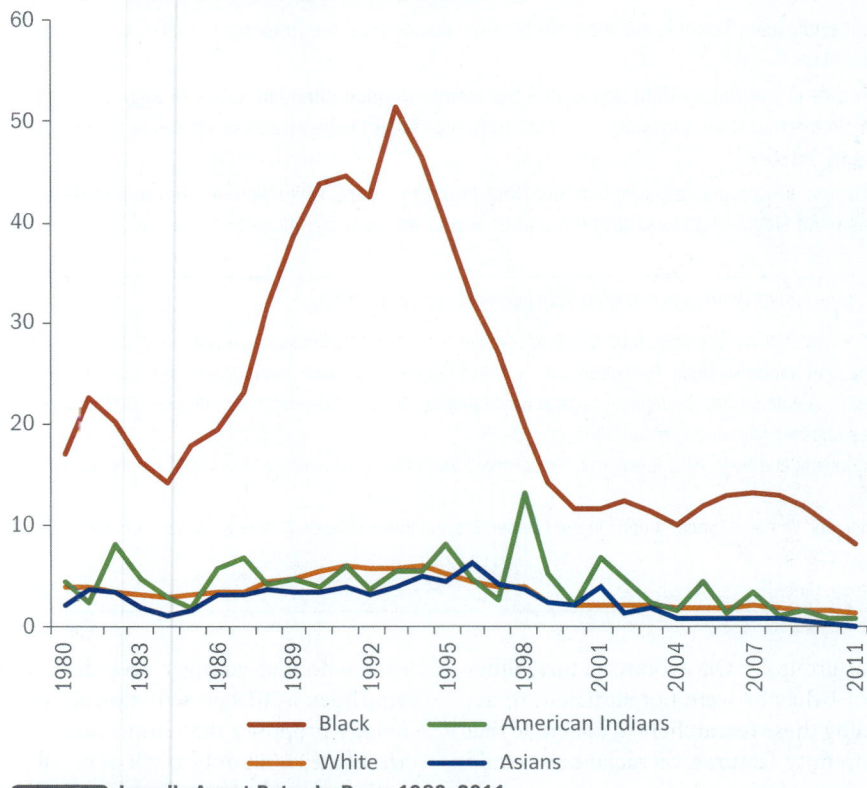

FIGURE 2-9 Juvenile Arrest Rates by Race, 1980–2011.
Source: Office of Juvenile Justice and Delinquency Prevention, *Statistical Briefing Book*, http://www.ojjdp.gov/ojstatbb/crime/JAR_Display.asp?ID=qa05262.

Social Class and Delinquency

Decades of debate still have not produced consensus on the true relationship between social class and delinquency. In particular,

- A review of 35 studies examining the relationship between class and crime concluded that very little support existed for the contention that delinquency is basically a lower-class phenomenon.[31]

- It is also charged that self-report studies overload their questionnaires with trivial offenses, so when middle- and upper-class youths record their participation in such offenses as swearing or violating

> **Research has been unable to find a clear relationship between social class and delinquency.**

curfew, they are found to be as delinquent as lower-class youths.[32]

- One study applied a new self-report measure deemed to be more representative of the full range of official acts for which juveniles could be arrested to a national probability sample of adolescents. These researchers reported class differences in the number of youth crimes in society (prevalence) and in the frequency of delinquent acts for serious offenses (incidence), and their study also revealed class differences in the incidence of nonserious offenses; class differences, according to these researchers, were more pervasive and stronger according to an incidence (as opposed to a prevalence) measure.[33]

In sum, research traditionally has been unable to find a clear relationship between social class and delinquency. It may be that lower-class youngsters vary not in the frequency of delinquent acts from middle- and upper-class youngsters but in the types of delinquent behaviors. It may also be that the delinquent acts of adolescents from lower-class backgrounds are more serious than those committed by youths from upper-class backgrounds.

▶ Length and Intensity of Juvenile Offending

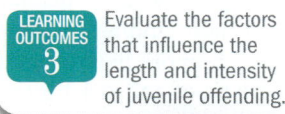

LEARNING OUTCOMES 3: Evaluate the factors that influence the length and intensity of juvenile offending.

One question we might ask is whether delinquency ends with adolescence or if offending behavior tends to continue throughout life. For some individuals, delinquency is strictly confined to their adolescent years, but other individuals, conversely, make a transition from delinquency during adolescence to crime during their adult years.

Developmental life-course criminology is particularly concerned with documenting and explaining individual changes in offending across the life course. This paradigm has greatly advanced knowledge about the measurement of criminal career features such as (1) age of onset, (2) continuation or persistence, (3) escalation of offenses, (4) specialization of offenses, (5) tendency toward chronic offending, (6) and length of criminal career. One of the reasons that developmental life-course criminology became important during the 1990s was the enormous volume of longitudinal research on offending that was published during that decade.[34]

Age of Onset

Several studies have found that the **age of onset** is one of the best predictors of the length and intensity of delinquent careers.[35] In particular,

> **Several studies have found that the age of onset is one of the best predictors of the length and intensity of delinquent careers.**

- Blumstein and colleagues' well-known study showed that one of the factors predicting those who became chronic offenders was offending at an early age.[36]
- Another study showed that those who were first convicted at the earliest ages (10 to 12 years old) offended consistently at a higher rate and for a longer period than did those first convicted at later ages.[37]
- The Seattle Social Development Project data showed that an early age of onset predicted a high rate of offending in both self-reports and court referrals. There was significant continuity of offending in both court referrals and self-reports, but continuity was greater in court referrals; the concentration of offending, as well as the importance of chronic offenders, was greater in self-reports.[38]
- Another study, examining the differences between early- and late-start youthful offenders in a sample of previously incarcerated youths in Oregon's juvenile justice system, determined that youths with foster care experience were four times more likely to be early-start offenders than those without foster care experience and that those youths who had family members convicted of a felony were two times more likely to be early-start delinquents than those with no family felons.[39]

Escalation of Offenses

The findings on **escalation of offenses**, or the increase in the frequency and severity of an individual's delinquent offenses, are more mixed than those on age of onset. In particular,

- Official studies of delinquency have generally found that the incidence of arrest accelerates at age 13 and peaks at about age 17, but this pattern is not so clearly evident in self-report studies.
- Rolf Loeber and colleagues' longitudinal study on the development of antisocial and prosocial behavior in 1,517 adolescent males in Pittsburgh found numerous correlates of escalation in offending among the three samples.[40] They identified three developmental pathways to a delinquent career:

  1. An early "authority conflict" pathway, which consists of a sequence of stubborn behavior, defiance, and authority avoidance
  2. A "covert" pathway, which consists of minor covert behaviors, property offenses, and moderate to serious forms of delinquent behavior
  3. An "overt" pathway, which consists of fighting, aggression, and violence[41]

They concluded that these pathways are interconnected; that is, youths may embark on two or three paths simultaneously. An

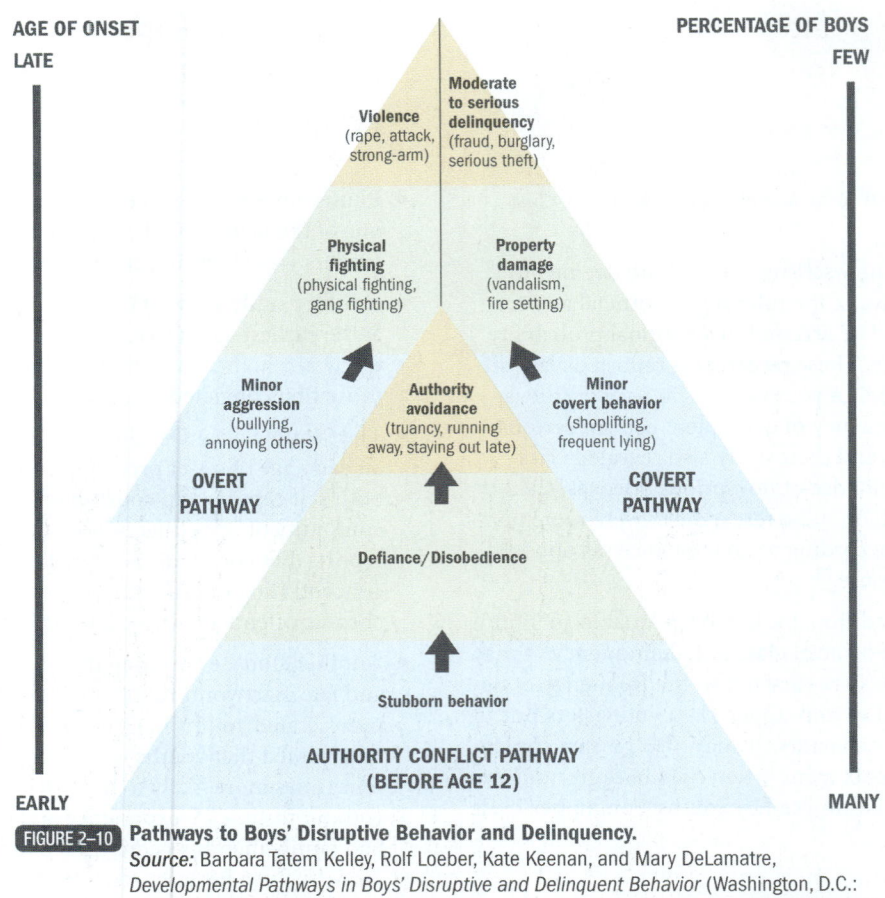

FIGURE 2–10 Pathways to Boys' Disruptive Behavior and Delinquency.
Source: Barbara Tatem Kelley, Rolf Loeber, Kate Keenan, and Mary DeLamatre, *Developmental Pathways in Boys' Disruptive and Delinquent Behavior* (Washington, D.C.: Office of Juvenile Justice and Delinquency Prevention, Bureau of Justice Statistics, 1997), p. 9.

implication of this research is that the youths' problem behaviors may escalate as youths become involved in more than one developmental pathway. See Figure 2–10 for a diagrammatic representation of these three pathways to boys' disruptive behavior and delinquency.[42]

In the mid-1990s, Terrie Moffitt differentiated the small group of early-onset persistent offenders from the much larger category of "adolescence-limited" delinquent males, contending that these two groups differ both in age-related profiles of offending and in patterns of early risk. For persistent offenders, risks center on individual vulnerabilities that were evident early in childhood; in contrast, later-onset adolescence-limited groups are characterized by more marginal levels of psychosocial and individual risks, and their adolescent difficulties are perceived to be prompted by experiencing frustration associated with an adolescent maturity gap and by copying with the behavior of deviant peers.[43] (See Chapter 3 for more discussion of Moffitt's theory.)

More recently, in 2007, Alex Piquero and colleagues, using data from the National Collaborative Perinatal Project, tested Moffitt's hypothesis that life-course-persistent offenders will be at high risk in mid-life for poor physical and mental health, early disease morbidity, and cardiovascular disease. This study found that compared to adolescence-limited offenders, life-course-persistent offenders are more likely to experience adverse physical and mental health outcomes, and they explained these findings by saying that life-course-persistent offenders are more likely than their counterparts to be involved in the type of antisocial lifestyles that increase the chances of adverse health outcomes.[44]

Specialization of Offenses

The majority of early studies found little or no specialization among delinquent populations, but several recent studies have found some evidence of specialization.

One study examined the interaction between gender and age at the onset of offending and asked how these factors relate to specialization. The study determined that offenders who initiated offending earlier in the life course demonstrated more versatility in their offending patterns and that delinquents who began offending at a later age tended to be more specialized. Early-onset females tended more toward offending diversity than early-onset males, whereas among late-onset groups, males tended more toward offending diversity than females.[45] Yet another study found that violent offenders are more likely to engage in additional violent offenses and that nonviolent offenders are more likely to continue nonviolent offense patterns.[46]

> **Think About It...**
>
> Chronic youthful offenders account for the majority of active delinquents. What implications does this fact hold for social policy and the control of delinquency?

D. Wayne Osgood and Christopher J. Schreck, using 2007 data from three studies, further concluded that there are substantial levels of specialization in violence, that specialization remains considerably stable over time, and that the consistent relationships of specialization are partly explained by gender, parental education, and risk seeking.[47]

Chronic Offending

Chronic offending is drawing increased attention for several reasons. Some believe that **chronic youthful offenders** constitute a majority of the active offenders, and the finding that a small number of chronic juvenile offenders accounts for a disproportionate share of all crimes also helps to explain this increased attention. To understand chronic youthful offenders, researchers examine their social background and criminal history and analyze potential predictors of chronic offending. In terms of social background, the vast majority of chronic offenders are identified by most cohort studies as coming from the ever-growing minority underclass that finds itself permanently trapped. As to criminal history, cohort studies consistently report that chronic offenders are more frequently involved in violence than are other juvenile offenders and that they are more likely than other youthful offenders to use crack cocaine or other hard-core drugs or are more likely to traffic drugs to other juveniles at school and in the neighborhood.[48]

Predictors of Chronic Offending

One of the most important but controversial issues is whether chronic juvenile offending can be predicted. In fact, several important studies have identified predictors of chronic offending with delinquent populations.

Blumstein and colleagues identified three population groups in their study: a group of "innocents" never involved with law enforcement, a group of "amateurs" with a relatively low recidivism probability, and a group of "persisters" with a relatively high recidivism probability. They discovered seven factors that distinguished the persisters (or chronics) from other convicted offenders: (1) conviction of crime before age 13, (2) low family income, (3) "troublesome" rating by teachers and peers at ages 8 to 10, (4) poor public school performance by age 10, (5) psychomotor clumsiness, (6) low nonverbal IQ, and (7) convicted sibling.[49]

Farrington and Hawkins found that persistence in crime between 21 and 32 years of age was predicted "by low paternal involvement with the boy in leisure activities, a low degree of commitment to school and low verbal IQ at ages eight to ten years," as well as by heavy drinking and unemployment during the adolescent years.[50]

However, Lila Kazemian and David P. Farrington's 2006 longitudinal study examined residual career length (average remaining number of years in criminal careers until the last offense) and residual number of offenses (average remaining number of offenses in criminal careers), concluding that official records make it difficult to accurately predict criminal career outcomes.[51]

Youth Crimes and Adult Criminality

The experience of having been institutionalized as a juvenile seriously compromises multiple life domains in adulthood, especially for females. Research shows that institutionalization is strongly predictive of premature, unstable, precarious, and unsatisfied conditions in multiple life domains, but is much less predictive of behavior outcomes.[52] In *A General Theory of Crime*, for example, Michael Gottfredson and Travis Hirschi concluded that competent research regularly shows that the best predictor of crime is prior criminal behavior.[53] James Q. Wilson and Richard Herrnstein also observed that "the offender offends not just because of immediate needs and circumstances but also because of enduring personal characteristics, some of whose traces can be found in his behavior from early childhood on."[54] Daniel S. Nagin and Raymond Paternoster, in examining the relationship between delinquency and adult criminality, suggested two interpretations of this relationship. The first is that "prior participation has a genuine behavioral impact on the individual. Prior participation may, for example, reduce inhibitions against engaging in delinquent activity."[55] Nagin and Paternoster referred to such an effect as "state dependence." Another explanation is that individuals have different propensities to delinquency and that each person's innate "propensity is persistent over time." This second explanation is similar to the findings of Gottfredson and Hirschi and of Wilson and Herrnstein.[56] Nagin and Paternoster, in using a three-wave panel set, found that the positive association between past and future delinquency is due to a state-dependent influence.[57] Sampson and Laub sought to explain both the continuity of delinquency into adult criminality and noncriminality (that is, a change) in adulthood for those who were delinquent as children using a basic threefold thesis:

1. Structural context mediated by informal family and school social control explains delinquency in childhood and adolescence.

2. In turn, there is continuity in antisocial behavior from childhood through adulthood in a variety of life domains.

TABLE 2–3 DIMENSIONS OF DELINQUENT BEHAVIOR

Dimension of Behavior	Finding	Consensus
Age of onset	It is the best predictor of length and continuity of delinquent behavior.	Strong
Escalation of offenses	Official studies have generally found that the incidence of arrest accelerates at age 13 and peaks at about age 17.	Mixed
Specialization	The majority of studies have found little or no evidence of specialization.	Fairly strong
Chronic offender	Members of a small group of offenders commit the most serious offenses.	Strong
Youth crimes and adult criminality	Some childhood factors have been identified as contributing to the continuity of criminality.	Very mixed
Lengths of criminal careers	Careers tend to be longer for violent offenders, for those with early convictions, and for minority offenders.	More studies needed to determine outcomes

3. Informal social bonds to work and family in adulthood explain changes in criminality over the life span despite early childhood propensities.[58]

Using life-history data drawn from the Gluecks' longitudinal study, Sampson and Laub found that although adult crime is connected to childhood behavior, both incremental and abrupt changes still take place through changes in adult social bonds, and the emergence of strong bonds to work and family among adults deflects early established behavior trajectories. Sampson and Laub also posited that the events that trigger the formation of strong adult bonds to work and family commonly occur by chance or luck.[59]

In sum, this section addresses some key issues important in evaluating developmental life-course theory. They include why delinquents start offending, how onset sequences are explained, why there is continuity in offending from adolescence to adulthood, why early onset predicts a long criminal career, whether there is versatility in offending, what the main factors are in predicting chronic offenders, and what we know about the lengths of criminal careers.[60] The studies revealed greater consensus on some of these dimensions of delinquent behavior than on others, but together, they do represent a helpful understanding of the nature of delinquent behavior. See Table 2–3 for a summary of these dimensions of delinquent behavior.

The experience of having been institutionalized as a juvenile seriously compromises multiple life domains in adulthood.

▶ Prevention and Control of Delinquency

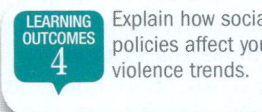

LEARNING OUTCOMES 4: Explain how social policies affect youth violence trends.

One of the most important issues in delinquency today is the continued reduction of youth violence. The national epidemic of youth violence began in the late 1980s, peaked in the 1990s, and then dropped to earlier levels, where it remains today. There is common agreement that this outburst of youth violence was as deadly as it was because more guns were carried and used than ever before. Homicide death rates of males 13 to 17 years old tripled in the 1990s, primarily because of gun assaults.[61]

The police have played a major role in the decline of gun use by juveniles. Their efforts have resulted in a reduction of firearm violence in major cities such as Atlanta, Boston, Detroit, Indianapolis, Los Angeles, and St. Louis. The Boston Gun Project has been one of the most successful efforts; the two main elements of its Operation Ceasefire were a direct law enforcement attack on illicit firearms traffickers supplying juveniles with guns and an attempt to generate a strong deterrent to gang violence. Youth homicides decreased dramatically following the first gang intervention in May 1996 and have remained low to the present.[62]

The Office of Juvenile Justice and Delinquency Prevention (OJJDP) implemented the Partnership to Reduce Juvenile

One of the most important issues in delinquency today is the continued reduction of youth violence.

Gun Violence Program to focus on gun violence and juveniles. Gun ownership, possession, and carrying have led to violence in drug transactions, schools, and gangs. After examining 400 gun violence programs throughout the United States, it was decided that implementation of the seven strategies shown in Figure 2–11 would be required if the program was to achieve its goals.

FIGURE 2–11 Seven Strategies to Reduce Juvenile Gun Violence.

THE CASE

The Life Course of Amy Watters, Age Eight

When Amy was eight years old she was in the third grade. One day, her teacher handed out a one-page questionnaire to all of the students in the class, and asked them to fill in circles with their pencils to answer the ten questions that it contained. Although Amy didn't know it, the anonymous questionnaire was actually a self-report social survey intended to give researchers at a local university insight into instances of early delinquent behavior. The researchers were attempting to identify situations in the lives of young children that might make them more crime-prone. They were also seeking to gain some understanding of the extent of unreported and undiscovered delinquency among the community's children in grades 3 through 6. The fourth survey question asked whether she had ever stolen anything. She answered "yes" to that question, and then circled "drugstore" to provide more details as to where she had stolen from. Although she'd only done it twice, she'd taken items from the beauty section of a Walgreen's pharmacy that she'd visited with her father. One time it was glue-on nails, and the second time it was nail polish. She'd told a couple of friends about it, but her father never knew. Most important, she hadn't been caught. Survey question 9 asked if she was thinking of stealing again, to which she answered "yes."

Discuss
1. What have been the most significant influences in Amy's young life?
2. What things might have happened differently, causing her life to take a different direction?

Learn more on the Web:
- Learn more about the self-report method for measuring delinquency and crime by visiting the National Criminal Justice Reference Service at NCJRS.gov and reading the publication numbered NCJ 185538.

Follow the continuing Amy Watters saga in the next chapter.

CHAPTER 2 The Measurement and Nature of Delinquency

LEARNING OUTCOMES 1

Give examples of the types of information provided by each major source of statistics on delinquency.

Official and unofficial statistics on juvenile delinquency come from the FBI's Uniform Crime Reporting Program, published juvenile court statistics, cohort studies, self-reports, and victimization surveys. They tell us, for example, that youth crime is widespread in U.S. society, and that juveniles today are committing more violent crimes than their counterparts did in the past. It is important to note, however, that juvenile homicide rates have been decreasing since 1994.

1. What are the major sources of delinquency statistics?
2. What do these statistics tell us about the nature and extent of juvenile delinquency in America?

Uniform Crime Reporting (UCR) Program The Federal Bureau of Investigation's program for compiling annual data about crimes committed in the United States.

juvenile court statistics The data about youths who appear before the juvenile court, compiled annually by the National Center for Juvenile Justice.

cohort studies Research that usually includes all individuals who were born in a specific year in a particular city or country and follows them through part or all of their lives.

prevalence of delinquency The percentage of the juvenile population involved in delinquent behavior.

cohort A generational group as defined in demographics, in statistics, or for the purpose of social research.

incidence of delinquency The frequency with which delinquent behavior occurs.

validity The extent to which a research instrument measures what it says it measures.

reliability The extent to which a questionnaire or interview yields the same answers from the same juveniles when they are questioned two or more times.

self-report study A study of juvenile crime based on surveys in which youths report on their own delinquent acts.

hidden delinquency Any unobserved or unreported delinquency.

LEARNING OUTCOMES 2

Explain how social factors such as gender, racial/ethnic background, peer pressure, and social class relate to delinquency.

Social factors relate to delinquency, with researchers noting that lower-class youths are involved in more frequent and more serious offending than are middle-class youths. Long-lasting serious youth crime is primarily found among the lower classes.

1. How do such social factors as gender, racial/ethnic background, peer pressure, and social class relate to delinquency?
2. Why do such factors appear to influence delinquent behavior?

LEARNING OUTCOMES 3

Evaluate the factors that influence the length and intensity of juvenile offending.

The length and intensity of juvenile offending are impacted by things such as the age of onset, an escalation in frequency and types of offending, the specialization of offenders, and a tendency toward chronic offending that continues into adulthood. In short, young people who begin offending early tend to have long delinquent careers; and at least some youthful offenders progress to increasingly serious forms of delinquency, with a handful of youthful offenders going on to become career offenders.

1. What factors influence the intensity of juvenile offending?
2. What factors influence its length?

age of onset The age at which a child begins to commit delinquent acts; an important dimension of delinquency.

escalation of offenses An increase in the frequency and severity of an individual's offenses—an important dimension of delinquency.

chronic youthful offender A juvenile who engages repeatedly in delinquent behavior. The Philadelphia cohort studies defined chronic offenders as youths who had committed five or more delinquent offenses. Other studies use this term to refer to youth involved in serious and repetitive offenses.

LEARNING OUTCOMES 4

Explain how social policies affect youth violence trends.

Gun control policy has the potential to affect youth violence trends because juveniles today are carrying far more guns than in the past. Likewise, the easy availability of handguns has contributed to a growing trend in youth violence in this country.

1. Why is gun control such an important topic within juvenile delinquency?
2. How might social policies regarding gun control affect trends in youth violence?

3

Individual Causes of Delinquency

"America's best hope for reducing crime is to reduce juvenile delinquency and youth crime."

—President's Commission on Law Enforcement and Administration of Justice, 1967

1. Elaborate on how the theoretical constructs of the classical school of criminology explain juvenile delinquency.
2. Summarize rational choice theory and the routine-activities approach and explain their views of delinquency.
3. Identify the three basic assumptions of positivism.
4. Evaluate contemporary biological and psychological positivism in terms of the contributions they make to understanding delinquency.
5. Compare three important developmental studies of delinquency.
6. Explain the importance of theoretical understandings in preventing delinquency.
7. Identify the factors affecting desistence from juvenile offending.

INTRO: CAN NAMES CAUSE DELINQUENCY?

A few years ago, researchers at Shippensburg University in Pennsylvania released results of a study showing that unpopular first names are frequently associated with juvenile delinquency for children of all races.[1] The researchers concluded that unpopular names are probably not the direct cause of crime but are instead correlated with socioeconomic factors that increase the tendency toward juvenile delinquency, such as a disadvantaged home environment, low income, place of residence, and acquisition of cultural values supportive of delinquency. At the same time, it is possible to imagine that some people are unconsciously influenced by the need to live up to their name. The study's authors reviewed other literature showing that job applicants with certain first names were more likely to receive calls back from potential employers, even when their skills and other qualifying attributes were similar to those of other job candidates. The authors suggested that juveniles with unpopular names may be treated differently by their peers, making it more difficult for them to form positive relationships, and may turn to crime or delinquency when their names result in a negative employment bias. Finally, as noted by the study authors, their findings have "potential implications for identifying . . . who may engage in disruptive behavior or relapse into criminal behavior."[2]

In this chapter we offer some possible explanations for delinquent behavior. In contrast to the unconscious influence exerted by unpopular first names described in this chapter's opening story, some authors suggest that much delinquency is caused not by factors beyond the offender's control, but by a conscious thought process that considers the costs and benefits of particular behavior and, with some degree of planning and foresight, reasons whether the behavior is desirable or not.[3]

On the other hand, if something as simple as a first name can impact people's behavior, then they might not be able to make fully conscious choices. This kind of deterministic view—that delinquents cannot stop themselves from committing socially unacceptable behavior because of some overpowering influences—builds on a perspective known as positivism, a major theoretical position in criminology.

A third explanation discussed in this chapter highlights the significance of developmental theories. A developmental approach suggests that while some young people have the opportunity to learn how to act legally and morally, others do not. In such cases, the effects of life circumstances and a lack of moral development can place adolescents on a trajectory with tragic consequences.

First grade children wearing name tags. What might cause some of these children to become delinquent as they enter adolescence?

DISCUSS Do you believe that a person's name can influence his or her life experiences? Can a name contribute to delinquency? Why or why not?

▶ The Classical School and Juvenile Delinquency

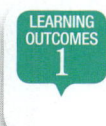

LEARNING OUTCOMES 1: Elaborate on how the theoretical constructs of the classical school of criminology explain juvenile delinquency.

The association between criminal behavior and the rationality of crime has roots in the eighteenth-century classical school of criminology. This school's founders were Charles de Secondat, Baron de Montesquieu; Cesare Bonesana, Marquis of Beccaria; and Jeremy Bentham (see accompanying timeline). These thinkers viewed humans as rational creatures who are willing to surrender enough liberty to the state so that society can establish rules and sanctions for the preservation of the social order; their contributions are as follows:[4]

- *Montesquieu.* In Charles de Secondat's 1747 book *On the Spirit of the Laws*, he argued that "the severity of punishment is fitter for despotic governments whose principle is terror, than for a monarchy or a republic whose strength is honor and virtue." Montesquieu added that under a moderate and lenient government, "the greatest punishment of a bad action is conviction."[5]

- *Beccaria.* In 1764, Cesare Bonesana, Marquis of Beccaria, published *On Crimes and Punishments*. Beccaria based the legitimacy of criminal sanctions on the **social contract**.

> The association between criminal behavior and the rationality of crime has roots in the eighteenth-century classical school of criminology.

TIMELINE: Founders of the Classical School

1747 — **Charles de Secondat, Baron de Montesquieu** argued against severe punishments for crime in his book, *On the Spirit of the Laws*.

1764 — **Cesare Bonesana, Marquis of Beccaria** developed notion of the social contract, and suggested that the purpose of punishment should be "to deter persons from the commission of crime and not to provide social revenge."

1780 — **Jeremy Bentham** contended that punishment would deter criminal behavior, provided it was made appropriate to the crime.

Beccaria saw punishment as a necessary evil and suggested that "it should be public, immediate, and necessary; the least possible in the case given; proportioned to the crime; and determined by the laws."[6] He then defined the purpose and consequences of punishment as being "to deter persons from the commission of crime and not to provide social revenge. Not severity, but certainty and swiftness in punishment best secure this result."[7]

- *Bentham.* In 1780, Englishman Jeremy Bentham published *An Introduction to the Principles of Morals and Legislation*, which further developed the philosophy of the classical school. Believing that a rational person would do what was necessary to achieve the most pleasure and the least pain, Bentham contended that punishment would deter criminal behavior, provided it was made appropriate to the crime. He stated that punishment has four objectives: (1) to prevent all offenses if possible, (2) to persuade a person who has decided to offend to commit a less rather than a more serious offense, (3) "to dispose [a person who has resolved on a particular offense] to do no more mischief than is necessary to his purpose," and (4) to prevent crime at as cheap a cost to society as possible.[8] See the Exhibit 3.1 for the basic theoretical constructs of the classical school of criminology.

According to the principles of the classical school, then, juveniles who commit serious crimes or continue to break the law are presumed to deserve punishment rather than treatment, because they possess free will and know what they are doing. Proponents of the classical school view delinquency as purposeful activity resulting from rational decisions in which offenders weigh the pros and cons and perform the acts that promise the greatest potential gains.[9]

▶ Rationality and Delinquency

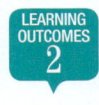

LEARNING OUTCOMES 2: Summarize rational choice theory and the routine-activities approach and explain their views of delinquency.

In the 1970s and 1980s, workers in a variety of academic disciplines, including the sociology of deviance, criminology, economics, and cognitive psychology, began to view crime as the outcome of rational choices and decisions.[10]

The ecological tradition in criminology and the economic theory of markets, especially, have applied the notion of rational choice to crime. Ecological researchers have inferred from the distribution of particular crimes that offenders make rational choices. For example, findings from several studies have revealed that homes on the borderline of affluent districts are at most risk of burglary.[11]

Economic analysis of criminal behavior argues that criminals, like noncriminals, are active, rational decision makers who respond to incentives and deterrents. In economic models of criminal decision making, crime is assumed to involve rational calculation and is viewed essentially as an economic transaction or a question of occupational choice.[12]

EXHIBIT 3.1 | Theoretical Constructs of the Classical School of Criminology

- Human beings are seen as rational creatures who, being free to choose their actions, could be held responsible for their behavior. This doctrine of **free will** was substituted for what previously had been the widely accepted concept of theological determinism, which saw humans as predestined to certain actions.
- Punishment is justified because of its practical usefulness, or utility. No longer was punishment acceptable for purposes of vengeful retaliation or as expiation on the basis of superstitious theories of guilt and repayment. According to **utilitarianism**, the aim of punishment is the protection of society, and the dominant theme is deterrence.
- The classical school sees the human being as a creature governed by a **felicific calculus**—an orientation toward obtaining a favorable balance of pleasure and pain.
- There should be a rational scale of punishment painful enough to deter the criminal from further offenses and to prevent others from following his or her negative example.
- Sanctions should be proclaimed in advance of their use; these sanctions should be proportionate to the offense and should outweigh the rewards of crime.
- Equal justice should be available to everyone.
- Individuals should be judged by the law solely for their acts, not for their beliefs.

> **Rational choice theory is based on the assumption that the delinquent or the criminal chooses to violate the law and has free will.**

Rational Choice Theory

Rational choice theory, borrowed primarily from the utility model in economics, is one of the hottest topics today in criminology, sociology, political science, and law.[13] It is based on the assumption that the delinquent or the criminal chooses to violate the law and has free will. Rational choice theory in its pure form can be seen, at least in part, as an extension of the deterrence doctrine found in the classical school, which includes incentives as well as disincentives and focuses on individuals' rational calculations of payoffs and costs before delinquent and criminal acts are committed.[14]

In a contribution to rational choice theory, some years ago Raymond Paternoster presented what he called a "deterrence/rational choice model" to examine a youth's decision to participate in, continue with, or desist from delinquent acts. Rational choice, according to Paternoster, recognizes that there are "choice-structuring" variables and that choices do not require complete information or rational analytic methods.[15] Similarly, in 2011 Carnegie Mellon University professor Shamena Aniwar and University of Maryland professor Thomas Loughran found that individuals will tend to increase the accuracy of their risk perceptions over time in response to cues they receive during their offending experiences.[16]

Recently, Jeffrey Fagan and Alex R. Piquero showed that both legal socialization and rational choice factors influence patterns of criminal offending over time. This study also shows that both developmental maturity and mental health moderate the effects of perceived crime risks and costs on criminal offending.[17]

The Routine-Activities Approach

Another approach to the rationality of crime is the **routine-activities approach**. This approach links variations in crime rates to changes in the routine-activity structure of U.S. society, and to a corresponding increase in target suitability and a decrease in the presence of "guardians" such as neighbors, friends, and family. For example, the decline of the presence of daytime adult caretakers in homes and neighborhoods, which is partly the result of a trend toward increased female participation in the labor force, has left homes and neighborhoods increasingly vulnerable to criminal activity during daytime hours. Some of the most important studies contributing to the routine-activities literature include the following theorists and their findings:

- Lawrence E. Cohen and Marcus Felson, guided by ecological concepts and the presumed rationality of offenders, developed a routine-activities approach for analyzing crime-rate trends and cycles. They believed that the volume and distribution of predatory crime are related to the interaction of three variables relating to the routine activities of U.S. life: the availability of suitable targets, the absence of capable guardians, and the presence of motivated offenders.[18]
- D. Wayne Osgood and colleagues, in analyzing individual changes in routine activities and deviance across five waves of data from a national sample, found that "unstructured socializing with peers in the absence of authority figures presents opportunities for deviance."[19]
- A 2010 study by Katherine Novak and Lizabeth Crawford examined the extent to which gender differences in delinquency can be explained by gender differences in participation in various routine-activity patterns. Although differential participation in routine activities by gender failed to explain males' high levels of deviance relative to those of females, participation in religious and community activities during the sophomore year in high school seemed to moderate the effect of gender on subsequent deviant behavior.[20]

Table 3–1 provides an explanation of rational choice and routine-activities theories or approaches.

Rational Choice and Delinquency

Some youthful offenders clearly engage in delinquent behavior because of the low cost or risk of such behavior. Much of delinquency can be interpreted as a form of problem-solving behavior in response to the pressures of adolescence. Finding themselves struggling with issues of perceived control; seeking positive evaluation of self; and facing the negative impact of others who punish, sanction, or reject them, delinquents address these problems by deriving short-term pleasures from delinquent

TABLE 3–1 | RATIONAL CHOICE AND ROUTINE-ACTIVITIES APPROACHES

Perspective	Theorist(s)	Principle(s)
Rational Choice	Paternoster	Rational choice does not require complete information for behavior to occur.
Routine Activities	Cohen and Felson	Availability of targets, absence of capable guardians, and presence of motivated offenders reflect the routine activities of life and have contributed to the rise of predatory crime.
Routine Activities	Messner and Tardiff	Their approach provided a useful framework for interpreting homicides in Manhattan.
Routine Activities	Osgood and others	Unstructured socializing with peers and absence of authority figures provide opportunities for crime and deviance.

involvements.[21] Conversely, offenders also may decide on rational grounds that the risks of continued delinquent behavior are not justified by the rewards. Even more to the point, most persistent offenders appear to desist from crime as they reach their late teens or early 20s, claiming that continued criminality is incompatible with the demands of holding a full-time job or settling down to marriage and a family.[22] Desistance from crime, or maturing out of crime, is a process of deciding that the benefits of crime are less than the advantages of ceasing to commit crime.

Yet there are important qualifications in assuming too much rationality in delinquent behavior. Rationality theory is based on the notion that delinquent behavior is planned—at least to some degree. Planning involves (1) formulating a scheme or a procedure for doing something before doing it or having an intention of acting, (2) assessing the possible alternative courses of action available, (3) choosing a particular course, and (4) constructing a complex set of acts to achieve the intended results. But many studies of delinquency have reported that most delinquent behavior is not planned; spur-of-the-moment decision making most frequently characterizes juvenile wrongdoing.[23]

The concept of rationality also assumes that individuals have free will and are not controlled by their emotions, but many youngsters do not appear to have such control. Youths who are mentally ill or who engage in obsessive-compulsive acts, such as compulsive arsonists, kleptomaniacs, and sex offenders, seem to be held in bondage by their emotions. Furthermore, in examining the actual process of rational choice, it is apparent that there are degrees of freedom for all juveniles and that juveniles' rationality is contextually oriented. The notion of degrees of freedom suggests, then, that delinquents "are neither wholly free nor completely constrained but fall somewhere between."[24] The contextual nature of rationality further suggests that in most situations delinquents do have some control over their acts but that in some situations they may have little or no control.

Emory University professor Robert Agnew's examination of hard and **soft determinism** led him to conclude that freedom of choice varies from one individual to another. It is dependent, he said, on factors—such as one's biological, psychological, or social nature—that exist prior to the choices that arise. For example, one individual may be forced to choose between two different alternatives because of psychological limits, but another may have six different alternatives available to him or to her because that person is less limited in his or her perceptions. The latter, Agnew says, has greater freedom of choice.[25]

Delinquency Prevention and the Philosophy of Punishment

If delinquency is rational behavior, then it stands to reason that it can be prevented by the goals and philosophy of punishment. The objectives of criminal punishment can be grouped into the distinct areas of general deterrence, specific deterrence, incapacitation, rehabilitation, restoration, redistribution/just deserts, and equity/restitution. The objectives of rehabilitation, restoration, and equity/restitution are discussed later, but general deterrence, specific deterrence, and incapacitation are briefly examined here.

General Deterrence

Deterrence is a goal of punishment designed to prevent others from committing similar crimes. The public application of punishment produces a **general deterrence** effect designed to signal the community at large that *crime or delinquency does not pay*. By severely punishing those juveniles convicted of delinquency, others who are contemplating delinquency will be frightened, deterred, and discoursed from their planned actions.

Specific Deterrence

The philosophy of **specific deterrence** focuses on the fact that individual offenders should learn firsthand that crime does not pay when they experience harsh delinquent or criminal penalties. What this position suggests is that the suffering caused by punishment should inhibit future criminal or delinquent activities.

Although a few research efforts have found that punishment in the form of specific deterrence can have a substantial impact on future criminal behavior, these studies are balanced by other research that has failed to uncover specific deterrence effects. Most prisoners (more than 80 percent) who are released from prison have had prior convictions, and the great majority (68 percent) will reoffend soon after they are released.[26] The fact that most convicted criminals reoffend weakens the argument that experiencing punishment produces a specific deterrent effect.

Incapacitation

Another goal of punishment is to incapacitate dangerous people so they do not have the opportunity to harm others. Offenders are sentenced to prison to restrain them physically so that society is protected during the time they are confined, a concept known as **incapacitation**. Sentencing for the purpose of incapacitation is embraced by both liberals and conservatives. According to liberals, prison was to be reserved for especially dangerous repeat offenders who require incapacitation to protect society while they are being treated and reformed. Conservatives may be less concerned about treatment but view incapacitation as a crime-prevention strategy that can reduce crime rates by imprisoning significant numbers of felons.

▶ Positivism and Delinquency

This section examines perspectives such as biological and psychological **positivism** to see how they might enhance our understanding of

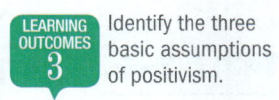

LEARNING OUTCOMES 3 — Identify the three basic assumptions of positivism.

Positivism became the dominant philosophical perspective of juvenile justice when the juvenile court was established in the last year of the nineteenth century.

Think About It...

Rational choice theories say that people make conscious and informed choices about their actions, and that—for whatever reasons—they sometimes choose crime or delinquency instead of conformity. Why might they make choices favoring delinquency? Aren't they concerned about the possible consequences of their choices?

why delinquent behavior occurs. Instead of viewing delinquency as a logical choice from among an available set of alternative behaviors, as rational choice theorists do, positivists argue that the social world operates according to laws or rules just as the physical world does. Hence, according to positivism, delinquents are affected by biological or psychological factors that (1) impair or alter their decision-making abilities and (2) can be identified through the use of social scientific techniques.

Positivism became the dominant philosophical perspective of juvenile justice at the time the juvenile court was established in the last year of the nineteenth century. During the **Progressive Era** (the period from about 1890 to 1920), the wave of optimism that swept through U.S. society led to the acceptance of positivism. The doctrines of the emerging social sciences assured reformers that through positivism their problems could be solved. The initial step was to gather all the facts of the case; equipped with these data, reformers were then expected to analyze the issues in scientific fashion and discover the right solutions.[27]

Armed with these principles, reformers set out to deal with the problem of delinquency, confident that they knew how to find its cause. Some progressives looked first to environmental factors, pinpointing poverty as the major cause of delinquency. Other progressives were attracted also to the doctrine of eugenics and believed that biological limitations drove youthful offenders to delinquency. But eventually the psychological origins of delinquency came to be more widely accepted than either the environmental or biological origins.[28] The positivist approach to youth crime is based on three basic assumptions, as Exhibit 3.2 shows.[29]

▶ Biological and Psychological Positivism and Delinquency

Biological, psychological, and sociological positivism are the three forms of positivism that have been used to explain delinquency. Each is explained here.

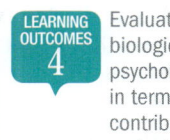

LEARNING OUTCOMES 4 — Evaluate contemporary biological and psychological positivism in terms of the contributions they make to understanding delinquency.

Early Forms of Biological Positivism

The belief in a biological explanation for criminality has a long history. For example, the study of physiognomy, which attempts to discern personal inner qualities through outward physical appearance, was developed by the ancient Greeks. Indeed, a physiognomist of that period charged that Socrates' face reflected a brutal nature.[30]

The attention given to **biological positivism** in the United States can be divided into two periods. The first period was characterized by (1) the nature–nurture debate during the latter part of the nineteenth century and the early twentieth century, and (2) the influence of Italian criminologist Cesare Lombroso's late-nineteenth-century theory of physical anomalies, genealogical studies, and theories of human somatotypes (body types) that represent early approaches relating crime and delinquency to biological factors.[31]

Frequently regarded as the founder of biological positivism, Lombroso is best known for his theory of the atavistic criminal. According to Lombroso, the **born criminal** was atavistic—that is,

---

EXHIBIT 3.2 | Three Assumptions of the Positivist Approach

- The character and personal backgrounds of individuals explain delinquent behavior. Positivism, relegating the law and its administration to a secondary role, looks for the cause of deviancy in the actor.
- The existence of **determinism** is a critical assumption of positivism. Delinquency, like any other phenomenon, is seen as determined by prior causes—it does not just happen. Because of this deterministic position, positivism rejects the view that the individual exercises freedom, possesses reason, and is capable of choice.
- The delinquent is seen as fundamentally different from the nondelinquent, so the task is to identify the factors that have made the delinquent a different kind of person. In attempting to explain this difference, positivism has concluded that wayward youths are driven into crime by something in their physical makeup, by aberrant psychological impulses, or by the meanness and harshness of their social environment.

he is someone who reverts to an earlier evolutionary form or level. Atavistic individuals, according to Lombroso, displayed the primitive characteristics of men and women in earlier evolutionary periods. Such characteristics, Lombroso said, would periodically reappear in certain individuals, leading them to crime because of the primitive impulses that they were also likely to possess.[32]

Around the same time, prominent American psychologist and eugenicist Henry Goddard found that at least half of all juvenile delinquents he studied were mentally defective. His findings sparked intense debate for more than a decade.[33] Goddard's findings conflicted with those of American criminologist Edwin Sutherland, who soon discouraged future investigations of the correlation between intelligence and delinquency.[34] Sutherland, in evaluating IQ studies of delinquents and criminals, concluded that the lower IQs of offenders were related more to testing methods and scoring than to the offenders' actual mental abilities.[35]

Finally, German medical researcher Ernst Kretscher advanced the idea that there are two body types: the schizothyme and the cyclothyme. Schizothymes were said to be strong and muscular, and, according to Kretscher, they were more likely to be delinquent than were the cyclothymes, who were soft-skinned and lacked muscle.[36]

Other famous social researchers of the early 1900s, such as Americans William Sheldon, Sheldon Glueck and Eleanor Glueck, and Juan B. Cortes and Florence M. Gatti, also supported the body-type theory. Cortes and Gatti even drew on the body-type theory to develop an extensive biopsychosocial theory of delinquency.[37]

Contemporary Biological Positivism: Sociobiology and Biosocial Criminology

Central to the second period of biological positivism was **sociobiology**, which stresses the interaction between the biological factors within an individual and the influence of the particular environment. Supporters of this form of biological positivism claim that what produces delinquent behavior, like other behaviors, is a combination of genetic traits and social conditions.[38]

Sociological research has examined the influence of environment and genetics through twin and adoption studies and has also addressed intelligence; neuropsychological factors, including brain functioning and temperament as well as learning disabilities; and biochemical factors in delinquency. Let's look at each of these areas of investigation.

Twin and Adoption Studies

The role of genetic influences on behavior has been suggested by numerous twin and adoption studies.[39] These studies were supported early on by research done in Denmark and other European countries, but more recently they have found support among researchers in the United States.

Twin Studies

The comparison of identical twins (monozygotic [MN]) with same-sex nonidentical (or fraternal) twins (dizygotic [DZ]) provides the most comprehensive data for exploring genetic influences on human variation. Identical twins develop from a single fertilized egg that divides into two embryos; hence, their genes are the same. Fraternal twins develop from two separate eggs that were both fertilized during the act of conception, so about half their genes are the same.[40]

Numerous twin studies have found support for genetic contributions to criminal behavior.

In one such early study, whose results were published in 1955, Scandinavian social scientist Karl O. Christiansen and University of Southern California professor S. A. Mednick reported on a sample of 3,586 twin pairs from Denmark who were followed between the years 1870 and 1920. The subset used by these researchers included almost all the twins born between 1881 and 1910 in a certain region of Denmark. An examination of criminal justice statistics for the period turned up 926 offenses involving the 7,172 twins, coming from 799 twin pars. Although the concordance rates (i.e., the frequency of both twins showing the same trait) in this study were lower than those in earlier surveys, they were still significant and indicated a genetic contribution to criminal behavior.[41]

Almost twenty years later, Thomas Bouchard, Jr., director of the Minnesota Center for Twin and Adoption Research at the University of Minnesota, examined three large data sets to assess the heritability of five basic personality traits: extroversion, neuroticism, agreeableness, conscientiousness, and openness. Bouchard concluded, "The similarity we see in the personality between biological relatives is almost entirely genetic in origin."[42]

In 2003, a study of 3,853 twin pairs undertaken by Dutch researcher M. J. H. Rietveld and colleagues found that shared environment, which is usually conceived of as the family environment, had little effect on a child's level of overactivity. This study adds weight to the literature supporting a significant role for genetic factors as determinants of human behavior.[43]

In 2009, an analysis of data taken from the Minnesota Twin Family Study of twins raised apart from each other found that identical (MZ) twin children have similar brain-wave patterns, become more similar in terms of abilities (arithmetic scores and vocabularies), and tend to die at about the same age. Fraternal twins become less similar in terms of abilities as they age, do not show as much similarity in brain-wave patterns, and are likely to die at different ages.[44]

Adoption Studies

The largest systematic adoption study of criminality examined all nonfamilial adoptions in Denmark from 1924 to 1947, a sample that included 14,427 male and female adoptees and their biological and adoptive parents. In that study, Danish researcher Christiansen concluded that criminality of the biological parents is more important than that of the adoptive parents, a finding that suggests genetic transmission of some factor or factors associated with crime.[45]

In sum, the evidence from these and other studies of twins and adoptees is impressive. However, the twin method has a number of weaknesses. The differences in MZ and DZ twin similarities tell us about genetic involvement only to the extent that the MZ–DZ difference is not related to environmental differences; also, the small number of twin pairs makes adequate statistical comparisons difficult. Further, it is not always easy to determine if twins are monozygotic or dizygotic. Finally, official definitions of crime and delinquency, with all their limitations, are exclusively used.[46]

Intelligence

With the growing acceptance of sociobiology in the 1960s and 1970s, researchers again turned their attention to intelligence as a possible factor in delinquent behavior. Numerous studies have been conducted, including one by sociologist Robert A. Gordon, who compared delinquency prevalence rates and delinquency incidence rates and concluded that minority juvenile males had higher arrest rates and court appearance rates than white males or females regardless of any specific geographic location, rural or urban. Gordon proposed that differences in IQ might provide the strongest explanation of these persistent differences in unlawful behavior.[47] In another paper, Gordon stated that "[lower] IQ was always more successful in accounting for the black-white differences [in crime] than income, education, or occupational status."[48]

Travis Hirschi and Michael Hindelang reexamined three research studies—including earlier data gathered by Hirschi from California, Marvin Wolfgang and associates' Philadelphia data, and Joseph Weis's data from the state of Washington—and found that "the weight of evidence is that IQ is more important than race and social class" in predicting delinquency. These researchers also rejected the contention that IQ tests are race and class biased, and said that such tests did not favor middle-class white youth over minorities. They concluded that low IQ, independent of race and ethnicity, affects school performance, resulting in an increased likelihood of delinquent behavior.[49]

In 2011 Tom Kennedy, Kent Burnett, and William Edmonds examined a population of juvenile offenders in order to identify which were more likely to be incarcerated for violent versus nonviolent offenses. They found that lower verbal intelligence, specifically reading ability as measured by school achievement tests, correlates strongly with offender status and can be used to correctly classify violent offenders.[50]

A recent study by Roos Koolhof, Rolf Loeber, Evelyn Wei, Dustin Pardini, and Annematt Collot D'Escury found that seriously delinquent boys are generally impulsive, but the higher-IQ serious delinquents seem to have better cognitive control systems. This study concluded that interventions aimed at boys with low IQs should focus on the remediation of behavioral impulsivity as well as cognitive impulsivity.[51]

Researchers today understand that whatever the correlation between IQ and delinquency may be, the association is further strengthened by environmental factors, such as the home environment, school performance, and peers.

Neuropsychological Factors

Some neuropsychological factors appear to be more directly related to delinquent behavior than others, and some have received wider attention than others in various studies, as discussed next.

The classic studies by German-British psychologist Hans Eysenck on the **autonomic nervous system** have their origins in the earlier attempts to understand the relationship between constitutional factors and delinquency. But his sociobiological theory goes one step further by noting the interactions of both biological and environmental factors. Eysenck contended that some children are more difficult to condition morally than others because of the inherited sensitivity of their autonomic nervous systems. He argued that individuals range from those in whom it is easy to excite conditioned reflexes and whose reflexes are difficult to inhibit to those whose reflexes are difficult to condition and easy to extinguish. Yet the moral conditioning of the child also depends on the quality of the conditioning the child receives within the family.[52]

Ronald Simons and colleagues' study used longitudinal data from a sample of several hundred African-American males and examined the manner in which variants in three genes—the 5 serotonin transporter gene (5-HTT), the dopamine receptor gene (DRD4), and the monoamine oxidase gene (MAOA)—modulate the effects of community and family adversity on adoption of the street code and aggression. They found that variants in any of these three genes made offenders more susceptive to the adoption of the street code and patterns of behavioral aggression.[53]

Brain Functioning and Temperament

A child's temperament is hard to define but can more easily be identified by the behaviors associated with it. Activity and emotionality are two of these behaviors. The term *activity* in this context refers to gross motor movements, such as moving the arms and legs, crawling, or walking.

It has been a standard finding that youth involved with juvenile courts often suffer from mental health difficulties and disorders, and these mental health disorders are a serious factor leading to participation in juvenile delinquent behaviors and activities. Patricia Stoddard-Dare and colleagues' study investigated which specific mental health disorders predicted detention for serious or violent crimes, and they found that youth with attention deficit–hyperactivity disorder and conduct disorder diagnoses were significantly less likely to commit personal crimes and experience subsequent detention; in contrast, youth with bipolar diagnoses were significantly more likely.[54]

Children who exhibit an inordinate amount of movement compared with peers are sometimes labeled "hyperactive" or are said to have **attention deficit–hyperactivity disorder (ADHD)**. **Emotionality** ranges from very little reaction to intense emotional reactions that are out of control.

The hyperactive child remains a temperamental mystery. This child's three behaviors are inattention (the child is easily distracted and does not want to listen), impulsivity (he or she shifts quickly from one activity to another), and excessive motor activity (he or she cannot sit still, runs about, is talkative and noisy). Educators note that children with ADHD have difficulty

Attention deficit–hyperactivity disorder (ADHD) is the most common neurobehavioral disorder of children.

> **Attention Deficit Hyperactivity Disorder—Impulsive Type**
> - Lacks attention to details or makes careless mistakes
> - Fails to sustain attention
> - Does not seem to listen
> - Has difficulty following through on instructions
> - Lacks organizational skills
> - Does not care for tasks that require continuous mental effort
> - Misplaces things
> - Can be easily distracted
> - Tends to be forgetful

FIGURE 3–1 Attention Deficit–Hyperactivity Disorder—Impulsive Type.

> **AD/HD Predominantly Hyperactive—Impulsive Type: (AD/HD-HI)**
> - Squirms in chair or fidgets with hands or feet
> - Has a problem remaining seated
> - Climbs or runs about excessively
> - Finds it difficult to quietly engage in activities
> - Is hyperactive in his or her movements
> - Talks excessively
> - Has difficulty not blurting out answers before questions are completed
> - Struggles to take turns or wait on others
> - Frequently interrupts or intrudes upon the rights of others

FIGURE 3–2 ADHD—Predominantly Hyperactive–Impulsive Type (ADHD-HI).

staying on task, sustaining academic achievement in the school setting, remaining cognitively organized, and maintaining control over their behavior.[55]

ADHD is the most common neurobehavioral disorder of children, with the condition affecting between 5 and 10 percent of the children in the United States.[56] One study showed that two-thirds of children with ADHD have at least one other condition, such as depression, anxiety, or learning disabilities.[57] There is also evidence that children with ADHD have other problem behaviors, in addition to those in school, and that these problem behaviors increase the likelihood that such youngsters will become involved in delinquent acts and perhaps even go on to adult crime.[58] Figure 3–1 provides additional information about ADHD.

Learning Disability (LD)

Some evidence points to a link between having a **learning disability (LD)** and being involved in delinquent behavior. An LD is a disorder that affects people's "ability . . . either [to] interpret what they see and hear or to link information from different parts of the brain. These limitations can show up in many ways—as specific difficulties with spoken and written language, coordination, self-control, or attention. Such difficulties extend to schoolwork and can impede learning to read or write or to do math."[59]

An LD can be a lifelong condition that affects many parts of an individual's life: school or work, family life, daily routines, and even friendships and play. Some people have many overlapping LDs, whereas others may have a single isolated learning problem that has little impact on other areas of their lives. LDs can be divided into three broad categories:

1. Developmental speech and language disorders
2. Academic skills disorders
3. Other (a catchall category including certain coordination disorders and learning handicaps not covered by the other classifications)[60]

The most common types of LDs are dyslexia, aphasia, and hyperkinesis. Dyslexia is expressed in reading problems, particularly the inability to interpret written symbols. Aphasia consists of speech difficulties, often resulting from both auditory and visual deficiencies. Hyperkinesis, frequently equated with hyperactivity, is excessive muscular movement.[61] (See Figure 3–2.)

The possibility of a link between LDs and delinquency has been the subject of considerable debate, but the research findings are mixed.[62] Although the link between LDs and delinquency is questionable, the fact is that youngsters with LDs frequently do fail in school, and officials of the justice system seem to be influenced by this evidence of school failure to process them through the juvenile justice system.

As noted, the most common types of LDs are dyslexia, aphasia, and hyperkinesis.[63] The dominant explanations for the cause of an LD lie in organic or neurological disorders, including birth injury or anything contributing to premature birth, infant or childhood disease, head injury, or lack of proper health care or nutrition.

A recent study examined the link between learning disabilities and delinquency. Social worker Karen Matta Oshima and colleagues, using empirical data from a midwestern state, found that youth with disabilities had higher rates of juvenile court petitions than similar low-income peers.[64]

Biochemical Factors

Research has shown that some delinquent behavior can be attributed to an **orthomolecular imbalance** in the body or to brain toxicity. (The term *orthomolecular* refers to "correct chemical balances in the body.") Biochemists suggest that when normal functioning is affected by diet, pollutants, and/or genetic deficiencies such as allergies, abnormal deficits or excesses in molecular brain concentrations of certain substances can lead to various mental and behavioral problems, including delinquency.[65]

A 2011 study, for example, examined propensity for violence and identified early health risk factors that influence negative behavioral outcomes. They were found to include prenatal and postnatal nutrition, tobacco use during pregnancy, maternal depression, birth complications, traumatic brain injury,

> Some delinquent behavior can be attributed to an orthomolecular imbalance in the body or to brain toxicity.

lead exposure, and child abuse. The framework developed by this emphasized the pre-perinatal and postnatal periods, when a child's development is crucial and the opportunity for behavioral and environmental modification is high.[66]

In sum, there is some support for the idea that chemical imbalances in the body, resulting from faulty nutrition, allergies, and exposure to substances such as lead, are related to delinquent behavior. At best, however, the link is very weak. Although faulty diet and vitamin deficiencies may affect how a juvenile feels, it does not necessarily follow that the adolescent will become involved in delinquent behavior.

The Biosocial Perspective

Within the last decade or two, a new biological perspective on delinquency has emerged. Known as **biosocial criminology**, it sees the interaction between biology and the physical and social environments as key to understanding human behavior, including delinquency and criminality. Whereas traditional biological approaches share overlapping areas of interest with biosocial researchers, current studies in biosocial criminology do not seek to identify a criminal gene or to find a particular area of the brain that causes delinquency. Instead, they attempt to evaluate many different aspects of human physiology and to assess how the human organism interacts with the environment around it to produce behavior. Although recognizing the role of human DNA, heritability, environmental contaminants, nutrition, hormones, physical trauma (especially to the brain), and body chemistry in human cognition, feeling, and behavior, biosocial theorists emphasize that it is the interaction between biology and the cultural and social environments that produces behavior, and that both conformity and criminality are a consequence of such interaction.

Some biosocial theories, including those offered by University of Pennsylvania criminologist Adrian Raine, stress the importance of the interaction between a cluster of biological markers—including brain dysfunction, glucose metabolism, poor nutrition, and physiological reactivity (such as skin resistance and heart rate)—and the social environment in producing deviance and criminality.[67] Raine argues that measurements of biological indicators and observations of the social environment can be used to accurately predict which people will turn to crime in later life.

Although discussion of the entire scope of biosocial criminology is beyond the ability of this text to encompass, it should be noted that brain development in children and teenagers is a central area for biosocial investigations. Recently, for example, Elizabeth Cauffman, a professor of psychology and social behavior at the University of California, Irvine, asked an audience of state lawmakers, "Why do most adolescents drive like they're missing part of their brain?" Her answer: "Because they are."[68] Cauffman was describing the latest findings from the field of developmental neurobiology that show the prefrontal cortex—the part of the brain that allows for impulse control and that experiences emotion—is not fully formed in human beings until around the age of 25. Although the human brain develops the ability to process sensory inputs early on in life, along with the ability to control bodily functions, the last mental component to develop is a solid sense of judgment. The story with which this book began (see Chapter 1) reviewed recent understandings of human neural development and the impact they have had on U.S. Supreme Court decisions involving adolescents. Hence, recent understandings of human neural development have had an impact on U.S. Supreme Court decisions involving adolescents. Exhibit 3.3 reports the results of one study on functional impairment in delinquent youth.

Psychological Positivism

Some theories claim that juveniles commit delinquent acts because they have underlying emotional problems or disturbances. According to these theories, juveniles may not have received adequate nurturing at home, and with that emotional deprivation, they find it difficult to function in social contexts,

---

EXHIBIT 3.3 | Functional Impairment in Delinquent Youth

A longitudinal study of youth detained at the Cook County Juvenile Temporary Detention Center in Chicago reveals that delinquents have trouble functioning in society. Participants were part of the Northwestern Juvenile Project (NJP), a longitudinal study of 1,829 youths (ages 10 to 18) arrested and detained between November 20, 1995, and June 14, 1998. The authors presented the results of their examination of the participants' functional impairment, as assessed three years following their release from detention. Key findings include the following:

- Only 7.5 percent of youth had no notable impairment in functioning.
- Approximately one of every five youth had markedly impaired functioning.
- Markedly impaired functioning was much more common in males than in females, but females were more likely to be severely impaired in the moods/emotions and self-harm domains than males.
- Among males living in the community, African Americans and Hispanics were more likely to be severely impaired in school and work than non-Hispanic whites.

This study is consistent with others finding that most youth in the juvenile justice system have social, academic, and psychiatric difficulties.

Critical Thinking Question: If delinquents are as impaired as a group, as this and other studies propose, what are the implications?

Source: Karen W. Adams, Jeanne Y. Chase, James W. Washburn, Eric G. Remano, Linda A. Teplin, and Elena R. Bassett, *Functional Impairment in Delinquent Youth*, Juvenile Justice Bulletin (Washington, DC: U.S. Department of Justice, Northwestern Juvenile Project, December 2013), pp. 1–9.

such as school, sports, or community activities. Thus, psychological positivism differs from both classical and contemporary biological positivism because its focus is more on the emotional makeup of the personality than on the biological nature of the individual. At first, psychoanalytic (Freudian) theory was widely used with delinquents, but more recently other behavioral and humanistic schools of psychology have been applied to the problem of youth crime.

Psychoanalytic Explanations

In the early part of the twentieth century, Sigmund Freud developed his famed **psychoanalytic theory**, which contributed three insights that have shaped the handling of juvenile delinquents throughout most of the last century: (1) Children who have not yet learned to control the primitive drive of the id (raw instincts and primitive drives) have difficulty distinguishing socially acceptable behavior from socially unacceptable behavior.[69] (2) Children must learn to control their sexual and aggressive drives, which create inner tensions that a child must learn to resolve in socially acceptable ways.[70] (3) What a child has experienced emotionally by the age of five affects that child for the rest of his or her life. Emotional traumas experienced in childhood are especially likely to cause lifelong psychological problems.[71]

Other psychologists have taken the insights of psychoanalysis and applied them to the situations of delinquents:

- Pioneer theorist William Healy focused on mental conflicts that originate in unsatisfactory family relationships.[72]
- Viennese-born psychoanalyst August Aichhorn thought that delinquents had considerable hatred toward their parents because of the conflicted nature of family relationships and believed that they could transfer this hatred to other authority figures.[73]
- Austrian-born Kate Friedlander focused on the development of antisocial characteristics in the personality, such as selfishness, impulsiveness, and irresponsibility, which she defined as the results of disturbed ego development in early childhood.[74]

Sensation Seeking and Delinquency

Sensation seeking is a much different approach to psychological positivism. Derived from optimal arousal theory, sensation seeking can be defined as "an individual's need for varied, novel and complex sensations and experiences and the willingness to take physical and social risks for the sake of such experiences."[75]

Ideas about sensation seeking assume that organisms are driven or motivated to obtain an optimal level of arousal.[76] Could this desire for excitement be a factor in delinquency?

Several observers have noted that delinquency is an enjoyable activity.[77] In 2004 research, R. N. Robbins examined relationships between impulsive sensation seeking and future orientation. He found that individuals with more positive future orientations were less likely to use marijuana, hard drugs, and alcohol during sex, and had fewer alcohol problems than those with a less positive outlook. In contrast, more impulsive adolescents had more alcohol use and alcohol problems, condom use, and cigarette smoking.[78] In another 2004 article, M. D. Slater and colleagues examined the relationship between violent media and aggressiveness. Their findings indicated that this relationship is more robust among sensation-seeking students who are victimized by their peers.[79]

In his controversial book *Seductions of Crime*, UCLA sociologist Jack Katz conjectured that when individuals commit a crime, they become involved in "an emotional process" involving "seductions and compulsions that have special dynamics," and that it is this "magical" and "transformative" experience that makes crime "sensible," even "sensually compelling." For example, Katz stated that for many adolescents, shoplifting and vandalism offer "the attractions of a thrilling melodrama," because "quite apart from what is taken, they may regard 'getting away with it' as a "thrilling demonstration of personal competence, especially if it is accomplished under the eyes of adults."[80]

Katz argued that instead of approaching criminal or delinquent behavior from the traditional focus on background factors, we need to give more consideration to the foreground or situational factors that directly precipitate antisocial acts and reflect the crimes' sensuality. According to Katz, offenders' immediate social environment and experiences encourage them to construct crimes as sensually compelling.[81]

Reinforcement Theory

James Q. Wilson and Richard Herrnstein's *Crime and Human Nature* combined biosocial factors and psychological research with rational choice theory to redevelop reinforcement

> **The rewards of crime are found in the form of material gain, revenge against an enemy, peer approval, and sexual gratification.**

Think About It...

Some theorists have proposed that sensation seeking might be associated with a higher risk of delinquency, and that young people who go out of their way to seek excitement are more prone to delinquency than others. How might young sensation seekers be channeled into positive and productive activities?

theory.[82] Wilson and Herrnstein considered potential causes of crime and of noncrime within the context of **reinforcement theory**, the theory that behavior is governed by its consequent rewards and punishments, as reflected in the history of the individual.

The rewards of crime, according to Wilson and Herrnstein, are found in the form of material gain, revenge against an enemy, peer approval, and sexual gratification. The consequences of crime include pangs of conscience, disapproval of peers, revenge by the victim, and—most important—possibility of punishment. The rewards of crime tend to be more immediate, whereas the rewards of noncrime generally are realized in the future. Wilson and Herrnstein showed how gender, age, intelligence, families, schools, communities, labor markets, mass media, and drugs—as well as variations across time, culture, and race—greatly influence the propensity to become involved in criminal behavior, especially violent offenses.[83]

In 2011 Jennifer Stevens and colleagues, in research examining developmental models that explain different types of delinquency at different phases in the life course, found from their examination of data of incarcerated delinquents in a midwestern state that youths may begin their involvement in delinquency in pursuit of intrinsic gratification but continue that involvement because of the external gratification that they receive from their peers.[84]

Personality and Crime

A **trait-based personality model** offers another perspective on possible sources of criminal behavior.[85] Traits are essential personal characteristics of individuals that are relevant to a wide variety of behavioral domains, including delinquency and criminality.[86] Some researchers and their contributions in this area are as follows:

- Sheldon Glueck and EleanorGlueck's study *Unraveling Juvenile Delinquency* examined a sample of 500 juvenile offenders and 500 nonoffenders in an effort to discover significant distinctions in the personality traits of the two groups. They found that the delinquents were more defiant, ambivalent about authority, extroverted, fearful of failure, resentful, hostile, suspicious, and defensive than the nondelinquents.[87]

- Joshua D. Miller and Donald Lynam's meta-analysis of the basic models of personality identified certain traits that are more characteristic of antisocial personalities: hostility, self-centeredness, spitefulness, jealousy, and indifference to others. Antisocial individuals also typically lack ambition, perseverance, and motivation; hold nontraditional and unconventional values and beliefs (for example, are low in conscientiousness); and have difficulty controlling their impulses.[88]

- Rolf Loeber and Jeffrey Burke's 2011 article summarizes the empirical studies showing pathways in the development of delinquent behavior. One of its significant contributions is that it identifies pathways between different diagnoses of disruptive behavior disorders, including oppositional defiant disorder (ODD), conduct disorder (CD), and antisocial personality disorder (APD).[89]

The Psychopath

Hard-core juvenile delinquents are sometimes diagnosed as **psychopaths** (also called *sociopaths*). According to the fourth edition of the American Psychiatric Association's *Diagnostic and Statistical Manual of Mental Disorders* (DSM-IV), these individuals are usually diagnosed with a conduct disorder. The claim is made that the psychopath or sociopath is the unwanted, rejected child who grows up but remains an undomesticated "child" and never develops trust in or loyalty to other adults. Hervey Cleckley gave an early description of this type of personality, listing 16 characteristics he had noted in his practice.[90] More recently, Robert D. Hare and colleagues developed a new checklist for those with antisocial personality with a conduct disorder. Among the most significant items on the list are the following:

1. Conning and manipulativeness
2. Lack of remorse or guilt
3. Callousness and lack of empathy
4. Lack of realistic long-term goals
5. Impulsivity
6. Failure to accept responsibility for one's actions[91]

Psychologist Linda Mealey argued that there are two kinds of sociopaths: primary sociopaths and secondary sociopaths. *Primary sociopaths* have inherited traits that predispose them to illegal behavior; that is, they have a genotype that predisposes them to antisocial behavior. *Secondary sociopaths*, in contrast, are constitutionally normal but are influenced by such environmental factors as poor parenting. Thus, she argued that one type of sociopathic behavior has a genetic basis and the other is environmentally induced.[92]

Some interest has been expressed in measuring the relationship between psychopathy and violent behavior in juveniles. At least four instruments have been designed to assess psychopathic features among juveniles: the Psychopathy Checklist, Youth Version (PCL:YV); two versions of the Antisocial Processes Screening Device (APSD); and a Psychopathy Content Scale on the Millon Adolescent Clinical Inventory (MACI). In a recent study, Daniel C. Murrie and colleagues found that the PCL:YV scores were significantly correlated with the severity of prior violence, violent offense history, and institutional violence.[93] About the same time, Raymond R. Corrado and colleagues' study also revealed that the PCL:YV significantly predicted violent and general recidivism among male adolescent offenders.[94]

In 2012 Jason Neland and Michael Miner examined psychopathic traits in adolescent males who offend against children as well as those who offend against peers. They found that most psychopathy traits and antisocial behaviors are similar in all sexual offenders, whereas maternal dysfunction and narcissistic traits distinguish sexual offenders from delinquents involved in non-sex crimes.[95]

Cognitive Theory

Another psychological approach that has been applied to delinquent behavior is **cognitive theory**, which is indebted to the mid-twentieth-century Swiss psychologist Jean Piaget who proposed that children's reasoning processes develop in an orderly fashion. He asserted that children build cognitive abilities through self-motivated action in the world, and he proposed that children develop through four main periods: (1) the sensorimotor period (ages 0 to 2), (2) the preoperational period (ages 2 to 7), (3) the concrete operational period (ages 7 to 11), and (4) the formal operational period (ages 11 to adulthood). This final period is when children make the transition to adulthood and begin to effectively use abstract and logical thinking.[96]

Lawrence Kohlberg later adapted cognitive theory to moral development in children's decision making, using three levels and six stages. He interviewed 72 white boys in Chicago about the "dilemma of Heinz," asking the boys whether a fictional and financially strapped person named Heinz did right or wrong in stealing a drug for his dying wife. Kohlberg found that young children assumed they had no choice but to obey the rules handed down by authorities. Accordingly, Heinz was wrong to steal the drug, a child typically says in Stage 1, "because it is bad to steal" or "because it is against the law to steal." However, most children later become aware of dilemmas involved with making moral decisions from a position of self-interest (Stage 2). Improving individual relationships becomes the main concern in Stage 3, whereas by Stage 6, a person works for a moral society—for justice—to the point of disobeying unjust laws.[97]

Kohlberg later extended his studies to a population of criminals and found that they were significantly lower in moral judgment than noncriminals. The majority of criminals were classified in Stages 1 and 2, whereas the majority of nonoffenders could be placed in Stages 3 and 4.[98] In later studies of delinquents, he found that they were "stuck" in a state of moral immaturity and usually could be placed in any of the first three stages. Many hard-core delinquents, he further found, would be placed at the punishment stage (Stage 1), because they only believe something is right or wrong because it hurts if you do what society thinks is wrong.[99]

Aaron T. Beck, who has become a major spokesperson for cognitive theory, has also examined offenders and found that offenders' sense of personal vulnerability is seen in their hypersensitivity to specific kinds of social confrontations, including domination or disparagement. These individuals react by fighting back or by attacking a weaker adversary. Whether juveniles or adults, violent offenders see themselves as victims and others as victimizers. Offenders' thinking is shaped by such rigid beliefs as the following: authorities are controlling and punitive; spouses are deceitful, rejecting, and manipulative; outsiders are self-serving, hostile, and treacherous; and nobody can be trusted.[100]

In sum, several psychological theories have attempted to explain delinquency and crime. A literature review categorizes such explanations into five categories: (1) learning theories, (2) intelligence theories, (3) personality theories, (4) theories of psychopathy, and (5) cognitive and social development theories. An overview of psychological theories would conclude that most delinquents have psychological traits within the normal personality range but that some delinquents have acute emotional deficits. Table 3–2 summarizes the biological, sociobiological, and psychological theories of delinquency.

TABLE 3–2 SUMMARY OF BIOLOGICAL, SOCIOBIOLOGICAL, AND PSYCHOLOGICAL THEORIES OF DELINQUENCY

Theory	Proponents	Causes of Crime Identified	Supporting Research
Atavistic (or born) crimina	Lombroso	The atavistic criminal is a reversion to an earlier evolutionary form.	Weak
Genealogical studies	Dugdale, Goddard	Criminal tendencies are inherited.	Weak
Body type	Sheldon, Glueck and Glueck, Cortes, Gatti	Mesomorphic body type correlates with criminality.	Weak
Genetic factors	Christiansen and Mednick	Twin and adoption studies show a genetic influence on criminal tendencies.	Moderately strong
Biosocial factors	Adrian Raine, Kevin Beaver	The interaction between the human organism and the physical and social environments result in behavior.	Moderately strong
Intelligence	Hirschi and Hindelang	IQ is a meaningful factor in criminal behavior when combined with environmental factors.	Moderately strong
Autonomic nervous system	Eysenck	Insensitivity of the autonomic nervous system, as well as faulty conditioning by parents, may cause delinquent behavior.	Weak
Psychoanalytic theory	Freud	Unconscious motivations resulting from early childhood experiences lead to criminality.	Weak
Psychopathic or sociopathic personality	Cleckley	Inner emptiness as well as biological limitations cause criminal tendencies.	Moderately strong
Reinforcement theory	Wilson and Herrnstein	Several key constitutional and psychological factors cause crime.	Weak
Cognitive theory	Piaget, Kohlberg, and Beck	Lack of reasoning and moral development result in delinquent behavior.	Moderately strong

Developmental Theories of Delinquency

This section presents information about three well-known longitudinal studies of offenders and offending: (1) the Dunedin (New Zealand) Multidisciplinary Health and Development Study undertaken by Terrie E. Moffitt and colleagues, (2) the Montreal Longitudinal Experimental Study conducted by Richard E. Tremblay and colleagues, and (3) the Cambridge Study in Delinquent Development led by David P. Farrington. A fourth longitudinal study, published by Stacy Tzoumakis in 2012, analyzed female offending, but is not discussed here.[101]

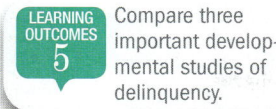

LEARNING OUTCOMES 5 — Compare three important developmental studies of delinquency.

The Dunedin Longitudinal Study

Terrie E. Moffitt, Donald R. Lynam, and Phil A. Silva, in their examination of the neuropsychological status of a thousand New Zealanders born in 1972, found that poor neuropsychological scores "were associated with early onset of delinquency [but were] unrelated to delinquency that began in adolescence."[102] The term *neuropsychological* refers to the relationship between the nervous system, especially the brain, and mental skills such as perception, memory, and language. Moffitt's developmental theory views the emergence of delinquency as proceeding along two developmental paths:

1. Children develop a lifelong tendency toward delinquency and crime at an age as early as three years, according to one path.[103] These **"life-course-persistent" (LCP) offenders**, according to Moffitt, are likely to continue to engage in illegal activity throughout their lives, regardless of the social conditions and personal situations they experience.[104]

2. Moffitt also identified a path wherein the delinquents start offending during their adolescent years and then begin to desist from delinquent behavior around their 18th birthday. Moffitt refers to these youthful offenders as **"adolescent-limited" (AL) offenders**, and it is this limited form of delinquency that characterizes most children who become involved in illegal activity.

Moffitt's Dunedin study is continuing today, and she is also following the development of 1,100 British twins born between 1994 and 1995 through the Environmental-Risk Longitudinal Twin Study.

Montreal Longitudinal Experimental Study

The Montreal Longitudinal Experimental Study (MLES) began in 1984. The principal investigator was Richard E. Tremblay, and it focused on aggressive seven- to nine-year-old children. Its original aim was to study the development of antisocial behavior from kindergarten to high school with a major focus on the role of parent–child interactions. The study initially assessed all kindergarten boys in 53 schools located in poor socioeconomic areas in Montreal in an effort to identify the most disruptive boys. Mother and teacher ratings and self-reported delinquency were the main instruments used to assess behavioral problems under the MLES. The study produced the following key findings:[105]

- Higher levels of disruptive behavior during kindergarten effectively predicted higher levels of delinquency before entry into high school.
- Physical aggression during kindergarten is the best behavioral predictor of later delinquency.
- No significant group of boys started to show chronic problems of physical aggression, opposition, or hyperactivity after their kindergarten year.
- Hyperactivity and anxiety significantly predicted the age of onset of smoking cigarettes, drinking to excess, and using drugs up to 15 years of age. Boys who had a high score on hyperactivity and a low score on anxiety were more likely to use substances at an early age.
- Boys exhibiting high levels of aggression and fighting between 5 and 12 years of age had generally lower heart rates at 11 and 12 years of age than other boys, controlling for pubertal status, body size, and level of family adversity.

Cambridge Study in Delinquent Development

The Cambridge Study in Delinquent Development, undertaken by principal investigator David P. Farrington at the Institute of Criminology at the University of Cambridge, England, was a 40-year longitudinal survey that followed the development of antisocial behavior in 411 South London boys, most of whom were born in 1953.[106] The study aimed to measure as many factors as possible that might contribute to the development of delinquency. Participants in the study were periodically interviewed from ages 8 to 46 years (i.e., between 1961 and 2001). They were also periodically tested in their schools, in their homes, and at the researchers' offices.[107] Teachers, parents, and significant others in the children's lives were interviewed as well. The study's chief findings were as follows:

- The prevalence of offending increased up to age 17 years and then decreased.
- The peak age of increase in the prevalence of offending was age 14.
- Persistence in offending was seen in the significant continuity of offending that took place from one age range to another.
- Most juvenile and young adult offenses resulting in convictions were committed with others, but the incidence of co-offending declined steadily with age.
- The most important risk factors of later offending were (1) antisocial behavior during childhood, including troublesomeness, dishonesty, and aggressiveness; (2) hyperactivity-impulsivity; (3) low intelligence; (4) poor school achievement; (5) family criminality; (6) family poverty; and (7) poor parenting.[108]

TABLE 3-3 COMPARISON OF THREE DEVELOPMENTAL STUDIES

	Moffitt	Cambridge	Tremblay
Sample	Followed 100 males and females from ages 3 to 29	Males born between 1951 and 1954	Followed Montreal children from birth
Delinquent Population	Two groups: adolescence-limited (AL) offenders and life-course-persistent (LCP) offenders	About one-third of the cohort	Potential for delinquency could be identified as early as kindergarten
Gender	Persistent path is extremely rare with females	Only boys in study	Only boys in study
Race	N/A	N/A	N/A
Chronic Offenders	N/A	6%; 23 boys of the 396 had six or more convictions	N/A
Patterns of Delinquent Behavior	AL delinquency may be as high as LCP delinquency during adolescence, but LCP continues into adult behavior.	Early discrimination and treatment of persistent delinquency can help prevent adult criminality.	Higher levels of disruptive behavior during kindergarten predict higher levels of delinquency before high school.

See Table 3–3 for a summary of the three developmental studies just discussed.

The Importance of Theory

The first chapter pointed out that theory and research are intertwined and that they need to be the foundation for policy recommendations to deal with juvenile delinquency in the United States (see Figure 3–3). Researchers have spent considerable time and effort trying to understand the causes and correlates of delinquency.[109] The question is, "What is the value of studying theories of delinquent behavior?" Perhaps the answer to this question can be found in the lives of those youngsters who come into contact with the juvenile justice system and are adjudicated delinquent.

In the lives of nearly every delinquent, questions can be raised: How did this person's family background influence the course of his or her behavior? How did success or failure in school influence subsequent behaviors? How was he or she affected by the environment? Why did he or she become involved in a youth gang? Why did this person become a drug user? What influenced this person to stop taking drugs or becoming involved in other illegal behaviors?

Delinquency theory, as will be discussed, is helpful in understanding why youngsters do what they do. With this understanding comes the ability to provide guidance and direction for those who work with delinquent youths. With understanding, parents can also have insight regarding how to provide

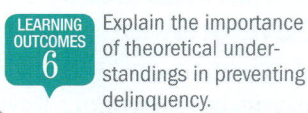

LEARNING OUTCOMES 6 — Explain the importance of theoretical understandings in preventing delinquency.

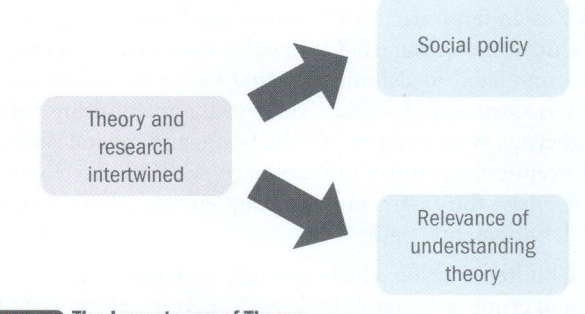

FIGURE 3-3 The Importance of Theory.

nurturance and acceptance to their children. Finally, with this understanding, researchers are able to design studies that will further the knowledge base regarding delinquent behavior.

Prevention and Control of Delinquency

An important consideration of life-course criminology is the matter of **desistance** from crime. One of the problems of establishing desistance is the difficulty of distinguishing between a gap in a delinquent career and true termination. There are bound to be crime-free intervals in the course of delinquent careers. To explain changes in offending over time, or desistance, theorists have proposed several explanations, which we'll consider by category:

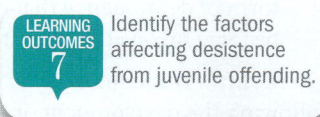

LEARNING OUTCOMES 7 — Identify the factors affecting desistence from juvenile offending.

- *Maturation and aging account for desistance.* The maturation process appears to be involved in desistance as youths or adults become aware either of the desirability of pursuing a conventional lifestyle or of the undesirability of continuing with unlawful activities.
- *Developmental accounts for desistance.* One developmental explanation of desistance is that identity changes account

Theory and research are intertwined and need to be the foundation for policy recommendations to deal with juvenile delinquency.

50 Chapter 3 Individual Causes of Delinquency

TABLE 3-4 PERSPECTIVES ON DESISTANCE

Perspective	Explanation
Maturation and Aging Account for Desistance	Delinquents grow up and decide not to pursue delinquent behavior anymore.
Development Accounts for Desistance	A cognitive process takes place and delinquents decide in their late teens that it is necessary to make changes in their lives if they want to be successful adults.
Rational Choice Accounts for Desistance	Delinquents decide that the cost is too great to continue with criminal activity.
Life-Course Perspective Accounts for Desistance	Desistance is a process rather than an event, in that individuals desist because of actions (choice) in conjunction with situational context and structural influences.

The decision to give up or continue with crime is based on a person's conscious reappraisal of the costs and benefits of criminal activity.

for reduction or cessation of crime. Edward Mulvey and John LaRosa, focusing on the period from ages 17 to 20 years—the period they call the time of "natural" recovery—found that desistance was linked to a cognitive process taking place in the late teens when delinquents realized that they were "going nowhere" and that they had better make changes in their lives if they were going to be successful as adults.[110]

- *Rational choice accounts for desistance.* The main idea of the rational choice framework is that the decision to give up or continue with crime is based on a person's conscious reappraisal of the costs and benefits of criminal activity. Proponents of this theory saw persisters and desisters as "reasoned decision makers."[111]

- *Life-course perspective accounts for desistance.* The major objective of the life-course perspective, whose framework was discussed in Chapters 1 and 2, is to link social history and social structure. Laub and Sampson perceived desistance as a process rather than an event—a process that operates simultaneously at different levels (individual, situational, and community) and across different contextual environments (especially family, work, and military service). They concluded that "offenders desist as a result of individual actions (choice) in conjunction with situational contexts and structural influences linked to key institutions that help sustain desistance."[112] (See Table 3-4.)

THE CASE

The Life Course of Amy Watters, Age Nine

When Amy turned nine years old, her father held a birthday party for her that included a number of invited guests from among Amy's school friends. The party was organized around a picnic table in the backyard of Amy's home. One of the guests, Cassandra—a girl of about the same age as Amy—gave Amy a first-grade reader as a birthday gift. It was never clear whether "Cassie," as the girl was known to Amy, meant to gift that particular book, or whether she had somehow confused the book with another. When Amy opened the present, however, she thought that it was meant as an insult. "How," she thought, "could anyone give me such a childish present?" Was Cassie trying to say that Amy was like a first grader? Feeling embarrassed in front of her friends, Amy flew into a rage immediately upon opening the present and attacked Cassie, grabbing her hair and dragging her to the ground. Her father had to pull a screaming Amy off of Cassie, as the two rolled in the backyard grass.

Discuss
- This chapter says, "The concept of rationality . . . assumes that individuals have free will and are not controlled by their emotions, but many youngsters do not appear to have such control." Why might Amy be lacking in self-control? What experiences can help build self-control among adolescents?

Learn more on the Web:
- Learn more about the impact of family and community structure on delinquency by visiting the National Criminal Justice Reference Service at NCJRS.gov and reading the publication numbered NCJ 215999.

Follow the continuing Amy Watters saga in the next chapter.

CHAPTER 3 Individual Causes of Delinquency

LEARNING OUTCOMES 1

Elaborate on how the theoretical constructs of the classical school of criminology explain juvenile delinquency.

In order to justify punishing delinquent juveniles, today theorists have turned to classical school principles or to rational choice theory, a perspective that builds on classical thought. Both perspectives assert that individuals have free will and should be held responsible for their behavior.

1. What contributions have the classical school of criminology made to the understanding of delinquency today?
2. What does felicific calculus have to teach us about human behavior? Do you believe that the basic assumptions of felicific calculus are correct? Why or why not?
3. Do people have free will, or are their actions determined largely by their biology and their environment?
4. What implications does a belief in free will have for the handling of delinquents?

social contract An unstated or explicit agreement between people and their government as to the rights and obligations of each.

free will The ability to make rational choices among possible actions and to select one over the others.

utilitarianism A doctrine that holds that the useful is the good and that the aim of social or political action should be the greatest good for the greatest number.

felicific calculus A method for determining the sum total of pleasure and pain produced by an act; also the assumption that human beings strive to obtain a favorable balance of pleasure and pain.

LEARNING OUTCOMES 2

Summarize rational choice theory and the routine-activities approach and explain their views of delinquency.

Rational choice theory is based on the assumption that the delinquent chooses to violate the law and has free will. Rational choice theory can be seen as an extension of the deterrence doctrine found in classical school thought. The routine-activities approach, another approach that points to the role of rationality in crime, links increases in crime rates since 1960 to changes in the routine-activity structure of U.S. society, including things such as a decrease in the influence of religion, neighbors, friends, and family.

1. Rational choice theory posits that crime and delinquency are the results of rational choices that people make. With this in mind, how might an increase in penalties associated with shoplifting impact the incidence of shoplifting in stores in your area?
2. To what extent do you believe that increased punishments would reduce the number of offenses? What does that say about the rationality of crime?
3. What are the implications of the routine-activities approach for delinquency control?

routine-activities approach The contention that crime-rate trends and cycles are related to the nature of everyday patterns of social interaction that characterize the society in which they occur.

soft determinism A perspective that holds that freedom of choice varies from one person or situation to another.

general deterrence The idea that punishing one person for his or her criminal or delinquent acts will discourage others from committing similar acts.

specific deterrence A goal of criminal sentencing that seeks to prevent a particular offender from engaging in repeat criminality.

incapacitation Isolating offenders to protect society.

LEARNING OUTCOMES 3

Identify the three basic assumptions of positivism.

Positivism is an approach to juvenile crime based on the assumptions that (1) the background and characteristics of juveniles explain delinquent behavior, (2) individuals are fully determined in their behavior and do not exercise freedom, and (3) individuals are not are capable of choice. In this sense, the delinquent is seen as fundamentally different from the nondelinquent.

1. The main assumption underlying positivism is that delinquents are determined to or cannot help but commit illegal behavior. Do you agree or disagree with this position? Why?
2. Describe the philosophical position known as *positivism*.

positivism The view that just as laws operate in the medical, biological, and physical sciences, laws govern human behavior and these laws can be understood and used.

Progressive Era The period from around 1890 to 1920, when a wave of optimism swept through American society and led to the acceptance of positivism.

determinism A philosophical position that suggests that individuals are driven into delinquent or criminal behavior by biological or psychological traits that are beyond their control.

LEARNING OUTCOMES 4

Evaluate contemporary biological and psychological positivism in terms of the contributions they make to understanding delinquency.

Biological positivism and psychological positivism point to biological and psychological factors within the individual as the most significant determinants of delinquency. These factors may be very elusive—such as a difficult-to-condition autonomic nervous system or an inadequately developed superego—or they may be more easily discernable—such as inappropriate interpersonal relationships.

1. Explain the theory of sociobiology. If the theory is valid, then what implications does it have for the control of crime and delinquency?
2. What are the characteristics of a psychopath? How might a psychopath behave? What are the implications of psychopathy for the study of delinquency?
3. Which of the positivist theories discussed in this chapter do you think makes the most sense in terms of understanding delinquent behavior? Why?

biological positivism The belief that juveniles' biological characteristics and limitations drive them to delinquent behavior.

born criminal An individual who is atavistic, who reverts to an earlier evolutionary level, and is unable to conform his or her behavior to the requirements of modern society—thus, an individual who is innately criminal.

sociobiology An expression of biological positivism that stresses the interaction between biological factors within an individual and the influence of the person's particular environment; also the systematic study of the biological basis of all social behavior.

autonomic nervous system The system of nerves that govern reflexes, glands, the iris of the eye, and activities of interior organs that are not subject to voluntary control.

attention deficit–hyperactivity disorder (ADHD) A cognitive disorder of childhood that can include inattention, distractibility, excessive activity, restlessness, noisiness, impulsiveness, and so on.

emotionality An aspect of temperament. It can range from a near absence of emotional response to intense, out-of-control emotional reactions.

learning disability (LD) A disorder in one or more of the basic psychological processes involved in understanding or using spoken or written language.

orthomolecular imbalance A chemical imbalance in the body, resulting from poor nutrition, allergies, or exposure to lead and certain other substances, which is said to lead to delinquency.

biosocial criminality The belief that a person's biological characteristics make them prone to certain forms of behavior when the surrounding environment encourages it.

psychoanalytic theory A theory based on Sigmund Freud's insights, which have helped to shape the handling of juvenile delinquents. They include these axioms: (1) The personality is made up of three components—id, ego, and superego; (2) a normal child passes through three psycho-sexual stages of development—oral, anal, and phallic; and (3) a person's personality traits are developed in early childhood.

reinforcement theory A perspective that holds that behavior is governed by its consequences, especially rewards and punishments that follow from it.

trait-based personality model A theory that attributes delinquent behavior to an individual's basic inborn characteristics.

psychopath An individual with a personality disorder, or a hard-core juvenile delinquent/adult criminal; also called a *sociopath*.

cognitive theory A perspective on human development that says children develop cognitive abilities through interaction with the physical and social worlds.

LEARNING OUTCOMES 5

Compare three important developmental studies of delinquency.

There are three important developmental studies of delinquency. In one, Terrie Moffitt identified life-course-persistent (LCP) and adolescent-limited (AL) paths, in which young people either engage in persistent crime violation or temporarily experiment with delinquency. In another, Richard Tremblay and colleagues' Montreal Longitudinal Experimental Study found that antisocial behavior was at its peak during the kindergarten years and that physical aggression during the kindergarten years is the best behavior predictor of later delinquency. In a third, the Cambridge Study in Delinquent Development, David P. Farrington found that the types of acts that lead to convictions tend to be components of a larger pattern of antisocial behavior.

1. Which of the three developmental studies of delinquency identified in this chapter appeal to you the most? Why?
2. What is the difference between adolescent-limited offenders and life-course persisters? How can we tell one from the other?
3. What are the implications of the developmental model for delinquency control?

life-course-persistent (LCP) offenders Offenders who begin offending early in life and persistently engage in criminal and antisocial activities over the duration of the life course.

adolescent-limited (AL) offenders Individuals who offend only for a very short period of time that is limited to the adolescent years.

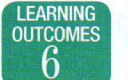

LEARNING OUTCOMES 6

Explain the importance of theoretical understandings in preventing delinquency.

Delinquency theory is helpful in understanding why youngsters do what they do. With understanding comes the ability to provide guidance and direction for those who work with delinquent youths. Similarly, parents who gain understanding can have insight regarding how to provide nurturance and acceptance to their children. Finally, with theoretical understanding, researchers are able to design studies that will further knowledge of delinquent behavior.

1. What is the importance of theoretical understanding in preventing delinquency?
2. Can workable delinquency prevention strategies be crafted without theoretical underpinnings?
3. What delinquency prevention strategies might you recommend based on what you have read in this chapter?

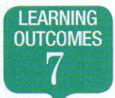

LEARNING OUTCOMES 7

Identify the factors affecting desistence from juvenile offending.

Desistance involves a juvenile quitting or "walking away from delinquency." There are a number of reasons for juveniles to desist from offending, including maturation and aging, personal characteristics, social experiences, the making of positive rational choices, and events in the life course.

1. Which of the desistance approaches do you find more compatible with your personal perspective? Why?
2. Why do some people persist in delinquent behavior, eventually turning to adult criminal activity?

desistance The termination of a delinquent career or behavior.

“When we speak of a delinquent subculture, we speak of a way of life that has somehow become traditional among certain groups in American society.”

—*Albert K. Cohen, Delinquent Boys*

4 Social Structural and Social Process Theories of Delinquency

1. Describe the social disorganization theory of delinquency.
2. Describe the cultural deviance approach to delinquency.
3. Explain strain and opportunity theories of delinquency.
4. Summarize the differential association theory of delinquency.
5. Summarize control theories of delinquency.
6. Explain the benefits of integrated theoretical explanations for delinquency.
7. Explain the structural and social processes that impact delinquency over time.
8. Summarize the goals and research strategies that characterize the Project on Human Development in Chicago Neighborhoods.

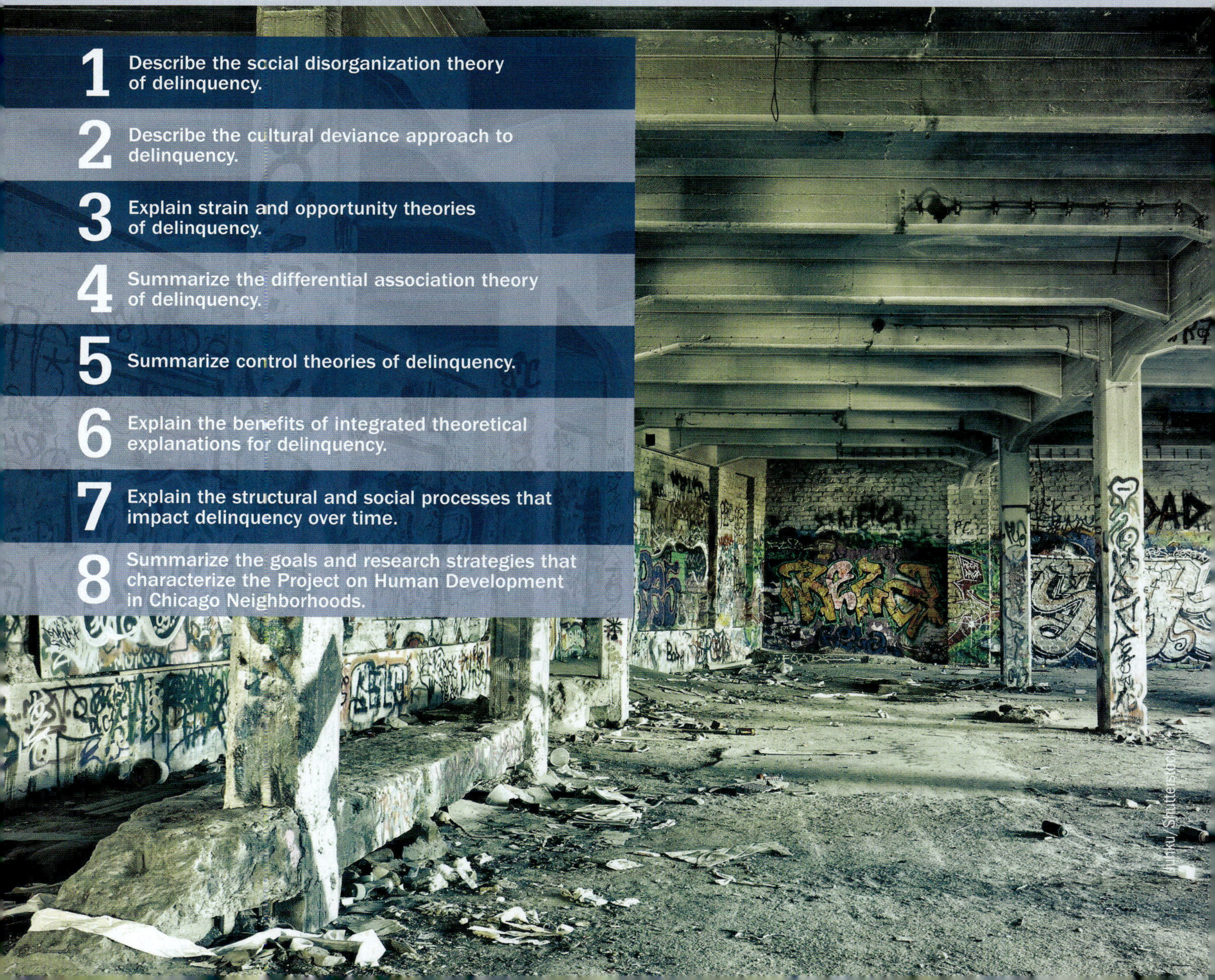

Jiriku/Shutterstock

INTRO: CHILDHOOD EXPOSURE TO VIOLENCE

In 2012, New York City police arrested a 12-year-old girl from Queens and charged her with selling marijuana and crack cocaine. Her arrest came as part of a city-wide sweep of drug dealers. Rahiem Newkirk, a youth program coordinator with the city, told television reporters that he knew the girl personally, "She is really a pretty nice young lady," he said. "I'm actually really, really, really surprised to hear that she's involved in this activity."[1]

Neighborhood residents, however, told a different story, saying that gangs run everything in the neighborhood, and that children as young as seven and eight years old routinely sell drugs and run guns for their older brothers and sisters.

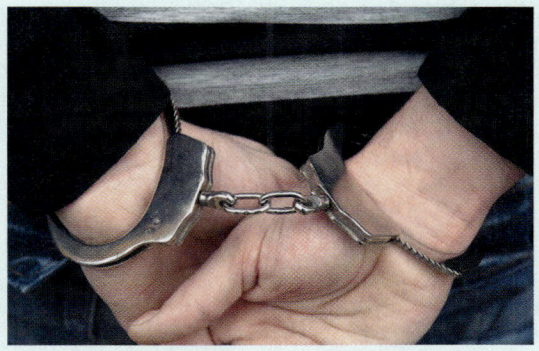

A handcuffed youthful offender. Criminal subculture is based on values supportive of illegal activities. How do some young people become socialized into criminal subculture?

DISCUSS How does exposure to violence during childhood affect children? Why does the social context surrounding such exposure matter?

Chapters 4 and 5 examine sociological explanations for delinquency. This chapter looks closely at features of the social environment, also known as *social structure*, that influence young people—causing some of them to commit delinquent acts—as well as social process theories that examine the interaction between individuals and their environments that can lead them to become delinquent.

The term **social structure** can have a variety of meanings. As used by sociologists, it can refer to entities or groups in relation to each other, to relatively enduring patterns of behavior and relationships within social systems, or to social institutions and norms embedded in social systems in such a way that they shape the behavior of actors within those systems. For our purposes, however, *social structure* can be defined as the relatively stable formal and informal arrangements that characterize a society, including its economic arrangements, social institutions, and values and norms. Social structure helps shape human behavior and is related to delinquency by way of such factors as child poverty, racial disparity, disorganized communities, and unemployment.

The various **social process theories** of delinquency, another focus of this chapter, *examine the interactions between individuals and their environments for clues to the root causes of delinquency.* Most youngsters are influenced by the family, the school experience, and their peers, all of which are discussed in the next section on delinquency and environment. It is the process of socialization occurring within these social institutions that, along with social structure, provides the forces that insulate youths from or influence them to commit delinquent acts (see Exhibit 4–1). Several theories focusing on social process have been widely used to explain juvenile delinquency—differential association, drift, and social control theories.

Social process theories look to the interaction between individuals and their environments for clues to the root causes of delinquency.

▶ Social Disorganization Theory

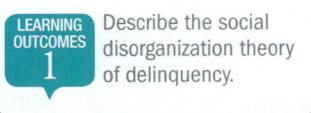

LEARNING OUTCOMES 1 Describe the social disorganization theory of delinquency.

Social disorganization is an important concept in any discussion of social structure. It can be defined as "the inability of a community structure to realize the common values of its residents and maintain effective social control."[2] **Social disorganization theory** suggests that macrosocial forces (for example, migration, segregation, structural transformation of the economy, housing discrimination) interact with community-level factors (concentrated poverty, family disruption, residential turnover) to impede social organization. This sociological viewpoint focuses attention on the structural characteristics and mediating processes of community social organization that help explain crime while also recognizing the larger historical, political, and social forces that shape local communities.[3]

EXHIBIT 4–1 | Elijah Anderson and the Code of the Street

Elijah Anderson's *Code of the Streets*, which grew out of the ethnographic work Anderson did in two urban communities in Philadelphia, focused on the theme of interpersonal violence between and among inner-city youths. In questioning why so many inner-city youths are inclined to commit aggression and violence toward one another, he concluded that in the economically depressed and crime- and drug-ridden communities in which they live, a "code of the streets" has replaced or at least weakened the rule of civil law.

A set of informal rules or prescriptions for behavior, focuses on a search for respect. What is understood as respect is sometimes called "props" in street code (or "proper due"). In street culture—according to Anderson—respect is difficult to win, can be easily lost, and requires constant vigilance. Respect is a form of social capital that is particularly valuable when other forms of capital are unavailable or have been lost.

The concept of "manhood" expresses respect and identity in the lives of these inner-city youths. This concept of manhood requires a certain ruthlessness and the ability to take care of oneself. It also requires having a sense of control, of being in charge, and of showing nerve. One's manhood must be communicated through words, gestures, and actions. Youths make it clear that everyone understands that if you mess with them, there will be "street justice or severe consequences because they are man enough to make you pay."

Sources: Elijah Anderson, *Code of the Streets: Decency, Violence, and the Moral Life of the Inner City* (New York: W. W. Norton, 1999); "The Code of the Street and African-American Adolescent Violence," *Research in Brief*, February 2009; Karen F. Parker and Amy Reckdenwald, "Concentrated Disadvantage, Traditional Male Role Models, and African-American Juvenile Violence," *Criminology* 46 (2008), pp. 711–735; Nikki Jones, "Working 'the Code': On Girls, Gender, and Inner-City Violence," *Australian and New Zealand Journal of Criminology*, 41 (2008), pp. 63–83; and Eric A. Stewart and Ronald L. Simons, "Race, Code of the Street, and Violent Delinquency: A Multilevel Investigation of Neighborhood Street Culture and Individual Norms of Violence," *Criminology* 48 (2010), pp. 569–603.

Think About It…

The social disorganization perspective says that delinquency results from a breakdown in mechanisms of social control and a disruption in the social order. Yet little looting occurred in Japan in 2011 in those areas devastated by earthquakes and tsunamis. Why did social order remain intact there?

justasc/Shutterstock

The intellectual antecedents of social disorganization theory can be traced to the work of Emile Durkheim; in Durkheim's view, **anomie**, or normlessness, resulted from society's failure to provide adequate regulation of its members' attitudes and behaviors. Loss of regulation was particularly likely when society and its members experienced rapid change and laws did not keep pace.[4]

Shaw and McKay

Social disorganization theory was developed by Clifford R. Shaw and Henry D. McKay during the first half of the twentieth century. Shaw and McKay focused specifically on the social characteristics of the community as a cause of delinquency.[5] Their pioneering investigations established that delinquency varied in inverse proportion to the distance from the center of the city, that it varied inversely with socioeconomic status, and that delinquency rates in a residential area persisted regardless of changes in the racial and ethnic composition of the area.[6]

> **Delinquent behavior came to be seen as an alternative mode of socialization through which youths who were part of disorganized communities were attracted to deviant lifestyles.**

Social Disorganization and the Community

Shaw and McKay viewed juvenile delinquency as resulting from the breakdown of social control among the traditional primary groups, such as the family and the neighborhood, because of the social disorganization of the community. Rapid industrialization, urbanization, and immigration processes contributed to the disorganization of the community. Delinquent behavior, then, became an alternative mode of socialization through which youths who were part of disorganized communities were attracted to deviant lifestyles.[7] The delinquent values and traditions, replacing traditional ones, were passed from one generation to the next.

Shaw and McKay turned to ecology to show this relationship between social disorganization and delinquency. Park and Burgess had earlier used the concept of ecology in explaining the growth of cities. Burgess, for example, suggested that cities do not merely grow at their edges but rather have a tendency to expand radially from their centers in patterns of concentric circles, each moving gradually outward.[8] Figure 4–1 is a diagram of the growth zones as Burgess envisioned them.

In 1929, Shaw reported that marked variations in rates of school truancy, juvenile delinquency, and adult criminality existed among different areas in Chicago. These rates varied inversely with the distance from the center of the city; that is, the nearer a given locality was to the center of the city, the higher its rates of delinquency and crime.[9] In 1942, Shaw and McKay published their classic work *Juvenile Delinquency and Urban Areas*, which developed these ecological insights in greater scope and

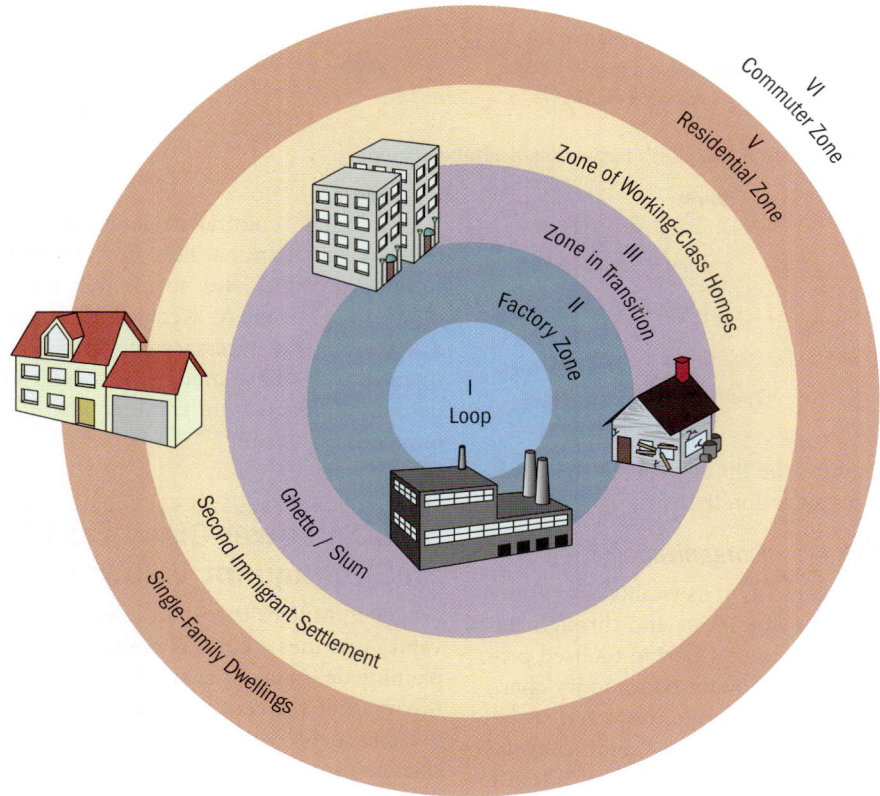

FIGURE 4–1 Concentric Zones in Chicago.

depth.[10] They discovered that over a 33-year period, the vast majority of the delinquent boys came either from an area adjacent to the central business and industrial areas or from neighborhoods along two forks of the Chicago River.

Then, applying Burgess's concentric zone hypothesis of urban growth, they constructed a series of concentric circles, like the circles on a target, with the bull's-eye in the central city. Measuring delinquency rates by zones and by areas within the zones, they found that in all three periods the highest rates of delinquency were in Zone I (the central city), the next highest were in Zone II (next to the central city), and so forth, in progressive steps outward to the lowest rates in Zone V. Significantly, although the delinquency rates changed from one period to the next, the relationships among the different zones remained constant, even though in some neighborhoods the ethnic compositions of the population had changed totally. During the first decade of the twentieth century, the largest portion of the population was German or Irish, but 30 years later it was Polish and Italian.[11]

Opportunity Structure and Delinquency

Shaw and McKay eventually refocused their analysis from the influence of social disorganization of the community to the importance of economics on high rates of delinquency. They found that the economic and occupational structures of the larger society were more influential in the rise of delinquent behavior than was the social life of the local community. They concluded that the reason members of lower-class groups remained in the inner-city community was less a reflection of their newness of arrival and their lack of acculturation to American institutions than a function of their class position in society.[12]

The consequences of this **differential opportunity structure** led to a conflict of values in local communities: Some residents embraced illegitimate standards of behavior, whereas others maintained allegiance to conventional values. Delinquent groups were characterized by their own distinctive standards, and Shaw and McKay became increasingly involved in examining the process through which delinquents came to learn and to pass on these standards.[13]

Cultural Transmission Theory

Shaw and McKay also elaborated on social disorganization theory by arguing that delinquent behavior became an alternative mode of socialization through which youths who were part of disorganized communities were attracted to deviant lifestyles.[14] This line of thought became known as the cultural deviance component of social disorganization theory.

Shaw and McKay further contended that the delinquent values and traditions that replaced traditional social standards were not the property of any one ethnic or racial group but were culturally transmitted from one generation to the next.[15] As evidence in support of this **cultural transmission theory**, these researchers found that certain inner-city areas continued to have the highest delinquency rates in Chicago despite shifts in the population of nearly all of these areas.

Shaw and McKay assumed that juvenile and adult gangs in these areas accounted for the transmission of this tradition of

FIGURE 4–2 Shaw and McKay's Social Disorganization Theory.

The necessary and sufficient cause of delinquency in cultural deviance models is socialization to subcultural values condoning as right conduct what the controlling legal system defines as crime.

delinquency. Figure 4–2 diagrams the theoretical constructs of Shaw and McKay's social disorganization theory.

Evaluation of Shaw and McKay's Disorganization Theory

Social disorganization theory lost much of its vitality as a prominent criminological theory in the late 1960s and through the 1970s because theory and research in that period focused primarily on individual rather than group and community characteristics.[16] Despite the criticisms it received, however, social disorganization theory experienced "a quiet, but significant revival" in the 1980s and later.[17] As the reemergence of interest in social disorganization theory shows, the work of Shaw and McKay and social ecology has had an enduring impact on the study of delinquency in the United States.

▶ Cultural Deviance Theory and Delinquency

Social disorganization theory focuses on the structural breakups of urban communities, but another perspective, **cultural deviance theory**, examines the delinquent values that are found in some lower-class cultures. Both perspectives, however, can be termed "cultural transmission theory" because both contribute to recurrent deviance

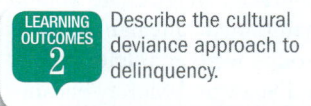

LEARNING OUTCOMES 2 — Describe the cultural deviance approach to delinquency.

Central to cultural deviance theory is the belief that delinquent and criminal behavior are expressions of conformity to cultural values and norms that are in opposition to those of the larger society. According to sociologist Ruth Rosner Kornhauser, the necessary and sufficient cause of delinquency in cultural deviance models "is socialization to subcultural values condoning as right conduct what the controlling legal system defines as crime."[18]

Miller's Lower-Class Culture and Delinquent Values

Walter B. Miller's theory of lower-class culture and delinquent values provides a cultural deviance theory that is useful in explaining delinquent behavior. In his version of cultural deviance theory, Miller, an anthropologist, argued that the motivation to become involved in delinquent behavior is endemic to lower-class culture:

> The cultural system which exerts the most direct influence on [delinquent] behavior is that of the lower-class community itself—a long-established, distinctively patterned tradition with an integrity of its own—rather than a so-called "delinquent subculture" which has arisen through conflict with middle-class culture and is oriented to the deliberate violation of middle-class norms.[19]

Focal Concerns of Lower-Class Culture

Miller argued that a set of **focal concerns of the lower class** characterizes this socioeconomic group (Exhibit 4–2). These concerns—trouble, toughness, smartness, excitement, fate, and autonomy—command widespread attention and a high degree of emotional involvement.[20]

Miller is contending that the lower class has a distinctive culture of its own and that its focal concerns, or values, make

---

EXHIBIT 4–2 | Miller's Focal Concerns

- **Trouble.** Miller contended that staying out of trouble represents a major challenge for lower-class citizens and that personal status is therefore often determined in terms of this law-abiding/non-law-abiding dimension.
- **Toughness.** Physical prowess, as demonstrated by strength and endurance, is valued in lower-class culture. In the eyes of lower-class boys, the tough guy who is hard, fearless, and undemonstrative as well as a good fighter is the ideal man.
- **Smartness.** The capacity to outsmart, outfox, outwit, con, dupe, and "take" others is valued in lower-class culture; in addition, a man also must be able to avoid being outwitted, duped, or "taken"

himself. Smartness also is necessary if people are to achieve material goods and personal status without physical effort.
- **Excitement.** The search for excitement or a thrill is another of the focal concerns of lower-class life.
- **Fate.** Lower-class individuals, according to Miller, often feel that their lives are subject to a set of forces over which they have little control; they may accept the concept of destiny and may sense that their lives are guided by strong spiritual forces.
- **Autonomy.** The desire for personal independence is an important concern, partly because the lower-class individual feels controlled so much of the time.

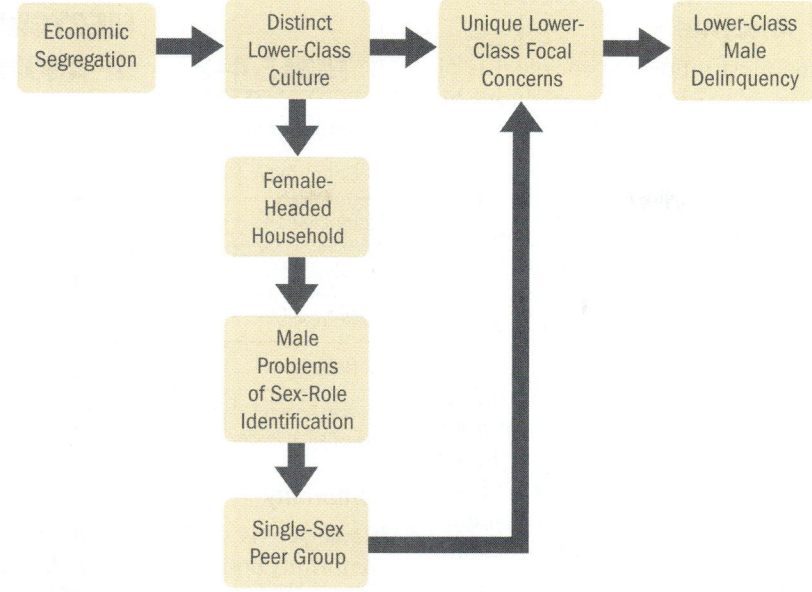

FIGURE 4-3 Miller's Theory of Lower-Class Culture.

lower-class boys more likely to become involved in delinquent behavior. These boys want to demonstrate that they are tough and are able to outwit the cops. They also look at the pursuit of crime as a thrill. Yet they are likely to believe that if an individual is going to get caught, there is nothing he or she can do about it. Crime, then, permits lower-class youths to show personal independence from the controls placed on them and also provides an avenue through which youths hope to gain material goods and personal status with a minimum of physical effort. See Figure 4-3 for the theoretical constructs of Miller's theory.

Evaluation of Miller's Theory

Miller's theory appears most plausible when applied to the behavior of lower-class gang delinquents. As researchers have noted, gangs appear to have their own values and norms, distinct from the norms and values of the larger culture. In keeping with this perspective, criminologists Marvin E. Wolfgang and Franco Ferracuti argued that a subculture of violence among young males in the lower social classes legitimates the use of violence in various social situations.[21]

Miller's contention that the lower classes have distinctive values has been widely criticized, however. Some critics argue that the evidence shows that lower-class youths hold the same values as those of the larger culture. For example, Richard A. Cloward and Lloyd E. Ohlin (discussed later in this chapter) as well as Albert K. Cohen have claimed that lower-class youths have internalized middle-class values and that their delinquent acts in fact reflect these middle-class values.[22] See Table 4-1 for cultural deviance theories.

▶ Strain and Opportunity Theories of Delinquency

Strain theory proposes that delinquency results from the frustrations that individuals feel when they are unable to achieve the goals they desire. 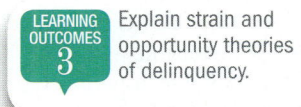 One of the most important strain theorists is Robert K. Merton.

TABLE 4-1 | CULTURAL DEVIANCE THEORIES OF CRIME

Theory	Cause of Crime Identified in the Theory	Supporting Research
Cultural Deviance Theories		
Shaw and McKay	Delinquent behavior becomes an alternative mode of socialization through which youths who are part of disorganized communities are attracted to delinquent values and traditions.	Moderate
Miller	Lower-class culture has a distinctive culture of its own, and its focal concerns, or values, make lower-class boys more likely to become involved in delinquent behavior.	Weak
Wolfgang and Ferracuti	Subcultures of violence exist among lower-class males and legitimize the use of violence.	Weak

Merton's Theory of Anomie

Robert K. Merton, one of the most influential sociologists of the twentieth century, saw deviant behavior as produced by various social structures. In his now-classic work *Social Theory and Social Structure,* Merton wrote:

> Socially deviant behavior is just as much a product of social structure as conformist behavior.... Our primary aim is to discover how some social structures exert a definite pressure upon certain persons in the society to engage in nonconforming rather than conforming behavior.[23]

In *Social Theory and Social Structure,* Merton considered two elements of social and cultural systems: **culturally defined goals** and **institutionalized means**. The first is the set of "culturally defined goals, purposes, and interests held out as legitimate objectives for all or for diversely located members of the society."[24] These are the goals that people feel are worth striving for; they may be considered cultural goals. A second important aspect "defines, regulates, and controls the acceptable means of reaching out for these goals."[25] Although a specific goal may be attained by a variety of means, the culture does not sanction all of these means. The acceptable method is referred to as the institutionalized means. Merton contended that the two elements must be reasonably well integrated if a culture is to be stable and run smoothly. If individuals believe that a particular goal is important, they should have a legitimate means to attain it, but when a culture lacks such integration, then a state of normlessness, or anomie, occurs. Merton further asserted that contemporary U.S. culture seemed to "approximate the polar type in which great emphasis upon certain success-goals occurs without equivalent emphasis upon institutional means."[26] For example, the lower classes are asked to orient their behavior toward the prospect of accumulating wealth, but they are largely denied the means to do so legitimately. The opposition of the cultural emphasis and the social structure creates intense pressure for deviation.

Merton developed a typology of the modes of adaptation that individuals may use when confronted with anomie. Table 4–2 lists five types of individual adaptation: conformity, innovation, ritualism, retreatism, and rebellion. A plus sign (+) signifies acceptance, a minus sign (–) signifies rejection, and a plus/minus sign (±) signifies a rejection of the prevailing values and a substitution of new ones. Merton's theory uses these modes of adaptation to explain how deviant behavior in general is produced by the social structure, but they can also be applied specifically to juvenile law-breaking.[27] The five types of adaption are explained more fully in the following paragraphs.

Strain theory says that delinquency results from the frustration individuals feel when they are unable to achieve the goals they desire.

TABLE 4–2 MERTON'S THEORY OF ANOMIE

Modes of Adaptation	Cultural Goal	Institutional Means
1. Conformity	+	+
2. Innovation	+	–
3. Ritualism	–	+
4. Retreatism	–	–
5. Rebellion	±	±

Source: Robert K. Merton, "Social Structure and Anomie," *American Sociological Review* 3 (1938), p. 676.

Conformity

If a society is well integrated and therefore anomie is absent, conformity both to cultural goals and to institutionalized means will be the most common adaptation. Conforming juveniles accept the cultural goals of society as well as the institutional means of attaining them; they work hard in legitimate ways to become a success.

Innovation

When adolescents accept cultural goals but reject the institutional means of attaining them, they may pursue other paths that are not legitimate in terms of accepted cultural values.

Ritualism

Although they may have abandoned approved cultural goals, some juveniles will continue to abide by the acceptable means for attaining them. Ritualism, then, consists of "individually seeking a private escape from the dangers and frustrations . . . inherent in the competition for major cultural goals by abandoning these goals and clinging all the more closely to the safe routines and institutional norms."[28]

Retreatism

Some people reject both culturally approved goals and means and retreat from society. Homeless people, survivalists, drug addicts, and some people with mental illness could be classified as retreatists.

Rebellion

Rebellion consists of rejecting the values and institutions of one's own culture and substituting a new set of goals and values for them. Anarchists and revolutionaries are the epitome of rebels in American society, although anyone who adopts a dramatically alternative lifestyle can also fit into this category.[29]

Merton argued that his theory of anomie was "designed to account for some, not all, forms of deviant behavior customarily described as criminal or delinquent."[30] Thus, instead of attempting to explain all the behaviors prohibited by criminal law, Merton focused attention on the pressure or strain resulting from the discrepancy between culturally induced goals and the opportunities inherent in the social structure.[31] See Figure 4–4 for the theoretical constructs of Merton's theory.

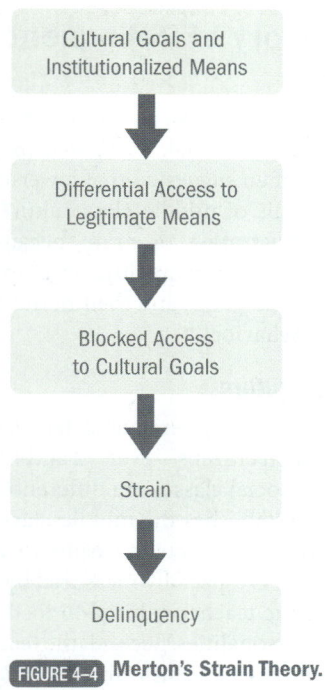

FIGURE 4–4 Merton's Strain Theory.

Institutional Anomie Theory

Twenty years ago, Steven Messner and Richard Rosenfeld authored a book called *Crime and the American Dream*. In it they developed a theory of institutional anomie. They agreed with Merton that that the success goal is widespread in society, and they described this as the "American dream," which they viewed as both a goal and a process. As a goal, the American dream involves accumulating materialistic goods and wealth. As a process, Americans are socialized to dream that this goal is attainable and are taught that they can obtain it. The desire to attain this goal generates pressures toward delinquency on those who don't have the required means to achieve success.[32]

According to Messner and Rosenfeld, what is unique about American society is that anomic conditions have been permitted to develop to such a high degree and that this, in turn, is what determines high rates of delinquency.[33] In a testing of cross-national data sets, University of Nebraska criminologist Jukka Savolainen found support for institutional anomie theory. Savolainen's study, which was international in scope, indicated that the demonstrable effects of economic inequality on the level of lethal violence are limited to nations characterized by weak collective institutions of social protection.[34]

Evaluation of Merton's Theory

One of the main emphases of Merton's theory—an emphasis that has been largely ignored—is that it is "a theory of societal *anomie*, not of individually felt strain."[35] Merton's revision of anomie theory has been called "the most influential single formulation in the sociology of deviance in the last 25 years and . . . possibly the most frequently quoted single paper in modern sociology."[36] This theory's influence on the later theoretical contributions of Richard A. Cloward and Lloyd D. Ohlin as well as Albert K. Cohen demonstrates its importance to delinquency theory.[37]

Strain Theory and the Individual Level of Analysis

Strain theory, especially in the form of anomie, dominated criminology in the 1960s before labeling theory gained acceptance in the late 1960s and early 1970s. A major reason for the widespread acceptance of strain theory was that its central thesis of **blocked opportunity** resonated with Americans' growing concern over equal opportunity, and with the fear that social injustice had deep cultural roots.[38]

Strain theory met increased criticism in the 1970s. Many commentators at the time argued that strain theory had little empirical support and ought to be abandoned as a causal explanation of crime.[39] Strain theory survived those attacks, although it now plays a more limited role in explaining crime and delinquency.[40] In the 1980s, Thomas J. Bernard defended strain theory as not having been tested adequately.[41]

Developed in the 1980s, Robert Agnew's revised strain theory of delinquency points to another source of frustration and strain: the blockage of pain/avoidance behavior (Table 4–3).[42] Agnew argued that when juveniles are compelled to remain in painful or aversive environments, such as dysfunctional families and schools in which they have little interest, the ensuing frustration is likely to lead to escape attempts or anger-based delinquent behavior. His examination of data from the Youth in Transition survey revealed that a juvenile's location in aversive environments in the school and family "has a direct effect on delinquency and an indirect effect through anger."[43]

TABLE 4–3 SUMMARY OF STRAIN THEORIES OF DELINQUENCY

Strain Theories	Features	Supporting Research
Agnew	Stress is a major source of criminal motivation.	High
Merton	Social structure exerts pressure on individuals who cannot attain the cultural goal of success, leading them to engage in nonconforming behavior.	Moderate
Cohen	Lower-class boys are unable to attain the goals of middle-class culture, and therefore they become involved in nonutilitarian, malicious, and negative behavior.	Weak

> **Think About It...**
>
> Reaction formation describes a psychological strategy for dealing with the frustration brought about by the inability to attain middle-class goals. How can such frustration be reduced?

Fundamental to Agnew's findings was his use of an autonomy scale by which he was able to accurately predict the amount of involvement in delinquency of boys two years following testing. The questionnaire he used included questions such as "One of my goals in life is to be free of the control of others." Boys who were most driven to achieve autonomy were more likely to turn to delinquency, regardless of their socioeconomic status or the presence or absence of social controls at home or at school.[44]

General Strain Theory

Agnew also developed a general strain theory of crime and delinquency that distinguishes three different sources of strain: "failure to achieve positively valued goals, . . . the removal of positively valued stimuli from the individual, [and] the presentation of negative stimuli."[45] Anger and frustration are negative emotions resulting from such strain, and juveniles may cope with these strains through delinquent behaviors. Delinquency may be a way of escaping from or reducing strain (for example, theft to achieve monetary goals in order to pay a debt). Certain strains are seen as more likely to lead to delinquency than others: (1) those high in magnitude, (2) those viewed as unjust, (3) those associated with lower self-control, and (4) those creating some pressure or incentive to engage in crime.[46] Agnew's general strain theory then presents guidelines, or a strategy, for measuring strain and explores under what conditions strain is likely to result in "nondelinquent and delinquent coping."[47]

John Rodriguez and Scott Belshaw's 2010 study of general strain theory examined how the approach may aid in explaining racial differences in offending. The study compared measures of general strain theory with levels of white and Latino juvenile delinquency. It found that even though Latino youth suffer from strain, they are less likely to commit delinquent acts due to strain than white American youth. In addition, the study found that white youth have a greater propensity to commit more serious acts of delinquency when strain is present than do Latino youths.[48]

In sum, after a period of neglect, individual-level strain theory has experienced a revival, primarily through the work of Robert Agnew, especially his general strain theory.[49] Subsequent studies examining the effects of strain have contributed to the revival of the individual-level strain theory.

Cohen's Theory of Delinquent Subcultures

In 1955 the famous American sociologist Albert K. Cohen published his well-received book *Delinquent Boys: The Culture of the Gang*. In it, Cohen suggested that lower-class youths are internalizing the goals of middle-class culture but that they experience **status frustration**, or strain, because they are unable to attain those goals. Consequently, strain explains their membership in delinquent gangs and their nonutilitarian, malicious, and negativistic behavior.[50]

Delinquent Subculture

The social structure in American society, Cohen claimed, has an immense hold on citizens—even 12 and 13-year-old children know about how social classes are differentiated.[51] The American class system establishes the middle-class values and norms that most children are expected to aspire to, and to achieve.

Status at school is especially measured by these middle-class standards. First, the teacher is hired to foster the development of middle-class personalities. Second, the teacher is likely to be a middle-class person who values ambition and achievement and quickly recognizes and rewards these virtues in others. Third, Cohen pointed out, the educational system itself favors "quiet, cooperative, 'well-behaved' pupils" who make the teacher's job easier, and it greets with disapproval the "lusty, irrepressible, boisterous youngsters who are destructive of order, routine, and predictability in the classroom."[52]

As mentioned previously, a pivotal assumption in Cohen's theory is that lower-class males internalize middle-class norms and values but then are unable to attain middle-class goals. Status frustration occurs, and the mechanism of **reaction formation** is used to release it. On the one hand, according to Cohen, the delinquent claims that the middle-class standards do not matter; but on the other hand, he or she *reacts* by directing irrational, malicious, unaccountable hostility toward the norms of the respectable middle-class society.[53]

Cohen defined nine norms that he said make up the middle-class "measuring rod":

1. Ambition
2. Individual responsibility
3. Achievement
4. Temperance
5. Rationality
6. Courtesy and likeability
7. Less physical aggression
8. Educational recreation
9. Respect for property[54]

See Figure 4–5 for the theoretical constructs of Cohen's theory.

As an alternative to unattainable positive social goals, the delinquent subculture offers lower-class males the status they cannot achieve in the larger culture, but demands of them conformity to lower-class values and patterns of behavior. As such, the status offered by the delinquent subculture is valuable only when seen through the eyes of fellow delinquents.[55]

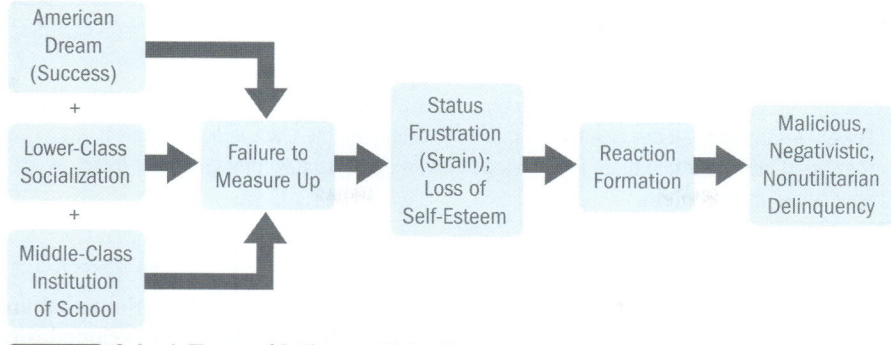

FIGURE 4–5 Cohen's Theory of Delinquent Subcultures.

Cohen added that delinquent subculture is nonutilitarian in that delinquents commit crime "for the hell of it" without necessarily intending to profit or gain from their illegal acts. Cohen also claimed that malice is frequently evident in the crimes fostered by delinquent subculture, that delinquents often display joy in the discomfort of others, and that delinquents often similarly delight in the defiance of others. Further, delinquent conduct is right by the standards of delinquent subculture precisely because it is wrong by the norms of the larger culture.[56] Moreover, the delinquent subculture demonstrates versatility in its delinquent behavior; members of this subculture do not specialize in any particular form of crime or deviance, as do many adult criminal gangs and "solitary" delinquents. Delinquent subculture is characterized by "short-run hedonism." Its members have little interest in planning activities, setting long-term goals, budgeting time, or gaining knowledge and skills that require practice, deliberation, and study. Instead, gang members literally hang around the corner waiting for something to turn up. A further characteristic of delinquent subculture is its emphasis on group autonomy, which makes gang members intolerant of any restraint except the informal pressures of the gang itself.[57]

Evaluation of Cohen's Theory

Cohen's *Delinquent Boys* made a seminal contribution to the delinquency literature. Cohen's theory is important because it views delinquency as a process of interaction between the delinquent youths and others rather than as the abrupt and sudden product of strain or anomie, as proposed by Merton's theory. Cohen contended that delinquency arises during a continuous interaction process whereby changes in the self result from the activities of others.[58] Although Cohen does not offer any empirical evidence to support his theory, and the vagueness of such concepts as reaction formation and lower-class internalization of middle-class values makes it difficult to test his theory, much of the delinquency research since the publication of *Delinquent Boys* has built on Cohen's findings.

Cloward and Ohlin's Opportunity Theory

Richard A. Cloward and Lloyd E. Ohlin sought to integrate the theoretical contributions of Merton and Cohen with the ideas of Edwin H. Sutherland. Although Merton argued that lower-class youths strive for monetary success and Cohen contended that they strive for status, Cloward and Ohlin conceptualized success and status as separate strivings that can operate independently of each other. In their **opportunity theory**, Cloward and Ohlin portrayed delinquents who seek an increase in status as striving for membership in the middle class, whereas other delinquent youths try to improve their economic position without changing their class position.

Cloward and Ohlin contended that the most serious delinquents are those who experience the greatest conflict with middle-class values, as they "are looked down upon both for what they do want (i.e., the middle-class style of life) and for what they do not want (i.e., 'crass materialism')."[59] Cloward and Ohlin use Merton's theory to explain the particular form of delinquency that youths commit. They assume that these youths have no legitimate opportunities to improve their economic position and therefore will become involved in one of three specialized gang subcultures: "criminal," "conflict," and "retreatist."[60] Each subculture is characterized by its own set of values and behavior, as we discuss next.

Criminal Subculture

The criminal subculture is primarily based on criminal values. Within this subculture, illegal acts such as extortion, fraud, and theft are accepted as means to achieve economic success. This subculture provides the socialization by which new members learn to admire and respect older criminals and to adopt their lifestyles and behaviors.[61] As new members master the techniques and acquire the values of the criminal world through criminal episodes, they become hostile toward and distrustful of representatives of the larger society, whom they regard as "suckers" to be exploited wherever possible.[62]

Conflict Subculture

Violence is the key ingredient in the conflict subculture, whose members pursue status (or "rep") through force or threats of force. Warrior youth gangs exemplify this subculture. The "gangster bopper," the basic role model, fights to win respect from other gangs and to demand deference from the adult world. Because of the role he plays in his subculture, he is expected to show great courage in the face of personal danger and always to defend his personal integrity and the honor of the gang.[63]

Retreatist Subculture

The consumption of drugs is the basic activity of the retreatist subculture. Feeling shut out from conventional roles in the family or occupational world, members of this subculture withdraw

TABLE 4–4 | OPPORTUNITY THEORY

Opportunity Theory	Features	Supporting Research
Cloward and Ohlin	Lower-class boys seek out illegitimate means to attain middle-class success goals if they are unable to attain them through legitimate means, usually through one of three specialized gang contexts.	Moderate

into an arena where the ultimate goal is the "kick," which may mean alcohol, marijuana, hard drugs, sexual experiences, hot music, or any combination of these.[64]

Cloward and Ohlin noted that although these subcultures exhibit essentially different orientations, the lines between them may become blurred.[65] Table 4–4 outlines the main theoretical constructs of Cloward and Ohlin's theory.

Evaluation of Cloward and Ohlin's Theory

Cloward and Ohlin's opportunity theory is important because of the impact it has had on the development of public policy and criminological theory.[66] However, the findings of several studies sharply disagree with the assumptions of Cloward and Ohlin's opportunity theory.[67] Still, the role of blocked opportunity, whether found in Merton or Cloward and Ohlin, has received considerable attention in the sociological analysis of male delinquency. See Table 4–4 for an overview of opportunity theory.

▶ Differential Association Theory

We now turn our attention to social process theories of delinquency. In one of the best-known social process theories to date, Edwin H. Sutherland's 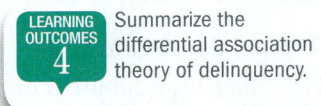 **differential association theory** proposed that delinquents learn crime from others. In developing the theory of differential association, Sutherland contended that individuals are constantly being changed as they take on the expectations and points of view of the people with whom they interact in intimate small groups.[68] Sutherland began with the notion that criminal behavior is to be expected of individuals who have internalized a preponderance of definitions that are favorable to law violations.[69] In 1939, he first developed the theory in his text *Principles of Criminology*, and he continued to revise it until its final form appeared in 1945. Figure 4–6 provides a look at the development of Sutherland's theory of differential association.

Propositions of Differential Association Theory

Sutherland's theory of differential association outlines seven propositions. These seven propositions consist of three interrelated concepts—normative (culture) conflict, differential association, and differential social organization. The interrelated concepts operate at two levels of the explanation: the society or group level and the individual level.[70]

Sutherland assumes that delinquents must be taught antisocial behavior. Those who do not engage in socially unacceptable behavior have been socialized or enculturated to conventional values, but those who become involved in delinquent behavior do so because they have been taught other values. Sutherland developed a quantitative metaphor, in which conventional and criminal value systems are composed of elementary units called "definitions." Each unit can be weighted by the modalities of frequency, priority, duration, and intensity of contact; delinquency or criminality is determined by the algebraic sum of these weighted units.[71]

> **Cloward and Ohlin said that the most serious delinquents are those who experience the greatest conflict with middle-class values.**

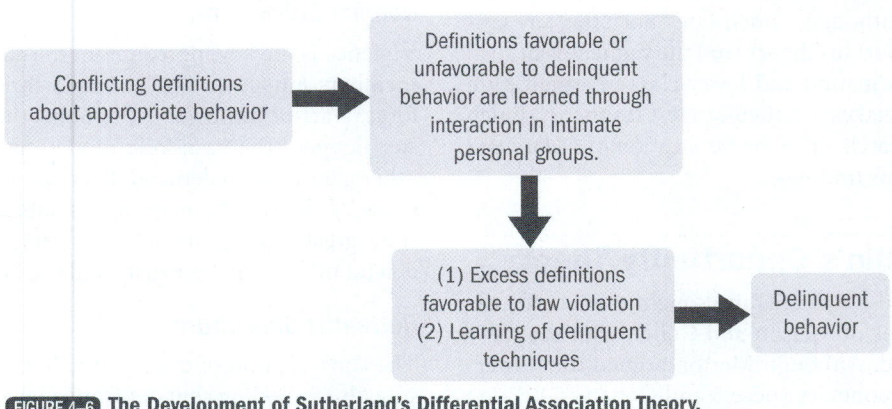

FIGURE 4–6 The Development of Sutherland's Differential Association Theory.

Differential association theory makes a strikingly simple claim: that delinquents learn crime from others who are already delinquent.

Evaluation of Differential Association Theory

Criminology was under heavy criticism before the theory of differential association was developed because it lacked a general theoretical perspective to integrate findings and guide research.[72] On balance, the theory of differential association still remains one of the best-known and most enduring theories of delinquent behavior.

▶ Control Theory and Delinquent Behavior

Differential association is a learning theory of crime, but **control theory** is focused more on an internal mechanism that helps youngsters avoid delinquent behavior. The core ideas of control theory have a long history going back at least to the nineteenth century. Control theorists agree on one especially significant point: Human beings must be held in check, or somehow controlled, if delinquent tendencies are to be repressed. Control theorists also generally agree that delinquency is the result of a deficiency in something and that juveniles commit delinquency because some controlling force is absent or defective.[73]

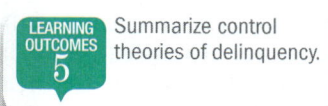

LEARNING OUTCOMES 5 — Summarize control theories of delinquency.

Early versions of control theory include Albert J. Reiss, Jr.'s theory of personal and social controls and F. Ivan Nye's family-focused theory of social control. Reiss described how the weak egos of delinquents lacked the personal controls to produce conforming behavior.[74] Nye added that the problem for the theorist was not to find an explanation for delinquent behavior; rather, it was to explain why delinquent behavior is not more common.[75] Walter C. Reckless's containment theory, which can explain both conforming behavior and deviancy, has two reinforcing elements: an inner control system and an outer control system (see Table 4–5). The assumption is that strong inner containment and reinforcing external containment provide insulation against deviant behavior.[76] Travis Hirschi's social control theory is the most developed example of control theory, and we'll examine it next.

Social Control Theory

American criminologist Travis Hirschi is the theorist most closely identified with **social control theory**, or bonding theory. In his book *Causes of Delinquency*, Hirschi linked delinquent behavior to the quality of the bond an individual has with society, stating that "delinquent acts result when an individual's bond to society is weak or broken."[77] In Hirschi's words, "We are all animals and thus all naturally capable of committing criminal acts."[78] Hence, he argues that humans' basic impulses motivate them to become involved in crime and delinquency unless there is reason for them to refrain from such behavior. Instead of the standard question "Why do they do it?" Hirschi asserts that the most important question becomes "Why don't they do it?"[79]

Hirschi theorized that individuals who are most tightly bonded to social groups such as the family, the school, and their peers are less likely to commit delinquent acts.[80] **Commitment to the social bond**, according to Hirschi, is made up of four main elements: attachment, commitment, involvement, as described in the following subsections.

Attachment

An individual's attachment to conventional others (that is, to other people who hold traditional values) is the first element of the social bond (Figure 4–7). Sensitivity toward others, argued Hirschi, relates to the ability to internalize norms and to develop a conscience.[81] Attachment to others also includes the ties of affection and respect children have to parents, teachers, and friends. The stronger his or her attachment to others, the more likely it is that an individual will take this into consideration when or if he or she is tempted to commit a delinquent act.[82] Attachment to parents is the most important variable insulating a child against delinquent behavior, and even if a family is broken by divorce or desertion, the child needs to maintain attachment to one or both parents. "If the child is alienated from the parent," Hirschi asserted, "he will not develop an adequate conscience or superego."[83]

Control theory focuses on internal mechanisms that help youngsters avoid delinquent behavior.

TABLE 4–5 | SUMMARY OF CONTAINMENT THEORIES OF DELINQUENCY

Theory	Proponents	Cause of Delinquency Identified in the Theory	Supporting Research
Containment	Walter Reckless	Strong inner containment and reinforcing external containment provide insulation against criminal behavior.	Moderate
Social control	Travis Hirschi	Criminal acts result when an individual's bond to society is weak or broken.	Strong

ELEMENTS OF THE SOCIAL BOND

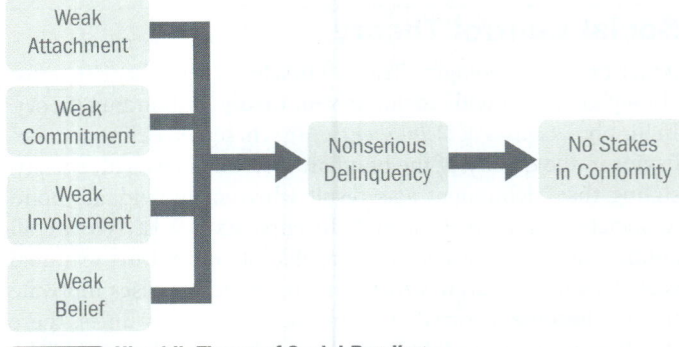

FIGURE 4–7 | Hirschi's Theory of Social Bonding.

Commitment

The second element of the social bond is commitment to conventional activities and values. An individual is committed to the degree that he or she is willing to invest time, energy, and self in attaining conventional goals such as education, property, or reputation. When a committed individual considers the cost of delinquent behavior, he or she uses common sense and thinks of the risk of losing the investment already made in conventional behavior.[84] Hirschi contended that if juveniles are committed to these conventional values and activities, they develop a stake in conformity and will refrain from delinquent behavior.

Involvement

Involvement also protects an individual from delinquent behavior. Because any individual's time and energy are limited, involvement in conventional activities leaves no time for delinquent behavior: "The person involved in conventional activities is tied to appointments, deadlines, working hours, plans, and the like," reasoned Hirschi, "so the opportunity to commit deviant acts rarely arises. To the extent that he is engrossed in conventional activities, he cannot even think about deviant acts, let alone act out his inclinations."[85]

Beliefs

The fourth element of the social bond is beliefs. Delinquency results from the absence of effective beliefs that forbid socially unacceptable behavior.[86] Such beliefs, for example, include respect for the law and for the social norms of society. This respect for the values of the law and legal system develops through intimate relations with other people, especially parents. Hirschi portrayed a causal chain "from attachment to parents, through concern for the approval of persons in positions of authority, to belief that the rules of society are binding on one's conduct."[87]

Evaluation of Social Control Theory

Hirschi tested his theory by administering a self-report survey to 4,077 junior high and high school students in Conta Costa County, California. He then used school-based files and police records to assess the data and the extent to which students' behavior was controlled by the social bond.

Although social control theory cannot explain all acts of delinquency, it still has more empirical support today than any other explanation of delinquency.[88] Unlike other theorists discussed in this chapter, Hirschi was able to test his theory with a population of adolescents. The basic theoretical constructs of control theory—concepts such as attachment to parents, involvement in school, and commitment to conventional activities—were found to be clearly defined and measurable.

▶ Integrated Theories of Delinquency

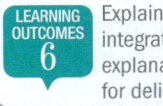

LEARNING OUTCOMES 6 — Explain the benefits of integrated theoretical explanations for delinquency.

The development of integrated theoretical explanations for delinquency has been one of the most highly praised concepts in criminology.[89] Theory integration generally implies the combination of two or more contexts, including existing theories, levels of theory, social contexts, or individual contexts, on the basis of their perceived commonalities.

Despite the daunting challenges of achieving integrated theories, several integrated theories for delinquent behavior have been developed (see Table 4–6).[90] Four of the most important are Michael R. Gottfredson and Travis Hirschi's **general theory of crime**, Delbert S. Elliott's integrated social process theory, Terence P. Thornberry's interactional theory, and J. David Hawkins and Joseph G. Weis's social development model.[91]

Gottfredson and Hirschi's General Theory of Crime

In their 1990 publication *A General Theory of Crime*,[92] Gottfredson and Hirschi defined lack of self-control as the common factor underlying problem behaviors. Thus, self-control is the degree to which an individual is "vulnerable to the temptations of the moment."[93] The other pivotal construct in this theory of crime is crime opportunity, which is a function of the structural or situational circumstances encountered by the individual. In combination, these two constructs are intended to capture the simultaneous influence of external and internal restraints on behavior[94] (see Figure 4–8).

More than two dozen studies have been conducted on the general theory of crime, and the vast majority of the research has been largely favorable.[95] Criticisms of the general theory of crime have focused largely on its lack of conceptual clarity.[96]

Elliott and Colleagues' Integrated Social Process Theory

Delbert Elliott and colleagues offer "an explanatory model that expands and synthesizes traditional strain, social control, and social learning perspectives into a single paradigm that accounts for delinquent behavior and drug use."[97] Integrating the strongest features of these theories into a single theoretical model, Elliott and colleagues contended that the experience of living in socially disorganized areas leads youths to develop weak bonds with conventional groups, activities, and norms. High levels of strain, as well as weak bonds with conventional groups, lead some youths to seek out delinquent peer groups, and these

TABLE 4-6 INTEGRATED THEORIES

Name of Theory	Proponent	Cause of Delinquency	Elements of the Theory	Strengths	Criticisms
General theory of crime	Hirschi and Gottfredson	Lack of self-control	Common factor under delinquent behavior	Wide support in research	Lack of conceptual clarity
Integrated social process theory	Elliott and colleagues	Strain, lack of social control, and negative social learning	Integrated the strongest features of strain, social control, and social learning theories	Moderate support	Applications to various types of delinquent behavior
Interactional theory	Thornberry	Negative events occurring in a developmental fashion	Social bonds, attachments to antisocial peers, and additional involvement in delinquent behavior	Moderate support	Neglects middle-class delinquency and ignores racial and gender issues
Social development model	Hawkins and Weis	Breakdown of social control	Integration of social control and cultural learning theories	Strong support	Does not deal as much with serious delinquency

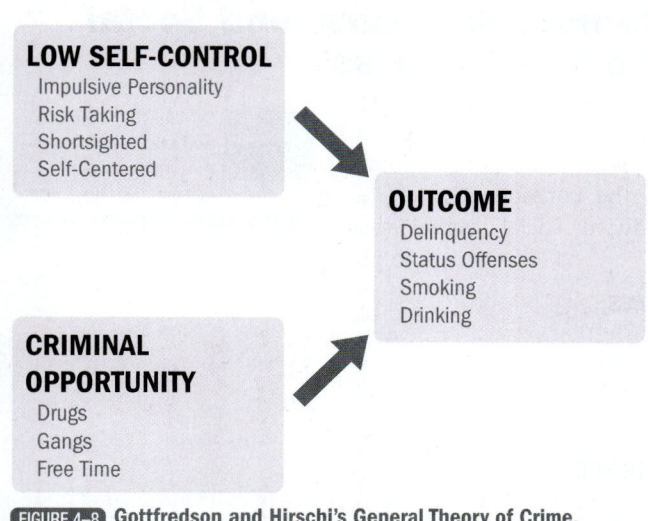

FIGURE 4-8 Gottfredson and Hirschi's General Theory of Crime.

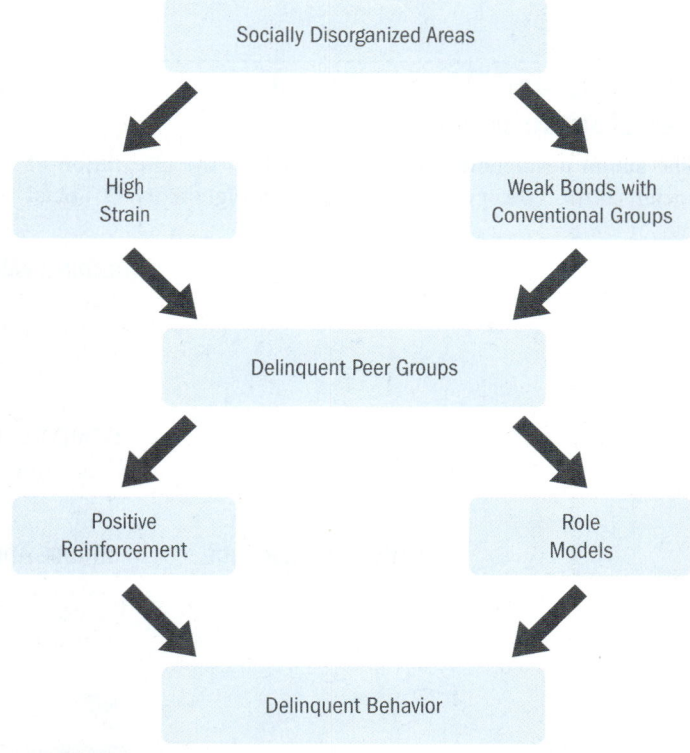

FIGURE 4-9 Elliott and Colleagues' Integrated Social Process Theory.

antisocial peer groups provide both positive reinforcement for delinquent behavior and role models for this behavior. Consequently, Elliott and colleagues theorized that there is a high probability of involvement in delinquent behavior when bonding to delinquent groups is combined with weak bonding to conventional groups[98] (see Figure 4-9).

Examinations of this theory have generally been positive, yet some doubt has been raised about its application to various types of delinquent behaviors. Questions have even been raised about its power and utility with different types of drug activity.[99]

Thornberry's Interactional Theory

In Thornberry's interactional theory of delinquency, the initial impetus toward delinquency comes from a weakening of the person's bond to conventional society, represented by attachment to parents, commitment to school, and belief in conventional values[100]—the most influential factor in bonding the youngster to conventional society and reducing delinquency. But as the youth matures and moves through middle adolescence, the world of friends, school, and youth culture becomes the dominant influence over his or her behavior. Finally, as the person enters adulthood, commitments to conventional activities and to family, especially, offer new avenues to reshape the person's bond to society and involvement with delinquent behavior.[101]

Moreover, this interactive process develops over the person's life cycle. During early adolescence, for example, the family is the most important socializing agent, but later loses its significance as young people mature and form peer bonds. Finally, interactional theory holds that these process variables are systematically related to the youngster's position in the social structure. Class, minority group status, and social disorganization of the community all affect the initial values of the interactive variables as well as the behavioral trajectories. It is argued that youths from the most socially disadvantaged backgrounds begin the process least bonded to conventional society and most exposed to the world of delinquency. The nature of the process increases the chances that they will continue on to a career of serious criminal involvement; on the other hand, youths from middle-class families enter a trajectory that is oriented toward conformity and away from delinquency (see Figure 4–10).

Interactional theory has several positive features, one of the most important is that interactional approaches are consistent with the social settings in which individuals live and interact with others.[102] Most significant of the shortcomings is that interactional theory fails to address the presence of middle-class delinquency and basically ignores racial and gender issues.[103]

Hawkins and Weis's Social Development Model

The **social development model** is based on the integration of social control theory and cultural learning theory.[104] Social control theory focuses on the individual characteristics that lead to delinquent behavior and the impact of the major socializing institutions on delinquency, whereas cultural learning theory examines the role of the community context in the process of learning criminal and delinquent attitudes and behaviors. Social control theory posits that youths become delinquent because of inadequate social controls; cultural learning theory adds that juveniles become socialized to delinquency in disorganized communities.

The social development model proposes that the development of attachments to parents will lead to attachments to school and a commitment to education, as well as a belief in and commitment to conventional behavior and the law. Learning theory describes the process by which these bonds develop: If juveniles are given adequate opportunities for involvement in legitimate activities and are able to acquire the necessary skills with a consistent reward structure, they will develop the bonds of attachment, commitment, and belief. Figure 4–11 presents a diagram of the social development model.

▶ Delinquency Across the life Course: Structural and Social Process Theories

An important structural explanation of delinquency across the life course points to the consequences of the reduced social capital that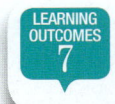

LEARNING OUTCOMES 7 Explain the structural and social processes that impact delinquency over time.

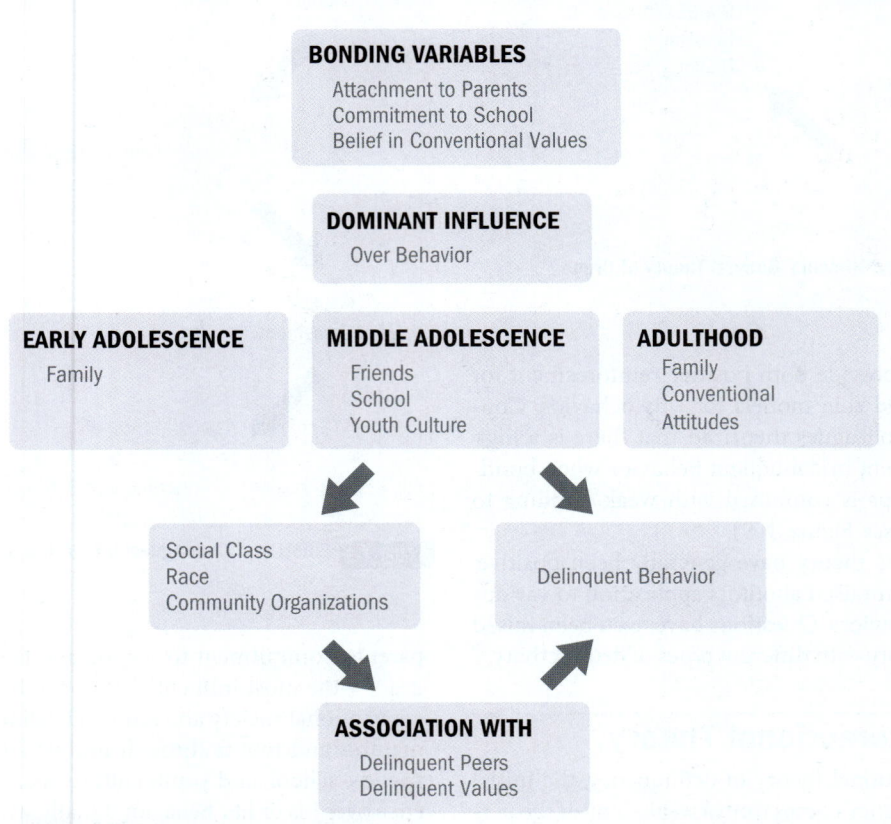

FIGURE 4–10 Thornberry's Interactional Theory.

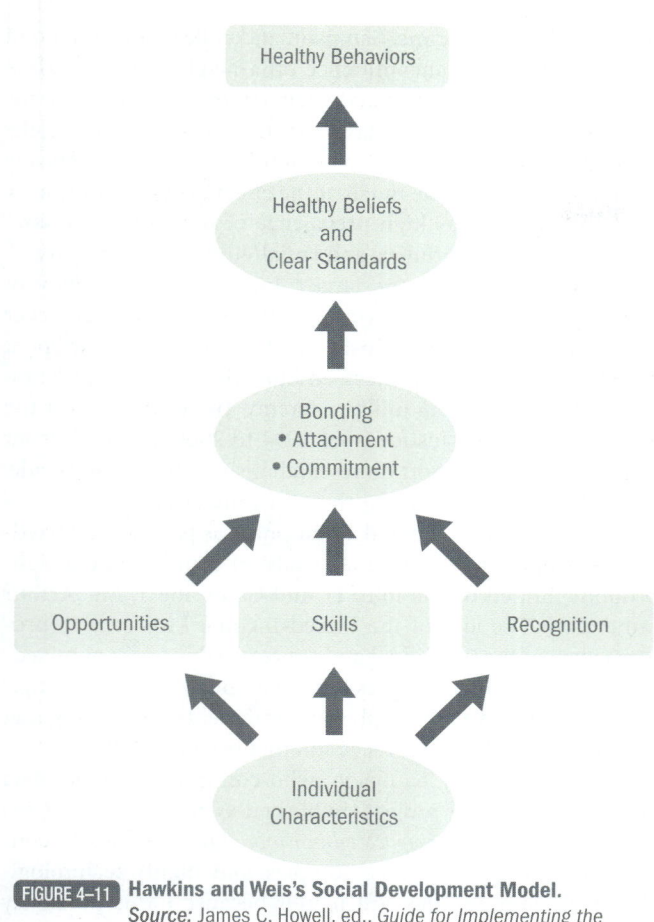

FIGURE 4-11 Hawkins and Weis's Social Development Model.
Source: James C. Howell, ed., *Guide for Implementing the Comprehensive Strategy for Serious, Violent, and Chronic Juvenile Offenders* (Washington, DC: Office of Juvenile Justice and Delinquency Prevention, 1995), p. 23.

lower-class children have, and a social process theory across the life course relates to cumulative disadvantage.

Reduced Social Capital

Lower-class youngsters often lack access to **social capital**—to the norms, networks, and supportive relationships they need if they are to realize their potential. They may be forced to struggle to meet their basic survival needs. Economic deprivation is first felt at home, and it is this deprivation that drives many youths to the streets.[105] Not surprisingly, the father frequently leaves, and the mother is gone much of the time simply trying to make ends meet. G. Roger Jarjoura, Ruth A. Triplett, and Gregory P. Brinker, using 14 years of longitudinal data for a national sample of younger adolescents, found that the exposure to poverty and the timing of such exposure are indeed related to an increased likelihood of delinquent involvement.[106]

Cumulative Disadvantage

Most juvenile delinquents' lives are not characterized by the kind of competence to plan that leads to one successful experience after another throughout the life course. Instead, delinquent youths often deal with personal deficits that lead to a series of cumulative disadvantages. For example, Thornberry

> **Delinquent youths often deal with personal deficits that lead to a series of cumulative disadvantages.**

and Krohn's examination of the Rochester data revealed that individuals who begin antisocial behavior early have individual deficits (that is, negative temperamental qualities) that both contribute to and are adversely affected by parental deficits (for example, explosive physical disciplinary styles and low affective ties). Over time, these researchers contended that these parents and children develop a coercive interaction, the result being children who express persistent patterns of oppositional and aggressive behavior.[107]

What this concept of cumulative disadvantage suggests is that each negative event in an offender's life tends to limit the positive options available to the individual and becomes a disadvantage in living a crime-free life. Incarceration, especially, leads to cumulative disadvantage in other areas. Thus, arrest and incarceration may spark failure in school, unemployment, and weak community bonds, which in turn increase adult crime.[108]

▶ Delinquency and Social Policy: PHDCN and Lafans

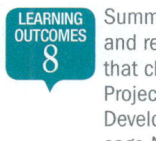

LEARNING OUTCOMES 8: Summarize the goals and research strategies that characterize the Project on Human Development in Chicago Neighborhoods.

The project on Human Development in Chicago Neighborhoods (PHDCN) is an interdisciplinary study of how families, schools, and neighborhoods affect child and adolescent development.[109] It was launched in the mid-1990s with major support from the National Institute of Justice and the John D. and Catherine T. MacArthur Foundation. PHDCN was led by Felton Earls, M.D., at the Harvard University School of Public Health and Medical School. Project directors represent a variety of disciplines and major universities.[110]

The project, whose data continue to be made available through the University of Michigan's Inter-university Consortium for Political and Social Research (ICPSR), is remarkable in both its scope and design. It combined (1) a longitudinal study of youths, with repeated interviews of more than 6,000 youths and their caregivers, along with (2) a neighborhood study that included a survey of almost 9,000 neighborhood residents and systematic observation of levels of social and physical disorder in 80 neighborhoods. Data collection was conducted based on four separate components that focused on a variety of individual and community characteristics:[111]

1. *Community survey.* The dynamic structure of the local community, neighborhood organizational and political structures, cultural values, informal and formal social controls, and social cohesion were measured.

2. *Systematic social observations.* A standardized approach for directly observing the physical, social, and economic characteristics of neighborhoods, one block at a time,

was applied to 80 to 343 neighborhoods (i.e., over 23,000 blocks) in the study. These observations were coded to assess neighborhood characteristics such as land use, housing, litter, graffiti, and social interactions.

3. *Longitudinal cohort study.* An accelerated longitudinal design with seven cohorts was separated by three-year intervals. These randomly selected cohorts of children, adolescents, and young adults and their primary caregivers were followed over a period of seven years to study changes in their personal characteristics and circumstances.

4. *Infant assessment unit.* As part of the longitudinal cohort study, 412 infants from the birth cohort and their primary caregivers were studied during wave 1 (1994–1997) to examine the effects of prenatal and postnatal conditions on their growth and health, cognitive abilities, and motor skills.

Early Findings from the PHDCN Study

Findings from the PHDCN's neighborhood study received widespread attention in both the professional and general media. For example, in a widely cited article published in *Science* in 1997 and summarized in a National Institute of Justice *Research Review*, Robert J. Sampson, Stephen Raudenbush, and Felton Earls found that neighborhood social processes had a significant impact on homicide and violence in the community. In particular, homicide and violent victimization rates were found to be lower in neighborhoods where residents shared values, had common expectations that neighbors would intervene in problem behavior, and had trust in each other. The researchers called this combination of shared values, trust, and expectations for social intervention "collective efficacy" to control crime and deviance. The level of collective efficacy, in turn, was strongly influenced by neighborhood conditions such as the extent of poverty and the lack of residential stability. Collective efficacy thus seems to be a mediating link between neighborhoods with similar conditions—those with greater collective efficacy experienced less violence.[112]

Robert J. Sampson, a Harvard University professor, and colleagues developed the concept of collective efficacy as characteristics of a community that they felt would work together to prevent and control crime. Sampson and colleagues contended that the most important influence on a neighborhood's crime is neighbors' willingness to act, when necessary or needed, for one another's benefit, especially for the benefit of one another's children. Several studies have found that collective efficacy does function to mediate much of the effect of such community structural variables as high prevalence of poverty, unemployment, single-parent families, and racial/ethnic heterogeneity.[113]

PHDCN is perhaps the largest interdisciplinary study of the complex influences exerted on human development ever undertaken. The National Institute of Justice has so far spent over $18 million on the project, and the MacArthur foundation has spent another $23.6 million. Jeremy Travis, director of the National Institute of Justice from 1994 to 2000, noted "It is far and away the most important research insight in the last decade. I think it will shape policy for the next generation."[114]

In 2001, PHDCN entered a new phase as part of the Mixed-Income Project, a longitudinal study of families and neighborhoods funded by the John D. and Catherine T. MacArthur Foundation. The aim of the Mixed-Income Project is to produce a view of the individual and aggregate dynamics of mixed-income housing, including residential mobility, housing change, job loss, and key aspects of physical and mental well-being that occurred during the great recession that began in 2008.[115]

In 2012, Robert J. Sampson, who continues to direct data gathering under the project, published *Great American City: Chicago and the Enduring Neighborhood Effect*. Sampson concluded that, even in today's complex and highly technological world, "communities still matter because life is decisively shaped [by] where you live."[116]

The Los Angeles Family and Neighborhood Survey (LAFANS), which builds on key PHDCN findings, is an ongoing project, begun in 2000, that seeks to answer the questions of "What makes a neighborhood a positive place to live?"[117] The survey gathered data on 3,000 families in 65 Los Angeles neighborhoods in two waves: one between 2000 and 2001, and another between 2006 and 2008. LAFANS, which is being conducted by the RAND Corporation and the UCLA School of Public Health, has resulted in numerous publications, including at least one that shows that members of racial/ethnic groups "appear to exhibit negative health risk behaviors when they reside in areas that are disproportionately populated with their co-ethnic peers."[118]

THE CASE

The Life Course of Amy Watters, Age Ten

If you could ask Amy what the most significant event that took place in the tenth year of her life had been, she would likely say that it was the day that the police called and said that her father, Simon, was in jail. He'd been arrested for driving while under the influence of an intoxicating substance (marijuana). Amy was frantic when she received the call because there was no adult in the house to whom she could turn for help. About an hour later, her father called from jail and asked Amy to phone Uncle Fred, who lived only a few miles away, for help. Fred would post bail, her dad said, and he could get out of jail. Sure enough, Uncle Fred came through, and Amy's dad came home later that same evening.

Discuss

1. Research suggests that delinquency is more likely to occur in those families in which parental self-control is low. One study, in particular (see the following link), seemed to demonstrate a significant link between parental low self-control and child low self-control. Moreover, that link was shown to be correlated with a greater incidence of delinquency among children raised in families exhibiting low parental self-control. Does the incident described in this box mean that Amy's father suffered from low self-control? If so, what might the consequences be for Amy?

Learn more on the Web:

- Read a classic overview of antisocial behavior among teenagers by visiting the National Criminal Justice Reference Service at NCJRS.gov and reading the publication numbered NCJ 059525.

Follow the continuing Amy Watters saga in the next chapter.

CHAPTER 4: Social Structural and Social Process Theories of Delinquency

LEARNING OUTCOMES 1

Describe the social disorganization theory of delinquency.

The social disorganization theory of delinquency, set forth by Clifford R. Shaw and Henry D. McKay, demonstrates the importance of social ecology, specifically the locations where young people live. Social disorganization theory is increasingly used today in terms of crime and community.

1. According to Shaw and McKay, what is the relationship among ecology, social disorganization, and transmission of deviant culture?
2. What is meant by the term *differential opportunity structure*? How do opportunity structures contribute to delinquency?
3. What's the difference between social structure and social process?

social structure The relatively stable formal and informal arrangements that characterize a society, including its economic arrangements, social institutions, and values and norms.

social process theories A theoretical approach to delinquency that examines the interactions between individuals and their environments, especially those that might influence them to become involved in delinquent behavior.

social disorganization theory An approach that posits that juvenile delinquency results when social control among the traditional primary groups, such as the family and the neighborhood, breaks down because of social disarray within the community.

anomie A condition of normlessness within a society.

differential opportunity structure The differences in economic and occupational opportunities open to members of different socioeconomic classes.

cultural transmission theory An approach that holds that areas of concentrated crime maintain their high rates over a long period, even when the composition of the population changes rapidly, because delinquent "values" become cultural norms and are passed from one generation to the next.

LEARNING OUTCOMES 2

Describe the cultural deviance approach to delinquency.

Cultural deviance theories of delinquency propose that delinquents and criminals have value systems or norms that differ from those of conformists. In effect, they say that lower-class youths do not aspire to middle-class values because they have their own lower-class values, or focal concerns, that encourage involvement in delinquent behavior. There is mixed support for the value of cultural deviance theories.

1. What are Walter B. Miller's focal concerns, or values, of lower-class delinquency?
2. Do you believe that lower-class youngsters aspire to middle-class values, or do they have their own values?
3. What are the implications of cultural deviance theory for delinquency prevention?

cultural deviance theory A theory wherein delinquent behavior is viewed as an expression of conformity to cultural values and norms that are in opposition to those of the larger U.S. society.

focal concerns of the lower class The values or focal concerns (toughness, smartness, excitement, fate, and autonomy) of lower-class youths that differ from those of middle-class youths.

LEARNING OUTCOMES 3

Explain strain and opportunity theories of delinquency.

Strain theories argue that delinquency results from the frustrations individuals feel when they are unable to achieve the goals they desire. This theory has been proposed by Robert Merton and Albert K. Cohen, and a recent version is general strain theory by Robert Agnew. There is strong support for the various versions of this theory.

1. How do you explain strain theory? What is the relationship between strain and delinquency?
2. What is meant by *reaction formation*? What leads to reaction formation?
3. List and describe some culturally approved goals. What alternative means might be used to achieve them?

culturally defined goals In Merton's strain theory, the set of purposes and interests a culture defines as legitimate objectives for individuals.

institutionalized means In Merton's theory, culturally sanctioned methods of attaining individual goals.

strain theory A theory that proposes that the pressure the social structure exerts on youths who cannot attain cultural success goals will push them to engage in nonconforming behavior.

blocked opportunity The limited or nonexistent chance of success; according to strain theory, a key factor in delinquency.

status frustration The stress that individuals experience when they cannot attain their goals because of their socioeconomic class.

reaction formation The psychological strategy for dealing with frustration by becoming hostile toward an unattainable object.

opportunity theory A perspective that holds that gang members turn to delinquency because of a sense of injustice about the lack of legitimate opportunities open to them.

LEARNING OUTCOMES 4

Summarize the differential association theory of delinquency.

Differential association theory suggests that individuals who are involved in antisocial groups are more likely to accept and internalize antisocial conduct norms and behavioral definitions. This theory has received considerable support through the years.

1. Why is differential association referred to as a learning theory?
2. Does differential association theory support the "nature" or "nurture" argument of crime causation? Explain your response.
3. What kinds of delinquency prevention programs might be based on differential association theory?

differential association theory The view that delinquency is learned from others and that delinquent behavior is to be expected of individuals who have internalized a preponderance of definitions that are favorable to law violations.

LEARNING OUTCOMES 5

Summarize control theories of delinquency.

The social disorganization theory of delinquency, set forth by Clifford R. Shaw and Henry D. McKay, demonstrates the importance of social ecology, specifically the locations where young people live. Social disorganization theory is increasingly used today in terms of crime and community.

1. What is meant by control theory? How do Reckless and Hirschi differ in their versions of control theory?
2. Social control approaches—including bonding theory—maintain that the more strongly adolescents are attached by positive social bonds, the more likely it is that they will refrain from delinquent behavior.

control theory Any of several theoretical approaches that maintain that human beings must be held in check, or somehow be controlled, if delinquent tendencies are to be repressed.

social control theory A perspective that delinquent acts result when a juvenile's bond to society is weak or broken.

commitment to the social bond The attachment that a juvenile has to conventional institutions and activities.

LEARNING OUTCOMES 6

Explain the benefits of integrated theoretical explanations for delinquency.

The development of integrated theoretical explanations for delinquency has been one of the most highly praised concepts in the field of criminology. Theory integration implies the combination of two or more existing theories on the basis of their perceived commonalities.

1. Which one of the four integrated theories discussed in this section makes the most sense to you? Why?
2. What are the advantages of integrated theory? What are its disadvantages?
3. What implications does theory integration hold for social policy in the area of crime and delinquency control?

general theory of crime A perspective that holds that lack of self-control is the common factor underlying problem behaviors.

social development model A perspective based on the integration of social control theory and cultural learning theory that holds that the development of attachments to parents will lead to attachments to school and a commitment to education, as well as a belief in and commitment to conventional behavior and the law.

LEARNING OUTCOMES 7

Explain the structural and social processes that impact delinquency over time.

The sociological viewpoint focuses attention on structural characteristics within a society and surrounding social processes to explain crime. Macrosocial forces (such as migration, segregation, structural transformation of the economy, and housing discrimination) can interact with community-level factors (such as concentrated poverty, family disruption, and residential turnover) to impede social organization and to create delinquency.

1. What is social capital?
2. How can social capital be enhanced? How might it be lost?
3. What consequences accrue to those who possess substantial social capital?

social capital The norms, networks, and supportive relationships that people need if they are to realize their potential.

LEARNING OUTCOMES 8

Summarize the goals and research strategies that characterize the Project on Human Development in Chicago Neighborhoods.

The Project on Human Development in Chicago Neighborhoods found that homicide and violent victimization rates were lower in neighborhoods where residents shared values, had common expectations that neighbors would intervene in problem behaviors, and trusted each other. The researchers called this "collective efficacy." It has received wide support as a mediating link between neighborhood conditions and crime and violence.

1. What are the goals of the Project of the Project on Human Development in Chicago Neighborhoods?
2. What is the concept of collective efficacy within the Project on Human Development in Chicago Neighborhoods? Why is it so important?

"We worry about what a child will become tomorrow, yet we forget that he is someone today."

—*Stacia Tauscher, National Center for Juvenile Justice,* Annual Report, *2003*

5

Social Interactionist Theories of Delinquency

1. Explain the significance of labeling as a cause of future behavior.
2. Summarize the symbolic interactionist theory of delinquency.
3. Explain the conflict theory of delinquency.
4. Describe restorative justice and peacemaking.
5. Summarize the contributions of the conflict perspective to social policy.

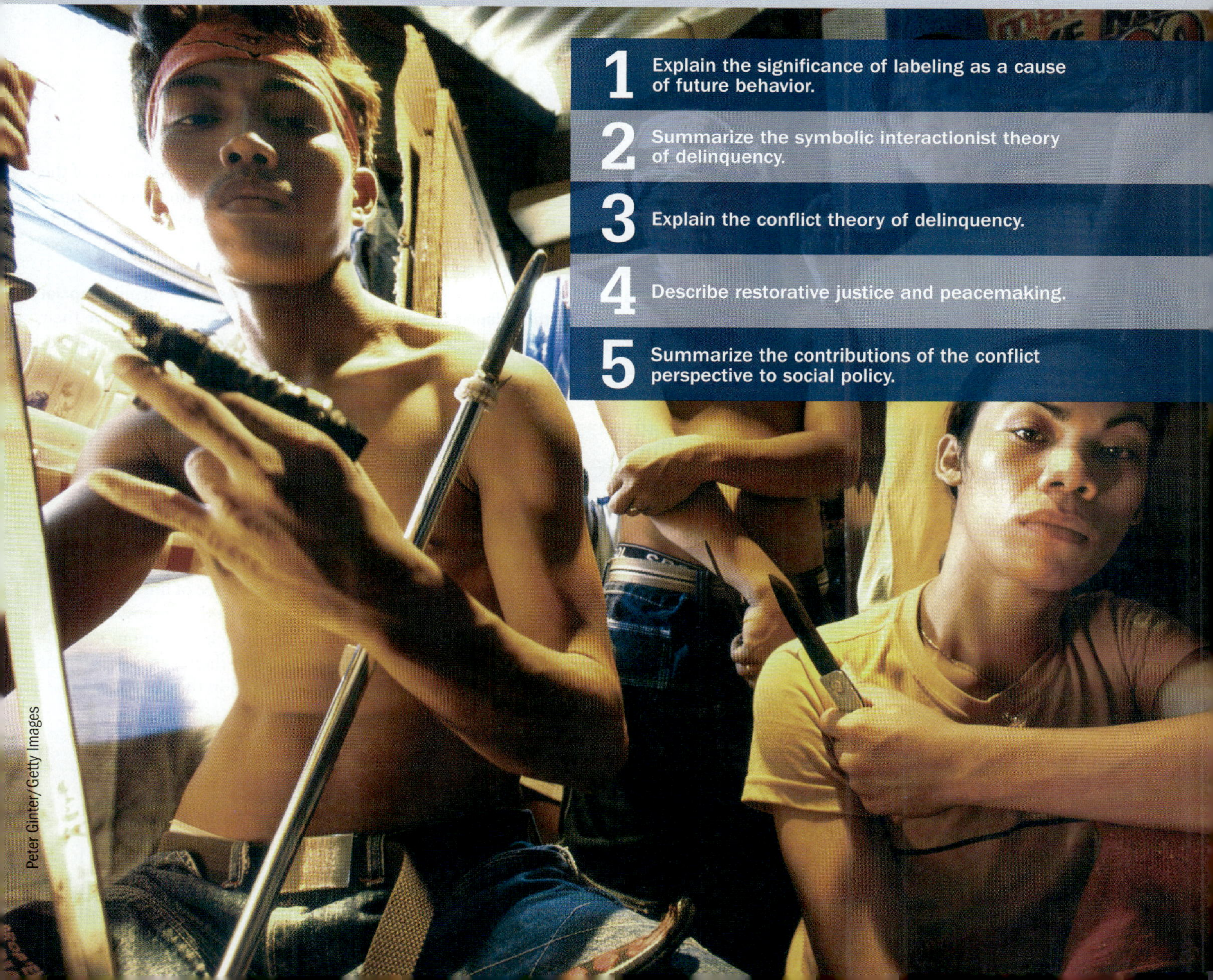

Peter Ginter/Getty Images

INTRO: ADOLESCENT BULLYING

Suicides by bullied adolescents are occurring with alarming frequency. On October 15, 2013, for example, Rebecca Ann Sedwick, age 12, jumped to her death in an old cement plant in Lakeland, Florida, after she had been bullied by more than a dozen youths. She was apparently made despondent by online social media comments from other youngsters, who sent her phrases such as "Go kill yourself"; and "Why are you still alive?" Terrorized before she committed suicide, she texted such questions as "How many over-the-counter drugs do you take to die?"[1] In another 2013 incident, after being repeatedly called names by peers, 12-year-old Jose Reyer brought a gun to school, shot two classmates, and killed a teacher before shooting himself. One witness reported that he told his victims, "You guys ruined my life so I'm going to ruin yours."[2] In still other recent incidents, a student in Sparks, Texas, and another in Albuquerque, New Mexico, who had just been bullied committed suicide, shortly after both had seen an anti-bullying video. Lewis, the father of one of the students, said, "All I know is that they were discussing the bullying, and showing kids bullying, and at the end of the show they showed pictures of kids that took their lives." Lewis said, "When a child or person is at the end of their rope, and they don't think there is anywhere to go, and they don't think anyone's doing anything about it, and they see something on video, they relate."[3]

A memorial to twelve-year-old Rebecca Ann Sedwick. The Florida girl committed suicide after being taunted by other youngsters on social media. How are bullying and suicide related?

DISCUSS Can anything be done to change a fatalistic child's view on life, especially a child growing up in poverty?

Bullying is a form of labeling, a perspective that this chapter discusses, and it can result in violent behavior toward one's self and others. In addition to labeling, this chapter also discusses symbolic theory, conflict theory, and restorative justice.

Labeling theory describes the labeling process and explains how labels are applied to people, and how such labeling influences the nature and extent of delinquency. Symbolic interactionist theory considers the process by which deviant or delinquent behavior is shaped by reference groups and peers, whereas conflict theory sees delinquency as a by-product of the conflict that results when groups or classes with differing interests interact with one another. Restorative justice focuses on the peacemaking process, and hopes to be able to provide equitable "justice" to all parties involved in a criminal event.

These four theoretical perspectives are termed **social interactionist theories** of delinquency because they derive their explanatory power from the give-and-take that continuously occurs between social groups and between individuals and society.

▶ Labeling Theory

During the 1960s and 1970s, the labeling perspective was one of the most influential approaches to understanding crime and delinquency.[4]

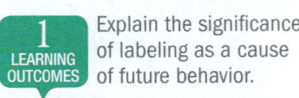

1 LEARNING OUTCOMES Explain the significance of labeling as a cause of future behavior.

Labeling theory or the labeling perspective, sometimes called the interactional theory of deviance or the social reaction perspective, is based on the premise that society creates deviants by branding those who are apprehended as different from other individuals when in reality they are different only because they have been tagged with a deviant label. Accordingly, labeling theorists focus on the processes by which individuals become involved in deviant behavior and stress the part played by social audiences and their responses to the norm violations of individuals.

The view that formal and informal social reactions to criminality can influence criminals' subsequent attitudes and behaviors has been recognized for some time. Frank Tannenbaum, Edwin M. Lemert, and Howard Becker, three of the chief proponents of the labeling perspective, focus on the process by which formal social control agents change the self-concept of individuals through these agents' reactions to their behavior. Recent work in labeling theory is also discussed in this section.

> **Labeling theory is based on the premise that society creates deviants by branding those who are apprehended as different from other individuals.**

78 Chapter 5 Social Interactionist Theories of Delinquency

Frank Tannenbaum: Dramatization of Evil

In 1938, Tannenbaum developed the earliest formulation of labeling theory in his book *Crime and the Community*. Tannenbaum examined the process whereby a juvenile came to the attention of the authorities and was labeled as different from other juveniles, and he theorized that this process produced a change in both how such individuals were then handled by the justice system and how they came to view themselves:

> The process of making the criminal, therefore, is a process of tagging, defining, identifying, segregating, describing, emphasizing, making conscious and self-conscious; it becomes a way of stimulating, suggesting, emphasizing, and evoking the very traits that are complained of.[5]

Tannenbaum called this process the "dramatization of evil," writing that the process of tagging a juvenile resulted in the youth becoming involved with other delinquents and that these associations represented an attempt to escape the society that was responsible for the negative labeling. The delinquent then became involved in a deviant career, and regardless of the efforts of individuals in the community and the justice system to change his or her "evil" behavior, the negative behavior became increasingly hardened and resistant to positive values. Tannenbaum proposed that the less the evil is dramatized, the less likely youths are to become involved in deviant careers.[6]

Edwin Lemert: Primary and Secondary Deviation

The social reaction theory developed by Edwin H. Lemert provided a distinct alternative to the social disorganization theory of Shaw and McKay, the differential association notion of Edwin H. Sutherland, and the social structural approach of Merton. Lemert focused attention on the interaction between social control agents and rule violators as well as on how certain behaviors came to be labeled criminal, delinquent, or deviant.[7]

Lemert's concept of primary and secondary deviation is regarded as one of the most important theoretical constructs of the labeling perspective. According to Lemert, **primary deviation** consists of the individual's behavior, and **secondary deviation** is society's response to that behavior. The social reaction to the deviant, Lemert charged, could be interpreted as forcing a change in status or role; that is, society's reaction to the deviant person resulted in a transformation in the individual's identity.[8] The social reaction to the deviant person, whether a disapproving glance or a full-blown stigmatization, is critical in understanding the **process of becoming deviant**.

The social reaction to deviance is expressed in this process of interaction. *Social reaction* is a general term that summarizes both the moral indignation of others toward deviance and the action directed toward its control. This concept also encompasses a social organizational perspective; as an organizational response, the concept of social reaction refers to the capacity of control agents to impose such constraints on the behavior of the deviant person as are reflected in terms such as *treat, correct,* and *punish*.[9]

Think About It...

Howard Becker argued that once a person is caught and labeled, that person gains a new social status—that of outsider. What are the consequences of being an outsider?

Howard Becker: Deviant Careers

Howard Becker, another major labeling theorist, conceptualized the relationship between the rules of society and the process of being labeled as an outsider:

> Social groups create deviance by making the rules whose infraction constitutes deviance, and by applying those rules to particular people and labeling them as outsiders. From this point of view, deviance is not a quality of the act the person commits, but rather a consequence of the application by others of rules and sanctions to an "offender." The deviant is one to whom that label has successfully been applied; deviant behavior is behavior that people so label.[10]

Becker argued that once a person is caught and labeled, that person becomes an outsider and gains a new social status, with consequences for both the person's self-image and his or her public identity. The individual is now regarded as a different kind of person.[11] Although the sequence of events that leads to the imposition of the label of "deviant" is presented from the perspective of social interaction, the analytical framework shifts to that of social structure once the label is imposed. In other words, before a person is labeled, he or she participates in a process of social interaction, but once labeling has occurred, the individual is assigned a status within a social structure.[12] For the relationship among the theoretical constructs that constitute labeling theory, see Figure 5–1.

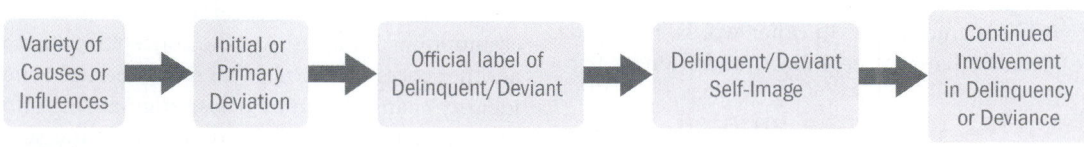

FIGURE 5–1 General Assumptions of Labeling Theory.

The Juvenile Justice Process and Labeling

There has long been wide support for the contention that the labeling found in the formal processing of youths through the juvenile justice system is what influences the secondary response of continued delinquent acts. Edwin Schur contended that most delinquent acts are insignificant and benign and that punishment is not needed. But when youths are arrested and brought before the juvenile court, they are stereotyped as different. Having acquired this label, they receive greater attention from authorities, and they are likely to be processed more deeply in the justice system because of this increased attention. Delinquency laws are actually counterproductive, Schur stated, because they produce more delinquency than they deter. In 1973, Schur went so far as to argue for a policy of **radical nonintervention**, which simply means to "leave the kids alone whenever possible."[13]

More recently, several studies have suggested that under certain circumstances, "official punishment appears to increase the likelihood of subsequent deviance as suggested by labeling theory."[14] One study found that the formal reaction to delinquency affects the likelihood of subsequent delinquent behavior but that these effects are related to the types of reactions and the types of deviance.[15] Another study investigated the relationship between prior and current youth court dispositions and found support for labeling theory; the findings indicated that prior juvenile court dispositions exerted a significant impact on current disposition, even with the control of relevant variables.[16]

New Developments in Labeling Theory

The early versions of labeling theory came under serious attack for theoretical flaws and lack of support.[17] Critics of this perspective charged that "labeling theorists had grossly exaggerated the role of labeling by suggesting that it is the only factor responsible for persistent deviance and by implying that it always increases the likelihood of subsequent rule breaking."[18] Assailed by these and other criticisms, the theory was under serious challenge by 1980 and was "pronounced dead by 1985."[19] However, the labeling perspective later enjoyed a resurgence because of its more sophisticated application, as discussed next.[20]

Recent Applications of Labeling Theory

Ruth Ann Triplett and G. Roger Jarjoura developed what they termed "new avenues for exploring the effects of labeling."[21] They separated labeling into formal and informal labeling: Formal labels, the emphasis of early labeling theorists, are the reactions by official agents of the justice system to illegal behaviors; in contrast, an informal label is "an attempt to characterize a person as a given 'type' . . . by persons who are not acting as official social control agents, and in social situations that are not formal social control 'ceremonies.'"[22] In other words, informal labels are those given by parents, neighbors, and friends. For example, John Braithwaite examined shaming in the family; his study showed that families use shaming, or reintegrative shaming, to bring an offender back into line with their beliefs.[23]

Triplett and Jarjoura also divided labels into subjective and objective labels. An audience's reaction to an actor is an objective label, whereas the actor's interpretation of that reaction is a subjective label. Although the importance of subjective labels has always been emphasized in symbolic interactionism, it has remained largely unexplored in labeling theory and research.[24] Triplett, using the four waves of Elliott's National Youth Survey, concluded that the informal labels of significant others (parents) affect delinquent behavior both directly and indirectly for whites, but that informal or subjective labels of significant others have no consistent direct or indirect effect on delinquent behavior for nonwhites.[25]

Robert J. Sampson and John Laub claimed that labeling is one indicator leading to "cumulative disadvantage" in future life chances (see Chapter 4), which increases the likelihood of a person's involvement in criminal acts. This *life-course approach* views public labeling as a transitional event pushing young people experiencing a transitory disadvantage into greater involvement in deviance and crime.[26] Other recent studies have also found support for the finding that labeling leads to continued criminality.[27]

Evaluation of Labeling Theory

The labeling perspective has consistently received mixed responses, but it does have several strengths:

- Labeling theory provides an explanation for why youths who become involved in the juvenile justice process frequently continue delinquent acts until the end of their adolescent years.

- Labeling theory emphasizes the importance of rule making and power in the creation of deviance. Consideration of the broader contexts of the labeling process lifts the focus of delinquency from the behavior of an individual actor to the interactions of an actor and his or her immediate and broader influences.

- As part of a larger symbolic interactionist perspective, labeling theory points out that individuals do take on the roles and self-concepts that are expected of them; this means that they can indeed become victims of self-fulfilling prophecies.

- The more sophisticated applications of labeling theory developed since the early 1990s have moved this explanation of delinquent behavior from a unidimensional focus to a perspective examining more contingencies of labeling effects, including both direct and indirect effects of labeling.

The labeling perspective has been criticized, however, because it fails to answer several critical questions raised by the assumptions it makes: Are the conceptions that we have of one another correct? Whose label really counts? When is a personal identity changed, and by whose stigmatizing effort is it altered? Does a bad name cause bad action? Is the social response to crime generated more by the fact of the crime or by the legally

> **Once a person is caught and labeled, that person becomes an outsider.**

TABLE 5–1 AN EVALUATION OF LABELING THEORY

Proponents	Theory	Outcome of Labeling	Strengths	Criticisms
Tannenbaum	Processed youths were labeled and viewed as different	Deviant career and dramatization of evil	Introduced the labeling concept	Did not consider secondary deviation of youths
Lemert	Concept of primary and secondary deviation	Transformation in the individual's identity	Identified the process of becoming deviant	Did not consider secondary deviation of youths
Becker	Conceptualized relationship between rules of society and process of becoming an outsider	Individual becomes an outsider	Outsiders are given a new status	Did not consider secondary deviation of youths
Schur	Labeled youths are processed more deeply in the justice system	Official punishment increases the likelihood of deviancy	Support in the literature	Did not consider secondary deviation of youths
Triplett and Jarjoura	Developed formal and informal labeling and exclusive and inclusive labeling	Examined more fully the effects of labeling	Expanded the effects of labeling	Did not consider secondary deviation of youths

irrelevant social characteristics of the offender? If official labels are so important, why do so many youths mature out of delinquency during their later adolescent years?[28] See Table 5–1 for an evaluation of labeling theory.

In sum, delinquency is clearly related to factors other than official labels, and it is extremely questionable to ascribe too much significance to the influence of the labeling process on adolescents' subsequent identities and behaviors.[29] Nevertheless, the resurgence of labeling theory in the late 1980s and 1990s proves that it remains alive and well. The theoretical refinements in labeling theory (for example, formal and informal labels, subjective and objective labels, and exclusive and inclusive social reactions) promise to offer fruitful avenues for examining delinquency in the future.

▶ Symbolic Interactionist Theory

The **symbolic interactionist theory** of delinquency was developed by sociologists Ross L. Matsueda and Karen Heimer.[30] This theory sees the social order as a dynamic process that is the ever-evolving product of an ongoing system of social interaction and communication.[31] It proposes to explain delinquent behavior in terms of self-development mediated by language—which is the central medium through which symbolic interaction occurs.[32] Of central importance is the process by which shared meanings, behavioral expectations, and reflected appraisals are built up through interaction and applied to behavior.[33] This interactionist perspective, according to Heimer, also has the "potential for illuminating the dynamic relationship among gender inequality, racial inequality, and law violation."[34]

2 LEARNING OUTCOMES Summarize the symbolic interactionist theory of delinquency.

Role Taking and Delinquency

Matsueda and Heimer built on the social act as the unit of analysis. They began with the immediate situation of delinquent behavior, which is made up of a social interaction between two or more individuals.[35] The situation can influence delinquency in two ways: First, the specific situation that juveniles encounter may present opportunities for delinquent behavior; second, and more important, the immediate situation influences delinquent behavior through its effects on the content and direction of social interaction.[36]

In analyzing social interaction, symbolic interactionists define the unit of analysis as the transaction that takes place in interaction between two or more individuals.[37] The important mechanism by which interactants influence each other is role taking, which Mead viewed as the key to social control.[38] According to Matsueda, role taking consists of the following:

> [It is] projecting oneself into the role of other persons and appraising, from their standpoint, the situation, oneself in the situation, and possible lines of action. With regard to delinquency, individuals confronted with delinquent behavior as a possible line of action take each other's roles through verbal and nonverbal communication, fitting their lines of action together into joint delinquent behavior.[39]

The transaction is built up through this process of reciprocal role taking, in which one person initiates a lawful or unlawful action and a second takes the role of the other and responds. The first person then reacts to the response, which continues until a jointly developed goal is reached, a new goal is substituted, or the transaction is ended. Through such reciprocal role taking, individual lines of action are coordinated, and concerted action is taken toward achieving the goal. This means that the initiated delinquent act of one juvenile might elicit a negative response from another juvenile, perhaps contributing to the group's searching for another, more suitable alternative. Matsueda suggested, "Whether or not a goal is achieved using unlawful means is determined by each individual's contribution to the direction of the transaction; those contributions, in turn, are determined by the individual's prior life experience or biography."[40]

Matsueda concluded that this discussion of role taking implies four features of a theory of the self and delinquent behavior. First, the self is formed by how an individual perceives that others view him or her and thus is rooted in symbolic interaction. Second, the self is an object that "arises partly endogenously within situations, and partly exogenously from prior situational self being carried over from previous experience." Third, the self as an object becomes a process that has been determined by the self at a previous point in time and by prior resolutions of problematic situations. Fourth, delinquent behavior takes place partly because habits are formed and partly because the stable perception of oneself is shaped by the standpoint of others.[41]

Using classic symbolic interactionist theory, Matsueda talked about the self as a consistent "me" that is relatively stable across situations. This self, which is called "a looking-glass self" by Charles H. Cooley[42] or the "self as an object" by Mead,[43] is a process that consists of three components: how others actually see us (others' actual appraisals), how we perceive the way others see us (reflected appraisals), and how we see ourselves (self-appraisals).[44] A person's self, then, is made up in part of a "reflected appraisal" of how significant others appraise or evaluate him or her.[45]

Matsueda used a sample from the National Youth Survey to test his theory. His findings supported a symbolic interactionist conceptualization of reflected appraisals and delinquency in a number of ways. Juveniles' reflected appraisals of themselves from the standpoint of parents, friends, and teachers "coalesced into a consensual self, rather than remaining compartmentalized as distinct selves."[46] This remained true whether the reflected appraisals were found in rule violators or socialized youths. In agreement with labeling theory, parental labels of youths as rule violators were more likely among nonwhites, urban dwellers, and delinquents. Delinquent youths' "appraisals of themselves are also strongly influenced by their parents' independent appraisals of them."[47] Moreover, prior delinquent behavior, both directly and indirectly, reflected appraisals of self. In addition, reflected appraisals as a rule violator exerted a large effect on delinquent behavior and mediated much of the effect of parental appraisals as a rule violator on delinquent behavior. Finally, age, race, and urban residence exerted significant effects on delinquency, most of which worked indirectly through prior delinquency and in part through the rule violator's reflected appraisal.[48]

Symbolic interactionists explain delinquent behavior in terms of interaction between the self and others, an interaction that is mediated by language—the primary symbolic medium.

Interactionist Perspectives on Gender, Race, and Delinquency

Heimer argued that "structural conflict gives rise to gender and race differences in motivations to break the law."[49] From the interactionist perspective, then, racial and gender inequalities are consequential for law violation because they restrict the positions of minorities and females and therefore constrain communication networks and the power needed to influence others.[50] She goes on to say the following:

> Hence, these forms of structural inequality influence definitions of situations because they partially determine the significant others and reference groups considered in the role-taking process. Through shaping definitions of situations, gender and racial inequality contribute to the patterning of crime and delinquency. Thus, consistent with the tradition of differential association in criminology, an interactionist theory of delinquency argues that there will be differences across groups in definitions of situations and the law to the extent that communication networks vary.[51]

Evaluation of Symbolic Interactionist Theory

The symbolic interactionist theory of delinquency has several strengths:

- It builds on symbolic interactionist theory, a great tradition in American sociology. This tradition has identified the locus of social control in the process of taking the role of the other and of linking with the broader social organization through role commitments, generalized others, and reference groups.[52]

- It builds on and adds to the insights of labeling theory. At a time in which labeling is being reformulated and is emerging in a more sophisticated form, the insights that Matsueda, Heimer, and their colleagues provide in relating symbolic interactionism and delinquency promise to further enrich labeling's contributions to our understanding of delinquency.

- The symbolic interactionist theory of delinquent behavior is insightful regarding how both law-abiding and delinquent youths form their conceptions of themselves and how these perceptions influence their decision making.

- This theory contributes helpful insights about the influence of delinquent peers and the group context on youths' self-appraisals. See Table 5–2 for a summary of symbolic interactionist theory.

An evaluation of symbolic interactionist theory, of course, is limited by the fact that it has been tested by Matsueda, Heimer, and colleagues in only a few settings.[53] At this point, it is uncertain how much delinquency it explains, even among group delinquents, and many of the criticisms aimed at labeling theory apply also to this theory. Nevertheless, symbolic interactionist theory is still a promising attempt to explain delinquent behavior.

TABLE 5–2 SUMMARY OF SYMBOLIC INTERACTIONIST THEORY

Proponents	Definition of Symbolic Interaction	Role Taking and Delinquency	Gender and Race	Strengths	Criticisms
Matsueda and Heimer	Dynamic process that is the ever-evolving product of an ongoing system of social interaction and communication	One person initiates an unlawful action and a second takes the role of the other and responds	Structural conflict gives rise to gender and racial differences in motivations to break the law	Builds on and adds to the strengths of labeling theory	Has been tested in only a few settings

▶ Conflict Theory

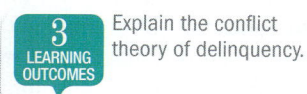

3 LEARNING OUTCOMES — Explain the conflict theory of delinquency.

Conflict theory sees social control as the end result of the differential distribution of economic and political power in any society, and conflict theorists view laws as tools created by the powerful for their own benefit.[54] The development of the conflict model is indebted to the concept of "dialectics." This concept, like that of order, can be traced back to the philosophers of ancient Greece. In antiquity, the term *dialectics* referred to the art of conducting a dispute or bringing out the truth by disclosing and resolving contradictions in the arguments of opponents.[55]

Dimensions of Conflict Criminology

A great deal of variation exists among the ideas of conflict criminologists. Some theories emphasize the importance of socioeconomic class, some focus primarily on power and authority relationships, and others emphasize group and cultural conflict.

Socioeconomic Class and Radical Criminology

Even though Karl Marx, a German philosopher and economist whom many have called the father of communism, wrote very little on the subject of crime as the term is used today, he inspired a new school of criminology that emerged in the early 1970s. This school is variously described as Marxist, critical, socialist, left-wing, or new criminology as well as **radical criminology**. Marx was concerned both with deriving a theory of how societies change over time and with discovering how to go about changing society. This joining of theory and practice is called "praxis."[56]

Marx saw the history of all societies as the history of class struggles and viewed crime as resulting from these class struggles.[57] He wrote in the *Communist Manifesto*,

> Freeman and slave, patrician and plebian, lord and serf, guildmaster and journeyman, in a word, oppressor and oppressed, stood in constant opposition to one another, carried on an uninterrupted, now hidden, now open

Conflict theorists see laws as tools created by the powerful for their own benefit.

fight, a reconstruction of society at large, or in the common ruin of the contending classes.[58]

Emerging with each historical period, according to Marx's theory, is a new class-based system of ranking. Marx contended that with **capitalism**, "society as a whole is more and more and more splitting up into two great classes directly facing each other—bourgeoisie [capitalist class] and proletariat [working class]."[59] The relations between the bourgeoisie and the proletariat become increasingly strained as the bourgeoisie comes to control more and more of society's wealth and the proletariat is increasingly pauperized. In this relationship between the oppressive bourgeoisie and the pauperized proletariat lie the seeds of the demise of capitalism.[60]

Mark Colvin and John Pauly developed an integrated structural theory of delinquency, the purpose of which was to provide "a comprehensive theoretical approach to understanding the social production of serious patterned delinquent behavior," and using the empirical findings of others to support their model, they contended that the power relations to which most lower-class workers are subjected are coercive.[61]

Herman Schwendinger and Julia Siegel Schwendinger also stated that capitalism produces a marginal class of people who are superfluous from an economic standpoint.[62] They went so far as to say that "the historical facts are incontrovertible: capitalism ripped apart the ancient regime and introduced criminality among youth in all stations of life."[63]

The Schwendingers further argued that socialization agents within the social system, such as the school, tend to reinvent within each new generation the same class system: "The children of families that *have* more *get* more, because the public educational system converts human beings into potential commodities."[64] The schools tend to be geared toward rewarding and assisting those youths who exhibit early indications of achieving the greatest potential success in institutions of higher learning and later in the job market, but this selection is made at the expense of those who do not exhibit such potential in their early encounters with the educational system.[65]

In the Marxist perspective, the state and the law itself are ultimately tools of the ownership class and reflect mainly the economic interests of that class. Capitalism produces egocentric, greedy, and predatory human behavior. The ownership class is guilty of the worst crime: the brutal exploitation of the working class. Revolution is a means to counter this violence and is

> **Think About It…**
>
> In the tradition of Karl Marx, radical criminologists see the history of all societies as the history of class struggles and view crime as a result of those struggles. Yet, communist societies were unable to eliminate crime. Why?

generally both necessary and morally justifiable. Conventional crime is caused by extreme poverty and economic disenfranchisement, products of the dehumanizing and demoralizing capitalist system.[66]

Power and Authority Relationships

A second important dimension of conflict criminology is the focus on power and authority relationships. Max Weber, Ralf Dahrendorf, Austin T. Turk, William J. Chambliss, John Hagan, Raymond Michaelowski, Robert M. Regoli, John D. Hewitt, and others have made contributions to this body of scholarship.

Weber's theory, like the Marxist perspective, contains a theory of social stratification that has been applied to the study of crime. Although Weber recognized the importance of the economic context in the analysis of social stratification, he did not believe that such a unidimensional approach could explain satisfactorily the phenomenon of social stratification. He added power and prestige to the Marxist emphasis on property and held these three variables responsible for the development of hierarchies in society. Weber also proposed that property differences led to the development of classes, power differences led to the creation of political parties and the development of classes, and prestige differences led to the development of status groups.[67] Further, Weber discussed the concept of "life chances" and argued that they were differentially related to social class; from this perspective, criminality exists in all societies and is the result of the political struggle among different groups attempting to promote or enhance their own life chances.[68]

Both Dahrendorf and Turk have extended the Weberian tradition in the field of criminology by emphasizing the relationships between authorities and their subjects. Dahrendorf contended that power is the critical variable explaining crime, arguing that although Marx built his theory on only one form of power, property ownership, a more useful perspective could be constructed by incorporating broader conceptions of power.[69]

Turk, constructing his analysis from the work of both Weber and Dahrendorf, argued that the social order of society is based on the relationships of conflict and domination between authorities and subjects.[70] Focusing on power and authority relationships, this perspective of conflict theory examines the relationships between the legal authorities who create, interpret, and enforce right–wrong standards for individuals in the political collectivity and those who accept or resist but do not make such legal decisions. Turk also made the point that conflicts

> **One form of culture conflict arises whenever society has diverging subcultures with differing conduct norms.**

between authorities and subjects take place over a wide range of social and cultural norms.[71]

John Hagan and his associates viewed the relationship between gender and nonserious delinquency as linked to power and control.[72] Using the data collected in Toronto, Ontario, they suggested that the presence of power among fathers and the greater control of girls explain why boys are delinquent more often than girls. Unlike Hirschi's control theory, Hagan and colleagues' **power-control thesis** based the measurement of class on the authority that parents have in their positions at work, and they assumed that the authority of parents at work translates into conditions of dominance in the household and in the degree of their parental control over their children.

Robert M. Regoli and John D. Hewitt's **theory of differential oppression** contends that in the United States, authority is unjustly used against children, who must "adapt to adults' conceptions of what 'good children' are." Children experience oppression, in this view, because they exist in a social world in which adults look on them as inferior and in which they lack social power relative to adults. Oppression takes place when adults use their power to prevent children from attaining access to valued resources or to prevent them from developing a sense of self as a subject rather than an object. Accordingly, children must submit to the power and authority of adults, and when children react negatively or fail to conform to these pressures, a process begins that results in delinquent acts.[73]

Regoli and Hewitt recognized that the oppression of children falls along a continuum and that some children are oppressed to a greater degree than others. The very basis of their theory hinges on the belief that children who are reared in highly oppressive family conditions are more likely to become delinquent than those who are not raised in such aversive environments.[74]

Group and Cultural Conflicts

Another dimension of conflict criminology is **culture conflict theory**, which focuses on group conflict. Thorsten Sellin and George B. Vold advocated this approach to the study of crime. Sellin argued that to understand the cause of crime, it is necessary to understand the concept of **conduct norms**,[75] a concept referring to the rules of a group concerning the ways its members should act under particular conditions. The violation of these rules arouses a group reaction.[76] Each individual is a member of many groups (family group, work group, play group, political group, religious group, and so on), and each group has its own particular conduct norms.[77]

Sellin noted that an individual experiences a conflict of norms "when more or less divergent rules of conduct govern the specific life situation in which a person may find himself."[78] The act of violating conduct norms is "abnormal behavior," and crime represents a particular kind of abnormal behavior distinguished by the fact that crime is a violation of the conduct norms defined by criminal law.[79]

Sellin also has developed a theory of "primary and secondary culture conflict." Primary culture conflict occurs when an individual or group comes into contact with an individual or group from another culture and the conduct norms of the two cultures are not compatible; secondary culture conflict refers to the conflict arising whenever society has diverging subcultures with different conduct norms.[80]

Vold, like Sellin, analyzed the dimension of group conflict. He applied group conflict to particular types of crimes, but he did not attempt to explain all types of criminal behavior. He stated that group members are constantly engaged in defending and promoting their group's status. As groups move into each other's territory or sphere of influence and begin to compete in those areas, intergroup conflict is inevitable. The outcome of a group conflict results in a winner and a loser, unless a compromise is reached—but compromises never take place when one group is decidedly weaker than the other. Vold believed that group loyalty develops and intensifies during group conflict.[81]

In sum, conflict criminologists can be divided into three basic groups: those emphasizing socioeconomic class, those emphasizing power and authority relationships, and those emphasizing group and cultural conflict. Those who emphasize socioeconomic class call themselves radical, Marxist, critical, humanist, or new criminologists and do not identify with the other two groups. Some significant differences do exist between radical criminologists and the other two groups: The non-Marxist conflict criminologists emphasize a plurality of interests and power and do not put a single emphasis on capitalism (as do the Marxist conflict criminologists), nor do the non-Marxist conflict criminologists reject the legal order as such or the use of legal definitions of crime.[82] Table 5–3 compares the three groups of conflict criminologists.

Evaluation of Conflict Theory

Conflict criminology's critiques of the social order do contribute two important pieces to the puzzle of why juveniles commit delinquent acts. First, the various conflict criminology perspectives call attention to the macrostructural flaws that contribute to high rates of juvenile delinquency. Second, radical humanism, also rooted in the structural inequalities of the social order, emphasizes the dignity of the person and is quick to identify instances where children experience oppression in the United States.[83] However, conflict theory leaves many unanswered questions, such as the following: How about middle-class delinquency? How about lower-class youths who do not become delinquent?

▶ The Social Context of Delinquency: Restorative Justice and Peacemaking

4 LEARNING OUTCOMES Describe restorative justice and peacemaking.

Advocates of restorative justice argue that after 25 years of relying on legal mechanisms, it is clear to many that legal standards are not sufficient to create healthy, ethical community behavior. The legal system is too distant from daily life to be effective and is too complicated and abstract for citizens to feel that they are a part of setting those standards or that they have responsibility for enforcing those standards in the community. In addition, because the legal system involves coercion and deprivation of liberty, it can set only minimum standards of behavior. Restorative justice processes that encourage cooperation and voluntary engagement can establish standards for maximum behavior.[84]

One of the lessons of restorative justice taught to youths is empathy development. According to Kay Pranis and other proponents of restorative justice, we have allowed enormous distance to develop between ourselves and the children of others. We have not come to know them and have not invested emotionally, materially, and spiritually in their well-being. Moreover, we have not taught them by example to understand the interconnectedness of all things and the need to understand the impact of our actions on others.[85] The development of empathy requires (1) regular feedback about how our actions affect others, (2) relationships in which we feel valued and our worth is validated, and (3) experience of sympathy from others when we are in pain.[86]

Restorative justice provides a framework for community members to reestablish a more appropriate relationship between community members and young people and to reduce the fear adults have of young people. The processes of restorative justice, especially face-to-face processes, involve the telling of personal stories in intimate settings. Stereotypes and broad generalizations about groups of people are difficult to sustain in the face of direct contact between youths and adults in a respectful setting. Restorative justice processes assume value in every human being and therefore present individuals to one another in a respectful way, which draws out human dignity in everyone.[87]

Restorative justice programs try to teach empathy to youthful offenders.

TABLE 5–3 COMPARISONS OF CONFLICT PERSPECTIVES

Perspective	Legal Definitions	Legal Order	Purpose of Conflict	Capitalism
Socioeconomic Class (Marxist)	Rejection	Rejection	Revolution	Rejection
Power and Authority Relationships	Acceptance	Acceptance	Reform	Acceptance
Group and Cultural Conflict	Acceptance	Acceptance	Reform	Acceptance

EXHIBIT 5–1 Restorative Justice and Related Treatment Interventions

Theory	Treatment Interventions
Provides a framework for community members to establish a communication network with young people to resolve minor disputes	Community Conferencing and Peacemaking
Makes it possible for victims, youths, and community members to resolve issues of youthful members' trespasses; following a healing circle, a sentencing circle decides on the behavioral consequences	Community Conferencing and Sentencing
Uses the family group decision-making model in order to try to stop family violence	Family Group Conferences (FGCs)
Involves a reparations program track designed for offenders who commit nonviolent offenses and who are considered at low risk for reoffense	Reparation and Restitution
Enables in-kind or actual return of what has been lost; it can be viewed within the larger context of "making amends"	Restitution Programs
Encourages one-on-one victim–offender reconciliation facilitated through a mediator	Victim–Offender Conferencing

Community Conferencing and Sentencing Circles

Community conferences make it possible for victims, youths, and community members to meet one another to resolve issues raised by an offender's trespass.[88]

How does a sentencing circle work? Participants in healing or sentencing circles typically speak out while passing around a "talking piece." Separate healing circles are initially held for the victim and the offender; after the healing circles meet, a sentencing circle (with feedback from the family, the community, and the justice system) determines a course of action, and other circles then follow up to monitor compliance, whether that involves, for example, restitution or community service.[89]

Evaluation of Restorative Justice

Restorative justice is rapidly gaining acceptance in juvenile and adult justice systems. Instead of relying on legal intervention to deal with youths' misbehavior and community conflicts, restorative justice groups are increasingly intervening and seeking to find reconciliation among offenders, victims, and the community. Its basic approach of valuing youngsters, affirming their strengths, and seeking communication with them has much in common with a school of thought known as peacemaking criminology. See Exhibit 5–1 for a description of restorative justice theory and the programs that have been developed from it.

Nancy Rodriguez used official juvenile court data from an urban area and found that youths who participated in a restorative justice program were less likely to recidivate than juveniles in a comparison group. Her study further revealed that male and female juveniles with a minimal offense history exhibited the most success from participating in these programs.[90] Another study of the long-term impact of restorative justice referrals on prevalence of reoffense, number of later official contacts, and seriousness of later offending behavior over several follow-up periods also found a positive impact of restorative justice programs in all of these categories.[91] Gwen Robinson and Joanna Shapland saw the possibility for restorative justice to be able to reduce recidivism.[92] Restorative justice appears to be one of the most hopeful approaches to juvenile crime, especially with minor forms of juvenile delinquency.

One of the major challenges is finding ways to break the cycle of the wasted lives of alienated youths going from the juvenile to the adult correctional system and frequently spending a majority of their lives in prison. Restorative justice is one possibility, PYD is another, and effective prevention programs would be a third possibility. In addition, those who work with youths in various types of programming—ranging from probation to residential treatment to institutional care—can sometimes be instrumental in helping youths turn their lives around.

▶ Delinquency and Social Policy: The Conflict Perspective

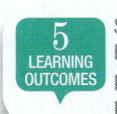

5 LEARNING OUTCOMES — Summarize the contributions of the conflict perspective to social policy.

The conflict perspective has several contributions to make to handling youth crime in America. Its emphasis on improving human rights is a reminder to policymakers, as well as to all interest groups for children, that the ability of youths to achieve their maximum potential in American society is very much affected by the larger issue of human rights. Similarly, women's rights affect the thousands of children across the nation reared in one-parent homes. Finally, children's rights promise that youths will be granted or guaranteed more of the basic rights that adults enjoy.

Conflict criminology also has much to teach children's advocacy groups about how power and domination affect the creation of policy. For example, these theories contend that in our society, control is gained by those groups that wield the most power and resources; that once a group achieves dominance over others, it seeks to use the available societal mechanisms to its advantage to maintain that dominance; that laws are formulated in the interests of the dominant groups, with the result

86 Chapter 5 Social Interactionist Theories of Delinquency

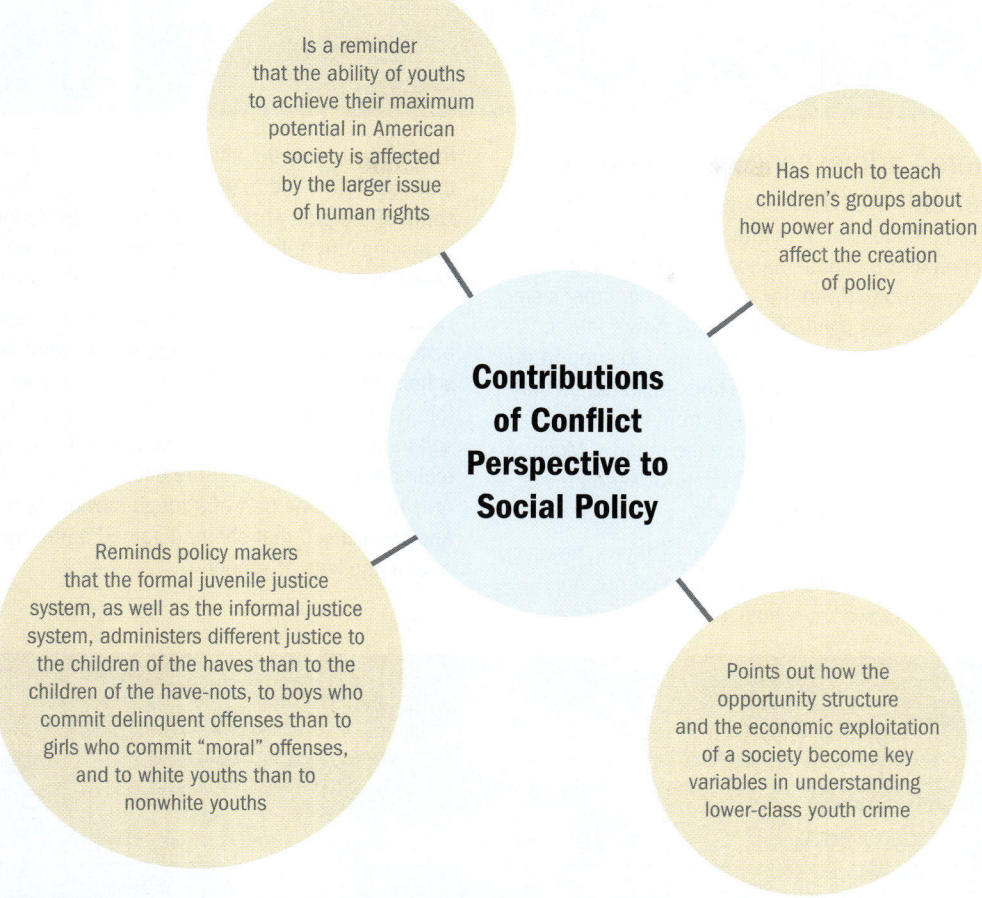

FIGURE 5–2 Contributions of Conflict Perspective to Social Policy.

that those behaviors common to the less powerful groups may be restricted; and that the law enforcement and control systems operate to process disproportionately the less powerful members of society.

Third, the conflict perspective points out that the opportunity structure and the economic exploitation of a society become key variables in understanding lower-class youth crime. Societies in which economic exploitation is extreme and in which opportunity is limited can be expected to have high rates of delinquency. Many of the stories in the *Voices of Delinquency* (which is a supplement to this text that can be read online), especially those of youths who have gone on to the adult correctional system, reveal backgrounds of economic deprivation and abuse; they felt powerless and dominated, and they struck out in retaliation. Finally, conflict criminologists argue that **social injustice** prevails in American society. These criminologists believe that the formal juvenile justice system, as well as the informal justice system, administers different sorts of justice to the children of the haves than to the children of the have-nots, to boys who commit delinquent offenses than to girls who commit "moral" offenses, and to white youths than to nonwhite youths.[93] Figure 5–2 describes the contributions that the conflict perspective can make to social policy.

THE CASE

The Life Course of Amy Watters, Age 11

As Amy entered adolescence she began to question her self-worth. Although she was not consciously aware of it, the loss of her mother had contributed to a sense of rejection and personal inadequacy. Amy found it hard to believe that anyone loved her, especially her older sister, Jordon, with whom she was fighting constantly. Amy's father, Simon, was rarely around, as he still worked hard to support the family. Jordon had assumed many of the household duties that a mother might otherwise have performed—from keeping the house clean to preparing meals and doing the laundry. Much to Amy's disgust, her father had also told Jordon to "keep an eye" on Amy, and to assign her chores to perform.

The worst thing that happened to Amy in her 11th year, however, was that a small group of bullies began picking on her. Amy was not part of the "in crowd" at school, and she didn't have the money to buy the kinds of clothes and electronic gadgets that might have led to greater social acceptance. As a result, some of the girls whom everyone seemed to look up to began harassing Amy, telling her that her hairstyle was an "unrecoverable disaster," and calling her names that really hurt.

Feeling unloved at home and threatened at school, Amy found acceptance with a crowd of adolescent troublemakers at her school. When she thought about it, which was only rarely, Amy told herself that she wasn't really like the people she found herself hanging out with, but reasoned that she needed their protection from the bullies. Sure enough, once it was known that Amy had become part of a tough crowd, the bullying ceased and she sensed that she had gained a new measure of respect among the kids at school.

Discuss

1. Why does Amy resent Jordan? What might her father do to lessen the stress between the girls? Why did Amy turn to a "tough" crowd? What alternatives might she have pursued?

Learn more on the Web:

- Learn more about *bullying in schools* by visiting the National Criminal Justice Reference Service at NCJRS.gov and reading the publication numbered NCJ 227422.

Follow the continuing Amy Watters saga in the next chapter.

CHAPTER 5: Social Interactionist Theories of Delinquency

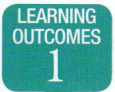

LEARNING OUTCOMES 1

Explain the significance of labeling as a cause of future behavior.

Labeling theory is based on the premise that society creates deviants by labeling those who are apprehended as different from other individuals, when in reality they are different only because they have been tagged with a deviant label. The perspective emphasizes the importance of rule making and social and legislative power in the creation of deviance.

1. What is the labeling perspective's explanation for why adolescents become delinquent?
2. How would labeling theory explain the process of becoming delinquent?
3. What is meant by *radical nonintervention*, and why might it be a workable strategy according to labeling theory?

social interactionist theory A theoretical perspective that derives its explanatory power from the give-and-take that continuously occurs between social groups and between individuals and society.

labeling theory The view that society creates the delinquent by labeling those who are apprehended as different from other youths when in reality they are different primarily because they have been tagged with a deviant label.

primary deviation According to labeling theory, the initial act of deviance that causes a person to be labeled a deviant.

secondary deviation According to labeling theory, deviance that is a consequence of societal reaction to an initial delinquent act.

process of becoming deviant In labeling theory, the concept that the process of acquiring a delinquent identity takes place in a number of steps.

radical nonintervention A policy toward delinquents that advises that authorities should "leave the kids alone whenever possible."

LEARNING OUTCOMES 2

Summarize the symbolic interactionist theory of delinquency.

Symbolic interactionist theory builds on labeling theory and has identified the locus of social control within the process of taking the role of the other and within the process of linking with the broader social organization through role commitments, generalized others, and reference groups. Labeling theory, on the other hand, emphasizes the symbolic nature of the "deviant" label once it has been applied. The more sophisticated applications of labeling theory developed since the early 1990s have moved the explanation of delinquent behavior from a unidimensional focus to a perspective examining more contingencies of labeling effects, including both direct and indirect effects of labeling.

1. How is the symbolic interactionist theory of delinquency an extension of, but different from, labeling theory?
2. What are the social policy implications of symbolic interactionist theory?

symbolic interactionist theory A perspective in social psychology that analyzes the process of interaction among human beings at the symbolic level and that has influenced the development of several social process theories of delinquent behavior.

LEARNING OUTCOMES 3

Explain the conflict theory of delinquency.

Conflict criminologists relate delinquency to alienation and powerlessness among youths, especially lower-class youths; to the dominant class's creation of definitions of crime to control subordinate classes; and to what they see as economic exploitation of the lower classes.

1. What are the explanations of delinquency according to conflict theory?
2. What insights are offered by the perspective known as radical criminology?
3. What does the theory of differential oppression say is the likely cause of delinquency and crime?

conflict theory A perspective that holds that delinquency can be explained by socioeconomic class, by power and authority relationships, and by group and cultural differences.

radical criminology A perspective that holds that the causes of crime are rooted in social conditions that empower the wealthy and the politically well organized but disenfranchise the less fortunate.

capitalism An economic system in which private individuals or corporations own and control capital (wealth and the means of production) and in which competitive free markets control prices, production, and distribution of goods.

power-control thesis The view that the relationship between gender and delinquency is linked to issues of power and control.

theory of differential oppression The view that in the United States, authority is unjustly used against children, who must adapt to adults' ideas of what constitutes "good children."

culture conflict theory A perspective that delinquency or crime arises because individuals are members of a subculture that has conduct norms that are in conflict with those of the wider society.

conduct norms The rules of a group governing the ways its members should act under particular conditions, and the violation of these rules arouses a group reaction.

LEARNING OUTCOMES 4

Describe restorative justice and peacemaking.

Restorative justice and the peacemaking process are the increasingly used form of communication between victims and youths, and between delinquent youths and members of the wider community. Restorative justice processes assume that every individual has value and therefore present individuals to one another in a respectful manner, which is intended to emphasize the human dignity present in everyone.

1. How does restorative justice provide a framework for community members to use in reestablishing appropriate relationships between community members and young people who violate the law?
2. How can the framework of restorative justice be used to achieve a reduction in the incidence of delinquent behavior?
3. Why do those who work within the area of restorative justice talk about human dignity? How is the concept relative to delinquency?

LEARNING OUTCOMES 5

Summarize the contributions of the conflict perspective to social policy.

The conflict perspective offers several contributions to handling youth crime, including an emphasis on children's rights, its reminder to children's advocacy groups about how power and domination affect the creation of policy, its position that the opportunity structure and the economic explanation of a society become key variables in understanding lower-class youth crime, and its reminder that social injustice continues to be present in the United States.

1. What is the conflict perspective?
2. What is meant by social injustice? Can you identify any situations in the United States that might be characterized as socially unjust?
3. What contributions does the conflict perspective offer for the handling of delinquent youth?
4. What social policy implications are inherent in the conflict perspective?

social injustice According to conflict-oriented criminologists, social injustice takes the form of unfairness in the juvenile justice system. It arises from poor youths being disproportionately represented, from female status offenders being subjected to sexist treatment, and from racial minorities being dealt with more harshly than whites.

"There has been growing concern that while most juvenile arrests have been decreasing, the number of female juvenile arrests in some offense categories (such as drug and alcohol violations) continues to rise."

—*Girls' Study Group (Research Triangle Institute)*

6

Gender and Delinquency

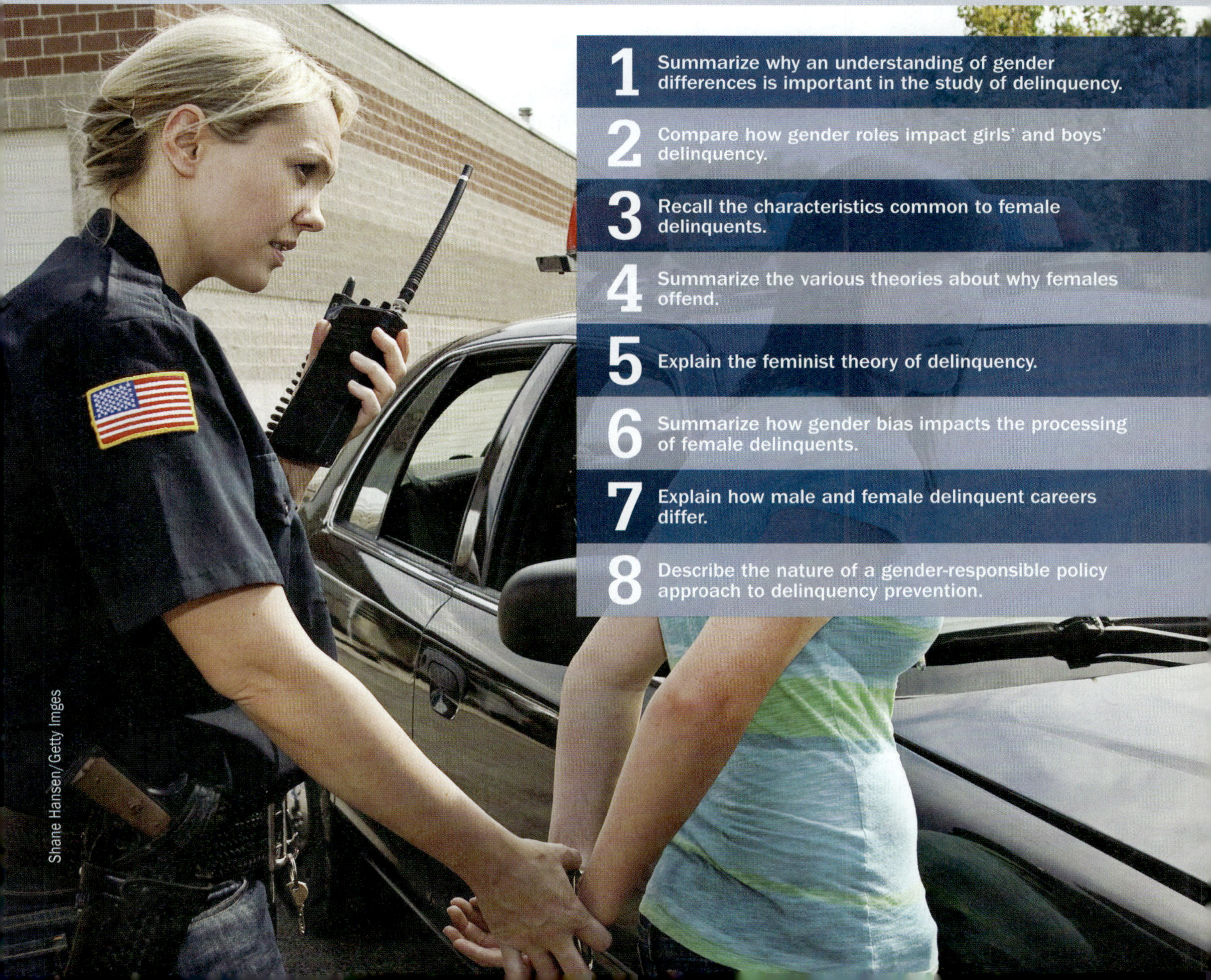

Shane Hansen/Getty Images

1. Summarize why an understanding of gender differences is important in the study of delinquency.
2. Compare how gender roles impact girls' and boys' delinquency.
3. Recall the characteristics common to female delinquents.
4. Summarize the various theories about why females offend.
5. Explain the feminist theory of delinquency.
6. Summarize how gender bias impacts the processing of female delinquents.
7. Explain how male and female delinquent careers differ.
8. Describe the nature of a gender-responsible policy approach to delinquency prevention.

INTRO: CHILD PROSTITUTION

On June 25, 2012, the Federal Bureau of Investigation (FBI) announced that its agents, working with local police officers in 57 cities, had arrested 104 alleged pimps and rescued 77 underage girls and 2 boys from lives of forced prostitution. The boys and girls, many of whom provided sexual services at truck stops, storefronts, casinos, and hotels, had been held against their will and were forced into prostitution by their adult captors who threatened to harm them and their families if they stopped cooperating. In announcing the arrests, FBI Assistant Director Kevin Perkins said, "Child prostitution remains a major threat to children across America. It is a violent and deplorable crime, and we are working with our partners to disrupt and put behind bars individuals and members of criminal enterprises who would sexually exploit children."[1]

Until recently, the study of delinquency had largely been the study of *male* delinquency. Meda Chesney-Lind, one of the country's most respected experts on female delinquency, says that the study of delinquency is gender biased and that delinquency theories are preoccupied with the delinquency of males. Consequently, she argues, the study of offending and of the juvenile justice process is shaped by male experiences and male understandings of the social world.[2]

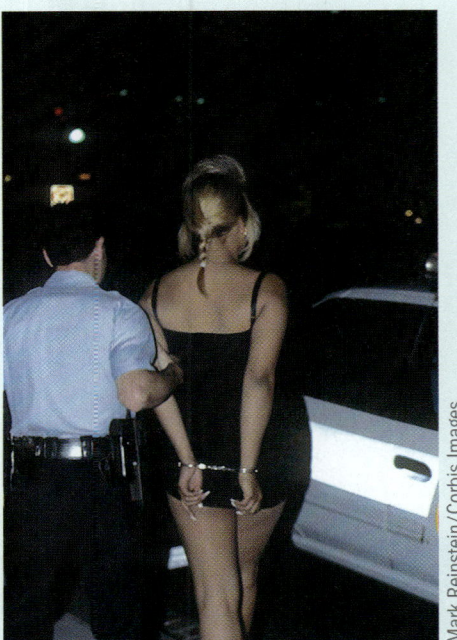

A young prostitute under arrest. How does the delinquency of girls differ from that of boys?

DISCUSS The feminist perspective is one in which women's experiences and ways of knowing are emphasized. How might a teenage girl's perspective differ from that of a teenage boy?

▶ The Gender Ratio in Offending

Although numerous studies of girls' delinquency followed the exhortations of feminists, things began to move much faster in 2003 when the federal Office for Juvenile Justice and Delinquency Prevention (OJJDP) awarded a grant to North Carolina's Research Triangle Institute (RTI) to study female delinquency and its consequences. Using funds provided by the OJJDP, the RTI formed the Girls' Study Group (GSG) with the avowed purpose of identifying sound theoretical strategies for combating female delinquency and violence.[3] Researchers and practitioners participating in the study group have been reviewing and analyzing existing literature as well as working to identify programs that effectively address the prevention and reduction of female offending. In recent years, the GSG has produced a number of publications and studies, some of which will be discussed later in this chapter.

Today's feminist criminologists agree on gender-based differences in adolescents' experiences, developmental rates, and the scope and motivation of male and female patterns of offending.[4] There is also general agreement that female adolescents enjoy greater social support and are more controlled than are males. Further, a review of available data shows that females are less disposed to crime than males and have fewer opportunities for certain types of crimes,[5] and researchers commonly accept that high self-esteem has the effect of discouraging favorable risk-taking situations among female adolescents while encouraging risk-taking situations in males.[6]

There is disagreement, however, in how to address the male-oriented approach to delinquency, thought by many to be both persistent and dominant. One approach focuses on the question of generalizability. Supporters of this gender-neutral position have examined such subjects as the family, social bonding, social learning, delinquent peer relationships, and, to a lesser degree, deterrence and strain.[7] These theorists argue that little evidence to date suggests that separate theories are needed to account for male and female delinquency. They also claim that female delinquency tends to operate through the same factors as male delinquency and add that empirical studies generally reveal that much more variation exists within each gender than between the sexes.[8] Thus, many feminist theorists would recommend that the subject of female delinquency be presented in textbooks as part of "a seamless whole rather than as a separate chapter."[9]

LEARNING OUTCOMES 1: Summarize why an understanding of gender differences is important in the study of delinquency.

In contrast, other feminist theorists argue that new theoretical efforts are needed to understand female delinquency and women's involvement in adult crime. Sociologist Eileen Leonard, for example, questioned whether anomie, labeling, differential association, subculture, and Marxist theories can be used to explain the crime patterns of women and concluded that these traditional theories do not work and that they are basically flawed.[10] Chesney-Lind's application of male-oriented theories to female delinquency has posited that existing delinquency theories are inadequate to explain female delinquency, and she suggested that there is a need for a feminist model of delinquency because a patriarchal context has shaped the explanations and the handling of female delinquents and status offenders. She argued that the sexual and physical victimizations of adolescent females at home—and the relationship between these experiences and females' crimes—have been systematically ignored.[11]

Leonard is one who has argued that new theoretical efforts to understand women's crime must include an analysis of the links among gender, race, class, and culture.[12] After accusing some feminists of ignoring racial, class, ethnic, religious, and cultural differences among women, Elizabeth V. Spelman concluded that it is only through an examination of such factors that oppression against women can be more clearly grasped and understood.[13] Chesney-Lind further extended this argument when she said that adolescent females and women are victims of "multiple marginality" because their gender, class, and race have placed them at the economic periphery of society. The labeling of a girl as delinquent takes place in a world, Chesney-Lind charged, "where gender still shapes the lives of young people in very powerful ways. Gender, then, matters in girls' lives and the way gender works varies by the community and the culture into which the girl is born."[14]

In the face of these two divergent positions—one seeking to explain away gender gaps and to be gender neutral, and the other focusing on the importance of gender in understanding delinquency and crime—Darrell Steffensmeier and Emilie Allen have attempted to put the two approaches together. They contended that "[there] is no need for gender-specific theories," although they acknowledge that "qualitative studies reveal major gender differences in the context and nature of offending."[15] These researchers go on to develop a "middle road position,"[16] which has not received much acceptance or support in the literature.

In 2006, Peggy C. Giordano and colleagues' review of the Ohio Serious Offender Study led them to conclude that "the either/or dichotomy suggested by the contrast between traditional and feminist frameworks is neither necessary nor helpful to the theory-building process."[17] They suggested that the Ohio study "indicates that the basic tenets of these seemingly opposing viewpoints are not in themselves fundamentally incompatible, and the results require a more integrated approach," finding that this was particularly true when the focus was on a small subgroup of girls with serious delinquent histories.[18]

During a follow-up study, Giordano suggested that a comprehensive understanding of delinquent actions requires that we enlist the help of both classic explanations of delinquency and contemporary perspectives that emphasize uniquely gendered processes. Within the life histories of girls, for example, there is ample evidence of the types of social dynamics that support both approaches. The study found that frequent themes that impact girls include disadvantaged neighborhoods, economic marginality, and an "excess of definitions favorable to the violation of law." At the same time, the study found, parents' criminal involvement and/or severe alcohol and drug problems can be identified early on, and that they continued throughout the women's childhood and adolescent years. The adult follow-up study further supported the idea that some processes associated with continued crime or desistance seem to be "generic" (that is, they have a good fit with both women's and men's life experiences), whereas others appear to be more gender specific.[19]

> ## Think About It...
>
> It is generally well established that females are considerably less likely than males to be involved in most forms of crime and delinquency. Why?
>
>

An understanding of gender differences in the study of delinquency is important because of the need to answer the following gender-related questions: (1) Why are females less likely than males to be involved in most crimes? (2) Conversely, why are males more crime-prone than females?, and (3) What explains gender differences in rates of offending?[20]

The issue of gender differences in rates of offending is sometimes called the "gender-ratio issue." It naturally leads to an inquiry into the factors that block or limit girls' or women's involvement in crime. It can be argued that this type of inquiry "reflects an androcentric [male-centered] perspective that makes men's behavior the norm from which women appear to deviate through their limited offending."[21]

Some feminist theorists propose treating gender as a key element of social organization rather than as an individual trait; thereby providing an approach that permits a more complex examination of the gender gap. Data on crime trends, for example, reveal that a gender gap is more persistent for some offenses than for others, fluctuates over time, and varies by class, race/ethnicity, and age.[22] Approaches that study the gender-ratio issue should use the opportunity to examine how causal factors differently shape men's and women's offending across important social dimensions. Miller and Mullins illustrate this point by noting evidence of a link between "underclass" conditions and African-American women's offending—a link that, however, fails to have explanatory power for women's offending in other social contexts.[23]

University of Iowa professor Karen Heimer and colleagues examined the "economic marginalization thesis," which proposes "that the gender gap in crime decreases and females

The economic marginalization thesis says that the gender gap in crime decreases and females account for a greater proportion of crime when women's economic well-being declines.

account for a greater proportion of crime when women's economic well-being declines."[24] "Not only are women more likely to live in poverty than men," they added, "but also the gender gap in poverty rates for women in the most crime-prone group continues to increase."[25] They concluded that continued economic oppression, instead of enhanced economic opportunities for women, may be the root cause of the narrowing of the gender gap in crime that has taken place over the past four decades.[26]

A promising avenue for exploring the complexities of the gender ratio of offending is found in a conceptual scheme offered by Daly and consists of these three areas of inquiry:

1. *Gendered pathways.* What trajectories propel females and males into offending? What social contexts and factors facilitate entrance to and desistance from offending, and how are they gendered?

2. *Gendered crime.* What are the ways in which street life, sex and drug markets, criminal opportunities, informal economics, and crime groups are structured by gender and other social features? What observed variation occurs in the sequencing and contexts of women and men's lawbreaking?

3. *Gendered lives.* How does gender affect the daily lives of females and males? How does gender structure identities and courses of action? How do these experiences intersect with lawbreaking?[27] See Figure 6–1.

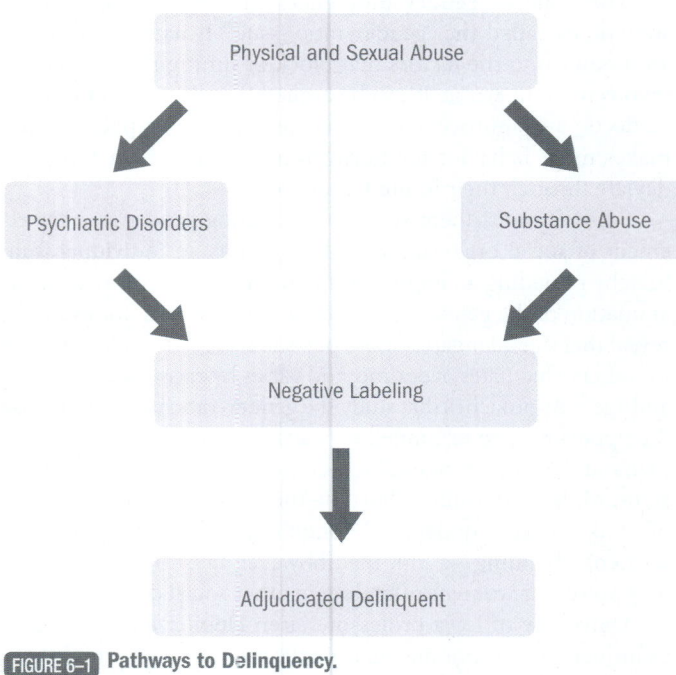

FIGURE 6–1 Pathways to Delinquency.

Social Context of Delinquency: Gender Roles and Delinquency

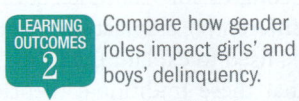

LEARNING OUTCOMES 2: Compare how gender roles impact girls' and boys' delinquency.

To a large degree, understandings of **gender** and gender-based roles are acquired through socialization. Children are socialized into preexisting gender arrangements and construct understandings of themselves and how they relate to others in terms of those frameworks. As Berkeley professor Barrie Thorne noted in her well-known book *Gender Play*,

> Parents dress infant girls in pink and boys in blue, give them gender-differentiated names and toys, and expect them to act differently. Teachers frequently give boys more classroom attention than girls. Children pick up the gender stereotypes that pervade books, songs, advertisements, TV programs, and movies. And peer groups, steeped in cultural ideas about what it is to be a girl or a boy, also perpetuate gender-typed play and interaction. In short, if boys and girls are different, they are not born but *made* that way.[28]

An empirically based landmark study by the American Association of University Women (AAUW), which included African-American girls and all social classes, examined the behavior and treatment of girls in the classroom. The most striking finding in this research was that Caucasian girls tend to lose their sense of self-esteem as they advance from elementary school to high school; African-American girls, in contrast, were found to maintain their self-esteem but too often would become dissociated from the school and schoolwork.[29]

Themes found to be unique to the high school-age girls in the AAUW study, and in the girls described in the book *Schoolgirls* by Orenstein, were obsession with physical appearance and popularity based on external characteristics rather than achievement, loss of freedom in later adolescence associated with budding sexuality, close attention to relationships, and intense mother–daughter patterns of communication. Inner-city African-American and Latina girls were found to have somewhat unique issues related to life in tough neighborhoods, and the development of a tough exterior was seen as vital for their protection from gangs and violence; early pregnancy was a reality for many of them. In short, girls' victimization—from sexual harassment either at school or on the streets to full-blown sexual assaults—was a fact of girls' lives and had an important impact on their personalities and later development.[30]

In their gender-specific guidelines written for the state of Oregon, P. Patton and M. Morgan suggested that although these statements may not be true of every girl and boy, generally speaking the following can be assumed:

- Girls develop their identity in relation to other people, whereas boys develop their identity in relation to the world.

- Girls resolve conflict based on relationships, whereas boys resolve conflict based on rules.

TABLE 6–1   GENDER ROLES

	Identity Development	Method for Resolving Conflict	Focus	Types of Aggression
Girls	In relation to other people	Based on relationships	Connectedness and independence	Relational aggression
Boys	In relation to the world	Based on rules	Independence and autonomy	Overaggression

Source: P. Patton and M. Morgan, "The Current State of Gender-Specific Delinquency Programming," *Journal of Criminal Justice* 36 (2008), pp. 262–269.

- Girls focus on connectedness and interdependence, whereas boys focus on independence and autonomy.
- Girls exhibit relational aggression, whereas boys exhibit overaggression.[31]

Although there has been a recent resurgence in recognizing the importance of biology in determining sex-linked behavior, it is also important to recognize that children in today's society continue to be effectively socialized into gender roles. Thorne reminds her readers that children have an active role in society and that the social construction of gender—an active and ongoing process in their lives—is most visible in play. When she observed children in middle school, she could identify gender separation and integration taking place within the classroom, in the lunchroom, and on the playground. Children's active role in constructing gender could be seen as they formed lines, chose seats, gossiped, teased, and sought access to or avoided particular activities. Sociologist Barrie Thorne particularly found extensive self-separation by gender on the playground, where adults have little control.[32]

In addition to the social construction of **gender roles**, there appears to be considerable evidence that girls develop differently than boys. Marty Beyer, a clinical psychologist who has examined adolescent males and females across the nation since 1980, said recently that research "has identified different vulnerabilities and protective factors in girls."[33] Girls, for example, have a greater tendency to internalize, and they experience higher rates of anxiety, depression, withdrawal, and eating disorders than boys do. Girls are also more focused on relationships than boys, Beyer claimed.[34]

See Table 6–1 for a comparison of gender roles.

The Female Delinquent

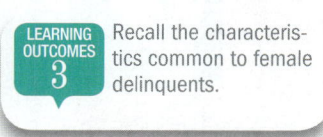
Recall the characteristics common to female delinquents.

- She is 13 to 18 years old.
- She has experienced academic failure, truancy, and dropping out.
- She has a history of repeated victimization, especially physical, sexual, and emotional abuse.
- She is from an unstable family background that includes involvement in the criminal justice system, lack of connectedness, and social isolation.
- She has a history of unhealthy dependent relationships, especially with older males.
- She has mental health issues, including a history of substance abuse.
- She is apt to be a member of a community of color.

FIGURE 6–2   **The Typical Female Juvenile Offender.**
Source: B. Bloom and S. Covington, "Effective Gender-Responsive Interventions in Juvenile Justice: Addressing the Lives of Delinquent Girls," paper presented at the Annual Meeting of the American Society of Criminology, Atlanta, Georgia, 2001.

Recently, a growing body of research has been devoted to the study of the characteristics of delinquent girls.[35] Researchers have identified basic demographic and offense patterns as well as background characteristics such as family dysfunction, trauma, physical abuse, mental health issues, substance abuse, risky sexual behavior, academic problems, and delinquent peers as common features among girls in custody.[36]

The profile of at-risk adolescent females that emerges identifies common characteristics, including stories of victimization, unstable family life, school failure, repeated status offenses, and mental health and substance-abuse problems.[37] B. Bloom and S. Covington have outlined a profile of a female juvenile offender (see Figure 6–2).

The Girls' Study Group, referred to at the start of this chapter, examines issues such as patterns of offending among adolescents and how they differ for girls and boys; risk and protective factors associated with gender, and the causes and correlates of girls' delinquency. See Exhibit 6–1 for a recent report by this study group.

According to Joanne Belknap and Kristi Holsinger, "The most significantly and potentially useful criminological research in recent years has been the recognition that girls' and women's pathways to offending" differ from those of boys and men.[38] The first step along females' pathway into the juvenile justice system is victimization. The ages at which interviewed adolescent girls reportedly were more likely to be beaten, raped, stabbed, or shot were 13 and 14 years old.[39] A large proportion of girls first entered the juvenile justice system as runaways, who frequently were attempting to escape abuse at home.[40]

Certain abuses follow these adolescent females even after they enter the juvenile justice system. Specific forms of abuse reportedly experienced by juvenile females include the consistent use of foul and demanding language by juvenile custodial

EXHIBIT 6–1 | Differences Between Girls' and Boys' Delinquency

A few years ago, the Girls' Study Group, a collaborative project funded by the Office of Justice Programs at the U.S. Department of Justice, released a 20-page report entitled "Causes and Correlates of Girls' Delinquency." That document summarized the findings of 1,600 studies that had been conducted on girls' delinquency during the past two decades. A baker's dozen of some of the most interesting findings are as follows:

- Research conducted to date suggests that subtle differences in certain biological functions and psychological traits may contribute to gender-related variations in responses to certain environmental conditions.
- On the whole, girls' delinquent acts are typically less chronic and often less serious than those of boys.
- There is evidence that girls experience a greater number of negative life events during adolescence than boys do, and they may, in turn, be more sensitive to their effects, especially when such events take place within the home.
- There is evidence that girls more often experience certain types of trauma, such as sexual abuse and rape, than boys do.
- Many studies of incidence of sexual abuse suggest that it is more pervasive among girls who engage in antisocial behavior, particularly those who engage in violent behavior, than among their male counterparts.
- In addition to gender differences in exposure to certain stressors, girls and boys may also vary in their sensitivity to the same stressor. For example, there is some suggestion that girls may be more sensitive to dysfunction and trauma within the home.
- Boys outnumber girls by a ratio of 3 to 1 in the diagnoses of attention deficit–hyperactivity disorder (ADHD) and other conduct disorders.
- Mental health problems linked to life stressors and experiences of victimization, such as anxiety, depression, and post-traumatic stress disorder, are diagnosed at much higher rates among girls than boys.
- Early maturation creates particular risks for girls because of the development of physical signs of maturity inconsistent with still largely undeveloped cognitive and emotional systems.
- Some studies have found that compared with other girls, early-maturing girls are more likely to engage in delinquency and other risk-taking behaviors such as substance abuse, truancy, and running away.
- Early maturation in girls further appears to be a risk factor in exposure to intimate partner violence in adolescence.
- Early puberty, especially when coupled with disadvantaged neighborhoods and family conflict, is a key gender-related factor in predicting girls' delinquency.
- Complex family processes, such as parental supervision, attachment, and maltreatment, are important factors that help explain the difference in the onset of delinquency between girls and boys.

The entire publication can be found online at http://www.ncjrs.gov/pdffiles1/ojjdp/226358.pdf.

Source: Margaret A. Zahn, Robert Agnew, Diana Fishbein, Shari Miller, Donna-Marie Winn, Gayle Dakoff, Candace Kruttschnitt, Peggy Giordano, Denise C. Gottfredson, Allison A. Payne, Barry C. Feld, and Meda Chesney-Ling, *Causes and Correlates of Girls' Delinquency* (Washington, DC: U.S. Department of Justice; Office of Juvenile Justice and Delinquency Prevention, 2010).

---

staff members; inappropriate touching, pushing, and hitting by staff; placement in isolation for trivial reasons; and withholding of clean clothing. Some girls have also been strip-searched in the presence of male officers.[41]

A second step along females' pathway into the juvenile justice system involves substance abuse. Substance use by females is highly correlated with early childhood sexual victimization, especially among white females, with the literature consistently reporting a strong link between childhood abuse and the later development of alcoholism and other drug problems.[42] Significantly, at about the same age as the victimization occurred (usually when the girls were between 13 and 14 years old), the girls started using addictive substances.

A third step along females' pathway into the juvenile justice system involves girls acting out at home or in school, through sexual activity, by engaging in law-violating acts, and through gang involvement. The emotional problems troubled girls usually have tend to influence their negative behaviors; as a result, they do poorly in school, are sometimes suspended or expelled, or they drop out. They run away from home and come before the juvenile court, or they are referred to the court for their involvement in gangs or delinquent behaviors.[43] The three pathways to delinquency in this discussion of the female delinquent are depicted in Figure 6–3.

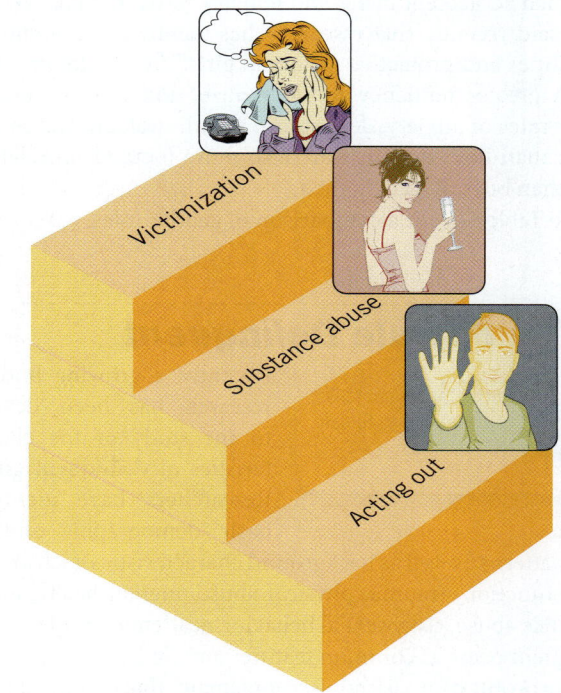

FIGURE 6–3 Three Pathways to Female Delinquency.

Explanations of Female Delinquency

4 LEARNING OUTCOMES Summarize the various theories about why females offend.

Criminologists come to vastly different conclusions concerning the question of whether female juveniles commit delinquent acts for reasons different from those of young males. Early explanations of female delinquency, which viewed adolescent females as having certain biological characteristics or psychological tendencies that made them more receptive to certain kinds of delinquency, focused on biological and psychological factors thought to be common to females. Today, however, many criminologists question some of the biological and psychological explanations of delinquency, and instead see troublesome adolescent females as the product of a male-led patriarchal society. Consequently, many recent explanations of female delinquency have placed much greater emphasis on sociological factors.

Some criminologists challenge whether gender-specific explanations for delinquency and crime are even needed because, they say, existing social scientific theories can account for both males' and females' delinquency.[44] Still others argue for gender-specific explanations because, they say, traditional sociological theories of delinquent behavior fail to adequately explain the experience of being female. Gender-specific theories are discussed later in this chapter.

Biological and Constitutional Explanations

Although sociological theories remain in the forefront of the delinquency literature, the focus has shifted recently to biopsychological vulnerability factors that may be related to girls' delinquency. Five general vulnerability factors have been considered: (1) stress and anxiety, (2) attention deficit–hyperactivity disorder (ADHD) and conduct disorder (CD), (3) intellectual deficits, (4) early pubertal maturation, and (5) mental health issues. Most of these factors apply also to boys' delinquency, but girls appear to have greater vulnerability to them.[45] For example, recently discovered gender-related differences may account for sex-related differences in reaction to stressors, and contribute to a heightened vulnerability to behavioral problems with females in responding to traumatic life events.[46] In other words, recent research has led some to the conclusion that girls may indeed be more sensitive—and react with heightened emotion—to negative events in their lives than are boys.

Psychological Explanations

Psychological explanations of female delinquency also vary between early and more recent explanations. Early studies

> **Some say that traditional sociological theories of delinquent behavior fail to adequately explain the experience of being female.**

addressed what was assumed to be "innate" female nature and its relationship to deviant behavior; but more recently the focus of study has been on social contexts as they contribute to female delinquency.

Gisela Konopka's early study of delinquent females, for example, linked a poor home life with a deep sense of loneliness and low self-esteem. Her conception of delinquency relied heavily on the notion of individual pathology, and she concluded that only a female who is "sick" can become delinquent.[47] Konopka identified four key factors contributing to female delinquency: (1) a uniquely dramatic biological onset of puberty, (2) a complex identification process because of a girl's competitiveness with her mother, (3) the changing cultural position of females and the resultant uncertainty and loneliness, and (4) the hostile picture that the world presents to some young females.[48]

A contemporary study, in contrast, focused on physical and sexual abuse of girls, and found that abused female delinquents tend to exhibit psychopathology, including post-traumatic stress disorder (PTSD), suicidal behavior, dissociative disorder, and borderline personality disorder.[49]

Sociological Explanations

General Strain Theory

General strain theory explains female delinquency by contending that many females experience strains conducive to delinquency, such as harsh discipline, parental rejection, peer abuse, negative secondary school experiences, homelessness, and a strong need for money.[50] Males, however, may be more likely to become involved in delinquency than females because males tend to experience strains conducive to delinquency and they tend to cope with strains through delinquency. Females, in turn, may experience certain forms of strains that lead to other-directed delinquency.

Blocked Opportunity Theory

The role of blocked, or limited, opportunity has received considerable attention in the sociological analysis of male delinquency (see Chapter 4). However, the usefulness of such variables in studying female delinquency has been largely ignored because males are seen as being concerned with achieving short- and long-term status and economic success, whereas juvenile females are frequently viewed as having no such aspirations, instead being satisfied to occupy a role dependent on males.[51] Several studies found that the perception of limited opportunity was more strongly related to female delinquency than it was to male delinquency. In some studies, both African-American and white female delinquents regarded their opportunities less positively than did the male delinquents in their sample; status offenders also perceived their opportunities as being less favorable than did nondelinquents.[52]

Social Learning Theory

Social learning theory contends that males have higher rates of delinquency than females primarily because they tend to be associated with delinquent peers and belong to gangs more often than do females. It is also argued that female peer groups are less conducive to delinquency than mixed-gender or all-male peer groups; males, in turn, have beliefs more favorable to delinquency than do females. However, according to social learning theory, some females are more likely than others to become involved in delinquent behavior because they tend to associate with others who provide exposure to delinquent models, reinforce delinquent behaviors, and teach identities that are favorable to delinquency.[53]

Social Control Theory

Proponents of social control theory contend that females are less involved in delinquency than males because **sex-role socialization** results in more ties and stronger social bonds for females than for males.[54] In addition, adolescent females may have less opportunity to engage in delinquent behavior because in general they are more closely supervised by parents. Females who are delinquent, according to social control theory, have less parental supervision, are less tied to their homes and families, are weakly bonded to parents and teachers, perform poorly in school, spend less time on homework, are involved in delinquent peer groups, and have less self-control.[55]

Differential Association Theory

Karen Heimer and Stacy De Coster found that emotional bonds to families were negatively related to the learning of violent definitions for girls but not for boys, coercive parental discipline and aggressive friends were positively related to the learning of violent definitions for boys but not for girls, and patriarchal beliefs about gender inhibited female violence without having any effect on male violence.[56]

Masculinity Hypothesis

Several studies of female delinquents have proposed a **masculinity hypothesis**. Freda Adler, for example, contended that as females are afforded more social opportunities previously only available to males, they would become more delinquent.[57] Francis Cullen and coworkers found that the more male and female adolescents possessed "male" personality traits, the more likely they were to become involved in delinquency, but that the relationship between masculinity and delinquency was stronger for males than for females.[58] William E. Thornton and Jennifer James found a moderate degree of association between masculine self-expectations and delinquency but concluded that males were still more likely to be delinquent than were females, regardless of their degree of masculinity.[59]

Power-Control Theory

John Hagan and colleagues (discussed in Chapter 5) proposed a power-control theory to explain female delinquency.[60] Using a class-based framework and data collected in Toronto, Ontario, they contended that as mothers gain power relative to their husbands (usually by employment outside the home), daughters and sons alike are encouraged to be more open to risk taking. Parents in egalitarian families, then, redistribute their control efforts so that daughters are subjected to controls more like those imposed on sons; in contrast, daughters in patriarchal families are taught by their parents to avoid risks.[61] Hagan and colleagues concluded that "patriarchal families will be characterized by large gender differences in common delinquent behavior while egalitarian families will be characterized by smaller gender differences in delinquency."[62] Power-control theory thus concludes that when daughters are freed from patriarchal family relations, they more frequently become delinquent.[63]

Labeling Theory

Labeling theorists claim that males are more likely to be labeled as delinquents than females both because the male cultural stereotype views males as troublemakers and because males engage in more delinquency. Labeling theory argues that some females are more delinquent than others because they have been informally labeled as delinquents by parents, teachers, and others as well as formally labeled by the juvenile justice system.[64]

Interactionist Theory of Delinquency

Heimer reported that delinquency for both females and males occurred through a process of role taking in which youths considered the perspectives of significant others; and, among both boys and girls, attitudes favoring deviance encouraged delinquency. She also found that "girls' misbehavior can be controlled by inculcating values and attitudes, whereas more direct controls may be necessary to control boys' deviance."[65]

Deterrence, Rational Choice, and Routine-Activities Theories

The explanation as to why females see the costs of crime as high and the benefits as low is related to their higher level of supervision, their moral beliefs, more self-control, less time spent in unstructured and unsupervised activities with peers, less association with delinquent peers, and less prior delinquency. Some females who see the costs of crime as low and the benefits as high differ from other females; for example, they may spend more unstructured and unsupervised time with peers. This is particularly true of those females who run away from home and spend a lot of time on the streets.[66]

Evaluation of Explanations of Female Delinquency

The discussion of female delinquency readily leads to the conclusion that biological explanations, although they may help explain why girls avoid law violation, are among the less predictive factors of delinquency involvement. Personal maladjustment hypotheses may have some predictive ability in determining the frequency of delinquency in girls, but sociological theories appear to be able to explain more of female delinquency and do it far more adequately. Some feminists are satisfied with the conclusion of sociological studies positing that males and females are differentially exposed to or affected by the same criminogenic associations.[67] Strain theory, general theory, social learning theory, social control theory, differential association theory,

> **The masculinity hypothesis says that as females share social opportunities more equally with men, they will become more delinquent.**

TABLE 6-2 | SUMMARY OF TYPES OF EXPLANATIONS OF FEMALE DELINQUENCY

Types	Explanation
Biological and Constitutional Explanations	Biopsychological vulnerability factors related to girls' delinquency
Psychological Explanations	Focus on psychiatric disorders
Sociological Explanations	Focus on social structure and relationships among groups
General Strain Theory	Females can experience strain, especially in the family and school, conducive to female delinquency.
Blocked Opportunity Theory	Some evidence has been found that the perception of limited opportunity is more strongly related to female delinquency than it is to male delinquency.
Social Learning Theory	Some females are more likely than others to become involved in delinquent behavior because of their exposure to delinquent models.
Social Control Theory	Females who are delinquent have less parental supervision and bonding to the school.
Differential Association	Emotional bonds to families are negatively related to the learning of violent definitions for girls but not for boys.
Masculinity Hypothesis	Some studies have found that as females become more malelike and acquire more masculine traits, they become more delinquent.
Power-Control Theory	When daughters are freed from patriarchal family relations, this theory concludes that they become more delinquent.
Labeling Theory	Males are more likely to be labeled as delinquent than females, but some females—especially the more delinquent girls—can be informally labeled by parents, the school, and the justice system.
Interactionist Theory of Delinquency	For both males and females, delinquency occurs through a process of role taking.
Deterrence, Rational Choice, and Routine-Activities Theories	Some females see the costs of crime as low and the rewards as high. They usually spend more time in unstructured and unsupervised activities with peers.

power-control theory, labeling theory, and symbolic interactionist theory all have received some support.[68] Other feminists (as the next two sections of this chapter will show) contend that the unique experiences of females require gender-specific theories.

See Table 6–2 for a summary of explanations for female delinquency.

▶ Feminist Theories of Delinquency

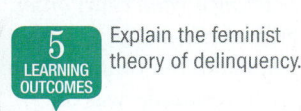

5 LEARNING OUTCOMES — Explain the feminist theory of delinquency.

Historically, feminist theory has at least seven expressions: liberal feminism, phenomenological feminism, socialist feminism, Marxist feminism, radical feminism, third-wave feminism, and postmodern feminism. Chesney-Lind's radical feminist theory of delinquency, which is discussed in this chapter, is one of the most exciting efforts to explain delinquent behavior in adolescent females.

The **feminist theory of delinquency** contends that girls' victimization and the relationship between that experience and girls' crime have been systematically ignored. Meda Chesney-Lind, one of the main proponents of this position, stated that it has long been understood that a major reason for girls' presence in juvenile courts is their parents' insistence on their arrest. Researchers and those who work with female status offenders are discovering today that substantial numbers are victims of both physical and sexual abuse.[69]

Chesney-Lind proposed that a feminist perspective on the causes of female delinquency include the following four propositions: First, girls are frequently the victims of violence and sexual abuse (estimates are that three-quarters of sexual abuse victims are girls), but unlike those of boys, girls' victimization and their response to that victimization are shaped by their status as young women. Second, their victimizers (usually males) have the ability to invoke official agencies of social control to keep daughters at home and vulnerable. Third, as girls run away from abusive homes characterized by sexual abuse and parental neglect, they are forced into the life of an escaped convict, unable to enroll in school or take a job to support themselves because they fear detection. Female runaways are forced to engage in panhandling, petty theft, and sometimes prostitution to survive. Fourth, it is no accident that girls who are on the run from abusive homes or are on the streets because of impoverished homes become involved in criminal activities that exploit their sexuality. Because U.S. society has defined physically "perfect" young women as desirable, girls on the streets—who have little else of value to trade—are encouraged to utilize this resource.

Girls are frequently the victims of sexual abuse.

Victimizers (often fathers) may utilize official agencies (like the police and the juvenile court) to keep victims at home and vulnerable.

As girls run away from home, they are forced to survive on the streets and become involved in various forms of crime.

On the streets, they become involved in various forms of criminal activity that exploits their sexuality.

FIGURE 6–4 Chesney-Lind's Four Propositions on the Feminist Theory of Delinquency.

Not surprisingly, the criminal subculture also views them from this perspective.[70]

Considerable research supports the frequent victimization of adolescent females. Mimi Silbert and Ayala M. Pines found that 60 percent of the street prostitutes they interviewed had been sexually abused as juveniles.[71] R. J. Phelps and colleagues, in a survey of 192 female youths in the Wisconsin juvenile justice system, discovered that 79 percent of these youths (most of whom were in the system for petty larceny and status offenses) had been subjected to physical abuse that resulted in some form of injury.[72] Chesney-Lind's investigation of the backgrounds of adult women in prison underscored the links between their victimization as children and their later criminal careers, with interviews revealing that virtually all of these women were victims of physical and/or sexual abuse as youngsters. Chesney-Lind's four propositions on the feminist theory of delinquency are noted in Figure 6–4.

▶ Gender Bias and the Processing of Female Delinquents

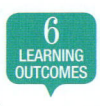
LEARNING OUTCOMES 6 Summarize how gender bias impacts the processing of female delinquents.

The underlying theme of this chapter is that adolescent females grow up in a culture that facilitates domination and control by males.[73] In this society, it is claimed that troublesome adolescent females are seen through lenses of discrimination, exploitation, and oppression.[74] Here are seven corollaries:

1. *Adolescent females receive discriminatory treatment because of society's disapproval of sexual activity.*[75] Krohn, Curry, and Nelson-Kilger's analysis of 10,000 police contacts in a midwestern city over a 30-year period found that adolescent females who were suspected of status offenses were more likely than their male counterparts to be referred to juvenile court for such offenses during all three decades.[76] Some studies have found that police officers adopt a more paternalistic and harsher attitude toward younger females to deter any further violation or inappropriate sex-role behavior.[77] Several studies have indicated that juvenile females are treated more harshly than boys because of their sexual history.[78]

2. *Offering another perspective, Rosemary C. Sarri concluded that juvenile law has long penalized females.* She claimed that although the law may not be discriminatory on its face, the attitudes and ideologies of juvenile justice practitioners administering it may result in violations of the Equal Protection Clause of the Fourteenth Amendment by leading them to commit females to longer sentences than males under the guise of "protecting" the female juveniles.[79] She added that "females have a greater probability of being detained and held for longer periods than males, even though the overwhelming majority of females are charged with status offenses."[80]

3. *Juvenile females, as numerous studies have documented, receive punitive processing through the juvenile justice system.* This results in their staying longer in detention and having longer stays in juvenile institutions than males for similar offenses.[81]

4. *According to another perspective, the oppressive treatment of adolescent females is hidden in the juvenile justice system.* Following the decriminalization of status offenses in 1979, Anne R. Mahoney and Carol Fenster reported that many girls appeared in court for criminal-type offenses that had previously been classified as status offenses, and they suggested that juvenile justice officials may have redefined these girls to be eligible for the kinds of protectionist sanctions that have been traditionally applied.[82]

5. *Another expression of the gender bias found in this "hidden justice" is that certain provisions of the Juvenile Justice and Delinquency Prevention Act provide that status offenders found in contempt of court for violating a valid court order may be placed in secure detention facilities, which permits juvenile judges to use their contempt power to confine repeat status offenders.* If a runaway girl, for example, was ordered by the court to remain at home but she chose to run away again, she might be found in contempt of court—a criminal-type offense. There is reason to believe that juvenile judges apply their contempt power more often to female status offenders than to their male counterparts.[83]

6. *The early studies, especially, found that police officers, intake personnel, and judges supported a sexual double standard. Female status offenders, as previously indicated, were more likely than their male counterparts to be petitioned*

> **The underlying theme of this chapter is that adolescent females grow up in a culture that facilitates domination and control by males.**

to formal court proceedings, to be placed in preadjudicatory detention confinements, and to be confined in juvenile institutions. But at the same time, males who committed delinquent acts frequently received harsher treatment than their female counterparts. Consistent with what is known as the "**chivalry factor**" or "paternalism" thesis, police were less likely to arrest females suspected of property or person crimes; if arrested, female delinquents were less likely than male delinquents to be formally charged with criminal offenses; and if charged, they were less likely than males to be incarcerated for their offenses.[84]

7. *The typical girl entering the juvenile justice system is a non-violent offender who is very often a low-risk, but high-need individual.* In *Improving the Juvenile Justice System for Girls*, Liz Watson and Peter Edelman presented the findings of the report *Marginalized Girls and Young Women* and conclude that this typical girl poses little risk to the public, but enters the system with significant and pressing personal needs.[85] Meda Chesney-Lind and Nikki Jones, in *Fighting for Girls*, which examines ten new investigations as well as findings from hundreds of other studies, add that girls are not more violent than in the past; if anything, they are less violent than in the past. At the same time, the authors add, they are being arrested and incarcerated in ever-greater numbers.[86]

On balance, some evidence does exist that the discriminatory treatment of female status offenders may be declining since passage of the Juvenile Justice and Delinquency Prevention Act.[87] No longer do many states send status offenders to training schools with delinquents. But the long tradition of sexism in juvenile justice will be difficult to change. Due process safeguards for female delinquents, as well as for female status offenders, must be established to ensure greater social justice for them in the juvenile justice system. The intrusion of extralegal factors into the decision-making process in the juvenile court has led to discrimination against the adolescent female that must become a relic of the past. Figure 6–5 provides a summary of seven corollaries of gender bias and the processing of female delinquents.

Think About It...

The underlying theme of this chapter is that adolescent females grow up in a culture that facilitates domination and control by males. Are there any societies in which that theme doesn't apply?

Influence of Class

As part of the female delinquent's "multiple marginality," class oppression is another form of exploitation that she experiences.[88] In many ways, powerful and serious problems of childhood and adolescence related to poverty set the stage for a young person's entry into homelessness, unemployment, drug use, survival sex and prostitution, and ultimately even more serious delinquent and criminal acts. Even those adolescents coming from middle-class homes may be thrust into situations of economic survival if they choose to run away from abusive environments.

Traditional theories also fail to address the life situations of girls on the economic and political margins, because researchers typically fail to examine or talk with these girls. For example, almost all urban females identified by police as gang members have been drawn from low-income groups.[89] Lee Bowker and Malcolm Klein's examination of data on girls in gangs in Los Angeles stated the importance of classism as well as racism:

> We conclude that the overwhelming impact of racism, sexism, poverty and limited opportunity structures is

Traditional theories fail to address the life situations of girls on the economic and political margins, because researchers typically fail to examine or talk with these girls.

1. Society's disapproval of sexual activity results in discriminatory treatment of juvenile females.
2. Juvenile law has long overly-penalized females.
3. Juvenile females are punitively processed throughout the juvenile justice system.
4. The oppressive treatment of adolescent females is hidden within the juvenile justice system.
5. Female status offenders are frequently found in contempt of court for violating a valid court order and then are placed in secure juvenile detention facilities.
6. Early studies found that police officers, intake personnel, and judges support a sexual double standard.
7. The typical girl entering the juvenile justice system is a non-violent offender who is very often low-risk, but high need individual.

FIGURE 6–5 Seven Corollaries of Gender Bias and the Processing of Female Delinquents.

likely to be so important in determining the gang membership and juvenile delinquency of women and girls in urban ghettos that personality variables, relations with parents and problems associated with heterosexual behavior play a relatively minor role in determining gang membership and juvenile delinquency.[90]

Class becomes important in shaping the lives of adolescent females in a number of other ways. Lower-class adolescent females tend to confront higher risk levels than middle- and upper-class adolescent females. They are more likely to have unsatisfactory experiences at school, to lack educational goals beyond high school, to experience higher rates of physical and sexual abuse, to deal with pregnancy and motherhood, to be involved in drug and alcohol dependency, to confront the risk of HIV/AIDS, and to lack supportive networks at home.[91] Although not all adolescent females at risk end up in the juvenile justice system, the likelihood of such a placement is greater for lower-class girls.[92]

Racial Discrimination

Young women of color, as well as other minority girls, often grow up in contexts very different from those of their white counterparts. An article by Lori D. Moore and Irene Padavic examines how gender-role ideology may affect racial/ethnic disparities, using data on African-American, white, and Hispanic female juvenile offenders in Florida. As expected, they found that African-American girls received harsher dispositions than white girls; but, contrary to what might be expected, they found that Hispanic girls' dispositions were no harsher than those of white girls. Further examination revealed that the effects of race/ethnicity depend largely on legal variables. Up to a certain threshold, white girls appear to be granted greater leniency than other racial groups, but as their offending severity and prior records increase, the juvenile justice system become increasingly intolerant. Sentencing decisions then become harsher for white girls than for African-American girls.[93]

Because racism and poverty often go hand in hand, these girls are forced by their minority status and poverty to deal early and regularly with problems of abuse, drugs, and violence.[94] They also are likely to be attracted to gang membership.[95] H. C. Covey and colleagues summarized the effect of ethnicity on gang membership:

> Racial differences in the frequency of gang formation such as the relative scarcity of non-Hispanic, white, ethnic gangs may be explainable in terms of the smaller proportion of the non-Hispanic European American population that [lives] in neighborhoods characterized by high rates of poverty, welfare dependency, single-parent households, and other symptoms that characterize social disorganization.[96]

Minority girls' strategies for coping with the problems of abuse, drugs, violence, and gang membership, as Chesney-Lind has noted, "tend to place them outside the conventional expectations of white girls," and it also increases the likelihood that they will come to the attention of the juvenile justice system.[97]

The Whole Is Greater Than the Sum of Its Parts

An examination of the experience of African-American women reveals the geometric effects of multiple forms of oppression involving gender, class, and race.[98] Diane Lewis has noted that because feminist theories of women's inequality "focused exclusively upon the effects of sexism, they have been of limited applicability to minority women subjected to the constraints of both racism and sexism."[99] Lewis further noted that "black women . . . tended to see racism as a more powerful cause of their subordinate position than sexism and to view the women's liberation movement with considerable mistrust."[100]

Daly summarized this argument by saying that "unless you consider all the key relations of inequality—class, race, gender (and also age and sexuality)—you have considered none," adding that "unless you consider the inseparability of these relations in the life of one person, you do not understand what we are saying."[101] Spelman conceptualized the independence and multiple natures of gender, class, and race by saying that "how one form of oppression is experienced is influenced by and influences how another form is experienced."[102]

This suggests that gender, class, and race are interlocking forms of oppression and that the whole is greater than its parts. Thus, female delinquents, like adult women, suffer the consequences of multiple types of oppression as they face processing by the justice system.[103]

Prevention of Delinquency

Formerly called the Girls Club of America, Girls Inc. is a nonprofit organization that inspires all girls to be strong, smart, and bold through a network of local organizations in the United States and Canada. Girls Inc. responds to the changing needs of girls and their communities through research-based programs and advocacy that empower girls to reach their full potential and to understand, assert, and value their rights. Girls Inc. sponsors a number of programs that are designed to enable young women to develop their capacities. They include the following:[104]

- *Preventing Adolescent Pregnancy.* Seeking to educate girls about the issues of sex and pregnancy, this program is designed to prepare girls to be able to decide when they want to engage in sexual practices.

- *Operation Start:* Aiming to increase the interest and abilities of girls in math, science, and technology, this program specifically seeks to prevent girls who show interest in these areas from adopting and attitude that technology and science are the exclusive arena of males and that females cannot excel in them.

- *Project Bold.* Teaching girls about violence and its prevention, this program is designed to help girls resist violence at home and the school. It further shows concrete examples of how to defend themselves.

- *Media Literacy.* Teaching girls to think critically about the images of women as presented by the media, this program focuses on issues such as body image and the dysfunctional manner in which the media portray the female body as a sexual object.

- *Economic Literacy.* Teaching girls how to handle money, this program presents the basic issues, such as debt, credit-card practices, interest rates, and the value of savings. This program focuses on teaching girls how to plan and control their own economic future.
- *National Scholars.* This program focuses on making it possible to provide scholarships for deserving young women. Lucille Miller Wright, a longtime supporter of Girls Inc., bequeathed $6.4 million from her estate to the organization to fund scholarships for young women members.

With its commitment to provide girls with a strong and healthy self-concept so that they can grow into competent women, Girls Inc. has developed the Girls' Bill of Rights®. It states:

- Girls have the right to be themselves and to resist gender stereotypes.
- Girls have the right to express themselves with originality and enthusiasm.
- Girls have the right to take risks, to strive freely, and to take pride in success.
- Girls have the right to accept and appreciate their bodies.
- Girls have the right to have confidence in themselves and to be safe in the world.
- Girls have the right to prepare for interesting work and economic independence.

▶ Delinquency Across the Life Course: Gender and Delinquency

7 LEARNING OUTCOMES Explain how male and female delinquent careers differ.

Independent researcher Jean Bottcher, in a study that targeted brothers and sisters of incarcerated teenagers, conceptualized gender as social practices and used these practices as the unit of analysis. Her study revealed a number of social factors that intertwined with delinquent activities, limiting female delinquency while at the same time enabling and rewarding male delinquency. They include male dominance, differences in routine daily activities, variations in both sexual interests and transition to adulthood, and an ideology that defined both crime as male activity and child care as female activity.[105]

Longitudinal studies reveal that delinquent careers differ by gender. Male careers tend to begin earlier and to extend longer into the adult years. Studies of youth gangs show that female members are more likely than male members to leave the gang

Longitudinal studies reveal that delinquent careers differ by gender.

if they have a child. According to Bottcher, conventional life patterns—especially marriage, parenting, and work—draw both males and females away from gangs and delinquency but do so more quickly and completely for females.[106]

Amy C. D'Unger and colleagues, in a follow-up of the second Philadelphia cohort study, found both life-course-persistent and adolescence-limited delinquency (see Terrie Moffitt's classification scheme in Chapters 2 and 3) among the males, with a high and low category for each group. Among the females in this study, there were comparable adolescence-limited groups, although with lower overall offending levels. The high-rate adolescence-limited female offenders did share marked similarities with low-rate chronic male offenders; however, the chronic or persistent category of offender was less prominent among the females.[107]

Rebecca S. Katz, using data from the National Longitudinal Study of Youth, found that, much as in other studies, childhood victimization, sexual discrimination, adult racial discrimination, and domestic violence largely explained women's involvement in crime and deviance. Katz found some support for revised strain theory as an explanation for female involvement in criminal behavior, but she concluded that female crime also may require a unique theoretical model that more directly takes into account females' social and emotional development in a racist and patriarchal society.[108]

Alex R. Piquero, Robert Brame, and Terrie E. Moffitt—using data from the Cambridge study of males and from the Dunedin, New Zealand, birth cohort—found that the vast majority of both males and females never experience a conviction, and for those who do, the number of convictions is quite small. They also stated that boys, more than girls, tend to become involved in crime when measured by conviction experience and that boys, once they are involved, exhibit more variations in conviction activity than do girls; the data further revealed that boys can be separated into low-, medium-, and high-frequency offender groups, whereas girls can be separated into low- and medium-frequency groups. Finally, their analysis found "that the process of continuity in criminal activity is formed by the end of adolescence similarly for both males and females" and that "there appear to be more similarities than differences across gender in how adolescent and adult patterns of offending are linked."[109]

At least three studies have examined the desistance process among women. I. Sommers, D. R. Baskin, and J. Fagan found that quality marriages led women to desist from crime, with some variation depending on the class and race of the women being studied.[110] A later study by Sommers and Baskin revealed that the desistance process was quite different for inner-city African-American women, who were more likely to desist when they received alcohol and drug treatment or because they grew tired or fearful of repeated imprisonments.[111] Finally, Peggy C. Giordano and colleagues followed up on a sample of serious adolescent female delinquents and found neither marital attachment nor job stability to be strongly related to female desistance; instead, desisters underwent a cognitive shift, or transformation, in which they experienced successful "hooks for change," which "facilitated the development of an alternative view of self that was seen as fundamentally incompatible with criminal behavior."[112]

▶ Delinquency and Social Policy: A Gender-Responsive Policy Approach

Describe the nature of a gender-responsible policy approach to delinquency prevention.

Another problem is that female offenders represent one of the least-serviced juvenile justice populations. There are only a few effective gender-specific programs nationally. The continuum of programs and services required to reduce females' entry into the juvenile justice system must be responsive both to gender and age and to developmental age.

A gender-responsive policy approach calls for a new vision for the juvenile justice system, one that recognizes the behavioral and social differences between female and male offenders that have specific implications for gender-responsive policy and practice.[113] Gender-responsive policy provides effective interventions that address the intersecting issues of substance abuse, trauma, mental health, and economic oppression, as Bloom and colleagues indicated; a focus on juvenile females' relationships with their family members is paramount as well.

Optimum environments for at-risk females of this age would be intensive family-based programs tailored to the needs of adolescent females.[114] Another possibility that has merit is a community-based all-girls school setting, anchoring such services as family counseling, substance-abuse prevention, specialized educational services (e.g., learning disabilities assessment), and mentoring services. A further gender-specific strategy is offering programs that provide the opportunity for the development of positive relationships between female offenders and their children.[115]

THE CASE

The Life Course of Amy Watters, Age 12

When Amy was 12, she made a terrifying discovery. One day, while undressing in front of the full-length mirror that her father had installed in her bedroom a few months earlier, she looked closely at one of the brackets holding the mirror in place on the wall. To her surprise she saw that a screw head on that bracket appeared to be missing. Upon further examination, she realized that what she was looking at was the lens of a tiny camera hidden within the bracket. Had someone been watching her as she undressed?

Amy hurriedly called her friends to talk about the discovery, and soon Sarah, Jake, and Mallory came over to her house to examine the mirror. Her father was away at work, and Jake disassembled the mirror, finding that Amy's suspicions had been correct. A small wireless camera, running on tiny batteries, was hidden in the mirror. When Jake, who was something of a geek, powered on her father's computer he quickly found that the wireless signal from the camera in the mirror fed into the home's router. Her father's computer screen displayed everything that went on in Amy's room, and provided an especially good close-up of activities taking place in front of the mirror.

Amy was horrified at the thought that her father had been watching her as she changed her clothes, and started thinking that he might have been selling live video feeds of her most intimate moments across the Internet. Before her friends could stop her, Amy packed a bag, gathered what money she could find in her father's desk drawers, and headed for the bus station. She didn't know where she was going, but she knew that she had to get away from home.

Discuss
What emotional impact did the discovery of the hidden camera have on Amy? Could her relationship with her father ever be the same again? What alternatives did Amy have to running away? Why didn't she take them? How was this event likely influenced by Amy's gender?

Learn more on the Web:
- A large body of literature has recently been developed that examines gender-specific pathways to offending. It shows, in part, that girls and boys may turn to delinquency for different reasons. One significant difference can often be found in the various forms of sexual victimization that some girls experience, causing them to leave home or to turn to their peers for support. See the following for more information:
- Learn more about *gender and delinquency* by visiting the National Criminal Justice Reference Service at NCJRS.gov and reading the publication numbered NCJ 238950.

Follow the continuing Amy Watters saga in the next chapter.

CHAPTER 6   Gender and Delinquency

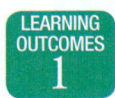

LEARNING OUTCOMES 1

Summarize why an understanding of gender differences is important in the study of delinquency.

An understanding of gender differences in the study of delinquency is important because of the need to answer the following gender-related questions: (1) Why are females less likely than males to be involved in most crimes? (2) Conversely, why are males more crime-prone than females? (3) What explains gender differences in rates of offending? Also, many criminologists argue that an understanding of gender is important in the study of delinquency because adolescent females are socially positioned in society in ways that make them especially vulnerable to male victimization, including physical and sexual abuse and the negative effects of poverty.

1. Why is an understanding of gender differences important in the study of delinquency?
2. What are the major differences that male and female adolescents are likely to face as they move through their teenage years?
3. What implications do such differences hold for individual behavior and delinquency?
4. How can delinquency prevention programs take advantage of what is known about the differences between the experiences of male and female adolescents?

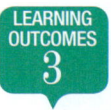

LEARNING OUTCOMES 2

Compare how gender roles impact girls' and boys' delinquency.

Gender roles impact male and female delinquents in different ways: Girls develop their identity in relation to other people, whereas boys develop their identity in relation to the world; girls resolve conflict based on relationships, whereas boys resolve conflict based on rules; girls focus on connectedness and interdependence, whereas boys focus on independence and autonomy; and girls exhibit relational aggression, whereas boys exhibit overt aggression.

1. How is gender learned? What does *learned gender* mean?
2. What is a gender role?
3. How much do early gender roles affect the development of adolescent males and females?

gender The personal traits, social positions, and values and beliefs that members of a society attach to being male or female.

gender role A societal definition of what constitutes either masculine or feminine behavior.

LEARNING OUTCOMES 3

Recall the characteristics common to female delinquents.

The characteristics common to female delinquents are a history of victimization, unstable family life, school failure, repeated status offenses, and mental health and substance-abuse problems.

1. What are some of the characteristics common to female delinquents?
2. How can the identification of the characteristics common to female delinquents help in the creation of delinquency prevention programs?

LEARNING OUTCOMES 4

Summarize the various theories about why females offend.

Biological explanations of female delinquency are frequently offered, but appear to be less predictive than a number of other perspectives. The personal maladjustment hypotheses, or psychological explanations, may have some predictive ability, but sociological theories appear to be able to explain more of female delinquency and do it far more adequately.

1. What are the main explanations of female delinquency?
2. Which of the sociological explanations for juvenile females' involvement in delinquency do you think is found most frequently in female offenders?
3. What are the policy implications of the various theories that have been offered to explain female delinquency?

sex-role socialization The process by which boys and girls internalize their culture's norms, sanctions, and expectations for members of their gender.

masculinity hypothesis The idea that as girls become more boylike and acquire more masculine traits, they become more delinquent.

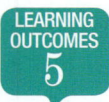

LEARNING OUTCOMES 5

Explain the feminist theory of delinquency.

The feminist theory of delinquency states that adolescent females' victimization at home causes them to become delinquent and that this fact has been systematically ignored. The perspective holds that gender bias influences the processing of female delinquents, and that it leads to discriminatory treatment within the juvenile justice system.

1. What is the feminist theory of delinquency?
2. What are the implications of the feminist theory of delinquency for delinquency prevention programs?

feminist theory of delinquency A theory that adolescent females' victimization at home causes them to become delinquent and that this fact has been systematically ignored.

LEARNING OUTCOMES 6

Summarize how gender bias impacts the processing of female delinquents.

Some studies have found that police officers adopt a more paternalistic and harsher attitude toward younger females to deter any further violation or inappropriate sex-role behavior. Similarly, other justice system personnel apparently tend to commit females to longer sentences than males in the interest of protecting them.

1. Why has gender bias played such a significant role in the processing of juvenile offenders?
2. Why are females often treated more harshly than males in the juvenile justice system?
3. How can greater gender equality within the juvenile justice system be achieved?

chivalry factor The idea that the justice system tends to treat adolescent females and women more leniently because of their gender.

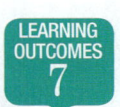

LEARNING OUTCOMES 7

Explain how male and female delinquent careers differ.

The careers of male delinquents tend to begin earlier and extend longer into the adult years. Moreover, boys, once they are involved in delinquency, exhibit greater variations in activity than do girls.

1. How do male and female delinquent careers differ?
2. What does it mean to say that boys exhibit greater variation in delinquent activity than do girls?

LEARNING OUTCOMES 8

Describe the nature of a gender-responsible policy approach to delinquency prevention.

The juvenile justice system can better serve adolescent female offenders through a gender-responsive policy that provides effective intervention to address the intersecting issues of substance abuse, trauma, mental health, and economic oppression, as well as a focus on juvenile female relationships with their family members.

1. What is meant by gender-responsiveness in the juvenile justice system?
2. Can you think of gender-responsive ways in which the juvenile justice system can more effectively serve adolescent female offenders?

7

Families and Delinquency

> "The number of abused and neglected children has special significance for the juvenile justice system because many of these children end up in the system."
> —Federal Advisory Committee on Juvenile Justice

1. Explain how problems in the family can contribute to delinquency.
2. Explain how the mass media can influence adolescent behavior.
3. Explain how neglect and child abuse contribute to delinquency.
4. Summarize the sequence of events that occurs as the community responds to child maltreatment.
5. Recall the family-related risk factors for delinquency.
6. Recall interventions that can help prevent and reduce the extent of child abuse and neglect.

Lisa F. Young/Shutterstock

INTRO: LEARNING SOCIAL ROLES

In what can only be described as strange, a number of videos appeared on YouTube and on various television networks a few years ago showing a two-year-old toddler in Indonesia who is addicted to cigarettes,[1] and a three-year old Chinese girl who not only smokes, but is a regular drinker.[2] Whereas the father of the Indonesian boy readily admitted to getting his son hooked on smoking, claiming that it did him no harm, the parents of the imbibing Chinese girl said that she indulged in such behavior only behind their backs. Although it is difficult to imagine a three-year-old having the presence of mind to hide her vices, it is important to recognize that in any culture the family is the primary agent for the socialization of children. It is the first social group a child encounters and it is the group with which most children have their most enduring relationships. The family gives a child his or her principal identity (even his or her name); teaches social roles, moral standards, and society's laws; and disciplines any child who fails to comply with those norms and values. The family either provides for or neglects children's emotional, intellectual, and social needs; as suggested above, the neglect of these basic needs can have a profound effect on the shaping of a child's attitudes and values.

A child smoking. How do early life experiences shape a person's later behavior?

DISCUSS How does childhood socialization determine what a person later becomes? Why is the family such an important factor in socialization?

This chapter discusses adolescents and family problems; the relationship between the family and delinquency; and the types and impact of child abuse and neglect, both at the time of their occurrence and across the life course.

▶ Social Context of Delinquency: Impact of Families on Delinquency

The importance of the family in understanding delinquent behavior can be seen in the fact that most theories of delinquency rely heavily on the parent–child relationship and parenting practices to explain delinquency.[3] Social disorganization theories, subcultural theories, social control theories, and life-course theories all have this emphasis.[4] The theoretical emphasis on family processes, in turn, is supported by findings that family relationships and parenting skills are directly or indirectly related to delinquent behavior.[5]

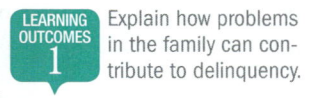

LEARNING OUTCOMES 1 Explain how problems in the family can contribute to delinquency.

A structure-versus-function controversy has been one of the important and continuing debates on the relationship between family and delinquency. The structural perspective focuses on factors such as parental absence, family size, and birth order, whereas the functional or quality-of-life view argues for the significance of parent–child interaction, the degree of marital happiness, and the amount and type of discipline.[6]

There are those who challenge whether parental behavior is related to delinquency among children. A strong proponent of this position is Judith Rick Harris. She claimed that a youth's conduct, including delinquency, is predominantly influenced by peers or group **socialization**. She maintained that the relationship between parental socialization and child outcomes is largely due to the genes that are shared between parent and offspring.[7] Harris's research has led to other studies that have questioned the association between family life and child outcomes, and most of these studies are driven by findings from behavioral genetic research.[8] This line of research has argued that once the effects that the child has on the family are taken into consideration, the relationship between family factors and child outcomes vanishes.[9]

Family Factors

Numerous family factors have been identified as having association with delinquency behavior, and these are covered in the following sections.

- *Broken Homes.* Early research found a direct relationship between **broken homes** and delinquency;[10] later studies, however, questioned the relationship between broken homes and delinquency.[11] Researchers have shed further light on this debate. It has been reported that the factor of broken homes affects adolescent females more than males,[12] that broken homes have a larger impact on delinquency among African Americans than on other racial groups,[13] and that the connection between broken homes and delinquency is more evident for status offenses than it is for more serious offenses.[14]

- *Birth Order.* Some evidence supports the significance of **birth order** in that delinquent behavior is more likely to be exhibited by middle children than by first or last children. The first child, according to this view, receives the undivided attention and affection of parents, and the last child benefits from the parents' experience in raising children as well as from the presence of other siblings, who serve as role models.[15]
- *Family Size.* Research findings on **family size** generally reveal that large families have more delinquency than do small families.[16]
- *Delinquent Siblings and Criminal Parents.* Some evidence exists that **delinquent siblings** learn crime from other family members.[17]
- *Quality of Home Life.* Studies have generally reported that poor quality of home life, measured by marital adjustment and harmony within the home, affects the rate of delinquent behavior among children more than whether or not the family is intact. Nye found the happiness of the marriage to be the key to whether or not children become involved in delinquent behavior.[18]
- *Family Rejection.* Several studies have found a significant relationship between **rejection by parents** and delinquent behavior.[19]
- *Discipline in the Home.* Inadequate **supervision and discipline** in the home have been commonly cited to explain delinquent behavior. John Paul Wright and Francis T. Cullen, in using data from the National Longitudinal Survey of Youth, advanced the concept of "parental efficacy" as an adaptation of Robert J. Sampson and colleagues' "collective efficacy" (see Chapter 4). They found that support and control are intertwined and that parental efficacy exerts substantive effects on reducing children's inappropriate behaviors.[20]

Ronald L. Simons and colleagues, using data from a sample of several hundred African-American caregivers and their children, found that increases in collective efficacy within a community over time were associated with increases in authoritative parenting, which is defined as parents combining warmth and support with firm monitoring and control.[21]

Conclusions

Conflicting findings make drawing conclusions about the relationship between delinquency and the family difficult, but the following seven observations have received wide support:

1. Family conflict and poor marital adjustment are more likely to lead to delinquency than is the structural breakup of the family.

Multiple risk factors within the family are associated with a higher probability of juvenile delinquency than are single factors.

2. Children who are intermediate in birth order and who are part of large families appear to be involved more frequently in delinquent behavior, but this is probably related more to parents' inability to provide the emotional and financial needs of these children than to birth position or family size.
3. Children who have delinquent siblings or criminal parents appear to be more prone to delinquent behavior than those who do not.
4. Rejected children are more prone to delinquent behavior than those who have not been rejected, and children who have experienced severe rejection are probably more likely to become involved in delinquent behavior than those who have experienced a lesser degree of rejection.
5. Consistency of discipline within the family seems to be important in deterring delinquent behavior.
6. Lack of mother's supervision, father's and mother's erratic/harsh discipline, parental rejection, and parental attachment appear to be the most important predictors of serious and persistent delinquency.[22]
7. The rate of delinquency appears to increase with the number of unfavorable factors in the home; that is, multiple risk factors within the family are associated with a higher probability of juvenile delinquency than are single factors.[23]

See Figure 7–1 for a representation of family factors and their relationship to delinquency. Exhibit 7–1 provides an overview of Multisystemic Therapy (MST), a community-based treatment strategy that is often employed with chronic and violent juvenile offenders.

Transitions and Delinquency

Divorced and single-parent families, poverty, homelessness, alcohol and drug abuse, and violence are some of the family problems that affect adolescents today. Adolescents experiencing such problems are at a high risk of becoming involved in socially unacceptable behaviors.

The high divorce rate in the United States translates into an increasing number of single-parent families. In 2012, 64 percent of children below the age of 18 years lived with two married parents, 28 percent with one parent, and 4 percent with no biological parents (see Figure 7–2).[24] Divorce has affected African-American families more than Caucasian families: As many as 40 percent of Caucasian children and 75 percent of African-American children will experience divorce or separation in their family before they reach 16 years of age. Many of these children will experience multiple family disruptions over the course of their childhood.[25]

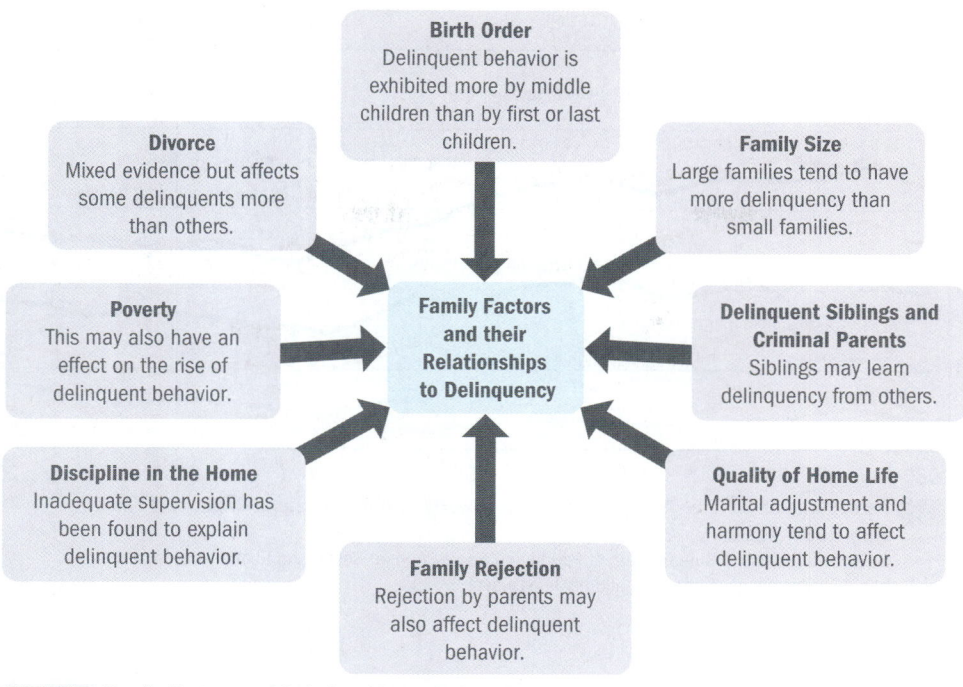

FIGURE 7-1 Family Factors and Relationships to Delinquency.

EXHIBIT 7-1 | Evidence-Based Practice: Multisystemic Therapy (MST)

MST provides cost-effective community-based clinical treatment of chronic and violent offenders who are at high risk for out-of-home placement. MST addresses the multiple determinants of serious antisocial behavior in juvenile offenders. It views individual behavior as being determined by a network of interconnected social systems (the family, the peer group, the school, and the neighborhood). To successfully treat the juvenile offender, intervention may be necessary in any one or in a combination of these systems. The overarching goal of the intervention is to help parents understand and help their children overcome the multiple problems contributing to antisocial behavior. Treatment generally lasts for about four months, which includes about 60 hours of therapist–family contact. Program evaluations have revealed 25 to 70 percent reductions in long-term rates of rearrest and 47 to 54 percent reductions in out-of-home placements. These and other positive results have been shown to last for at least four years after treatment ended.

Sources: Center for the Study and Prevention of Violence at the University of Colorado Boulder, *Blueprints: We Know What Works*, http://www.colorado.edu/cspv/blueprints/ (accessed May 11, 2014); and Office of Juvenile Justice and Delinquency Prevention, *Model Programs* Guide, http://www.ojjdp.gov/mpg (accessed May 11, 2014).

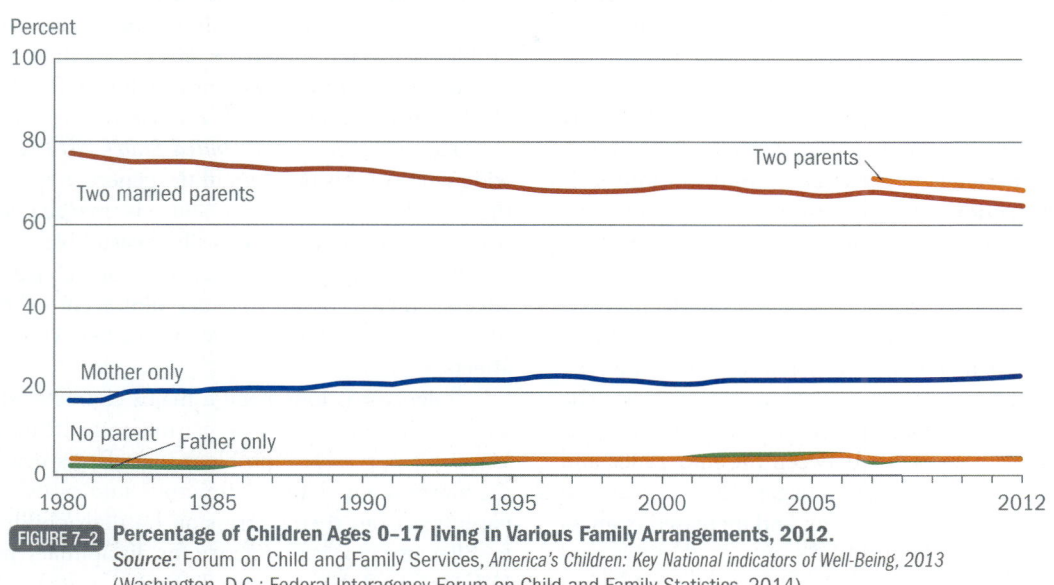

FIGURE 7-2 Percentage of Children Ages 0–17 living in Various Family Arrangements, 2012.
Source: Forum on Child and Family Services, *America's Children: Key National Indicators of Well-Being, 2013* (Washington, D.C.: Federal Interagency Forum on Child and Family Statistics, 2014).

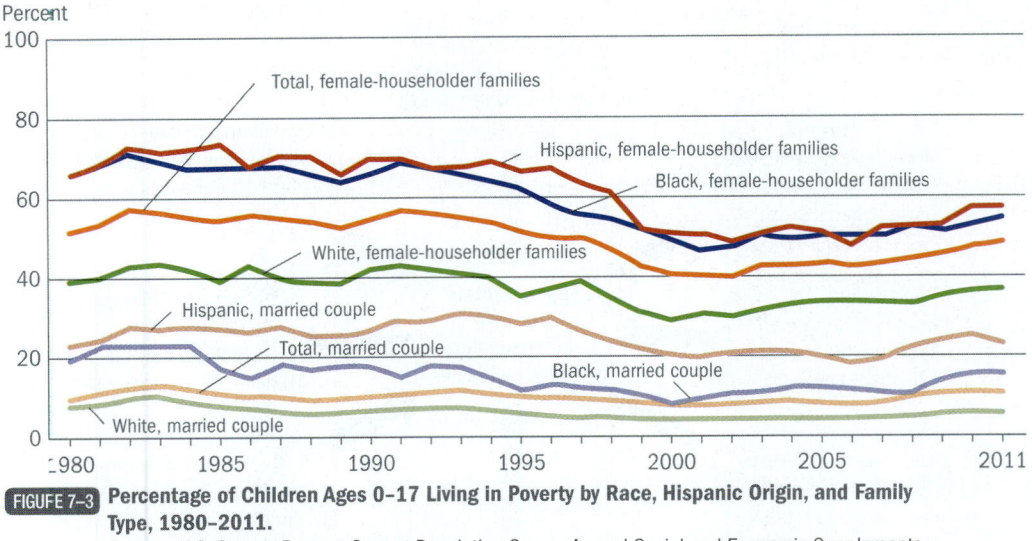

FIGURE 7-3 Percentage of Children Ages 0–17 Living in Poverty by Race, Hispanic Origin, and Family Type, 1980–2011.
Source: U.S. Census Bureau, Current Population Survey, Annual Social and Economic Supplements, http://childstats.gov/americaschildren/eco1a.asp.

Poverty is a serious problem in the lives of children. In 2011, 22 percent of children ages 0 to 17 (16.1 million) lived in poverty. This is up from a low of 16 percent in 2000 and 2001. Consistent with expectations related to the economic downturn, child poverty has increased annually since 2006, when the rate was 17 percent.[26] For children living in female-householder families, the poverty rate was 48 percent in 2011, an increase from 45 percent in 2009 (see Figure 7–3). Economic hardship and lack of access to opportunity tend to undermine marital and parental functioning; furthermore, adolescents who experience family transitions may have difficulty managing anger and other negative emotions that may contribute to their involvement with delinquency or drugs.

The majority of divorced parents remarry, and adolescents in these families must learn to adjust to a new parental figure. Blended families place stress on biological parents, stepparents, and children. In a typical blended family, the mother has custody of her children, and the stepfather lives with his wife's children; his biological children (if any) usually visit the home on an occasional or regular basis. Few adolescents escape the experience of a blended family without feeling resentment, rejection, and confusion. Some stepparents even subject their stepchildren to emotional, physical, or sexual abuse.

Childbearing is a life experience that many American female adolescents have. In some instances, children are wanted and adolescent mothers are married; more often than not, however, pregnancy in adolescence leads to abortion or adoption. The birth rate of unmarried women has risen sharply since 2002, after having been relatively stable between the mid-1980s and 2002.[27] The birth rate for unmarried teenagers 15 to 17 years old in 2006 rose from 62 to 92 percent today, and increased from 40 to 81 percent for those ages 18 and 19.[28]

Homelessness is a phenomenon that shapes the lives of an estimated 500,000 to 1.3 million young people each year. Many homeless youths leave their families after years of physical and sexual abuse, the addiction of a family member, strained interpersonal relations, and parental neglect. Homelessness, regardless of a child's age, is likely to expose him or her to settings permeated by substance abuse, promiscuity, pornography, prostitution, and crime.[29]

Unemployment also affects some family units in the United States. In 2011, the number of people 16 years old and older officially designated as unemployed was 8.9 percent. In 2011, the unemployment rate for whites 16 years and older was 7.9 percent. The unemployment rate for African-American men 16 years and older was 16.1 percent; and the unemployment rate for Hispanics 16 years and older was 11.3 percent.[30] The bad news for African-American and Hispanic families is that from 11 to 16 percent of the population is still experiencing unemployment and its ill consequences.[31]

Adolescents whose family members have substance-abuse problems also have their sad stories to tell. Neglect, abuse, and economic hardship are common factors in family settings where alcohol misuse and substance abuse are ordinary behavior. Arrest data in *Crime in the United States 2013* reflect the nationwide scope of this problem in the general population. But while the prevalence of substance abuse is unarguable, its actual impact on adolescents is not easily measurable, as it is simply not possible to display the impact on a "one abuse instance = one adverse impact on one or more adolescent(s)" basis.[32] The impact is clearly visible, however, in the behaviors of the youths it affects.

Violence has long been a major characteristic of the problem family, and it is no stranger to family life today. Marital violence is a pervasive problem that affects nearly one-third of the married population. Numerous studies also show that some parents act out their aggression on their children,[33] and some families use physical violence for disciplinary purposes. Karen Heimer found that coercive discipline strategies teach youths to rely on force and coercion to resolve problems.[34]

The Foster Family

The foster family; the adopted child; children with lesbian, gay, bisexual, and transgender parents; and cohabiting parents provide other family contexts for children.

Foster care can be defined as 24-hour substitute care for children outside their own homes. Foster care settings include, but are not limited to, relative foster homes (whether payments are being made or not), nonrelative foster family homes, emergency shelters, residential facilities, and preadoptive homes. The publication *Foster Care Statistics 2010* reveals a number of key findings:

- On September 30, 2010, there were an estimated 408,425 children in foster care.
- More than a quarter (26 percent) were in the homes of relatives, and nearly half (48 percent) were in nonrelative foster family homes.
- About half (51 percent) had the goal of reunification with their families.
- About half (51 percent) of the children left the system to be reunited with their parents or primary caretakers.
- Close to half of the children (46 percent) who left foster care in fiscal year 2010 were in care for less than one year.[35]

The 254,114 children who exited foster care during fiscal year 2010 spent time in care as follows:

- 13 percent in care for less than 1 month
- 33 percent in care for 1 to 11 months
- 24 percent in care for 12 to 23 months
- 12 percent in care for 24 to 35 months
- 10 percent in care for 3 to 4 years
- 7 percent in care for 5 or more years.[36]

One recent study found that children had better outcomes when they remained at home rather than entering foster care. This study found that 44 percent of the children in foster care were arrested, whereas only 14 percent were arrested when staying at home. Fifty-six percent of females became pregnant in foster care, but only 33 percent became pregnant while staying at home.[37] This study also suggests that children in foster care have a greater likelihood of difficult adjustments later in life and will require additional intervention if future problems occur.

The Adopted Child

About 120,000 children are adopted each year in the United States. Children with developmental, physical, or emotional handicaps who were once considered unadoptable are now being adopted ("special needs adoptions"). Adoptions provide the opportunity for many of these children to grow up in permanent families instead of in foster homes or institutions.[38]

An important issue in adoptions is the question of when (or whether) to tell children that they are adopted. Experts agree that children should learn of their adoption from the adoptive parents. If a child learns intentionally or accidentally from someone other than his or her adopted parents, the child may feel anger and mistrust toward the parents and as a result may view the adoption as shameful or bad because it was kept a secret. The struggle with their own identity, which is normal for all adolescents, may be even more intense for those children adopted from other countries or cultures. In addition, the adopted child may have an increased interest in his or her birth parents.[39] Some adoptive children may develop emotional or behavioral problems, which may or may not relate to insecurities related to being adopted.[40]

Children with Lesbian, Gay, Bisexual, and Transgender Parents (LGBT)

Millions of children in the United States have gay, lesbian, bisexual, and/or transgender (LGBT) parents. Some of these children were conceived in heterosexual relationships or marriages. An increasing number of LGBT parents have conceived children and/or raised them from birth, either in ongoing committed relationships or as single parents.[41]

In contrast to what is commonly believed, children of LGBT parents:

- Are not more likely to be gay than children with heterosexual parents.
- Do not reveal differences in whether they think of themselves as male or female (gender identity).
- Are not more likely to be sexually abused.
- Do not show differences in their male and female behaviors (gender-role behavior).[42]

Although research shows that children with gay and lesbian parents are often as well adjusted as children who have heterosexual parents, they can still face challenges. Some LGBT families face discrimination in their communities, and children may be teased or bullied by their peers. Parents can help their children cope with such pressures by preparing them to handle questions about their background or family, by helping their children come up with and practice appropriate responses to teasing or mean remarks, and by considering living in a community where diversity is more accepted.[43]

Cohabitating Parents

The rates of divorce are going down, and the numbers of cohabiting parents are rapidly increasing. Before 12 years of age, children are more likely to live with unmarried parents than to have married parents separate or divorce.[44]

Some children must deal with a variety of partners, usually mothers' boyfriends, moving into or out of the home. Over time, the child's parent may have lived with dozens or even hundreds of partners. Some stay a short period of time, whereas others may be a part of the child's life for years. Eventually the relationship may lead to marriage.

Another recent study found that a quarter of American women with multiple children conceived them with multiple partners.[45] Psychologist John Gottman, a coauthor of the study, says such instability can have a negative impact on kids in various ways. He claims that, on average, children of cohabitating parents tend to be both aggressive and depressed.[46] Another study found that cohabitation is associated with children's simultaneous increases in offending.[47]

▶ The Mass Media and Delinquent Behavior

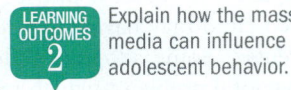

LEARNING OUTCOMES 2 Explain how the mass media can influence adolescent behavior.

Part of the challenge of being a parent today is dealing effectively with the influence that the mass media have on children. For our purposes, the term *mass media* refers to the Internet, radio, television, commercial motion pictures, videos, CDs, music, and the press (newspapers, journals, and magazines).[48]

Think About It...

Adolescents are strongly influenced by today's media, including Internet-based services such as social networking. How might social networking contribute to delinquency?

Monkey Business Images/Shutterstock

Violent TV Programs and Movies

Most people today watch a lot of television, and many seem to depend on media programming for their understandings of the surrounding world.[49] Consequently, criminologists have shown considerable interest in assessing the relationship between delinquent behavior and the exposure to violence viewed on television. Researchers in the area of delinquency generally conclude that TV violence is most likely to negatively impact the behavior of those children who are already predisposed toward violence and that it seems to have much less influence on young people who are not so predisposed.[50]

The influence of television and motion pictures also extends to the phenomenon of contagion. An example of the contagion effect of motion pictures can be seen in the movie *Colors*, whose showing in theaters across America led gang members nationwide to begin wearing their groups' colors; prior to seeing the movie, most gang members had not been wearing their gang colors.[51]

Some evidence exists to indicate that there is connection between parental responsibility and the access children have to violent media content. Gregory Zimmerman and Greg Pogarsky's study investigated differences in parent and child estimates of the child's exposure to violence. Using data from the Project on Human Development in Chicago Neighborhoods, most parents (66 percent) underestimated their children's exposure to violence and its impact on the child's psychosocial functioning. Parental underestimates of children's exposure to violence reflected lower levels of family support, which led to more internalizing and externalizing problems and delinquency for the child.[52]

Violent Video Games

Video games involving violent scenarios, such as "Postal 2," "MadWorld," "Gears of War 2," "God of War 2" and "Asheron Call 2," are the focus of considerable controversy today. Some people accuse video-game makers of promoting values that support violence. Not surprisingly, the software entertainment industry, with its annual $28 billion in sales paced by a nation's thirst for action, claims that their games are offered only for entertainment purposes.[53]

In August 2005, members of the American Psychological Association (APA) adopted a resolution calling for less violence in video and computer games marketed to children. One APA panelist, Keven M. Kieffer, reported research showing that playing violent video games tends to make children more aggressive and less prone to helping behaviors.[54] Craig A. Anderson, one of the pioneers of research in this area, adds, "There really isn't any room for doubt that aggressive game playing leads to aggressive behavior"[55]

In the fall of 2005, the Federal Trade Commission (FTC) launched an investigation into the system used for rating video games, particularly what some saw as undeservedly low ratings that made the violent and sexually themed game "Grand Theft Auto" available to teens. Around the same time, a group of bipartisan senators proposed that the National Institutes of Health oversee a comprehensive $90 million study on the effects of violent media, including video games, on children's development.[56]

Recently, researchers C. L. Olson and D. W. Warner conducted focus groups with 42 boys ages 12 to 14 to determine how children are influenced by violent interactive games. Boys, they found, typically used games to fantasize about power and fame, to work through angry feelings or relieve stress, and to explore and master what they perceived as exciting and realistic environments. The boys in this study group did not believe that they have been negatively impacted by violent games, although they were concerned that younger children might imitate game behavior, particularly swearing.[57]

Internet-Initiated Crimes

Internet access is easily available to nearly everyone in the United States today, and the Web has become a new frontier for innovative forms of cybercrime. One source of Internet-initiated crime is the supremacist and hate groups that target young people through the Web. In like manner, youthful perpetrators of violent crimes are sometimes influenced by information collected or contacts made on the Internet, and child sexual abuse in which initial contacts are made through the Web now accounts for up to 4 percent of all arrests for sexual assaults against juveniles.[58]

Gangsta Rap

Gangsta rap is a form of hip-hop music that some believe negatively influences young people by devaluing human life, the

> **Part of the challenge of being a parent today is dealing effectively with the influence that the mass media have on children.**

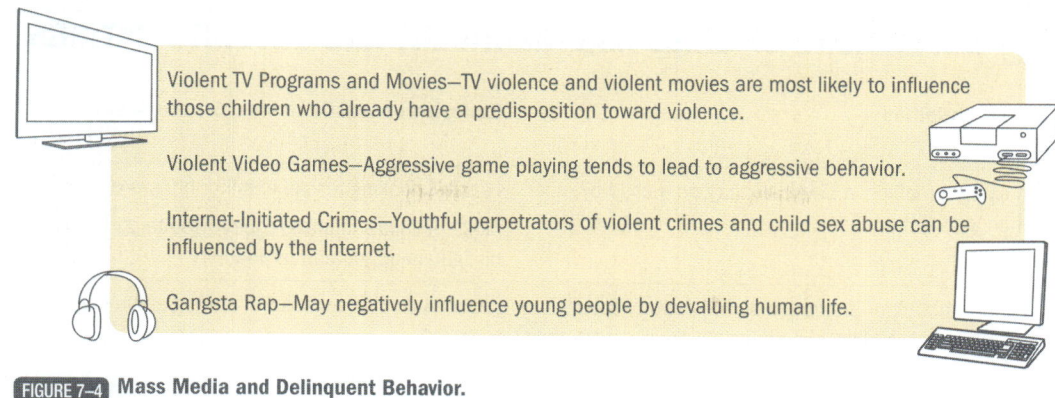

- Violent TV Programs and Movies—TV violence and violent movies are most likely to influence those children who already have a predisposition toward violence.
- Violent Video Games—Aggressive game playing tends to lead to aggressive behavior.
- Internet-Initiated Crimes—Youthful perpetrators of violent crimes and child sex abuse can be influenced by the Internet.
- Gangsta Rap—May negatively influence young people by devaluing human life.

FIGURE 7–4 Mass Media and Delinquent Behavior.

family, religious institutions, schools, and the justice system.[59] Gangsta rap, pioneered by Ice-T and other rappers influenced by Schoolly D's hard-core rap, portrays the lifestyles of inner-city gang members, and its lyrics relate stories of violence-filled lives. Guns play a prominent part in those lyrics and are frequently depicted as a means for attaining manhood and status.

Today's rap music has its origins in the hip-hop culture of young, urban, working-class African Americans.[60] The subject matter of this music, which is available to children via television (especially MTV), the Internet, radio (including satellite radio), and retail CDs and DVDs, has created considerable controversy, with critics charging that the messages it espouses include misogyny, homophobia, racism, and materialism. Gangsta rappers usually defend themselves by pointing out that they are describing the reality of inner-city life and claim that when they are rapping, they are merely playing a character.[61]

Brown University Professor Tricia Rose's 2006 book *Hip-Hop Wars* claims that hip-hop is in crisis, because its lyrics are becoming increasingly saturated with themes involving thugs, pimps, black gangsters, and "hos" (promiscuous women). She raises a number of important questions about hip-hop: Does hip-hop cause violence, or does it merely reflect a violent ghetto culture? Is hip-hop sexist, or are its detractors merely anti-sex? Does the portrayal of black culture in hip-hop undermine black social advancement? Rose calls for a more accurate reflection in the music of a richer cultural space, including anger, politics, and sex, than the current images in sound and video provide.[62]

In summary, today's parents must face the reality that their children's minds are being bombarded with extensive disturbing stimuli. Violence permeates movies and TV screens; video games are no less violent, and the most popular ones among teenagers are probably the most violent. Supremacist and hate groups are targeting young people through their Web sites; the Internet offers opportunities for the sexual abuse of vulnerable adolescent males and females. Finally, gangsta rap is filled with violence, appears to devalue human life, and contains lyrics promoting homophobia, misogyny, racism, and materialism. See Figure 7–4 for the types of media and a brief explanation of how they can influence adolescent behavior.

▶ Neglect and Child Abuse

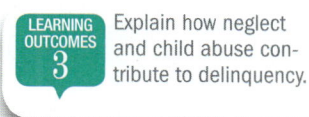

Neglect and **child abuse**, like the other family problems addressed in this chapter, have a profound influence on shaping the behavior and attitudes of adolescents and adults.[63] Various categories of child abuse and neglect, also referred to as *child maltreatment*, are identified in Table 7–1.[64]

LEARNING OUTCOMES 3 Explain how neglect and child abuse contribute to delinquency.

Cathy Spatz Widom's initial study of abuse and neglect found that 29 percent of those abused and neglected as children had a nontraffic criminal record as adults, compared with 21 percent of the control group.[65] Widom and Michael G. Maxfield's updated study, which followed 1,575 cases from childhood through adolescence and into young adulthood, was able to examine the long-term consequences of abuse and neglect:[66]

1. Being abused or neglected as a child increased the likelihood of arrest as a juvenile by 59 percent, as an adult by 29 percent, and for a violent crime by 30 percent.
2. Maltreated children were younger at the time of their first arrest, committed nearly twice as many offenses, and were arrested more frequently.
3. Physically abused and neglected (versus sexually abused) children were the most likely to be arrested later for a violent crime.
4. Abused and neglected females also were at increased risk of arrest for violence as juveniles and adults.
5. Caucasian abused and neglected children were no more likely to be arrested for a violent crime than their nonabused and nonneglected Caucasian counterparts; in contrast, African-American abused and neglected children showed significantly increased rates of violent arrests compared with African-American children who were not maltreated.[67]

Neglect and child abuse have a profound influence on shaping the behavior and attitudes of adolescents and adults.

TABLE 7–1 DEFINITIONS OF CHILD MALTREATMENT AND SEVERITY RATINGS

Types of Maltreatment	Brief Definition	Examples of Least and Most Severe Cases
Physical Abuse	A caregiver inflicts a physical injury on a child by other than accidental means.	Least—Spanking results in minor bruises on a child's arm. Most—A child's injuries require hospitalization, cause permanent disfigurement, or lead to a fatality.
Sexual Abuse	Sexual contact or attempted sexual contact occurs between a caretaker (or responsible adult) and a child for the purposes of the caretaker's sexual gratification or financial benefit.	Least—A child is exposed to pornographic materials. Most—A caretaker uses force to make a child engage in sexual relations or prostitution.
Physical Neglect	A caretaker fails to exercise a minimum degree of care in meeting a child's physical needs.	Least—Food is not available for a child's regular meals, a child's clothing is too small, or a child is not kept clean. Most—A child suffers from severe malnutrition or severe dehydration due to gross inattention to his or her medical needs.
Lack of Supervision or Moral Neglect	A caretaker does not take adequate precautions (given a child's particular emotional and developmental needs) to ensure his or her safety in and out of the home.	Least—An eight-year-old is left alone for short periods of time (for example, less than three hours) with no immediate source of danger in the environment. Most—A child is placed in a life-threatening situation without adequate supervision.
Emotional Maltreatment	Thwarting of a child's basic emotional needs (such as the need to feel safe and accepted) occurs persistently or at an extreme level.	Least—A caretaker often belittles or ridicules a child. Most—A caretaker uses extremely restrictive methods to bind a child or places a child in close confinement such as a closet or trunk for two or more hours.
Educational Maltreatment	A caretaker fails to ensure that a child receives an adequate education.	Least—A caretaker allows a child to miss school up to 15% of the time when the child is not ill and there is no family emergency. Most—A caretaker does not enroll a child in school or provide any educational instruction.
Moral–Legal Maltreatment	A caretaker exposes a child to or involves a child in illegal or other activities that may foster delinquency or antisocial behavior.	Least—A child is permitted to be present for adult activities, such as drunken parties. Most—A caretaker causes a child to participate in felonies such as armed robbery.

Source: Adapted from Barbara Tatem Kelley et al., "In the Wake of Childhood Maltreatment," *Juvenile Justice Bulletin* (Washington, DC: U.S. Department of Justice, Office of Juvenile Justice and Delinquency Prevention, 1997), p. 4. See Figure 7–5 for victimization rates by maltreatment types.

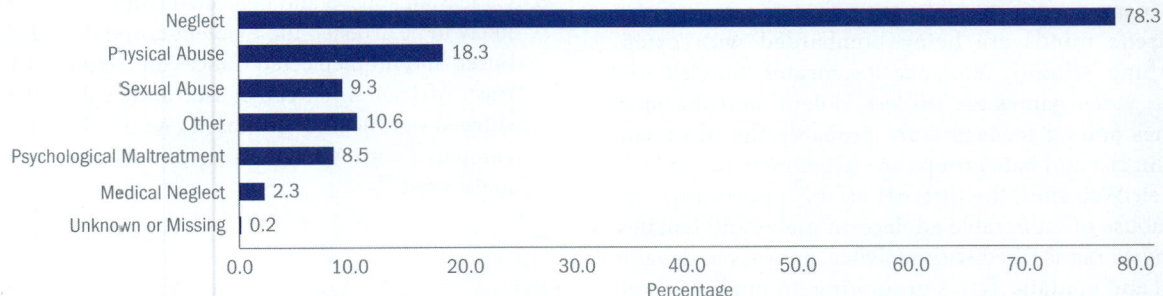

FIGURE 7–5 Child Victimization Rates by Maltreatment Type, 2012.
Source: Children's Bureau, *Child Maltreatment 2012* (Washington, DC: U.S. Department of Health and Human Services, 2013), p. 40.

EXHIBIT 7-2 | Child Maltreatment Victimization Statistics

Following are some figures from 2012:

- More than 75 percent of child maltreatment victims suffered neglect.
- More than 18 percent suffered physical abuse.
- Less than 10 percent suffered sexual abuse.
- Less than 10 percent suffered psychological maltreatment.[69]

Extent and Nature of the Problem

The passage of legislation in all 50 states in the late 1960s requiring mandatory reporting of child abuse and neglect cases focused attention on these problems, as did the passage by Congress of the Child Abuse Prevention and Treatment Act and the establishment of the national Office on Child Abuse and Neglect in 1974. As an indication of the extent of maltreatment of children, an estimated 3.3 million referrals involving the maltreatment of approximately 6 million children were made to child protective services (CPS) during the fiscal year 2008, and of that number an estimated 772,000 children were found to be victims.[68] For recent victimization statistics see Exhibit 7-2

Younger children make up the largest percentage of victims. Nearly 33 percent (32.6 percent) of all victims of maltreatment were younger than 4 years of age, an additional 23.6 percent were ages 4 to 7, and 18.9 percent were ages 8 to 11. Victimization was split almost evenly between the sexes: 51.5 percent of the victims were girls and 48.2 percent were boys. Nearly one-half (46.1 percent) of all victims were Caucasian, one-fifth (21.7 percent) were African American, and one-fifth (20.8 percent) were Hispanic. Figure 7-6 shows the age and gender of victims for the year 2008.[70]

Child fatalities represent the most tragic consequences of maltreatment. In a recent year:

- An estimated 1,740 children died due to child abuse or neglect.
- More than 30 percent (31.9 percent) of child fatalities were attributed to neglect only, but physical abuse was also a major contributor to child fatalities.
- More than three-quarters (79.8 percent) of the children who died because of child abuse and neglect were younger than four years old.
- Infant boys (younger than one year) had the highest rates of fatalities, 19.31 deaths per 100,000 boys of the same age in the national population.
- Infant girls less than one year of age had a rate of 17.32 deaths per 100,000 girls of the same age.[71]

Perpetrators of Maltreatment

Statistics show that nearly 80 percent of child maltreatment victims are abused by their parents, with another 6.5 percent abused by other relatives. Women comprise a larger percentage of perpetrators than men—56.2 percent compared to 42.6 percent. Nearly 75 percent of all perpetrators are younger than age 40.[72]

Neglect

The word *neglect* generally refers to disregard for the physical, emotional, or moral needs of children or adolescents. The Children's Division of the American Humane Association established a comprehensive definition of neglect, stating that physical, emotional, and intellectual growth and welfare are jeopardized when a child can be described in the following terms:

- Malnourished, ill-clad, dirty, without proper shelter or sleeping arrangements

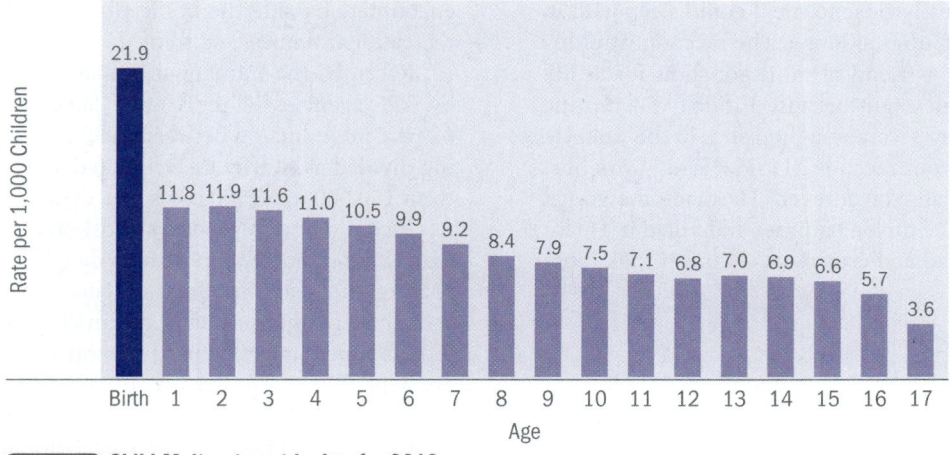

FIGURE 7-6 Child Maltreatment by Age for 2012.
Source: Children's Bureau, *Child Maltreatment 2012* (Washington, DC: U.S. Department of Health and Human Services, 2013), p. 20.

- Unsupervised, unattended
- Ill, lacking essential medical care
- Denied normal experiences that produce feelings of being loved, wanted, secure, and worthy (emotional neglect)
- Failing to attend school regularly
- Exploited, overworked
- Emotionally disturbed due to constant friction in the home, marital discord, or mentally ill parents
- Exposed to unwholesome, demoralizing circumstances[73]

Child Abuse

There are several types of child abuse, including physical, emotional, and sexual abuse. The term *physical abuse* refers to intentional behavior directed toward a child by the parent or caretaker to cause pain, injury, or death.

Murray A. Straus has been one of the strongest proponents of defining corporal punishment as physical abuse. Straus examined the extent of physical abuse using data from a number of sources, notably the 3,300 children and 6,000 couples in the National Family Violence Survey, and he found that 90 percent of U.S. citizens used physical punishment to correct misbehavior. He claimed that although physical punishment may produce conformity in the immediate situation, its long-run effect is to increase the probability of delinquency in adolescence and violent crime inside and outside the family.[74]

Emotional abuse is more difficult to define than physical abuse because it involves a disregard for the psychological needs of a child or adolescent. Emotional abuse encompasses a lack of expressed love and affection as well as deliberate withholding of contact and approval and may include a steady diet of put-downs, humiliation, labeling, name-calling, scapegoating, lying, demands for excessive responsibility, seductive behavior, ignoring, fear-inducing techniques, unrealistic expectations, and extreme inconsistency.[75] Randy, a 16-year-old boy, tells about the emotional abuse he suffered:

> My father bought me a baby raccoon. I was really close to it, and it was really close to me. I could sleep with it, and it would snug up beside me. The raccoon wouldn't leave or nothing. A friend of mine got shots for it. My father got mad one night because I didn't vacuum the rug, and there were seven or eight dishes in the sink. He said, "Go get me your raccoon." I said, "Dad, if you hurt my raccoon I'll hate you forever." He made me go get my raccoon, and he took a hammer and killed it. He hit it twice on the head and crushed its brains. I took it out and buried it.[76]

Nature of Child Abuse

Stephanie Amedeo and John Gartrell's study of 218 abused children found that the characteristics of parents, including being mentally ill and having been abused themselves, have the greatest explanatory power of predicting abuse; this study also revealed that triggers or stressors, such as alcohol and drug use, perform as factors that precipitate abuse.[77]

Research findings disagree concerning the age at which a child is most vulnerable to parental abuse. The National Incidence and Prevalence of Child Abuse and Neglect study found that the incidence of physical abuse increased with age.[78] Gil found that half the confirmed cases of abuse involved children over six years of age and that nearly one-fifth were teenagers.[79] Yet although many adolescents may experience child abuse, the more serious cases still occur with infants and young children. Child abuse also seems to be more prevalent in urban areas than in suburban or rural settings. The fact that urban areas have better resources to detect child abuse does not entirely explain why so many more cases are reported to urban police. Obviously, the congested populations and poverty of the city, which lead to other social problems, partly account for abuse being predominantly an urban problem.

The abusive situation is often characterized by one parent who is aggressive and one who is passive. The passive parent commonly defends the aggressive one, denies the realities of the family situation, and clings to the intact family and to the abusive partner. The passive parent behaves as though he or she is a prisoner in the relationship, condemned to a life sentence, and usually does not consider the option of separating from the aggressive partner because he or she is committed to the relationship, no matter how miserable the home situation may be.[80]

Children and adolescents may be victimized by either nonfamilial sexual abuse or incestuous sexual abuse. **Sexual abuse** of a child is intentional and wrongful physical contact with a child that entails a sexual purpose or component. Oral–genital relations, fondling of erogenous areas of the body, mutual masturbation, and intercourse are typical sexually abusive acts.[81]

Incest, according to the Office on Child Abuse and Neglect, is "intrafamily sexual abuse which is perpetrated on a child by a member of that child's family group and includes not only sexual intercourse, but also any act designed to stimulate a child sexually or to use a child for sexual stimulation, either of the perpetrator or of another person."[82] Incestuous sexual abusers may include a parent, grandparent, stepparent, sibling, aunt, uncle, or other member of the child's extended family. Nonfamilial sexual abusers may include any unrelated adult the child encounters outside the home (for example, at school, church, recreational venues, and so on).

Recently, the number of sexual abuse cases substantiated by CPS agencies in the United States underwent a dramatic 62 percent reduction between 1992 and 2012, with opinion being divided as to why the estimated annual incidence dropped from 150,000 to 56,500 cases (see Figure 7–7).

Incest reportedly occurs most frequently between a biological father or stepfather and a daughter but also may involve brother and sister, mother and son, and father and son.[83] Although stepfathers sexually victimize stepdaughters, biological fathers appear to be involved in more cases of sexual abuse than are stepfathers.[84] The average incestuous relationship lasts about three and one-half to four years.[85] The completed act of intercourse is more likely to take place with adolescents than with younger children.

Helen, a 16-year-old, was sexually victimized by her father for three years, and she had great difficulty getting anyone to

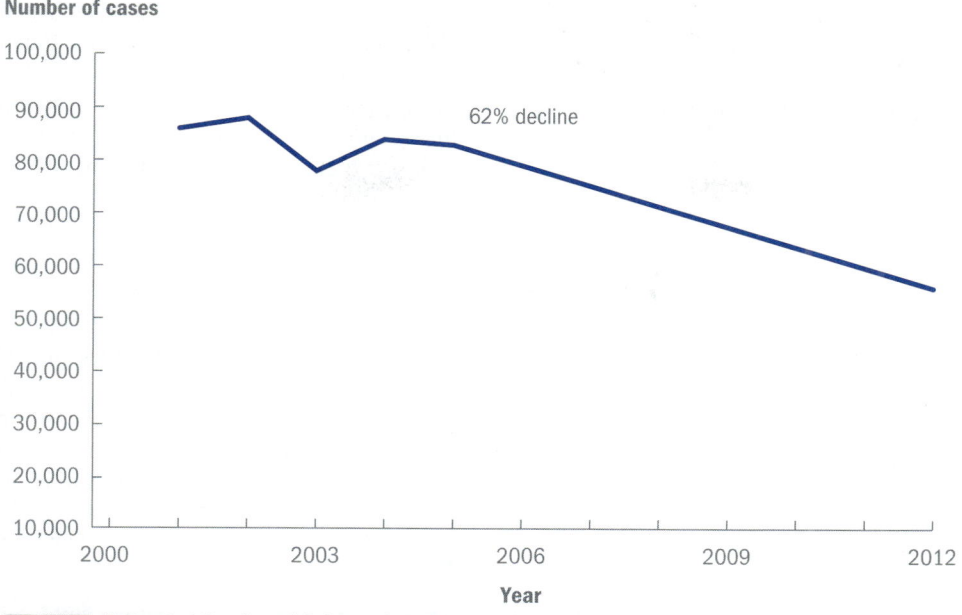

FIGURE 7-7 Estimated Number of Substantiated Cases of Child Sexual Abuse in the United States.
Source: David Finkelhor and Lisa M. Jones, *Explanations for the Decline in Child Sexual Abuse Cases* (Washington, DC: Office of Juvenile Justice and Delinquency Prevention, 2004) citing data from 1990–2000 National Child Abuse and Neglect Data System (NCANDS) reports (U.S. Department of Health and Human Services, 1992–2002); and Children's Bureau, *Child Maltreatment 2012* (Washington, DC: U.S. Department of Health and Human Services, 2013), p.20.

believe that her father was committing incest. When the father was finally prosecuted, she made this statement:

> When I was thirteen, my father started coming into my room at night. He usually did it when he was drinking. He would force me to have sex with him. I told my mother. I told my teachers at school. But nobody would believe me.[86]

Some evidence exists that **brother–sister incest** takes place more frequently than **father–daughter incest**, but its long-term consequences are usually less damaging because it does not cross generational boundaries and often occurs as an extension of sex play.[87] But brother–sister incest can have damaging consequences for the sister if the act is discovered and she is blamed for being sexually involved with her brother. If the girl feels she has been seduced or exploited, then the damage may be even greater.

Mother–son incest is less common and only rarely reported, largely because of the strong stigmas and taboos attached to the idea of sex between boys and their mothers.[88] Mother–son incest usually begins with excessive physical contact, which eventually becomes sexually stimulating. "Don't leave me" or "Don't grow up" messages are communicated to the son as the mother seeks ways to prolong physical contact with him by sleeping with him, bathing him, or dressing him.[89]

Father–son incest also is rarely reported, largely because it violates both the moral code against incest and the taboo against homosexuality. The stress of an incestuous relationship, as well as the threat to masculinity, often results in serious consequences for the boy when father–son incest does occur. Sons who are involved in father–son incest usually experience acute anxiety because they feel damaged, dirty, and worthless, and

Think About It...
Child abuse and delinquency appear to be closely correlated. Why might abuse lead to delinquency?

they may cope by retreating into their own world and losing contact with reality.[90]

The National Center on Child Abuse and Neglect has identified five factors that are usually present when father–daughter incest takes place: (1) the daughter's voluntary or forced assumption of the mother's role, (2) the parents' sexual incompatibility, (3) the father's reluctance to seek a partner outside the family unit, (4) the family's fear of disintegration, and (5) the unconscious sanctioning by the mother.[91]

Neglect, Child Abuse, and Delinquency

Research findings have revealed that a neglected or abused child is more likely to become involved in delinquency or status offenses. Neglect or abuse may have a negative impact on the emotional development of the child; it may lead to truancy and disruptive behavior in school or **running away** from home, or it may generate so much pain that alcohol and drugs are sometimes viewed as a needed escape. Neglect or abuse may cause so much self-rejection, especially in victims of incest, that these youths may vent the need for self-destructive activities through

TABLE 7–2 THE CONNECTION BETWEEN CHILD NEGLECT AND ABUSE AND DELINQUENCY

Consequences of Abuse and Neglect
Victims of child abuse and neglect often show psychological damage.
Victims of child abuse and neglect frequently run away from home.
Some research supports that neglected and abused children have greater difficulty in school.
Many abused and neglected children turn to drug and alcohol abuse.
Evidence exists that sexual abuse victims themselves may become involved in deviant sexual behavior.
Children who have experienced abusive and violent childhoods are likely to grow up and express violent behavior.

prostitution or may even commit suicide. Neglect or abuse may also create so much anger that abused youngsters later commit aggressive acts against others.

There is some evidence that childhood maltreatment that does not persist into adolescence has minimal correlation with adolescent delinquency.[92] The negative influence of severe maltreatment, such as sexual abuse by parents or caretakers, is commonly seen as carrying into adulthood and perhaps even throughout the life course. However, Peggy Giordano, Stephen A. Cernkovich, and Jennifer L. Rudolph's study of women across the life course is a reminder that female offenders who suffered extremely abusive childhoods can still have cognitive transformations as adults and can desist from criminal behaviors.[93] See Table 7–2 for the possible consequences of neglect and child abuse on delinquency.

▶ Child Abuse and the Juvenile Justice System

The term *child protective services* (CPS) usually refers to services that are provided by an agency authorized to act on behalf of a child when parents are unwilling or unable to do so. In all states, these agencies are required by law to conduct assessments or investigations of reports of child abuse and neglect and to offer treatment services to families where maltreatment has taken place or is likely to occur.[94]

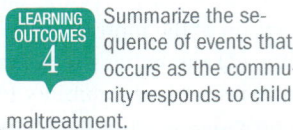

LEARNING OUTCOMES 4: Summarize the sequence of events that occurs as the community responds to child maltreatment.

Sexual abuse victims themselves often become involved in deviant sexual behavior.

Although the primary responsibility for responding to reports of abuse and neglect rests with state and local CPS agencies, the prevention and treatment of child maltreatment can involve professionals from many organizations and disciplines. Jurisdictions do differ in their procedures, but community responses to child maltreatment generally include the following sequence of events.

Identification

- Individuals who are likely to identify abuse are often those in a position to observe families and children on a regular basis. These include educators, medical professionals, police officers, social services personnel, probation officers, day-care workers, and the clergy. Family members, friends, and neighbors also may be able to identify abuse.

Reporting

- Some individuals—educators, child-care providers, medical and mental health professionals, social services providers, police officers, and clergy—often are required by law to report suspicions of abuse and neglect.
- CPS or law enforcement agencies generally receive the initial report of alleged abuse or neglect.

Intake and Investigation

- Protective services staff members are required to determine whether the report constitutes an allegation of abuse or neglect and how urgently a response is needed.
- In some jurisdictions, a police officer always accompanies the social worker on the child abuse or neglect investigation to protect the social worker, to help if the parents become assaultive, to use legal authority to take the child out of an abusive home if necessary, to gather evidence and take pictures if admissible evidence is present, and to permit the social worker to focus on the family rather than being preoccupied with the legal investigation.
- Caseworkers usually respond to reports of abuse and neglect within two to three days. An immediate response is required if it is determined that the child is at imminent risk of injury or impairment.
- If the decision is made to take the child out of the home, the juvenile court judge must be called for approval as soon as the social worker and police officer leave the house.
- Following the initial investigation, the protective services agency usually draws one of the following conclusions: (1) There is sufficient evidence to support or substantiate the allegation of maltreatment or risk of maltreatment; (2) there is insufficient evidence to support maltreatment; or (3) maltreatment or the risk of maltreatment appears to be present, although there is insufficient evidence to conclude or substantiate the allegation.

Assessment

- Protective services staff members are responsible for identifying the factors that contributed to the maltreatment and for addressing the most critical treatment needs.

Case Planning

- Case plans are developed by protective services, other treatment providers, and the family to alter the conditions and/or behaviors that result in child abuse or neglect.

Treatment

- Protective services and other treatment providers have the responsibility to implement a treatment plan for the family.

Evaluation of Family Progress

- After implementing the treatment plan, protective services and other treatment providers evaluate and measure changes in family behaviors and conditions that led to child maltreatment.

Case Closure

- Some cases are closed because the family resists intervention efforts and the child is seen as being at low risk of harm. Other cases are closed when it has been determined that the risk of abuse or neglect has been eliminated or reduced to the point that the family can protect the child from maltreatment without additional intervention.
- If the determination is made that the family will not protect the child, the child may be removed from the home and placed in foster care. If the decision is made that a child cannot be returned home within a reasonable time, parental rights may be terminated so that permanent alternatives can be found for the child.

Involvement of Juvenile or Family Court

- An adjudication (fact-finding) hearing is held if a petition of abuse or neglect has been filed by the department of social services.
- States vary in the standard of proof needed to substantiate allegations of child abuse and neglect: 6 states rely on the caseworker's judgment, 18 states on some credible evidence, 11 states on credible evidence, and 12 states on the preponderance of evidence; and 3 states have no official reporting means. About 30 percent of all child abuse and neglect reports in the country are substantiated, which varies somewhat by type of maltreatment and by state.[95]

Self-control theory argues that the principal cause of individuals' low self-control is ineffective parenting.

Termination of Parental Rights

- In the most serious cases of child maltreatment, the state moves to terminate parental rights and to place a child for adoption.

Prosecution of Parents

- The prosecution of parents in criminal court depends largely on the seriousness of the injury to the child and on the attitude of the district, county, or state attorney's office toward child abuse. The cases most likely to be prosecuted are those in which a child has been seriously injured or killed and those in which a father or stepfather has sexually abused a daughter or stepdaughter. The most common charges in prosecutions are simple assault, assault with intent to commit serious injury, and manslaughter or murder. See Figure 7–8 for the sequence of events from child abuse to court processing.

▶ Delinquency Across the Life Course: Family-Related Risk Factors for Delinquency

LEARNING OUTCOMES 5 — Recall the family-related risk factors for delinquency.

With the emergence of the life-course perspective, there has been increased empirical and theoretical interest in the role played by family relations both in fostering and in protecting against delinquency and drug involvement. Studies have documented the family-related risk factors that increase delinquency propensity. Some of those risk factors and linked outcomes are ineffective parenting and low self-control; links between corporal punishment and delinquent behavior; family structure at the time of adolescence, such as single-parent families; physical abuse early in life cycle; and links between being married and reduction in delinquency.[96]

▶ Prevention of Delinquency and Social Policy: Child Maltreatment

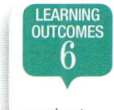
LEARNING OUTCOMES 6 — Recall interventions that can help prevent and reduce the extent of child abuse and neglect.

Child maltreatment is a serious issue in the United States. This maltreatment can be inflicted from a variety of contexts: abusive or neglectful parents or caretakers, the Internet (in terms of child pornography), teachers or classmates, or even religious leadership.

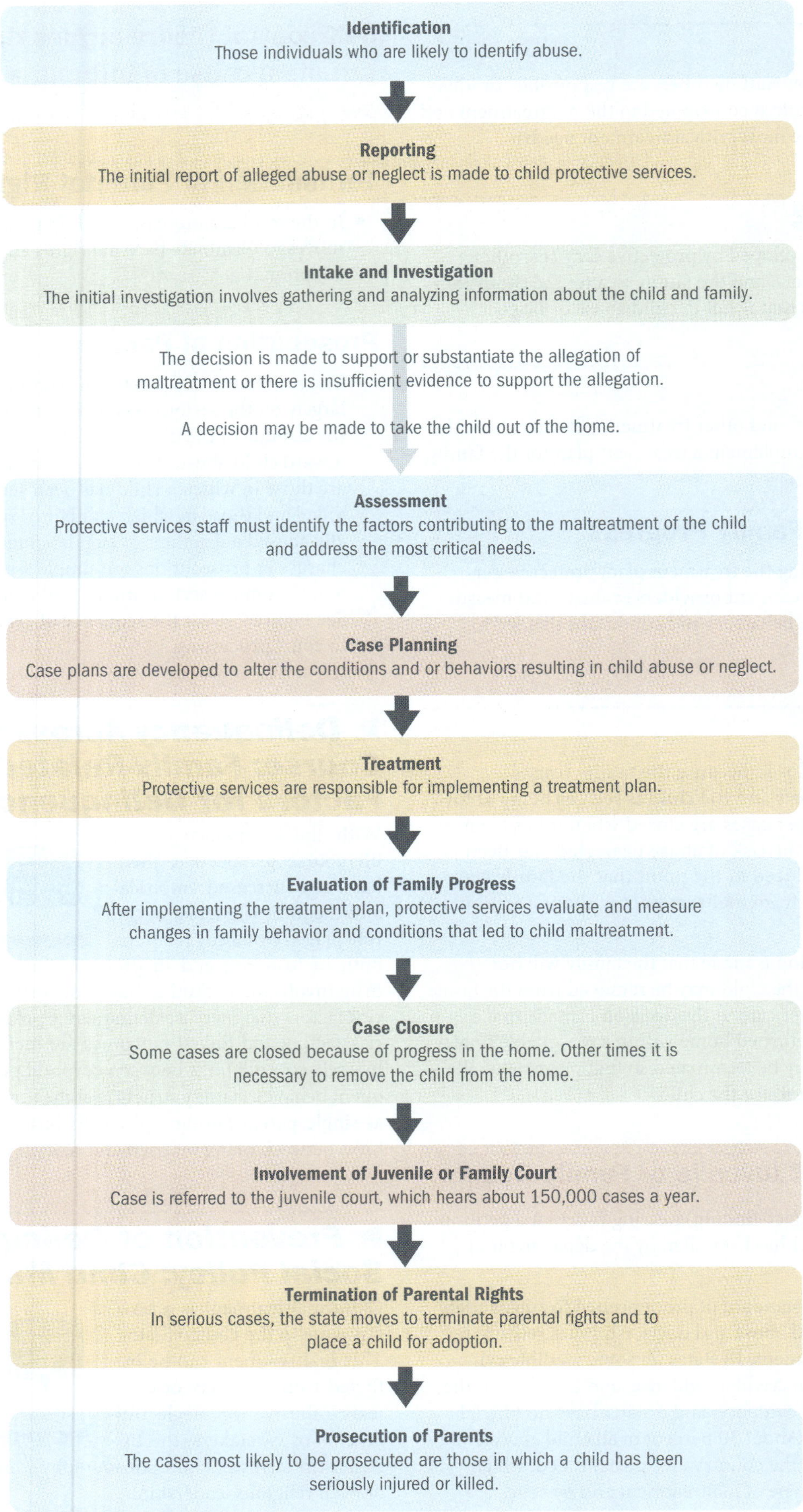

Identification
Those individuals who are likely to identify abuse.

Reporting
The initial report of alleged abuse or neglect is made to child protective services.

Intake and Investigation
The initial investigation involves gathering and analyzing information about the child and family.

The decision is made to support or substantiate the allegation of maltreatment or there is insufficient evidence to support the allegation.

A decision may be made to take the child out of the home.

Assessment
Protective services staff must identify the factors contributing to the maltreatment of the child and address the most critical needs.

Case Planning
Case plans are developed to alter the conditions and or behaviors resulting in child abuse or neglect.

Treatment
Protective services are responsible for implementing a treatment plan.

Evaluation of Family Progress
After implementing the treatment plan, protective services evaluate and measure changes in family behavior and conditions that led to child maltreatment.

Case Closure
Some cases are closed because of progress in the home. Other times it is necessary to remove the child from the home.

Involvement of Juvenile or Family Court
Case is referred to the juvenile court, which hears about 150,000 cases a year.

Termination of Parental Rights
In serious cases, the state moves to terminate parental rights and to place a child for adoption.

Prosecution of Parents
The cases most likely to be prosecuted are those in which a child has been seriously injured or killed.

FIGURE 7–8 The Sequence of Events from Child Abuse to Court Processing.

We know that child maltreatment can be an influential factor leading to such undesirable outcomes as emotional trauma, running away, disruptive and truant behavior in school, drug and alcohol abuse, sexual behavior, and violence and abuse. The more serious the maltreatment of a child, the more likely it is that he or she will become involved in these behaviors, which can have extremely negative consequences for his or her life course. The abused child, if seriously abused, can even become involved in taking a parent's life.

To reduce the extent of child abuse and neglect in the United States, numerous strategies or interventions are needed. Widom recommended the following six principles:

1. "The earlier the intervention, the better."
2. "Don't (continue to) neglect neglected children."
3. "One size does not fit all," which means that "what works for one child in one context may not work for a different child in the same setting, the same child in another setting, or the same child in another period in his or her development."
4. "Surveillance is a double-edged sword," meaning that intervention agents must be sensitive to the possibilities of differential treatment on the basis of race or ethnic background and take steps to avoid such practices.
5. "Interventions are not one-time efforts."
6. "Resources should be accessible."[97]

There is emerging evidence of the effectiveness of early family-based programs designed to address some the familial risk factors for delinquency.[98] For example, Piquero and colleagues conducted a meta-analysis of the effects of early family/parent training programs for young children and found that early family/parent training is an effective intervention for reducing antisocial behavior.[99]

THE CASE

The Life Course of Amy Watters, Age 13

After she left home, Amy spent almost a year on the run. During that time she didn't attend school and had no contact with her father. She lived under a highway overpass in a city about an hour away from her home with new "friends" that she had made. They were other kids who, like herself, had left home for one reason or another. During that time she became especially close to Damon, a 15-year-old boy who had left a Mormon family in Utah and spent his days earning a small income doing odd jobs for people who didn't ask about his background. Physical closeness had been natural, as staying warm at night meant snuggling up with Damon. After only a couple of nights, Amy found herself having sex. It quickly turned into a regular occurrence and Amy, who had begun menstruating a year earlier, became concerned that she would get pregnant. At the same time, she didn't want to disappoint Damon, who seemed to greatly enjoy their encounters, and she soon learned to find pleasure in their nightly activities. Not long after they had pledged themselves to one another, however, Amy learned that Damon had begun to sell sexual services to men whom he met by hanging around bars in the city's seedy downtown district. One of the men, Damon told her, wanted to take naked pictures of him and sell them on the Internet. The money was sure to be good, Damon said.

DISCUSS

1. What is the likely relationship between Amy's early sexual activity and other forms of delinquency? Generally speaking, why might early sex and delinquency be associated with one another?

Learn more on the Web:

- Some studies have shown that early sexual activity may lead teens into delinquency. See, for example:
- Developmental Patterns in Exposure to Violence: http://justicestudies.com/developmental.pdf.

Follow the continuing Amy Watters saga in the next chapter.

CHAPTER 7 Families and Delinquency

LEARNING OUTCOMES 1

Explain how problems in the family can contribute to delinquency.

Studies of the relationship between the family and delinquency have generally concluded that the quality of life within the home is a more significant deterrent of delinquent behavior than the presence of both parents; that parental rejection is associated with delinquent behavior; and that inconsistent, lax, or severe discipline is associated with increased delinquency. Similar research concludes that delinquent behavior among children increases proportionately with the number of problems within the family. Divorced and single-parent families, blended families, births to unmarried women, alcohol and drug abuse, poverty, and violence are problems that some families encounter. The failure of a family to provide for the needs of its children can have an effect on the attitudes and behaviors of those children that can last into their adult years—and even for the rest of their lives.

1. How is the family the primary agent for the socialization of children?
2. What are the most serious problems facing the American family today? What are their effects on children?
3. What conditions within the family are more likely to result in delinquent behavior?

socialization The process by which individuals come to internalize their culture; through this process, an individual learns the norms, sanctions, and expectations of being a member of a particular society.

broken home A family in which parents are divorced or are no longer living together.

birth order The sequence of births in a family and a child's position in it, whether the firstborn, middle, or youngest child.

family size The number of children in a family—a possible risk factor for delinquency.

delinquent sibling A brother or sister who is engaged in delinquent behaviors—an apparent factor in youngsters' involvement in delinquency.

rejection by parents The disapproval, repudiation, or other uncaring behavior directed by parents toward children.

supervision and discipline The parental monitoring, guidance, and control of children's activities and behavior.

LEARNING OUTCOMES 2

Explain how the mass media can influence adolescent behavior.

The mass media can influence delinquent behavior as adolescents are exposed to a variety of seemingly negative media influences, including violent movies, TV shows, and video games; Internet pornography; and gangsta rap and other forms of music carrying violent themes.

1. Why do the mass media impact the behavior of juveniles so powerfully?
2. What can parents do to counterbalance the negative effects of the mass media?
3. What social programs and policies might be based on an understanding of how the mass media influence adolescent behavior?

LEARNING OUTCOMES 3

Explain how neglect and child abuse contribute to delinquency.

Children who have been neglected and abused may experience psychological problems, run away from home, become involved in truancy and disruptive behavior in school, and turn to drug and alcohol abuse. Some neglected and abused youngsters become involved in deviant sexual behavior and assume an aggressive stance toward others. Moreover, research findings show at least a partial link between child abuse and neglect and delinquent behavior and status offenses.

1. What is neglect? What are some examples of neglect within the home?
2. What are physical and emotional abuse? What are some examples of physical and emotional abuse within the home?
3. What is incest? What different kinds of incest exist? What type of father is most likely to become involved in incest?
4. How are child abuse and neglect related to status offenses and delinquent behavior?

neglect A disregard for the physical, emotional, or moral needs of children. Child neglect involves the failure of the parent or caregiver to provide nutritious food, adequate clothing and sleeping arrangements, essential medical care, sufficient supervision, access to education, and normal experiences that produce feelings of being loved, wanted, secure, and worthy.

child abuse The mistreatment of children by parents or caregivers. Physical abuse is intentional behavior directed toward a child by the parent or caregiver to cause pain, injury, or death. Emotional abuse involves a disregard of a child's psychological needs. Sexual abuse is any intentional and wrongful physical contact with a child that entails a sexual purpose or component, and such sexual abuse is termed *incest* when the perpetrator is a member of the child's family.

emotional abuse A disregard for the psychological needs of a child, including lack of expressed love, withholding of contact or approval, verbal abuse, unrealistic demands, threats, and psychological cruelty.

sexual abuse The intentional and wrongful physical contact with a person, with or without his or her consent, that entails a sexual purpose or component.

incest Any intrafamily sexual abuse that is perpetrated on a child by a member of that child's family group that includes not only sexual intercourse but also any act designed to stimulate a child sexually or to use a child for sexual stimulation, either of the perpetrator or of another person.

brother–sister incest Sexual activity that occurs between brother and sister.

father–daughter incest Sexual activity that occurs between a father and his daughter. Also refers to incest by stepfathers or the boyfriend(s) of the mother.

mother–son incest Sexual activity that occurs between a mother and her son. Also refers to incest by stepmothers or the girlfriend(s) of the father.

father–son incest Sexual activity between father and son. Also refers to incest by stepfathers or the boyfriend(s) of the mother.

running away The act of leaving the custody and home of parents or guardians without permission and failing to return within a reasonable length of time; a status offense.

LEARNING OUTCOMES 4

Summarize the sequence of events that occurs as the community responds to child maltreatment.

Community responses to child maltreatment generally include the following sequence of events: identification, reporting, intake and investigation, assessment, case planning, treatment, evaluation of family progress, case closure. The response might also extend to the involvement of juvenile or family court, the termination of parental rights, and the prosecution of parents.

1. What are typical types of community responses to child maltreatment?
2. How do child protective service agencies work with juvenile court officials?

LEARNING OUTCOMES 5

Recall the family-related risk factors for delinquency.

Family-related risk factors associated with an increase in the propensity for delinquency include the following: (1) ineffective parenting and low self-control, (2) the use of corporal punishment, (3) family structure, (4) early physical abuse, and (5) marital status.

1. What are the family-related risk factors associated with an increase in the propensity for delinquency?
2. What implications for social policy and for the prevention and control of delinquency would a realistic assessment of family-related risk factors for delinquency have?

LEARNING OUTCOMES 6

Recall interventions that can help prevent and reduce the extent of child abuse and neglect.

Strategic interventions that can help prevent and reduce the extent of child maltreatment include early intervention, available community resources, and individualized programs.

1. What kinds of early intervention can be employed in order to prevent and/or reduce the extent of child abuse and neglect that might otherwise occur?
2. What community resources can be used to prevent and/or reduce the extent of child abuse and neglect?

8

"If we want to deal with youth crime, adult crime, and street gangs, we must go back to the family unit, must improve our schools, and must make our neighborhoods more desirable."

—*John Walker*

Schools and Delinquency

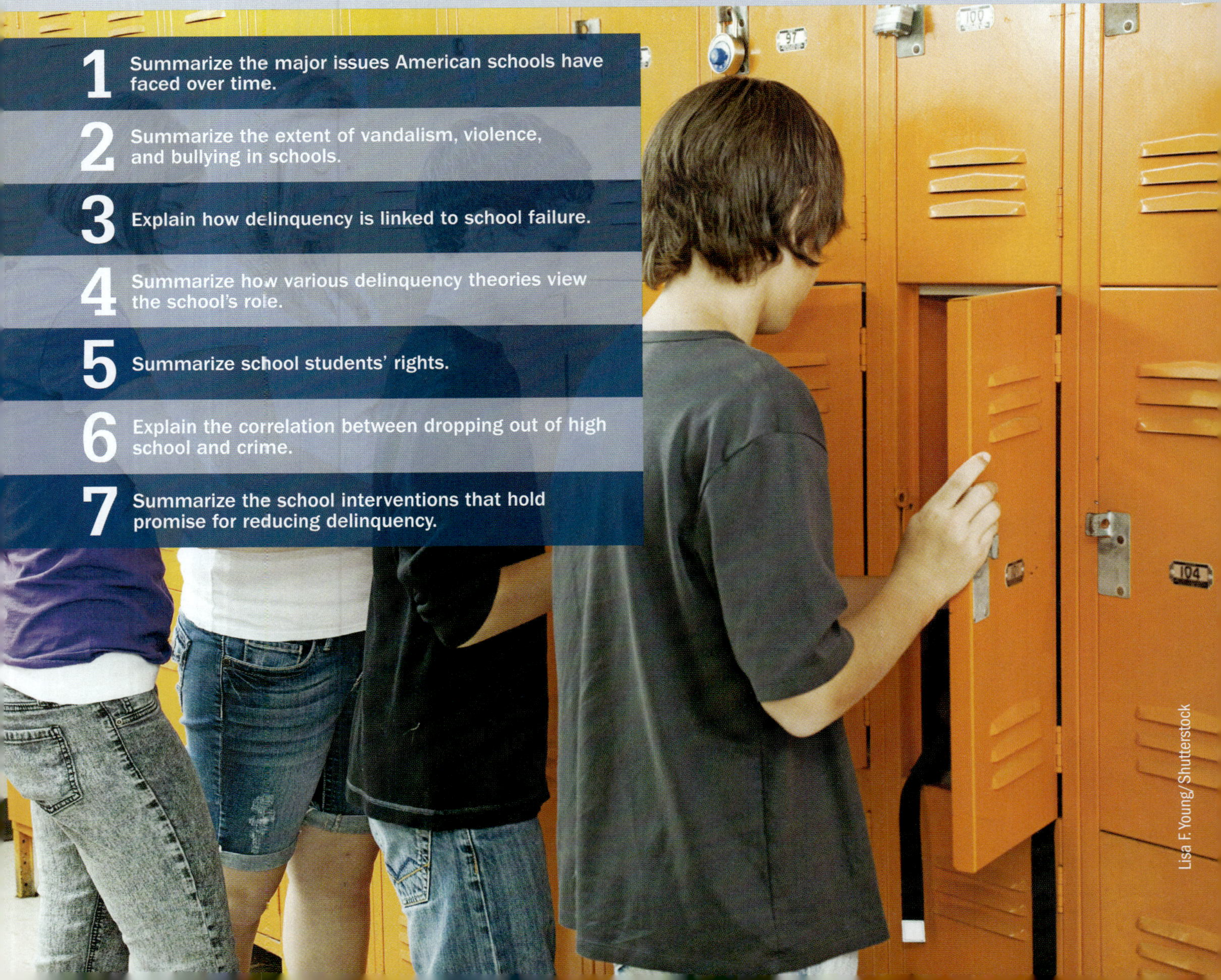

1. Summarize the major issues American schools have faced over time.
2. Summarize the extent of vandalism, violence, and bullying in schools.
3. Explain how delinquency is linked to school failure.
4. Summarize how various delinquency theories view the school's role.
5. Summarize school students' rights.
6. Explain the correlation between dropping out of high school and crime.
7. Summarize the school interventions that hold promise for reducing delinquency.

Lisa F. Young/Shutterstock

INTRO: SCHOOL DELINQUENCY

A recent national study of delinquency prevention in schools found that minor forms of problem behavior are common in schools.[1] The study discovered, for example, that 27 percent of teachers reported that student problem behavior kept them from teaching effectively "a fair amount or a great deal." In a quarter of all schools participating in the study, 42 percent or more of teachers reported that student problem behavior kept them from teaching "at least a fair amount."

The study also found that more serious forms of problem behavior, such as physical attacks or fights involving a weapon, robberies, or threats involving a knife or a gun, occur much less frequently than the relatively pervasive kinds of minor student misconduct. But these events happen often enough that they pose major problems for schools. Almost 7 percent of schools participating in the study reported at least one incident of physical attack or fight involving a weapon to law enforcement officials. In the case of middle schools and junior high schools the percentage was 21 percent.

From the student perspective, the study found that being threatened or attacked in school is a relatively common experience. Nineteen percent of students participating in the study reported being threatened and 14 percent reported having been attacked. Study authors wrote that "a startling 5% of students" reported having been threatened with a knife or a gun.

Teachers, on the other hand, rarely experience being attacked and are not often threatened. Although 20 percent of secondary school teachers (and 31 percent of urban middle school teachers) reported to researchers that they had been threatened by remarks made by a student, only 0.5 percent reported having had a weapon pulled on them. Of all teachers in the study, only 0.07 percent reported having been attacked and having to see a doctor as a result of the attack.

There is no question that an examination of delinquency in the United States must take a long look at the school experience. J. Feldhusen, J. Thurston, and J. Benning's longitudinal study found school relationships and experiences to be the third most predictive factor in delinquency, exceeded only by family and peer-group relationships.[2]

A Third-Grade Classroom. What is the Relationship between Schools and Child Misbehavior?

Delbert S. Elliott and Harwin L. Voss stated, "the school is the critical social context for the generation of delinquent behavior."[3] Arthur L. Stinchcombe believed that failure in school leads to rebelliousness, which leads to more failure and negative behaviors.[4] More recently, Eugene Maguin and Rolf Loeber's meta-analysis found that "children with lower academic performance offended more frequently, committed more serious and violent offenses, and persisted in their offending."[5]

In sum, there is considerable evidence that the school has become an arena for learning delinquent behavior. This chapter will look at the history of education in the United States, at the nature of crime in the schools, at different aspects of the relationship between the school setting and delinquent behavior, at the issue of students' rights, and at interventions used by some schools to prevent and control delinquency within school settings.

DISCUSS How does problem behavior in schools impact students' educational opportunities? How should such behavior be handled?

▶ A Brief History of American Education

The U.S. Constitution says nothing about public schools, but by 1850 nearly all the northern states had enacted laws mandating free education. By 1918, education was both free and compulsory in nearly every state in the union. The commitment to public education arose largely from the growing need for a uniform approach to

1 LEARNING OUTCOMES Summarize the major issues American schools have faced over time.

socialization of the diverse groups immigrating to this country. Joel H. Spring, a historian, writes of this movement:

> Education during the nineteenth century has been increasingly viewed as an instrument of social control to be used to solve the social problems of crime, poverty, and Americanization of the immigrant. The activities of public schools tended to replace the social training of

The need to establish a safe learning atmosphere is a serious issue in public education today.

Think About It...

School relationships and experiences tend to be one of the most highly predictive factors in delinquency. What aspects of the school experience are most likely to influence a young person's social development?

other institutions, such as the family and church. One reason for the extension of school activities was the concern for the education of the great numbers of immigrants arriving from eastern and southern Europe. It was feared that without some form of Americanization immigrants would cause a rapid decay of American institutions.[6]

During most of the nineteenth century, U.S. schools were chaotic and violent places where teachers unsuccessfully attempted to maintain control over unmotivated, unruly, and unmanageable children through novel and sometimes brutal disciplinary methods.[7] For example, Horace Mann reported in the 1840s that in one school with 250 pupils, he saw 328 separate floggings in one week of five school days, an average of over 65 floggings a day.[8]

Widespread dissatisfaction with the schools at the turn of the twentieth century was one of the factors leading to the Progressive education movement. Its founder, John Dewey, advocated reform in classroom methods and curricula so students would become more questioning, creative, and involved in the process of their own education. Dewey was much more concerned about individualism and personal growth than rigid socialization.[9]

The 1954 U.S. Supreme Court decision that ruled racial segregation in public schools unconstitutional was a pivotal event in the history of American education—it obligated the federal government to make certain that integration in schools was achieved "within a reasonable time limit."[10] The busing of children to distant schools, which arose out of the Supreme Court decision and has resulted in the shift from neighborhood schools, remains a hotly debated issue.

During the 1960s, open classrooms, in which the teacher served as a "resource person" who offered students many activities from which to choose, were instituted as an alternative to the earlier teacher-oriented classrooms. As was the case with the Progressive education movement, the concept of the open classroom was accepted more widely in private schools than in public schools.

The baby boom of the 1950s resulted in increased enrollments and more formalized student–teacher contacts in public schools in the 1960s and early 1970s. Public education also became more expensive in the 1970s, because the increasing numbers of children in the classroom meant that more equipment (including expensive items such as computers, scientific equipment, and audiovisual aids) had to be purchased. At the same time, teachers' unions took a firmer stance during contract talks, and many larger cities experienced teachers' strikes during this decade.

Since at least the mid-1980s, instead of optimism, dire warnings have been issued by all sides concerning the state of education. An expert on schools put it this way in 1984:

> American schools are in trouble. In fact, the problems of schooling are of such crippling proportions that many schools may not survive. It is possible that our entire public education system is nearing collapse. We will continue to have schools, no doubt, but the basis of their support and their relationship to families, communities and states could be quite different from what we have known.[11]

See the accompanying timeline.

▶ School Crime

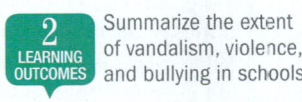

2 LEARNING OUTCOMES — Summarize the extent of vandalism, violence, and bullying in schools.

Crime in the schools, especially public schools, is a serious problem now facing junior and senior high schools across the nation. This high crime rate expresses itself through **vandalism**, **violence**, drug trafficking, and gangs. Vandalism and violence are examined in this section, and Chapters 9 and 10 will explore the challenges that youth gangs and drugs bring to the school setting.

TIMELINE — Major Issues American Schools Have Faced during Various Time Periods

1850	1896	1900	1918	1954
Nearly all of the northern states had enacted mandatory free education.	**John Dewey's** advocation of reforms led to the Progressive education movement.	**Schools were** chaotic and violent places where teachers used sometimes brutal measures to maintain control.	**Education was** both free and compulsory in nearly every state in the union.	**The U.S. Supreme Court** ruled racial segregation in public schools was unconstitutional.

130 Chapter 8 Schools and Delinquency

Vandalism and Violence

The need to establish a safe learning atmosphere is a serious issue in public education today, but the added security features of many public schools make them appear even more like prisons. Uniformed police are stationed in many schools; other schools have their own security staff. Students must submit to a metal detector search to enter some schools, electronically locked doors are becoming more common, and locker searches for drugs and weapons are everyday occurrences in many schools. Identification tags or photo ID badges for students and silent panic buttons for teachers are other means schools are using to regain control of the environment. Until it was ruled unconstitutional by the courts, a school in Boston even gave a drug test (urinalysis) to every student during the physical examination performed by the school physician at the start of each academic year.[12]

In 2013, the National Center for Education Statistics published its 15th annual report on school crime, *Indicators of School Crime and Safety: 2012*, which profiled school crime and safety and described the characteristics of the victims of these crimes (see the following discussion for the report's basic findings). It can be argued that schools are safer for children than other areas because children experience higher rates of violence away from school than they experience when they are at school (as well as coming to or leaving school).

School Bullying

Bullying in school is a worldwide problem. Even though most of the research on bullying has taken place in Great Britain, Japan, and Scandinavian countries, it is a topic of concern in schools everywhere. Bullying consists of such direct behaviors as teasing, threatening, taunting, hitting, and stealing that have been initiated by one or more aggressive students against a weaker victim. In addition to such direct attacks, bullying may also be more indirect, causing a student to be socially isolated through intentional exclusion. Boys typically are involved in more direct bullying methods, whereas girls utilize more subtle strategies, such as spreading rumors and enforcing social isolation. Whether the bullying is direct or indirect, its key component is repeated physical or psychological intimidation that creates an ongoing pattern of harassment and abuse.[13]

According to bullying statistics, about 2.7 million students are bullied each year by about 2.11 million other students taking on the role of the bully. Bullying statistics further reveal that about one in every seven students in grades kindergarten through 12th grade is either a bully or has been a victim of bullying. A teen or child who has been bullied may in turn become the bully in retaliation. Physical bullying increases in elementary school, peaks in middle school, and declines in high school; verbal abuse, on the other hand, tends to remain constant.[14]

Bullying in schools can create a climate of fear and discomfort.

Cyberbullying

Cyberbullying is a form of teen violence that can do lasting harm to young people. Cyberbullying involves using technology, such as cell phones and the Internet, to bully or harass another person. Cyberbullying can take many forms:

- Spreading rumors online or through texts
- Sending mean messages or threats to a person's email account or cell phone
- Stealing a person's account information to break into his or her account and send damaging messages
- Posting hurtful or threatening messages on social networking sites or Web messages
- Pretending to be someone else online to hurt another person
- Sexting, or circulating sexually suggestive pictures or messages about a person
- Taking unflattering pictures of a person and spreading them via cell phone on the Internet[15]

Cyberbullying can lead to depression, anxiety, or suicide. Also, once things have circulated on the Internet, they may never disappear, and hence can resurface at later times to renew the path of cyberbullying.

How Bullying Impacts the School Environment

Numerous studies have documented how bullying in schools can create a climate of fear and discomfort:

- One study first summarized the literature, stating that bullying can be understood as both a dyadic and a peer-group phenomenon, primarily situated in the heads (thinking) of those involved, in a lack of skill or experience, or in the delinquency of a bully who needs to be reformed.

1960s	1970s	1980s	2010s
Open classrooms in which teachers served as resource persons were instituted as an alternative to the teacher-oriented classrooms.	**Increased enrollments** and more formalized student–teacher contacts grew out of the baby boom.	**Public education** became more expensive.	**Dire warnings** began to be issued concerning the state of education.	**American schools** in trouble is an increasingly articulated position.

School Crime

TABLE 8-1 FINDINGS FROM INDICATORS OF SCHOOL CRIME AND SAFETY: 2012

Violent Deaths at School

- Of the 31 students, staff, and nonstudent school associated violent deaths occurring between July 1, 20 2010 through June 30, 2011, there were 11 homicides and 3 suicides of school-aged youth (5–18) at school.
- During the school year 2010–2011, there were 1,396 homicides among school-age youth ages 5–18. During the 20117 calendar year, there were 1,456 suicides of youth ages 5–18.

Nonfatal Student Victimization

- In 2011, students ages 12–18 were victims of 1,246,000 million nonfatal crimes at school, including thefts and violet crimes.
- In 2011, more students ages 12–18 were victims of theft at school than away from school.

Nonfatal Teacher Victimization

- A greater percentage of secondary school teachers (8%) reported being threatened with injury by a student than elementary school teachers (7%). However, a greater percentage of elementary school teachers (6%) reported having been physically attacked than secondary school teachers (2%).

School Environment

- In 2009–2010, 85% of public schools reported that one or more incident of crime had taken place at public school, amounting to an estimated 1.9 million crimes.
- During the 2009–2010 school year, 16% of public schools reported that bullying occurred among students on a daily or weekly basis. In 2009, 23 percent of students ages 12–18 reported having been bullied at school during the academic year.
- In 2011, 18% of students ages 12–18 reported that street gangs were operating in their school. In 2011, 23 percent of urban schools, 16 percent of suburban schools, and 12 percent or rural schools reported gang presence in their schools. During 2011, 19 percent of public schools and only 2 percent of private schools reported the presence of gangs.
- In 2011, 26% of students in grades 9–12 reported that someone had offered, sold, or given them an illegal drug on school property in the past 12 months. This had decreased from 32 percent in 1995.
- In 2011, 9% of students ages 12–18 reported that someone at school had used hate-related words against them, and more than one-third (28%) reported seeing hate-related graffiti at school. This had decreased from 12 percent in 2001, and was far lower than the 36 percent who reported seeing hate-related graffiti at school in 1999.
- In 2011, about 26 percent of males reported carrying a weapon anywhere compared to 7 percent of females, and 8 percent of males carried a weapon on school property compared to 2 percent females.
- In 2011, 33 percent of students reported that they had been involved in a physical fight over the previous 12 months, and 12 percent were involved in a fight on school property.

 If violence in public schools is declining, why do so many teachers feel unsafe in the school setting? What can be done to make public schools safer?

Source: Simone Roberts, Jijun Zhang, and Jennifer Truman, *Indicators of School Crime and Safety: 2012* (Washington, DC: U.S. Departments of Education and Justice, U.S. Government Printing Office, 2013).

This study added that, unfortunately, typical anti-bullying strategies often simply train bullies to be better at bullying (meaning that they learn to bully more covertly and more expertly so as to inflict the same devastation without adult detection).[16]

- Another study performed a meta-analysis and posited that an association existed between bullying and psychosomatic problems.[17]
- Still another study found that students with mild disabilities were more likely to be perceived as bullies by both teachers and peers; in addition, teachers rated students with mild disabilities as being bullied by their peers significantly more often. Academically gifted students were seen by teachers as having the lowest rates of both bullying and being bullied.[18]
- The data from a survey of 24,345 youths on the evidence of racial/ethnic differences in children's self-report of being a victim of bullying revealed that African-American youths who were victimized tended to underreport being a victim of bullying.[19]
- According to recent bullying statistics, gay and lesbian teens who are bullied are two to three times more likely to commit suicide than other youths facing similar circumstances. About 30 percent of all completed suicides have been related to gay identity crises. Students who fall into the gay, bisexual, lesbian, or transgendered identity group

Think About It...

Kate Middleton, who married England's Prince William in 2011, admitted that she had once been a victim of school bullying, and asked her royal wedding guests to donate to an anti-bullying charity. What are the roots of bullying? What can be done to prevent it?

▶ Delinquency and School Failure

Lack of academic achievement, low social status at school, and dropping out are factors frequently cited as being related to involvement in delinquency. This section will look at the first two factors, and dropping out is considered later in the chapter.

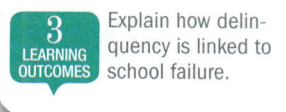

Explain how delinquency is linked to school failure.

Achievement

Considerable evidence indicates that, whether measured by self-report or by official police data, both male and female delinquency is associated with poor **academic performance** at school.[21] Travis Hirschi claimed that the causal chain shown in Figure 8–1 may eventually lead to delinquent behavior.[22] Numerous researchers have pointed out that delinquents' lack

report being five times more likely to miss school because they feel unsafe after being bullied due to their sexual orientation. About 28 percent of these students claim that this is a major contributor to school dropout.[20]

See Exhibit 8–1 for a description of bullying problems and for information on intervention strategies that can reduce bullying in schools.

EXHIBIT 8–1 | Bullying Fact Sheet

Facts About Bullying

- Bullying is often blamed as an important factor in school-related deaths.
- Membership in either bullying or victim groups is associated with dropping out of school, psychosocial adjustment problems, delinquent activity, and other long-term consequences.
- Physical bullying increases in elementary school, peaks in middle school, and declines in high school; verbal abuse, on the other hand, tends to remain constant.
- Over two-thirds of students believe that schools respond poorly to bullying.
- Only 25 percent of teachers see nothing wrong with bullying or put-downs and, as a result, intervene in only 4 percent of bullying incidents.

What Can Schools Do?

- **Early intervention.** Researchers advocate intervening in elementary or middle school or even as early as preschool. Social skills training is highly recommended, as are counseling and systematic aggression interventions for students demonstrating bullying and victim behaviors.
- **Parent training.** Parents must learn to reinforce their children's positive behavior patterns and must demonstrate appropriate interpersonal interactions.
- **Teacher training.** Training can help teachers identify and respond to potentially damaging victimization as well as implement positive feedback and modeling to address inappropriate social interactions. Support services personnel who work with administrators can be helpful in designing effective teacher training modules.
- **Attitude change.** Researchers maintain that society must stop defending bullying behavior as part of growing up or by assuming the attitude that "kids will be kids." School personnel should never ignore bullying behaviors.
- **Positive school environment.** Schools with easily understood rules of conduct, smaller class sizes, and fair discipline practices report less violence and bullying behaviors.

What Can Parents Do?

- Parents should contact the school social worker, counselor, or school psychologist and ask for help with bullying or victimization concerns.
- Parents can provide positive feedback to their children for appropriate social behaviors that do not include aggression or bullying.
- Parents should use alternatives to physical punishment, such as the removal of privileges, as consequences for bullying behavior.
- Parents should stop bullying behavior when it takes place and help their children develop more appropriate social skills.

Source: Adapted from Andrea Cohn and Andrea Canter, *Bullying: Factors for Schools and Parents*, http://www.naspcenter.org/factsheets/bullying_fs.html. Copyright 2003 by the National Association of School Psychologists, Bethesda, Md. Reprinted with permission of the publisher.

FIGURE 8–1 Hirschi's Causal Chain.
Source: Adapted from Travis Hirschi, *Causes of Delinquency* (Berkeley: University of California Press, 1969), pp. 131–132, 156.

> Both male and female delinquency is associated with poor academic performance.

of achievement in school is related to other factors besides academic skills. For example, several studies have found that delinquents are more rejecting of the student role than are nondelinquents.[23] Delinquents' performance in school may be further affected by their relationships with classmates and teachers; several studies have concluded that the relationship between school performance and delinquency is mediated by peer influence.[24]

Low Social Status

Albert K. Cohen's influential study of delinquent boys was one of the most comprehensive analyses ever undertaken of the role of the school in the development of delinquent subcultures. According to Cohen's theory, working-class boys (as discussed in Chapter 4) feel status deprivation when they become aware that they are unable to compete with middle-class youths in the school. Although avoiding contact with middle-class youths might solve the problem, working-class boys cannot do this because they are forced to attend middle-class schools established on middle-class values; consequently, they reject middle-class values and attitudes and form delinquent subcultures that provide them with the status denied in school and elsewhere in society.[25] John C. Phillips proposed steps by which low status in school can lead to deviant behavior (see Figure 8–2).[26] However, the proposed relationship between social class and delinquency in the school has been challenged. For example, one study found that any adolescent male who does poorly in school, regardless of class background, is more likely to become involved in delinquent behavior than one who performs well in school.[27]

In short, most of the evidence points to three conclusions: Lack of achievement in school is directly related to delinquent behavior, most delinquents want to succeed in school, and the explanations for poor academic achievement are more complex than lack of general aptitude or intelligence. Although the existence of a relationship between social class and delinquency in the school has mixed support, a relationship between school achievement and delinquency is much clearer.

School Failure

A number of observations can be made about the relationship between school failure and delinquency. First, it can be claimed that school failure is directly related to delinquency. Those students who fail in school seek out peers who also are not succeeding in school. School failure brings disapproval from family, teachers, and the community. Second, school failure can create psychological problems for youth, and these negative self-feelings can lead to delinquent acts. Third, school failure and delinquency, it can be argued, share a common cause, such as poverty, drugs, family disruption, or gangs. Fourth, the school has a role in school failure. The school can contribute to students' alienation, and many have charged that school tracking—which is dividing students into groups according to achievement level and ability—has been a contributing cause of delinquent behavior.

School failure is one of the contributing causes to dropping out of school, and the high rate of dropouts is one of the most serious issues facing schools in the United States. School dropouts, as discussed later in this chapter, contribute to high rates of unlawful behavior and delinquency across the life course.

Theoretical Perspectives on School and Delinquency

Most major theories of delinquency see the school as a factor contributing to delinquent behavior. Blocked opportunity theory, strain theory, cultural deviance theory, social control theory, labeling theory, radical criminology, general theory of crime, and interactionist theories all make contributions to understanding delinquency in schools.

The majority of studies focusing on blocked opportunity have found that those most likely to commit delinquent acts are young people who do poorly in school or who believe that they have little chance of graduation. Observers say that when youthful offenders are unable to perform satisfactorily in school, they become disruptive, decide to drop out, or are suspended—all of which further reinforces involvement in deviant behavior.[28] Strain theorists contend that youngsters from certain social classes are denied legitimate access to culturally determined goals and opportunities and that the resulting frustration leads to either the use of illegitimate means to obtain society's goals or the rejection of those goals. Strain theory views the school as a middle-class institution in which lower-class children are frequently unable to perform successfully; these youths then turn to delinquency to compensate for feelings of status frustration, failure, and low self-esteem.[29]

Cultural deviance theorists argue that children learn delinquent behavior through being exposed to others and by

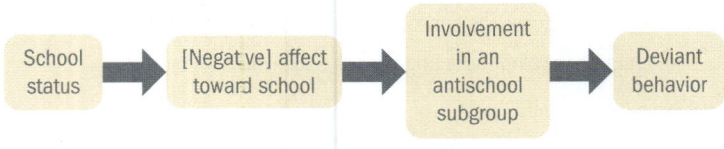

FIGURE 8–2 Phillips's Steps Leading to Deviant Behavior.

mimicking or modeling others' actions—children may come to view delinquency as acceptable because of their exposure to others whose definitions of such behavior are positive. Because schools tend to reflect the characteristics of the community of which they are a part, attending school in high-crime areas increases the likelihood of association with delinquent peers.[30]

Social control theorists believe that delinquency varies according to the strength of a juvenile's bond to the social order. Social control theorists also posit that the school is one of the major socializing institutions, providing youths with structure, incentives, expectations, and opportunities for social bonding, and that delinquency is likely to result when a strong bond to school does not develop.[31]

Labeling theorists argue that once students are defined as deviant, they adopt a deviant role in response to their lowered status. Early on, schools attach labels on the basis of achievement and behavior, and these labels may influence the subsequent treatment of youths. For example, when students are labeled as aggressive, difficult to manage, or slow learners at an early stage, they may be put in a slow track for the remainder of their schooling. According to labeling theorists, this differential treatment contributes to delinquent identities and behaviors.[32]

Some radical criminologists view the school as a means by which the privileged classes maintain power over the lower classes. Subjected to the controlling forces of the state, lower-class children are exploited as they experience powerlessness and alienation, and they are more likely than middle- and upper-class children to be placed in the lowest tracks, to receive poor grades, to be suspended for disciplinary reasons, and to drop out of school. According to radical theorists, lower-class children are essentially being trained to accept menial roles in the social order.[33]

In the general theory of crime, once self-control has formed in childhood, it affects adolescents in the choices they make in peer relations, school conduct and achievement, drug and alcohol use, and delinquent activities. Thus, students with self-control will be able to abstain from activities in school that would affect teachers' negative evaluations; from unwholesome peer relations in and out of school that would affect their desire to succeed, including gang participation; and from behaviors that would garner the attention of the police and juvenile justice system officials.[34]

Interactional theory, as developed by Thornberry and colleagues, is an integrated theory that can be applied to the school. It originally stated that attachment to parents and commitment to school are important buffers against delinquency, so adolescents who are emotionally bonded to parents and who succeed at school are unlikely candidates for serious delinquency. Later versions of this theory have found that while weakened bonds to family and school do cause delinquency, delinquent behavior further reduces the strength of the bonds to family and school, thereby establishing a behavioral trajectory toward increasing delinquency.[35]

Another integrated theory related to the school is one developed by Wayne N. Welsh, Jack R. Greene, and Patricia H. Jenkins that draws on control theory, school climate theory, and social disorganization theory to examine the influence of individual, institutional, and community factors on misconduct in Philadelphia middle schools. One of the strong conclusions reached by these researchers is that the simplistic assumption that bad communities typically produce "bad children" or "bad schools" is unwarranted.[36] See Table 8–2 for the theoretical perspectives on school and delinquency.

TABLE 8–2 THEORETICAL PERSPECTIVES ON SCHOOL AND DELINQUENCY

Blocked Opportunity Theory	Those most likely to commit delinquent acts are those who do poorly in school or who believe they have little chance of graduation.
Strain Theory	The school is viewed as a middle-class institution in which lower-class children are frequently unable to perform successfully, and they turn to delinquency to compensate for feelings of status frustration, failure, and low self-esteem.
Cultural Deviance Theory	Because schools tend to reflect the characteristics of the community of which they are a part, attending school in high-crime areas increases the likelihood of association with delinquent peers.
Social Control Theory	The school is seen as one of the major socializing institutions, providing students with structure, incentives, expectations, and opportunities for social bonding; delinquency is likely to result when a strong bond to school does not develop.
Labeling Theory	This theory argues that once students are defined as deviant, they adopt a deviant role in response to their lowered status.
Radical Criminology	Some radical criminologists view the school as a means by which the privilege classes maintain power over the lower classes.
General Theory of Crime	Students with self-control are able to abstain from activities in school that would attract them to delinquent behavior and that would gain the negative attention of teachers and the juvenile justice system.
Interactional Theory	Delinquency behavior reduces the strength of the bonds to family and school, thereby establishing a behavioral trajectory toward increased delinquency.

Students' Rights

5 LEARNING OUTCOMES — Summarize school students' rights.

The school's authority over students comes from two principal sources: the concept of *in loco parentis* and state-enabling statutes.[37] E. Edmund Reutter, Jr., summarized *in loco parentis* as follows:

> The common law measure of the rights and duties of school authorities relative to pupils attending school is the *in loco parentis* concept. This doctrine holds that school authorities stand in the place of the parent while the child is at school. Thus, school personnel may establish rules for the educational welfare of the child and may inflict punishments for disobedience. The legal test is whether a reasonably knowledgeable and careful parent might so act. The doctrine is used not only to support rights of school authorities but also to establish their responsibilities concerning such matters as injuries that may befall students.[38]

State-enabling statutes authorize local school boards to establish reasonable rules and regulations, which do not necessarily have to be in written form, for operating and keeping order in schools.[39]

The courts have become involved with schools in a number of important areas: procedural due process, freedom of expression, hair and dress codes, school searches, and safety.[40]

Procedural Due Process

Dixon v. *Alabama State Board of Education* (1961) was a major breakthrough for students' rights because the appeals court held for the first time that due process requires a student to receive notice and some opportunity for a hearing before being expelled for misconduct.[41] In 1969, the U.S. Supreme Court issued its far-reaching decision in *Tinker* v. *Des Moines Independent School District*, declaring that students do not shed their constitutional right of freedom of speech at the schoolhouse door. The issue that was involved in this case was whether students had the right to wear black armbands to protest the Vietnam War, and the Court ruled that school authorities did not have the right to deny free speech, even the expression of an unpopular view, unless they had reason to believe that it would interfere with the school operations.[42] In the 1986 *Bethel School District No. 403* v. *Fraser* case, the Court upheld a school system's right to suspend or discipline a student who uses profane or obscene language or gestures, reasoning that the use of lewd and offensive speech undermined the basic educational mission of the school.[43] In a 1988 decision, *Hazelwood School District* v. *Kuhlmeier*, the Court ruled that the principal could censor articles having to do with pregnancy and parental divorce in a student publication; the Court's majority justified this censorship because such publications were perceived to be part of the educational curriculum of the school.[44]

In January 1975, the U.S. Supreme Court took up the problem of **due process rights** in the schools, stating in *Goss* v. *Lopez* that schools may not summarily suspend students, for even one day, without following fundamentally fair fact-finding procedures.[45] In suspensions of ten days or less, a student is entitled to oral or written notice of the charges, an explanation of the evidence, and an opportunity to be heard. The *Wood* v. *Strickland* ruling, issued a month after the *Goss* decision, found that school officials may be subject to suit and held financially liable for damages if they deliberately deprive a student of his or her clearly established constitutional rights.[46]

The issue of corporal punishment came before the U.S. Supreme Court in the 1975 *Baker* v. *Owen* and *Ingraham* v. *Wright* cases.[47] Although *Baker* v. *Owen* merely affirmed a lower-court ruling, *Ingraham* v. *Wright* held that reasonable corporal punishment is not cruel and unusual punishment under the Eighth Amendment to the U.S. Constitution.[48]

Freedom of Expression

Several court cases have defined students' rights to freedom of religion and expression in schools. In *West Virginia State Board of Education* v. *Barnette*, the Supreme Court held that students could not be compelled to salute the flag if that action violated their religious rights.[49] In *Tinker*, the wearing of black armbands was declared symbolic speech and therefore within the protection of the First Amendment.[50]

Hair and Dress Codes

Court cases testing the power of school administrators to suspend students for violations of hair and dress codes were widespread in the late 1960s and early 1970s. In *Yoo* v. *Moynihan*, a student's right to style his or her hair was held to be under the definition of the constitutional right to privacy;[51] then, in *Richards* v. *Thurston*, the Court ruled that a student's right to wear long hair derived from his or her interest in personal liberty.[52] In *Crossen* v. *Fatsi*, a dress code prohibiting "extreme style and fashion" was ruled unconstitutionally vague and unenforceable as well as an invasion of the student's right to privacy.[53] Other decisions have held that schools cannot prohibit the wearing of slacks,[54] dungarees,[55] or hair "falling loosely about the shoulders."[56]

School Searches

The use of drugs and weapons is changing the nature of police–student relations in schools. In the 1990s, the police began to enforce the 1990 federal Gun-Free School Zones Act and increasingly, in communities across the nation, began to enforce drug-free school zone laws. Drug-free zones usually include the school property along with the territory within a 1,000-foot radius of its perimeter. Alabama has the most aggressive law in

> **Court cases testing the power of school administrators to suspend students for violations of hair and dress codes were widespread in the late 1960s and early 1970s.**

this nation: Territory within three miles of a school is declared drug free.[57]

The use of drug-sniffing dogs, Breathalyzers™, hidden video cameras, and routine **school searches** of students' pockets, purses, school lockers, desks, and vehicles on school grounds appears to be increasing as school officials struggle to regain control over their schools. In some cases, school officials conduct their own searches; in other cases, the police are brought in to conduct the searches.

In the *New Jersey* v. *T.L.O.* decision (1985), the U.S. Supreme Court examined the issue of whether Fourth Amendment rights against unreasonable searches and seizures apply to the school setting.[58] On March 7, 1980, a teacher at Piscataway High School in Middlesex County, New Jersey, discovered two adolescent females smoking in a bathroom. He reported this violation of school rules to the principal's office, and the two females were summoned to meet with the assistant vice principal. When one of the females, T.L.O., claimed that she had done no wrong, the assistant principal demanded to see her purse; on examining it, he found a pack of cigarettes and cigarette rolling papers, some marijuana, a pipe, a large amount of money, a list of students who owed T.L.O. money, and letters that implicated her in marijuana dealing. T.L.O. confessed later at the police station to dealing drugs on school grounds.[59]

The juvenile court found T.L.O. delinquent and sentenced her to a year's probation, but she appealed her case to the New Jersey Supreme Court on the grounds that the search of her purse was not justified under the circumstances of the case. When the New Jersey Supreme Court upheld her appeal, the state appealed to the U.S. Supreme Court, which ruled that school personnel have the right to search lockers, desks, and students as long as they believe that either the law or school rules have been violated. The legality of a search, the Court stated, need not be based on obtaining a warrant or on having probable cause that a crime has taken place; rather, the legality of the search depends on its reasonableness, considering the scope of the search, the student's gender and age, and the student's behavior at the time.[60]

The significance of this decision is that the Supreme Court opened the door for greater security measures because it gave school officials and the police the right to search students who are suspected of violating school rules.[61] Of 18 cases in the years 1985–1991 that were decided by state appellate decisions applying the *T.L.O.* decision, school officials' intervention was upheld in 15 of them.[62]

In its 1995 *Vernonia School District 47J* v. *Acton* decision, the U.S. Supreme Court extended schools' authority to search by legalizing a random drug-testing policy for student athletes. This decision suggests that schools may employ safe-school programs, such as drug-testing procedures, as long as the policy satisfies the reasonableness test.[63]

In the 2002 *Board of Education of Independent School District No. 92 of Pottawatomie County* v. *Earls* decision, the U.S. Supreme Court reversed the judgment of the court of appeals and upheld the right of the school district to test students who participated in extracurricular activities; the Court found this to be a "reasonably effective means of addressing the School District's legitimate concerns in preventing, deterring, and detecting drug use by students."[64] The Court in *Pottawatomie* expanded the *Vernonia* decision by extending the drug testing of student athletes to the testing of students involved in extracurricular activities, which is an especially important issue, given the recent concern over steroid use on the part of professional, college, and high school athletes.

Safety

Court-imposed limitations on schools concerning the rules under which youths can be disciplined (*Tinker*) and the requirements for procedural due process relating to school administrators taking disciplinary action (*Goss*, *Ingraham*, and others) have made local school authorities increasingly wary of using tough methods to discipline students. Principals have become reluctant, for example, to suspend youths for acts such as acting insubordinately, wearing outlandish clothing, loitering in halls, and creating classroom disturbances; only a few decades earlier, such conduct would have drawn a quick notice of suspension. Increased judicial intervention in the academic area has contributed to (but not caused) an increase in unruly behavior, thereby reducing the safety of students in the public schools.[65] See Table 8–3 for a summary of the landmark cases that have had significant impact on students' rights.

In sum, judicial intervention in schools over the past three decades has had both positive and negative impacts. Students' rights are less likely to be abused than in the past because the courts have made it clear that students retain specific constitutional rights in school settings. However, school administrators who perceive themselves as handcuffed by court decisions have become reluctant to take firm and forceful action against disruptive students, and violence and delinquency in the schools have increased.

School Discipline

Both public and private schools have a responsibility to provide a safe environment for students and teachers, and to promote an environment conducive to learning. Consequently, it is sometimes necessary to discipline students who endanger others or create a negative learning environment.

Security Measures

Schools typically have a number of security measures to address things such as fights on campus, vandalism, thefts, drugs, alcohol, weapons, bomb threats, teacher safety, parking lot problems, fire alarms, and outsiders on campus. Each of these situations usually has a number of associated sub-security measures.

Corporal Punishment

An important security issue concerns whether a teacher or school official can legitimately inflict corporal punishment on a misbehaving child. By law, more than half of the states do not permit corporal punishment. Even so, the U.S. Supreme Court upheld the use of corporal punishment in public schools as a legitimate disciplinary measure.[66] Still, in those states that permit corporal punishment, school officials are understandably concerned about its use.

TABLE 8–3 SUMMARY OF LANDMARK CASES AND STUDENTS RIGHTS

Category of Rights	Name and Date of Case	Summary of the Case and Decision
Procedural Due Process	Dixon v. Alabama State Board of Education (1961)	This case specified that due process requires a student to receive notice of and opportunity for a hearing before being expelled for misconduct.
Procedural Due Process	Tinker v. Des Moines Independent School District (1969)	The issue was whether students had the right to wear black armbands to protest the Vietnam War. The U.S. Supreme Court ruled that school authorities did not have the right to deny free speech, even the expression of an unpopular view, unless they had reason to believe that it would interfere with the school operations.
Procedural Due Process	Bethel School District No. 403 v. Fraser (1986)	The Court upheld a school system's right to suspend or discipline a student who uses profane or obscene language or gestures, reasoning that the use of lewd and offensive speech undermined the basic educational mission of the school.
Freedom of Expression	West Virginia State Board of Education v. Barnette (1943)	Students could not be compelled to salute the flag if the action violated their religious rights.
Hair and Dress Clothes	Yoo v. Moynihan (1969)	A student's right to style his or her hair was held to be under the definition of the constitutional right to privacy.
School Searches	New Jersey v. T.L.O. (1985)	School personnel have the right to search lockers, desks, and students as long as they believe that either the law or school rules have been violated. The significance of this decision is that the Supreme Court opened the door for greater security measures because it gave school officials and the police the right to search students who are suspected of violating school rules.
School Searches	Vernonia School District 47J. v. Acton (1995)	The Supreme Court extended schools' authority to search by legalizing a random drug-testing policy for student athletes. This decision suggests that schools may employ safe-school programs, such as drug testing procedures, as long as the policy satisfies the reasonableness test.
School Searches	Board of Education of Independent School District No. 92 of Pottawatomie County v. Earls (2002)	The Court reversed the judgment of the court of appeals and upheld the right to test students of the district who participated in extracurricular activities.

- Investigating Incidents
- Identifying Suspects
- Controlling Campus Access
- Searching for Drugs and Weapons

FIGURE 8–3 The Role of the School Resource Officer.

Out-of-School Suspensions

Between 79 and 94 percent of schools have policies known as "zero-tolerance"—a term that is given to a school or district policy that mandates certain punishment for various student offenses.[67] In 2009–2010, for example, California schools issued 400,000 out-of-school suspensions based on things like zero-tolerance for bullying, weapons possession, and drugs.[68]

Expulsion from School

The main difference between a suspension and expulsion from school is the amount of time that a student must stay out of school. A suspension may only last a few days but an expulsion can extend up to a year. The local board of education makes expulsion decisions and will usually appoint an impartial hearing officer when expulsion is being considered. Typical charges leading to expulsion are:

1. Possessing a gun or other deadly weapon on school grounds or at a school activity.
2. Using a firearm or other deadly weapon to commit a crime off school grounds.

3. Selling or attempting to sell illegal drugs, on or off school grounds.[69]

Delinquency Across the Life Course: Factors Involved in Dropping Out of School

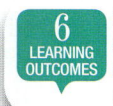

6 LEARNING OUTCOMES — Explain the correlation between dropping out of high school and crime.

High school dropout rates have become a major crisis in the United States, with one student in five dropping out of school. Nearly 5 million 18- to 24-year-olds lack a high school diploma. In addition, the United States currently ranks 20 out of 28 among industrialized democracies on high school graduation rates.[70] Students tend to drop out of school for four reasons, which are frequently interrelated: (1) academic failure, which involves failing courses; (2) disinterest in school, which often results in poor attendance; (3) problematic behavior inside or outside of the school setting that interferes with learning; and (4) life events, such as getting a job, becoming pregnant, or caring for an ill family member.[71]

One study that related the school to a life-course perspective was undertaken by Zeng-yin Chen and Howard B. Kaplan. Using a longitudinal panel data set collected at three developmental stages (early adolescence, young adulthood, and middle adulthood), Chen and Kaplan investigated how early school failure influenced status attainment at midlife, concluding that "early negative experiences set in motion a cascade of later disadvantages in the transition to adulthood, which, in turn, influences SES [socioeconomic status] attainment later in the life course."[72]

Wendy Schwartz analyzed information from the Educational Resource Information Center and determined the following:

- In the last 20 years, the earnings level of **dropouts** doubled, whereas it nearly tripled for college graduates.
- Recent dropouts will earn $200,000 less than high school graduates and over $800,000 less than college graduates over the course of their lives.
- Dropouts comprise nearly half of all heads of households on welfare.
- Dropouts comprise nearly half of the nation's prison population.[73]

John Sampson and John Laub have demonstrated that high school can be a turning point in an individual's life course (see Chapter 2).[74] Richard Arum and Irenee R. Beattie assessed the effects of high school educational experiences on the likelihood of adult incarceration.[75] Using event history analysis and the National Longitudinal Survey of Youth data, they found that high school educational experiences have a lasting effect on an individual's risk of incarceration. This study offered specifications of the high school context to identify how high school experiences can serve as a defining moment in an adolescent's life trajectory.[76]

Delinquency and Social Policy: Promising Interventions

7 LEARNING OUTCOMES — Summarize the school interventions that hold promise for reducing delinquency.

Several intervention strategies promise to benefit schools in the United States: improved quality of the school experience; increased use of mentors for students who are encountering difficulties or experiencing problems; greater use of alternative schools for students who cannot adapt to the traditional education setting; reduction of the crime control and punitiveness in public schools; development of a comprehensive approach to school success that includes home, school, church/synagogue, parents, and other institutions and persons who participate in school processes affecting students' lives; effective school-based violence-prevention programs; and more effective programs to prevent dropping out of school. See Figure 8–4 for a summary of this information.

Improving the Quality of the School Experience

For students, a good school experience begins with good teaching. Good teachers can make students feel wanted and accepted and can encourage students to have more positive and successful experiences in the classroom. Safety is another of the important prerequisites of effective involvement in the educational process; unless students feel safe, they are unlikely to involve themselves very deeply in the school experience.

Mentoring Relationships

In 2005, 3 million adults had formal one-to-one mentoring relationships with young people, an increase of 19 percent since 2002.[77] Youth development experts generally agree that

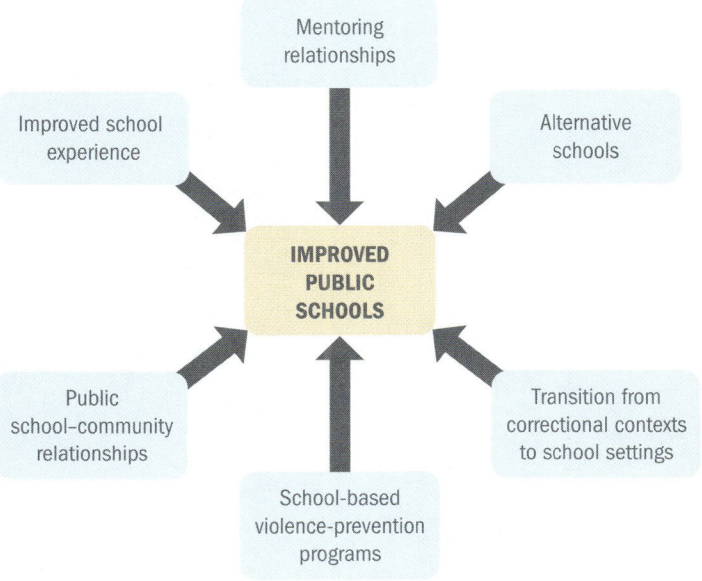

FIGURE 8–4 Intervention Strategies to Improve Schools.

mentoring is a critical component in a child's social, emotional, and cognitive development and that it has the potential to build a sense of industry and competency, boost academic performance, and broaden horizons.[78] School-based mentoring is one of the most promising types of youth mentoring taking place today and is experiencing rapid growth.

Alternative Schools

Disruptive behavior is a very serious problem in many of this nation's classrooms. School administrators often suspend or expel students who cause trouble;[79] however, this policy of swift suspension stigmatizes troublemakers as failures and reinforces their negative behaviors. **Alternative schools** are deemed a much more satisfactory way of dealing with young people whom public schools cannot control or who are doing unsatisfactory work in a public school setting. The juvenile court sometimes requires disruptive students to attend an alternative school, but more frequently, students are referred by the public school system. In 2000–2001, 39 percent of public school districts had alternative schools and programs and served approximately 613,000 at-risk students in about 10,900 alternative schools and programs in the United States. In addition to dealing more effectively with disruptive students than the public school system does, alternative schools tend to reduce absenteeism and dropout rates.[80]

Positive School–Community Relationships

In contrast to efforts at reducing delinquency in the school by investing in hardware and preventive technology, an alternative intervention strategy is the development of a comprehensive, or multicomponent, approach that includes home, school, and other persons and institutions that participate in the social processes affecting the students' lives. Delinquency and the quality of the public school experience, then, must be analyzed within the larger context of school–community relationships.[81]

> **Disruptive behavior is a very serious problem in many of our nation's classrooms.**

Reduce High School Dropouts

The 2009 National Governors Association publication *Achieving Graduation for All* offers a number of action steps to establish a more effective prevention and recovery agenda for school dropout. The action steps are (1) promoting high school graduation for all; (2) targeting youth at risk of dropping out; (3) reengaging youth who have dropped out of school; and (4) providing rigorous, relevant options for earning a high school diploma.[82] Together, says the report, "these strategies form a comprehensive approach to dropout prevention and recovery."

Reduction of the Crime-Control Model in Public Schools

Despite decreases in student delinquency, student drug use, violent school victimization, and school-related deaths, formal social control has intensified in public schools during the past two decades. Examples of harsher forms of student discipline and punishment include more teacher referrals to the principal, more in-school and out-of-school detentions, and more expulsions. In addition, schools are becoming more and more prison-like. Many schools hire uniformed security guards or uniformed and armed security resources officers (SROs); some schools also perform regular locker searches, install security cameras, and use drug-sniffing dogs (Figure 8–3).[83] Furthermore, as part of the crime-control model in public schools, there are increased research findings that schools with a larger proportion of African-American students are likely to implement harsh disciplinary practices toward these students.[84]

THE CASE

The Life Course of Amy Watters, Age 14

Amy's life as a runaway came to an abrupt end on a cold February night, when Damon didn't come back to her as he normally did. Earlier, he had told her that he was going out on a "photo shoot," as he liked to call the time he spent posing for photographers pandering to portions of the gay community's desire for images of underage boys. Desperately cold and hungry, Amy made her way to a homeless shelter, where workers quickly identified her as a runaway and called social services workers. A lady with the Florida Department of Children and Families (DCF) interviewed Amy, determined her identity, and made a few phone calls to some of Amy's relatives. Following a hot meal and a one-night stay at the shelter, Amy was put on a bus for the two-hour trip to her Aunt Ellen's place. When she got there, Ellen was waiting at the bus station for her, and took her underwing with many kind and loving words. Ellen was Amy's father's sister, and after a few days spent with Ellen, Amy's father arrived to take her home.

Amy and her father never spoke about why Amy had run away, nor did the topic of the camera hidden in the mirror ever come up. Amy was thankful to get back to her own home and, after a night spent in her own bed, did a thorough search of her room for hidden viewing devices. Satisfied that there were none, she settled back into a somewhat normal routine and resumed her schooling.

Amy was now in junior high school, however, and the atmosphere at the school was far different from what it had been at the school she had left. Many of the students seemed haughty and boastful, whereas others were outright troublemakers. Very few students seemed concerned about their grades, and all of them hung in small gangs that didn't accept outsiders. Amy wasn't a member of any particular group, and she soon found herself being picked on by girls her own age who made fun of her on any pretext. One day they taunted Amy because of the clothes she wore, saying that they were "Walmart's finest." On another day, they criticized her looks, telling her that she was ugly and that it was a waste of renewable resources (a topic that was under study in class) having her on the planet. Amy felt socially isolated and soon became distraught. Although she wanted to, she was unable to concentrate on her studies until she remembered her experience of three years earlier when she had had to join a tough crowd in order to end the bullying to which she had been subjected. Given the sexual experience she had gained as a runaway, Amy found it easy to gain favor among the school's most admired athletes. With surprisingly little effort, Amy soon became the girlfriend of the football team's star running back, who people called CJ. CJ, who had failed his freshman year and was 17 years old, had a rough-and-tumble personality that attracted Amy. "I was never the kind of person to play by the rules," he told her one day. "The more someone tells me not to do something the more I want to do it." The word soon went out on campus, "Don't nobody touch this girl; she belongs to CJ." In no time, the girls who had taunted Amy were seeking her attention.

Discuss

1. How could the school environment have been better structured so as to protect Amy from bullying? Generally speaking, are there aspects of the high school environment that inadvertently contribute to (or support) delinquent activity?

Learn more on the Web:

- Toward Safe and Orderly Schools—The National Study of Delinquency Prevention in Schools: http://justicestudies.com//delinquency_in_schools.pdf.

Follow the continuing Amy Watters saga in the next chapter.

CHAPTER 8 Schools and Delinquency

Summarize the major issues American schools have faced over time.

The major issues American schools have faced over time include whether or not to require mandatory free education, how teachers could maintain control in the classrooms without resorting to brutal measures, the overcoming of racial discrimination, how to handle increased enrollments, and how to deal with the rising costs of education.

1. What are some of the major issues that American schools have faced over time?
2. Of the issues American schools have faced over time, which have been the most challenging?
3. How have those issues been addressed?

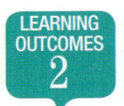
Summarize the extent of vandalism, violence, and bullying in schools.

American schools experience a small number of homicides each year, but over 1.7 million nonviolent crimes occur at school. A greater percentage of secondary school teachers than elementary school teachers reported being threatened with injury by a student, 85 percent of public schools reported one or more violent incidents of crime during the 2007–2008 school year, one-fourth of public schools reported that students were bullied on a daily or weekly basis during the 2007–2008 school year, and about one-fourth of students reported gangs in their school or that someone had offered them drugs during the 2007–2008 school year.

1. Why is violence a more serious problem in urban schools than in nonurban schools?
2. What can be done to lower the incidence of bullying in schools?
3. How do gangs influence schools?

vandalism The act of destroying or damaging, or attempting to destroy or damage, the property of another without the owner's consent or destroying or damaging public property (except by burning).

violence A forceful physical assault with or without weapons. It includes many kinds of fighting, rape, other attacks, gang warfare, and so on.

bullying The hurtful, frightening, or menacing actions undertaken by one person to intimidate another (generally weaker) person to gain that person's unwilling compliance, and/or to put him or her in fear.

cyberbullying Bullying that involves using technology, such as cell phones and the Internet, to bully or harass another person.

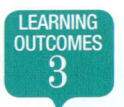
Explain how delinquency is linked to school failure.

Delinquency is linked to school failure through the lack of academic achievement, low social status at school, and dropping out of school.

1. Which factors related to school failure do you think are most common?
2. How can such factors be effectively addressed and curtailed or eliminated?

academic performance Achievement in schoolwork as rated by grades and other assessment measures. Poor academic performance is a factor in delinquency.

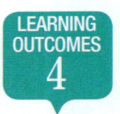
Summarize how various delinquency theories view the school's role.

Blocked opportunity theory, strain theory, cultural deviance theory, social control theory, labeling theory, radical criminology, general theory of crime, and interactional theory constitute the various delinquency theories that have examined the relationship between delinquency and the school.

1. Which delinquency theory is most helpful in understanding school failure? Explain your reasoning.
2. How might delinquency theories shape social policies designed to prevent delinquency in schools?

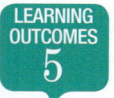

Summarize school students' rights.

Several landmark cases that have examined students' rights have ensured that students receive due process rights, unless it would interfere with school operations.

1. What legal rights do public school students have?
2. Do you believe students in public schools have the rights they need or do they need greater protection? Explain your position.

in loco parentis The principle according to which a guardian or an agency is given the rights, duties, and responsibilities of a parent in relation to a particular child or children.

due process rights The constitutional rights that are guaranteed to citizens—whether adult or juvenile—during their contacts with the police, their proceedings in court, and their interactions with the public schools.

school search The process of searching students and their lockers to determine whether drugs, weapons, or other contraband is present.

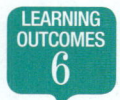

Explain the correlation between dropping out of high school and crime.

Dropping out of school influences later success in life by reducing income, making jobs harder to attain, making it more likely to have to rely on welfare, and setting in motion later disadvantages in the transition to adulthood.

1. There are a number of reasons why students drop out of school. Which factor do you believe contributes to more students dropping out?
2. How can high school dropout rates be reduced?
3. Why is it important to reduce dropout rates?

dropout A young person of school age who, of his or her own volition, no longer attends school.

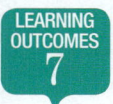

Summarize the school interventions that hold promise for reducing delinquency.

Research has identified school interventions that hold promise for reducing delinquency. These include improved school experiences, mentoring relationships, alternative schools, positive school–community relationships, school-based violence-prevention programs, and interventions to reduce school dropout.

1. Which school intervention strategies do you consider most fruitful for reducing delinquency in public schools?
2. What is an alternative school? How might alternative schools help reduce delinquency?

disruptive behavior Unacceptable conduct at school. It may include defiance of authority, manipulation of teachers, inability or refusal to follow rules, fights with peers, destruction of property, use of drugs in school, and/or physical or verbal altercations with teachers.

alternative school A facility that provides an alternative educational experience, usually in a different location, for youths who are not doing satisfactory work in the public school setting.

9

Gangs and Delinquency

"Gang members' mutual support of criminal activities, and possession of a value system which condones such behavior, distinguishes gang members and gangs from all other offenders and groups."

—Michael K. Carlie, Into the Abyss

1. Summarize what is known about the nature and extent of gang activity in the United States.
2. Summarize theories of how gangs form.
3. Describe how the life-course perspective views gang membership.
4. Summarize strategies for preventing and controlling gangs.

Bob Ingelhart/Getty Images

FLASH MOBS

In what has become an Easter tradition, flocks of gang-bangers filled New York City's Time Square in April—harassing pedestrians and bursting into stores, where they grabbed merchandise off of shelves and ran away.[1] Whereas New York's City's experience appears to be related to rites of gang initiation, Philadelphia has recently experienced the same kind of phenomenon. Using text messages and email postings, teenagers organize themselves into what Philadelphia's police commission calls *flash mobs*—groups of violent and marauding young people that form at a moment's notice, seeming to come out of nowhere.[2]

A flash mob of pillow fighters in London. The event was organized by social media. How can flash mobs serve criminal purposes?

DISCUSS Why do young people join gangs? What does the gang provide its members that other social institutions don't?

Street Gangs and Organized Crime

Over the past 30 years, urban street gangs—armed with Israeli-made Uzis, Soviet AK-47s, diverted U.S. military M-16s, and other automatic weapons—have evolved into small criminal empires fighting for control of thriving narcotics, auto theft, prostitution, gun running, and extortion operations. Illegal drugs form the backbone of most gang money-making criminal operations, with the manufacture and sale of **crack**, or rock cocaine, providing the bulk of the business. The crack trade, more than anything else, transformed street gangs into ghetto-based for-profit criminal organizations. Although most such gangs are led by adults, juveniles often play a central role in their day-to-day activities.[3]

As street gangs have become more business-like, they have formed associations with other organized crime groups, including Mexican drug cartels, Asian criminal groups, and Russian organized crime families. Gangs and their members are also becoming more sophisticated in their use of technology, including computers, cell phones, and the Internet. These new high-tech tools are frequently used to facilitate criminal activity and avoid detection by the police. Although some sources say that the number of gang members is in decline across the United States, some Hispanic gangs, such as *Mara Salvatrucha* (MS-13) are experiencing an influx of new members.[4]

This chapter focuses on youths who are involved in gangs. Youth gangs have become a problem in many nations and are widespread in the United States in urban, suburban, and rural areas.

1 LEARNING OUTCOMES Summarize what is known about the nature and extent of gang activity in the United States.

Nature and Extent of Gang Activity

For a brief overview of the development of gangs in the twentieth and early twenty-first century, see the accompanying timeline, which reveals how gangs have emerged from highly transitory social groups to supergangs and violent and drug-trafficking gangs.

2 LEARNING OUTCOMES Summarize theories of how gangs form.

According to the 2011 National Youth Gang Survey, an estimated 782,500 gang members and 29,900 gangs were active in the United States. As revealed in Figure 9–1, nearly one-third of all responding law enforcement agencies reported gang activity in 2011. Overall, an estimated 3,300 jurisdictions served by city (population of 2,500 or more) and county law enforcement agencies experienced gang problems in 2011.[5]

Knowledge of the gang world requires an examination of the definition of gangs and the profile of gang members as well as an understanding of gangs' intimidation of the school environment, of the structure and leadership of urban street gangs, of emerging gangs in small communities across the nation, of the racial and ethnic backgrounds of gangs, and of female delinquent gangs.

Nature and Extent of Gang Activity **145**

TIMELINE — Development of Gangs in the Twentieth and Early Twenty-First Century

1920s–1940s
Gangs were largely transitory social groups in Chicago and elsewhere, and gang membership was a type of rite of passage.

1940s–1950s
Teenage gangs became established in Boston, New York, and Philadelphia. Members hung out together, partied together, and gangs fought each other over "turf."

1960s
Drugs began to influence gang activity, "supergangs" in Chicago and Los Angeles emerged, and some Chicago gangs became involved in social betterment programs.

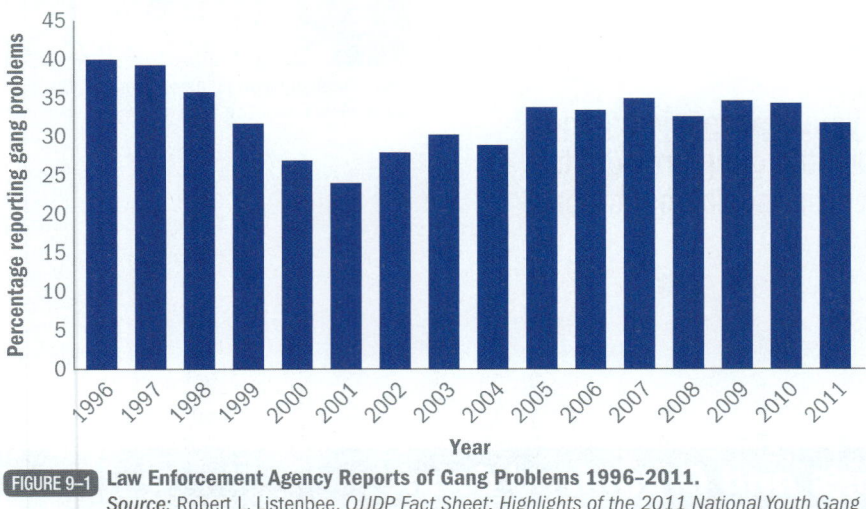

FIGURE 9–1 Law Enforcement Agency Reports of Gang Problems 1996–2011.
Source: Robert L. Listenbee, *OJJDP Fact Sheet: Highlights of the 2011 National Youth Gang Survey* (Washington, D.C.: Office of Juvenile Justice and Delinquency Prevention, 2013), p. 2.

Definitions of Gangs

Thrasher's 1927 gang study was one of the first attempts to define a youth **gang**:

> A gang is an interstitial group originally formed spontaneously and then integrated through conflict. It is characterized by the following types of behavior: meeting face-to-face, milling, movement through space as a unit, conflict, and planning. The result of this collective behavior is the development of tradition, unreflective internal structure, esprit de corps, solidarity, morale, group awareness, and attachment to local territory.[6]

Thrasher does not specify that a gang's definition must include illegal activity, but Finn-Aage Esbensen and most other gang researchers do. Whereas Thrasher's definition focused on group interaction, Esbensen was interested in clarifying group demographics (age range, sense of identity, and permanence within a specific area). Combining all three definitions could provide a useful and comprehensive definition of a youth gang.

Profiles of Gang Members

Gang profiles have at least four important dimensions: age of gang membership, size of the gang, commitment to the gang, and attraction of the gang.

Age of Gang Membership

The smaller the community, the more likely it is that its gang members will be juveniles.

Esbensen and colleagues, in their examination of gang members in 11 locations, found that youth make up the following percentage of gang members: Milwaukee, Wisconsin, 15 percent; Phoenix, Arizona, 12.6 percent; Omaha, Nebraska, 11.4 percent; Las Cruces, New Mexico, 11.0 percent; Kansas City, Missouri, 10.1 percent; Orlando, Florida, 9.6 percent; Philadelphia, Pennsylvania, 7.7 percent; Terrance, California, 6.3 percent; Providence, Rhode Island, 6 percent; Porcello, Idaho, 5.6 percent; and Will County, Oregon, 3.8 percent.[7]

Juveniles become involved in gangs at as young as eight years of age, running errands and carrying weapons or messages. They are recruited as lookouts and street vendors and join an age-appropriate junior division of the gang. Gangs use younger and smaller members to deal cocaine out of cramped "rock houses," which are steel-reinforced fortresses. Gangs have long known that youngsters are invaluable because their age protects them against the harsher realities of the adult criminal justice system.[8]

> **The smaller the community, the more likely it is that its gang members will be juveniles.**

1970s–1988	1989–1999	2000–present
Leadership of gangs was assumed by adults, street gangs became involved in more unlawful behaviors and drug trafficking, and gangs became increasingly more violent.	**The number of** youth gangs exploded across the United States.	**Gang membership** and the number of gangs have begun to slightly decline, with some ethnic gangs skyrocketing in numbers. Gangs have spread worldwide.

Think About It…

Gang life is a significant part of the adolescent experience for many. What attracts some young people to gangs?

Size of the Gang

Gangs vary in size depending on whether they are traditional or specialty gangs in urban areas or emerging gangs in smaller cities or communities. Large and enduring traditional (territorial) gangs in urban areas average about 180 members, whereas drug-trafficking gangs average only about 25 members. Some urban gangs (for example, the supergangs of Chicago) have thousands of members, but gangs in emerging areas usually number less than 25 or so members.[9]

Commitment to the Gang

Gang members have varying degrees of commitment to the gang. A typology of gang commitment is contributed by Ira Reiner, who identified five different levels of commitment to the gang: at risk youth, wanabes, associates, hard-core, and original gangsters.[10]

Youth gang members in a dark alley. Why do young people join gangs?

Attraction of the Gang

Why do young people join gangs? Willie Lloyd, legendary leader of a gang called the Almighty Unknown Vice Lords, explained why he became involved with gangs:

> I grew up on the streets of Chicago. When I was growing up, the Lords had a big impact on me. I never saw it as a gang but a cohesive and unified principle on which a person could organize his life. Even as a kid of nine, I was intrigued by the Lords when I first saw them outside of the Central Park Theater. It was the first time I had ever witnessed so many black people moving so harmoniously together. They were motored by the same sense of purpose and they all wore similar dress and insignia. There were over a hundred guys, all in black, with capes and umbrellas. To my young eyes, it was the most beautiful expression I had ever seen. They all seemed so fearless, so proud, so much in control of their lives. Though I didn't know one of them at the time, I fell in love with all of them. In retrospect, I made up my mind the very first time I saw the Vice Lords to be a Vice Lord.[11]

Mike Carlie, in his national overview of youth gangs, expanded on the question of why youths join gangs, asking why gangs form and what gangs offer to those who join them (see Table 9–1).

Gangs in Schools

Schools have become fertile soil for violent youth gangs. The violence perpetrated by gangs across the nation tends to vary from one school to the next, depending on the economic and social structures of the community, the gang tradition within that school, the gang's stage of development, and the extent of drug trafficking taking place. See Figure 9–2 for the percentages of students ages 12 through 18 years of age who reported that street gangs were present at school in 2011.

Gangs perpetrate school violence in a number of ways. For example, George W. Knox, David Laske, and Edward Tromanhauser reported that high school students who are gang members are significantly more likely than nongang members to carry a firearm to school for purposes of protection.[12] Joseph F. Sheley and James D. Wright also found higher rates of ownership and carrying of firearms among gang members than among nongang members.[13] Furthermore, Charles M. Callahan and Ira Rivara determined that gang members are nearly three times as likely as nongang members to say firearm access is "easy."[14]

Nature and Extent of Gang Activity **147**

TABLE 9-1 ATTRACTION OF GANGS

Why Gangs Form	What Gangs Offer	Why Youths Join
Social discrimination or rejection	Acceptance	To avoid being discriminated against and to seek acceptance and a sense of belonging
Absence of a family and its unconditional love, positive adult role models, and proper discipline	Surrogate family	To be in a family and to have unconditional love, positive adult role models, and discipline
Feelings of powerlessness	Power	To overcome their powerlessness
Abuse, fear, and lack of security	Security	To reduce their feelings of fear and to feel secure
Economic deprivation	Means of earning money	To gain economically
School failure and delinquency	Alternative to school	To vent their frustration
Low self-esteem	Opportunities to build high self-esteem	To acquire high self-esteem
Lack of acceptable rites of passage into adulthood	Rite of passage to adulthood	To accomplish their passage from childhood to adulthood
Lack of legitimate free-time activities	Activity	To keep from being bored
Pathological needs	Setting in which to act out aggression	To vent their anger
Influence of migrating gang members	Any of the aforementioned	To get any of the aforementioned
Mass media portrayals of gangs and gang members	Any of the aforementioned	To get any of the aforementioned
Choice to follow in others' footsteps	Any of the aforementioned	To follow tradition and to gain acceptance
Ability to join	Any of the aforementioned	To get any of the aforementioned

Source: Adapted from Mike Carlie, *Into the Abyss: A Personal Journey into the World of Street Gangs*, http://people.missouristate.edu/MichaelCarlie. Reprinted with permission from Michael K. Carlie.

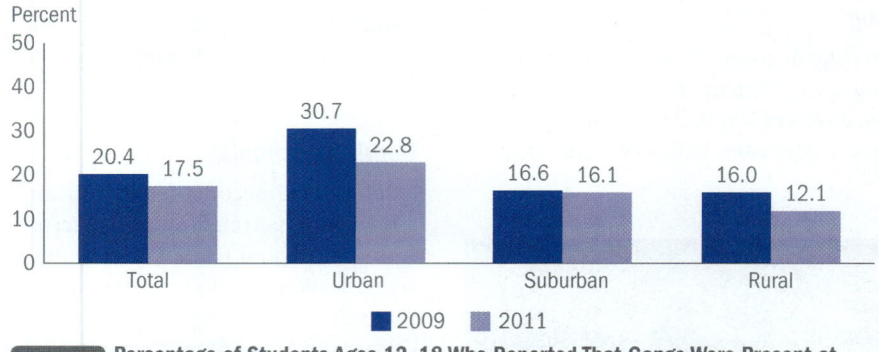

FIGURE 9-2 Percentage of Students Ages 12-18 Who Reported That Gangs Were Present at School During the School Year, 2009 and 2011.
Source: Simone Robers, Jana Kemp, Jennifer Truman, and Thomas D. Snyder, *Indicators of School Crime and Safety: 2012* (Washington, D.C.: National Center for Education Statistics, 2013).

Gangs are also constantly recruiting new members, and nongang members are likely to be physically assaulted if they refuse to join. An African-American male who grew up in Chicago, went to college on a football scholarship, and graduated from law school told how he avoided gang membership: "They were always on me to join a gang. The only way I kept from getting beaten up all the time was to run home from football practice and to run to school every morning. I kept moving all the time, but I kept out of the gangs."[15]

Moreover, because more than one gang is typically present in a high school, conflict among gangs takes place on a regular basis. This conflict may be based on competition over the drug market, or it may relate to individual gangs within the school that are seeking to expand their turf. Fights may erupt in the school hallways, in the cafeteria, or during dances. Warring gang youths sometimes start a mass riot, with stabbings and shootings occurring during these altercations. The use of deadly weapons, of course, increases the likelihood of injuries or fatalities.

Finally, conflict among rival gangs in different schools also leads to violence. Fights commonly take place during athletic contests between competing schools. A drive-by shooting is one of the most serious types of violence that can erupt among rival gangs in the school setting. What usually happens is that a gang youth is killed, and the victim's gang deems it necessary to retaliate; so before school, during lunch recess, or following school, a car speeds by—its occupants spraying bullets.[16]

Gangs, Schools, and Drugs

Gangs in schools today have an economic base (drug dealing), which was not true in earlier years. Gangs have a number of techniques for selling drugs in schools. In some schools, gang members prop doors open with cigarette packs and then signal from windows to nonstudents waiting to enter the building.[17] Some gang members sell drugs in the bathrooms, in the lunchrooms, or in parking lots. Gangs also use younger children in their drug trafficking: The children first serve as lookouts, but as they get older, they can become couriers (runners), who work as conduits between dealers and buyers.[18]

Gang Recruitment and Initiation Rites

Gangs regularly go on recruiting parties, using three basic recruitment strategies (Figure 9–3).

The recruitment of younger members is generally easy, because the life of a gang member looks very glamorous. Recruitment begins early in the grade school years; adolescent males are most vulnerable in the junior high years.[19] But even if a youth has enough support systems at home to resist joining a gang, it is very difficult to live in a neighborhood that is controlled by a street gang and not join. A gang leader explained, "You had two choices in the neighborhood I grew up in—you could either be a gang member or [be] a mama's boy. A mama's boy would come straight home from school, go up to his room and study, and that was it."[20]

Urban gangs have several methods of initiation:

- A new member may be "blessed-in" to a gang. Those who are blessed-in to a gang usually have older brothers, fathers, mothers, or other relatives who are already in the gang.

- A new male member more typically must be "jumped-in," that is, he must fight other members. He may have to fight a specified number of gang members for a set period of time and demonstrate that he is able to take a beating and fight back, he may have to stand in the middle of a circle and fight his way out, or he may have to run between lines of gang members as they administer a beating (under the latter circumstances, he is expected to stay on his feet from one end of the line to the other).

- A female is usually initiated into male-dominated gangs by providing sexual services for one or more gang members.

- A new member is often expected to participate in illegal acts, such as committing thefts or larcenies.

Three gang recruitment strategies

1. In the "fraternity" type of recruitment, the gang presents itself as an organization that is the "in" thing to join.

2. The "obligation" recruitment strategy involves members who attempt to persuade potential members that it is their duty to join.

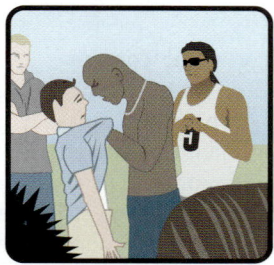

3. The "coercive" type of recruitment strategy uses physical and/or psychological pressure on potential members and threatens that either they or their family will be attacked if they fail to join.

FIGURE 9-3 Three Gang Recruitment Strategies.
Source: Martin Jankowski, *Islands in the Street* (Oakland: University of California Press, 1991).

- A new member is frequently expected to assist in trafficking drugs.
- A new member in some gangs is expected to participate in "walk-up" or "drive-by" shootings.
- A new member is sometimes expected to commit a gang-assigned murder. Completing the procedure has sometimes been called a "blood-in," but is rarely part of initiation rites today.[21]

Law-Violating Behaviors and Gang Activities

Despite the fluidity and diversity of gang roles and affiliations, it is commonly agreed that core gang members are involved in more serious delinquent acts than are situational or fringe members.[22] The 2011 National Youth Gang Survey shows seven main factors contributing to local gang violence.[23] The two highest rated factors across survey years are drug-related factors and intergang conflict (see Figure 9–4).

Core gang members are involved in more serious acts of delinquency than are fringe members.

Nature and Extent of Gang Activity **149**

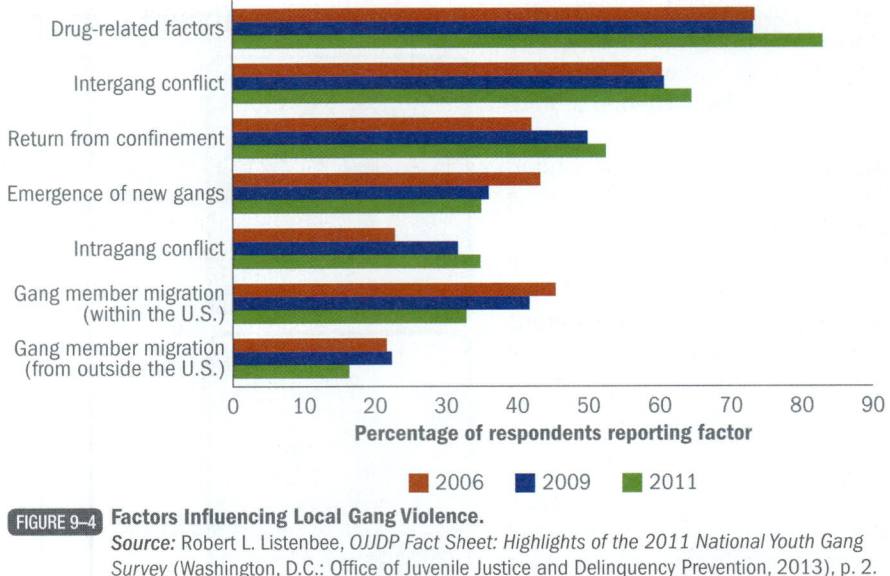

FIGURE 9–4 Factors Influencing Local Gang Violence.
Source: Robert L. Listenbee, *OJJDP Fact Sheet: Highlights of the 2011 National Youth Gang Survey* (Washington, D.C.: Office of Juvenile Justice and Delinquency Prevention, 2013), p. 2.

Gangs are increasingly using technology in the commission of crime. The most frequently reported use of technology involves cell phones with walkie-talkie or push-to-talk functions. Walkie-talkie cell phones enable gang members to alert one another to the presence of law enforcement officers or rival gang members. Gang members also use pay-as-you-go cell phones and call forwarding to insulate themselves from police; in addition, gang members make use of police scanners, surveillance equipment, and equipment for detecting microphones or bugs to insulate their criminal activity and to impede police investigations.[24]

Gangs are also making increased use of computers and the Internet. According to the *2011 National Gang Threat Assessment*, gangs use personal computers, laptops, handhelds, and other devices to produce ledgers and maintain records of their criminal enterprises.[25] In addition, some evidence exists that gangs are using the Internet to track court proceedings and to identify witnesses; armed with publicly available records of legal proceedings, gangs can then identify and victimize witnesses. The Internet is sometimes used for soliciting sexual acts (a form of Internet-supported prostitution), and it provides a venue for the sale of gang-related clothing, music, and other paraphernalia; gangs are also using the Internet to become more involved in the pirating of movies and music.[26]

Studies of large urban samples found that gang members are responsible for a large proportion of violent offenses. In Rochester, New York, gang members made up 30 percent of the sample but self-reported committing 68 percent of all adolescent violent offenses, which is about seven times as many serious and violent acts as nongang youths.[27] A study in Columbus, Ohio, analyzed the arrest records of 83 gang leaders in the years 1980–1994; during these 15 years, the 83 gang leaders accumulated 834 arrests, 37 percent of which were for violent crimes (ranging from domestic violence to murder). The researchers theorized that violent crimes tended to increase as the gangs began engaging in drug activity and may have been connected to the establishment of a drug market.[28]

A final dimension of law-violating behaviors of urban street gangs is the extent to which they are becoming organized crime groups. Scott Decker, Tim Bynum, and Deborah Weisel interviewed members of African-American and Hispanic gangs in San Diego and Chicago and found that only the GDs in Chicago are assuming the attributes of organized crime groups.[29] It can be argued that aspects of organized crime groups are found in such drug-trafficking gangs as the Bloods and Crips in Los Angeles, the Miami Boys of southern Florida, and the Jamaican Posses of New York and Florida. Beginning in the mid-1980s, these street gangs appeared to become criminal entrepreneurs, supplying illicit drugs, and in a brief period of several years, many of these street gangs developed intrastate and interstate networks for the purpose of expanding their illegal drug-market sales.

Gangs in Small Communities

Since the early 1990s, nearly every city, many suburban areas, and even some rural areas across the nation have experienced the reality of youths who consider themselves gang members. Thrasher's finding that no gangs he studied were alike appears to be true for these **emerging gangs** as well.[30] Curry and colleagues' 1992 national survey found that cities with emerging gangs reported that 90 percent of the gangs were made up of juveniles.[31]

This nationwide expansion began in the late 1980s and appeared to be fueled by four different situations. First, in some communities it took place when ghetto-based drug-trafficking gangs sent ranking gang members to a community to persuade local youths to sell crack cocaine; second, gang-related individuals operating on their own established drug-trafficking networks among community youths. Third, urban gang members whose families had moved to these communities were instrumental in developing local chapters of urban gangs; and fourth, youths in communities with little or no intervention from outsiders developed their own versions of gangs. The latter two

FIGURE 9-5 Stages of Gang Development.

and experience a sense of camaraderie, yet their primary motivation is still to make money from selling drugs. One midwestern youth claimed that he was making $40,000 a month selling crack for the Unknown Vice Lords when he was arrested and institutionalized.[34] Conflict inevitably arises as drug-trafficking gangs attempt to expand their markets, usually in the same neighborhoods. Fights may break out during school functions, at athletic events and shopping centers, and in parks and other common gathering places. Weapons may be used at this time, and the number of weapons increases dramatically in the community.

3. *Organization and consolidation.* In stage 3, youths identifying with a certain gang attempt to develop a group culture. The leadership is assumed by one or more members of the core group as well as by young adult males from the community. The increased visibility of the gang attracts a sizable number of "wannabes." The gang may be larger but is still relatively unorganized, consisting primarily of a group of males hanging around together. Recruitment is emphasized, and considerable pressure is put on young minority males to join the gang. One of these males noted, "If you are black, age 12 or so, they really put pressure on you to join. It's hard not to."[35]

4. *Gang intimidation and community reaction.* Several events typically take place during stage 4. Some whites join the minority gangs, and other whites form gangs of their own. One youth represented the spirit of this white reaction when he said, "The blacks ain't going to push us around."[36] Minority gangs are still more likely to wear their colors and to demonstrate gang affiliation. Drugs are also increasingly sold in the school environment, and gang control becomes a serious problem in the school. A high school teacher expressed her concern: "I've never had any trouble teaching in this school. Now, with these gang kids, I'm half afraid to come to school. It's becoming a very serious situation."[37] Gangs become more visible in shopping centers, and older people begin to experience some fear of shopping when gang youths are present. Equally disturbing—and much more serious in the long run—is that gangs become popular among children in middle school, with some allegiance being given to gangs among young children in first and second grades.

5. *Expansion of drug markets.* Drugs are openly sold in junior and senior high schools, on street corners, and in shopping centers during the fifth stage. Crack houses are present in some minority neighborhoods. Extortion of students and victimization of both teachers and students takes place frequently in the public schools. The gangs are led by adults who remain in the community, the organizational structure is more highly developed, and the number of gang members shows a significant increase. Outsiders have been present all along, but during this stage they seem to be continually coming into and going out of the community. Men in their mid-20s roll into the community driving high-status automobiles, wearing expensive clothes and jewelry, and flashing impressive rolls of money.

types were less likely to become involved in drug trafficking than were the first two types.

Behind the first wave of nationwide gang expansion was urban gang leaders' knowledge that a lot of new markets were ripe for exploitation and that crack cocaine would command a high price in these new areas. To introduce the drug in these new markets, the representatives of most urban gangs promised the possibility of a gang satellite—that is, the emerging local gang would be connected by both name and organizational ties to the parent gang. However, urban gangs had neither the intent nor the resources to develop extensions in the emerging gang community, and the promise of being a gang satellite was only a carrot to persuade local youths to sell crack cocaine for the urban gang. The development of emerging gangs involved in drug trafficking throughout the nation has seven possible stages, and the degree and seriousness of gang activity in a community depend on the gang's stage of development (Figure 9–5):[32]

1. *Implementation.* The first stage begins when an adult gang member, usually a high-ranking officer, comes to a city that has no gangs. On arriving, this gang member goes to a low-income minority neighborhood where he recruits several juveniles to sell crack and be members of the new gang. The recruited juveniles are assured of a percentage of the money they make from the sale of crack; although the exact percentage seems to vary from gang to gang, it is typically about 10 percent.[33] The representative from the urban gang returns on a regular basis to supply drugs and pick up the money.

2. *Expansion and conflict.* In the second stage, the adult who came to the community tells the recruited juveniles enough about his gang that they are able to identify with it. They start to wear the proper clothing, learn gang signs,

6. *Gang takeover.* Communities that permit the gangs to develop to stage 6 discover that gangs are clearly in control in minority neighborhoods, in the schools, at school events, and in shopping centers. The criminal operations of gangs also become more varied and now include robberies, burglaries, aggravated assaults, and rapes. Drive-by shootings begin to occur on a regular basis, and citizens' fear of gangs increases dramatically. The police, whose gang units usually number several officers, typically express an inability to control drug trafficking and violence.

7. *Community deterioration.* The final stage is characterized by the deterioration of social institutions and the community itself because of gang control. Citizens move out of the city, stay away from shopping centers, and find safer schools for their children. When an emerging gang community arrives at this stage of deterioration, it is fully experiencing the gang problems of urban communities.

In sum, although a community's reaction greatly affects the seriousness of the problem, nongang and sometimes low-crime communities across the nation in the late 1980s and early 1990s began to experience the development of gangs. These emerging gangs developed along different trajectories, but the most toxic to a community was the process, described earlier, that would take hold when ghetto-based drug-trafficking gang members were able to persuade minority youths to sell crack cocaine for them, and these youths, in turn, developed what they thought would be a satellite to the parent gang.

Racial and Ethnic Gangs

Hispanic/Latino, African-American, Asian, Caucasian, and Native American gangs constitute the basic types of racial and ethnic gangs in the United States. Hispanic/Latino and African-American gangs are generally more numerous and have more members than other racial/ethnic gangs. Almost 50 percent of all gang members are of Hispanic/Latino origin (see Figure 9–6).

Hispanic/Latino Gangs

Hispanic/Latino gangs are divided into Mexican-American (or Chicano), Cuban, Puerto Rican, Dominican, Jamaican, and Central American members. According to the *2005 National Gang Threat Assessment*, law enforcement agencies across the nation reported that the most prominent Hispanic/Latino gangs in their jurisdictions were the Los Surenos (Sur 13), Latin Kings, MS-13, 18th Street, Nortenos, and La Raza, with more than 50 percent of reporting agencies indicating that Sur 13 was present in their jurisdiction and nearly 40 percent reporting moderate to high Sur 13 gang activity (Sur 13 was found to be present in 35 states).[38] Hispanic/Latino gang members frequently dress distinctively, display colors, communicate through graffiti, use monikers, and bear tattoos.[39]

African-American Gangs

African-American gangs have received more attention in this chapter than any other racial or ethnic group because most of the ghetto-based drug-trafficking gangs that have established networks across the nation are African American. For example, the Bloods and Crips from Los Angeles, the People and Folks from Chicago, and the Detroit gangs are all mostly African American. African-American gangs usually identify themselves by adopting certain colors in addition to other identifiers, such as the common hand signs shown in Figure 9–7.

Asian Gangs

There are varieties of Asian gangs in California, including Chinese, Vietnamese, Filipino, Japanese, and Korean groups. The Chinese gangs, especially, have spread to other major cities in the nation, and some of the other gangs also are active outside California. Asian gangs tend to be more organized and to have

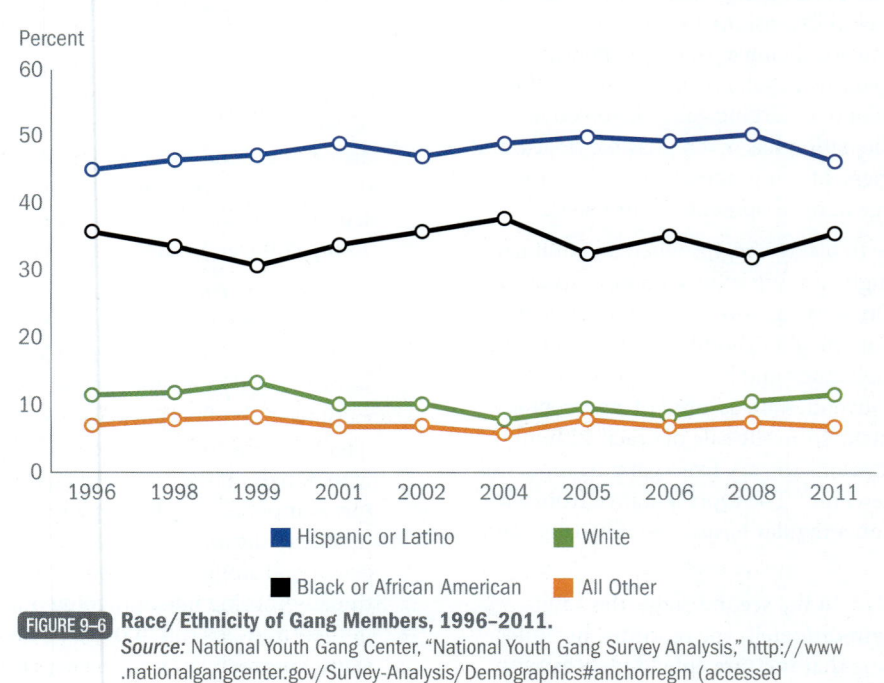

FIGURE 9–6 Race/Ethnicity of Gang Members, 1996–2011.
Source: National Youth Gang Center, "National Youth Gang Survey Analysis," http://www.nationalgangcenter.gov/Survey-Analysis/Demographics#anchorregm (accessed September 4, 2014).

FIGURE 9-7 Common Gang Hand Signs.
Source: Information gathered from Durham (NC) Police Department, *Gang Awareness Booklet,* http://www.durhampolice.com/pdf/gang_awareness_booklet.pdf.

more of an identifiable leadership than is true of other street gangs. Ko-Lin Chin's examination of Chinese gangs found them to be involved in some of the nation's worst gang-related violence as well as heroin trafficking, but unlike other ethnic gangs, Chinese gangs are closely tied to the social and economic life of their rapidly developing and economically robust communities.[40] A study of Vietnamese youth gangs in southern California found that these youths experienced much marginality but attained the American dream by robbing Vietnamese families of large amounts of cash that such families keep at home.[41]

Caucasian Gangs

Until the closing decades of the twentieth century, most gangs were made up of Caucasian youths. Today, according to Reiner, Caucasian youths make up about 10 percent of the gang population in the United States.[42] However, student surveys generally reveal a much larger representation of Caucasian adolescents among gang members.[43] For example, a survey of nearly 6,000 eighth graders in 11 sites showed that 25 percent of the Caucasians said they were gang members.[44] In the 1990s, the West Coast saw the solidification of lower- and middle-class Caucasian youths into groups who referred to themselves as stoners. These groups frequently abused drugs and alcohol and listened to heavy metal rock music, and some members practiced Satanism, which included grave robbing, desecration of human remains, and sacrifice of animals.[45] Stoner groups can be identified by their mode of dress: colored T-shirts with decals of their rock music heroes or bands, Levis, and tennis shoes. They may also wear metal-spiked wrist cuffs, collars, and belts as well as satanic jewelry. The emerging Caucasian gangs across the nation have used many of the symbols of the stoner gangs, especially the heavy metal rock music and the satanic rituals, but they are not as likely to call attention to themselves with their dress, may refer to themselves as neo-Nazi skinheads, and are involved in a variety of hate crimes in addition to drug trafficking.[46]

Native American Gangs

Attention also has been given to Navajo youth gangs.[47] In 1997, the Navajo Nation estimated that about 60 youth gangs existed in Navajo country. Gang values have encouraged such risky behaviors as heavy drinking and drug use, frequently leading to mortality from injuries and alcohol. A small percentage of Navajo male youths were involved in these groups, and at most 15 percent were peripherally affiliated with gangs. Many gang activities involved hanging around, drinking, and vandalizing, but gang members also robbed people, bootlegged alcohol, and sold marijuana.[48]

Female Delinquent Gangs

Traditional sociologists once considered female gangs to be almost a contradiction in terms. Recent decades, however, have brought increased awareness of adolescent girls who join gangs.

- A few studies have identified female gangs in Philadelphia and New York, with some of the gangs being extremely violent.[49]

- Some studies have found that adolescent females are connected to adolescent male gangs. The planning is done by the males, who usually exclude the females, but the female gang members participate in violent crimes and drug-related gang activities.[50]

- Loyalty to the gang rivaled loyalty to the family, and most friends came from within the gang. The gang, according to Quicker, offered warmth, friends, loyalty, and socialization as it insulated its members from the harsh environment of the barrio.[51]

- Finn-Aage Esbensen, Elizabeth Piper Deschenes, and L. Thomas Winfree, Jr., found from their analysis of the Denver Youth Survey that girl gang participants committed a wide variety of offenses at only a slightly lower frequency than boys involved in gangs,[52] and Carl S. Taylor found that women were frequently represented in drug-trafficking gangs in Detroit.[53]

- Beth Bjerregaard and Carolyn Smith determined that involvement in gangs for both females and males was associated with increased levels of delinquency and substance abuse.[54] Joan Moore and John Hagedorn's 2001 summary of the research on female gangs reported that delinquency rates of female gang members are lower than those of male

Nature and Extent of Gang Activity **153**

TABLE 9–2 CHARACTERISTICS OF VARIOUS TYPES OF GANGS

Type of Gang	Description
Urban Gangs	Located in urban areas, made up largely of adults who are involved in law-violating activities, including drug trafficking
Emerging Gangs	Located in smaller cities and communities across the nation, made up almost entirely of juveniles, and focused on hanging out and some law-violating activities
Racial and Ethnic Gangs	Hispanics/Latino, African American, Asian, Caucasian, and Native American constitute the main types of these gangs. These gangs tend to be made up of adults, and their law-breaking activities differ from one type of racial and ethnic gang to another.
Female Delinquent Gangs	These gangs are found primarily in urban areas and are made up more of adults than juveniles. Most of these gangs serve as adjuncts to male gangs.

gang members but higher than those of nongang females and males.[55]

- Esbensen and colleagues' findings also failed to support the notion that girls involved in gangs were mere sex objects and ancillary members, and they also showed that girls aged out of gangs before boys and that girls received more emotional fulfillment from their involvement with gang activity.[56]
- From research conducted in St. Louis, Missouri, and Columbus, Ohio, Jody Miller found that a female in a mixed-gender gang—an environment that supports gender hierarchies and the exploitation of young women—must learn to negotiate to survive in the gang milieu.[57]

In sum, most studies found that female gangs still serve as adjuncts to male gangs, yet an increasing number of important studies show that female gangs provide girls with the necessary skills to survive in their harsh communities while allowing them a temporary escape from the dismal future awaiting them.[58] What these studies revealed is that females join gangs for the same basic reasons that males do—and share with males in their neighborhood the hopelessness and powerlessness of the urban underclass.[59] See Table 9–2 for the characteristics of various types of gangs.

▶ **Theories of Gang Formation**

The classical theories about the origins of juvenile gangs and gang delinquency date from research done in the 1950s and were formulated by Herbert A. Bloch and Arthur Niederhoffer; Richard Cloward and Lloyd Ohlin; and Albert Cohen, Walter B. Miller, and Lewis Yablonsky.

- Bloch and Niederhoffer's theory was based on the idea that joining a gang is part of the experience male adolescents need to grow up to adulthood, so the basic function of the gang is to provide a substitute for the formalized puberty rites that are found in other societies.[60]
- Cloward and Ohlin's theory used the notion that lower-class boys interact with and gain support from other alienated individuals and that these youngsters pursue illegitimate means to achieve the success they cannot gain through legitimate means.[61]
- Cohen's theory stated that gang delinquency represents a subcultural and collective solution to the problem that faces lower-class boys of acquiring status when they find themselves evaluated according to middle-class values in the schools.[62]
- Miller held that there is a definite lower-class culture and that gang behavior is an expression of that culture; he saw gang leadership as based mainly on smartness and toughness and viewed the gang as very cohesive and highly conforming to delinquent norms.[63]
- Finally, Yablonsky suggested that violent delinquent gangs arise out of certain conditions, which are found in urban slums, that encourage the development of the sociopathic personality in adolescents, and such sociopathic individuals become the core leadership of these gangs.[64]

These classical theories of gangs focused on sociological variables such as strain (Cloward and Ohlin), subcultural affiliation (Miller and Cohen), and social disorganization (Yablonsky). Cohen, Cloward and Ohlin, and Miller also stressed the importance of the peer group for gang membership.[65] Each of the five theories of gang formation has received both support and criticism, but research into current expressions of gang activity is needed, because the existing theories were based primarily on 1950s gangs.[66]

Other theories of gangs are associated with social disorganization theory.[67] This theory is based on the assumptions that poor economic conditions cause social disorganization, that there is a deficiency of social control, and that this lack of social control leads to gang formation and involvement because youths in low-income neighborhoods seek the social order and security that gangs offer.[68]

More recently, underclass theory has been widely used to explain the origins of gangs.[69] In the midst of big-city ghettos and barrios filled with poverty and deprivation, it is argued, gangs are a normal response to an abnormal social setting.[70] Part of the underclass's plight, according to Fagan, is being permanently excluded from participating in mainstream labor market occupations, so members of the underclass are forced to rely on other economic alternatives, such as low-paying temporary jobs, part-time jobs, some form of welfare, or involvement in drug trafficking, prostitution, muggings, and extortion.[71] Jankowski contended that gang violence and the defiant attitude of young men are connected with the competitive struggle in poor communities and that being a product of their environment, they adopt a "Hobbesian view of life in which violence is an integral part of the state of nature."[72]

TABLE 9-3 THEORIES OF WHY JUVENILES JOIN GANGS

Type of Theory	Proponents	Brief Description
Normal Part of Growing Up	Block and Niederhoffer	Joining the gang is part of the experience adolescents need to grow up to adulthood.
Strain Theory	Cloward and Ohlin	Youngsters pursue gangs to achieve the success they cannot achieve through legitimate means.
Subcultural Affiliation and Strain Theory	Cohen	Gang delinquency represents a subcultural and collective solution to the problems facing lower-class boys.
Subcultural Affiliation	Miller	There is a definite lower-class culture and gang behavior is an expression of that culture.
Social Disorganization	Yablonsky	Violent delinquent gangs arise out of certain conditions, which are found in urban slums.
Underclass Theory	Fagan and others	Excluded from participation in labor market occupations, members of the underclass are attracted to other economic alternatives, such as gangs.
Larger Context of Pulls and Pushes	Decker and Van Winkle	Pulls relate to the attractiveness of gangs and pushes come from the social, economic, and cultural forces of the larger society.

Moreover, Decker and Van Winkle stated that an explanation of why youths join gangs must be seen in the larger context of pulls and pushes.[73] Pulls relate to the attractiveness and benefits that the gang is perceived to offer a youth, and the benefits frequently cited are enhanced prestige or status among friends, excitement, and monetary profits from drugs. The pushes of gang membership come from the social, economic, and cultural forces of the larger society. See Table 9–3 for a summary of the theories of why juveniles join gangs.

▶ Delinquency Across the Life Course: Gang Membership

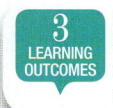

3 LEARNING OUTCOMES — Describe how the life-course perspective views gang membership.

The life-course perspective offers a number of insights regarding the study of gangs and their members. The most basic is that gang membership can be thought of as a trajectory, with some youngsters entering it and others avoiding it. Those who do enter it stay for varying lengths of time and become more or less involved in gang activities and behaviors. If gang membership is conceived as a trajectory with behavioral consequences, why some people enter it and some do not is an important consideration. The life-course perspective is a reminder that the origins of gang membership are found in several domains; are multidimensional; and include childhood risk factors, the social structural position of the family, family relationships, and unfolding influences of adolescence. Moreover, the life-course orientation suggests that for many people gang membership may act as a turning point with the potential to alter or redirect basic life-course pathways. Finally, the life-course perspective suggests that the duration of gang membership should intensify its consequences.[74]

Thornberry and colleagues contributed an important life-course orientation in their analysis of the gang behavior of

> **Gang membership exhibits a trajectory, with some youngsters entering it and others avoiding it.**

Rochester youths as they aged into their young adult years. Following the sample in the Rochester Youth Development Study from ages 13 to 22, these researchers were able to separate selection effects (the extent to which delinquents seek out the gang) from facilitation effects (the extent to which the gang fosters delinquent behavior in its members). They have done this analysis for a variety of illegal behaviors related to gang activity, delinquency, drug use, drug selling, violence, and gun carrying and use, and have found that gang membership seems to have a pronounced impact on facilitating all of these behaviors.[75]

Thornberry and colleagues also explored the longer-term consequences of joining a street gang. Does involvement in this strongly deviant form of adolescent social network exact a toll in the later life of the person, or is gang membership merely a transitory adolescent phenomenon with few (if any) long-term consequences?

▶ Delinquency and Social Policy: Prevention and Control of Youth Gangs

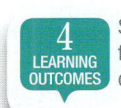

4 LEARNING OUTCOMES — Summarize strategies for preventing and controlling gangs.

Irving Spergel and colleagues' report on 45 cities with gang problems identified five strategies of intervention: (1) community organization, mobilization, and networking; (2) social intervention, focusing on individual behavioral and value change; (3) opportunities provision, emphasizing the improvement of basic education, training, and job openings for youths; (4) suppression, focusing on arrest, incarceration, monitoring, and supervision of gang members; and (5) organizational development and change, or the creation of special units and procedures.[76]

In examining the implementation of these strategies, Spergel and colleagues found that suppression was most frequently used (44 percent), followed by social intervention (31.5 percent), organizational development (10.9 percent), community organization (8.9 percent), and opportunities provision (4.8 percent).[77] Community organization was more likely to be used by programs in emerging gang cities, whereas social intervention and opportunity provision tended to be the favored strategic approaches in cities with chronic gang problems, but only 17 of the 45 cities saw any evidence of improvement in their gang situation.[78]

Spergel and colleagues, in developing a model for predicting general effectiveness in intervention strategies, stated the following:

> A final set of analyses across all cities [indicates] that the primary strategies of community organization and provision of opportunity along with maximum participation by key community actors [are] predictive of successful efforts at reducing the gang problem.[79]

Spergel and colleagues expanded their approach into the Comprehensive Community-Wide Approach to Gang Prevention, Intervention, and Suppression Program. This model contains several program components for the design and mobilization of community efforts by school officials, employers, street outreach workers, police, judges, prosecutors, probation and parole officers, and corrections officers.[80] The Gang Violence Reduction Program, an early pilot of this model, was implemented in Chicago, and after three years of program operations, the areas assessed in the preliminary evaluation of this project—lower levels of gang violence, few arrests for serious gang crimes, and hastened departures of youths from gang activities—were positive among the targeted group.[81]

The program was later implemented in five jurisdictions: Mesa, Arizona; Tucson, Arizona; Riverside, California; Bloomington, Illinois; and San Antonio, Texas.[82] These sites initially undertook the process of community mobilization as they identified or assessed the nature and extent of the gang problem; they then planned for program development and implementation in a problem-solving framework. It was not long thereafter that they began to implement appropriate interrelated strategies to target gang violence and its causes while they continued to reassess the changing nature and extent of the gang problem. Their strategies consisted of a combination of community mobilization, social intervention and outreach, provision of social and economic opportunities for youths, suppression or social control, and organizational change and development.[83]

What these efforts by Spergel and colleagues demonstrate is that only an integrated, multidimensional community-oriented effort is likely to have any long-term effect in preventing and controlling gangs in the United States. Such gang prevention, intervention, and control models must have several components: (1) The community must take responsibility for developing and implementing the model; (2) the model must take very seriously the structural hopelessness arising from the unmet needs of underclass children; (3) prevention programs, especially in the first six years of school, must be emphasized; (4) supporters must coordinate all the gang intervention efforts taking place in a community; and (5) sufficient financial resources must be available to implement the model. One of the exciting intervention efforts with gangs is found in Homewood Industries and the work of Father Greg Boyle; see Exhibit 9–1.

EXHIBIT 9–1 Father Greg Boyle, S. J., A Man with a Vision

One of the most remarkable and influential people who has ever worked in gang intervention is Father Greg, as he is known. He was born in Los Angeles, one of eight children, and after graduating from high school in Los Angeles, he decided to become a priest and was ordained.

When he was a priest in a small congregation in Dolores Mission Church, Father Greg and the local community developed positive alternatives to gang membership, including establishing a day-care program and an elementary school and finding legitimate employment for youth.

In 1982, as a response to civil unrest in Los Angeles, Father Greg launched the first business, Homeboy Bakery. One of its purposes was to enable gang members to work side by side. The success of the bakery laid the groundwork for other businesses that followed.

Father Greg is a nationally known speaker, and in 2005 was a featured speaker at the White House Conference on Youth at the personal invitation of Mrs. George Bush. In addition to all the committees he serves on, he has received much recognition and many awards, including the California Peace Prize, on behalf of Homeboy Industries and for his work with former gang members. In 2008, he received the Civic Metal of Honor from the Los Angeles Chamber of Commerce. In 2010, he published *Tattoos on the Heart: The Power of Boundless Compassion*, recalling his 20 years in the barrio of Los Angeles.

Father Greg, like others across the nation, is attempting to make a difference by giving gang youth hope and providing a means of support for them to leave the gang.

Source: Carol Ann Morrow, "Jesuit Greg Boyle, Gang Priest," *St. Anthony Messenger*, August, 1999, http://www.americancatjoc.org/Messenger/Aug1999/feature1.asn (accessed July 18, 2014).

Think About It...

Membership in youth gangs can affect people long after they have grown up. What are some of the possible long-term consequences of membership in street gangs?

© Hemis / Alamy

THE CASE

The Life Course of Amy Watters, Age 14

Amy soon learned that her new boyfriend, CJ, was a member of a street gang whose influence extended throughout the school. The gang was called the Splitter Boyz, and rumor had it that the Boyz made a lot of money by selling marijuana and other drugs to students throughout the city. Most sales took place during the school day and handoffs of money and drugs were concealed in exchanges of backpacks, lunches, and homework folders—and even secreted into laptops, iPads, and the like.

Amy soon learned that the Boyz were led by a man called Jake. Jake, whom CJ had never actually met, was said to be in his 30s and to be wealthy beyond belief. "He can buy anything—or ANYONE—he wants," CJ told her. "I'm going to be like that some day," he said. Right now, however, CJ was pretty low in the gang's hierarchy, and was striving to work his way up. CJ's assignment, said to have been handed down directly from Jake, was to turn as many of the school's football team players into regular customers as he could. Thanks to CJ, marijuana was soon the recreational drug of choice at team parties and pep rallies, although one golden rule remained: "No smoking before games," CJ told her. "Sex," he told her, "well, now that's a different story."

Other than marijuana, some team members were anxious to purchase steroids, which CJ made available to them at what he called "discount prices." Amy once asked CJ if he ever used steroids. "Hell no," he answered. "Who knows what's in that sh*t!"

Discuss

1. Why is CJ affiliated with a gang? Generally speaking, what is the attraction of street gangs for young people? How do gangs contribute to delinquency?

Learn more on the Web:

- National Gang Center: http://www.nationalgangcenter.gov

Follow the continuing Amy Watters saga in the next chapter.

CHAPTER 9 Gangs and Delinquency

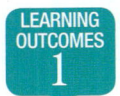

Summarize what is known about the nature and extent of gang activity in the United States.

The extent of gang activity, according to the 2011 National Youth Gang Survey, was an estimated 782,500 gang members and 29,900 gangs throughout the United States. In cities with populations larger than 50,000, gangs have remained about the same in size, but gangs have decreased in numbers in smaller communities.

1. Why do so many adolescents find gang membership attractive?
2. Why has the appeal of gangs apparently declined in small communities?
3. Why are so many gangs involved in illegal activities?
4. How might a member of a gang from one community interest youths in an area without gangs to become involved in gang activity?

crack A less expensive but more potent form of cocaine.

gang A group of youths who are bound together by mutual interests, have identifiable leadership, and act in concert to achieve a specific purpose that generally includes the conduct of illegal activity.

emerging gang Any youth gang that formed in the late 1980s and early 1990s in communities across the nation and that is continuing to evolve.

Summarize theories of how gangs form.

The classical theories of why youths join gangs, which focus on sociological variables, have been joined by more recently developed social disorganization application, underclass theory, competitive struggle in poor communities, and the context of pulls and pushes. Gangs are extending their influence in smaller communities, and generally move through the following stages of development: implementation, expansion conflict, organization and consolidation, gang intimidation and community reaction, expansion of drug markets, gang takeover, and community deterioration.

1. Which of the theories discussed in this section do you think offers the best explanation as to why youths become involved in gangs?
2. What are the stages of gang formation that have been identified?

Describe how the life-course perspective views gang membership.

The life-course perspective offers a number of insights regarding the study of gangs and their members. The most basic is that gang membership can be thought of as a trajectory, with some youngsters entering it and others avoiding it. Those who do enter stay for varying lengths of time and become more or less involved in gang activities and behaviors. The life-course perspective is a reminder that the origins of gang membership are multidimensional and include childhood risk factors, the social structural position of the family, family relationships, and the unfolding influences of adolescence.

1. How does the life-course perspective on delinquency differ from other perspectives?
2. Why do some people enter a trajectory that includes delinquency, whereas others do not?
3. How might life-course trajectories that involve delinquency be avoided?

Summarize strategies for preventing and controlling gangs.

Irving Spergel and colleagues identified five strategies of intervention from the 45 cities they studied: (1) community organization, mobilization, and networking; (2) social intervention; (3) opportunities provision; (4) suppression; and (5) organizational development and change. They found that suppression was most frequently used.

1. Why have communities relied on suppression as a major strategy for controlling gangs, especially emerging gangs?
2. How can social intervention be used to prevent gang development?
3. How can community mobilization be used to prevent gang development?

"For the foreseeable future, American youngsters will be aware of the psychoactive potential of many drugs and, in general, will have relatively easy access to them."

—*Monitoring the Future Survey*

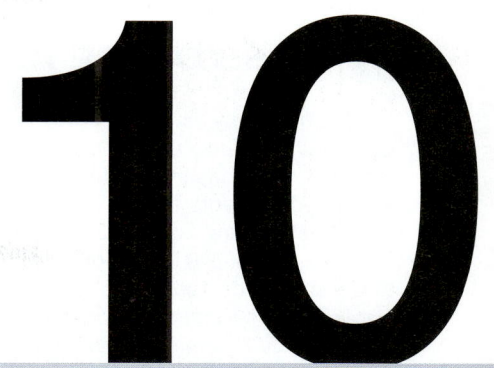

10

Drugs and Delinquency

1. Summarize recent trends in adolescent drug use.
2. Recall the main types of drugs used by adolescents.
3. Explain the relationship between drug abuse and delinquency.
4. Summarize the explanations for the onset of drug abuse.
5. Explain the impact drug use can have on a person's life.
6. Evaluate various efforts to prevent and control adolescent drug use.

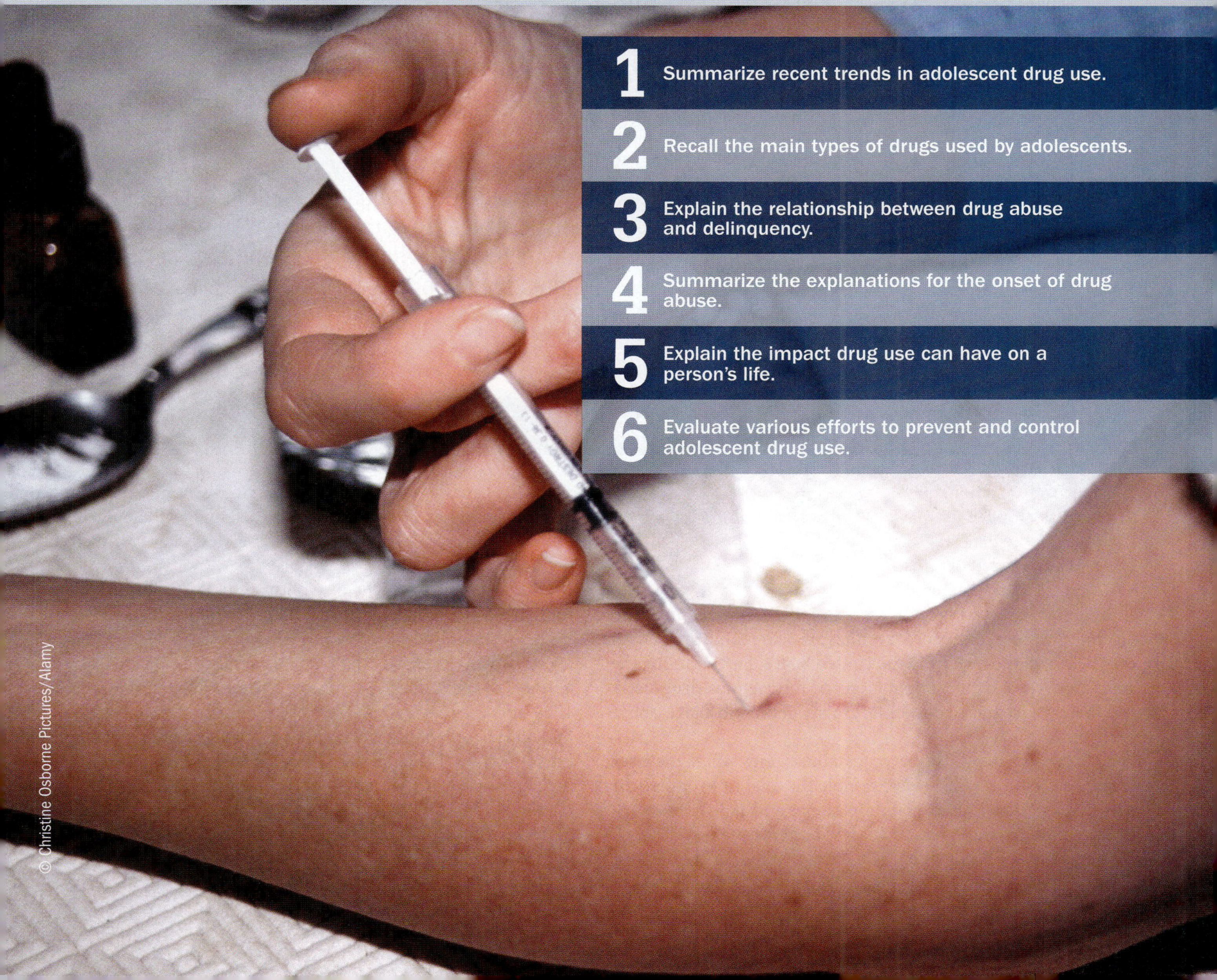

© Christine Osborne Pictures/Alamy

INTRO: SUBSTANCE ABUSE AMONG ADOLESCENTS

A recent report by the Office of Juvenile Justice and Delinquency Prevention (OJJDP) drew attention to the fact that research has consistently found that substance abuse among adolescents is linked to serious juvenile offending.[1] That finding was further supported by research from the ongoing OJJDP-sponsored Pathways to Desistance study. The "pathways" study is a large collaborative, multidisciplinary project that is currently following 1,354 serious juvenile offenders (both male and female) ages 14 to 18 for seven years after their adjudication as delinquent. The study is exploring factors that lead youths who have committed serious offenses to continue offending, or to desist from offending. Some of those factors include individual maturation, drug involvement, life changes, and involvement with the criminal justice system. A significant major finding of the study to date is that substance-abuse treatment reduces both the use of illegal substances and criminal offending.

The adolescent offenders profiled in the Pathways to Desistance study initially self-reported very high levels of substance use and substance-use problems. The use of illegal substances was linked to other illegal activities that were also engaged in by the study participants. As such, substance abuse was found to be "a strong, prevalent predictor of offending." The presence of a drug or alcohol disorder and the level of substance use were both shown to be strongly and independently related to the level of self-reported offending and the number of arrests. "The good news," say researchers involved in the study, "is that treatment appears to reduce both substance use and offending." According to those authors, "Youth whose treatment lasted for at least 90 days and included significant family involvement showed significant reductions in alcohol use, marijuana use, and offending over the following 6 months."

A teenager smoking marijuana. Studies have consistently shown that drug use among adolescents is linked to more serious juvenile offending. What is the link between the two?

DISCUSS What is the likely connection between the use of illicit substances by adolescents and their involvement in delinquency? What can be done to break that connection?

Drug Use Among Adolescents

LEARNING OUTCOMES 1: Summarize recent trends in adolescent drug use.

Substance abuse among adolescents has dropped dramatically since the late 1970s.[2] The bad news is that drug use has significantly increased among high-risk youths and is becoming commonly linked to juvenile lawbreaking.[3] More juveniles are also selling drugs than ever before in the history of the United States. Furthermore, the spread of AIDS within populations of intravenous drug users and their sex partners adds to the gravity of the substance-abuse problem.[4]

Adolescent drug use becomes abuse only when the user becomes dysfunctional (for example, is unable to attend or perform in school or to maintain social and family relationships; exhibits dangerous, reckless, or aggressive behavior; or endangers his or her health). The drug-dependent compulsive user's life usually revolves around obtaining, maintaining, and using a supply of drugs.[5] And as this chapter will show, drug use not only causes harm in itself but also is closely linked to delinquency.

Society tends to focus on youths' use of harder drugs, although alcohol remains the drug of choice for most adolescents. Drug use among adolescents was extremely high during the late 1960s and into the 1970s, reaching epidemic proportions. Overall rates of illicit drug use appeared to peak sometime around 1979 and then leveled off, but even with the leveling off that took place, rates of illicit drug use among youths remained high for some time. Then, in 2001, there was a significant downturn in drug-use levels.[6] According to the most recent 2013 Monitoring the Future study, overall illicit drug use by youths continued to decline until 2009, after which increased use of some drugs began to occur.[7]

Alcohol remains the drug of choice for most adolescents.

Illicit drugs include marijuana/hashish, cocaine (including crack), heroin, hallucinogens, inhalants, and prescription-type psychotherapeutic drugs used for nonmedical purposes. In 2012, an estimated 23.9 million Americans aged 12 or older were current illicit drug users, meaning they had used an illicit drug during the month prior to the survey interview. This estimate represents 9.2 percent of the population aged 12 or older. The overall rate of current illicit drug use among persons aged 12 or older in 2012 (9.2 percent) was similar to the rates in 2009 to 2011 (ranging from 8.7 to 8.9 percent), but it was higher than the rates in the years from 2002 to 2008. In 2012, marijuana was the most commonly used illicit drug, with 18.9 million users. It was used by 79.0 percent of current illicit drug users. About two-thirds (62.8 percent) of illicit drug users used only marijuana in the past month. Also, in 2012, 8.9 million persons aged 12 or older were current users of illicit drugs other than marijuana (or 37.2 percent of illicit drug users aged 12 or older).[8]

The National Survey on Drug Use and Health documented increases in the specific categories of prescription drugs, marijuana, MDMA (Ecstasy), and methamphetamine. The increase in the use of illicit drugs was driven by a significant increase in current use of marijuana. See Figure 10–1, which gives details on users of an illicit drug in 2012.

In 2012, males had higher rates of illicit drug use among persons aged 12 or older than females (11.6 percent versus 6.9 percent). Males were more likely than females in the past month to use marijuana (9.6 percent versus 5.0 percent), but males and females had similar rates for stimulants, methamphetamine, and sedatives.[9]

Think About It...

Studies tell us that although fewer adolescents appear to be experimenting with drugs today than in years past, those who use them tend to do so more frequently. What attracts some young people to drugs?

Current drug use among persons age 12 years or varied by race/ethnicity in 2012. The lowest rate was among Asians (3.7 percent). Rates were 14.8 percent for persons reporting two or more races, 12.7 percent among American Indians or Alaska Natives, 7.8 percent among Native Hawaiians or Other Pacific Islanders, 11.3 percent among African Americans, 9.2 percent among whites, and 8.3 percent among Hispanics.[10]

Adolescents vary, of course, in terms of how frequently they use drugs and the type of drugs they use (Table 10–1). The variables of age, gender, urban or rural setting, social class, and availability strongly affect the types of drugs used and have some effect on the frequency of drug use. Some users take drugs only at parties and on special occasions, some reserve them for

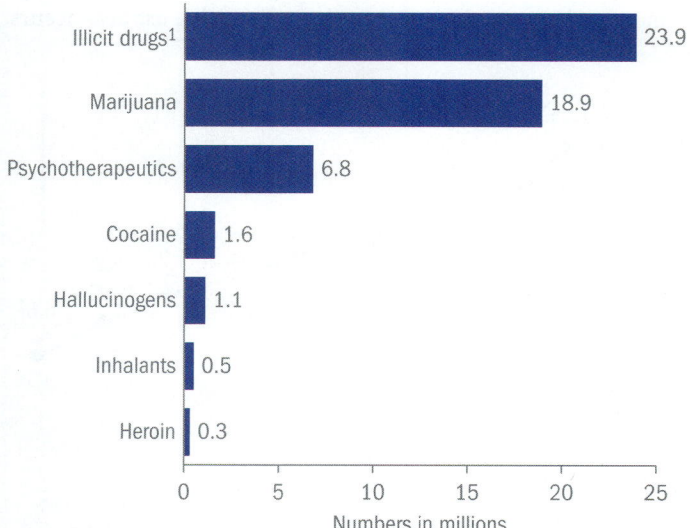

FIGURE 10–1 Illicit Drug Use 2012.
Note: [1] Illicit Drugs include marijuana/hashish, cocaine (including crack), heroin, hallucinogens, inhalants, or prescription type psychotherapeutics used nonmedically.
Source: Results from the 2012 National Survey on Drug Use and Health: National Findings (Rockville: Substance Abuse and Mental Health Services Administration, September 2013), p. 14.

TABLE 10–1 PERCENTAGES OF STUDENTS REPORTING USE OF SPECIFIC DRUGS, FOR GRADES 8, 10, AND 12 COMBINED, BY TYPE, 1999–2013

	1999	2001	2010	2013
Lifetime marijuana use	36.4%	35.3%	30.4%	32.0%
30-day marijuana prevalence	16.9	16.6	14.8	15.6
Lifetime cocaine use	7.2	5.9	3.8	3.1
30-day cocaine prevalence	1.9	1.5	0.9	0.8
Lifetime inhalant use	17.5	15.3	12.1	8.9
30-day inhalant prevalence	3.3	2.8	2.4	1.5
Lifetime heroin use	2.2	1.7	1.4	1.0
Lifetime methamphetamine use	6.5	5.8	2.2	1.5
Lifetime MDMA (Ecstasy) use	5.3	8.0	5.5	4.7

Source: Adapted from Lloyd D. Johnston, Patrick M. O'Malley, Jerald G. Bachman, and John E. Schulenberg, Monitoring the Future: National Results on Adolescent Drug Use (Washington, D.C.: National Institutes of Health, 2014), Tables 1, 3.

TABLE 10–2 PERCENTAGES OF HIGH SCHOOL STUDENTS REPORTING DRUG USE, 2013

Student Drug Use	Eighth Grade	Tenth Grade	Twelfth Grade
Past-month use	8.5%	19.4%	25.5%
Annual use	14.9	31.8	40.3
Lifetime use	20.3	38.8	50.4

Source: Adapted from Lloyd D. Johnston, Patrick M. O'Malley, Jerald G. Bachman, and John E. Schulenberg, *Monitoring the Future: National Results on Adolescent Drug Use* (Washington, D.C.: National Institutes of Health, 2014), Tables 5, 6 and 7.

Rates of illicit drug use in this nation remain high, especially among high-risk youths.

weekends, and some use drugs every day. Table 10–2 lists the percentages of students reporting drug use in the past month, in the past year, and over their lifetime.

Studies indicate that although fewer adolescents appear to be experimenting with drugs, those who use them tend to do so more frequently. Heavy users tend to be those who are male and white as well as youths who do not plan to attend college; and in schools, low achievers abuse drugs more than do high achievers.[11] Substance abuse is more common on the East and West Coasts than in the middle of the country.

In sum, although drug use among adolescents peaked during the late 1970s, rates of illicit drug use in this nation remain high, especially among high-risk youths.

▶ Types of Drugs

Recall the main types of drugs used by adolescents.

The licit and illicit drugs used by adolescents, in decreasing order of frequency, are alcohol, tobacco, marijuana, cocaine, methamphetamine, inhalants, sedatives, stimulants (amphetamines and hallucinogens), steroids, prescription drugs, and heroin. The licit drugs are those permitted for users who are of age (age 18 and older for tobacco and aged 21 and older for alcohol); the illicit drugs are those forbidden by law (exceptions being drugs prescribed by a physician and marijuana in jurisdictions that permit the use of this drug). A number of illicit drugs can take control of adolescents' lives when they become addicted. **Drug addiction**, according to noted drug-abuse researcher James A. Inciardi, is "a craving for a particular drug, accompanied by physical dependence, which motivates continuing usage, resulting in tolerance to the drug's effects and a complex of identifiable symptoms appearing when it is suddenly withdrawn."[12]

Alcohol and Tobacco

The seriousness of **alcohol** use among adolescents can be seen in the data from the 2014 Monitoring the Future research. According to this study, binge drinking (five or more drinks in a row during the prior two-week interval) has been a problem since the collection of data on adolescence and the use of alcohol.[13]

The use of cigarettes by adolescents is also a national public health concern. Due largely to efforts designed to steer young people away from the use of tobacco, cigarette smoking has declined sharply among American adolescents. From 2002 to 2012, the rate of current cigarette smoking among youths decreased for both males and females (Figure 10–2).[14]

Marijuana

Marijuana, made from dried hemp leaves and buds, is the most frequently used illicit drug. An interesting indicator of the popularity of marijuana is the number of street terms that have been used to designate the substance: *a-bomb, Acapulco gold, African black, ashes, aunt mary, baby, bammy, birdwood, California red, Colombian gold, dope, giggleweed, golden leaf, grass, hay, joints, Mexican brown, Mexican green, Panama gold, pot, reefer, reefer weed, seaweed, shit, stinkweed, Texas tea,* and *weed*.[15]

Cocaine

Cocaine, the powder derivative of the South American coca plant, is replacing other illegal drugs in popularity. Snorting (inhaling) is the most common method of using cocaine, but freebasing (smoking) cocaine became popular in the 1980s. Freebase cocaine is derived from a chemical process in which the purified cocaine is crystallized; the crystals are crushed and smoked in a special heated glass pipe. Smoking freebase cocaine provides a quicker, more potent rush and a more powerful high than regular cocaine gives. Intravenous cocaine use also occurs,

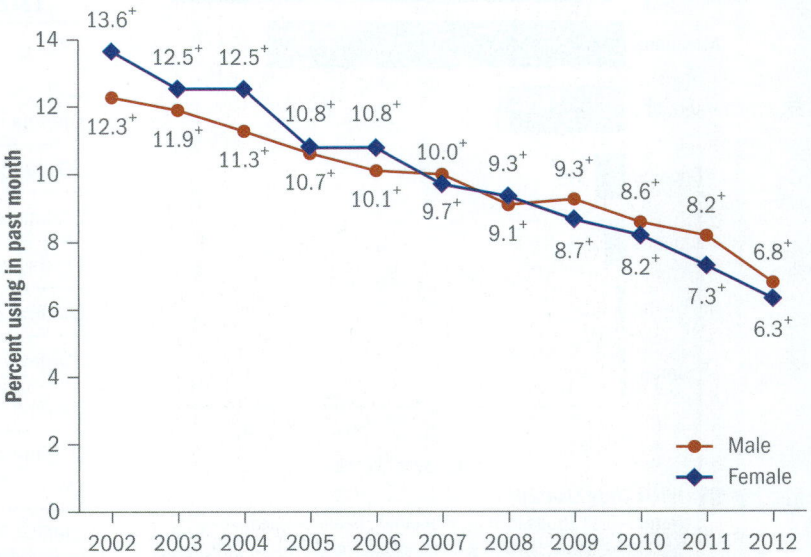

FIGURE 10–2 Cigarette Use Among Youths Aged 12 to 17, by Gender: 2002–2012.
Source: Results from the 2012 National Survey on Drug Use and Health: National Findings (Rockville: Substance Abuse and Mental Health Services Administration, September 2013), p. 46.

Dried marijuana flowers and stems. What are the effects of marijuana? Should it be classified as a "dangerous drug?"

Crack cocaine. Efforts have recently been made to legalize certain controlled substances. Would you be in favor of allowing recreational use of cocaine or crack cocaine in private?

producing a powerful high, usually within 15 to 20 seconds. The method of speedballing (the intravenous use of cocaine in combination with another drug) intensifies the euphoric effect but can be quite dangerous.[16]

Methamphetamine

Crystal methamphetamine. Why are some people drawn to illicit drug use?

Methamphetamine is a synthetic drug otherwise known by its street names: *chalk, crank, crystal meth, glass, ice,* and *meth* (to name just a few). It is a highly addictive stimulant that can be injected, smoked, or snorted, whose effects last up to eight hours (with an initial rush at the beginning and a less intense high for the duration). This drug makes a user feel awake, aware, and happy but also agitated and paranoid. Methamphetamine is one of many of the so-called club drugs. See Table 10–3 for the percentages of students reporting the use of methamphetamine in 2004 and 2013.

Inhalants

Many types of **inhalants** are used by adolescents, but what these drugs have in common is that youths have to inhale the vapors to receive the high that they seek. One frequently used inhalant is butyl nitrite, commonly called *RUSH*, which is packaged in small bottles and can often be found in adult bookstores as well as on the street.

The use of these drugs brings about a feeling of excitement that is often followed by disorientation accompanied by slurred speech and a feeling of sleepiness. The use of inhalants can also be followed by mild to severe headaches and/or nosebleeds. Chronic use of some inhalants is associated with neurological damage and injury to the liver and kidneys.[17]

Sedatives

Like inhalants, many different **sedatives**, or barbiturates, are used by young people. The common factors among all sedatives are that they are taken orally and that they affect the user by depressing the nervous system and inducing a drowsy condition.

Adolescents often abuse prescription drugs. Benzodiazepines (minor tranquilizers or sedatives) are among the most widely prescribed of all drugs. Valium, Librium, and Equanil are commonly prescribed for anxiety or sleep disorders, so to obtain them, some adolescents simply raid their parents' medicine cabinets. Adolescents can also get these prescription drugs from older teens or young adults or purchase them from Internet-based sources. The National Association of Boards of Pharmacy has identified about 200 websites that dispense prescription drugs but do not offer online prescribing services.

Amphetamines

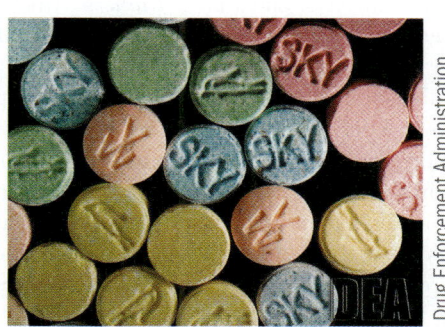

Amphetamines, or "uppers." Who's most likely to use non-prescribed amphetamines?

TABLE 10-3 PERCENT OF STUDENTS REPORTING METHAMPHETAMINE USE, 2004 AND 2013

	8th Grade		10th Grade		12th Grade	
	2004	2013	2004	2013	2004	2013
Past-month use	0.6%	0.4%	1.3%	0.4%	1.4%	0.4
Past-year use	1.5	1.0	3.0	1.0	3.4	0.9
Lifetime use	2.5	1.4	5.3	1.6	3.4	1.5

Source: Adapted from Lloyd D. Johnston, Patrick M. O'Malley, Jerald G. Bachman, and John E. Schulenberg, *Monitoring the Future: National Survey Results on Drug Use, 1975–2013*, Volume I (Washington, D.C.: National Institutes of Health, 2014), Tables 5, 6, and 7.

Amphetamines were first made in Germany in the 1880s, but it was not until World War II that they were used by Americans. In the 1990s, **Ecstasy**, the common name for MDMA, became popular on college campuses and with adolescents and was widely used at parties. Ecstasy is usually ingested orally in tablet or capsule form, is sometimes snorted, and is occasionally smoked; it is reported to produce profound pleasurable effects, such as acute euphoria and positive changes in attitude and self-confidence.[18] Ecstasy and various other substances are sometimes called **club drugs**.

Hallucinogens

A parade of **hallucinogens** has been available over the years to adolescents interested in embracing mind-expanding experiences. Phencyclidine (PCP), a nervous system excitant that has analgesic, anesthetic, and hallucinogenic properties, was introduced in the late 1960s and became popular during the 1970s. First marketed as the PeaCe Pill, PCP was also known as *angel dust, animal tank, aurora borealis, buzz, devil dust, DOA, dummy dust, elephant, elephant juice, goon, rocket fuel,* and *THC.* Concern over PCP mounted during the 1970s,[19] as its dangerousness became apparent.[20] Use of PCP declined during the 1980s, with national samples of high school seniors who had used PCP at least once dropping from 13 percent in 1979 to less than 3 percent by 1990.[21]

Anabolic Steroids

Currently, 100 different types of **anabolic steroids** have been developed, and each requires a prescription to be used legally in the United States. Street terms include *Arnolds, gym candy, juice, pampers, stackers,* and *weight trainers.* Anabolic steroids can be taken orally, injected intramuscularly, or rubbed on the skin in the form of creams or gels. Steroids are often used in patterns called *cycling,* which involves taking multiple doses of the drugs over a period of time, stopping for a period, and then starting again; users also often combine several different types of steroids in a process known as *stacking.* A further method of steroid use is called *pyramiding,* a process in which users slowly escalate steroid use, reaching a peak amount at mid-cycle and gradually lowering the dose toward the end of the cycle.[22]

Results from the 2013 Monitoring the Future study, which surveyed students in 8th, 10th, and 12th grades, showed that 1.1 percent of 8th graders, 1.3 percent of 10th graders, and

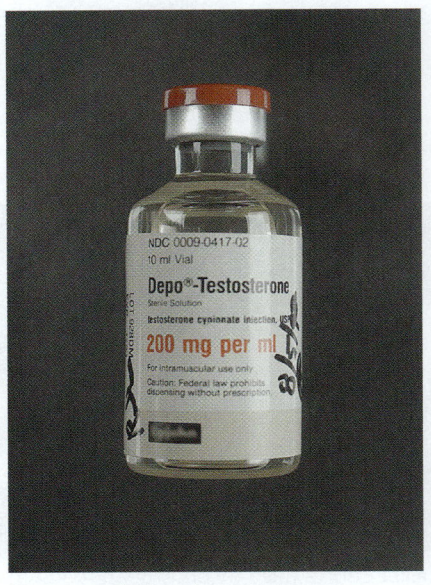

Pharmaceutical grade testosterone. Anabolic steroids, often used illegally in body building and to enhance athletic performance, have a number of legitimate medical uses. What are the dangers of unsupervised use?

2.1 percent of 12th graders reported using steroids at least once in their lifetime (see Table 10–4).

Heroin

Opium, which is derived from certain poppy species, is the source of heroin, morphine, paregoric, and codeine, some of which are still used medically today. **Heroin**, a refined form of morphine, was introduced about the turn of the twentieth century, and its street names include *black tar, boy, brown, H, harry, henry, horse, shit,* and *smack.*[23]

Chronic heroin use, unlike the use of most other drugs, appears to produce relatively minor direct or permanent physiological damage. Nevertheless, street heroin users typically neglect themselves and, as a result, report such disorders as heart and lung abnormalities, scarred veins, weight loss, malnutrition, endocarditis (a disease of the heart valves), stroke, gynecological problems, hepatitis, local skin infections, and abscesses.[24]

TABLE 10–4 REPORTED STEROID USE BY GRADE LEVEL

	8th Grade	10th Grade	12th Grade
Past-month use	0.3%	0.4%	1.0%
Past-year use	.06	.08	1.5
Lifetime use	1.1	1.3	2.1

Source: Adapted from Lloyd D. Johnston, Patrick M. O'Malley, Jerald G. Bachman, and John E. Schulenberg, *Monitoring the Future: National Results on Adolescent Drug Use* (Washington, D.C.: National Institutes of Health, 2014), Tables 3, 5, and 7.

Table 10–5 lists types of drugs along with a description of each.

▶ Drug Use and Delinquency

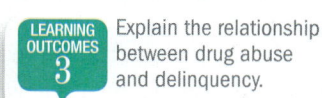

LEARNING OUTCOMES 3 Explain the relationship between drug abuse and delinquency.

An issue that has long been debated is whether drugs cause delinquency or delinquency leads to drug use, or whether some other factors precede both delinquency and the onset of drug use.[25] Considerable research has found that delinquency tends to precede the use of drugs.[26] Other research suggests that what might appear to be a causal association is in fact a product of shared antecedents.[27] It is possible that a common factor, or syndrome, exists that underlies both delinquent behavior and drug use; this common factor may explain the frequency and type of drug use.[28]

An important question is whether drugs cause delinquency or delinquency leads to drug use, or whether some other factors precede both delinquency and the onset of drug use.

Since the early 1990s, consensus has been increasing on the findings that explain the onset and continuing use of illicit drugs:

- There is widespread agreement that a sequential pattern of involvement in drug use during adolescence exists.[29] Denise B. Kandel and colleagues, using cross-sectional research and longitudinal data, proposed a developmental model for drug-use involvement: Alcohol use follows a pattern of minor delinquency and exposure to friends and parents who drink; the use of marijuana follows participation in minor delinquency and adoption of beliefs and values that are consistent with those held by peers but opposed by parents' standards; and adolescents' drug use proceeds to other illicit drugs if relationships with parents are poor and there is increased exposure to peers who use a variety of illegal drugs.[30]

- In examining drug use, it is important to identify in which of three major groups users belong. In the first group, youths or adults experiment once or twice and then discontinue drug use, whereas members of the second group continue drug use into young adulthood but do not allow drug use to interfere with their lives in any major ways; those in the third group become addicted or dependent on drugs, their entire lifestyle is likely to be designed around acquiring drugs daily, and they frequently commit crimes to maintain their drug supply.

TABLE 10–5 DRUG USE BY DECREASING ORDER OF FREQUENCY

Type of Drug	Description
Alcohol and Tobacco	Both are considered licit drugs because their use by juveniles is prohibited. Their wide use is considered a serious social problem.
Marijuana	The most frequently used illicit drug, marijuana is known by a variety of street names and is usually smoked.
Cocaine	Snorting (inhaling) is the most common method of using cocaine, but freebasing (smoking) cocaine has gained some popularity.
Methamphetamine	This highly addicted stimulant can be injected, smoked, or snorted. This is one of the many so-called club drugs.
Inhalants	With these drugs, youths need to inhale the vapors to receive the high they seek.
Sedatives	The common factor of sedatives is that they are taken orally and depress the nervous system, inducing a drowsy condition.
Ecstasy	Sometimes called a club drug, Ecstasy can be ingested orally, is sometimes snorted, and is occasionally smoked.
Hallucinogens	LSD was used in the 1960s and 1970s, but PCP, a nervous system excitant, has been more recently used by adolescents.
Anabolic Steroids	It is believed that steroids can produce an effect on muscle size; the 100 different types can be taken orally, injected intramuscularly, or rubbed on the skin in the form of creams or gels.

- Numerous risk factors appear to be related to delinquency and drug use. Early factors consist of perinatal difficulties, minor physical abnormalities, and brain damage, and later developmental risk factors are found in the family environment, including a family history of alcoholism, poor family management practices, and family conflict; other risk factors are early antisocial behavior and academic failure. Community risk factors include living in economically deprived areas and disorganized neighborhoods. According to J. David Hawkins, Richard F. Catalano, and Devon D. Brewer, the more of these risk factors a child has, the more likely it is that he or she will become involved in drug abuse.[31]

- There is little debate that youths who use hard drugs are more likely to engage in chronic delinquent behavior.[32] Elliott and Huizinga found that nearly 50 percent of serious juvenile offenders were also multiple drug users, that 82 percent of these offenders reported use (beyond experimentation) of at least one illicit drug, that rates of alcohol use among serious offenders were 4 to 9 times those of nonoffenders, and that rates of marijuana use among serious offenders were 14 times those of nonoffenders.[33] Jeffrey Fagan and colleagues' survey of inner-city youths also determined that heavy substance use was more prevalent and frequent among serious delinquents but that the type of substance used was more strongly associated with delinquency than was the frequency of drug use.[34]

▶ Explanations for the Onset of Drug Abuse

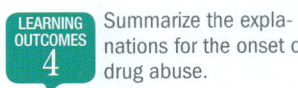

LEARNING OUTCOMES 4: Summarize the explanations for the onset of drug abuse.

Some adolescents never use drugs, others use drugs from time to time on an experimental or recreational basis, and still others go through a period of experimentation with substance use and become committed to continuous use. This latter group is physically and/or emotionally addicted to the continued use of drugs.

There are at least two issues that can help us understand juveniles who use drugs. The first is determining whether it is the onset of drug use, the escalation of drug use, the addiction to drug use, or the cessation of drug use that is being addressed. We might ask: Why do some juveniles never try drugs? Why do some juveniles experiment with drugs from time to time but do not become addicted? Why do other adolescents go from the beginning stages of drug use to more serious stages? Why do still other juveniles become addicted to drugs? Why are some of those who become addicted able to quit, whereas other addicts seem unable or unwilling to terminate drug use?

The second issue is that there is no single comprehensive picture of what causes adolescents' use of drugs. Simons, Conger, and Whitbeck made this point when they said that "while research has established a number of correlates of drug use, no theoretical model has been developed which specifies the causal ordering of these associations and explicates their relationship to each other."[35] To express this another way, we might be aware of many of the reasons why juveniles become involved in drug use, but we do not know how all of the pieces of the puzzle fit together.[36]

The following sections specifically address adolescents' initial use of drugs by focusing on theories that attempt to explain substance use among adolescents.

Cognitive-Affective Theories

Some theories have focused on how perceptions about the costs and benefits of drug use contribute to adolescents' decisions to experiment with these substances. Such models share two assumptions: (1) The decision to use substances rests in substance-specific expectations and perceptions held by adolescents, and (2) the effects of all other variables (for example, adolescents' personality traits or their involvement with peers who use substances) are mediated through substance-specific cognitions, evaluations, and decisions.[37] The theory of reasoned action, which holds that the most important determinant of a person's behavior is behavioral intent, is the most encompassing of these cost-benefit/decision-making models.[38]

Addictive Personality Theory

Another explanation for the onset and continued use of drugs says that the typical addict has an addiction-prone personality and suffers from some deep-rooted personality disorder or emotional problem.

Stress Relief Theory

The desire to get high, which is seen as a way to relieve stress, depression, or the boredom of everyday life, is common in adolescent peer culture. The desire to drink alcohol and get high is very much related to the desire to feel good, to be comfortable in social situations, and to gain acceptance in peer culture. This explanation for the appeal of substance abuse says that stress relief provides a sought-after high or peak experience.

> ### Think About It…
> Youths who use hard drugs are more likely to engage in chronic delinquent behavior than those who don't. Do drugs cause delinquency or does delinquency lead to drug use? Or do some other factors precede both delinquency and the onset of drug use?
>
>

Social Learning Theory

Social learning theory posits that an adolescent's involvement in substance abuse has three sequential effects: It begins with the observation and imitation of substance-specific behaviors; it continues with social reinforcement, such as encouragement and support for drug use; and it culminates in a juvenile's expectation of positive social and physiological consequences from continued drug use. These anticipated consequences might be primarily social in nature, such as acceptance or rejection by peers during experimental use and then become largely physiological in nature, such as positive or negative physiological reactions to the substances themselves during subsequent stages. Social learning theory essentially says that an adolescent who anticipates that using substances will produce more personal benefits than costs will be at risk for continued use.[39]

Social Control Theories

Travis Hirschi's social control theory and Hawkins and Weis's social development model both assume that emotional attachments to peers who use substances is a primary cause of substance abuse. Unlike social learning theories, however, these two approaches pay specific attention to weak conventional bonds to society and to the institutions and individuals who might otherwise discourage deviant behavior.[40] Hirschi asserted that the deviant impulses that most adolescents share are held in check or controlled by strong bonds to conventional society, families, schools, and religions; however, adolescents who do not have such controlling influences will not feel compelled to adhere to convention or to engage in socially acceptable behaviors.[41]

The social development model proposes that adolescents become attached to substance-using peers if they feel uncommitted either to conventional society or to positive role models. Unlike Hirschi's social control theory that focuses largely on social systems, the social development model focuses more on individuals, their social development and their social interactions. This focus shifts developmentally, with parents dominating the preschool years, teachers dominating the preadolescent phase, and peers dominating the adolescent stage.[42]

> **Adolescents become attached to substance-using peers if they feel uncommitted either to conventional society or to positive role models.**

Social Disorganization Theory

Social disorganization theory explains the onset and escalation of adolescents' drug use by claiming that a bleak economic environment for certain disenfranchised groups has created a generation of young adults in urban inner cities who regularly experience doubt, hopelessness, and uncertainty. According to this perspective, the hopelessness of the poor leads them to seek relief. Hence, drug use and alcohol abuse provide an immediate fix for hopelessness but, in the long run, create other problems.[43]

Integrated Theories

Delbert S. Elliott and colleagues offer a model that expands traditional strain, social control, and social learning theories into a single perspective that accounts for delinquent behavior and drug use.[44] They described the mechanisms by which neighborhood disorganization, attachment to families, and social values contribute to involvement with drugs.[45] This model was initially created to explain the causes of delinquency, but it was later more fully developed to explain adolescents' drug-using behavior.[46] See Exhibit 10–1, "Explanations for the Onset of Drug Abuse."

▶ Delinquency Across the Life Course: Drug Use

Two basic pathways are possible for substance-abusing youths. They may restrict themselves to substance abuse

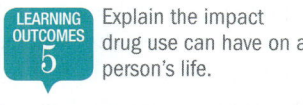

LEARNING OUTCOMES 5 — Explain the impact drug use can have on a person's life.

EXHIBIT 10–1 | Explanations for the Onset of Drug Abuse

Types of Explanation Description

- **Cognitive-Affective Theories** —These theories relate to how the perceptions about the costs and benefits of drug use contribute to adolescents' decision to experiment with these substances.
- **Addictive-Personality Theory** —The typical addict has an addiction-prone personality and suffers from some deep-rooted personality disorder or emotional problems.
- **Stress Relief Theory** —The desire to get high—as a means to relieve stress, depression, or the boredom of everyday life—is common in adolescent culture.
- **Social Learning Theory** —This theory postulates that an adolescent's involvement in substance abuse begins with observation and imitation of substance-specific behaviors, continues with social reinforcement, and cultivates in a juvenile's expectation of positive social and physiological consequences from continued drug use.
- **Social Control Theories** —Emotional attachment to peers who use substances is a primary cause of substance abuse.
- **Social Disorganization Theory** —The bleak economic environment has resulted in those situated in these settings to experience doubt, hopelessness, and uncertainty, and, as a result, they seek relief in drugs.
- **Integrated Theories** —Elliott and colleagues use strain, social control, and social learning theories to form a perspective that accounts for delinquent behavior and drug use.

and not become involved in other delinquent activities; these offenders may desist from substance abuse after their adolescent years or continue to use drugs as adults. Alternatively, substance-abusing youths who also participate in other delinquent activities may desist from one or both types of activity during adolescence or continue to be involved in one or both as adults.

There is some evidence showing that about two-thirds of substance-abusing youths continue to use drugs after reaching adulthood but that about half desist from other forms of criminality. Researchers in the 1980s found that drug abusers who persisted in both crime and substance abuse as adults typically came from poor families, did poorly in school, used multiple types of drugs, were chronic offenders, and had an early onset of both drug use and delinquent behavior.[47]

Marvin D. Krohn, Alan J. Lizotte, and Cynthia M. Perez, in their 1997 analysis of the Rochester data, found that the use of alcohol and drugs in early adolescence increases a youngster's risk of becoming pregnant or impregnating someone, becoming a teenage parent, dropping out of school, and prematurely living independently from parents or guardians; in turn, the process of experiencing these early transitions increases the chances that individuals will use alcohol and drugs when they become young adults.[48] Krohn and colleagues suggested that the cumulative impact of experiencing various early transitions may be detrimental to the successful movement, or transition, to adult status and adult roles.[49] It is not surprising that an early or unsuccessful transition in one area will have implications for other trajectories.[50] Off-time and out-of-order transitions can be especially disruptive because the individual may not be prepared for the added responsibilities and obligations that frequently accompany these transitions, and precocious transitions can further lead to problematic consequences because of the increased economic burdens and reduced economic prospects facing those who experience them. For example, teenage parenthood can disrupt the order of transitions by leading youths to enter full-time employment before completing high school, which can derail career development. The person who leaves school before graduation may not have any choice but a low-paying unskilled job, which in turn produces job instability and ongoing economic disadvantages.[51]

Gary M. McClelland, Linda A. Teplin, and Karen M. Abram highlighted several generalizations about drug use and adolescent development that are widely recognized and accepted:

- Substance use commonly follows a sequence from tobacco and alcohol to marijuana and then to more dangerous substances.
- Substance use and abuse that begin in early adolescence are associated with more serious delinquency and longer deviant careers, antisocial personality disorders in later life, and more numerous risky behaviors.
- Substance abuse is associated with poor academic performance.
- More severe substance abuse and dependence are associated with serious criminal offenses in general.
- Substance use and abuse are associated with higher rates of psychiatric disorders and with disorders of greater severity.[52]

Kandel and colleagues reported that significant status changes, including marriage and parenthood, were correlated with the cessation of marijuana smoking among users in their middle to late 20s.[53] L. A. Goodman and W. H. Kruskal found that reasons for cessation involved the imposition of both internal controls and external controls.[54] L. Thomas Winfree, Jr.; Christine S. Sellers; and Dennis L. Clason examined the reasons for adolescents' cessation of and abstention from substance use and determined that social learning variables clearly distinguished abstainers from current users, but they were less able to distinguish former users from current users or former users from abstainers.[55] Ryan D. Schroeder, Peggy C. Giordano, and Stephen A. Cernkovich investigated the impact of drug use on desistance processes using a sample of previously institutionalized youth and found that social network effects, particularly partner criminality, explain some of the negative impacts of drug use on life-course patterns of criminal offending.[56]

▶ Delinquency and Social Policy: Solutions to the Drug Problem

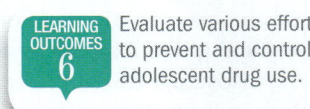

LEARNING OUTCOMES 6 — Evaluate various efforts to prevent and control adolescent drug use.

Prevention programs, treatment interventions, strict enforcement (Figure 10–3), and harm reduction are all possible means of controlling drug use among adolescents. Prevention and treatment appear to be the most effective means of controlling drug abuse, but there is abundant evidence showing that deterrence tactics, such as the federal "war on drugs" (involving mostly strict enforcement), have been largely ineffective with both juveniles and adults.

Prevention Programs

The 1990s saw dramatic developments in drug-prevention programs. The Center for the Study and Prevention of Violence at

FIGURE 10–3 Strict Enforcement.

the University of Colorado began an initiative called Blueprints for Violence Prevention, in which researchers evaluated 600 programs designed to prevent violence and drug abuse and to treat youths with problem behaviors.[57] The investigators were able to identify 11 model programs and 21 promising programs. Following are some of the more noteworthy: Life Skills Training (LST), which is designed to prevent or reduce the use of "gateway" drugs such as tobacco, alcohol, and marijuana;[58] (2) Midwestern Prevention Project (MPP), which is a comprehensive three- to five-year community-based prevention program targeting gateway use of alcohol, tobacco, and marijuana;[59] and (3) Project Toward No Drug Abuse (PROJECT TND), which targets high school youths who are at risk for drug abuse.[60] Significantly, Blueprints for Violence Prevention reported that both model programs and promising programs had positive outcome assessments when evaluated over a period of several years.[61]

Police departments across the country conduct at least three substance-abuse-prevention programs in schools: Drug Abuse Resistance Education (D.A.R.E.), School Program to Educate and Control Drug Abuse (SPECDA), and Project Alert. The D.A.R.E. program is a widely replicated effort to prevent substance abuse. Although Chapter 12 notes that recent evaluations of D.A.R.E. are less than encouraging, it is the most popular school-based drug-education program in the United States and operates in about 70 percent of our nation's school districts, reaching 25 million students; it has also been adopted in 44 other countries.[62] New York City's Project SPECDA, a collaborative project of the city's police department and board of education, is another highly praised drug-prevention program.[63] Project Alert, a program originating in middle schools in California and Oregon, appears to have had some success in teaching students to avoid drugs and to resist peer pressure to use tobacco and alcohol.[64]

Effective programs need to incorporate early childhood and family interventions, school-based interventions, and comprehensive community-wide efforts. The important dimension of drug-prevention interventions, as is continually emphasized throughout this text, is a multidimensional approach centering on the family, school, and community.

Treatment Interventions

Treatment for drug abusers takes place in psychiatric and hospital settings for youngsters whose parents can afford it or have the needed insurance benefits. Other youths, especially those substance abusers who have committed minor forms of delinquency, receive treatment in privately administered placements, which vary tremendously in the quality of program design and implementation. Substance abusers who are involved in serious forms of delinquency will likely be placed in county or state facilities whose basic organizational goals are custodial and security oriented, and they generally receive some substance-abuse counseling, especially in group contexts.

Substance-abusing youths with multiple typical problems may be more malleable than adult offenders, but there is little evidence that the majority of substance-abuse programs are any more successful than those for adult substance abusers. Élan in Maine; Rocky Mountain in Colorado; Provo Canyon in Utah; and Cascade, Cedu, and Hilltop in California are privately administered therapeutic schools or emotional growth programs that may be better than the average substance-abuse program for juveniles.[65]

Drug courts are another fairly recent treatment innovation for those who have a history of drug use. To address alcohol and drug problems, treatment services in drug courts have been based on formal theories of drug dependence and abuse. They also attempt to employ the best therapeutic tools and to provide participants with the opportunities needed to build cognitive skills. Research findings generally show that drug courts can reduce recidivism and promote other positive outcomes, but research has been unable to uncover which court processes affect which outcomes and for what types of offenders.[66]

The balanced and restorative justice model (discussed further in Chapter 11) has been used as a form of treatment intervention with drug- and alcohol-abusing adolescents. It forms the guiding philosophy in 12 states and builds on restorative justice conferencing that takes place in informal settings where voluntary negotiating encounters include victims, offenders, and their relevant communities.[67] Restorative justice conferencing can also use more coerced restorative obligations, such as restitution or community service imposed by formal proceedings. What makes these processes and obligations "restorative," rather than rehabilitative or retributive, is the restorative intent underlying their imposition.[68]

Drug and alcohol abuse interventions have also been developed in a number of community-based and institutional settings. Some training schools, for example, conduct group sessions for those with histories of drug use. A social worker may conduct ongoing drug- and alcohol-abuse groups, and members from outside groups, such as Alcoholics Anonymous (AA) or Narcotics Anonymous (NA), may come into the institution and hold sessions.

Strict Enforcement

The "war on drugs" has not been won with juveniles any more than it has with adults. A disastrous consequence of this "war" is that increasing numbers of minority youths who were involved in using or selling crack cocaine have been brought into the justice system for extended periods of time. Some have even argued that the war on drugs has been a factor contributing to the spread of youth gangs.[69] Strict enforcement, however, has seemed to make a difference in several ways:

- The destruction of overseas drug-producing crops has probably had some impact on the availability of drugs in the United States, raising prices and making some drugs harder to find.

- Heavy penalties associated with the sale of illicit drugs appear to have been at least somewhat effective in deterring both juvenile and adult offenders.

The "war on drugs" has not been won with juveniles any more than it has been with adults.

- Law enforcement's targeting of dealers has had some success in getting those offenders off the streets.
- The policing of the sale of tobacco products, especially cigarettes at convenience stores and other places, has made it more difficult for minors to purchase or obtain tobacco products.
- The strict enforcement of no-drug zones around schools has discouraged or at least reduced the number of persons trafficking drugs to school-age children.
- Strict enforcement of laws against adolescent drug trafficking at school and in neighborhoods may have reduced the availability of drugs to young people.

Harm Reduction

Harm reduction is an approach designed to reduce the harm done to youths by drug use and by the severe penalties resulting from drug use and sales. Numerous harm-reduction strategies have been employed:

- Programs in which health professionals administer drugs to addicts as part of a treatment and detoxification regimen
- Drug-treatment facilities that are available for those drug addicts wishing to enter treatment
- Needle-exchange programs that are intended to slow the transmission of HIV and that provide educational resources about how HIV is contracted and spread

Juvenile drug users generally find a wide variety of treatment programs and facilities. Treatment programs are usually more readily available to middle- and upper-class youths than to lower-class youths, partially because wealthier parents can afford to pay for the care of their dependent children. The legalized administration of drugs to addicts and needle-exchange programs are more typically found when working with adult drug users than with juveniles. See Table 10–6 for a summary of the types of efforts, as well as brief descriptions of the efforts and comments on their effectiveness.

TABLE 10–6 | PROPOSED SOLUTIONS TO THE DRUG PROBLEM

Type of Effort	Brief Description	Evaluation
Prevention Programs	More than 600 programs have been developed to prevent and treat drug abuse.	A few have promise, but most have been ineffective.
Treatment Interventions	These usually take place in psychiatric and hospital settings for parents who can afford it or have third-party insurance benefits.	Little evidence of being successful
Strict Enforcement	The "war on drugs" campaign waged against juveniles.	With juveniles, no evidence of success, but it has had some impact in deterring drug trafficking.
Harm Reduction	This approach was designed to reduce the harm done to youths by drug use and by the severe penalties resulting from drug use and sales.	Programs more widely spread with adults than with juveniles

THE CASE

The Life Course of Amy Watters, Age 15

Amy's father, Simon, had always been a drinker. He had consumed both alcohol and marijuana for as long as she could remember, and he was often tipsy or high, and sometimes clearly drunk. He made no excuses for his behavior, and frequently told Amy that his father had given him his first drink when he was only eight years old. Children who learned to drink early, he said, had far less trouble handling alcohol and other substances later in life than those to whom alcohol was forbidden.

One night when her father was clearly intoxicated, he asked Amy if she'd like to have a drink with him. Until now, he'd separated the part of his life that involved drinking from Amy—except, of course, for the unintended influence that it had had on her to see him drunk. Now, however, he told Amy that it was always nice to have a drinking partner, and that she was old enough to drink, anyway. Of course, alcohol was not new to Amy and she had sometimes engaged in binge drinking while away from home. Amy was no stranger to illicit drugs, either, having smoked marijuana and experimented with cocaine with her former boyfriend, Damon, on quite a few occasions.

So, after a few more words of encouragement from her father, she sat down in front of the television and started drinking Scotch—her father's drink of choice. As the evening wore on she became increasingly intoxicated and passed out on the couch.

She woke up the next day with a headache, but feeling strangely liberated—as though she had somehow entered an adult world in which she had the freedom to make choices previously unavailable to her. Or at least choices that were somehow now acceptable. Alcohol itself, she realized, was also liberating, and she vaguely remembered telling her father closely guarded secrets that she had kept to herself since running away.

Discuss

1. What kind of a role model is Amy's father? Why are alcohol consumption and delinquency closely associated?

Learn more on the Web:

- Studies have shown that children of heavy drinkers are at greater risk of having emotional problems than are children whose parents are not alcoholics. Moreover, most children of alcoholics have experienced various forms of neglect and abuse.
- Learn more about alcohol and crime by visiting the National Criminal Justice Reference Service at NCJRS.gov and reading the publication numbered NCJ 231685.

Follow the continuing Amy Watters saga in the next chapter.

CHAPTER 10 Drugs and Delinquency

LEARNING OUTCOMES 1

Summarize recent trends in adolescent drug use.

With a few exceptions—specific categories of prescription drugs, marijuana, Ecstasy, and methamphetamine—drug use continues to decline among adolescents in the United States.

1. Identify and describe recent trends in adolescent drug use.
2. What explains the recent trends in adolescent drug abuse?

LEARNING OUTCOMES 2

Recall the main types of drugs used by adolescents.

In decreasing order of frequency, the licit and illicit drugs used by adolescents are alcohol, tobacco, marijuana, cocaine, methamphetamine, inhalants, sedatives, stimulants (amphetamines and hallucinogens), steroids, prescriptions drugs, and heroin.

1. What drugs are most used by adolescents? Why are some more widely used than others?
2. How does marijuana affect the mind and body?
3. How does heroin impact the mind and body?
4. What are anabolic steroids, and why are they used?

drug addiction The excessive use of a drug, which is frequently characterized by physical and/or psychological dependence.
alcohol A drug made through a fermentation process that relaxes inhibitions.
marijuana The most frequently used illicit drug; usually smoked, it consists of dried hemp leaves and buds.
cocaine A coca extract that creates mood elevation, elation, grandiose feelings, and feelings of heightened physical prowess.
methamphetamine A synthetic drug that is a highly addictive stimulant; it can be injected, smoked, or snorted.
inhalant A volatile liquid that gives off a vapor, which is inhaled, producing short-term excitement and euphoria followed by a period of disorientation.
sedative A drug that is taken orally and affects the user by depressing the nervous system, causing drowsiness.
amphetamine A stimulant drug that occurs in a variety of forms.
Ecstasy A form of amphetamine (MDMA) that began to be used by adolescents in the United States in the 1980s and 1990s and is now rather widespread.
club drug A synthetic psychoactive substance often found at nightclubs, bars, raves, and dance parties. Club drugs include MDMA (Ecstasy), ketamine, methamphetamine (meth), GBL (gamma-Butyrolactone), gamma-Hydroxybutyrate, phencyclidine (PCP), and Rohypnol.
hallucinogen A drug that causes perceptual distortions of time and place, including possible visual and auditory hallucinations.
anabolic steroid A drug derived from the male sex hormone testosterone; often used as a performance enhancer or to build muscle mass.
heroin A refined form of morphine that was introduced around the beginning of the twentieth century.

LEARNING OUTCOMES 3

Explain the relationship between drug abuse and delinquency.

The relationship between drug abuse and delinquency is complex but there seems to be a sequential pattern of involvement in drug use during adolescence. Adolescents vary in the frequency with which they use drugs, and certain risk factors appear to be related to drug abuse. Moreover, adolescents who use hard drugs appear to be those most likely to be involved in chronic delinquent behavior.

1. What is the relationship between drug use and delinquency?
2. What are some risk factors associated with drug use among adolescents?
3. What is the relationship between the use of hard drugs and chronic delinquency?

LEARNING OUTCOMES 4

Summarize the explanations for the onset of drug abuse.

The explanations for the onset of drug abuse include cognitive-affect theories, addictive personality theory, stress relief theory, social learning theory, social control theories, social disorganization theory, and integrated theories.

1. What are the various theories for the onset of drug use among adolescents and adults? In your mind, what theory makes the most sense? Why?
2. How does social learning theory explain the onset of drug use?
3. How does social disorganization theory explain the onset of drug use among adolescents?

LEARNING OUTCOMES 5

Explain the impact drug use can have on a person's life.

The impact that drug use can have on a person's life not only includes present dysfunction but also its destructiveness over the span of the life course.

1. Why is drug use frequently so destructive over a person's life course?
2. How does illegal drug use impact the life of a juvenile?

LEARNING OUTCOMES 6

Evaluate various efforts to prevent and control adolescent drug use.

Of the various efforts to prevent and control drug abuse, consisting of prevention programs, treatment interventions, strict enforcement, and harm reduction, none has been particularly effective in treating the individual problem of drug abuse but some have had some impact on reducing the availability of drugs.

1. What approaches have been tried to solve the drug problem? Which one appears to have the greatest promise? Explain your answer.
2. How do drug-prevention programs differ from strict enforcement strategies?
3. What do harm reduction programs focus on?

11

An Overview of Juvenile Justice in America

> "The overarching goal of the juvenile justice system is to support prosocial development of youth who become involved in the system and thereby ensure the safety of communities."
>
> —National Research Council (2014)

1. Summarize the development of the juvenile justice system.
2. Identify examples of prevention programs.
3. Identify examples of diversion programs.
4. Explain the structure of today's juvenile justice system.
5. Summarize the stages of delinquency case processing.
6. Compare the basic correctional models of juvenile justice.
7. Identify therapeutic methods used in juvenile facilities.
8. Summarize attempts that have been made to address minority overrepresentation in the juvenile justice process.
9. Describe some comprehensive delinquency prevention strategies.
10. Summarize possible future trends in juvenile justice.

INTRO: RISK ASSESSMENT AND JUVENILE DETENTION

In 2011, the New York–based Vera Institute of Justice released a report on New York City's risk assessment instrument (RAI), a tool that had been created in 2007 to help family court judges make informed decisions about whether arrested youth are likely to reoffend or fail to appear if allowed to go home before their cases could be adjudicated in court. The Vera study came amidst a crisis in the city's ability to place children awaiting final disposition by the court. The crisis began in 2006, when the New York City Department of Probation shut down the city's only alternative to juvenile detention—a program that provided schooling, counseling, and supervision to youths who had been ordered to remain at home until their cases had been heard. That program had been built around alternative to detention (ATD) centers, which operated daily from eight in the morning until four o'clock in the afternoon. The ATDs closed, however, after claims that they were not reaching the right juveniles, and that youths were being held in the program for much longer than needed. The city's juvenile court judges were left with no alternative but to detain offenders whom they deemed at-risk youth prior to adjudicatory hearings.

Five years after the closing of the ATD centers, the Vera report found that under the new RAI, "the overall rate of rearrest for youth during the time their cases are pending . . . dropped by about one-third." Researchers also noted that far fewer low-risk youth were being ordered into detention at their first court appearance. "The RAI," says

A juvenile in detention. What alternatives to detention might be available to juveniles processed by the justice system?

Annie Salsich, director of Vera's Center on Youth Justice, "gives judges objective data to consider when making detention decisions."[1]

DISCUSS What is meant by "alternatives to juvenile detention"? What kinds of programs might be included under this rubric? When should such alternatives be employed?

▶ Development of the Juvenile Justice System

1 LEARNING OUTCOMES Summarize the development of the juvenile justice system.

Society has long considered how best to process and treat juvenile offenders. One of the most significant questions has been how to determine at what age a person is able to form the mental intent necessary for the commission of a crime. Some observers suggest children are too immature to form the "evilness" required to plan and commit certain acts of violence and therefore deserve compassion.[2] However, in support of the position of "get tough with juveniles," the argument is frequently made that society has some 15-, 16-, and 17-year-old youthful offenders who function on adult levels; traditional treatment, this position contends, does not hold much promise in dealing with these kids.

The juvenile justice system is responsible for controlling and correcting the behavior of law-violating juveniles. The system's inability to accomplish its basic mission has resulted in massive criticism from all sides. Indeed, both liberals and conservatives want to reduce the scope of the juvenile court's responsibilities: Conservatives want to refer serious youthful offenders to the adult court, whereas some liberals recommend divesting the juvenile court of its jurisdiction over status offenders.

The juvenile justice system is responsible for controlling and correcting the behavior of law-violating juveniles.

This chapter examines juvenile justice through the lenses of the past, the present, and the future. Beginning with the early handling of juveniles and the development of juvenile justice in the United States, the juvenile justice system's structures, functions, and issues are discussed, and future possibilities are suggested.

Colonial Period (1636–1823)

The history of juvenile justice in the United States actually begins in the colonial period. The colonists saw the family as a source and primary means of social control of children. In colonial times the law was uncomplicated, and the family was the cornerstone of the community.[3] Town fathers, magistrates, sheriffs, and watchmen were the only law enforcement officials, and the only penal institutions were jails for prisoners awaiting trial or punishment.

TIMELINE

Timeline of Community-Based Corrections for Juveniles in the United States

1820s — **Superintendents of** houses of refuge had the power to release juveniles from the institution.

1840s — **States set up** inspection procedures to supervise those with whom juveniles were placed.

1841 — **John Augustus** began to supervise juvenile and adult offenders in Boston.

Juvenile lawbreakers did not face a battery of police, probation, or parole officers, nor would the juvenile justice system try to rehabilitate them; instead, young offenders were sent back to their families for punishment. If they were still recalcitrant after harsh whippings and other forms of discipline, they could be returned to community officials for more punishment, such as public whippings, dunkings, or the stocks, and in more serious cases, expulsion from the community or even the use of capital punishment.

Houses of Refuge

In the nineteenth century, reformers became disillusioned with the family and looked for a substitute that would provide an orderly, disciplined environment similar to that of the ideal Puritan family.[4] Houses of refuge were proposed as a solution; there, discipline was to be administered firmly and harshly. These facilities were intended to protect wayward children from "weak and criminal parents," "the manifold temptations of the streets," and "the peculiar weakness of [the children's] moral nature."[5] Houses of refuge reflected a new direction in juvenile justice, for no longer were parents and family the first line of control for children; the authority of families had been superseded by that of the state, and wayward children were placed in facilities presumably better equipped to reform them.

Houses of refuge flourished for the first half of the nineteenth century; but by the middle of the century, reformers were beginning to suspect that these juvenile institutions were not as effective as had been hoped. Some had grown unwieldy in size and discipline, care, and order had disappeared from most. Reformers also were aware that many youth were being confined in institutions—jails and prisons—that were filthy, dangerous, degrading, and ill equipped to manage juveniles effectively. A change was in order, and reformers proposed the juvenile court as a way to provide for more humane care of law-violating juveniles.

Origins of the Juvenile Court

The first juvenile court was founded in Cook County (Chicago), Illinois, in 1899 when the Illinois legislature passed the Juvenile Court Act. The *parens patriae* doctrine provided a legal catalyst for the creation of the juvenile court, furnishing a rationale for the use of informal procedures for dealing with juveniles and for expanding state power over children. *Parens patriae* was also used to justify the juvenile court's authority to determine the causes of delinquent behavior and to make decisions on the disposition of cases. The kindly parent—the state—could thus justify relying on psychological and medical examinations rather than on trial by evidence. Once the *parens patriae* rationale was applied to juvenile proceedings, the institution of the juvenile court followed.

In his book *The Child Savers*, Anthony Platt discussed the political context of the origin of the juvenile court, claiming that the juvenile court was established in Chicago and later elsewhere because it satisfied several middle-class interest groups. He saw the juvenile court as an expression of middle-class values and of the philosophy of conservative political groups. In denying

> **During the first half of the nineteenth century, houses of refuge reflected a new direction in juvenile justice; the authority of families had been superseded by that of the state.**

> **The first juvenile court in the United States was founded in Cook County (Chicago), Illinois, in 1899.**

TIMELINE

Timeline of Juvenile Institutionalization

1825 — **The New York House** of Refuge was opened.

1854 — **The cottage** system was introduced.

1850s–1860s — **Juvenile facilities** were called training schools or industrial schools.

1880–1899 — **The public became** disillusioned, realizing that training schools were primarily custodial institutions and not rehabilitative.

1869	1890	1950	1980s–present
The Commonwealth of Massachusetts established a visiting probation agent system that supervised youthful offenders.	**Juvenile probation was** established statewide in Massachusetts.	**The Highfields** Project was established.	**Retrenchment** took place in community-based corrections.

that the juvenile court was revolutionary, Platt contended that the behaviors the **child savers** deemed worthy of penalty—such as engaging in sex, roaming the streets, drinking, fighting, frequenting dance halls, and staying out late at night—were found primarily among lower-class children. Therefore, juvenile justice from its inception, he argued, reflected class favoritism that resulted in the frequent processing of poor children through the system while middle- and upper-class children were more likely to be excused.[6]

Emergence of Community-Based Corrections

The first application of community-based corrections for juveniles grew out of juvenile aftercare, or parole, used to supervise juveniles after their institutionalization. Such programs are nearly as old as juvenile correctional institutions. By the 1820s, superintendents of houses of refuge had the authority to release juveniles when they saw fit; some juveniles were returned directly to their families, and others were placed in the community as indentured servants and apprentices who could reenter the community as free citizens once they finished their terms of service. This system became formalized only in the 1840s, when states set up inspection procedures to monitor the supervision of those with whom youths were placed.

Juvenile **aftercare** was influenced by the development of adult parole in the late 1870s. Zebulon Brockway, the first superintendent of Elmira Reformatory in New York State, permitted parole for carefully selected prisoners. When they left the institution, parolees were instructed to report to a guardian on arrival, to write immediately to the superintendent, and to report to the guardian on the first of each month.

Juvenile aftercare programs spread throughout the United States in the early decades of the twentieth century and took on many of the features of adult parole. Juveniles were supervised in the community by aftercare officers, whose jobs were similar to those of parole officers in the adult system. The parole board did not become a part of juvenile corrections, for in more than two-thirds of the states, institutional staff continued to decide when youths would return to the community.

Probation, as an alternative to institutional placement for juveniles, arose from the effort of John Augustus, a Boston cobbler, in the 1840s and 1850s. Augustus, who is called "the father of probation," spent considerable time in the courtroom and in 1841 persuaded a judge to permit him to supervise an offender in the community rather than sentencing the offender to an institution. Over the next two decades, Augustus worked with nearly 2,000 individuals, including both adult and juvenile offenders. As the first probation officer, Augustus initiated several services still used in probation today: investigation and screening, supervision, educational and employment services, and provision of aid and assistance.[7]

Expansion and Retrenchment in the Twentieth Century

In the twentieth century, probation services spread to every state and were administered by both state and local authorities. The use of volunteer probation workers had disappeared by the turn of the twentieth century, only to return in the 1950s. Probation became more treatment oriented: Early in the twentieth century, the medical treatment model was used; later, in the 1960s and 1970s, probation officers became brokers who delivered services to clients. The upgrading of standards and training also was emphasized in the 1960s and 1970s.

Residential programs, the third type of community-based juvenile corrections to appear, had their origins in the Highfields Project, a short-term guided-interaction group program.

> **Probation as an alternative to institutional placement for juveniles arose from the effort of John Augustus, a Boston cobbler, in the 1840s and 1850s.**

1900–1950s	1960s–1970s	Late 1970s	Late 1980s–present
Training schools underwent a period of reform, especially with the introduction of varied methods of treatment.	**Training schools** came under great criticism for not reforming juveniles under their care.	**Training schools** underwent another period of reform.	**Training schools** became overcrowded, grew more violent, and confined increased numbers of minority youths.

Think About It...

The principles of the juvenile court are over 100 years old. What are those principles? Is it time to reconsider them?

Known officially as the New Jersey Experimental Project for the Treatment of Youthful Offenders, this project was established in 1950 on the former estate of Colonel and Mrs. Charles Lindbergh. The Highfields Project housed adjudicated youths who worked during the day at the nearby New Jersey Neuro-Psychiatric Institute and met in two guided-interaction groups five evenings a week at the Highfields facility. Similar programs were initiated in the 1960s across the nation. In the late 1980s and 1990s, a decline in federal funding, along with the "get-tough" mood of society, meant the closing of some residential and day-treatment programs. Although probation remained the most widely used judicial disposition, both probation and after-care services were charged to enforce a more hard-line policy with juvenile offenders. See the accompanying timeline of the most important events in the evolution of community-based corrections for juveniles.

Development of Juvenile Institutions

The development of the **cottage system** and the construction of these juvenile institutions outside cities were two reforms of the mid-nineteenth century. The cottage system, which was introduced in 1854 and quickly spread throughout the nation, housed smaller groups of youths in separate buildings, usually no more than 20 to 40 youths per cottage. Early cottages were log cabins; later cottages were built from brick or stone. Now called **training schools** or industrial schools, these juvenile facilities were usually constructed outside cities so that youths would be reformed through exposure to the simpler rural way of life. It was presumed that residents would learn responsibility and new skills as they worked the fields and took care of the livestock, and their work would enable the institution, in turn, to provide its own food and perhaps even realize a profit.

Twenty First-Century Changes

In spite of the improvements in many reform schools, as well as the truly experimental efforts in a few, the story of the twenty first-century training school is one of scaled-down prisons for juveniles. Chapter 14 documents how training schools have become overcrowded and violent. Members of minorities made up a greater proportion of the population of juvenile correctional institutions, especially for drug offenses. (See the accompanying timeline of juvenile institutionalization.)

▶ Juvenile Prevention Programs

The prevention of delinquency is certainly a desired goal. Three different levels of **delinquency prevention** have been identified. **Primary prevention** is focused on modifying conditions in the physical and social environment that lead to delinquency. **Secondary prevention** is intervention in the lives of juveniles or groups identified as being in circumstances that dispose them toward delinquency. Secondary prevention also takes place in diversionary programs in which youngsters in trouble are diverted from formal juvenile justice programs. **Tertiary prevention** is directed at the prevention of recidivism,[8] and takes place in traditional rehabilitation programs.

Promising Prevention Programs

The Blueprints for Violence Prevention study, developed by the Center for the Study and Prevention of Violence at the University of Colorado–Boulder and supported by the Office of Juvenile Justice and Delinquency Prevention, identified 11 model programs that have received rigorous evaluation.[9] The following discussion will briefly describe the 11 model programs.

Big Brothers Big Sisters of America (BBBSA)

With a network of more than 500 local agencies throughout the United States that maintain more than 145,000 one-to-one relationships between youths and volunteer adults, Big Brothers Big Sisters of America (BBBSA) operates as the best-known and largest mentoring program in the nation. The program serves youths ages 6 to 18, a significant number of whom are from single-parent and disadvantaged households. An 18-month evaluation found that, compared with a control group waiting for a match, youths in this mentoring program were 46 percent less likely to start using drugs, 27 percent less likely to start drinking, and 32 percent less likely to hit or assault someone. They also were less likely to skip school and more likely to have improved family relationships.[10]

Bully Prevention Program

This model program aims to restructure the social environment of primary and secondary schools in order to provide fewer opportunities for bullying and to reduce the peer approval and support that reward bullying behavior. Adults in the school setting are seen as the driving force of this program; the program seeks to ensure that adults in the school are aware of bullying problems and are actively involved in their prevention.[11] This program has proved effective in large samples evaluated in

> The development of the cottage system and the construction of juvenile institutions outside of cities were two reforms of the mid-nineteenth century.

Norway and South Carolina. In rural South Carolina, for example, children in 39 schools in grades 4 through 6 reported that they experienced a 25 percent decrease in the frequency at which they felt bullied by other children.[12]

Functional Family Therapy (FFT)

This is a short-term, family-based prevention and intervention program that has been successfully applied in a variety of contexts to treat high-risk youths and their families from various backgrounds. Specifically designed to help underserved and at-risk youth ages 11 to 18, this multisystemic clinical program provides 12 one-hour **family therapy** sessions spread over three months. More difficult cases may receive up to 30 hours of therapy.[13] The success of this program has been demonstrated and replicated for more than 25 years. Evaluations using controlled follow-up periods of one, three, and five years have demonstrated significant and long-term reductions in the reoffending of youths, ranging from 25 percent to 60 percent.[14]

Incredible Years: Parent, Teacher, and Child Training Series

The Incredible Years model program has a comprehensive set of curricula designed to promote social competence and to prevent, reduce, and treat conduct problems in young children. The target population of this program is children ages two to eight who exhibit or are at risk for conduct problems.[15] This program has received positive evaluations as far as meeting its original goals.[16]

Life Skills Training (LST)

LST's lessons emphasize social resistance skills training to help students identify pressures to use drugs. This intervention is meant to be implemented in school classrooms by teachers but also has been taught successfully by health professionals and peer leaders.[17] Using outcomes from more than a dozen studies, evaluators have found LST to reduce tobacco, alcohol, and marijuana use by 50 to 75 percent in intervention students compared to control students.[18]

Midwestern Prevention Project (MPP)

This project includes school normative environment change as one of the components of a comprehensive three- to five-year community-based prevention program that targets gateway use of alcohol, tobacco, and marijuana.[19] Researchers followed students from eight schools who were randomly assigned to treatment or control groups for three years and found that the program brought net reductions of up to 40 percent in adolescent smoking and marijuana use, with results maintained through high school graduation.[20]

Multidimensional Treatment Foster Care (MTFC)

For adolescents who have had problems with chronic antisocial behavior, delinquency, and emotional disturbance, MTFC has been a cost-effective alternative to group or residential treatment, confinement, or hospitalization.[21] Evaluations of MTFC demonstrated that youths who participated in the program had significantly fewer arrests (an average of 2.6 offenses versus 5.4 offenses) and spent fewer days in lockup than youths placed in other community-based programs.[22]

Multisystemic Therapy (MST)

Multisystemic Therapy, or MST, provides cost-effective, community-based clinical treatment to chronic and violent juvenile offenders who are at high risk of out-of-home placement. MST specifically targets the multiple factors contributing to antisocial behavior. The overarching goal of the intervention is to help parents understand and help their children overcome their behavior problems.[23] Program evaluations have revealed 25 to 70 percent reductions in long-term rates of rearrest and 47 to 64 percent reductions in out-of-home placements. These and other positive results were maintained for nearly four years after treatment ended.[24]

Nurse–Family Partnership

Formerly called Prenatal and Infancy Home Visitation by Nurses, this model program sends nurses to the homes of lower-income, unmarried mothers, beginning during pregnancy and continuing for two years following the birth of the child.[25] Follow-up showed that this program's positive outcomes had long-term effects for both mothers and children.[26]

Project Toward No Drug Abuse (Project TND)

Project TND targets high school youths (ages 14 to 19) who are at risk for drug abuse.[27] At a one-year follow-up, participants in 42 schools revealed reduced usage of cigarettes, alcohol, marijuana, and hard drugs.[28]

Promoting Alternative Thinking Strategies (PATHS)

A comprehensive program for promoting social and emotional competencies, PATHS focuses on the understanding, expression, and regulation of emotions. The yearlong curriculum is designed to be used by teachers and counselors with entire classrooms of children in kindergarten through fifth grade. Lessons include such topics as identifying and labeling feelings, assessing the intensity of feelings, expressing feelings, managing feelings, and delaying gratification.[29] Evaluations of this program have found positive behavioral changes related to peer aggression, hyperactivity, and conduct problems.[30]

These prevention programs are promising in their diversity and range of offerings. They work to prevent delinquency through family-, school-, peer-group-, and community-based interventions.

Diversion From the Juvenile Justice System

In the late 1960s and early 1970s, **diversion programs** sprouted up across the nation. *Diversion*, a term that refers to keeping juveniles outside the formal justice system, can be attempted either through the police and the courts or through agencies outside the juvenile justice system. The main characteristic of diversion initiated by the courts or police is that the justice subsystems retain control over youthful offenders, and youths who fail to respond to such a program

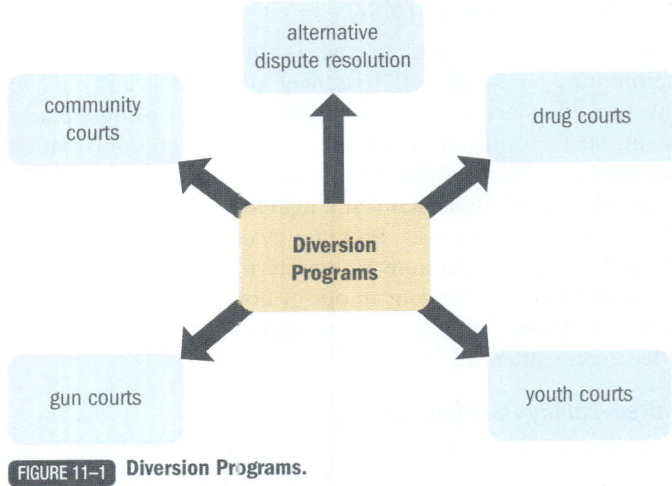

FIGURE 11-1 Diversion Programs.

Youth courts are juvenile justice programs in which youths are sentenced by their peers.

ages 11 to 17 years old who are charged with nonviolent misdemeanor offenses. The offender has typically acknowledged his or her guilt and participates in a youth court voluntarily rather than going through the more formal juvenile justice procedures.[31] In 2010, more than 1,050 youth-court programs were in operation in 49 states and the District of Columbia.[32] Annually, about 110,000 youths volunteer to hear more than 115,000 juvenile cases, and more than 20,000 adults volunteer to be facilitators for peer justice in youth-court programs.[33] Figure 11-3 shows four possible case-processing models used in youth courts.

Youth courts usually handle first-time offenders who are charged with offenses such as theft, misdemeanor assault, disorderly conduct, and possession of alcohol. The majority of these teen courts (87 percent) reported that they rarely or never accepted any juveniles with prior arrest records. The most common disposition used by these courts is community service, followed (in level of use) by victim apology letters (86 percent), apology essays (79 percent), teen-court jury duty (75 percent), drug/alcohol classes (59 percent), and monetary restitution (34 percent).[34]

usually will be returned to the juvenile court for continued processing within the system.

In the 1990s, new forms of diversion developed in the United States and included community courts, alternative dispute resolution, gun courts, youth courts, and drug courts (Figure 11-1). Youth courts and drug courts are described in more detail in the following discussion.

Youth Courts

Youth courts, also known as *teen courts, peer courts,* or *student courts,* are juvenile justice programs in which youths are sentenced by their peers (see Figure 11-2 for a history of youth courts). Established and administered in a variety of ways, most youth courts are used as a sentencing option for first-time offenders

Juvenile Drug-Court Movement

In 1989 the nation's first drug court began operation in Miami-Dade County, Florida. By 2003, approximately 300 juvenile drug courts had opened, and many more exist today. The juvenile drug-court movement is part of an expanding adult drug-court movement that has been stimulated by Title V of the Violent Crime Control and Law Enforcement Act of 1994, an act that authorizes the attorney general to make grants to

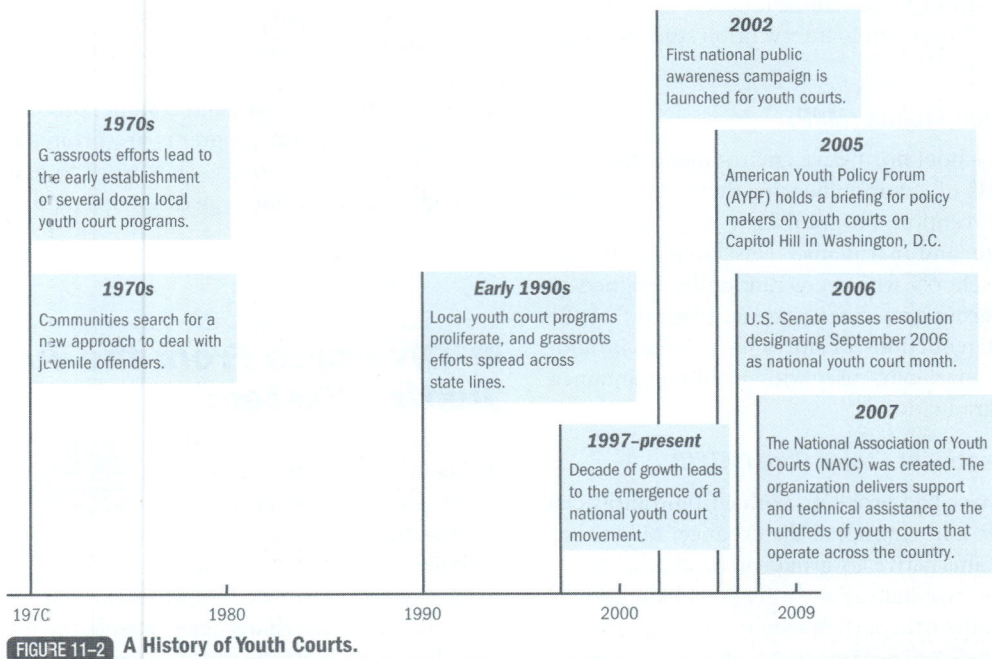

FIGURE 11-2 A History of Youth Courts.
Source: Adapted from Scott B. Peterson and Jill Beres, *Report to the Nation, 1993 to 2008: The Global Youth Justice Movement—15-Year Update on Youth Courts and Teen Courts* (Highland Hills: Global Issues Resource Center, 2008).

various agencies to establish drug courts. These agencies include states, state and local courts, units of local government, and Indian tribal governments.[35]

Certain strategies are common to juvenile drug courts as compared with traditional juvenile courts:

- Much earlier and much more comprehensive intake assessments
- Much greater focus on the functioning of the juvenile and the family throughout the juvenile court system
- Much closer integration of the information obtained during the assessment process as it relates to the juvenile and the family
- Much greater coordination among the court, the treatment community, the school system, and other community agencies in responding to the needs of the juvenile and the court
- Much more active and continuous judicial supervision of the juvenile's case and treatment process
- Increased use of immediate sanctions for noncompliance and incentives for progress for both the juvenile and the family[36]

The National Drug Court Resource Center says that 438 juvenile drug courts are in operation nationwide. The Escambia County Juvenile Drug Court in Pensacola, Florida, began operating in April 1996. It is a 12-month, three-phase approach to treating substance use and abuse, with Phase I lasting about two months, Phase II lasting four months, and Phase III lasting six months. The drug-court judge supervises treatment of up to 40 offenders by reviewing reports from treatment personnel to determine the need for either positive or negative incentives to encourage participation and involvement.[37]

The most positive characteristic of diversion programs is that they minimize the penetration of youthful offenders into the justice system, but empirical studies of diversion generally have not demonstrated that doing something (treatment or services)

1. *Adult judge.* An adult serves as judge and rules on legal terminology and courtroom procedures. Youths serve as attorneys, jurors, clerks, bailiffs, and so forth.

2. *Youth judge.* This is similar to the adult judge model except that a youth serves as the judge.

3. *Tribunal.* Youth attorneys present the case to a panel of three youth judges, who decide the appropriate disposition for the defendant. A jury is not used.

4. *Peer jury.* This model does not use youth attorneys. The case is presented to a youth jury by a youth or adult, and the youth jury then questions the defendant directly.

FIGURE 11–3 Youth Courts: Four Possible Case-Processing Models.
Source: Scott B. Peterson and Jill Beres, *Report to the Nation, 1993 to 2008: The Global Youth Justice Movement—15-Year Update on Youth Courts and Teen Courts* (Highland Hills: Global Issues Resource Center, 2008).

is necessarily better than doing nothing. Researchers warn that the overlooked negative consequences of diversion challenge the viability of this concept.[38] Some of these negative effects include widening the net of juvenile justice by increasing the number of youths under the control of the system, increasing the size of the system (budget and staff), ignoring clients' due process rights or constitutional safeguards, and labeling minor offenders.[39]

Juvenile Justice System Today

LEARNING OUTCOMES 4 Explain the structure of today's juvenile justice system.

Like most systems (private or public), the juvenile justice system is most concerned with maintaining its equilibrium and institutional survival. The system is able to survive by maintaining internal harmony while simultaneously managing environmental inputs. The police and the juvenile court, juvenile probation, residential and day-treatment programs, detention facilities, long-term juvenile institutions, and aftercare are all closely interrelated, so changes in one organization have definite consequences elsewhere within the system.

Structure and Functions

The juvenile justice system is made up of three basic subsystems—police, juvenile court, and corrections—that consist of between 10,000 and 20,000 public and private agencies, with annual budgets totaling hundreds of millions of dollars.

The juvenile justice system is made up of three basic subsystems—police, juvenile court, and corrections.

Think About It...

Teen courts are a relatively new innovation in which minor cases involving juvenile offenders are heard by their peers. What are the advantages of such courts?

© Marmaduke St. John/Alamy

Many of the 40,000 police departments across the nation have juvenile divisions, and over 3,000 juvenile courts and about 1,000 juvenile correctional facilities exist in the United States.[40] Of the 50,000 employees in the juvenile justice system, more than 30,000 are employed in juvenile correctional facilities, 6,500 are juvenile probation officers, and the remaining personnel are aftercare (parole) officers and staff members who work in residential programs. In addition, several thousand more employees work in diversion programs and private juvenile correctional systems.[41]

The functions of the three subsystems differ somewhat. The basic work of the police is maintaining order and enforcing the law. The function of maintaining order, which occupies most of police officers' time, involves such responsibilities as settling family disputes, providing emergency ambulance service, directing traffic, furnishing information to citizens, preventing suicides, giving shelter to drunks, and checking the homes of families on vacation. The law enforcement function requires that the police deter crime, make arrests, obtain confessions, collect evidence for strong cases that can result in convictions, and increase crime clearance rates. The police must also deal with juvenile lawbreaking and provide services juveniles need.

The juvenile courts are responsible for disposing of cases referred to them by intake divisions of probation departments (see Chapter 13), supervising juvenile probationers, making detention decisions, dealing with child neglect and dependency cases, and monitoring the performance of youths who have been adjudicated delinquent or status offenders. The *parens patriae* philosophy of the juvenile court charges the court with treating rather than punishing youngsters appearing before juvenile judges, but the treatment arm of the juvenile court goes only so far, and youths who commit serious crimes or persist in juvenile lawbreaking may be sent to training schools or transferred to adult court.

The corrections system is charged with the care of youthful offenders sentenced by the courts. Juvenile probation, the most widely used judicial disposition, supervises offenders released to probation by the courts, ensuring that they comply with the conditions of probation imposed by the courts and desist from delinquent behavior in the community. Day-treatment and residential programs (see Chapter 14) are charged with preparing youths for their return to the community, with preventing unlawful behavior in the program or in the community, and with providing humane care for youths directed to the programs. Long-term juvenile correctional institutions have similar responsibilities, but the officials of these programs also are charged with deciding when each youth is ready to be released to the community. Officials of long-term institutions must also ensure that residents receive their constitutional and due process rights. Aftercare officers, the final group in the juvenile justice system, have the responsibility of supervising youths released from long-term juvenile correctional institutions; like probation officers, aftercare officers are expected to make certain that youthful offenders fulfill the terms of their aftercare agreements and avoid delinquent behavior. (See Figure 11–4.)

▶ Stages in the Juvenile Justice Process

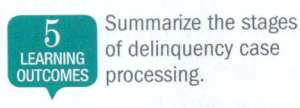

5 LEARNING OUTCOMES Summarize the stages of delinquency case processing.

The means by which juvenile offenders are processed by juvenile justice agencies are examined throughout this text. The variations in the juvenile justice systems across the nation make it difficult to succinctly describe this process, but Figure 11–5 provides a flowchart of the juvenile justice system that shows what these systems have in common. The process begins when the youth is referred to the juvenile court. Some jurisdictions permit a variety of agents to refer the juvenile, whereas in others the police alone are charged with this responsibility. The more common procedure is that the youth whose alleged offense has already been investigated is taken into custody by the police who have made the decision to refer the juvenile to the juvenile court.

The intake officer, usually a probation officer (see Chapter 13), must decide whether the juvenile should remain in the community or be placed in a shelter or detention facility. As indicated in Figure 11–5, the intake officer has a variety of options in determining what to do with a youth, but in more serious cases, the juvenile generally receives a petition to appear before the juvenile court.

The juvenile court judge (or the referee in many jurisdictions) hears the cases of juveniles referred to the court. If the juvenile is to be transferred to adult court, this must be done before any juvenile proceedings take place; otherwise, an adjudicatory hearing, the primary purpose of which is to determine whether the juvenile is guilty of the delinquent acts alleged in the petition, takes place. The court hears evidence on these allegations. *In re Gault* (see Chapter 13) usually is interpreted to guarantee to juveniles the right to representation by counsel, freedom from self-incrimination, and the right to confront and

The juvenile justice process begins when a youth is referred to the juvenile court.

Subsystem	Function
Police	Maintaining order and enforcing the law
Juvenile Court	Disposing of cases referred to them by intake divisions of probation departments, supervising juvenile probationers, making detention decisions, dealing with cases of child neglect and dependency, monitoring the performance of youths who have been adjudicated delinquent or status offenders
Corrections	Caring for youthful offenders sentenced by the courts, supervising offenders released to probation by the courts, and using day-treatment and residential programs, as well as short- and long-term juvenile facilities, to prepare youths for release to the community

FIGURE 11–4 Basic Subsystems of the Juvenile Justice System.

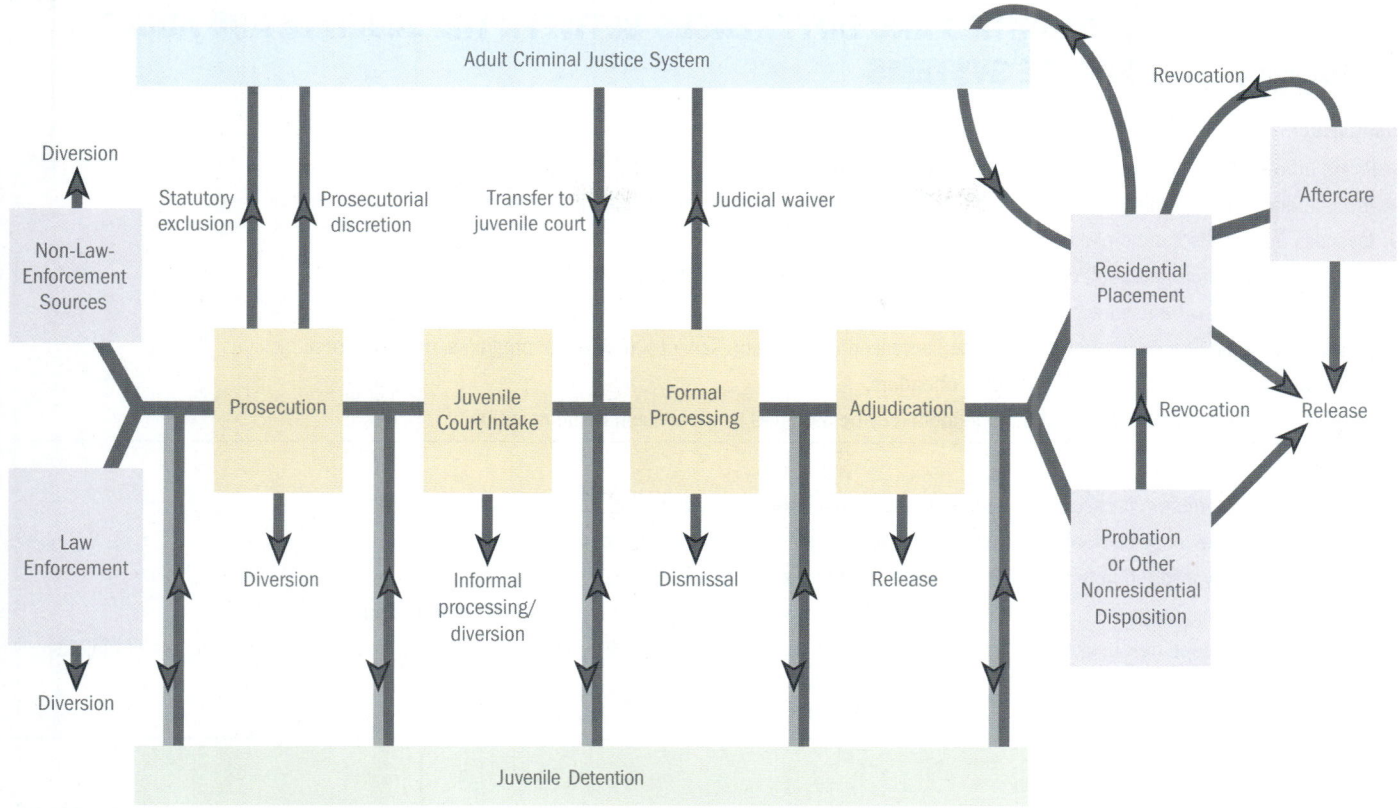

FIGURE 11–5 Stages of Delinquency Case Processing in the Juvenile Justice System.
Note: This chart gives a simplified view of case flow through the juvenile justice system. Procedures vary among jurisdictions.
Source: Adapted from Howard N. Snyder and Melissa Sickmund, *Juvenile Offenders and Victims: 2006 National Report* (Washington, D.C.: Office of Juvenile Justice and Delinquency Prevention, 2006), p. 205.

cross-examine witnesses, and some states also give juveniles the right to a jury trial.

A disposition hearing takes place when a juvenile has been found delinquent in the adjudicatory stage. Most juvenile court codes now require that the adjudicatory and disposition hearings be held at different times. The number of dispositions juvenile judges have available to them varies from one jurisdiction to the next. In addition to the standard disposition of warning and release, placement on juvenile probation, or adjudication to the department of youth services or corrections, some judges can place juveniles in a publicly or privately administered day-treatment or residential program, and some jurisdictions even grant juvenile judges the authority to send a juvenile to a particular correctional facility.

The juvenile adjudicated to a training school is generally treated somewhat differently in small states than in large states. In small states with one training school for males and (usually) one for females, a youth adjudicated to a training school usually is sent directly to the appropriate school, but large states that have several facilities for males and perhaps more than one for females may send the youth to a classification (or diagnostic) center to determine the proper institutional placement. Training school residents currently are not confined as long as they were in the past and frequently are released within a year. Institutional release takes place in a variety of ways, but the juvenile released from the training school is generally placed on aftercare status. To be released from this supervision, the juvenile must fulfill the rules of aftercare and must avoid unlawful behavior.

Comparison of the Juvenile and Adult Justice Systems

There is much similarity between the juvenile and adult justice systems (see Table 11–1). Both systems are made up of three basic subsystems (police, court, and corrections) and numerous interrelated agencies. The flow of justice in both is supposed to progress from law violation to police apprehension, judicial process, judicial disposition, and rehabilitation in correctional agencies. The basic vocabulary is usually the same in the juvenile and adult systems, but even when the vocabulary differs, the intent remains the same (see Table 11–2).

A disposition hearing takes place when a juvenile has been found delinquent in the adjudicatory stage.

TABLE 11-1 SIMILARITIES AND DIFFERENCES BETWEEN THE JUVENILE AND ADULT JUSTICE SYSTEMS

Similarities
- Police officers use discretion with both juvenile and adult offenders.
- Juvenile and adult offenders receive *Miranda* warnings and other constitutional rights at time of arrest.
- Juveniles and adults can be placed in pretrial facilities.
- The juvenile court and the adult court use proof beyond a reasonable doubt as the standard for evidence.
- Plea bargaining may be used with both juvenile and adult offenders.
- Convicted juvenile and adult offenders may be sentenced to probation services, residential programs, or institutional facilities.
- Boot camps are used with juvenile and adult offenders.
- Released institutional juvenile and adult offenders may be assigned to supervision in the community.

Differences
- Juveniles can be arrested for acts that would not be criminal if they were adults (status offenses).
- Age determines the jurisdiction of the juvenile court; age does not affect the jurisdiction of the adult court.
- Parents are deeply involved in the juvenile process but not in the adult process.
- Juvenile court proceedings are more informal, whereas adult court proceedings are formal and open to the public.
- Juvenile court proceedings, unlike adult proceedings, are not considered criminal. Juvenile records are generally sealed when the age of majority (usually age 16 or 17) is reached. Adult records are permanent.
- Juvenile courts cannot sentence juveniles to jail or prison; only adult courts may issue such sentences.

Both juvenile and adult systems are under fire to "get tough on crime," especially on offenders who commit violent crimes. Both must deal with case overloads and institutional overcrowding; both must operate on fiscal shoestrings; and both face the ongoing problems of staff recruitment, training, and burnout. Table 11-1 further describes the common ground and differences between the juvenile and adult justice systems.

TABLE 11-2 JUVENILE AND ADULT JUSTICE SYSTEM TERMS

Juvenile Terminology	Adult Terminology
Adjudicatory hearing	Trial
Aftercare	Parole
Commitment	Sentence to confinement
Detention	Holding in jail
Dispositional hearing	Sentencing hearing
Juvenile court officer	Probation officer
Offender	Defendant
Petition	Indictment
Petitioner	Prosecutor
Respondent	Defense attorney
Taking into custody	Arrest

▶ Basic Correctional Models

To correct the behavior of the juvenile delinquent, there have traditionally been four basic correctional models applicable to the juvenile justice system: (1) the rehabilitation model, (2) the justice model, (3) the balanced and restorative justice model, and (4) the crime-control model.

- *Rehabilitation Model.* The goal of the **rehabilitation model** is to change an offender's character, attitudes, or behavior patterns to diminish his or her propensities for youth crime.[42] The three variations of the rehabilitation model—the medical model, the adjustment model, and the reintegration model—all are expressions of rehabilitative philosophy.

- *Justice Model.* The **justice model** holds to the belief that punishment should be the basic purpose of the juvenile justice system. Among the variants of the justice model for youth crime are those proposed by David Fogel, by the Report of the Committee for the Study of Incarceration, and by the Report of the Twentieth Century Fund.[43] The concept of **just deserts** is the pivotal philosophical basis of the justice model. According to Fogel's model of **justice as fairness**, offenders are volitional and responsible human beings, so they deserve to be punished if they violate the law because punishment shows that the delinquent is blameworthy for his or her conduct.[44]

- *Balanced and Restorative Justice Model.* The **balanced and restorative justice model** is an integrated effort to reconcile the interests of victims, offenders, and communities through programs and supervision practices. The word *balanced* refers to system-level decision making by administrators to ensure accountability to crime victims, to increase competency in offenders, and to enhance community safety[45] (see Figure 11–6). These three goals are summarized in accountability, competency, and community protection. The balanced and restorative justice model is based on a balanced approach between treatment and punishment. It is also much more focused on accountability than has been the case in the past. The juvenile justice system, in implementing the balanced and restorative justice model, uses many of the same principles as the justice model to develop effective systems for the supervision of juvenile offenders in the community.[46]

- *Crime-Control Model.* The public has become increasingly intolerant of serious youth crime and is more and more receptive to the **crime-control model**, which emphasizes punishment as the remedy for juvenile misbehavior. The crime-control model is grounded on its adherents' conviction that the first priority of justice should be the protection of the life and property of the innocent, and supporters of the crime-control model, which is based on the classical school of criminology (examined in Chapter 3), charge that punishment is the preferred correctional model because it both protects society and deters crime. Youthful offenders are taught not to commit further crimes, and noncriminal youths receive a demonstration of what happens to a person who breaks the law.[47]

> **The public has become increasingly intolerant of serious youth crime and is more and more receptive to the crime-control model, which emphasizes punishment as the remedy for juvenile misbehavior.**

FIGURE 11–6 The Balanced and Restorative Justice Model.
Source: Gordon Bazemore and Mark S. Umbreit, *Balanced and Restorative Justice* (Washington, D.C.: Office of Justice and Delinquency Prevention, 1994), p. 1.

Comparison of the Four Models

The rehabilitation model is more concerned that juvenile delinquents receive therapy than that they be institutionalized; the crime-control model, on the other hand, is a punishment model that contends juveniles must pay for their crimes. Those who back the crime-control model also claim that punishment has social value for both offenders (deterrence) and society (protection). The justice model strongly advocates that procedural safeguards and fairness be granted to juveniles who have broken the law, yet proponents of this model also firmly hold that juveniles should be punished according to the severity of their crimes. The balanced and restorative justice model is an accountability model that is focused on recognizing the needs of victims, giving proper attention to the protection of society, and providing competency development for juveniles entering the system. Table 11–3 compares the four models.

TABLE 11–3 COMPARISON OF KEY ELEMENTS OF THE REHABILITATION, JUSTICE, BALANCED AND RESTORATIVE, AND CRIME-CONTROL MODELS

Elements	Models			
	Rehabilitation	Justice	Balanced and Restorative	Crime Control
Theory of why delinquents offend	Behavior is caused or determined; based on positivism	Free will; based on the classical school	Free will; based on the classical school	Free will; based on the classical school
Purpose of sentencing	Change in behavior or attitude	Justice	Community protection	Restoration of law and order
Type of sentencing advocated	Indeterminate	Determinate	Determinate	Determinate
View of treatment	Goal of correctional process	Voluntary but necessary in a humane system	Voluntary but necessary in a humane system	Ineffective and actually coddles offenders
Crime-control strategy	Use therapeutic intervention to eliminate factors causing crime	Provide fairness for victims, for offenders, and for practitioners in the system	Make juvenile offenders accountable for their behavior	Declare war on youth crime by instituting "get-tough" policies

Source: Reprinted with permission from Clemens Bartollas.

TABLE 11-4 PHILOSOPHICAL GOALS IN JUVENILE CODE PURPOSE CLAUSE

Prevention/Diversion/Treatment	Punishment	Both Prevention/Diversion/Treatment and Punishment	
Arizona*	Arkansas	Alabama	New Hampshire
District of Columbia	Georgia	Alaska	New Jersey
Kentucky	Hawaii	California	New Mexico
Massachusetts	Illinois	Colorado	New York
North Carolina	Iowa	Connecticut	North Dakota
Ohio	Louisiana	Delaware	Oklahoma
South Carolina	Michigan	Florida	Oregon
Vermont	Missouri	Idaho	Pennsylvania
West Virginia	Rhode Island	Indiana	Tennessee
		Kansas	Texas
		Maryland	Utah
		Maine	Virginia
		Minnesota	Washington
		Mississippi	Wisconsin
		Montana	Wyoming
		Nebraska	
		Nevada	

- Most states seek to protect the interests of the child, the family, the community, or some combination of the three.
- In 17 states, the purpose clause incorporates the language of the balanced and restorative justice philosophy, emphasizing offender accountability, public safety, and competency development.
- Purpose clauses also address court issues such as fairness, speedy trials, and even coordination of services. In nearly all states the code also includes protections of the child's constitutional and statutory rights.

*Arizona's statutes and court rules did not contain a purpose clause; however, the issue is addressed in case law.

Source: Adapted from Patricia Torbet and Linda Szymanski, State Legislative Responses to Violent Juvenile Crime: 1996–97 Update, Office of Juvenile Justice and Delinquency Prevention, "1999 National Report Series," Juvenile Justice Bulletin (Washington, D.C.: U.S. Department of Justice, 1999), p. 3.

Emergent Approaches to Handling Youthful Offenders

Until recently there was wide-spread support for using the crime-control model with serious and violent juvenile offenders. For example, from 1992 through 1997, legislatures in 47 states and the District of Columbia enacted laws that made their juvenile justice systems more punitive[48] (Many states added to the purpose clauses of their juvenile codes such phrases as "provide effective deterrents"; "hold youths accountable for criminal behavior"; "balance attention to youthful offenders, victims, and the community"; and "impose punishments consistent with the seriousness of the crime."[49]

In Table 11-4, it can also be seen that in 1997 about as many states were emphasizing prevention/diversion/treatment philosophical goals as were advocating punishment philosophical goals. At the same time, nearly twice as many states placed importance on both sets of goals in their juvenile codes. The trend toward a balanced and restorative approach also was seen in the late 1990s, and by the start of the twenty-first century, 17 states had adopted the language of the balanced and restorative justice philosophy, emphasizing offender accountability, public safety, and competency development.[50]

▶ Treatment in Juvenile Justice

This section presents a description of selected therapeutic methods—both individual and group—that have been used nationally in juvenile community-based and correctional facilities. It also identifies some of their more salient features.

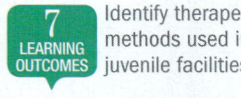

LEARNING OUTCOMES 7: Identify therapeutic methods used in juvenile facilities.

Individual-Level Treatment Programs

The number of different individual techniques include insight-based therapy, behavioral therapy, and cognitive-behavioral therapy. These are reviewed next.

Insight-Based Therapy

It is common for training schools today to employ insight-based therapy techniques for the treatment of mental and emotional disorders. There are many different types of **insight-based therapy** techniques, but in general the therapist utilizes insight, persuasion, suggestion, reassurance, and instructions so that residents can see themselves and their problems more realistically and can develop a desire to cope effectively with their fears and problems.

Psychiatrists, clinical psychologists, and psychiatric social workers have used various forms of insight-based therapies in training schools since the early twentieth century. Residents are encouraged to talk about past conflicts that cause emotional problems. The insight that residents gain from this therapy supposedly helps resolve the conflicts and unconscious needs that drove them to crime. At the conclusion of therapy, it is hoped that the resident will become responsible for his or her own behavior.

Insight-based therapies have some fundamental limitations in a training school context. For instance, residents usually do not see themselves as having emotional problems and are reluctant to share their inner thoughts.

Behavioral Therapy

A second form of individual treatment, behavioral therapy, rests on the assumption that desirable behaviors that are rewarded immediately and systematically will increase, whereas undesirable behaviors that are not rewarded or punished will diminish or be extinguished. Behavioral therapy uses what it terms "positive and negative reinforcement" in order to encourage desirable and extinguish undesirable behavior. **Behavioral modification** is the principal technique used in behavioral therapy, and it is practiced informally in a great many training schools. It works like this: Residents receive additional privileges as they become more accepting of the institutional rules and procedures, and as they demonstrate more positive attitudes. Conversely, bad attitudes and bad behavior result in loss of privileges.

Cognitive-behavioral therapy (CBT) for offenders is based on the assumption that the foundations for criminal behavior are dysfunctional patterns of thinking. The intent is that by altering routine misinterpretations of life events, offenders can modify antisocial aspects of their personality and consequential behavior. The goal of these interventions is to identify cognitive deficits linked to delinquency, such as impulsivity, personal impairments, self-defeating behavior, egocentricity, inability to reason critically, interpersonal problem-solving skills, and a preoccupation with self.[51]

CBT in offender treatment targets the thoughts, choices, attitudes, and meaning systems that are associated with antisocial behavior as well as deviant lifestyles. It generally uses a training approach to teach new skills in areas where offenders showed deficits, such as generating alternative solutions, rather than reacting on the first impulse; interpersonal problems awareness; opening up and listening to other perspectives; evaluating consequences; resisting; soliciting feedback; taking others' well-being in to account; and deciding on what is the most beneficial course of action.[52]

The most widely adopted of the cognitive-behavioral interventions is the **Cognitive Thinking Skills Program (CTSP)** developed by Robert Ross and Elizabeth Fabiano, which is now a core program in the Canadian correctional system and has been implemented in the United States, New Zealand, Australia, and some European countries.[53]

CTSP was developed through a systematic review of all published correctional programs that were associated with reduced criminal recidivism. The researchers identified 100 evaluations of effective programs and discovered they all were designed to target offenders' thinking. Rigid thinking could be minimized by teaching participants creative thinking skills and providing them with prosocial alternative to use when reporting on or responding to interpersonal problems. A core component of CTSO is the belief that teaching offenders techniques of self-control could improve their social adjustments.[54]

A review of the literature leads to the conclusion that combining elements of cognition and behavior approaches is found in the principle of self-reinforcement. This concept says that behavior and cognitive changes reinforce each other. When cognitive changes lead to change in behavior, what results is a sense of well-being that strengthens positive thinking and, as a result, further strengthens behavioral changes. This self-reinforcing feedback process is key to the cognitive behavior approach and is a basis for helping offenders understand the cognitive-behavior process.[55]

A considerable amount of research shows positives effects for the use of cognitive-behavioral approaches with offenders:[56]

- A meta-analysis of 69 studies covering both behavioral and cognitive-behavioral problems determined that the cognitive-behavioral programs are more effective in reducing rates of recidivism than the behavioral programs. The mean reduction was about 39 percent for the treated offenders.[57]

- Another meta-analysis of correctional treatment concluded that cognitive-behavioral methods constituted critical aspects of effective correctional treatment.[58]

- Another study determined that the most effective interventions are those that employed cognitive-behavioral techniques to improve cognitive function.[59]

- There is strong evidence that positive results are more likely to take place among certain subgroups. For example, CTSP seems to be more effective with offenders over age 25 and with property offenders.[60]

Group Programs

In addition to individual-level therapies, most training schools maintain group counseling programs. The most popular of these programs are guided group interaction, positive peer culture, and drug and alcohol treatment programs.

Guided Group Interaction

Guided group interaction (GGI) is probably the most widely used treatment modality. It has been used in at least 11 states: Florida, Georgia, Illinois, Kentucky, Maryland, Michigan, Minnesota, New Hampshire, New Jersey, South Dakota, and West Virginia. Since the 1950s, when this modality was first used, it has been based on the assumption that youths could confront their peers and force them to face the reality of their behavior more effectively than could staff.

The GGI approach is characterized by a non-authoritarian atmosphere, intensity of interaction, group homogeneity, and an emphasis on group structure. Residents in many residential GGI programs, for example, are given considerable say in when a group member will be released, granted a home furlough, or approved for off-campus visits; in how a group member will be punished; and in whether the outside door will be locked or left open at night.

Giving residents responsibility for decision making, of course, is a different approach to child care from that followed in most correctional settings. The adult leader constantly refers the decision making back to the group. When informed by a youth that a group member planned to run away, for example, one staff member retorted: "So what do you want me to do? He's your buddy; he's part of your group. You can talk to him if you have to; but it's up to all of you to help one another."[61]

Although the research findings on GGI have been mixed, the general picture that emerges is that a GGI experience in a nonresidential program is at least as effective as and much less costly than confinement in a state facility and that a GGI experience in an institutional program seems to have more positive impact on less delinquent youngsters.[62]

Positive Peer Culture

The concept of **positive peer culture (PPC)** generated considerable excitement in juvenile corrections, especially in the 1970s. Developed by Harry Vorrath and associates as an outgrowth of GGI, PPC has been implemented in all of the juvenile state institutions in Michigan, Missouri, and West Virginia.[63]

Vorrath believes that PPC "is a total system for building positive youth subcultures."[64] The main philosophy of PPC is to "turn around" the negative peer culture and to mobilize the power of the peer group in a positive way. PPC does this by teaching group members to care for one another; caring is defined as wanting what is best for a person. Vorrath believes that once caring becomes "fashionable" and is accepted by the group, "hurting goes out of style."[65]

Although Vorrath believes that the basic assumptions of these youths can be changed, few people change many of their background assumptions over the period of a lifetime—much less when they are stripped of their freedom and are in therapy. For this modality to be properly evaluated more research is needed. But its present successes should remind both followers and critics that PPC remains one of the most promising ways to treat, change, correct, and rehabilitate juvenile offenders.

Drug- and Alcohol-Abuse Interventions

Drug and alcohol abuse by juveniles, as well as their involvement in drug trafficking in the community, constitutes a serious social problem today. A director of guidance in a training school acknowledged the seriousness of the problem when he said, "Rarely do we get a boy who doesn't have some history of drug or alcohol abuse in his background."[66]

Drug and alcohol abuse interventions increasingly are being developed in community-based and institutional settings to assist those who need help with such problems. These groups are being conducted in training schools in at least three ways: First, institutionalized juveniles assessed to have a problem with alcohol and/or drugs are placed in a separate cottage or in a chemical-abuse group. Specialized staff are hired to work in these cottages or lead these groups. Second, in other training schools, the social worker or another cottage staff member conducts ongoing drug- and alcohol-abuse groups. Third, outside groups, such as Alcoholics Anonymous (AA) or Narcotics Anonymous (NA), come into the institution and hold sessions for interested residents.

Considering the extensiveness of the problem of drug use and trafficking among juvenile offenders, there are still too few programs being offered in juvenile placements. The programs that are offered tend to be relatively unsophisticated and lacking in adequate theoretical design, treatment integrity, and evaluation follow-up. Treatment studies conducted on prison populations have found that when drug programs are well integrated and use effective program elements that have been implemented carefully, these programs:

- Reduce relapse
- Reduce criminality
- Reduce inmate misconduct
- Reduce mental illness
- Reduce behavioral disorders
- Increase the level of the inmates' stake in societal norms
- Increase levels of education and employment upon return to the community
- Improve health and mental health symptoms and conditions
- Improve relationships[67]

Unquestionably, development of effective alcohol- and drug-abuse programs represents one of the most important challenges of juvenile justice today.

What Works for Whom and in What Context

The overall quality of treatment in the juvenile justice system is not impressive. Enforcing offender rehabilitation has sometimes resulted in making delinquents worse rather than better through treatment. The frequent criticism that offender rehabilitation is defective in theory and is a disaster in practice has been true on too many occasions. Program designs often have given little consideration to what a particular program can realistically accomplish with a particular group of offenders and frequently have relied on a single cure for a variety of complex problems. In addition, programs generally have lacked integrity, because they have not delivered the service they claimed with sufficient strength to accomplish the goals of treatment. Furthermore, the research on offender rehabilitation generally has been inadequate, with many projects and reports on rehabilitation almost totally lacking in well-developed research designs.[68]

Still, some progress has been made. Various meta-analyses and literature reviews from the 1980s indicated that treatment programs had somewhat more positive findings than earlier studies had revealed.[69] The emerging picture that received increased support in the 1990s was that "something" apparently works, although no generic method or approach, as distinct from individual programs, especially shines.[70] Or, to state this differently, several methods appear promising, but none had produced major reductions in recidivism.

This was to change with the work of Mark W. Lipsey. He pointed out the limitations of individual studies and advocated the value of the systematic analysis of a body of research.[71] Beginning with his study of diversion in Southern California, Lipsey reported evidence that juveniles in treatment groups had recidivism rates approximately 10 percent lower than those of untreated groups, and that the best intervention programs produced a 20 to 30 percent reduction in recidivism rates.[72]

Beginning in the 1990s and continuing until the present day, and certainly influenced by the work of Mark Lipsey, evidence-based programs and practices have been increased substantially. The federal Office of Juvenile Justice and Delinquency Prevention (OJJDP) was one of the most enthusiastic supporters of evidence-based programs. In this text, several examples of evidence-based programs are discussed. It is anticipated that these increasing numbers of evidence-based programs will give the field a better understanding of what works.

The fact still remains that correctional treatment must discover what works for which offenders in what context. In other words, correctional treatment could be more effective if amenable offenders were offered appropriate treatments by matched workers in an environment that is conducive to producing positive effects.

Matching up individual offenders with the treatments most likely to benefit them is no easy task. In recognizing offenders' needs, researchers recommend using "template matching techniques" to create a set of descriptors (or a "template") of the kinds of people who are most likely to benefit from a particular treatment according to the theory or basic assumptions underlying it.[73]

Graduated Sanctions in Juvenile Justice

In adult corrections, increased attention has been given to intermediate sanctions, and in recent decades these intermediate sanctions have included a system of graduated sanctions, ranging from fines, daily reporting centers, and drug courts to intensive probation and residential placement.

This same movement has gained some momentum in juvenile justice, but in juvenile justice the system of graduated sanctions is focused on serious, violent, and chronic juvenile offenders. These offenders are moving along a continuum through a well-structured system that addresses both their needs and the safety of the community. At each level, juvenile offenders are subject to more severe sanctions if they continue in their delinquent offenses.[74]

Core Principles of a System of Graduated Sanctions

A model "graduated system" combines youth discipline with humane, reasonable, and appropriate sanctions. It offers a continuum of care that consists of diverse programs. Included in this continuum are intermediate sanctions within the community both for the first-time nonviolent offenders and for more serious offenders, secure care programs for the most violent offenders, and aftercare programs that provide high levels of both social control and treatment services.

Each of the graduated sanctions is intended to consist of graduations, or levels, that together with appropriate services constitute an integrated approach. This approach is designed to stop the youthful offender's further participation in the system by inducing law-abiding behavior as early as possible through the commendation of treatment sanctions and appropriate interventions. The family must be involved in each level in the continuum. Aftercare must be actively involved in supporting the family and integrating the youth into the community. Programs will need to use risk and needs assessments to determine appropriate placement for the offender. The effectiveness of interventions depends on their being swift and certain, and incorporating increased sanctions, including the possible loss of freedom. As the severity of the sanctions increases, so must the intensity of the treatment. Such sanctions could ultimately mean confinement in a secure setting, ranging from a secure community-based facility to a public or private training school, camp, or ranch. The programs are most effective for hard-to-handle youth and address key areas of risk in their lives, provide adequate support and supervision, and offer youths a long-term stake in the community.

▶ Race and Juvenile Justice

One of the most disturbing issues facing the juvenile justice system today is the long-standing and pronounced disparities in the processing of white and minority youths. Northeastern University's Donna Bishop concluded: "Despite decades of research, there is no clear consensus on why minority youths enter and penetrate the juvenile justice system at such disproportionate rates."[75] According to Bishop, two explanations have been given: "The first is that minority overrepresentation reflects race and ethnic differences in the incidence, seriousness, and persistence of delinquent

LEARNING OUTCOMES 8 Summarize attempts that have been made to address minority overrepresentation in the juvenile justice process.

One of the most disturbing issues facing the juvenile justice system today is the long-standing and pronounced disparities in the processing of white and minority youths.

involvement (the 'differential offending' hypothesis)" and "the second is that overrepresentation is attributable to inequities—intended or unintended—in juvenile justice practice (the 'differential treatment hypothesis')."[76]

University of Missouri–St. Louis Professor Janet L. Lauritsen, in examining what is known about racial and ethnic differences in juvenile offending, offered the following conclusions that have wide support in the literature:

- Rates of juvenile homicide are higher for minorities than for white youthful offenders. Similarly, variations exist in rates of lethal violence between minority groups.
- Official data suggest disproportionate involvement in nonlethal violence on the part of African-American youths. When arrest data are restricted to specific forms of nonlethal violence, African-American youths appear to be disproportionately involved in robbery, aggravated assault, and rape.
- Juvenile property crime data show that African-American youths are slightly more involved in such offenses than white youths, although the level of involvement varies by type of property crime.
- Arrest data show that white youths are disproportionately involved in alcohol offenses and that American Indian youths are slightly more likely than African-American or Asian-American youths to be arrested for these crimes.
- African-American youths are disproportionately arrested for drug-abuse violations and illicit drug use, but self-report data from juveniles on their own drug involvement do not confirm the difference between African-American and white youths suggested by arrest data. In fact, white youths are somewhat more likely to report using marijuana, selling any drug, and selling marijuana.
- Weapons violations arrest data indicate that African-American youths are disproportionately likely to be arrested for weapons possession or use.[77]
- Although the most commonly occurring crimes exhibit few group differences, the less frequent and serious crimes of violence show generally higher levels of African-American and Latino-American involvement.[78]

Lauritsen concluded that this kind of empirical evidence suggests that the relationship between race and ethnicity and juvenile involvement in delinquency is complex and contingent on the type of offense. In contrast, Bishop suggested that minority overrepresentation in the juvenile justice system is attributable to inequities in system practices rather than differences in the incidence, seriousness, or persistence of offending.

Minorities are overrepresented among youths held in secure detention, petitioned to juvenile court, and adjudicated delinquent. Among those who are adjudicated delinquent, minorities are more often committed to the "deep end" of the juvenile system: When confined, they are more likely to be housed in large public institutions rather than in privately run specialized treatment facilities or group homes, and prosecutors and judges seem quicker to relinquish jurisdiction over minorities, transferring them to criminal court for prosecution and punishment.[79]

Disproportionate Minority Confinement

Carl E. Pope and William H. Feyerherm's highly regarded assessment of the issue of discrimination against minorities revealed that two-thirds of the studies they examined found "both direct and indirect race effects or a mixed pattern (being present at some states and not at others)."[80] They added that selection can take place at any stage and that small racial differences may accumulate and become more pronounced as minority youths are processed through the juvenile justice system.[81]

The Coalition for Juvenile Justice (then the National Coalition of State Juvenile Justice Advisory Groups) brought national attention to the problem of **disproportionate minority confinement** in its 1988 annual report to Congress. In that same year, Congress responded to evidence of disproportionate confinement of minority juveniles in secure facilities by amending the Juvenile Justice and Delinquency Prevention Act (JJDPA) of 1974 to provide that states must determine whether the proportion of minorities in confinement exceeded their proportion in the population of the state; if there was overrepresentation, states must demonstrate efforts to reduce it.[82]

During the 1992 reauthorization of the JJDPA, Congress substantially strengthened the effort to address disproportionate confinement of minority youths in secure facilities. Elimination of disproportionate minority confinement was elevated to the status of a "core requirement" alongside deinstitutionalization of status offenders, removal of juveniles from adult jails and lockups, and separation of youthful offenders from adults in secure institutions. The 2002 reauthorization of the JJDPA also changed the disproportionate minority confinement (DMC) mandate to reduce minority contact with the system.

▶ Prevention of Delinquency: Comprehensive Delinquency Prevention Strategy

Based on research spearheaded and funded by the OJJDP, a consensus developed that the most effective strategy for juvenile corrections is to focus comprehensive prevention

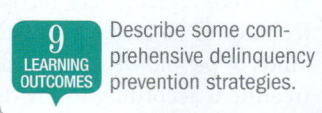
9 LEARNING OUTCOMES Describe some comprehensive delinquency prevention strategies.

and diversion efforts on high-risk juveniles who are involved in violence; these juveniles—the ones whom officials are quick to dump into the adult system—commit the most frequent and more serious delinquent acts. At the same time that the seriousness of their behaviors was effecting changes in juvenile codes across the nation, research was beginning to find that these high-risk youths can be impacted by well-equipped and well-implemented prevention and treatment programs.[83]

Such programs are based on the assumption that the juvenile justice system does not see most serious offenders until it is too late to intervene effectively.[84] This strategy also presumes that if the goal is to reduce the overall violence in American society, it is necessary to successfully intervene in the lives of high-risk youthful offenders, who commit about 75 percent of all violent juvenile offenses.[85]

Several general characteristics are found in these comprehensive programs: They address key areas of risk in youths' lives, they seek to strengthen the personal and institutional factors contributing to healthy adolescent development, they provide adequate support and supervision, and they offer youths a long-term stake in the community.[86] These prevention programs for high-risk youths must be integrated with local police, child welfare, social services, school, and family preservation programs because comprehensive approaches to delinquency prevention and intervention require strong collaborative efforts between the juvenile justice system and other service provision systems, including health, mental health, child welfare, and education. An important component of a community's comprehensive plan is to develop mechanisms that effectively link these service providers at the program level.[87]

The comprehensive or multi-systemic aspects of these programs are designed to deal simultaneously with many aspects of youth' lives. They are intensive, often involving weekly or even daily contacts with at-risk youths, and build on youths' strengths rather than focusing on their deficiencies. These programs operate mostly (although not exclusively) outside the formal justice system under a variety of public, nonprofit, or university auspices. Finally, they combine accountability and sanctions with increasingly intensive rehabilitation and treatment services, which are achieved through the system of graduated sanctions in which an integrated approach is used to stop the penetration of youthful offenders into the system.[88]

In 1996, three communities—Lee and Duval Counties in Florida and San Diego County in California—collaborated with the OJJDP to apply the processes and principles set forth in the OJJDPP's comprehensive strategy statement; initial evaluations of the three pilot projects reported that each of the three sites had benefited significantly from the comprehensive planning process.[89] The following were among the accomplishments identified in a 2000 report:

- Enhanced community-wide understanding of prevention services and sanction options for juveniles
- Expanded networking capacity and better coordination among agencies and service providers
- Institution of performance measurement systems
- Hiring of staff to spearhead ongoing comprehensive strategy planning and implementation efforts
- Development of comprehensive five-year strategic action plans.[90]

Trends for the Future

Several changes are taking place in juvenile justice today that will likely continue in the future:

- *Expansion of restorative justice.* As mentioned in several chapters of this text, restorative justice is one of the most exciting movements in corrections today, and it has recently been coupled with intermediate sanctions.  From the grassroots level to local and state headquarters, restorative justice is rapidly gaining momentum within the United States. Victim–offender conferencing (sometimes called mediation) is the oldest and most widely used expression of restorative justice, with more than 1,300 programs in 18 countries.[91] While stressing accountability for offenses committed, restorative strategies operate with the goal of repairing injuries to victims and to communities in which crimes have taken place. Whether these conferences occur before, during, or after adjudication, they promote education and transformation within a context of respect and healing. These models neither are mutually exclusive nor compete in and of themselves and can be combined or adapted depending on the specific situation at hand.[92]

- *Increased use of technology.* Rather than rely on traditional methods of security and control, the correctional system is now entering a new phase of technocorrections, which involves using technology rather than personnel to monitor probation, aftercare, and institutional populations. Today, technology-driven security is designed to maintain security, both in the community and in institutions. Community corrections has relied for quite some time on technology to monitor offenders; for example, electronic monitoring (EM) has been increasingly used in probation services. Now, new methods of technology are being explored to provide probation and parole officers with tools to better manage their caseloads and do their jobs more effectively and efficiently.

- *Greater use of evidence-based practice principles and approaches.* Evidence-based practice principles are increasingly used in juvenile justice today. It is contended that programs that go by the following principles have a better chance of succeeding than those that do not: (1) target criminogenic needs, (2) target programs to high-risk offenders, (3) base design and implementation on a proven theoretical model, (4) use a cognitive-behavioral approach, (5) disrupt the delinquency network, (6) provide intensive services, (7) match the offender's personality and learning style with appropriate program settings and approaches, (8) include a prevention component in release decisions, (9) integrate juvenile justice with community-based services, and (10) reinforce integrity of services. Effective programs continually monitor program development, organizational structure, staff development and training, and other core organizational processes, and an important part of this effective offender intervention treatment approach is program evaluation.[93]

Clearly, some of these changes are more likely to occur than others, and resources may constrain certain agencies from fully implementing all of them.[94]

THE CASE

The Life Course of Amy Watters, Age 15

It never occurred to Amy (not seriously, at least) that she might be arrested. One day, however, after smuggling drugs into the school in a couple of tampon containers that she carried in her purse, Amy was called to the office. When she got there, she was ushered into the principal's conference room, where she faced the principal, a school counselor, and a female deputy sheriff. Her boyfriend, CJ, was also seated at the table, looking very uncomfortable.

The sheriff's office, Amy was told, had been conducting a county-wide investigation into the use of illegal drugs in the county's high schools. Video surveillance, it turned out, had implicated both Amy and CJ in a series of drug transfers. She was shown one of the videos, a black-and-white stream from an overhead camera in one of the school's hallways, that clearly showed her handing freezer bags full of what looked like marijuana (the pictures were a bit grainy) to CJ.

Although the investigators did not yet know the extent of her involvement, it quickly became clear to Amy that she and CJ had been caught red-handed. Amy was told that her backpack was being confiscated by deputies, and that it would be searched for drugs or drug residue. Her father was on his way to the school, the principal told her, along with CJ's parents, and once they got there she and CJ were to be questioned by the female officer.

Amy and CJ were told to wait in a small area off of the conference room, to await the arrival of their parents. While there, the two talked about their situation, and Amy told CJ that it would be best if they admitted what they had been doing. CJ was adamant in proclaiming that he would deny everything. He had to protect the Boyz (his gang of friends) at all costs, he said. He would never rat them out. Besides, he said, "I'm going to be 19 soon, and a senior. If I get busted, I'm going to criminal court."

DISCUSS

1. Why hadn't Amy realistically considered the possibility of arrest? Should young people placed under arrest have all of the same rights as an adult? Why or why not?

Learn more on the Web:

- juvenile justice case flow processing at ww.ojjdp.gov/ojstatbb/structure_process/case.html

Follow the continuing Amy Watters saga in the next chapter.

CHAPTER 11 An Overview of Juvenile Justice in America

Summarize the development of the juvenile justice system.

Beginning with the colonial period and parents' control of children, the juvenile justice system has developed into community-based corrections, juvenile institutions, and aftercare.

1. Who were the child savers? What was the focus of the child savers movement?
2. Would it be better if parents had more control over the behavior of their children, as they did in the colonial era? Why or why not?
3. What various aftercare options are available to juvenile court judges?

child savers A name given to an organized group of progressive social reformers of the late nineteenth and early twentieth centuries that promoted numerous laws aimed at protecting children and institutionalizing an idealized image of childhood innocence.

aftercare The supervision of juveniles who are released from correctional institutions so that they can make an optimal adjustment to community living; also, the status of a juvenile conditionally released from a treatment or confinement facility and placed under supervision in the community.

probation A court-ordered nonpunitive juvenile disposition that emphasizes community-based services and treatment and close supervision by an officer of the court. Probation is essentially a sentence of confinement that is suspended so long as the probationer meets the conditions imposed by the court.

residential program A program conducted for the rehabilitation of youthful offenders within community-based and institutional settings.

cottage system A widely used treatment practice that places small groups of training school residents into cottages.

training school A correctional facility for long-term placement of juvenile delinquents; may be public (run by a state department of corrections or youth commission) or private.

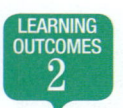

Identify examples of prevention programs.

Examples of effective prevention programs include Multisystemic Therapy (MST), Nurse–Family Partnership Bullying Prevention Program, and Big Brothers Big Sisters of America.

1. Of the various prevention programs cited in this chapter, which do you believe offer greater chances of success?
2. What are the differences between primary, secondary, and tertiary prevention?

delinquency prevention An organized effort to forestall or prevent the development of delinquent behavior. See also *primary prevention*, *secondary prevention*, and *tertiary prevention*.

primary prevention The effort to reduce delinquency by modifying conditions in the physical and social environments that lead to juvenile crime.

secondary prevention The intervention in the lives of juveniles or groups identified as being in circumstances that dispose them toward delinquency.

tertiary prevention A program directed at the prevention of recidivism among youthful offenders.

family therapy A counseling technique that involves treating all members of a family; a widely used method of dealing with a delinquent's socially unacceptable behavior.

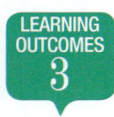

Identify examples of diversion programs.

Examples of diversion programs include drug courts and youth courts.

1. What are diversion programs, and how are they relevant to the processing of juveniles through the justice system?
2. How can you evaluate drug courts and teen courts as to their effectiveness as diversionary programs?

diversion programs Dispositional alternatives for youthful offenders that exist outside of the formal juvenile justice system.

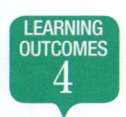

Explain the structure of today's juvenile justice system.

The juvenile justice system, similar to the adult justice system, is made up of law enforcement, courts, and corrections.

1. Does society really need a juvenile justice system that is separate from the adult system used with criminals? Explain your answer.
2. What is a petition, and what role does it play in juvenile justice system processing?
3. What is the purpose of a juvenile dispositional hearing?

LEARNING OUTCOMES 5

Summarize the stages of delinquency case processing.

The stages of the juvenile justice system proceed from the arrest of the juvenile, to handling by the courts, and to either release or further disposition by the justice system in institutions or community-based corrections.

1. How is juvenile case processing similar to the processing of adult criminal cases? How is it different?
2. As juveniles are processed through the juvenile justice system, do they receive too many breaks?

adjudicatory hearing The stage of juvenile court proceedings that usually includes the youth's plea, the presentation of evidence by the prosecution and by the defense, the cross-examination of witnesses, and a finding by the judge as to whether the allegations in the petition can be sustained.

commitment A determination made by a juvenile judge at the disposition stage of a juvenile court proceeding that a juvenile is to be sent to a juvenile correctional institution.

detention The temporary restraint of a juvenile in a secure facility, usually because he or she is acknowledged to be dangerous either to him- or herself or to others.

dispositional hearing The stage of the juvenile court proceedings in which the juvenile judge decides the most appropriate placement for a juvenile who has been adjudicated a delinquent, a status offender, or a dependent child.

juvenile court officer A probation officer who serves juveniles (the term is used in some but not all probation departments).

petition A document filed in juvenile court alleging that a juvenile is a delinquent and asking that the court assume jurisdiction over the juvenile or asking that an alleged delinquent be waived to criminal court for prosecution as an adult.

petitioner In the juvenile justice system, an intake officer (prosecutor) who seeks court jurisdiction over a youthful offender.

respondent The defense attorney in the juvenile court system.

taking into custody The process of arresting a juvenile for socially unacceptable or unlawful behavior.

LEARNING OUTCOMES 6

Compare the basic correctional models of juvenile justice.

In terms of correctional models of juvenile justice, the rehabilitation model is more concerned that juvenile delinquents receive therapy than be institutionalized; the crime-control model, on the other hand, is a punishment model that contends juveniles must pay for their crimes. The justice model strongly advocates that procedural safeguards and fairness be granted to juveniles who have broken the law, yet proponents of this model also firmly hold that juveniles should be punished according to the severity of their crimes. The balanced and restorative justice model is an accountability model that is focused on recognizing the needs of victims, giving proper attention to the protection of society, and providing competency development for juveniles entering the system.

1. The juvenile justice system has devised four ways to deal with delinquency: the rehabilitation model, the justice model, the balanced and restorative justice model, and the crime-control model. Which do you think works best? Why?
2. Why is the balanced and restorative justice model gaining such popularity nationwide?
3. What is the medical model of juvenile justice?

rehabilitation model A correctional model's goal is to change an offender's character, attitudes, or behavior so as to diminish his or her delinquent propensities. The medical, adjustment, and reintegration models are variants of this model because they are all committed to changing the offender.

justice model A contemporary model of imprisonment based on the principle of just deserts.

just deserts A pivotal philosophical underpinning of the justice model that holds that juvenile offenders deserve to be punished and that the punishment must be proportionate to the seriousness of the offense or the social harm caused.

justice as fairness A justice model that advocates that it is necessary to be fair, reasonable, humane, and constitutional in the implementation of justice.

balanced and restorative justice model An integrative correctional model that seeks to reconcile the interests of victims, offenders, and communities through programs and supervision practices.

crime-control model A correctional model supporting discipline and punishment as the most effective means of deterring youth crime.

LEARNING OUTCOMES 7

Identify therapeutic methods used in juvenile facilities.

Therapeutic strategies can be grouped into two categories: individual-level treatment programs, and group-level programs. Individual-level techniques include insight-based therapy, behavioral therapy, and cognitive-behavioral therapy. Group-level programs generally include guided group interaction, positive peer culture, and drug and alcohol treatment programs.

1. What individual-level strategies for working with youth in juvenile facilities are identified in this chapter?
2. What group-level strategies for working with youth in juvenile facilities are identified in this chapter?

insight-based therapy Treatment designed to encourage communication of conflicts and insight into problems, with the goal of symptoms relief, change in behavior, and personality growth.

behavioral modification A technique in which rewards and punishments are used to change a person's behavior.

Cognitive-behavioral therapy (CBT) Therapy based on the assumption that the foundations for criminal behavior are dysfunctional patterns of thinking.

Cognitive Thinking Skills Program (CTSP) A cognitive-behavioral intervention program designed to improve offenders' thinking processes.

Guided Group Interaction (GGI) A treatment modality based on the assumption that youths can confront their peers and force them to face the reality of their behavior more effectively than staff can. GGI is the most widely used treatment modality in juvenile corrections.

positive peer culture (PPC) A system for building positive youth subcultures. Its main goal is to turn around negative peer cultures and to mobilize the power of the peer group in positive ways.

LEARNING OUTCOMES 8

Summarize attempts that have been made to address minority overrepresentation in the juvenile justice process.

Because of minority overrepresentation in the justice system, especially in juvenile institutions, the Juvenile Justice and Delinquency Prevention Act has called attention to disproportionate confinement, and states failing to comply with this requirement are denied justice system funding.

1. What social factors likely explain minority overrepresentation in the juvenile justice system?
2. What is meant by disproportionate confinement?
3. How can issues of disproportionate confinement be addressed?
4. The juvenile justice system has had success in reducing and in some states eliminating status offenders from being housed with delinquents, but juvenile institutions are still vastly overrepresented by minority offenders. What more can be done in addition to the various enactments of the Juvenile Justice and Delinquency Prevention Act?

disproportionate minority confinement (DMC) The court-ordered confinement, in juvenile institutions, of members of minority groups in numbers disproportionate to their representation in the general population.

LEARNING OUTCOMES 9

Describe some comprehensive delinquency prevention strategies.

The most effective strategy for prevention is to focus comprehensive prevention and diversion efforts on high-risk juveniles who are involved in violence. These juveniles—the ones whom officials are quick to dump into the adult system—commit the most frequent and more serious delinquent acts. Several general characteristics are found in these comprehensive programs: They address key areas of risk in youths' lives, they seek to strengthen the person and institutional factors contributing to healthy adolescent development, they provide adequate support and supervision, and they offer youths a long-term stake in the community.

1. What are some of general characteristics found in comprehensive delinquency prevention programs?

LEARNING OUTCOMES 10

Summarize possible future trends in juvenile justice.

The three most likely changes in juvenile justice that can be anticipated as likely to occur in the future are expansion of restorative justice, increased use of technology, and greater use of evidence-based practice principles and approaches.

1. What trends in juvenile justice can you identify?
2. Do the future trends of juvenile justice appear to be positive changes in how juveniles are handled in the United States?

12

"The vast majority of youth are good citizens who have never been arrested for any type of crime."

—*Shay Bilchik, President, Child Welfare League of America*

Police and the Juvenile

1. Summarize police–juvenile relations.
2. Summarize how juvenile offenders are processed.
3. Summarize the legal rights of juveniles in encounters with police.
4. Explain police efforts to deter delinquency.
5. Explain how police can avoid contributing to the ongoing delinquency of juveniles.
6. Evaluate the D.A.R.E. program.

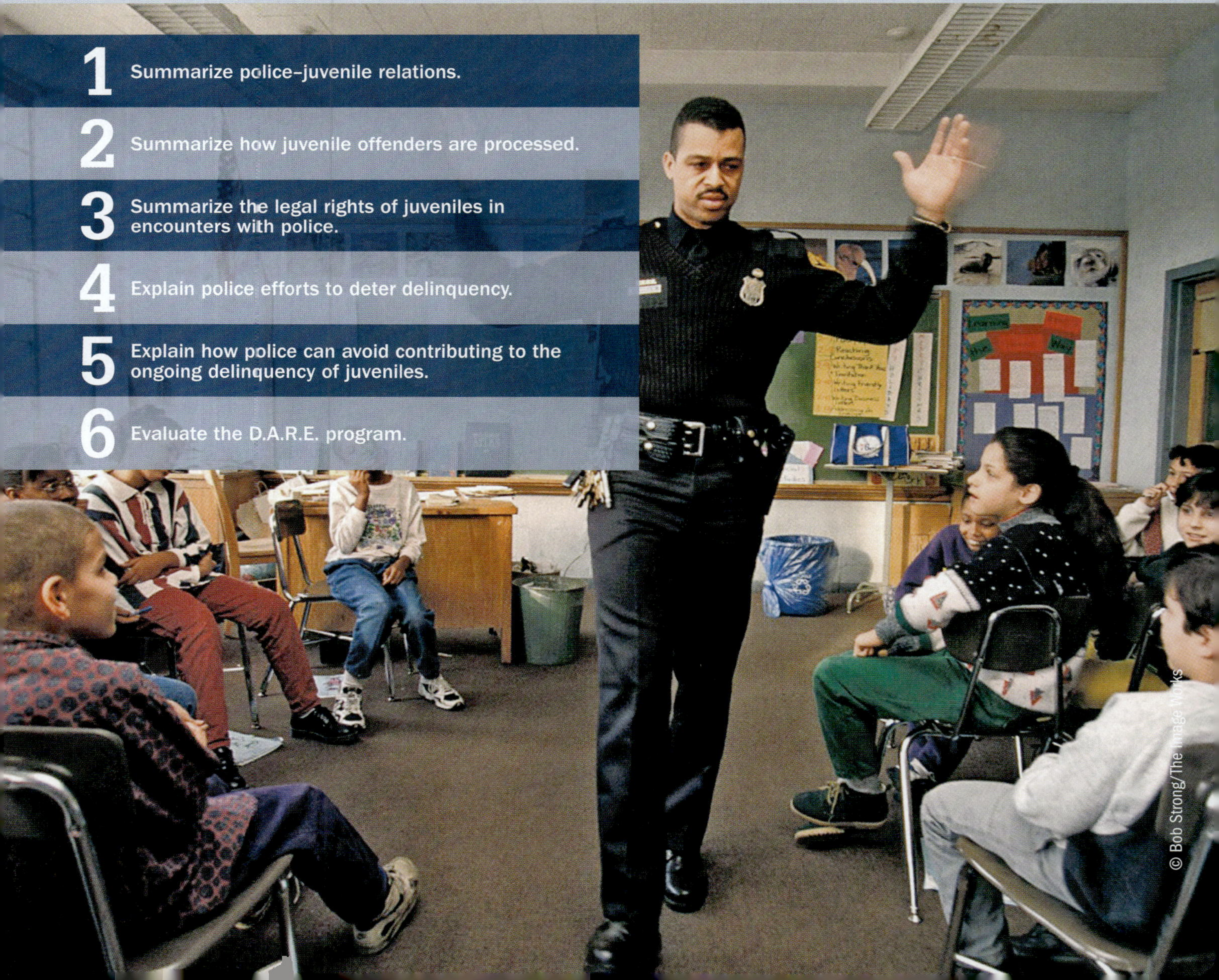

© Bob Strong/The Image Works

INTRO: POLICING CHILDREN

In April of 2011, an eight-year-old boy named Aiden was pepper sprayed by Lakewood, Colorado, police officers responding to a call for assistance from teachers at Glennon Heights Elementary School. Aiden, it seems, had flown into a violent rage, throwing furniture and threatening to kill his teachers. When police arrived they found him wielding a sharp piece of wooden trim that he had torn off a wall and was using like a spear—threatening to stab those around him. Rather than risk a physical encounter, responding officers sprayed the boy with pepper spray. The incident was the third time that police had been called to deal with Aiden's apparent temper tantrums. Even so, the boy's mother criticized police for using what she saw as excessive force. They treated him "like a common criminal," she later told reporters.[1]

A child sitting in a corner as punishment. If you were a police officer, how would you deal with the situation described in this chapter's opening story?

DISCUSS Should police officers exercise restraint when dealing with juveniles? If so, how much restraint might be necessary?

▶ Juveniles' Attitudes Toward the Police

LEARNING OUTCOMES 1 Summarize police–juvenile relations.

Juvenile crime represents one of the most demanding and frustrating areas of police work. A common complaint of police officers is that arrested juvenile offenders are back on the streets before the officers have had a chance to complete the necessary paperwork. Also, with the rise of youth gangs and with increased numbers of juveniles carrying weapons, policing juveniles is much more dangerous than it used to be. Finally, police departments give little status to those dealing with youth crime because they regard arresting a juvenile as a poor "bust."

Policing juveniles is similar in some ways to policing adults, yet in other ways it is quite different. It is similar in that both juveniles and adults have constitutional protections; that juveniles can be as hostile to the police as adults can be; that armed juveniles, of course, are as dangerous as armed adults; that both juveniles and adults are involved in gangs, some of which are involved in drug trafficking; and that alcohol and drugs affect the functioning of both juveniles and adults. A major difference is the belief that juveniles are more salvageable than adults—few would argue against the widely held tenet that juveniles are more likely than adults to experience a turning point where they can walk away from crime.

Accordingly, the importance of police–juvenile relations cannot be minimized. The police are usually the first contact a youth has with the juvenile justice system. As the doorway into the system, the police officer can use his or her broad discretion to either detour youths or involve them in the system. In a real sense, the police officer becomes an on-the-spot prosecutor, judge, and correctional system when dealing with a juvenile offender.

The subject of juveniles' attitudes toward the police has received considerable attention in recent decades. Several studies have reported that juveniles who have had contact with the police have more negative attitudes toward them than those who have not had contact.[2] This seems to be especially true of African-American youths whose culturally accepted view of police is independent of their arrest experience.[3] Some of the most important studies are described in the list that follows:

- Scott H. Decker's 1981 review of the literature on attitudes toward the police concluded that youths had more negative attitudes toward the police than did older citizens and that race, the quality of police services, and previous experiences with the police also affected citizens' attitudes.[4]

- Komanduri S. Murty, Julian B. Roebuck, and Joann D. Smith found in a 1990 Atlanta study that "older, married, white-collar, educated, and employed respondents reported a more positive image of the police than their counterparts—younger, single, blue-collar, low-educated, unemployed/underemployed respondents."[5]

- Michael J. Leiber, Mahesh K. Nalla, and Margaret Farnworth's 1998 study challenged the traditional argument that juveniles' interactions with the police are the primary or sole determinant of youths' attitudes toward the police. Instead, according to these authors, "[juveniles'] attitudes toward authority and agents of social control develop in a larger sociocultural context, and global attitudes toward police affect youths' assessment of specific police contacts."[6]

- Susan Guarino-Ghezzi and Bryan Carr contend, on the basis of a study conducted in Boston, "that the way police interact with juveniles alienates youths who are already alienated from the wider society," and that those feelings are incorporated into the youths' subculture. This sets the stage for what Guarino-Ghezzi and Carr call a cycle of alienation.[7]

- In 2005 Terry Nihart and colleagues found that juveniles' attitudes toward the police are positively correlated with the youths' attitudes toward parents and teachers.[8] In a different type of study, Nihart found that rural youths are more positive toward the police than are urban youths, with whites not significantly more positive than African Americans.[9]

- A 2007 study by Yolander G. Hurst at Ohio's Xavier University found that the attitudes of rural youth toward the police were generally more supportive than those of their metropolitan counterparts.[10]

In general, most youths appear to have positive attitudes toward the police. Younger juveniles are more positive than older ones, white juveniles are more positive than African Americans, and female juveniles are more positive than males. A positive attitude also seems to be influenced by social class, because middle-class youths tend to be more positive than lower-class youths. Generally, juveniles who have not had contact with the police are more positive than those who have had police contact. The most hostile attitudes are typically those of youths with extensive histories of law-violating activities, who have had contact with the police, or who are involved in youth gangs (see Table 12–1).

Most youths appear to have positive attitudes toward the police.

TABLE 12–1 ATTITUDES TOWARD THE POLICE

Favorable Attitudes Toward Police	Less Favorable Attitudes Toward Police
younger children	older children
Caucasians	African Americans
girls	boys
middle- and upper-class youngsters	lower-class youngsters

▶ Processing of Juvenile Offenders

LEARNING OUTCOMES 2 — Summarize how juvenile offenders are processed.

The Baltimore Outward Bound Police Insight Program is a unique one-day police–youth program that brings officers and middle school students together for a day to participate in team-building activities. A qualitative study of the Police Insight Program, which uses Intergroup Contact Theory (ICT) as a framework to assess the program, notes that it facilitates stereotype reduction between officers and youth. When officers and youth share equal status and common goals, must cooperate to succeed, and share the support of authority figures, it was found that the program did reduce stereotyping of the opposite group and increase a desire for future positive interactions.

The one-day Police Insight Programs runs on a monthly basis. Each Insight Program brings together all of the officers who work a given shift from one district (20 to 25 officers) with an equal number of students from a middle school located in that same district. Students participate voluntarily and are invited to take part in the program at the direction of teachers and school administrators. The program day consists of small groups of students and officers, generally five of each, working together on a series of game and group challenges led by Outward Bound facilitators at the Baltimore Chesapeake Bay Outward Bound base. It was further found that establishing optimal contact conditions may create the potential for improved long-term interaction.[11]

When responding to juvenile lawbreakers, police are influenced by a variety of individual, sociocultural, and organizational factors. They can choose a more or less restrictive response to an individual offender.

Factors Influencing Police Discretion

Police discretion can be defined as the choice a police officer makes between two or more possible means of handling a situation. Discretion needs to be both professional and personal. Discretion is important, for the police actually act as a court of first instance in initially categorizing a juvenile. The police officer thus becomes a legal and social traffic director who can use his or her wide discretion to detour juveniles from the justice system or involve them in it.

Police discretion has come under attack because many believe the police abuse their broad discretion, but most police contacts with juveniles are impersonal and nonofficial and consist simply of orders to "get off the corner," "break it up," or "go home." Studies generally estimate that only 10 percent to 20 percent of police–juvenile encounters become "official" contacts.[12] In 2004, Stephanie M. Myers, reporting on data collected for the Project on Policing Neighborhoods (POPN), a study of police in Indianapolis, Indiana, and St. Petersburg, Florida, found that 84 (13 percent) of the 654 juvenile suspects were arrested.[13]

The point can also be made that the juvenile justice system could not function without police discretion. Urban courts, especially, are overloaded; probation officers' caseloads are entirely too high; and many juvenile correctional institutions are jammed to capacity. If police were to increase by two to three times the number of youths they referred to the system, the resulting backlog of cases would be unmanageable.

The police officer's disposition of the juvenile offender is mainly determined by 11 factors: (1) offense, (2) citizen complaints, (3) gender, (4) race, (5) socioeconomic status, (6) individual characteristics of the juvenile, (7) police–juvenile interactions, (8) demeanor, (9) police officer's personality, (10) departmental policy, and (11) external pressures (see Table 12–2).

Offense

The most important factor determining the disposition of the misbehaving juvenile is the seriousness of the offense.[14]

Citizen Complaints

Studies have found that the presence of a citizen or the complaint of a citizen is an important determining factor in the disposition of an incident involving a juvenile.[15] If a citizen initiates a complaint, remains present, and wishes the arrest of a juvenile, chances are that the juvenile will be arrested and processed.[16] If the potential arrest situation results from police patrol, the chances are much greater that the youth will be warned and released.

> **The presence of a citizen or the complaint of a citizen is an important determining factor in the police disposition of a juvenile.**

TABLE 12–2 | FACTORS INFLUENCING DISPOSITION

Individual Factors
Personality characteristics of the juvenile
Personality characteristics of the police officer
Interaction between the police officer and the juvenile

Sociocultural Factors
Citizen complaints
Gender of the juvenile
Race/ethnicity of the juvenile
Socioeconomic status of the juvenile
Influence of cultural norms in the community and values of the wider society on both juveniles and police officers
External pressures in the community to arrest certain types of juvenile offenders

Organizational Factors
Nature of the offense
Departmental policy

Gender

Traditionally, girls have been less likely than boys to be arrested and referred to the juvenile court for criminal offenses, but there is some evidence of the erosion of police "chivalry" in the face of youthful female criminality.[17] Yet, as Chapter 6 noted, girls are far more likely to be referred to the court if they violate traditional role expectations for girls through behaviors such as running away from home, failing to obey parents, or being sexually promiscuous.[18]

Race

Studies differ on the importance of race in determining juvenile disposition. On the one hand, several studies (after results were corrected to account for offense seriousness and prior record) have found that the police are more inclined to arrest minority juveniles[19]; however, several other studies failed to find much evidence of racial bias. It is difficult to appraise the importance of race in the disposition of cases involving juveniles, because African Americans and members of other minority groups appear to be involved in serious crimes more often than Caucasians. Nonetheless, it does seem that racial bias makes minority juveniles special targets of the police.[20]

Socioeconomic Status

Substantiating the effect of class on the disposition of cases involving juveniles is difficult because most studies examine race and socioeconomic status together, but lower-class youngsters, according to many critics of the juvenile justice system, receive different "justice" than middle- or upper-class youths. What the critics mean by this is that lower-class youths are dragged into the net of the system for the same offenses for which middle- and upper-class juveniles often are sent home.

Individual Characteristics of the Juvenile

Such individual factors as prior arrest record, previous offenses, age, peer relationships, family situation, and conduct of parents also have a bearing on how the police officer handles each juvenile.[21] A juvenile who is older and has committed several previous offenses is likely to be referred to the juvenile court.[22] The family of the juvenile is also an important variable.

Police–Juvenile Interactions and Demeanor

Some studies have found that a juvenile's deference to a police officer is influential in determining disposition.[23] As would be expected, these studies show that juveniles who act with disrespect are most likely to be arrested.[24]

> **Think About It...**
> The police handling of juvenile offenders is determined by a number of factors. What factors does this chapter identify?

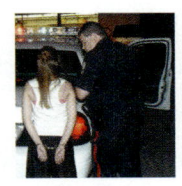
Jack Dagley/Shutterstock

Processing of Juvenile Offenders **199**

Police Officer's Personality

The factor of police officer personality has received some support for shaping the nature of police–juvenile interactions. An officer who has little tolerance for adolescents may more frequently become involved in a confrontation requiring an official contact.

Departmental Policy

Police departments vary in their policies on handling misbehaving juveniles.[25] James Q. Wilson found that the more professional police departments had higher numbers of juveniles referred to the juvenile court because they used discretion less often than departments that were not as professional.[26]

External Pressures

The attitudes of the press and the public, the status of the complainant or victim, and the philosophy and available resources of referral agencies usually influence the disposition of juvenile lawbreakers.

In sum, sufficient numbers of studies have been done to provide the outline of an empirical portrait of the policing of juveniles. Of the 11 factors influencing police officers' dispositions of juveniles, the seriousness of the offense and complaints by citizens appear to be more important than the other 9 factors. However, individual factors, departmental policy, and external pressures also are highly influential in determining how police–juvenile encounters are handled (see Table 12–3).

Informal and Formal Dispositions

Studies on police discretion reveal many inconsistencies. There is common agreement that the fair handling of juveniles should not be influenced by factors such as the friendliness of juveniles and their race, sex, social class, or community reputations. Nevertheless, personal biases do sometimes influence individual police officers. Unquestionably, police typically come into contact daily with many different types of juveniles in various situations. Some youths have mental illnesses; some come from families torn apart by alcohol, drugs, and other addictive disorders; some youths are neglected; and some are abused physically, emotionally, or sexually. Some youths have no family members to turn to in times of need, and some find school a frightening, frustrating, and valueless experience. Conversely, many find gang experiences rewarding and emotionally satisfying, and use them as a way to gain the respect of peers. Police officers must deal effectively with all of these types of youths.

A patrol officer or **juvenile officer** has at least five options when investigating a complaint against a juvenile or arriving at the scene of law-violating behavior:

1. *Warning and release.* The least severe sanction is applied when the patrol officer decides merely to question and release the youth. Commonly, this occurs when a juvenile is caught committing a minor offense.

2. *Station adjustment.* The juvenile can be taken to the station, where the juvenile will have his or her contact recorded, will be given an official reprimand, and then will be released to the parents. In a **station adjustment**, the first thing the department does when the juvenile is brought to the station is to contact the parents.[27]

3. *Referral to a diversion agency.* The juvenile can be released and referred to a diversion agency. In some jurisdictions, the police operate their own diversion program; more

TABLE 12–3 | FACTORS INFLUENCING POLICE DISCRETION

Factor	Explanation
Offense	Seriousness of the offense
Citizen Complaints	Presence or complaint of a citizen
Gender	Girls are less likely to be referred to the court, unless they violate traditional role expectations for girls.
Race	Race, and there is conflicting evidence, does appear to make minority juveniles special targets of the police.
Socioeconomic Status	In the midst of conflicting evidence, lower-class youngsters do appear to receive different "justice" than higher-class youths.
Individual Characteristics of the Juvenile	Age, peer relationships, family situation, and conduct of parents are some of the individual factors bearing on how police handle juveniles.
Police–Juvenile Interactions	Youths' deference to a police officer is influential in determining disposition.
Demeanor	The demeanor of the youth has influence in this process.
Police Officer's Personality	The officer's personality sometimes influences discretion.
Departmental Policy	Police departments also vary in their policies on handling the misbehavior of juveniles.
External Pressures	A number of external pressures, such as public attitude, can influence the disposition of juvenile misbehavior.

TABLE 12–4 PERCENTAGES OF DELINQUENCY CASES REFERRED TO COURT BY LAW ENFORCEMENT, 2010

Most Serious Offense	Percent
Delinquency	83%
Person	88%
Property	90%
Drugs	91%
Public order	64%

Source: Charles Puzzanchera and Sarah Hockenberry, *Juvenile Court Statistics 2010* (Washington, D.C.: National Center for Juvenile Justice, 2013).

typically, juveniles are referred to agencies such as Big Brothers Big Sisters, a runaway center, or a mental health agency.

4. *Citation and referral to juvenile court.* The police officer can issue a **citation** and refer the youth to the juvenile court. Law enforcement agencies refer more than four-fifths of the delinquency cases handed by juvenile courts. Table 12–4 gives the percentages of various types of delinquency cases referred to juvenile court by police agencies in 2010.

5. *Detention.* The police officer can issue a citation, refer the youth to the juvenile court, and take him or her to a detention center. An intake worker at the detention center then decides whether the juvenile should be returned to the parents or left at the detention center. A juvenile is left in detention when he or she is thought to be dangerous to self or others in the community or has no care in the home. Taking youths out of their homes and placing them in detention facilities clearly must be a last resort.

Legal Rights of Juveniles

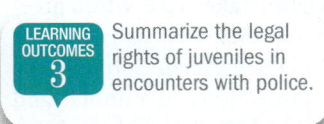

LEARNING OUTCOMES 3: Summarize the legal rights of juveniles in encounters with police.

Juveniles were at the mercy of the police for much of the twentieth century. Few or no laws protected juveniles in trouble because of the rehabilitative ideal in juvenile justice. Police officers, whose primary mission was to maintain law and order, used whatever tactics seemed appropriate to restore the peace. Friendliness, persuasion, threats, coercion, and force were all used to gain the compliance of juveniles. If these tactics failed, juveniles were taken into juvenile court or, depending on the laws of the state and the seriousness of the crimes, to adult court for prosecution. Few protections were granted to juveniles in the areas of search and seizure, interrogation, fingerprinting, lineups, or other procedures. In the 1960s, the U.S. Supreme Court's decisions began to change this relationship between the police and juveniles. Although not all police departments have endorsed or adhered to the guidelines laid down by the courts, most departments have made a conscientious effort to abide by the standards of justice and fairness implied by these decisions,[28] and juveniles who are under **arrest** have nearly all the due process safeguards accorded to adults.

Search and Seizure

The Fourth Amendment to the Constitution of the United States protects citizens from unauthorized **search and seizure**. In 1961, the Supreme Court decision in *Mapp* v. *Ohio* affirmed Fourth Amendment rights for adults, stating that evidence gathered in an unreasonable search and seizure—that is, evidence seized without probable cause and without a proper search warrant—was inadmissible in court.[29] In *State* v. *Lowry* (1967), the Supreme Court applied the Fourth Amendment ban against unreasonable searches and seizures to juveniles.[30]

Juveniles therefore are protected from unreasonable searches and seizures. Juveniles must be presented with a valid search warrant unless they have either waived that right, have consented to having their person or property searched, or have been apprehended in the act. If these conditions have not been met, courts have overturned rulings against juveniles. For example, evidence was dismissed in one case when police entered a juvenile's apartment at 5:00 a.m. without a warrant to arrest him.[31] In another case, Houston police discovered marijuana on a youth five hours after he had been stopped for driving a car without lights and a driver's license. Confined to a Texas training school for this drug offense, the youth was ordered released by an appellate court because the search took place too late to be related to the arrest.[32] The least right to privacy is on the street, followed generally by the automobile and school; the greatest right to privacy is in the home.[33]

Interrogation Practices

The Fourteenth Amendment of the Constitution affirms that police must adhere to standards of fairness and due process in obtaining confessions. Current standards also require that the courts must take into consideration the totality of circumstances under which a confession was made in determining the appropriateness of the confession.

The Supreme Court decision *Haley* v. *Ohio* is an early example of excesses in **police interrogation**.[34] In the *Haley* case, a 15-year-old youth was arrested at his home five days after a store robbery in which the owner was shot. Five or six police officers questioned the boy for about five hours; he then confessed after being shown what were alleged to be the confessions of two other youths. No parent or attorney was present during the questioning. The Supreme Court invalidated the confession, stating the following:

> The age of the petitioner, the hours when he was grilled, the duration of his quizzing, the fact that he had no friend or counsel to advise him, the callous attitude of the police toward his rights combine to convince us that this confession was wrung from a child by means which

TIMELINE
Important Supreme Court Cases on the Police Interrogation of Juveniles

1936	1948	1966	1967	1979	1989	2011
Brown v. Mississippi: Confessions cannot be extracted by police violence.	**Haley v. Ohio:** Methods used in obtaining juvenile's confession violated the Due Process Clause of the Fourteenth Amendment.	**Miranda v. Arizona:** This prohibits the use of a confession in court unless the individual was advised of his or her rights before interrogation.	**In re Gault:** This made the right against self-incrimination and the right to counsel applicable to juveniles.	**Fare v. Michael C.:** This applied the "totality of the circumstances" approach to the interrogation of juveniles.	**Commonwealth v. Guyton:** No other minor, not even a relative, can act as an interested adult (acting *in loco parentis*).	**J.D.B. v. North Carolina:** Extended *Miranda* warnings to children and held that a child's age must be considered in assessing whether a suspect is aware of his or her rights.

the law should not sanction. Neither man nor child can be allowed to stand condemned by methods which flout constitutional requirements of due process of law."[35]

The Supreme Court also ruled in *Brown* v. *Mississippi* that police may not use force to obtain confessions[36]; in this case, police had used physical force to extract a confession. Other confessions have been ruled invalid because the accused was too tired; was questioned too long; and/or was not permitted to talk with his or her spouse, friends, or lawyer either while he or she was being interrogated or until he or she confessed.[37]

Juveniles taken into custody are entitled to the rights stated in the 1966 decision of **Miranda v. Arizona**. This Supreme Court decision prohibits the use of a confession in court unless the individual was advised of his or her rights before interrogation, especially the right to remain silent, the right to have an attorney present during questioning, and the right to be assigned an attorney by the state if the individual cannot afford one.[38] *In re Gault* (see Chapter 13) made the right against self-incrimination and the right to counsel applicable to juveniles.[39] However, the *Gault* decision failed to clarify whether or not a juvenile could waive the protection of the *Miranda* rules and also failed to specify what is necessary for a juvenile to waive his or her *Miranda* rights intelligently and knowingly. For example, is a juvenile's ability to waive *Miranda* rights impaired if the youth is under the influence of drugs or alcohol or in a state of shock?

The 1979 *Fare v. Michael C.* decision applied the "totality of the circumstances" approach to the interrogation of juveniles. The circumstances behind this case were that Michael C. was implicated in a murder that took place during a robbery, so the police arrested the 16-year-old youth and brought him to the station. After he was advised of his *Miranda* rights, he requested to see his probation officer; when this request was denied, he proceeded to talk to the police officer, implicating himself in the murder. The Supreme Court ruled in this case that Michael C. appeared to understand his rights and that when his request to talk with his probation officer was denied, he expressed his willingness to waive his rights and continue the interrogation.[40]

Thomas Grisso, who studied juveniles interrogated by the St. Louis police in 1981, found that virtually all of them had waived their *Miranda* rights, so he questioned whether juveniles were even "capable of providing a meaningful waiver of the rights to avoid self-incrimination and to obtain legal counsel."[41]

After surveying a sample of juveniles, Grisso found that almost everyone younger than 14 years of age and half the juveniles in the 15- to 16-year-old age bracket had a less-than-adequate understanding of what their *Miranda* rights entailed.

Several court cases have held that the minority status of a juvenile is not an absolute bar to a valid confession. A California case upheld the confession of two juveniles from Spanish-speaking families; although both had been arrested before, one had an IQ of 65–71 with a mental age of 10 years and 2 months.[42] Similarly, a North Carolina court of appeals approved the confession of a 12-year-old youth who was charged with shooting out a window in a camper truck.[43] A Maryland appellate court approved the confession of a 16-year-old youth, a school dropout with an eighth-grade education, who was charged with fire-bombing and burning both a store and a school during a racial confrontation.[44]

To protect juveniles against police interrogation excesses, many jurisdictions have a statutory requirement that a parent, someone acting *in loco parentis* for the child, or counsel for the child must be present at police interrogations in order for a confession to be admissible. In *Commonwealth v. Guyton* (1989), the Massachusetts court held that no other minor, not even a relative, can act as an interested adult.[45] Other courts have ruled that the interested adult may be a child's relative.[46] Some states attempt to protect the juvenile by requiring that the youth be taken to the juvenile detention center or to juvenile court if he or she is not returned immediately to the parents' custody, obviously preferring that police interrogation take place within juvenile facilities rather than at a police station.[47]

Finally, in 2011, in the case of *J.D.B. v. North Carolina*, the U.S. Supreme extended *Miranda* protections to minors, and held that a child's age must be considered in assessing whether a suspect is aware of his or her rights. In *J.D.B.*, Justice Sotomayor, writing for the majority, said that "the law has historically

> **Many jurisdictions have a statutory requirement that a parent, someone acting *in loco parentis* for the child, or counsel for the child must be present at police interrogations.**

reflected the same assumption that children characteristically lack the capacity to exercise mature judgment and possess only an incomplete ability to understand the world around them."[48]

Fingerprinting

Fingerprinting, along with other pretrial identification practices, has traditionally been highly controversial in juvenile corrections. Some juvenile court statutes require that a judge approve the taking of fingerprints of juveniles, control access to fingerprint records, and provide for fingerprint destruction under certain circumstances.[49] In many other jurisdictions, the police department determines policy, with some police departments routinely fingerprinting all juveniles taken into custody and suspected of serious wrongdoing. The Juvenile Justice and Delinquency Prevention Act of 1974 recommended that fingerprints be taken only with the consent of the judge, that juvenile fingerprints not be recorded in the criminal section of the fingerprint registry, and that the records be destroyed after their purpose has been served.

A 1969 Supreme Court decision that reversed a Mississippi ruling is the most important case dealing with juvenile fingerprints. In this case, the U.S. Supreme Court ruled, among other things, that fingerprints taken by the police could not be used as evidence. The youth in question was detained by the police without authorization by a judicial officer, was interrogated at the time he was first fingerprinted, and was fingerprinted again at a later date; the Court ruled that the police should not have detained the youth without authorization by a judicial officer, that the youth was unnecessarily fingerprinted a second time, and that the youth should not have been interrogated at the first detention when he was fingerprinted.[50]

Pretrial Identification Practices

Among other **pretrial identification practices**, both photographing and placing juveniles in lineups are highly controversial. Another recent practice is to notify the school district regarding juveniles who have been convicted of serious or violent crimes.

A lineup consists of the police placing a number of suspects in front of witnesses or victims, who try to identify the person who committed the crime against them. If no one can be identified, the suspects are released to the community, but if one of the persons is identified as the perpetrator, the police then proceed with their prosecution. The courts have been careful to set standards for the police to follow because innocent youths could end up labeled as delinquents and confined in an institution; one important standard is that the offender must have an attorney at the initial identification lineup in order to ensure that the identification of the offender is not tainted.

In one important case, *United States* v. *Wade* (1967), the Supreme Court ruled that the accused has a right to have counsel present at post-indictment lineup procedures.[51] In *Kirby* v. *Illinois* (1972), the Court went on to add that the defendant's right of counsel during post-indictment lineup procedures goes into effect as soon as the indictment has been issued.[52] In the *In re Holley* decision (1970), a juvenile accused of rape had his conviction reversed by the appellate court because of the lack of counsel during the lineup identification procedure.[53]

At the end of 1997, 45 states and the District of Columbia had statutes permitting photographing of juveniles under certain circumstances for criminal history record purposes, and juvenile codes in 42 states allowed names—and sometimes even pictures and court records—of juveniles who were involved in delinquency proceedings to be released to the media.[54] Since 1997, still more states have permitted similar pretrial identification practices.

Photographs also can play an important part in the identification of offenders. For example, in one case, a rape victim was shown a photograph of one suspect only, and she could not identify the offender from that photograph but then later identified her attacker in the probation office. A California appellate court noted that permitting the identification of offenders on the basis of only one photograph was inappropriate because it could prejudice the victim.[55]

Another problem with photographs is their permanency and potential stigmatizing effects on youths in the community. Because photographs are filed and frequently reviewed by police officers, the police examine these photographs whenever something happens in the community, so innocent youths may never be able to escape the stigma of such labeling. For these reasons some states require that judges give the police written consent to take photographs, that the photographs not be published in the media, and that the photographs be destroyed when the youths become adults.

Table 12–5 summarizes the legal rights of juveniles.

TABLE 12–5 | LEGAL RIGHTS OF JUVENILES

Category	Brief Description of Juvenile Rights Within Each Category
Search and Seizure	Juveniles, like adults, are protected from unauthorized search and seizure.
Interrogation Practices	Police must adhere to standards of fairness and due process in obtaining confessions.
Fingerprinting	Police handle the fingerprinting of juveniles in a wide variety of ways; however, there is more consistency in how they destroy the records after their purpose has been served.
Pretrial Identification Practices	The photographing and placing of juveniles in lineups are controversial but are more frequently taking place today than in the past.

Community relations are a major focus of police officers who work with juveniles.

▶ Social Context of Delinquency: The Police and the Prevention of Juvenile Offenses

Explain police efforts to deter delinquency.

Three ways in which police departments are attempting to implement community-based policing in the prevention and deterrence of youth crime are community-based, school-based, and gang-based interventions (see Figure 12–1).

Community-Based
Community relations are a major focus of police officers who work with juveniles.

Gang-Based
The number of street gangs rose dramatically across the nation beginning in the late 1980s.

School-Based
Developing effective delinquency prevention programs in schools is one of the most important challenges facing the police today.

FIGURE 12–1 Three Police Interventions.

Community-Based Interventions

Community relations are a major focus of police officers who work with juveniles. They must cultivate good relations with school administrators and teachers, with the staff of community agencies, with the staff of local youth organizations and youth shelters, with the juvenile court, and with merchants and employees at popular juvenile hangouts. Of course, juvenile police officers also must develop good relations with parents of youthful offenders as well as with the offenders themselves. The officer who has earned the respect of the youths of the community will be aware of what is happening in the community and will be likely called on for assistance by youths in trouble.

One of the important challenges the police face today is finding missing children. The AMBER Alert system began in 1996 when Dallas–Fort Worth broadcasters teamed with local police departments to develop an early-warning system to assist in finding abducted children, which they called the Dallas AMBER Plan. AMBER, which stands for America's Missing: Broadcast Emergency Response, was named in memory of nine-year-old Amber Hagerman, who was kidnapped and brutally murdered while riding her bicycle in Arlington, Texas, in 1996. Other states and communities soon set up their own alert plans, and the AMBER Alert network was adopted nationwide.[56]

The police are called on to intercede in a variety of juvenile problems. These include enforcing the curfew ordinances that more and more communities across the nation are passing,[57] enforcing drug laws,[58] preventing hate crimes committed by teenagers against minority groups (Jews, other ethnic groups, and homosexuals),[59] focusing attention on serious habitual offenders, enhancing the quality and relevance of information that is exchanged through active interagency collaboration, and controlling gun-related violence in the youth population.

In many larger cities, police departments form special juvenile units to address youth crime.

In many larger cities, police departments form special juvenile units to address youth crime.

TABLE 12–6 SPECIAL UNITS TARGETING JUVENILE JUSTICE CONCERNS

	Type of Agency	
Type of Special Unit	**Local Police**	**State**
Drug education in schools	70%	30%
Juvenile crime	62	10
Gangs	45	18
Child abuse	46	8
Domestic violence	45	10
Missing children	48	31
Youth outreach	33	6

Source: Office of Juvenile Justice and Delinquency Prevention, *Juvenile Offenders and Victims: 2006 National Report* (Washington, D.C.: U.S. Government Printing Office, 2006), p. 153.

A 2000 survey of law enforcement agencies with 100 or more sworn officers reported that a large proportion of these agencies had special units targeting juvenile justice concerns (see Table 12–6).[60]

Developing effective delinquency prevention programs in schools is one of the most important challenges facing the police today.

> ### Think About It...
> Developing effective delinquency prevention programs in schools is one of the most important challenges facing the police today. How might such programs be designed?
>
>

School-Based Interventions

Developing effective delinquency prevention programs in schools is one of the most important challenges facing the police today. Community predelinquent programs have included courses in high school, junior high school, and elementary school settings addressing school safety, community relations, drug and alcohol abuse, city government, court procedures, bicycle safety, and juvenile delinquency. The Officer Friendly Program and McGruff "Take a Bite Out of Crime" were established throughout the nation to develop better relations with younger children.

More recently, popular prevention programs have included Gang Resistance Education and Training (G.R.E.A.T.) and Law-Related Education (LRE). Since the program began in 1991, more than 12,000 law enforcement officers have been certified as G.R.E.A.T. instructors and close to 6 million students have graduated from the G.R.E.A.T. program.[61] The program is found in all 50 states and in the District of Columbia and is in use in more than 500 communities across the United States. During 1999–2000, the program underwent an extensive curriculum review, which placed more emphasis on active learning and increased teacher involvement. The G.R.E.A.T program currently consists of a 13-week middle school curriculum, an elementary curriculum, a summer program, and family training.

Evaluations have been done in 1999, 2001, 2004, and 2012. From all the surveys conducted, the consistent finding was that G.R.E.A.T. has not reduced youth involvement in gangs and delinquent behavior, but it did help young people to develop positive relations with law enforcement.[62]

Law Enforcement Education (LRE), another prevention program, is designed to teach students the fundamental principles and skills needed to become responsible citizens in a constitutional democracy.[63] One of the few studies evaluating LRE programs found that these programs, when properly conducted, can reduce tendencies toward delinquent behavior and improve a range of attitudes related to responsible citizenship, and it found that successful students were also less likely to associate with delinquent peers and to use violence as a means of resolving conflict.[64]

Today, the need for substance-abuse-prevention programs demands creativity and involvement on the part of the police. The Drug Abuse Resistance Education (D.A.R.E.) program (discussed in the following section on social policy) is a widely replicated effort by the police to prevent substance abuse. New York City's School Program to Educate and Control Drug Abuse (Project SPECDA), which is a collaborative effort of the city's police department and board of education, is another highly praised drug-prevention program; in this project, a 16-session curriculum, with the units split evenly between the fifth and sixth grades, imparts basic information about the risks and effects of drug use, makes students aware of the social pressures that cause drug use, and teaches acceptable methods of resisting peer pressure to experiment with drugs.[65]

In addition to drug-prevention programs, the police respond to incidents ranging from student fights and assaults to drug and weapon possession. Officers also regularly drive by schools during night and weekend patrol to prevent vandalism and burglary to school property, and the police are responsible for providing security and safety to the school. In some schools, this requires conducting searches of students as they come into the school, monitoring the halls, doing conflict mediation when necessary, and protecting students as they come to and go home from school. The police are frequently called on to assist the school in searching for weapons and drugs on school property and are charged to enforce drug-free school-zone laws and the federal Gun-Free School Zones Act. The police are also expected to enforce school attendance programs in a few school districts across the nation.

The federal Office of Community-Oriented Policing Services (COPS) has awarded almost $715 million to more than 2,900 law enforcement agencies to fund more than 6,300 school resource officers (SROs) through the COPS in Schools (CIS) program. In addition, COPS has appropriated nearly $21 million to train COPS-funded SROs and school administrators in partnering schools or school districts to work more collaboratively through the CIS program. SROs in schools can serve in a variety of ways: They may function not only as a law enforcement officers but as problem solvers, LRE educators, and community liaisons; they may teach classes in crime prevention, substance-abuse awareness, and gang resistance; they may monitor and assist troubled students through mentoring programs; and they may promote social and personal responsibility by encouraging student participation in community service activities. Moreover, these officers help schools develop policies to address delinquent activity and school safety.[66]

Gang-Based Interventions

The number of street gangs rose dramatically across the nation beginning in the late 1980s. The characteristics of these gangs

> **Police–juvenile relations take place in the larger context of community-oriented policing, which has focused on developing a cooperative relationship between police officers and communities.**

vary widely from one city to another. Some of the gangs are simply groups of adolescents who hang around together and who seldom get into any serious trouble, other gangs engage in extensive drug activity, and some have become involved in violent drive-by shootings in which innocent citizens have been killed.

Drugs and violence have made gangs a problem for the police. For example, police officers caught a group of Los Angeles Crips conducting a drug sales seminar in St. Louis, Missouri.[67] Once a community becomes aware of the seriousness of the gang problem—usually after a violent gang incident has taken place—then pressure is typically put on the police to solve the problem. Police departments have frequently responded to this pressure by setting up one of three types of intervention units to work with gangs.[68]

The Youth Service Program, which is one such unit, is formed to deal with a specific gang problem and is not a permanent unit within the police department; officers continue to perform their regular duties and are not exclusively concerned with gang problems. The gang detail is a second type of unit, and the officers in these units generally are pulled from detective units or juvenile units. The gang detail differs from the Youth Service Program in that its officers are assigned solely to gang problems and do not routinely work on other assignments. The **gang unit** is the third type of unit, and the members of these permanent units see themselves as specialists who are working on gang problems; for example, many gang units will develop extensive intelligence networks with gang members in the community.[69]

▶ Delinquency Across the Life Course: Effects of Police Discretion

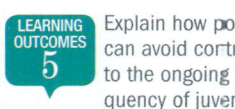
Explain how police can avoid contributing to the ongoing delinquency of juveniles.

The police are the first line of contact with law-violating juveniles. They frequently have the discretion to divert a youth or refer him or her to the attention of the juvenile justice system, especially when the juvenile is involved in a minor offense. As repeatedly stated in this text, there is no question that the juvenile who has an early onset of crime and comes to the attention of the justice system is more likely to be involved with the justice system longer and go on to the adult system more than the youth who is diverted from the system or begins his or her onset of crime at a later date in adolescence. With that in mind, the police must try everything possible to avoid contributing to the ongoing delinquency and later criminality of individuals (Figure 12–2).

▶ Delinquency and Social Policy: Project D.A.R.E.

The most popular school-based drug-education program in the nation is Drug Abuse Resistance Education (D.A.R.E), a program that receives over $200 million annually in public funding despite strong evidence of its ineffectiveness.

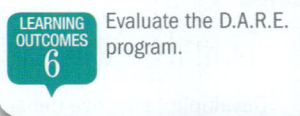
Evaluate the D.A.R.E. program.

This program is designed to equip elementary school children with skills for resisting peer pressure to experiment with tobacco, drugs, and alcohol. Using a core curriculum consisting of 17 hour-long weekly lessons, D.A.R.E. gives special attention to fifth and sixth graders to prepare them for entry into junior high and high school, where they are most likely to encounter pressure to use drugs. Since it was founded, D.A.R.E. has expanded to encompass programs for middle and high school students, gang prevention, conflict resolution, parent education, and after-school recreation and learning. As the most popular school-based drug-education program in the United States, it is administered in about 75 percent of this nation's school districts, reaching 26 million, and has been adopted in more than 50 countries.[70]

It has been widely evaluated, and there are several disappointing findings:

- The D.A.R.E. program has some immediate beneficial effects on student knowledge of drugs, social skills, attitudes about drug use, and attitudes toward the police, but these effects dissipate quickly and are typically gone within one to two years.

- The effects of D.A.R.E. on drug-use behavior (measured in numerous ways) are extremely rare.

- The identified effects tend to be small in size and also dissipate quickly.[71]

Dennis Rosenbaum summarized this collective evidence:

In sum, the results were very disappointing despite high expectations for the program. Across more than 30 studies, the collective evidence from evaluations with reasonably good scientific validity suggests that the core

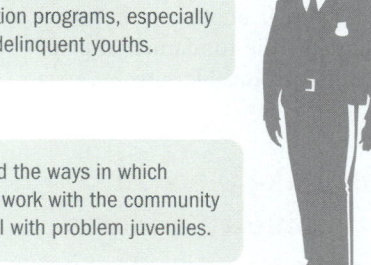

FIGURE 12–2 Police Activities to Combat Delinquency.

D.A.R.E. program does not prevent drug use in the short term, nor does it prevent drug use when students are ready to enter high school or college. Students who receive D.A.R.E. are indistinguishable from students who do not participate in the program.[72]

Rosenbaum raised a question that has been widely raised elsewhere—"How can we reconcile this state of knowledge with the reality of worldwide support for D.A.R.E.?"—and goes on to say, "The irony for the drug prevention field (and other fields as well) is that a program known to be ineffective receives millions of dollars in support, whereas programs known to be effective or promising are sidelined and remain unfunded."[73]

Dozens of communities in the 1990s and early 2000s have dropped the D.A.R.E. program, but the debate whether to continue funding has been waged both nationally and internationally. Proponents of D.A.R.E. are a strong interest group and presently are able to maintain federal funding for this drug-prevention program.

THE CASE

The Life Course of Amy Watters, Age 16

Things had not gone well when Amy and CJ were questioned by the deputy. To ensure fairness all around, the deputy had said, a tripod-based video camera would be used to create a record of the interviews. First the deputy interviewed Amy while she had CJ wait in a separate room—one well out of ear-shot of the interrogation room. Before the session started, however, Amy was advised of her rights in front of her father and asked whether she wanted to continue to answer questions. Her father was also told he could stop the interview process at any time and hire a lawyer to represent his daughter; the process would then resume at a later time.

Amy's father talked briefly with his daughter, and began to suggest that Amy stay silent, as was her right. Amy protested, however, saying that she wanted to admit her involvement in the scheme to bring drugs into the school. "Dad," she said to her father, "I didn't take any money for anything. I'm really not THAT guilty of doing anything wrong."

Amy's father didn't want to argue with his daughter, and wasn't sure that he could afford a lawyer anyway, so he went along with her request. So, as he watched, the deputy proceeded to ask Amy a series of questions, and Amy slowly admitted her involvement in the drug-smuggling scheme—eventually revealing what she knew of its scope and the extent of CJ's involvement in it. CJ, she said, wasn't really making any money from drug sales, and everybody on the football team wanted the marijuana that he sold them. The officer seemed unconvinced by her attempts to minimize the harm done, and told her that dealing drugs on school grounds was a serious offense. That night Amy slept in a juvenile confinement facility, waiting to be taken for a hearing before a juvenile court judge the next day.

Discuss
1. Why did Amy decide to confess? What would have happened if she hadn't?

Learn more on the Web:
- police encounters with juvenile suspects by visiting the National Criminal Justice Reference Service at NCJRS.gov and reading the publication numbered NCJ 205124.

Follow the continuing Amy Watters saga in the next chapter.

CHAPTER 12 Police and the Juvenile

Summarize police–juvenile relations.

Police–juvenile relations seem to be improving, but they still depend on such factors as class, gender, and race and whether juveniles have had previous unfavorable contacts with the police.

1. Overall, how do juveniles feel about the police?
2. Why do the attitudes of minority and white youths toward the police tend to differ?
3. Why would youthful offenders feel differently toward the police than nonoffenders?
4. Have your personal experiences with the police made a difference in how you feel about the police?

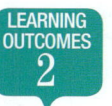

Summarize how juvenile offenders are processed.

The police officer has five options available when investigating a complaint against a juvenile or arriving at the scene of law-violating behavior: warning and release, station adjustment, referral to a diversion agency, citation and referral to juvenile court, or taking the youth to detention.

1. What are the most important factors affecting the processing of juveniles?
2. How does police discretion impact the processing of juveniles by the justice system?
3. What is meant by the term *station adjustment*?

police discretion A police officer's ability to choose from among a number of alternative dispositions when handling a situation.

juvenile officer In some police departments, a police officer who has received specialized training to work effectively with juveniles, and who is tasked primarily with such work.

station adjustment One of several disposition options available to a police officer whereby a juvenile is taken to the police station following a complaint, the contact is recorded, and the juvenile is given an official reprimand and then released to his or her parents or guardians.

citation A summons to appear in juvenile court.

Summarize the legal rights of juveniles in encounters with police.

When it comes to search and seizure and interrogation, the juvenile has constitutional rights similar to those of adults, but fingerprinting and pretrial identification practices do vary in some jurisdictions where there is more consideration given to protecting juveniles.

1. What are the most important legal rights of juveniles?
2. How is the case of *Miranda* v. *Arizona* relevant in the area of juvenile justice?
3. How do the due process rights of juveniles who are under arrest compare to those of adults?

search and seizure The police procedure used in the investigation of crimes for the purpose of gathering evidence.

police interrogation The process of interviewing a person who has been arrested with the express purpose of obtaining a confession.

Miranda* v. *Arizona The landmark 1966 U.S. Supreme Court ruling that suspects taken into police custody must, before any questioning can take place, be informed that they have the right to remain silent, that anything they say may be used against them, and that they have the right to legal counsel.

fingerprinting A pretrial identification procedure used with both juveniles and adults following arrest.

pretrial identification practices The procedures such as fingerprinting, photographing, and placing juveniles in lineups for the purpose of identification prior to formal court appearance.

arrest The process of taking a person into custody for an alleged violation of the law. Juveniles who are under arrest have nearly all the due process safeguards accorded to adults.

Explain police efforts to deter delinquency.

The police attempt to prevent delinquency through community-based efforts, school-based interventions, and gang-based interventions.

1. How do the police attempt to prevent and deter delinquency?
2. What police efforts to prevent and deter delinquency are likely to be the most successful? Why?

gang unit A specialized unit established by some police departments to address the problem of gangs.

LEARNING OUTCOMES 5

Explain how police can avoid contributing to the ongoing delinquency of juveniles.

The police can contribute to preventing delinquency across the life course when they develop positive relationships with juveniles, when they avoid abusive treatment toward juveniles, and when they expand community-wide ways to work with juveniles.

1. Can you think of ways that police can contribute to the long-term delinquency of a juvenile?
2. Why is the police role in working with juveniles more difficult today than it was in the past?
3. Is "by-the-book" policing the wisest course of action to prevent charges of discrimination? Explain your response.

LEARNING OUTCOMES 6

Evaluate the D.A.R.E. program.

The highly popular D.A.R.E. project, a program that receives over 200 million annually, has been widely evaluated and the findings are extremely disappointing regarding its effects on the drug-using behavior of juveniles.

1. What is your evaluation of D.A.R.E.?
2. Did you participate in a D.A.R.E. program in high school? If so, did it make a difference in your using or not using drugs?

"Under our Constitution the condition of being a boy does not justify a kangaroo court."

—In re Gault, 387 U.S. 1 (1967)

13

Juvenile Court

1. Recall the basic ideals on which juvenile court was founded.
2. Explain how constitutionalists have influenced juvenile justice.
3. Summarize the pretrial procedures involved in juvenile court proceedings.
4. Summarize the trial proceedings that take place in juvenile court.
5. Recall the various forms of sentencing available to a juvenile court judge.
6. Compare recidivism among juveniles transferred to adult court to that of those who are retained in juvenile court.
7. Recall the principles of juvenile court excellence.

INTRO: THE JUVENILE COURT IDEAL

As discussed in Chapter 11, the idea of a juvenile court, separate in principle from adult criminal courts, had its beginnings in Chicago in 1899. The juvenile court ideal, which inspired juvenile justice system workers in this country for over 100 years, was, however, disgraced by the actions of a corrupt Pennsylvania judge in the early 2000s. In 2009, former Luzerne County (Pennsylvania) juvenile court judge Mark Ciavarella, 61, was convicted by a federal jury of 12 counts of racketeering and conspiracy for accepting cash payoffs totaling nearly $1 million to place juvenile offenders into privately owned detention facilities. Following Ciavarella's conviction, the Pennsylvania Supreme Court quickly dismissed thousands of juvenile convictions that he had issued, saying that Ciavarella had run his courtroom with "complete disregard for the constitutional rights of the juveniles" who came before him, including the right to legal counsel and the right to intelligently enter a plea.[1]

DISCUSS Is the idea of a juvenile court a good one? That is, should courts for juveniles differ from adult criminal courts? If so, how?

Disgraced former Luzerne County (Pennsylvania) juvenile court judge Mark Ciavarella. Ciavarella was convicted by a federal jury of accepting cash for placing juvenile offenders into privately owned facilities. What differences exist between adult and juvenile courts?

▶ Juvenile Court

LEARNING OUTCOMES 1 Recall the basic ideals on which juvenile court was founded.

Ciavarella's conviction strongly contrasts with the idealistic perspective of Roscoe Pound, the dean of American jurisprudence, who called the juvenile court "the most significant advance in the administration of justice since the Magna Carta."[2] Many contemporary advocates of the **juvenile court** continue to insist that the informal setting of the court and the parental demeanor of the judge enable wayward youths to be saved or rescued from possible lives of crime.

Critics eventually challenged such idealistic views of the juvenile court, claiming that the court ideal had not succeeded in rehabilitating youthful offenders, in bringing justice and compassion to them, or even in providing them with their due process rights.[3] Some investigators even accused the juvenile court of doing great harm to the juveniles who appeared before it.[4]

Today three different positions have emerged concerning the role of the juvenile court. One position continues to support the *parens patriae* philosophy, or the state as parent, and holds to standard of the "best interest of the child" for decision making. A second position proposes that the justice model (see Chapter 11) should replace the *parens patriae* philosophy as the basis of juvenile court procedures. In the 1980s, proposed procedural changes such as the decriminalization of status offenses, determinate sentencing, mandatory sentencing, and opening up of juvenile proceedings and records struck at the very heart and core of traditional juvenile court proceedings.[5] Barry Feld is one of the most articulate spokespeople for this position, arguing that an integrated criminal court with a youth discount (juveniles would receive lesser sentences than adults for similar violations of the law) would provide youthful offenders with greater protections and justice than they currently receive in the juvenile justice system and with more proportional and humane consequences than judges currently inflict on them as adults in the criminal justice system.[6]

In sum, significant changes are sweeping through the 116-year-old corridors of the juvenile court. In the second decade of the twenty-first century, what is actually taking place is that all three positions are represented: For minor offenses, as well as for status offenses in most states, the position of the "best

Significant changes are sweeping through the 116-year-old corridors of the juvenile court.

interest of the child" is the guiding standard of juvenile court decision making; for offenders who commit more serious delinquent acts, the principles of the justice model are increasingly used in adjudicatory and disposition hearings; and repetitive or violent youthful offenders are commonly transferred quickly to the adult court and handled as adults. Perhaps the question is not whether the traditional juvenile court will change, but whether the court will survive.

The concept of the juvenile court was rapidly accepted across the nation—31 states had instituted juvenile courts by 1905, and by 1928, only 2 states did not have a juvenile court statute. In Cook County, the amendments that followed the original act brought the neglected, the dependent, and the delinquent together under one roof. The "delinquent" category comprised both status offenders and actual violators of criminal law.

Reformers further advocated that the juvenile judge sit at a desk rather than on a bench and that he occasionally "put his arm around [the delinquent's] shoulder and draw the lad to him."[7] But the sympathetic judge was instructed not to lose any of his judicial dignity. The goals of the court were defined as investigation, diagnosis, and prescription of treatment. Lawyers were deemed unnecessary because these civil proceedings were not adversary trials but informal hearings in which the best interests of the youths were the chief concern.

In short, the juvenile court was founded on several basic ideals: that the court should function as a social clinic designed to serve the best interests of youths in trouble; that youths who were brought before the court should be given the same care, supervision, and discipline as would be provided by a good parent; that the aim of the court is to help, to restore, to guide, and to forgive; that youths should not be treated as criminals; and that the rights to shelter, protection, and proper guardianship are the only rights of youths.[8] See Figure 13–1, "The Ideals of the Juvenile Court."

1. Youths should be given the same care as that provided by a good parent.
2. The aim of the court is to restore, help, and forgive.
3. Youths should not be treated as criminals.
4. The rights of youths are the rights to shelter, protection, and proper guardianship.

FIGURE 13–1 The Ideals of the Juvenile Court.

A series of decisions by the U.S. Supreme Court in the 1960s and 1970s demonstrated the influence of the constitutionalists on juvenile justice.

▶ Changes in Legal Norms

U.S. Supreme Court Decisions of Special Relevance

In the twentieth century, the group known as the **constitutionalists**, one of the most formidable foes of the juvenile court, contended that the juvenile court was unconstitutional because under its system the principles of a fair trial and individual rights were denied. A series of decisions by the U.S. Supreme Court in the 1960s and 1970s demonstrated the influence of the constitutionalists on juvenile justice.

LEARNING OUTCOMES 2: Explain how constitutionalists have influenced juvenile justice.

As Figure 13–2 shows, some of the most important cases include *Kent* v. *United States* (1966), *In re Gault* (1967), *In re Winship* (1970), *McKeiver* v. *Pennsylvania* (1971), and *Breed* v. *Jones* (1975), each of which is described briefly in the following discussion.

Kent v. United States (1966)

Kent is the first decision in which the U.S. Supreme Court dealt with a juvenile court case dealing with the matter of **transfer** (see Juvenile Law 13.2). The juvenile judge did not rule on the motions of Kent's counsel and held no hearings, nor did he confer with Kent, Kent's mother, or Kent's counsel. The judge instead entered an order saying that after full investigation he was transferring jurisdiction to the adult criminal court; he made no findings and entered no reasons for the waiver.

On appeal, the U.S. Supreme Court, holding that the juvenile court proceedings were defective, found that during a transfer hearing, Kent should have been afforded an evidential hearing; that he should have been present when the court decided to waive jurisdiction; that his attorney should have been permitted to examine the social worker's investigation of the youth, which the court used in deciding to waive jurisdiction; and that the judge should have recorded a statement of reasons for the transfer.

In re Gault (1967)

In May 1967, the U.S. Supreme Court reversed the conviction of a minor in *In re Gault*. This influential and far-reaching decision represented a new dawn in juvenile court history because, in effect, it brought the light of

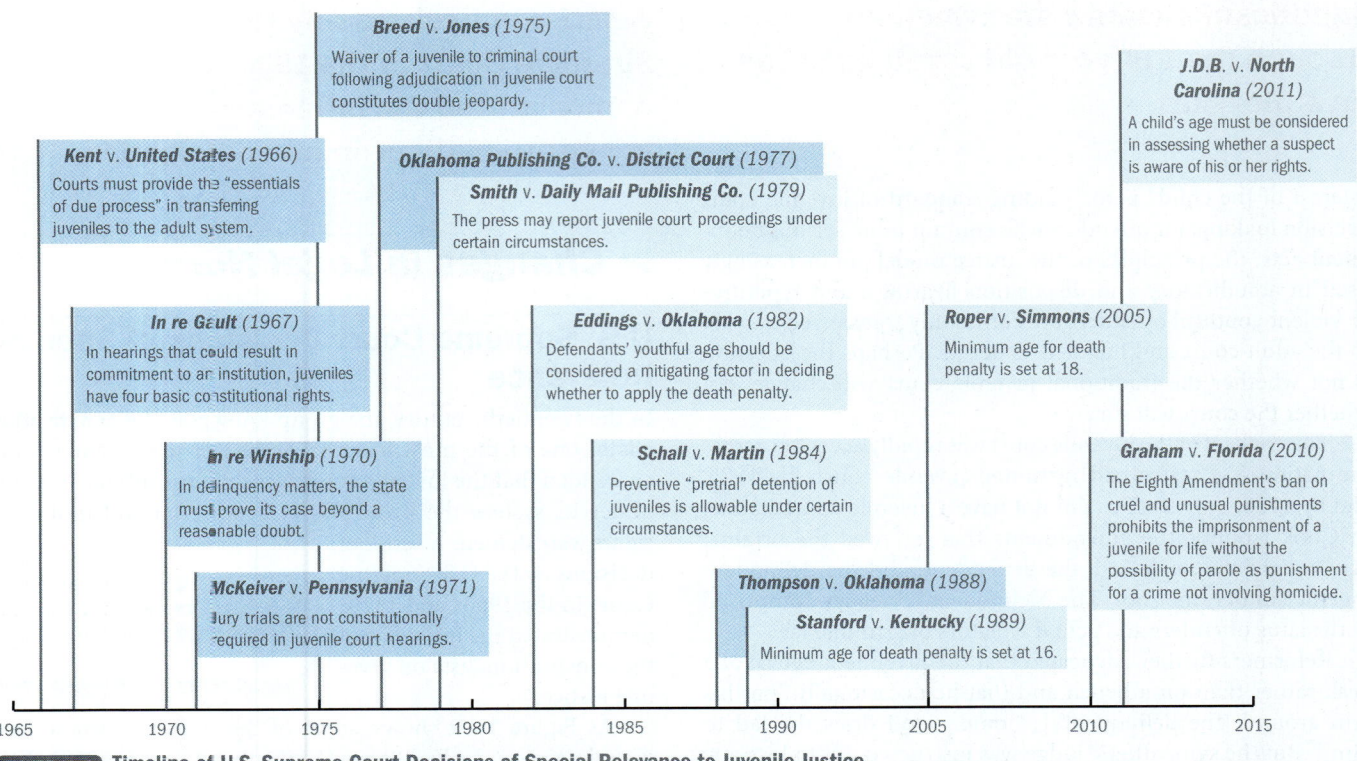

FIGURE 13-2 Timeline of U.S. Supreme Court Decisions of Special Relevance to Juvenile Justice.
Source: Adapted from Office of Juvenile Justice and Delinquency Prevention, *Juvenile Offenders and Victims: 2006 National Report* (Washington, D.C.: OJJDP, 2006), p. 101.

constitutional procedure into juvenile courts—no longer could due process and procedural safeguards be kept out of the adjudication proceedings.

In *Gault*, the U.S. Supreme Court overruled the Arizona Supreme Court for its dismissal of a writ of habeas corpus that had sought Gerald Gault's release from a training school.[9] The *In re Gault* decision affirmed that a juvenile has the right to due process safeguards in proceedings in which a finding of delinquency can lead to institutional confinement. The decision also established that a juvenile has the right to notice of the charges, right to counsel, right to confrontation and cross-examination, and privilege against self-incrimination. However, the Court did not rule that juveniles have the right to a transcript of the proceedings or the right to appellate review.

In choosing not to rule on these two latter rights, the Court clearly did not want to turn the informal juvenile hearing into an adversary trial. The cautiousness of this decision was underlined by a footnote stating that the decision did not apply to preadjudication or postadjudication treatment of juveniles.

In re Winship (1970)

In *Winship*, the Supreme Court decided that juveniles are entitled to proof **beyond a reasonable doubt** during the adjudication proceedings[10] (Juvenile Law 13.4 presents the facts of this case). In ruling that "preponderance of evidence" is not a sufficient basis for a decision when youths are charged with acts that would be criminal if committed by adults, the *Winship* decision not only expanded *Gault* but also reflected other concerns of the justices. The Court desired both to protect juveniles at adjudicatory hearings and to maintain the confidentiality, informality, flexibility, and speed of the juvenile process in the prejudicial and postadjudicative states. The Court obviously did not want to bring too much rigidity and impersonality to the juvenile hearing.

McKeiver v. Pennsylvania (1971)

During the 1969 through 1971 sessions, the Supreme Court heard three cases together (*McKeiver v. Pennsylvania*, *In re Terry*, and *In re Barbara Burrus*) concerning whether the due process clause of the Fourteenth Amendment guaranteeing the right to a jury trial applies to the adjudication of a juvenile court delinquency case.[11] The decision, which was issued in *McKeiver v. Pennsylvania*, denied the right of juveniles to have jury trials.

The Supreme Court gave the following five reasons for its ruling:

1. Not all rights that are constitutionally assured for the adult are to be given to the juvenile.
2. The jury trial, if required for juveniles, may make the juvenile proceedings into a fully adversary process and will put an end to what has been the idealistic prospect of an intimate, informal protecting proceeding.
3. A jury trial is not a necessary part of every criminal process that is fair and equitable.
4. The jury trial, if injected into the juvenile court system, could bring with it the traditional delay, the formality, and the clamor of the adversary system.

5. There is nothing to prevent an individual juvenile judge from using an advisory jury when he or she feels the need. For that matter, there is nothing to prevent individual states from adopting jury trials.[12]

Some states do permit jury trials for juveniles, but most adhere to the constitutional standard set by the Supreme Court. Surveys of states report that juveniles choose jury trials in only about 1 percent to 3 percent of cases.[13] The significance of the *McKeiver* decision is that the Court indicated an unwillingness to apply further procedural safeguards to juvenile proceedings, especially during the preadjudicatory and postadjudicatory treatment of juveniles.

Breed v. Jones (1975)

The question of transfer to an adult court, first considered in the *Kent* case, was taken up again in the *Breed v. Jones* decision.[14] This case raised the issue of **double jeopardy**, questioning whether a juvenile could be prosecuted as an adult after an adjudicatory hearing in the juvenile court. The increased use of transfers, or the binding over of juveniles to the adult court, makes this decision particularly significant today.

The U.S. Supreme Court ruled that Breed's case did constitute double jeopardy—a juvenile court cannot adjudicate a case and then transfer the case over to the criminal court for adult processing on the same offense. The significance of *Breed* is that **prosecutors** must determine which youthful offenders they want to transfer to the adult court before juvenile court adjudication; otherwise, the opportunity to transfer, or certify, those youths is lost.[15]

Today nearly every state has defined the specific requirements for transfer proceedings in its juvenile code (discussed in more detail later in this chapter). At present, when a transfer hearing is conducted in juvenile court, due process law usually requires (1) a legitimate transfer hearing, (2) a sufficient notice to the juvenile's family and defense attorney, (3) the right to counsel, and (4) a statement of the court order regarding transfer.

Some evidence exists that youths who have counsel may get more severe dispositions than those without counsel.[16] When it exists, there are two possible explanations for this positive relationship between counsel and punitive dispositions: First, the juvenile judge is punishing youths who choose to be represented by counsel; second, the youths who have committed more serious crimes are the ones requesting counsel and are the ones most likely to be adjudicated to training school or transferred to adult court. Although the former may have been true in the past, the latter is typically true today.

▶ Pretrial Procedures

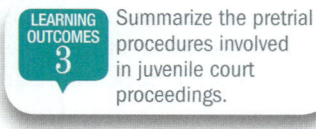
Summarize the pretrial procedures involved in juvenile court proceedings.

The types of cases that are under the jurisdiction of the juvenile court vary widely among and even within states, but they generally include those involving delinquency, neglect, and dependency. In 2010, juvenile courts handled an estimated 1,368,200 delinquency cases.

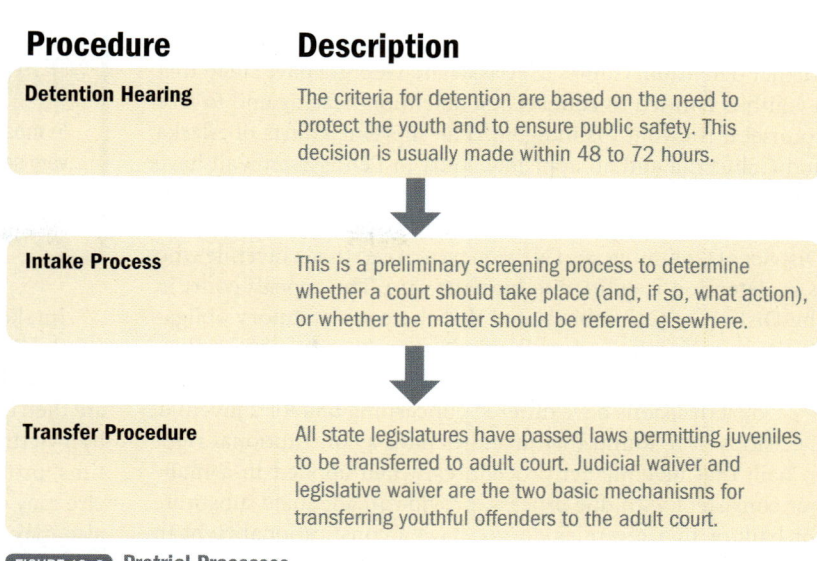

FIGURE 13–3 Pretrial Processes.

Procedure	Description
Detention Hearing	The criteria for detention are based on the need to protect the youth and to ensure public safety. This decision is usually made within 48 to 72 hours.
Intake Process	This is a preliminary screening process to determine whether a court should take place (and, if so, what action), or whether the matter should be referred elsewhere.
Transfer Procedure	All state legislatures have passed laws permitting juveniles to be transferred to adult court. Judicial waiver and legislative waiver are the two basic mechanisms for transferring youthful offenders to the adult court.

Between 1960 and 2010, juvenile court delinquency caseloads increased more than 300 percent.[17] Juvenile courts also may deal with cases involving adoption, termination of parental rights, appointment of guardians for minors, custody, contributing to delinquency or neglect, and nonsupport.

Pretrial procedures (Figure 13–3) in the juvenile justice system include the detention hearing, the intake procedure, and the transfer procedure, all of which take place before the adjudication stage of juvenile court proceedings.

Detention Hearing

Legislative acts that govern the juvenile court normally require that the police either take a youth to an intake officer of the court or a detention facility or release the youth to his or her parents. At a **detention hearing**, the criteria for detention are based on the need to protect the youth and to ensure public safety. The decision to detain must be made within a short period of time, usually 48 to 72 hours, excluding weekends and holidays. Urban courts, which have intake units on duty 24 hours a day for detention hearings, frequently act within a few hours.[18]

The **detention center** (detention hall or detention home) physically restricts youths for a short period, whereas **shelter care** is physically nonrestrictive and is available for those who have no homes or who require juvenile court intervention. A third type of placement is **jail** or police lockup. A fourth is **home detention**; in-home detention restricts a juvenile to his or her home and is supervised, normally by a paraprofessional staff member. Finally, **attention homes** offer services and staff support in a nonrestrictive setting.

Five states have legislated a hearing on probable cause for detained youths, and appellate cases in other states have moved

Pretrial procedures in the juvenile justice system include the detention hearing, the intake procedure, and the transfer procedure.

in the direction of mandating a probable cause hearing to justify further detention. Courts in Alaska and Georgia have ruled that a youth is entitled to counsel at a detention hearing and to free counsel if the youth is indigent. The supreme courts of Alaska and California and an appellate court in Pennsylvania all have overturned cases in which no reason or inadequate reason was stated for continuing detention. Finally, courts in Baltimore, the District of Columbia, and Nevada have ruled that a juvenile who is in detention is entitled to humane care. The appeals court in the District of Columbia stated that there is a statutory obligation to provide a juvenile with care "as nearly as possible equivalent to that which should have been given him by his parents."[19]

Court decisions have differed concerning **bail** for a juvenile. Decisions have found that juveniles have a constitutional right to bail; that juvenile act procedures, when applied in a manner consistent with due process, provide an adequate substitute for bail; or that juveniles do not have a constitutional right to bail. Nine states (Arkansas, Colorado, Connecticut, Georgia, Massachusetts, Nebraska, Oklahoma, South Dakota, and West Virginia) have enacted laws granting juveniles the right to bail; on the other hand, Hawaii, Kentucky, Oregon, and Utah deny juveniles the right to bail.

The U.S. Supreme Court decision in the *Schall* v. *Martin* (1984) case represented a fundamental change in detention practices.[20] The plaintiffs originally filed a lawsuit in federal district court claiming that the New York Family Court Act was unconstitutional because it allowed for the preventive detention of juveniles.

The Supreme Court, however, reversed the decision of the appeals court. Justice William H. Rehnquist, in writing the opinion for the majority, declared that the "preventive detention under the statute serves the legitimate state objective held in common with every State, of protecting both the juvenile and the society from the hazards of pretrial crime."[21] Some experts believe that the Court's ruling may encourage a significant expansion of preventive, or secure, detention for juveniles.

Intake Process

Intake essentially is a preliminary screening process to determine whether a court should take action—and, if so, what action—or whether the matter should be referred elsewhere. Larger courts usually handle this function through a specialized intake unit, and probation officers or other officers of the court screen incoming cases in smaller courts.[22]

Between 1985 and 2010, the likelihood that a delinquency case would be handled informally (without filing a petition for adjudication) decreased.[23] Although the overall delinquency caseload increased 17 percent between 1985 and 2010, the number of nonpetitioned cases decreased 1 percent and the number of petitioned cases increased 38 percent.

Intake essentially is a preliminary screening process to determine whether a court should take action—and, if so, what action.

Think About It...

In most jurisdictions, juveniles who commit very serious offenses can be transferred to an adult criminal court for trial. What are the consequences of such a transfer?

Intake procedures follow **complaints** to authorities against youths. Juvenile law varies from state to state regarding who is permitted to sign such a complaint. Typically, most complaints are filed by the police, although they may be initiated and signed by a victim or by the youth's parents. In some states, parents, victims, probation staff, social services staff, neighbors, or anyone else may go directly to the court to file a complaint. Complaints also may be brought by school officials and truant officers.

After the intake officer receives the complaint, he or she must first decide whether the court has statutory jurisdiction. If the statutory guides are unclear, the intake officer should seek the advice of the prosecuting attorney. Once legal jurisdiction is established, the second step is to conduct a preliminary interview and investigation to determine whether the case should be adjudicated nonjudicially or petitioned to the court. This evaluation procedure varies from jurisdiction to jurisdiction, principally because so many juvenile courts have failed to provide written guidelines, so the intake officer usually has broad and largely unregulated discretion in making the intake decision.

Options for the Disposal of Cases

The intake unit, especially in larger urban courts, may have up to five options for the disposal of cases: (1) outright dismissal of the complaint, (2) informal adjustment (chiefly diversion to a nonjudicial agency), (3) informal probation, (4) consent decree, and (5) filing of a petition.

Outright dismissal of the complaint takes place when legal jurisdiction does not exist or when the case is so weak that the intake officer questions the feasibility of petitioning the youth to the juvenile court. **Informal adjustment** means that the intake officer requires restitution from the youth (see Chapter 14), warns him or her, and then dismisses the case or diverts the youth to a social services agency. The diversion agency supervises such referrals and generally reports to the intake unit on the youth's progress; status offenders and juveniles charged with minor offenses typically are dealt with under this option.

Informal probation, which has been under increased criticism since the 1970s, involves the casual supervision of a youth by a volunteer or probation officer who reserves judgment on the need for filing a petition until the intake officer (or other designated person) sees how the youth fares during the informal probation period.

A **consent decree** is a formal agreement between the youth and the court in which he or she is placed under the court's supervision without a formal finding of delinquency. Consent decrees provide an intermediate step between informal handling and probation; the consent decree is used less often than the other options that are currently open to the intake officer. The consent decree, it should be noted, comes after the petition but before the adjudication hearing.

If none of these options is satisfactory, the intake officer can choose to file a petition. Unfortunately, the broad discretionary power given to intake workers has often been abused. For example, Duran Bell, Jr., and Kevin Lang's study of intake in Los Angeles County revealed the importance of extralegal factors, especially cooperative behavior, in reducing the length of detention and the effect of age in increasing the length of detention.[24]

Transfer Procedure

All state legislatures have passed laws permitting juveniles to be transferred to **adult court**. The peak year for the number of delinquency cases waived to criminal court was 1994, but this increase was followed by a 42 percent decline between 1994 and 2001; then between 2001 and 2008, the number of judicially waived delinquency cases increased by 13 percent.[25] In a 2010 study, Megan C. Kurlychek and Brian D. Johnson found "that even after rigorous statistical matching procedures, juvenile offenders are published more severely than their young adult counterpart."[26]

Some states have implemented transfer procedures by lowering the age of judicial waiver, some by excluding certain offenses from juvenile court jurisdiction, and others by passing legislation aimed at the transfer of serious juvenile offenders. During the mid-1990s, 41 states passed laws that facilitated trying juveniles in adult court.[27]

Every state currently has some provision for transferring juvenile offenders to adult criminal courts. Montana (at age 12), along with Georgia, Illinois, and Mississippi, can transfer youths at very young ages. More states make it possible to transfer youths at 14 years old than at any other age, and seven states transfer youths at either 15 or 16 years of age.

Several states grant prosecutors, rather than juvenile court judges, the nonreviewable discretionary power to determine the court before which juveniles will be required to appear. For example, in the early 1980s the state of Florida expanded the discretionary power of prosecutors in dealing with juveniles who are 16 years old or older.[28] Table 13–1 indicates which states allow prosecutors to try juveniles in either juvenile or criminal court.

Every state currently has some provision for transferring juvenile offenders to adult criminal courts.

TABLE 13–1 | STATES PERMITTING PROSECUTORIAL DISCRETION

Concurrent Jurisdiction Offense and Minimum Age Criteria, 2011

State	Minimum Age for Concurrent Jurisdiction	Any Criminal Offense	Certain Felonies	Capital Crimes	Murder	Certain Person Offenses	Certain Property Offenses	Certain Drug Offenses	Certain Weapon Offenses
Arizona	14		14						
Arkansas	14		16	14	14	14			
California	14		14	14	14	14	14	14	
Colorado	14		14		14	14	14		
Dist. of Columbia	16				16	16	16		
Florida	NS	16	16	NS	14	14	14		14
Georgia	NS			NS					
Louisiana	15				15	15	15	15	
Michigan	14		14		14	14	14	14	
Montana	12				12	12	16	16	16
Nebraska	NS	16	NS						
Oklahoma	15		16		15	15	15	16	15
Vermont	16	16							
Virginia	14				14	14			
Wyoming	14		14		14	14	14		

Note: Ages in the minimum age column may not apply to all offense restrictions but represent the youngest possible age at which a juvenile's case may be directly filed in criminal court. "NS" indicates that in at least one of the offense restrictions indicated, no minimum age is specified.

In states with concurrent jurisdiction, the prosecutor has discretion to file certain cases in either criminal court or juvenile court.

Source: Office of Juvenile Justice and Delinquency Prevention, *Statistical Briefing Book*, http://www.ojjdp.gov/ojstatbb/structure_process/qa04111.asp?qaDate=2011 (accessed April 28, 2014).

In 15 states, murder is excluded from juvenile court jurisdiction; 10 states exclude rape, 8 exclude armed robbery or robbery, 6 exclude kidnapping, and 3 exclude burglary. A total of 11 states use a combination of offense categories.[29]

Judicial waiver and legislative waiver (also called *remand*, *certification*, and *waiver of jurisdiction*) are the two basic mechanisms for transferring juvenile offenders to the adult criminal justice system. Judicial waiver, the more common of the two, takes place after a judicial hearing on a juvenile's amenability to treatment or his or her threat to public safety.[30]

Judicial waiver, as previously discussed in regard to the *Kent* v. *United States* and *Breed* v. *Jones* decisions, contains certain procedural safeguards for youthful offenders. The criteria that are used to determine the **binding-over** (transfer) decision typically include the age and maturity of the youth; the seriousness of the referral incident; the youth's past record; the youth's relationship with parents, school, and community; and the dangerousness of the youth. Court officials also decide if they believe the youth may be helped by juvenile court services. Most juvenile court judges appear to be influenced primarily by the youth's prior record and the seriousness of the present offense.

Legislative waiver is accomplished in five ways. The first occurs when legislatures simply exclude certain offenses from juvenile court jurisdiction, meaning that any juvenile who commits a specified offense automatically goes before the adult court. The second lowers the age over which the juvenile court has jurisdiction; for example, if a state's age of juvenile court jurisdiction is 18 years old, the legislature may lower the age to 16 years old. The third form of legislative waiver specifies that juveniles of specific ages who commit specific crimes are to be tried by adult court, a method of legislative waiver that focuses as much on the offense as it does on the age of the offender. The fourth method of legislative waiver involves statutes that simply state that anyone who commits a specific crime may be tried in adult court—an approach that is attractive to those who believe that any youth who violates the law should receive an appropriate punishment. The fifth method is for state legislatures to give both the juvenile and the adult courts concurrent jurisdiction over all juveniles who are under the jurisdictional age of the juvenile court.

Reverse waiver and **blended sentencing** must also be considered in discussing waiver. In reverse waiver, some state laws permit youths who are over the maximum age of jurisdiction to be sent back to the juvenile court if the adult court believes the case is more appropriate for juvenile court jurisdiction; for a reverse waiver, defense counsel and prosecutors attempt to make their case for their desired action, with some evidence and testimony being allowed and arguments being presented. When each side has had a chance to present its case and to rebut the opponents' arguments, the judge makes the decision.[31]

In blended sentencing, some states permit juvenile court judges at the disposition hearing to impose both an adult and a juvenile sentence concurrently. In these cases, the juvenile is given both sentences but is ordered first to fulfill the requirements of the juvenile disposition. If the juvenile meets the requirements of this disposition satisfactorily, then the adult disposition is suspended, but if the juvenile does not fulfill the conditions of the juvenile disposition, then he or she is required to serve the adult sentence. In some states, the juvenile may be ordered to abide by the requirements of the juvenile disposition until reaching the age of majority; at this point, the juvenile begins serving the adult sentence minus the time already spent under juvenile court supervision.[32]

In sum, although waivers are still relatively infrequent, they remain an important issue in juvenile justice. Significantly, juveniles waived to adult court are not always the most serious or violent offenders. Examinations of waivers have found that little consensus exists as to which criteria should be used in making waiver decisions.[33] Furthermore, although remanded youths are receiving severe penalties, waivers generally do not result in more severe penalties for juvenile offenders than they would have received in juvenile court. Several states have attempted to develop a process that might identify juveniles unfit for retention in juvenile court; using such criteria as age, offense, and prior record, for example, Minnesota has codified transfer procedures to be followed by judges and prosecutors.[34] With adult courts' massive caseload and their limited judicial experience in sentencing juveniles, little evidence exists that adult judges know what to do with juveniles who appear before them.[35]

▶ Juvenile Trial Proceedings

The trial stage of juvenile court proceedings is divided into the adjudicatory hearing, the disposition hearing, and judicial alternatives. There is usually also a (statutory) right to appeal.

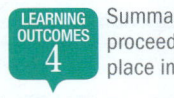

LEARNING OUTCOMES 4: Summarize the trial proceedings that take place in juvenile court.

Adjudicatory Hearing

Adjudication is the fact-finding stage of the court's proceedings. The adjudicatory hearing usually includes the following steps: the youth's plea, the presentation of evidence by the prosecution and by the defense, the cross-examination of witnesses, and the judge's finding. The number of cases in which the juvenile was adjudicated delinquent rose steadily from 1960 to 2000, but then leveled off and began a small decline around 2008—except for property cases, which began declining in the late 1990s[36] (see Figure 13–4).

The steps followed in the adjudicatory hearing serve as protections to ensure that youths are provided with proof beyond a reasonable doubt when they are charged with an act that would constitute a crime if it had been committed by an adult, and that the judge follows the rules of evidence and dismisses hearsay from the proceedings. Hearsay is dismissed because it can be unreliable or unfair, inasmuch as it cannot be held up for cross-examination. The evidence must be relevant and must contribute to the belief or disbelief of the act in question.

Prosecutors in most juvenile courts begin the adjudication proceedings by presenting the state's case. The arresting officer

> **The trial stage of juvenile court proceedings is divided into the adjudicatory hearing, the disposition hearing, and judicial alternatives.**

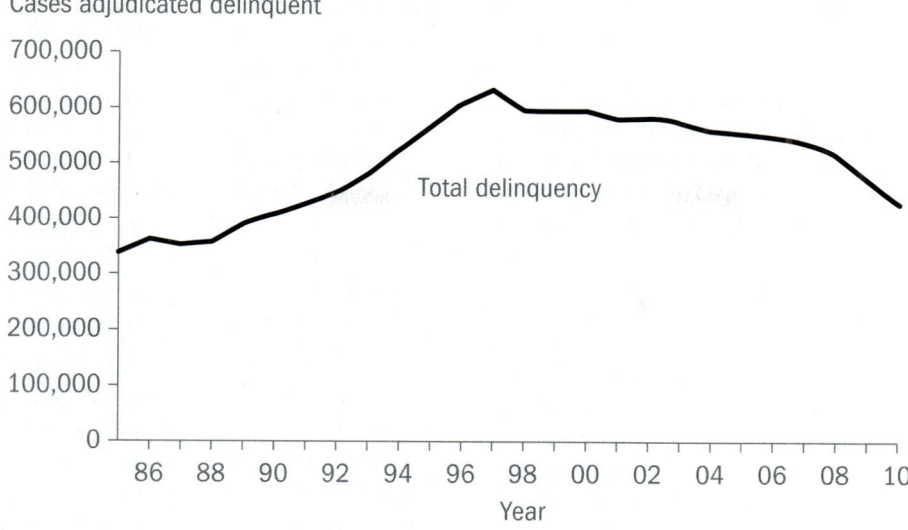

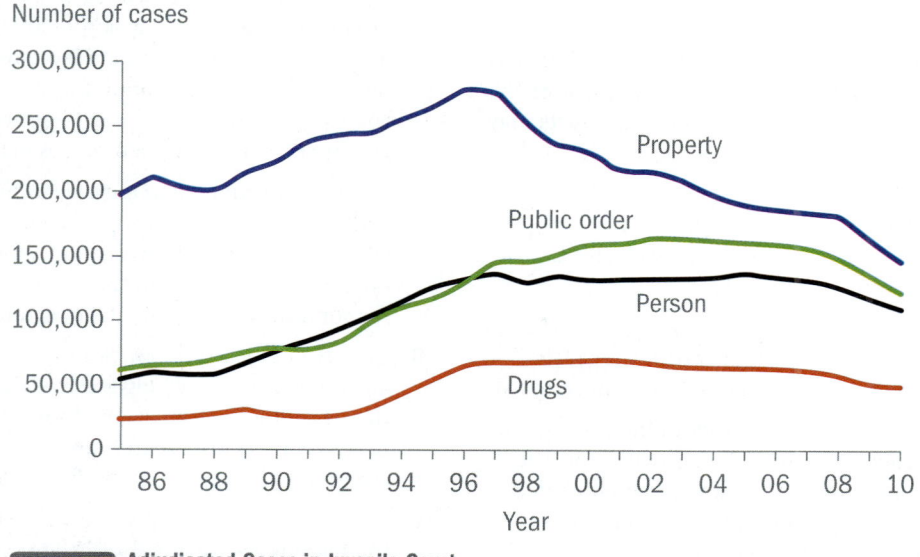

FIGURE 13-4 **Adjudicated Cases in Juvenile Court.**
Source: Adapted from Charles Puzzanchera and Crystal Robson, *Juvenile Court Statistics 2010* (Washington, D.C.: OJJDP, 2014).

and witnesses at the scene of the crime testify, and any other evidence that has been legally obtained is introduced. The defense attorney then cross-examines the witnesses. Defense counsel also has the opportunity at this time to introduce evidence that is favorable to the client, and the youth may testify on his or her own behalf; the prosecutor then cross-examines the defense witnesses. The prosecution and the defense present summaries of the case to the judge, who reaches a finding or a verdict.

There are 10 states that provide for a **jury trial** for juveniles, but jury trials are seldom demanded. Statutory provisions often close juvenile hearings to the general public, although this decision varies from one jurisdiction to the next. The right to a speedy trial has been provided by state court decisions and by statutes that limit the amount of time that can elapse between the filing of a complaint and the actual hearing.[37]

In sum, the typical adjudication hearing has come a long way since the *In re Gault* decision. Although some judges and defense attorneys are exemplary in the support they give to the due process protection of juveniles during this stage of the court's proceedings, other judges and defense attorneys fall short in living up to either the spirit or the letter of post-*Gault* juvenile law. This is particularly true of defense attorneys who lack knowledge of juvenile court procedures or the juvenile law itself. Significantly, largely because of the changing standards for transfer to the adult court, the prosecutor has become a prominent figure at these proceedings.

Disposition Hearing

Once a youth has been found delinquent at the adjudicatory stage, some juvenile court codes still permit judges to proceed immediately to the disposition (sentencing) hearing. However, the present trend is to hold a **bifurcated hearing**, or a split adjudicatory and dispositional hearing, because a split hearing gives the probation officer appointed to the case an opportunity to prepare a social study investigation of the youth.

The disposition stage of the court's proceedings normally is quite different from the fact-finding stage, especially when it is held at a different time. The traditional purpose has been to administer individualized justice and to set in motion the rehabilitation of the delinquent; therefore, the judge is not limited by constitutional safeguards as much as he or she was at the adjudication hearing. Rules of evidence are relaxed, parties and witnesses are not always sworn in, and hearsay testimony may be considered.[38] The starting point of the disposition hearing is usually the written social study of the juvenile prepared by the probation officer, a report that examines such factors as school attendance and grades, family structure and support, degree of maturity and sense of responsibility, relationships with peers, participation in community activities, and attitudes toward authority figures. In this final stage of the proceedings, juveniles are permitted to have legal counsel, and the *Kent* decision ensures the right of counsel to challenge the facts of the social study.

Judicial Alternatives

The alternatives that are available to different juvenile courts vary significantly. Large urban courts have all or most of the following 11 alternatives at their disposal, but rural courts may have only a few:

1. *Dismissal.* Dismissal is certainly the most desired disposition for juveniles. The fact-finding stage may have shown the youth to be guilty, but the judge can decide, for a variety of reasons, to dismiss the case.
2. *Restitution.* Also usually very desirable is restitution, where youths may be required to work off their debt with a few hours each week, but their lives are not seriously interrupted.
3. *Outpatient psychiatric therapy.* Whether in the court clinic, in the community mental health clinic, or with a private therapist, outpatient therapy is a treatment-oriented decision and is often reserved for middle-class youths to keep them from being sent to "unfitting" placements.
4. *Probation.* As the most widely used disposition, probation seems to be a popular decision with delinquents and a good treatment alternative for the court. Probation is sometimes set for a specific length of time, usually a maximum of two years. The judge can direct the probation officer to involve the youth in special programs, such as alternative schools, speech therapy, or learning disability programs.
5. *Foster home placement.* Foster home placements are more restrictive, inasmuch as youths are removed from their natural homes. These placements are used most frequently for status offenders and dependent and neglected youths.
6. *Day-treatment program.* Day-treatment programs are a popular alternative with juveniles because the youths who are assigned to these programs return home in the evening, but these programs are few in number and are available in only a few states.
7. *Community-based residential program.* There are different types of community-based residential programs, such as group homes and halfway houses, that are available to many judges. These residential facilities may be located in the community or in a nearby community, but they are not as desirable as community-based day-treatment programs because youths are taken from their homes to live in these facilities.
8. *Institutionalization in a mental hospital.* Institutionalization may be seen as appropriate for a youth's needs but requires a psychiatric evaluation; after the evaluation, the doctor may recommend that the court initiate proceedings for commitment to a mental hospital.
9. *County or city institution.* Some county or city institutions are available to a few judges across the nation. Placement in these facilities may be deemed appropriate for a youth who needs more security than probation offers but who does not require long-term placement in the state training school.
10. *State or private training school.* The state or private training schools are usually reserved for youths who have committed serious crimes or for whom everything else has failed. In some states, state training schools include minimum-security (forestry camps, farms, and ranches), medium-security, and maximum-security institutions.
11. *Adult facility or youthful offender facility.* In a few states, if the youth has committed a serious offense and is seen as too hard-core for a juvenile correctional institution, he or she is placed in an adult facility or a youthful offender facility.

Right to Appeal

Although juveniles do not yet have a constitutional right to make an **appeal** of their cases to a higher judiciary,

---

FORMAL
 (1) The recommendation of the probation officer and the information contained in the social study investigation
  a. The recommendation of the probation officer is usually followed by the juvenile judge.
 (2) The seriousness of the delinquent behavior and previous contacts with the court
  a. This has the greatest impact on judicial decision making at this stage. Studies of the juvenile courts in Colorado, Pennsylvania, and Tennessee also indicated that prior decisions by juvenile court personnel were related more strongly to disposition than any other factor.
 (3) The available options
  a. The most desirable placement may not be available in that jurisdiction, or the desired placement may have no space for the youth.

INFORMAL
 (1) The values and philosophy of the judge
  a. Some judges work from a legal model, some from an educational model, and some from a medical model, and the model that a particular judge emphasizes will, of course, affect his or her handling of juvenile delinquents.
 (2) The social and racial background of the youth, as well as his or her demeanor
 (3) The presence or absence of a defense counsel
 (4) The potential political repercussions of the delinquent acts

Juveniles do not have a constitutional right to appeal, but practically all states grant them that right.

practically all states grant them the right to appeal by statute. The states are following the lead of the U.S. Supreme Court, which pointed out in *Gault* that juveniles should have the same absolute right to appeal as do adults under the equal protection clause of the Constitution. Since that ruling, most state legislatures have passed laws granting juveniles the right to appeal; state courts have also ruled that state statutes granting the right to appeal for juveniles must be applied uniformly to all juveniles, a decision that effectively undermines the past practice in which some courts gave judges the discretion to determine which juvenile cases could be appealed. The common practice today is to give juveniles the same rights to appeal that adults have.[39]

The right to appeal is limited for the most part to juveniles and their parents. States may appeal in some circumstances, but this right is seldom exercised, and few cases have come before the courts. Another issue of appeal concerns the type of orders that may be appealed—although states generally permit the appeal of final orders, what is "final" varies from state to state. Most state statutes call for the case to be appealed to an appellate court, but a few states call for a completely new trial. Other common statutory rights of juveniles at appeal are the right to a transcript of the case and the right to counsel.[40]

Organizational factors limit the use of the **appellate review** of juvenile court decisions. Many juveniles lack counsel at trial who can make a record and obtain a transcript, and even more juveniles lack access to appellate counsel. In addition, juvenile public defenders' caseloads frequently preclude the luxury of filing appeals; many public defenders neither authorize their clients to file appeals nor advise their clients of the possibility of an appeal. The only study that compared rates of appeals by criminal defendants and juvenile delinquents found that convicted adults appealed more than ten times as often as did juveniles.[41] See Figure 13–5, "Trial Proceedings in the Juvenile Court."

▶ Juvenile Sentencing Structures

Determinate sentencing (fixed sentences for specified offenses) is a new form of sentencing in juvenile justice, and in some jurisdictions it is replacing the traditional form, **indeterminate sentencing** (sentencing at the judge's discretion). In addition, increasing numbers of juvenile courts are using a blended form of sentencing.

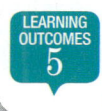

LEARNING OUTCOMES 5: Recall the various forms of sentencing available to a juvenile court judge.

Criticism of the decision-making outcomes of juvenile courts has increased since the 1970s. Early on, the criticism focused on the arbitrary nature of the decision making that violated the due process rights of juveniles; more recently, this criticism has been based on the belief that the juvenile court is too "soft" on crime. This latter criticism, especially, has led to a number of attempts to change sentencing and other juvenile procedures.

In the 1990s, nearly every state enacted **mandatory sentencing** for violent and repetitive juvenile offenders. The development of graduated, or accountability-based, sanctions was another means that states used in the 1990s to ensure that juveniles who are adjudicated delinquent receive an appropriate disposition by the juvenile court. Several states have created a blended sentencing structure, which is a mechanism for holding juveniles accountable for their offenses—specifically for cases involving repeat and serious juvenile offenders. This expanded sentencing authority allows criminal and juvenile courts to impose either juvenile or adult sentences—or at times both—in cases involving juveniles.[42] See Figure 13–6 for blended sentencing options.

ADJUDICATORY HEARING
This is the fact-finding stage of the court's proceedings and usually includes the youth's pleas, the presentation of evidence by the prosecution and defense, the cross-examination of witnesses, and the judge's finding.

DISPOSITION HEARING
The traditional purpose is to administer individualized justice and to set in motion the rehabilitation of the delinquent. Accordingly, the judge is not limited by constitutional safeguards as much as he or she was at the adjudication hearing.

JUDICIAL ALTERNATIVES
These alternatives available to juvenile courts vary significantly from one court to another, but most courts have a variety of choices.

RIGHT TO APPEAL
Juveniles do not have a constitutional right to make an appeal of their cases to a higher judiciary, but nearly all states permit the right to appeal by statute.

FIGURE 13–5 Trial Proceedings in the Juvenile Court.

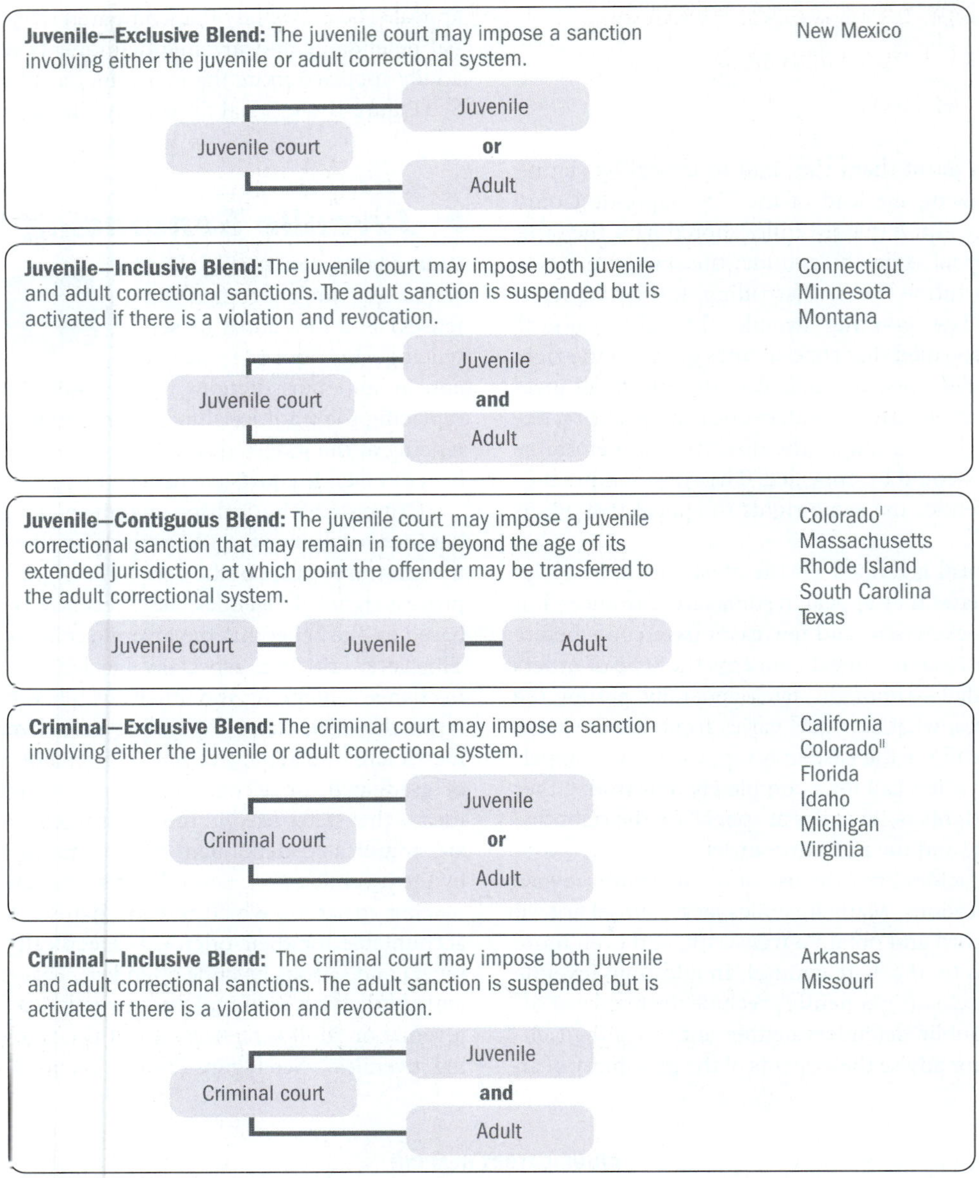

Juvenile—Exclusive Blend: The juvenile court may impose a sanction involving either the juvenile or adult correctional system.

Juvenile court → Juvenile or Adult

New Mexico

Juvenile—Inclusive Blend: The juvenile court may impose both juvenile and adult correctional sanctions. The adult sanction is suspended but is activated if there is a violation and revocation.

Juvenile court → Juvenile and Adult

Connecticut
Minnesota
Montana

Juvenile—Contiguous Blend: The juvenile court may impose a juvenile correctional sanction that may remain in force beyond the age of its extended jurisdiction, at which point the offender may be transferred to the adult correctional system.

Juvenile court — Juvenile — Adult

Colorado[I]
Massachusetts
Rhode Island
South Carolina
Texas

Criminal—Exclusive Blend: The criminal court may impose a sanction involving either the juvenile or adult correctional system.

Criminal court → Juvenile or Adult

California
Colorado[II]
Florida
Idaho
Michigan
Virginia

Criminal—Inclusive Blend: The criminal court may impose both juvenile and adult correctional sanctions. The adult sanction is suspended but is activated if there is a violation and revocation.

Criminal court → Juvenile and Adult

Arkansas
Missouri

Note: Blends apply to a subset of juveniles specified by state statute.
[I] Applies to those designated as "aggravated juvenile offenders."
[II] Applies to those designated as "youthful offenders."

FIGURE 13–6 Blended Sentencing Options in Juvenile Cases.
Source: Adapted from Office of Juvenile Justice and Delinquency Prevention, *1999 National Report Series* (Washington, D.C.: U.S. Department of Justice, 1999), p. 19.

Blended sentencing allows juvenile court judges to impose both an adult and a juvenile sentence on a delinquent concurrently.

▶ Delinquency Across the Life Course: the Impact of Transfer on Juveniles

The process of transferring juveniles to the adult court has generated considerable debate in juvenile justice circles and has raised a number of questions: Who should be transferred? What are the

Think About It...

Blended sentencing allows juvenile court judges to impose both an adult and a juvenile sentence on a delinquent concurrently, and creates a middle ground between traditional juvenile and adult sanctions. How does blended sentencing work and what are its advantages?

222 Chapter 13 Juvenile Court

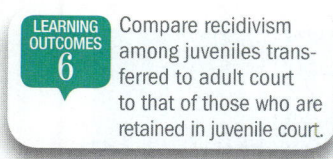

LEARNING OUTCOMES 6: Compare recidivism among juveniles transferred to adult court to that of those who are retained in juvenile court.

consequences in terms of criminal sanctions, as compared to juvenile court sanctions? What effect does the prison system have on juveniles? What are the consequences of transfer to the individuals involved? The answers to these questions help determine how transfer affects delinquents across the life course.

Richard E. Redding proposed that juveniles tried as adults have higher recidivism rates because of the stigmatization and other negative effects, the sense of resentment and injustice juveniles feel about being tried and convicted as adults, the learning of criminal mores and behaviors in prison, and the decreased focus on rehabilitation and family support in the adult system.[43] What Redding does not mention is that juveniles are more likely to be victimized, including sexually assaulted, in the adult system than they are in the juvenile system (something that is discussed in Chapter 14). It can be argued that at least juveniles who commit a violent crime before they are 18 years old can no longer be executed—but as this text goes to press they still can be placed in prison for life.

The sentence of life without parole is an option that has been used in most states to deal with convicted adults as well as juvenile offenders. Sometimes, juveniles as young as 13 or 14 years old receive what amounts to being sentenced to die in prison. An organization known as the Equal Justice Initiative has documented 74 cases where children 14 years of age or younger have been given this sentence.[44] In November 2009, the U.S. Supreme Court agreed to hear two cases that challenge the constitutionality of life sentences for juveniles. One of the cases involved 34-year-old Joe Sullivan, a Florida prisoner, who was sent away for life for raping an elderly woman when he was 13. The other case involved Terrance Graham, now 22, who was convicted of armed robberies that were committed when he was 16 and 17 years old. Bryan Stevenson, one of the defense attorneys appearing before the Court, told reporters that his basic argument is "to say to any child of 13 that you are only fit to die in prison is cruel," and cruel and unusual punishments are prohibited by the U.S. Constitution.[45]

▶ Prevention of Delinquency and Social Policy: Excellence in Juvenile Courts

The meaning of excellence in the juvenile court is one of the topics that often merits discussion among today's policymakers. The National Council of Juvenile and Family Court Judges provides an answer to this question, taking a somewhat broad approach and identifying the functions of the court and its judges (see Figure 13–7).[46]

LEARNING OUTCOMES 7: Recall the principles of juvenile court excellence.

Excellence in Juvenile Courts

Applies to the entire system
- Juvenile justice systems must have adequate staff, facilities, and program resources.

Applies specifically to judges
- Judges should engage in judicial leadership and encourage system collaboration.
- Status should be the same as other judges and judge should have multiple-year or permanent assignment.
- Judges should make certain that cases are diverted to alternative systems whenever possible and appropriate.
- Judges should make certain that victims have access to services they need.
- Judges should make certain that court depositions are individualized and that they include graduated sanctions and incentives.
- Judges should ensure that effective post-dispositions are provided to each youth.
- Judges should ensure accountability among courtroom participants.
- Judges should ensure that an adequate information system is available to evaluate performance.
- Judges are responsible to see that all court staff are adequately trained.

Apply to other staff members
- All members of the court team should treat youths, families, crime victims, witnesses, and others with respect, dignity, courtesy, and cultural understanding.
- Youths charged in the delinquency court should have qualified and adequately compensated legal representation.
- Staff should encourage family members to participate in the development and implementation of the youth's intervention plan.

Apply to the court
- Delinquency courts and juvenile abuse courts should have integrated one-family-one-judge case assignments.
- Courts should render timely and just decisions, and trials should conclude without continuances.

FIGURE 13–7 Principles of Excellence.

THE CASE

The Life Course of Amy Watters, Age 16

In Florida, the state where Amy lives, juvenile court jurisdiction extends to a person's 19th birthday. As a consequence of her involvement in the transportation and sale of controlled substances, Amy found herself facing formal processing by the juvenile court. At a hearing before a judge specializing in juvenile matters, Amy was adjudicated delinquent and ordered to be sent to a residential facility for serious juvenile offenders, and to be held there for six months. During that time, the judge told her that she had to participate in and successfully complete a drug-education program that the facility offered. While there, the judge said Amy would be expected to attend an on-site school (she was in the 10th grade), and to maintain at least a "C" average in the courses she took. Any sign of further misbehavior, the judge told Amy, could result in her being held at the facility until she turned 19.

Because Amy's boyfriend, CJ, was already 19 at the time of his arrest, he was treated as an adult and taken before a state criminal court judge. CJ, who did not have any money, and whose parents were poor, was provided with a public defender to represent him; but he held true to his word that he would not implicate anyone else in the crimes with which he had been charged. After a month spent in jail for lack of bail money, CJ's attorney convinced him to plead guilty to charges involving the sale and distribution of a controlled substance. Because his criminal activities occurred on school grounds, however, he was also charged with violating the state's Drug Free School Zone statute. Upon entering a plea of guilty, he received a five-year sentence, and was immediately taken to a prison within the state to serve his time. Federal drug-trafficking proceedings against CJ were being contemplated by federal prosecutors. If found guilty under federal law, he could be ordered to spend additional time in prison—this time in a federal confinement facility.

Discuss
1. How would Amy have been treated differently in court had she been an adult? What is likely to happen to CJ?

Learn more on the Web:
- Learn more about the self-report method for measuring delinquency and crime by visiting the National Criminal Justice Reference Service at NCJRS.gov and reading the publication numbered NCJ 185538.

Follow the continuing Amy Watters saga in the next chapter.

CHAPTER 13 Juvenile Court

LEARNING OUTCOMES 1

Recall the basic ideals on which juvenile court was founded.

The juvenile court was built on the following ideals: Youths should be given the same care as that provided by a good parent; the aim of the court is to restore, to help, and to forgive; youths should not be treated as criminals; and the only rights of youths are the rights to shelter, protection, and proper guardianship.

1. What does the idea of the juvenile court have to offer the justice process?
2. What are the most valid criticisms of the juvenile court?
3. Can you imagine ways in which it might be possible to improve the juvenile court concept?

juvenile court Any court that has jurisdiction over matters involving juveniles.

LEARNING OUTCOMES 2

Explain how constitutionalists have influenced juvenile justice.

The constitutionalist influence can be seen in a number of U.S. Supreme Court cases that granted youths procedural rights in the juvenile court.

1. What was the most important U.S. Supreme Court case concerning the rights of juveniles during the court process?
2. What did each of the U.S. Supreme Court cases discussed in this section contribute to American juvenile justice?
3. How do transfer procedures differ from one state to another?
4. What is the legal standard that needs to be met in order to adjudicate a young person delinquent by the juvenile court during the adjudicatory stage of the court's proceedings?

constitutionalists The name given to a group of twentieth-century reformers who advocated that juveniles deserve due process protections when they appear before the juvenile court.

Kent v. United States A 1966 U.S. Supreme Court decision on the matter of transfer; the first decision in which the Supreme Court dealt with a juvenile court case.

In re Gault A 1967 U.S. Supreme Court case that brought due process and constitutional procedures into juvenile courts.

In re Winship A 1970 case in which the U.S. Supreme Court decided that juveniles are entitled to proof beyond a reasonable doubt during adjudication proceedings.

McKeiver v. Pennsylvania A 1971 U.S. Supreme Court case that denied juveniles the right to trial by jury.

Breed v. Jones A 1975 double jeopardy case in which the U.S. Supreme Court ruled that a juvenile court cannot adjudicate a case and then transfer the case to the criminal court for adult processing of the same offense.

transfer The process of certifying a youth over to adult criminal court. It takes place by judicial waiver and legislative waiver.

beyond a reasonable doubt A legal standard establishing the degree of proof needed for a juvenile to be adjudicated a delinquent by the juvenile court during the adjudicatory stage of the court's proceedings.

double jeopardy A common law and constitutional prohibition against a second trial for the same offense.

prosecutor The representative of the state in court proceedings. Also called *county's attorney*, *district attorney*, or *state attorney*.

LEARNING OUTCOMES 3

Summarize the pretrial procedures involved in juvenile court proceedings.

The pretrial proceedings include the detention hearing, which decides whether or not to detain a youth; the intake process, which is a screening process to determine what action should be taken with the youth; and the transfer procedure, which permits a youth to be transferred to the adult court.

1. What are the three important hearings that take place during pretrial procedures, and why are they important?
2. What transpires during the juvenile court's intake process?
3. What is meant by blended sentencing? When are blended sentences most appropriate?

detention hearing A hearing, usually conducted by an intake officer of the juvenile court, during which the decision is made as to whether a juvenile will be released to his or her parents or guardians or be detained in a detention facility.

detention center A facility that provides custodial care for juveniles during juvenile court proceedings. Also called *juvenile halls* and *detention homes*, detention centers were established at the end of the nineteenth century as an alternative to jails for juveniles.

shelter care A facility that is used primarily to provide short-term care for status offenders and for dependent or neglected youths.

jail A police lockup or county holding facility for adult offenders. Jails have few services to offer juveniles.

home detention House arrest. This form of detention is used in some jurisdictions, and an adjudicated juvenile remains at home under the supervision of juvenile probation officers.

attention home An innovative form of detention facility, found in several locations across the nation, that is characterized by an open setting.

bail The money or property pledged to the court or actually deposited with the court to effect the release of a person from legal custody. Juveniles do not have a constitutional right to bail, as do adults.

intake The first stage of juvenile court proceedings, in which the decision is made whether to divert the juvenile being referred or to file a formal petition in juvenile court.

complaint A charge made to an intake officer of the juvenile court that an offense has been committed.

informal adjustment An attempt to handle a youthful offender outside of the formal structures of the juvenile justice system.

informal probation An arrangement in which, instead of being adjudicated as a delinquent and placed on probation, a youth is informally assigned to the supervision of a probation officer.

consent decree A formal agreement between a juvenile and the court in which the juvenile is placed under the court's supervision without a formal finding of delinquency.

adult court Criminal courts that hear the cases of adults charged with crimes, and to which juveniles who are accused of having committed serious offenses can be waived (transferred). In some states, adult criminal courts have jurisdiction over juveniles who are accused of committing certain specified offenses.

judicial waiver The procedure of relinquishing the processing of a particular juvenile case to adult criminal court; also known as *certifying* or *binding over* to the adult court.

binding over The process of transferring (also called *certifying*) juveniles to adult criminal court. Binding over takes place after a judicial hearing on a juvenile's amenability to treatment or his or her threat to public safety.

legislative waiver A legislative action that narrows juvenile court jurisdiction, excluding from juvenile courts those youths charged with certain offenses.

reverse waiver A provision that permits a juvenile who is being prosecuted as an adult in criminal court to petition to have the case transferred to juvenile court for adjudication or disposition.

blended sentencing The imposition of juvenile and/or adult correctional sanctions on serious and violent juvenile offenders who have been adjudicated in juvenile court or convicted in criminal court.

LEARNING OUTCOMES 4

Summarize the trial proceedings that take place in juvenile court.

The trial stage of juvenile court proceedings is divided into the adjudicatory hearing, which is the fact-finding state of the court's proceedings; disposition hearing, which is the sentencing stage of the proceeding; and judicial alternatives, in which the judge decides on the placement for the youth.

1. What takes place during the trial stage of juvenile court proceedings?
2. What does the term *adjudicated* mean when applied to a juvenile?
3. What is a bifurcated hearing, and how can it be useful?
4. Do juveniles have the right to a jury trial? Why or why not?

adjudication The court process wherein a judge determines if the juvenile appearing before the court committed the act with which he or she is charged. The term *adjudicated* is analogous to *convicted* in the adult criminal justice system and indicates that the court concluded that the juvenile committed the act.

jury trial The court proceeding in which a panel of the defendant's peers evaluates evidence and renders a verdict. The U.S. Supreme Court has held that juveniles do not have a constitutional right to a jury trial, but several jurisdictions permit juveniles to choose a jury trial.

bifurcated hearing A split adjudication and disposition hearing, which is the present trend of the juvenile court.

appeal The review of juvenile court proceedings by a higher court. Although no constitutional right of appeal exists for juveniles, the right of adjudicated juveniles to appeal has been established by statute in some states.

appellate review The review of the decision of a juvenile court proceeding by a higher court. Decisions by appellate courts, including the U.S. Supreme Court, have greatly affected the development of juvenile court law and precedent.

LEARNING OUTCOMES 5

Recall the various forms of sentencing available to a juvenile court judge.

The juvenile judge has the following options available: indeterminate sentencing, which is sentencing at the judge's discretion; determinate sentencing, which has fixed sentences for specified offenses; or blended sentencing, which creates a middle ground between traditional juvenile and adult sanctions.

1. How have juvenile sentencing structures changed in many jurisdictions?
2. What is determinate sentencing, and how does it apply to juvenile justice?
3. What is indeterminate sentencing, and how does it apply to juvenile justice?

determinate sentencing A model of sentencing that provides fixed terms of sentences for criminal offenses. Terms are generally set by the legislature rather than determined by judicial discretion.

indeterminate sentencing In juvenile justice, a sentencing model that encourages rehabilitation through the use of general and relatively unspecific sentences. Under the model, a juvenile judge has wide discretion and can commit a juvenile to the department of corrections or youth authority until correctional staff members make the decision to release the juvenile. This type of sentencing is used with juveniles in most jurisdictions other than those who have mandatory or determinate sentencing.

mandatory sentencing The requirement that individuals who commit certain offenses be sentenced to a specified length of confinement if found guilty or adjudicated delinquent.

LEARNING OUTCOMES 6

Compare recidivism among juveniles transferred to adult court to that of those who are retained in juvenile court.

The recidivism rates for those transferred to the adult court seem to be higher than those for youths retained in the juvenile system.

1. What is recidivism? How can recidivism be measured?
2. Why would transfer to adult court result in higher rates of recidivism versus the rates of those over whom jurisdiction is retained by the juvenile court?

LEARNING OUTCOMES 7

Recall the principles of juvenile court excellence.

The 16 principles of excellence proposed by the National Council of Juvenile and Family Court Judges are intended to ensure a higher level of performance by the juvenile court judges and staff.

1. Of the principles of excellence proposed by the National Council of Family Court and Judges, which two or three do you believe are the most important in upgrading the role and performance of the juvenile court?
2. What other principles of excellence can you imagine?

14

Juvenile Corrections

> "Our society is fearful of our kids. I think we don't know how to set limits on them. They begin to behave in severely outrageous ways, and nobody stops them."
> —David York, Cofounder of Tough Love International

1. Define probation.
2. Summarize how probation operates in juvenile corrections.
3. Summarize the types of residential and day-treatment programs that are available.
4. Summarize the types of institutional placements that are available.
5. Summarize training school experiences for boys and girls.
6. Summarize the rights of confined juveniles.
7. Recall the objectives of juvenile aftercare.
8. Summarize the administration of juvenile aftercare.
9. Explain the impact of institutionalization on juveniles.
10. Recall the risk factors for higher levels of sexual violence during institutionalization.

INTRO: JUVENILE INCARCERATION

Child advocates have harshly condemned the conditions under which youth offenders are housed in institutional care. California juvenile facilities, according to a recent report, are failing the state's children. They have little chance of leaving improved, the report says, and some are worse off than when they arrived.[1] In March of 2007, responding to the reports of sexual abuse of youths at the Texas Youth Commission institutions, Texas Governor Rick Perry placed the Texas Youth Commission under conservatorship to guide reform of the agency. A report documents the violence, sexual abuse, and lack of accountability in the juvenile facilities of this state.[2] The Connecticut Juvenile Training School has been a headache for state authorities since its opening in 2001. Its high-security perimeter fence, thick steel doors, and small cells with slits for windows make it feel more like a prison than a rehabilitation facility for juveniles.

The problems increased in 2010, as Connecticut raised the maximum age for juvenile offenders from 15 to 17 years old, moving many of the 250 to 300 16- and 17-year-olds who previously went to adult prisons each year into juvenile facilities.[3] The U.S. Justice Department (DOJ) has filed lawsuits against facilities in 11 states for supervision that is either abusive or harmfully negligent. Although the DOP does not have the power to shut down juvenile correctional facilities, through litigation it can force a state to improve its facilities and protect the civil rights of jailed youth.[4] In a nationally conducted survey, the Associated Press contacted each state agency that oversees juvenile correctional centers and asked for information on the numbers of deaths as well as the numbers of allegations and confirmed cases of physical, sexual, and emotional abuse by state members since January 1, 2004. According to this survey, more than 13,000 claims of abuse were identified in juvenile correctional facilities around the nation from 2004 through 2007—a disturbing number given that the total population of detained youth was about 46,000 at the time the states were surveyed.[5]

Institutionalized juveniles listening to a talk about acquiring work skills. How can facilities for juveniles be improved?

DISCUSS What is the role of juvenile detention facilities in the justice system? How do such facilities differ from adult correctional institutions?

▶ Probation

LEARNING OUTCOMES 1 Define probation.

This chapter examines juvenile corrections, including corrections both in the community and in long-term institutions. The basic forms of **community-based corrections** are probation, residential and day-treatment programs, and aftercare. These services are alternatives to institutional placements and keep juvenile delinquents out of training schools, jails, and adult prisons. This chapter also focuses on long-term juvenile institutional placements, which include reception and diagnostic centers, ranches and forestry camps, boot camps, and public and private training schools. Juveniles may also be sent to adult prisons. Finally, this chapter considers aftercare and transition services back to the community for juveniles as they are released from institutional care.

Probation, the history of which is discussed in Chapter 11, permits juvenile offenders to remain in the community under the supervision of a probation officer, subject to certain conditions imposed by the court. Probation, which many consider to be the brightest hope of corrections, has several different connotations in the juvenile justice system: It is a legal system in which an adjudicated delinquent can be placed, an alternative to institutionalization, and a subsystem of the juvenile justice system.

The *Desktop Guide to Good Juvenile Probation Practice*, a publication of the National Center for Juvenile Justice, stated that "good juvenile probation practice is mission-driven, performance-based, and outcome-focused."[6] "Mission-driven" means that "the work of juvenile probation must be directed at clearly articulated and widely shared goals" that must guide everyday procedures, budget allocations, and staff assignments;[7] "performance-based" means that it should move from general goals to specific objectives and should designate "concrete activities that are calculated to achieve its goals and hold itself responsible for performing them."[8] "Outcome-focused" means that it "systematically measures the tangible results of its interventions, compares those results to its goals, and makes itself publicly accountable for any differences."[9]

Think About It...

Juvenile and adult probation share similarities, but there are some important differences. What are those differences?

Operation of Probation Services

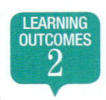 **LEARNING OUTCOMES 2** Summarize how probation operates in juvenile corrections.

The basic functions of probation services—intake, investigation, and supervision—operate using an increasingly "get-tough" approach to juvenile crime. In intake, the initial decision is made about what to do with the law-violating juveniles. Preparation of the social history report, which assists the juvenile judge at the disposition stage of the court proceedings, is the most important process during investigation. The supervisory function is divided into managing a caseload, providing treatment services, and maintaining surveillance.

Intake

The intake officer is usually a **probation officer**, although larger probation departments may have separate intake units in which intake officers are not probation officers. Regardless of the organizational structure, the intake officer is the chief decision maker for juveniles prior to the juvenile court proceeding and has two important decisions to make: what to do with the case and whether to detain the youth until a detention hearing can be scheduled.

Investigation

Investigation requires that probation officers prepare a **social history report** on a youth ruled delinquent to aid the judge in making the correct disposition. If a juvenile court uses a bifurcated hearing (separate adjudicatory and disposition stages), the judge orders a social history when a juvenile is found delinquent at the adjudicatory or fact-finding stage, but if the court combines the adjudicatory and disposition stages, the social history must be completed before a juvenile appears in front of the judge, who waits until the youth has been found delinquent to read the report.

Supervision

When a juvenile judge sentences a youth to probation, the probation officer generally takes the youth aside and explains the meaning of probation. The probationer is informed of

> **Investigation requires that probation officers prepare a social history report on a youth ruled delinquent to aid the judge in making the correct disposition.**

how frequently he or she will report to the probation officer and of the importance of complying with the conditions of probation. The length of time a youth must spend on probation varies from state to state. In some states, the maximum length is until the juvenile reaches the age of majority (normally 16 or 18 years old, but sometimes 21 years old).

The supervisory function is divided into casework management, treatment, and surveillance. Effective casework management requires that a probation officer keep an up-to-date casework file, carry out periodic reviews, decide how each client is to be handled, and divide probationers into several categories, depending on their needs and the risk they present to the community. Those with more serious needs and who present a greater risk to the community are required to report to their probation officers more frequently.

Surveillance requires that the probation officer make certain that probationers comply with the conditions of probation and that they do not break the law. The probation officer has a number of opportunities to observe the behavior of probationers in the office, at home, and perhaps at school, and also visits the probationer's parents. If a probationer's behavior is unacceptable, the probation officer is likely to receive reports from school or from law enforcement agencies. See Figure 14–1 for the three basic functions of probation.

Risk Control and Crime Reduction

The current emphasis in juvenile probation, as in adult probation, is on programs fostering risk control and crime reduction, including restitution and community service, intensive supervision, house arrest, and electronic monitoring (EM).

Probation
Permits juvenile offenders to remain in the community under the supervision of a probation officer, subject to certain conditions imposed by the court

Intake
What to do with the offender

Supervision
Responsible for behavior of youth violating probation

Investigation
Requires social history report

FIGURE 14–1 Basic Functions of Probation.

The main goals of **restitution** and community service programs are to hold youthful offenders responsible for their crimes. Over the past 30 years, restitution programs and community service orders have had significant growth, much of it resulting from the Office of Juvenile Justice and Delinquency Prevention (OJJDP). In 1977, the OJJDP launched a major restitution initiative by spending $30 million to fund the use of restitution in 85 juvenile courts throughout the United States, and the OJJDP followed this initiative with the National Restitution Training Program in 1983 and the Restitution Education, Specialized Training, and Technical Assistance (RESTTA) Project in 1985. These initiatives are directly responsible for most of the growth of restitution programs.[10]

When it comes to making restitution and overseeing community service work, probation officers are key players, and in many jurisdictions it is up to these officers to do some or all of the following:[11]

- Determine participation eligibility.
- Calculate appropriate amounts of restitution to be made.
- Assess offenders' ability to pay.
- Determine payments/work schedules.
- Monitor performance.
- Close cases.

With community work restitution, juveniles are generally ordered to perform a certain number of work hours at a private, nonprofit, or government agency. Some large probation departments have established up to 100 sites where this service may be performed, and these sites typically include public libraries, parks, nursing homes, animal shelters, community centers, day-care centers, youth agencies, YMCAs and YWCAs, and local streets. Some restitution programs involve supervised work crews; in these situations, juveniles go to a site and work under the supervision of an adult.

Intensive Supervision

As the twentieth century came to a close probation continued to be criticized as a lenient measure that allowed offenders to escape punishment, intensive supervision programs (ISPs) became more widely used in juvenile probation. Georgia, New Jersey, Oregon, and Pennsylvania were the leaders in experimenting with ISP programs for juveniles.[12] But more and more juvenile judges, especially in metropolitan juvenile courts, are placing high-risk juveniles on small caseloads and assigning them more frequent contact with a probation officer than would be true of traditional probation.

Some criminologists have sought to develop an integrated social control (ISC) model of intensive supervision addressing the major causal factors identified in delinquency theory and research. This proposed model—which integrates the central components of strain, control, and social learning theories—contends that the combined forces of inadequate socialization, strains between educational and occupational aspirations and expectations, and social disorganization in the neighborhood lead to weak bonding to conventional values and activities in the family, community, and school; weak bonding, in turn, can lead youths to delinquent behavior through negative peer influence. Figure 14–2 shows a diagram of this model.[13]

House Arrest and Remote Location Monitoring

House arrest is a sentence imposed by the court whereby youths are ordered to remain confined in their own homes for the length of their sentence, although they may be allowed to leave their homes for medical reasons, school, employment, and approved religious services. They may also be required to perform community service. **Remote location monitoring (RLM)** may or may not be used to monitor juveniles' presence in a residence where they are required to remain.

Recently, OJJDP estimated that 20% of all persons supervised in the community were on RLM. Nearly every state has adults on RLM, although the courts in some states limited the use of RLM by banning certain types of monitoring equipment

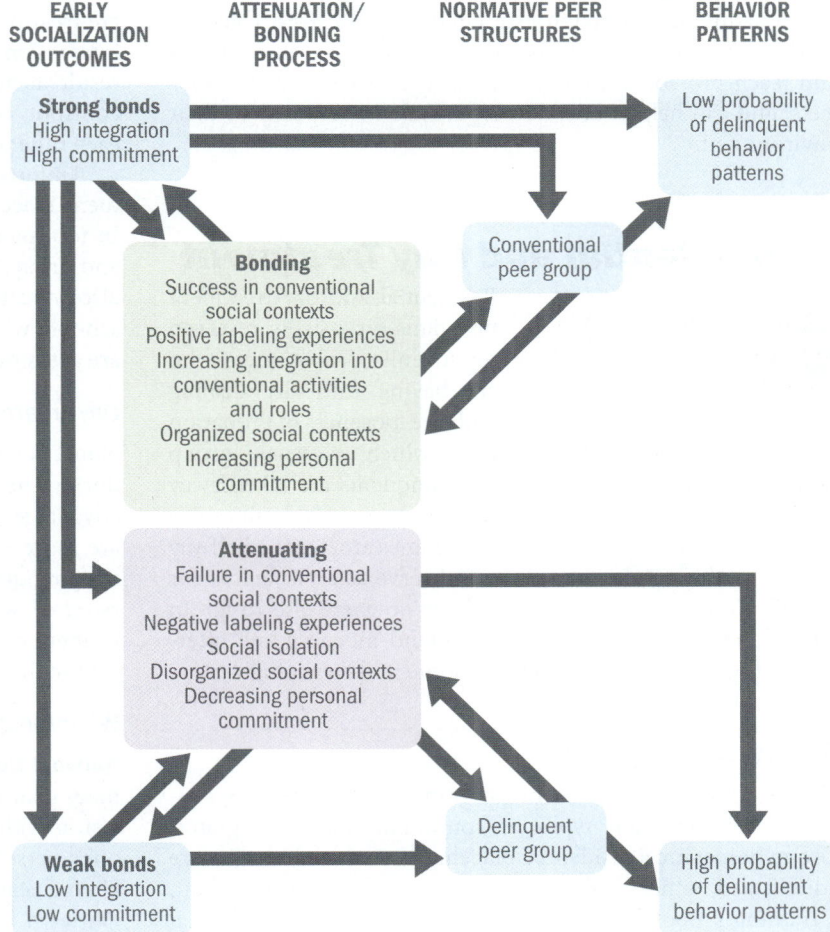

FIGURE 14-2 An Integrated Strain–Control Paradigm.
Source: Barry Krisberg et al., *Juvenile Intensive Planning Guide* (Washington, D.C.: Office of Justice and Delinquency Prevention, 1994), p. 7.

and allowing monitoring only by consent.[14] The use of RLM in juvenile justice has been gradually gaining acceptance. For example, according to a November 1988 survey, only 11 juvenile programs used RLM;[15] today, however, RLM programs are routinely used in juvenile justice programs throughout the United States.

RLM tends to be more effective when used as a tool in conjunction with other programs rather than when operating alone as a supervision program, yet there seems to be no consistent finding that successful completion of RLM programs leads to a decrease in recidivism.[16]

Volunteer Programs

As stated earlier, probation was initially staffed with volunteers, and professional staff did not begin appearing until the turn of the twentieth century. Today, over 2,000 court-sponsored **volunteer programs** are in operation, using volunteers to assist probation officers in a variety of ways, and the use of volunteers has become one of the most valuable ways to help offenders adjust to community life.

The National Information Center on Volunteers in Court has identified several areas in which **community volunteers** can work effectively with juvenile offenders. They can provide a one-to-one support relationship for the youth with a trustworthy adult; can function as a child advocate with teachers, employers, and police; can be good role models; can set limits and teach pro-social values; can teach skills or academic subjects; and can help youths develop a realistic response to their environment.

▶ Residential and Day Treatment

LEARNING OUTCOMES 3 — Summarize the types of residential and day-treatment programs that are available.

Residential and day-treatment programs are usually reserved for juvenile probationers who are having difficulty dealing with the looseness of probation supervision. In residential programs, which are usually group homes or **foster care** placements, delinquents are taken away from the supervision of parents and are assigned 24 hours a day to their new placement. Some group homes are like the halfway houses used in adult corrections and serve as a placement for juveniles on aftercare status who have nowhere else to go. In day-treatment programs, juveniles attend morning and afternoon program sessions and return home in the evening.

Types of Programs

Group homes, day-treatment programs, and wilderness programs are the main types of community-based programs. Group homes are a residential placement to which juveniles are adjudicated, either while on probation or when released from a training school. Day-treatment programs are nonresidential programs that juveniles attend during the day, returning home in the evening. Wilderness programs, sometimes called "survival programs," take place in such settings as the mountains,

Group homes, day-treatment programs, and wilderness programs are the main types of community-based programs.

the woods, the sea, and the desert, and the intent of these survival programs is to improve youths' self-confidence and sense of self-reliance.

Group Homes

Such terms as *group residence*, *halfway house*, *group home*, and *attention home* are used in various parts of the United States to identify a small facility serving about 13 to 25 youths. These types of **group homes** fulfill several purposes: They provide an alternative to institutionalization; they serve as a short-term community placement, wherein probation and aftercare officers can deal with youths' community problems; and they serve as a "halfway-in" setting for youths having difficulty adjusting to probation and as a "halfway-out" placement for delinquents who are returning to the community but lack an adequate home placement.

Intake criteria, treatment goals, length of stay, target population services, available services, physical facilities, location in reference to the rest of the city, and house rules of group homes throughout the United States are extremely diverse. Some homes are treatment oriented, using a modality such as guided group interaction (GGI) to generate a supportive environment among residents and staff. In GGI, residents are expected to support, confront, and be honest with one another so that they can help each other deal with their problems.[17]

Unfortunately, such exciting programs as the Achievement Place are not typical of group homes across the nation. In too many group homes, beds (vacancies) are hard to find, and group homes may even have long waiting lists. Residents also typically have longer stays than they would have in training schools, which raises real questions about whether group homes are a less punitive placement than juvenile institutions.

Day-Treatment Programs

Nonresidential **day-treatment programs** multiplied nationwide during the early 1970s. Their popularity can be traced to the advantages they offer community-based corrections: They are more economical because they do not provide living and sleeping quarters, they make parental participation easier, they require fewer staff members, and they are less coercive and punishment oriented than residential placements. See Figure 14–3 for the three types of community programs.

Wilderness Programs

Outward Bound is the most widely used wilderness program. Its main goal is to use the overcoming of a seemingly impossible task to gain self-reliance, to prove one's worth, and to define one's personhood.[18] The first Outward Bound program in the United States was established in Colorado in 1962, and today Outward Bound offers 750 wilderness courses, including rock climbing, kayaking, dog sledding, sailing, rappelling, backpacking, and more, to adults, teens, and youths. Over 10,000 students participate in wilderness courses. Outward Bound offers

Group Home
Residential placement into which juveniles are assigned, either while on probation or when released from a training school

Day-Treatment Programs
Nonresidential programs that do not provide living and sleeping quarters

Wilderness Programs
Use the wilderness, desert, sea, and urban areas in order to allow participants to gain self-reliance, to prove one's worth, and to define one's personhood

FIGURE 14–3 Three Types of Community Programs.

multiyear partnerships with 125 schools across the United States, and it encourages over 30,000 students and 4,000 teachers to reach high levels of achievement and to discover their potential. Outward Bound also has urban programs in Atlanta, Baltimore, Boston, New York, and Philadelphia.[19]

▶ Types of Institutional Placement

LEARNING OUTCOMES 4 Summarize the types of institutional placements that are available.

Youthful offenders who do not adequately adjust to community-based programs or who commit another offense while under community supervision may be placed in a public or private institution. Public institutional facilities are sometimes administered by the county, but the vast majority of them are under state control. Reception and diagnostic centers, ranches, forestry camps, boot camps, and training schools are the main forms that juvenile correctional institutions take. Private facilities play a somewhat significant role in the long-term custody of juveniles; although there are more than twice as many privately operated juvenile facilities as publicly operated ones, private facilities hold less than half as many youths as do public facilities.[20]

In 2011, more than 68,815 young persons were detained in around 2,000 residential placement facilities throughout the United States.[21] The rate of juvenile detention in 2011 was 225 youths per every 100,000 in the American population. On a positive note, the number of juvenile offenders in custody has declined by one-third since 1997. Juvenile offenders held for delinquency offenses accounted for 86 percent of all residents, and those held for status offenses accounted for 4 percent. Of all juveniles who were detained (for any valid reason), 90 percent

Reception and diagnostic centers, ranches, forestry camps, boot camps, and training schools are the main forms that juvenile correctional institutions take.

were in public facilities. For committed (or adjudicated) juveniles, 61 percent were in public facilities. Among those in residential placement as part of a diversion agreement in lieu of adjudication, 51 percent were in public facilities. Overall, there was a 33 percent decrease in the number of juvenile offenders in residential placement between 1997 and 2010. Public facilities housed more than three-quarters of those held for violent crimes (i.e., criminal homicide, rape, robbery, and aggravated assault), other public-order crimes, and technical violations of probation or parole. In contrast, fewer than six in ten juvenile offenders held for drug offenses were in public facilities. Nevertheless, public and private facilities had fairly similar offense profiles in 2010. Females accounted for 13 percent of offenders in residential placement.

The recent report *Implementing Reform in California* reveals the skyrocketing cost of juvenile institutional care. It costs California $115,129 per year to institutionalize each juvenile resident. California's average length of stay is 25.9 months—nearly three times as long as the average of 19 states that participated in a nationwide survey. It should be noted, however, that juvenile offenders in California may be kept in institutional care until they are 24 years old, something that has contributed significantly to the average length of stay for those sentenced to juvenile facilities in California.[22]

Reception and Diagnostic Centers

The purpose of **reception and diagnostic centers**, which are managed and operated by either public or private agencies, is to determine which treatment plan suits each adjudicated youth and which training school is the best placement.

Forestry Camps and Ranches

Minimum-security institutions, such as **forestry camps** and **ranches**, are typically reserved for youths who have committed minor crimes and for those who have been committed to the youth authority or private corrections for the first time. In forestry camps, which are popular in a number of states, residents usually do conservation work in a state park, including cleaning up, cutting grass and weeds, and doing general maintenance. Treatment programs usually consist of group therapy, individual contacts with social workers and the child-care staff, and one or two home visits a month. Residents also may be taken to a nearby town on a regular basis to make purchases and to attend community events. Escapes are a constant problem because of the nonsecure nature of these facilities.

Boot Camps

Boot camps for youthful offenders, like those for adult offenders, developed in the mid-1980s and 1990s. Emphasizing military discipline, physical training, and regimented activity for periods typically ranging from 30 to 120 days, these programs endeavor to shock juvenile delinquents out of committing further crimes.

Boot camp programs for juveniles emphasize military discipline, physical training, and regimented activity for periods typically ranging from 30 to 120 days.

A fair assessment may be that the quality of boot camps depends largely on how much they tailor their programs to participants' maturity levels and how effective they are in implementing and sustaining effective aftercare services. The combined disappointing recidivism results, as well as the charges of abuse, have prompted Arizona, Georgia, Maryland, and South Dakota to shut down or reevaluate the "get-tough-with-juveniles" approach popularized in the early 1990s. Arizona removed 50 juveniles from the boot camp in which Anthony Haynes died in 2009. He had been forced to eat mud, deprived of food and water, and forced to stand in the sun for hours in black clothing without water.[23] Maryland shut down one boot camp and suspended the military regimens at its other two facilities after reports of systematic assaults, and the charges of abuse led to the ouster of the state's top five juvenile justice officials.[24]

Public and Private Training Schools

Some training schools look like prisons, others resemble college campuses, and still others have a homelike atmosphere, yet regardless of what they look like, training schools are used more today than they were in the 1970s and 1980s. Youth gangs are becoming a serious problem in some training schools.

The larger states, such as California, Illinois, Michigan, and New York, have several training schools each.[25] Smaller states commonly have one training school for boys and another for girls, but Massachusetts and Vermont have no training schools. Coeducational institutions gained some acceptance in the 1970s, when several states opened one or more coeducational campuses, but that trend seems to have passed.

The physical structure of training schools ranges from the homelike atmosphere of small cottages to open dormitories with little privacy to fortress-like facilities with individual cells and fences. The level of security is usually higher for public than for private facilities because most public facilities are detention centers designed to control residents' movement through staff monitoring and physical restrictions, such as fences.[26]

Programs and Services

The programs that public and private training schools offer are superior to those of other juvenile institutions. The medical and dental services that residents receive tend to be very good, and most larger training schools have a full-time nurse on duty during the day and a physician who visits one or more days a week. Although institutionalized delinquents frequently complain about the medical and dental care they receive, most youths still receive far better care than they did before they were confined.

The rehabilitation of juvenile delinquents remains the avowed purpose of most training schools. In the twentieth century, seemingly every conceivable method was used in the effort to rehabilitate residents so they would refrain from unlawful behavior. The treatment technologies still in use include classification systems, treatment modalities, skill development, and prerelease programs, and the most widely used treatment modalities are transactional analysis, reality therapy, psychotherapy, behavior modification, GGI, positive peer culture, and drug and alcohol treatment. Rational therapy, sometimes called the "errors-in-thinking modality" or Cognitive Thinking Skills Program (CTSP), is a relatively recent treatment modality in juvenile corrections that has been implemented in a number of

Think About It…

It is expensive to institutionalize juveniles, but those who commit serious acts of delinquency are frequently placed into residential settings. What types of juvenile offenders most need to be institutionalized?

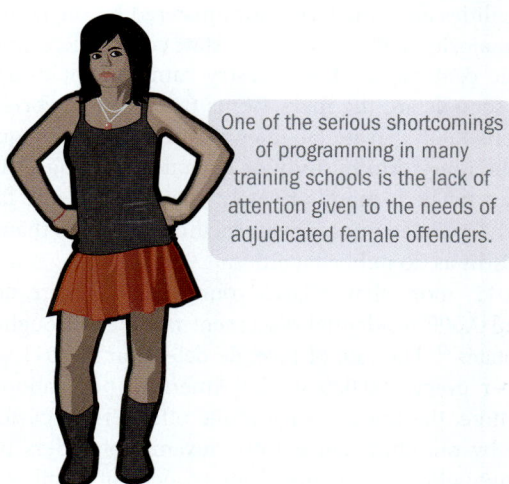

One of the serious shortcomings of programming in many training schools is the lack of attention given to the needs of adjudicated female offenders.

One of the serious shortcomings of programming in many training schools is the lack of attention given to the needs of adjudicated female offenders.

TABLE 14–1 COMPARISON OF TREATMENT TYPES IN ORDER OF EFFECTIVENESS

Noninstitutionalized Offender Treatments	Institutionalized Offender Treatments
Positive Effects, Consistent Evidence	
Individual counseling	Interpersonal skills
Interpersonal skills	Teaching family homes
Behavioral programs	
Positive Effects, Less Consistent Evidence	
Multiple services	Behavioral programs
Restitution, probation/parole	Community residential
	Multiple services
Mixed But Generally Positive Effects, Inconsistent Evidence	
Employment-related training	Individual counseling
Academic programs	Guided group counseling
Advocacy/casework	Group counseling
Family counseling	
Group counseling	
Weak or No Effects, Inconsistent Evidence	
Reduced caseload, probation/parole	Employment-related training
	Drug abstinence
	Wilderness/challenge
Weak or No Effects, Consistent Evidence	
Wilderness/challenge	Milieu therapy
Early release, probation/parole	
Deterrence programs	
Vocational programs	

Source: Mark W. Lipsey et al., *Effective Intervention for Serious Juvenile Offenders* (Washington, D.C.: Office of Juvenile Justice and Delinquency Prevention, 2000), p. 5.

public and private training schools across the nation. Table 14–1 compares treatment types in order of effectiveness with both noninstitutionalized and institutionalized offenders.

One of the serious shortcomings of programming in many training schools is the lack of attention given to the needs of adjudicated female offenders. The 1992 Amendment to the 1974 Juvenile Justice and Delinquency Prevention Act addressed the issue of gender bias, requiring states to analyze the need, types, and delivery of gender-specific services. As an example of gender-biased treatment, a comparative study of 348 violent juvenile females and a similar number of males reported in 1992 that half the males were admitted to rehabilitative or alternative programs, but only 29.5 percent of females received treatment in any form.[27]

Evaluation of Public Versus Private Training Schools

One of the debates that has raged for years concerns the comparison of public and private training schools. Privately administered training schools are usually better known to the public than are state institutions because private institutions' soliciting of funds has kept them in the public eye. Proponents of private institutions claim that they are more effective than public training schools; they have a limited intake policy, which allows them to choose whom they want to admit, and they can be more flexible and innovative.

A fair assessment of private placements is that, with some glaring exceptions, private training schools are usually more flexible and innovative than state facilities. The smaller size of private training schools is somewhat balanced by the fact that one-half of them still house 100 or more residents, numbers that are too large for effective work with institutionalized juveniles. Perhaps the old adage is right after all: The best institutions are private ones, and the worst juvenile institutional placements are also private ones. See Table 14–2 for the types of juvenile placements.

▶ Social Context: Training School Life

The nature of the **residential social system** (the social hierarchy established by inmates) is an important factor in the quality of life in a training school. The many empirical studies on the residential social system have consistently challenged the efficacy of juvenile institutionalization. Too many of these studies present a frightening picture of what a juvenile experiences during confinement, and these studies also have found that there are more similarities than differences in residential life in single-sex and coeducational institutions.

LEARNING OUTCOMES 5 — Summarize training school experiences for boys and girls.

Training Schools for Boys

Many studies of training schools for boys reflect an inmate society in which the strong take advantage of the weak.[28]

Following the passage and signing of the Prison Rape Elimination Act (PREA) of 2003, three major government-sponsored research effectors have provided additional insights about the conditions and scope of sexual victimization of confined juveniles. Although there are many exceptions to the lawless environment described in these studies, an environment in which

TABLE 14–2 | TYPES OF JUVENILE PLACEMENTS

Type	Goals	Characteristics
Reception and Diagnostic Centers	Evaluation and placement	Used to evaluate juveniles for possible placement in other facilities
Forestry Camps and Ranches	Minimum-security placement	Involves informal contact with staff, and a less secure placement than training schools
Boot Camps	Shock treatment	Short term and emphasizes military discipline
Public and Private Training Schools	Longer and more secure institutional placement	Larger physical facilities, longer terms of stay, and sometimes violent residential life

the strong take advantage of the week, the fact is that the quality of life for residents in too many training schools is extremely problematic. Even more troubling are the high rates of staff member involvement in the sexual victimization of residents.[29]

Training Schools for Girls and Coeducational Institutions

Until 1960, studies on confined juvenile girls were as numerous as those on incarcerated adult females. The early studies found that girls in training school became involved in varying degrees of lesbian alliances and pseudo-family relationships. Since 1970, only three major studies have been done on females' adjustment to training school.[30]

More recently, Christopher M. Sieverdes and Clemens Bartollas's study of six coeducational institutions in a southeastern state drew the following conclusions: Females adhered more strongly to inmate groups and peer relationships than did males, they felt more victimized by peers than did males, they did not harass or manipulate staff members as much as males did, and they were more satisfied with institutional life than were males.[31] Unlike Propper's study, these researchers found that pseudo-families existed among girls but were based much less on homosexual alliances than were those in all-girls training schools.[32] Status offenders, who made up 70 percent of the girls and 30 percent of the boys, were the worst victims in these training schools and had the most difficulty adjusting to institutional life.[33] Caucasian males and females experienced high rates of personal intimidation and victimization by African-American and Native American youths.

▶ Rights of Confined Juveniles

LEARNING OUTCOMES 6 — Summarize the rights of confined juveniles.

The rights of institutionalized juveniles have been examined by the federal courts and addressed in the Civil Rights of Institutionalized Persons Act (CRIPA). CRIPA gives the Civil Rights Division of the U.S. Department of Justice (DOJ) the power to bring actions against state or local governments for violating the civil rights of institutionalized persons.

> **U.S. courts have mandated three major rights for juveniles: the right to treatment, the right to be free from cruel and unusual punishment, and the right to access to the courts.**

U.S. Courts

The U.S. courts long paid less attention to juvenile institutions than to adult prisons because juvenile facilities were assumed to be more humane and to infringe less on the constitutional rights of offenders. However, deteriorating conditions in juvenile correctional facilities, including the overcrowded living conditions, the frequent assaults among residents and against staff, and the growing presence of gang youths, led to a wave of litigation in the latter decades of the twentieth century. The courts have mandated three major rights: the **right to treatment**, the right to be free from **cruel and unusual punishment**, and the right to access to the courts. See Figure 14–4.

CRIPA and Juvenile Correctional Facilities

Through November 1997, the Civil Rights Division had investigated 300 institutions under CRIPA; 73 of these institutions, or about 25 percent, were juvenile detention and correctional facilities. The Civil Rights Division was monitoring conditions in 34 juvenile correctional facilities through consent decrees in Kentucky, New Jersey, and Puerto Rico. The consent decree filed in Kentucky included all 13 juvenile facilities in the state, the decree in New Jersey was with 1 facility, and the decree in Puerto Rico was with 20 facilities.[34]

▶ Juvenile Aftercare

Parole, or **juvenile aftercare**, as it is usually called, is concerned with the release of a youth from an institution when he or she can best benefit from release and can make an optimal adjustment to community living. A major concern in juvenile justice

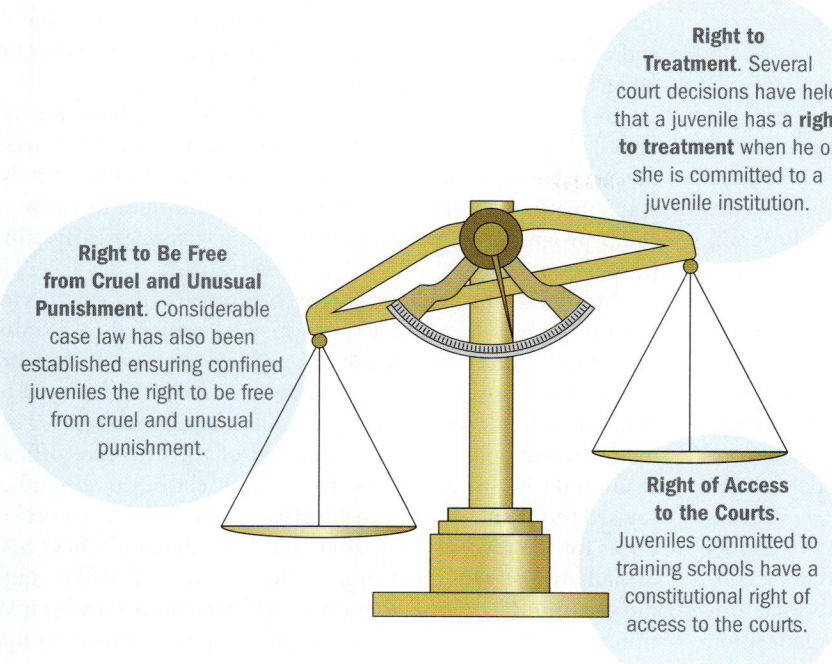

FIGURE 14–4 The Three Major Rights of Juveniles.

Juvenile aftercare is concerned with the release of a youth from an institution when he or she can best benefit from release and can make an optimal adjustment to community living.

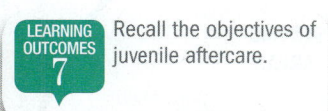

Recall the objectives of juvenile aftercare.

in the past 40 years has been the development of a workable philosophy and concept of aftercare. Numerous objectives for juvenile aftercare or parole have been developed through the years, as illustrated in Figure 14–5.

Once a youth is adjudicated to a state training school, the state normally retains jurisdiction until his or her release. The authority to make the decision about when to release a youth from training school is usually given to institutional staff members, although a number of states give other agencies and boards the authority to parole juveniles. Often the cottage staff members will review the progress of each youth at designated intervals, and when they recommend release, the recommendation is reviewed by a board made up of staff members from throughout the institution. If this board concurs, the recommendation must be approved by an institutional coordinator at the youth authority or youth commission.

Administration and Operation of Aftercare Services

Aftercare is the responsibility of the state and is administered by the executive branch in 44 states. In four states, aftercare is under the organization of the probation department and is administered by probation officers, and in the remainder of states other means of organizing and administering aftercare are used.[35]

LEARNING OUTCOMES 8 — Summarize the administration of juvenile aftercare.

The aftercare or probation officer (probation officers in many jurisdictions have aftercare youths as part of their caseloads) who is responsible for the case sometimes corresponds with or may even visit the institutionalized youth in training school. In many states, a youth cannot be released until the aftercare officer approves the home placement plan submitted by the institutional home worker, which usually involves a visit to the home by the officer to make certain that the home is a good placement. At other times, the aftercare officer must locate an alternate placement, such as a foster home, group home, or **halfway house**.

An **interstate compact** is sometimes initiated when a youth has no acceptable home placement within his or her own state. The institutional social worker usually contacts the appropriate agency in another state where the youth has a possible placement and submits an interstate compact for the transfer of the youth to that state after release from training school. The state of original jurisdiction retains authority over the youth and is kept advised of the juvenile's status.

1. Release residents from confinement at the most favorable time for community adjustment.
2. Prepare youths for their successful community completion of aftercare.
3. Reduce the crimes committed by released juveniles.
4. Reduce the violent acts committed by released offenders.
5. Increase the confidence of the community in the system of parole.
6. Alleviate overcrowding of training schools.
7. Monitor youthful offenders as they refrain from trafficking in or abusing drugs.
8. Discourage the return of youths to street gangs.

FIGURE 14–5 Juvenile Aftercare Objectives.

Risk Control and Crime Reduction

The current emphasis in aftercare is on short-term behavior control. The OJJDP has developed an intensive aftercare program that incorporates the principles of preparing youths for release to the community, facilitating youth–community interaction and involvement, and monitoring youths' reintegration into the community.[36]

The current emphasis in aftercare is on short-term behavior control.

Similar to juvenile probation, ISPs are being increasingly used—as of 1992, there were over 80 aftercare ISPs in the United States.[37] The most noteworthy of these intensive programs are the ones in the 30 counties of Pennsylvania; "Lifeskills 95," the Violent Juvenile Offender Research and Development Program in Boston, Memphis, Newark, and Detroit; the Skillman Intensive Aftercare Project; the Michigan Nokomis Challenge program; the PARJO program in New York; and OJJDP's Intensive Aftercare Program (IAP).

There has also been a focus on developing an integrated theoretical framework for guiding intensive supervision of chronic juvenile offenders. Based largely on combinations of social control, strain, and social learning theories, the IAP model focuses on the reintegrative process.[38] Figure 14-6 shows the program elements of this model. Underlying assumptions of this model are that chronic and serious delinquency is related to weak controls produced by social disorganization, inadequate socialization, and strain; that strain is produced by social disorganization independent of weak controls; and that peer-group influences intervene as a social force between youths with weak bonds and/or strain on the one hand and delinquent behaviors on the other.[39]

In-house detention and RLM programs still have not received the attention that they deserve in juvenile aftercare.[40] Juvenile aftercare also emphasizes drug and alcohol urinalyses (sometimes called "drug drops") and continues to use boot camp programs as a means of releasing juveniles early from training schools.

In both traditional and intensive aftercare, if a rule is violated or a law is broken, a youth may be returned to a training school. Although guidelines for the **revocation of aftercare** (see Exhibit 14-1) for juveniles have not been formulated by court decisions, revocation of a youth's aftercare status is no longer based solely on the testimony of the aftercare officer, who could be influenced by personality clashes or prejudice toward the client. Today, most jurisdictions have formal procedures for the revocation of aftercare. The aftercare officer may initially investigate the charge; if the finding is that the youth did commit the offense, the officer will report the parole violation to the supervisor. The supervisor may review the case and

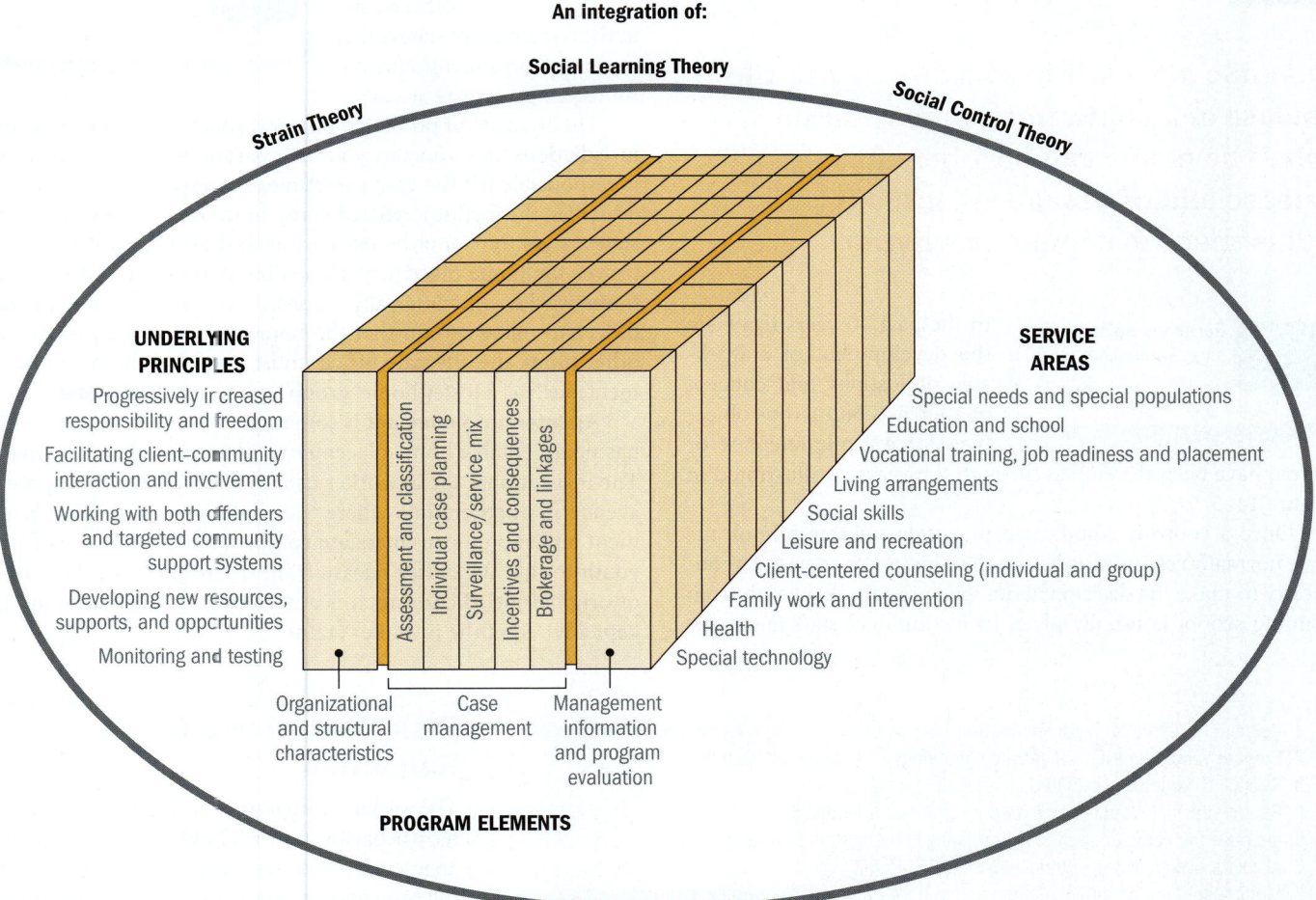

FIGURE 14-6 Intervention Model for Juvenile Intensive Aftercare.
Source: David Altschuler et al., *Reintegration, Supervised Release, and Intensive Aftercare* (Washington, D.C.: Office of Justice and Delinquency Prevention, 1999).

EXHIBIT 14-1 | Administration of Aftercare

Objective —The main objective is to release residents from confinement at the most favorable time for community adjustment.

Placement Options —The options are home placements or an alternative placement, such as a foster home, group home, or halfway house.

Supervision —An aftercare officer supervises the youth on aftercare or parole status but sometimes the youth is placed on intensive supervision, such as ISP, in which the youth is supervised on a more frequent basis.

Revocation —Formal procedures are initiated with a youth's violation of the law or rules of aftercare, and a revocation committee will actually revoke aftercare.

---

make the decision, or a revocation committee may examine the violation. The aftercare officer may be required to submit a written recommendation for revocation but is not allowed to testify, and the youth is permitted to speak in his or her own defense.

Juveniles in Adult Prisons

Juveniles who end up in prison have usually been transferred to the adult court and been given a prison sentence. They soon discover that adult correctional institutions are a world apart from nearly all training schools: Prisons are much larger, some containing several thousand inmates, and can cover acres of ground; life on the inside is typically austere, crowded, and dangerous; and the violent and exploitative relationships that are found in adult correctional institutions make this disposition a hard one for juveniles (Figure 14–7), who are particularly vulnerable to sexual victimization and physical assault.[41]

Some variations on the practice of confining juveniles in adult institutions exist among the states. In some jurisdictions, judges have no alternative but to place juveniles in adult institutions if the law requires it, but judges in a few states (under special circumstances) can place youths in either juvenile or adult institutions; judges in some other states can refer juveniles back to juvenile court, but they are then transferred to adult institutions when they come of age.[42]

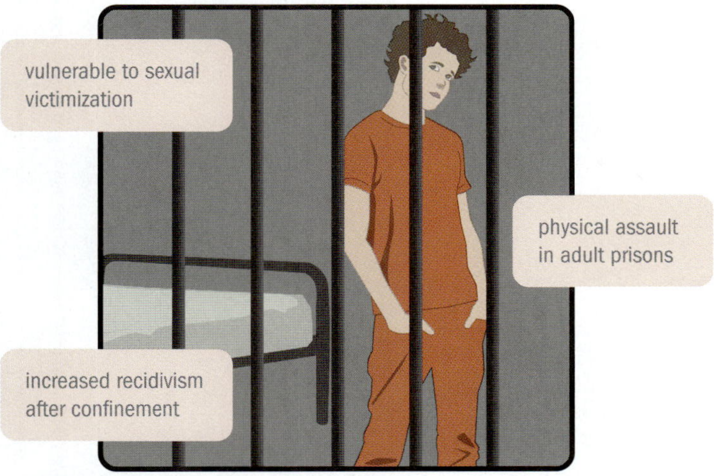

Every year, an estimated 4,100 new court commitments involving juveniles younger than 18 years old are sent to adult state prison. Between 1985 and 2002, the annual number of new court commitments to state prisons involving juveniles younger than age 18 increased 22 percent, with new commitments overall increasing 114 percent.[43]

In one study, Kelly Dedel Johnson, director of One in 37 Research, Inc., in Portland, Oregon, found that 13 states permit the transfer of juveniles to adult facilities: California, Colorado, Hawaii, Indiana, Kentucky, Massachusetts, New Jersey, New York, Rhode Island, South Carolina, Texas, Washington, and Wisconsin. The court has authority to make such transfers in one-third of these states, the commitment agency has authority in one-third, and the transfer decision is a joint agreement between two authorities (for example, agency and court or juvenile and adult agency) in one-third. The reasons for such transfers include age of the offender, seriousness of the offense, failure to benefit from the program, and poor institutional adjustment. A violent attack on a staff member by an older resident with an initial serious offense, for example, would be the type of case most likely leading to a transfer from a juvenile facility to an adult prison.[44]

▶ Delinquency Across the Life Course: Juvenile Institutionalization

For policymakers, one of the most serious issues related to juvenile institutionalization is providing for the safety of residents. The Prison Rape Elimination Act (2003) is a reminder of the importance of residents' safety, and emphasizes the possibility of sexual victimization during institutionalization. Various studies have identified a number of factors related to higher levels of sexual violence.

The National Prison Rape Elimination Commission has proposed a set of standards designed to create zero-tolerance policies for juvenile correctional institutions. These 2008 standards emphasized the need for heightened protection of those youths identified as vulnerable to sexual assault without restricting their access to the programs and other rights and privileges of the other confined youths, and they specifically rejected the policies of some facilities of placing lesbian, gay, bisexual, and

FIGURE 14–7 Vulnerabilities of Juveniles Confined in Adult Prisons.
- vulnerable to sexual victimization
- physical assault in adult prisons
- increased recidivism after confinement

transgender youths in segregation housing or in isolation. The standards go on to say that whenever possible, facilities should transfer victims of sexual abuse to outside health care providers for forensic medical exams to avoid a conflict of interest or a potential conflict and that all juvenile residents should have access to outside victim advocates and mental health professionals for the emotional support that is needed to deal with sexual abuse. Moreover, upon receiving an allegation of sexual abuse, the head of the juvenile facility must report the allegation to the head of the juvenile agency, the juvenile court that adjudicated the victim's case, and the parents or guardians of the victims (in most cases).[45]

▶ Delinquency and Social Policy: How to Make Juvenile Facilities Better

LEARNING OUTCOMES 10 — Recall the risk factors for higher levels of sexual violence during institutionalization.

Numerous recommendations for the management of a juvenile facility are offered below. These recommendations have been tested in the field and are intended to facilitate a humane and effective juvenile facility.

- *Pursue excellence in the facility.* Successful administrators set high standards. They not only expect excellence. They do it.
- *A meaningful residential program requires a carefully thought-out plan of activity or strategy.* Administrators must determine where they want to go (their vision) and how it is possible to get there (implementation of their vision).
- *Management should be proactive.* An anticipatory and preventative approach is fundamental in maintaining instrumental control.
- *Professionalism should be held up as a goal for all staff.* Staff development and training are important steps in staff members seeing themselves as professionals.
- *Cleanliness and orderliness of the facility are absolute necessities.* Cleanliness shows that the staff members are in control.
- *The institutional environment must be safe for youths and staff.* If an institution is not a safe environment, few positive outcomes can be accomplished.
- *Both residents and staff must be treated with dignity and respect.* The norm for staff is that they treat residents as they want their sons or daughters to be treated.
- *Good programming by committed staff must be available for those youths who want to make positive changes in their lives.* Treatment programs must be delivered effectively to those interested residents, especially those with addictions and anger management issues.
- *An effective system of accountability for both staff and youths is necessary.* Sufficient consequences are required for inappropriate behavior, especially when rules are broken.
- *The services that are promised must be delivered to youths when they are scheduled to be delivered.* It is important for the system to be predictable and trusted to do what is promised.
- *Facilities, as much as possible, must have the following characteristics.* They should be as close as possible to juveniles' facilities, smaller with personalized services, family friendly, and managed in a caring manner.
- *The administrator must be a model of integrity in every way,* both inside and outside the facility.
- *Accreditation is an important process in a juvenile residential facility,* offering humane confinement and mission effectiveness.[46]

THE CASE

The Life Course of Amy Watters, Age 17

After being adjudicated delinquent for her role in a school-based drug sales conspiracy, Amy was taken to a state-run residential facility for girls. Upon arrival at the facility, she was interviewed, given a battery of written tests, and assigned to live in a small cottage that was also home to five other girls. All of the girls were around the same age as Amy, although they were of different ethnic backgrounds and came from different parts of the state.

Amy seemed to have no trouble fitting in, and she soon became friends with her roommates. The cottage had individual beds, lockers for clothes, and a small cosmetics area in the shared bathroom for each girl to keep her personal items in. There was only one television, however, so when the girls weren't attending classes or participating in other programs, they had to agree on what programs they wanted to watch. Lights went out at 10 p.m., and came on again at 6 a.m. Breakfast was at 7 a.m., and the girls were required to attend. The school day started at 8 in the morning, and went until 4 in the afternoon. Amy soon learned, however, that the curriculum differed quite a bit from that in the public schools she had previously attended; it contained options allowing the girls to learn trades. Amy selected a couple of beautician courses, and soon found herself learning hairdressing and the art of makeup application. She even received training in how to give pedicures and manicures—something she very much enjoyed. When they had nothing else to do, the women who taught the course allowed Amy and her friends to practice what they had learned on each other, and the time spent giving and receiving beauty treatments made the girls feel good about themselves. One of the teachers, a middle-aged woman whom the girls called Mrs. Woods, took a special interest in Amy, and told her about how enjoyable a career as a beautician could be. She also encouraged Amy to think seriously about her future, and advised her to avoid getting back in with the wrong crowd when she went home. Soon, Amy began to think about attending beauty school when she was released, and started figuring out ways of paying for it.

Before she knew it, six months had passed and Amy was released back into her father's care.

Epilogue: Amy made good on her plan to become a cosmetologist. She found a part-time job working in a local eatery and, with supplementary funds provided by her father, was able to attend a local beauty college. After a few months she became licensed as an esthetician, and took on full-time work as a beauty specialist in a spa associated with a large retail store where she specialized in performing microdermabrasions (a peeling away of the outer layer of the skin to allow for healthy new skin to grow). She never saw her old boyfriend CJ again, but was soon able to afford her own apartment. The distance between Amy and her father, Simon, grew, and she rarely saw him once she was on her own. More important, she stayed away from drugs, and began dating a clean-cut young man who had recently received a two-year degree in criminal justice from the local Palm Beach State College. It appeared as though Amy had finally gotten her life on the right track.

Discuss

1. What aspects of the residential placement setting that Amy experienced might have helped turn her life around? What role did trade training likely play? How important might the personal attention she received from Mrs. Woods have been?

Learn more on the Web:

- Census of Juveniles in Residential Placement Databook: www.ojjdp.gov/ojstatbb/ezacjrp/

CHAPTER 14 Juvenile Corrections

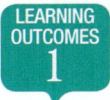

LEARNING OUTCOMES 1

Define probation.

Probation is a court sentence that permits juvenile offenders to remain in the community under the supervision of a probation officer, subject to certain conditions imposed by the court.

1. What is probation?
2. What is the purpose of probation?
3. What kinds of probation conditions might be imposed by juvenile courts?

community-based corrections A corrections program that includes probation, residential and day-treatment programs, and parole (aftercare). The nature of the linkages between community programs and their social environments is the most distinguishing feature of community-based corrections. As frequency, duration, and quality of community relationships increase, the programs become more community based.

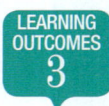

LEARNING OUTCOMES 2

Summarize how probation operates in juvenile corrections.

Probation functions through intake, investigation, and supervision. The main task of intake is to define what to do with the juvenile, investigation usually leads to a social history report, and supervision depends on the surveillance of the juvenile on probation.

1. What are the three basic functions of probation services?
2. What are the duties of a probation officer?
3. What are the features of a social history report, and what is its purpose?

probation officer An officer of the court who is expected to provide social history investigations, to supervise individuals who have been placed on probation, to maintain case files, to advise probationers on the conditions of their sentences, to perform any other probationary services that a judge may request, and to inform the court when persons on probation have violated the terms of that probation.

social history report A written report of a juvenile's social background that probation officers prepare for a juvenile judge to assist the court in making a disposition of a youth who has been ruled delinquent.

surveillance The observation of probationers by probation officers, intended to ensure that probationers comply with the conditions of probation and that they do not break the law.

restitution The court-ordered repayment to the victim; often used together with community service as a condition of juvenile probation.

remote location monitoring (RLM) The use of electronic equipment to verify that an offender is at home or in a community correctional center during specified hours or to track his or her whereabouts; also called *electronic monitoring*.

volunteer program The use of unpaid adult community members to assist probation officers in a variety of ways.

community volunteer An individual who donates his or her time to work with delinquents in the community.

LEARNING OUTCOMES 3

Summarize the types of residential and day-treatment programs that are available.

Community placements for juveniles include group homes, a residential placement; day-treatment, a nonresidential program that occurs during the day; and wilderness programs, survival programs that usually take place in the woods but can also be found on the sea, in desert settings, or even in urban environments.

1. What is a day-treatment program?
2. What are the three types of residential and day-treatment programs? How does each function?

foster care A home setting for juveniles who are lawfully removed from their birth parents' homes.

group home A placement for youths who have been adjudicated by the court that serves a group of about 13 to 25 youths as an alternative to institutionalization; also called *group residence*, *halfway house*, or *attention home*.

day-treatment program A court-mandated, community-based corrections program that juveniles attend in the morning and afternoon. They return home in the evening.

Outward Bound A wilderness-type survival program that is popular in many states as an alternative to the institutionalization of juveniles.

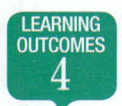

Summarize the types of institutional placements that are available.

Institutional placements for juveniles include reception and diagnostic centers, used for classification and placement; forestry camps and ranches, typically reserved for youths who have committed minor crimes; boot camps, which emphasize a strong military-like discipline in a short-term placement; and public and private training schools, which are long-term placements for youths considered deserving of such punishment.

1. What is the purpose of a boot camp for juvenile offenders? Are such programs likely to be effective?
2. What are the main types of juvenile institutions? How do these types differ?

reception and diagnostic center A facility where juveniles who have been committed to correctional institutions frequently are first sent. This type of center diagnoses youths' problems and develops individualized treatment plans.

forestry camp A correctional facility where residents usually do conservation work in state parks, including cleaning, cutting grass and weeds, and doing general maintenance.

ranch A public or private juvenile correctional institution that, like a forestry camp, is usually less secure than a training school and that has a more normal atmosphere.

boot camp A military-style facility used as an alternative to prison in order to deal with prison crowding and public demands for severe punishment.

Summarize training school experiences for boys and girls.

Training school experiences are similar for boys and girls, with male residents sometimes exposed to a more violent youth culture.

1. Why is youth culture sometimes so violent in training school?
2. Why do male residents sometimes experience a more violent environment than girls?

residential social system The social hierarchy that is established by residents in an institution.

Summarize the rights of confined juveniles.

The courts have mandated that institutionalized juveniles have the right to treatment, to be free from cruel and unusual punishment, and to have access to the courts.

1. Why are the legal rights of confined youths so important?
2. What are the legal rights of confined youths?
3. What evidence do we have that the legal rights of confined youths are sometimes violated?

right to treatment The entitlement of a juvenile who has been committed to a training school to receive any needed services (for example, therapy, education).

cruel and unusual punishment A guarantee provided by the Eighth Amendment to the U.S. Constitution against inhumane punishments. Accordingly, juveniles in correctional custody must not be treated with unnecessary harshness.

Recall the objectives of juvenile aftercare.

The objectives of aftercare include the following: (1) release residents from confinement at the most favorable time for community adjustment, (2) prepare youths for their successful community completion of aftercare, (3) reduce the number and seriousness of crimes committed by released juveniles, (4) reduce the number of violent acts committed by released offenders, (5) increase the confidence of the community in the system of parole, (6) alleviate overcrowding of training schools, (7) monitor youthful offenders as they refrain from trafficking in or abusing drugs, and (8) discourage the return of youths to street gangs.

1. What are the objectives of juvenile aftercare?
2. How can the various objectives of juvenile aftercare be achieved?

juvenile aftercare The supervision of juveniles who are released from correctional institutions so that they can make an optimal adjustment to community living.

LEARNING OUTCOMES 8

Summarize the administration of juvenile aftercare.

The administration of aftercare begins with tracking the progress of youths in institutional placements, continues with deciding on home placement (either at home or an alternative placement, such as a halfway house), follows with supervising the youth in the community, and ends when the youth is released from aftercare or aftercare is revoked.

1. What is juvenile aftercare? What is its purpose?
2. Why is the successful transition of an institutionalized youth to the community so important?
3. Why is it difficult to know when to release a youth from aftercare?

halfway house A residential setting for adjudicated delinquents, usually those who need a period of readjustment to the community following institutional confinement.

interstate compact The procedure for transferring a youth on probation or aftercare/parole from one state to another.

revocation of aftercare The cancellation of parole and return of the offender to an institution. It takes effect if a juvenile on aftercare commits another offense or violates the conditions of parole.

LEARNING OUTCOMES 9

Explain the impact of institutionalization on juveniles.

There is sufficient evidence to support the belief that institutionalization has a questionable impact on residents and may even contribute to high rates of recidivism.

1. How does institutionalization affect juveniles?
2. Why might the institutionalization of juveniles be related to increased rates of recidivism for some youths?

LEARNING OUTCOMES 10

Recall the risk factors for higher levels of sexual violence during institutionalization.

The following factors have been identified as related to higher levels of institutional sexual violence: Being in a long-term secure facility, having been physically assaulted, having been robbed in the facility, being under 14 years of age, being female, having a longer term of commitment (but victimization is most likely early in the resident's stay), having a gang presence in the facility, being a member of a gang, having serious charges (those with the most serious charges in their units have the highest risk of victimization), being of mixed or "other" race, and having high amounts of contraband in the facility.

1. What risk factor do you think would make a youth most vulnerable to sexual assault in a juvenile institution?
2. How can the risk of victimization be reduced?

Glossary

academic performance Achievement in schoolwork as rated by grades and other assessment measures. Poor academic performance is a factor in delinquency.

adjudication The court process wherein a judge determines if the juvenile appearing before the court committed the act with which he or she is charged. The term *adjudicated* is analogous to *convicted* in the adult criminal justice system and indicates that the court concluded that the juvenile committed the act.

adjudicatory hearing The stage of juvenile court proceedings that usually includes the youth's plea, the presentation of evidence by the prosecution and by the defense, the cross-examination of witnesses, and a finding by the judge as to whether the allegations in the petition can be sustained.

adolescence The life interval between childhood and adulthood; usually the period between the ages of 12 and 18 years.

adolescent-limited (AL) offenders Individuals who offend only for a very short period of time that is limited to the adolescent years.

adult court Criminal courts that hear the cases of adults charged with crimes, and to which juveniles who are accused of having committed serious offenses can be waived (transferred). In some states, adult criminal courts have jurisdiction over juveniles who are accused of committing certain specified offenses.

aftercare The supervision of juveniles who are released from correctional institutions so that they can make an optimal adjustment to community living; also, the status of a juvenile conditionally released from a treatment or confinement facility and placed under supervision in the community.

age of onset The age at which a child begins to commit delinquent acts; an important dimension of delinquency.

alcohol A drug made through a fermentation process that relaxes inhibitions.

alternative school A facility that provides an alternative educational experience, usually in a different location, for youths who are not doing satisfactory work in the public school setting.

amphetamine A stimulant drug that occurs in a variety of forms.

anabolic steroid A drug derived from the male sex hormone testosterone; often used as a performance enhancer or to build muscle mass.

anomie A condition of normlessness within a society.

appeal The review of juvenile court proceedings by a higher court. Although no constitutional right of appeal exists for juveniles, the right of adjudicated juveniles to appeal has been established by statute in some states.

appellate review The review of the decision of a juvenile court proceeding by a higher court. Decisions by appellate courts, including the U.S. Supreme Court, have greatly affected the development of juvenile court law and precedent.

arrest The process of taking a person into custody for an alleged violation of the law. Juveniles who are under arrest have nearly all the due process safeguards accorded to adults.

attention deficit–hyperactivity disorder (ADHD) A cognitive disorder of childhood that can include inattention, distractibility, excessive activity, restlessness, noisiness, impulsiveness, and so on.

attention home An innovative form of detention facility, found in several locations across the nation, that is characterized by an open setting.

autonomic nervous system The system of nerves that govern reflexes, glands, the iris of the eye, and activities of interior organs that are not subject to voluntary control.

bail The money or property pledged to the court or actually deposited with the court to effect the release of a person from legal custody. Juveniles do not have a constitutional right to bail, as do adults.

balanced and restorative justice model An integrative correctional model that seeks to reconcile the interests of victims, offenders, and communities through programs and supervision practices.

behavioral modification A technique in which rewards and punishments are used to change a person's behavior.

beyond a reasonable doubt A legal standard establishing the degree of proof needed for a juvenile to be adjudicated a delinquent by the juvenile court during the adjudicatory stage of the court's proceedings.

bifurcated hearing A split adjudication and disposition hearing, which is the present trend of the juvenile court.

binding over The process of transferring (also called *certifying*) juveniles to adult criminal court. Binding over takes place after a judicial hearing on a juvenile's amenability to treatment or his or her threat to public safety.

biological positivism The belief that juveniles' biological characteristics and limitations drive them to delinquent behavior.

biosocial criminology A perspective that holds that a person's biological characteristics make them prone to certain forms of deviant or criminal behavior when the surrounding environment encourages it.

birth order The sequence of births in a family and a child's position in it, whether the firstborn, middle, or youngest child.

blended sentencing The imposition of juvenile and/or adult correctional sanctions on serious and violent juvenile offenders who have been adjudicated in juvenile court or convicted in criminal court.

blocked opportunity The limited or nonexistent chance of success; according to strain theory, a key factor in delinquency.

boot camp A military-style facility used as an alternative to prison in order to deal with prison crowding and public demands for severe punishment.

born criminal An individual who is atavistic, who reverts to an earlier evolutionary level, and is unable to conform his or her behavior to the requirements of modern society—thus, an individual who is innately criminal.

Breed v. Jones A 1975 double jeopardy case in which the U.S. Supreme Court ruled that a juvenile court cannot adjudicate a case and then transfer the case to the criminal court for adult processing of the same offense.

broken home A family in which parents are divorced or are no longer living together.

brother–sister incest Sexual activity that occurs between brother and sister.

bullying The hurtful, frightening, or menacing actions undertaken by one person to intimidate another (generally weaker) person to gain that person's unwilling compliance, and/or to put him or her in fear.

capitalism An economic system in which private individuals or corporations own and control capital (wealth and the means of production) and in which competitive free markets control prices, production, and distribution of goods.

child abuse The mistreatment of children by parents or caregivers. Physical abuse is intentional behavior directed toward a child by the parent or caregiver to cause pain, injury, or death. Emotional abuse involves a disregard of a child's psychological needs. Sexual abuse is any intentional and wrongful physical contact with a child that entails a sexual purpose or component, and such sexual abuse is termed *incest* when the perpetrator is a member of the child's family.

child savers A name given to an organized group of progressive social reformers of the late nineteenth and early twentieth centuries that promoted numerous laws aimed at protecting children and institutionalizing an idealized image of childhood innocence.

chivalry factor The idea that the justice system tends to treat adolescent females and women more leniently because of their gender.

chronic youthful offender A juvenile who engages repeatedly in delinquent behavior. The Philadelphia cohort studies defined chronic offenders as youths who had committed five or more delinquent offenses. Other studies use this term to refer to youth involved in serious and repetitive offenses.

citation A summons to appear in juvenile court.

club drug A synthetic psychoactive substance often found at nightclubs, bars, raves, and dance parties. Club drugs include MDMA (Ecstasy), ketamine, methamphetamine (meth), GBL (gamma-Butyrolactone), gamma-Hydroxybutyrate, phencyclidine (PCP), and Rohypnol.

cocaine A coca extract that creates mood elevation, elation, grandiose feelings, and feelings of heightened physical prowess.

cognitive-behavioral therapy (CBT) Therapy based on the assumption that the foundations for criminal behavior are dysfunctional patterns of thinking.

cognitive theory A perspective on human development that says children develop cognitive abilities through interaction with the physical and social worlds.

Cognitive Thinking Skills Program (CTSP) A cognitive-behavioral intervention program designed to improve offenders' thinking processes.

cohort A generational group as defined in demographics, in statistics, or for the purpose of social research.

cohort studies Research that usually includes all individuals who were born in a specific year in a particular city or country and follows them through part or all of their lives.

commitment A determination made by a juvenile judge at the disposition stage of a juvenile court proceeding that a juvenile is to be sent to a juvenile correctional institution.

commitment to the social bond The attachment that a juvenile has to conventional institutions and activities.

community volunteer An individual who donates his or her time to work with delinquents in the community.

community-based corrections A corrections program that includes probation, residential and day-treatment programs, and parole (aftercare). The nature of the linkages between community programs and their social environments is the most distinguishing feature of community-based corrections. As frequency, duration, and quality of community relationships increase, the programs become more community based.

complaint A charge made to an intake officer of the juvenile court that an offense has been committed.

conduct norms The rules of a group governing the ways its members should act under particular conditions, and the violation of these rules arouses a group reaction.

conflict theory A perspective that holds that delinquency can be explained by socioeconomic class, by power and authority relationships, and by group and cultural differences.

consent decree A formal agreement between a juvenile and the court in which the juvenile is placed under the court's supervision without a formal finding of delinquency.

constitutionalists The name given to a group of twentieth-century reformers who advocated that juveniles deserve due process protections when they appear before the juvenile court.

control theory Any of several theoretical approaches that maintain that human beings must be held in check, or somehow be controlled, if delinquent tendencies are to be repressed.

cottage system A widely used treatment practice that places small groups of training school residents into cottages.

crack A less expensive but more potent form of cocaine.

crime-control model A correctional model supporting discipline and punishment as the most effective means of deterring youth crime.

cruel and unusual punishment A guarantee provided by the Eighth Amendment to the U.S. Constitution against inhumane punishments. Accordingly, juveniles in correctional custody must not be treated with unnecessary harshness.

cultural deviance theory A theory wherein delinquent behavior is viewed as an expression of conformity to cultural values and norms that are in opposition to those of the larger U.S. society.

cultural transmission theory An approach that holds that areas of concentrated crime maintain their high rates over a long period, even when the composition of the population changes rapidly, because delinquent "values" become cultural norms and are passed from one generation to the next.

culturally defined goals In Merton's strain theory, the set of purposes and interests a culture defines as legitimate objectives for individuals.

culture conflict theory A perspective that delinquency or crime arises because individuals are members of a subculture that has conduct norms that are in conflict with those of the wider society.

cyberbullying Bullying that involves using technology, such as cell phones and the Internet, to bully or harass another person.

day-treatment program A court-mandated, community-based corrections program that juveniles attend in the morning and afternoon. They return home in the evening.

deinstitutionalization of status offenders (DSO) The remove of status offenders from secure detention facilities.

delinquency prevention An organized effort to forestall or prevent the development of delinquent behavior. See also *primary prevention*, *secondary prevention*, and *tertiary prevention*.

delinquent sibling A brother or sister who is engaged in delinquent behaviors—an apparent factor in youngsters' involvement in delinquency.

delinquent youth A young person who has committed a crime or violated probation.

desistance The termination of a delinquent career or behavior.

detention The temporary restraint of a juvenile in a secure facility, usually because he or she is acknowledged to be dangerous either to him- or herself or to others.

detention center A facility that provides custodial care for juveniles during juvenile court proceedings. Also called *juvenile halls* and *detention homes*, detention centers were established at the end of the nineteenth century as an alternative to jails for juveniles.

detention hearing A hearing, usually conducted by an intake officer of the juvenile court, during which the decision is made as to whether a juvenile will be released to his or her parents or guardians or be detained in a detention facility.

determinate sentencing A model of sentencing that provides fixed terms of sentences for criminal offenses. Terms are generally set by the legislature rather than determined by judicial discretion.

determinism A philosophical position that suggests that individuals are driven into delinquent or criminal behavior by biological or psychological traits that are beyond their control.

developmental life-course (DLC) theory A theory concerned with four main issues in the study of delinquency: (1) the development of offending and antisocial behavior, (2) protective factors, (3) the risk of offending at different ages, and (4) the effects of life events on the course of a person's social and personal development.

differential association theory The view that delinquency is learned from others and that delinquent behavior is to be expected of individuals who have internalized a preponderance of definitions that are favorable to law violations.

differential opportunity structure The differences in economic and occupational opportunities open to members of different socioeconomic classes.

dispositional hearing The stage of the juvenile court proceedings in which the juvenile judge decides the most appropriate placement for a juvenile who has been adjudicated a delinquent, a status offender, or a dependent child.

disproportionate minority confinement (DMC) The court-ordered confinement, in juvenile institutions, of members of minority groups in numbers disproportionate to their representation in the general population.

disruptive behavior Unacceptable conduct at school. It may include defiance of authority, manipulation of teachers, inability or refusal to follow rules, fights with peers, destruction of property, use of drugs in school, and/or physical or verbal altercations with teachers.

diversion programs Dispositional alternatives for youthful offenders that exist outside of the formal juvenile justice system.

double jeopardy A common law and constitutional prohibition against a second trial for the same offense.

dropout A young person of school age who, of his or her own volition, no longer attends school.

drug addiction The excessive use of a drug, which is frequently characterized by physical and/or psychological dependence.

due process rights The constitutional rights that are guaranteed to citizens—whether adult or juvenile—during their contacts with the police, their proceedings in court, and their interactions with the public schools.

Ecstasy A form of amphetamine (MDMA) that began to be used by adolescents in the United States in the 1980s and 1990s and is now rather widespread.

emerging gang Any youth gang that formed in the late 1980s and early 1990s in communities across the nation and that is continuing to evolve.

emotional abuse A disregard for the psychological needs of a child, including lack of expressed love, withholding of contact or approval, verbal abuse, unrealistic demands, threats, and psychological cruelty.

emotionality An aspect of temperament. It can range from a near absence of emotional response to intense, out-of-control emotional reactions.

escalation of offenses An increase in the frequency and severity of an individual's offenses—an important dimension of delinquency.

family size The number of children in a family—a possible risk factor for delinquency.

family therapy A counseling technique that involves treating all members of a family; a widely used method of dealing with a delinquent's socially unacceptable behavior.

father–daughter incest Sexual activity that occurs between a father and his daughter. Also refers to incest by stepfathers or the boyfriend(s) of the mother.

father–son incest Sexual activity between father and son. Also refers to incest by stepfathers or the boyfriend(s) of the mother.

felicific calculus A method for determining the sum total of pleasure and pain produced by an act; also the assumption that human beings strive to obtain a favorable balance of pleasure and pain.

feminist theory of delinquency A theory that adolescent females' victimization at home causes them to become delinquent and that this fact has been systematically ignored.

fingerprinting A pretrial identification procedure used with both juveniles and adults following arrest.

focal concerns of the lower class The values or focal concerns (toughness, smartness, excitement, fate, and autonomy) of lower-class youths that differ from those of middle-class youths.

forestry camp A correctional facility where residents usually do conservation work in state parks, including cleaning, cutting grass and weeds, and doing general maintenance.

foster care A home setting for juveniles who are lawfully removed from their birth parents' homes.

free will The ability to make rational choices among possible actions and to select one over the others.

gang A group of youths who are bound together by mutual interests, have identifiable leadership, and act in concert to achieve a specific purpose that generally includes the conduct of illegal activity.

gang unit A specialized unit established by some police departments to address the problem of gangs.

gender The personal traits, social positions, and values and beliefs that members of a society attach to being male or female.

gender role A societal definition of what constitutes either masculine or feminine behavior.

general deterrence The idea that punishing one person for his or her criminal or delinquent acts will discourage others from committing similar acts.

general theory of crime A perspective that holds that lack of self-control is the common factor underlying problem behaviors.

group home A placement for youths who have been adjudicated by the court that serves a group of about 13 to 25 youths as an alternative to institutionalization; also called *group residence*, *halfway house*, or *attention home*.

Guided Group Interaction (GGI) A treatment modality based on the assumption that youths can confront their peers and force them to face the reality of their behavior more effectively than staff can. GGI is the most widely used treatment modality in juvenile corrections.

halfway house A residential setting for adjudicated delinquents, usually those who need a period of readjustment to the community following institutional confinement.

hallucinogen A drug that causes perceptual distortions of time and place, including possible visual and auditory hallucinations.

heroin A refined form of morphine that was introduced around the beginning of the twentieth century.

hidden delinquency Any unobserved or unreported delinquency.

home detention House arrest. This form of detention is used in some jurisdictions, and an adjudicated juvenile remains at home under the supervision of juvenile probation officers.

in loco parentis The principle according to which a guardian or an agency is given the rights, duties, and responsibilities of a parent in relation to a particular child or children.

In re Gault A 1967 U.S. Supreme Court case that brought due process and constitutional procedures into juvenile courts.

In re Winship A 1970 case in which the U.S. Supreme Court decided that juveniles are entitled to proof beyond a reasonable doubt during adjudication proceedings.

incapacitation Isolating offenders to protect society.

incest Any intrafamily sexual abuse that is perpetrated on a child by a member of that child's family group that includes not only sexual intercourse but also any act designed to stimulate a child sexually or to use a child for sexual stimulation, either of the perpetrator or of another person.

incidence of delinquency The frequency with which delinquent behavior occurs.

indeterminate sentencing In juvenile justice, a sentencing model that encourages rehabilitation through the use of general and relatively unspecific sentences. Under the model, a juvenile judge has wide discretion and can commit a juvenile to the department of corrections or youth authority until correctional staff members make the decision to release the juvenile. This type of sentencing is used with juveniles in most jurisdictions other than those who have mandatory or determinate sentencing.

informal adjustment An attempt to handle a youthful offender outside of the formal structures of the juvenile justice system.

informal probation An arrangement in which, instead of being adjudicated as a delinquent and placed on probation, a youth is informally assigned to the supervision of a probation officer.

inhalant A volatile liquid that gives off a vapor, which is inhaled, producing short-term excitement and euphoria followed by a period of disorientation.

insight-based therapy Treatment designed to encourage communication of conflicts and insight into problems, with the goal of symptoms relief, change in behavior, and personality growth.

institutionalized means In Merton's theory, culturally sanctioned methods of attaining individual goals.

intake The first stage of juvenile court proceedings, in which the decision is made whether to divert the juvenile being referred or to file a formal petition in juvenile court.

interstate compact The procedure for transferring a youth on probation or aftercare/parole from one state to another.

jail A police lockup or county holding facility for adult offenders. Jails have few services to offer juveniles.

judicial waiver The procedure of relinquishing the processing of a particular juvenile case to adult criminal court; also known as *certifying* or *binding over* to the adult court.

jury trial The court proceeding in which a panel of the defendant's peers evaluates evidence and renders a verdict. The U.S. Supreme Court has held that juveniles do not have a constitutional right to a jury trial, but several jurisdictions permit juveniles to choose a jury trial.

just deserts A pivotal philosophical underpinning of the justice model that holds that juvenile offenders deserve to be punished and that the punishment must be proportionate to the seriousness of the offense or the social harm caused.

justice as fairness A justice model that advocates that it is necessary to be fair, reasonable, humane, and constitutional in the implementation of justice.

justice model A contemporary model of imprisonment based on the principle of just deserts.

juvenile A youth at or below the upper age of juvenile court jurisdiction in a particular state.

juvenile aftercare The supervision of juveniles who are released from correctional institutions so that they can make an optimal adjustment to community living.

juvenile court Any court that has jurisdiction over matters involving juveniles.

juvenile court officer A probation officer who serves juveniles (the term is used in some but not all probation departments).

juvenile court statistics The data about youths who appear before the juvenile court, compiled annually by the National Center for Juvenile Justice.

juvenile delinquency An act committed by a minor that violates the penal code of the government with authority over the area in which the act occurs.

Juvenile Justice and Delinquency Prevention (JJDA) Act of 1974 A federal law that established a juvenile justice office within the existing Law Enforcement Assistance Administration to provide funds for the prevention and control of youth crime.

juvenile officer In some police departments, a police officer who has received specialized training to work effectively with juveniles, and who is tasked primarily with such work.

Kent* v. *United States A 1966 U.S. Supreme Court decision on the matter of transfer; the first decision in which the Supreme Court dealt with a juvenile court case.

labeling theory The view that society creates the delinquent by labeling those who are apprehended as different from other youths when in reality they are different primarily because they have been tagged with a deviant label.

learning disability (LD) A disorder in one or more of the basic psychological processes involved in understanding or using spoken or written language.

legislative waiver A legislative action that narrows juvenile court jurisdiction, excluding from juvenile courts those youths charged with certain offenses.

life-course-persistent (LCP) offenders Offenders who begin offending early in life and persistently engage in criminal and antisocial activities over the duration of the life course.

mandatory sentencing The requirement that individuals who commit certain offenses be sentenced to a specified length of confinement if found guilty or adjudicated delinquent.

marijuana The most frequently used illicit drug; usually smoked, it consists of dried hemp leaves and buds.

masculinity hypothesis The idea that as girls become more boylike and acquire more masculine traits, they become more delinquent.

McKeiver* v. *Pennsylvania A 1971 U.S. Supreme Court case that denied juveniles the right to trial by jury.

methamphetamine A synthetic drug that is a highly addictive stimulant; it can be injected, smoked, or snorted.

Miranda* v. *Arizona The landmark 1966 U.S. Supreme Court ruling that suspects taken into police custody must, before any questioning can take place, be informed that they have the right to remain silent, that anything they say may be used against them, and that they have the right to legal counsel.

mother–son incest Sexual activity that occurs between a mother and her son. Also refers to incest by stepmothers or the girlfriend(s) of the father.

neglect A disregard for the physical, emotional, or moral needs of children. Child neglect involves the failure of the parent or caregiver to provide nutritious food, adequate clothing and sleeping arrangements, essential medical care, sufficient supervision, access to education, and normal experiences that produce feelings of being loved, wanted, secure, and worthy.

Office of Juvenile Justice and Delinquency Prevention (OJJDP) A federal agency that works to provide national leadership, coordination, and resources to prevent and respond to juvenile delinquency and victimization.

opportunity theory A perspective that holds that gang members turn to delinquency because of a sense of injustice about the lack of legitimate opportunities open to them.

orthomolecular imbalance A chemical imbalance in the body, resulting from poor nutrition, allergies, or exposure to lead and certain other substances, which is said to lead to delinquency.

Outward Bound A wilderness-type survival program that is popular in many states as an alternative to the institutionalization of juveniles.

parens patriae A medieval English doctrine that sanctioned the right of the Crown to intervene in natural family relations whenever a child's welfare was threatened. The philosophy of the juvenile court is based on this legal concept.

petition A document filed in juvenile court alleging that a juvenile is a delinquent and asking that the court assume jurisdiction over the juvenile or asking that an alleged delinquent be waived to criminal court for prosecution as an adult.

petitioner In the juvenile justice system, an intake officer (prosecutor) who seeks court jurisdiction over a youthful offender.

police discretion A police officer's ability to choose from among a number of alternative dispositions when handling a situation.

police interrogation The process of interviewing a person who has been arrested with the express purpose of obtaining a confession.

positive peer culture (PPC) A system for building positive youth subcultures. Its main goal is to turn around negative peer cultures and to mobilize the power of the peer group in positive ways.

positivism The view that just as laws operate in the medical, biological, and physical sciences, laws govern human behavior and these laws can be understood and used.

power-control thesis The view that the relationship between gender and delinquency is linked to issues of power and control.

pretrial identification practices The procedures such as fingerprinting, photographing, and placing juveniles in lineups for the purpose of identification prior to formal court appearance.

prevalence of delinquency The percentage of the juvenile population involved in delinquent behavior.

primary deviation According to labeling theory, the initial act of deviance that causes a person to be labeled a deviant.

primary prevention The effort to reduce delinquency by modifying conditions in the physical and social environments that lead to juvenile crime.

probation A court-ordered nonpunitive juvenile disposition that emphasizes community-based services and treatment and close supervision by an officer of the court. Probation is essentially a sentence of confinement that is suspended so long as the probationer meets the conditions imposed by the court.

probation officer An officer of the court who is expected to provide social history investigations, to supervise individuals who have been placed on probation, to maintain case files, to advise probationers on the conditions of their sentences, to perform any other probationary services that a judge may request, and to inform the court when persons on probation have violated the terms of that probation.

process of becoming deviant In labeling theory, the concept that the process of acquiring a delinquent identity takes place in a number of steps.

Progressive Era The period from around 1890 to 1920, when a wave of optimism swept through American society and led to the acceptance of positivism.

prosecutor The representative of the state in court proceedings. Also called *county's attorney*, *district attorney*, or *state attorney*.

psychoanalytic theory A theory based on Sigmund Freud's insights, which have helped to shape the handling of juvenile delinquents. They include these axioms: (1) The personality is made up of three components—id, ego, and superego; (2) a normal child passes through three psycho-sexual stages of development—oral, anal, and phallic; and

psychopath An individual with a personality disorder, or a hard-core juvenile delinquent/adult criminal; also called a *sociopath*.

radical criminology A perspective that holds that the causes of crime are rooted in social conditions that empower the wealthy and the politically well organized but disenfranchise the less fortunate.

radical nonintervention A policy toward delinquents that advises that authorities should "leave the kids alone whenever possible."

ranch A public or private juvenile correctional institution that, like a forestry camp, is usually less secure than a training school and that has a more normal atmosphere.

reaction formation The psychological strategy for dealing with frustration by becoming hostile toward an unattainable object.

reception and diagnostic center A facility where juveniles who have been committed to correctional institutions frequently are first sent. This type of center diagnoses youths' problems and develops individualized treatment plans.

rehabilitation model A correctional model's goal is to change an offender's character, attitudes, or behavior so as to diminish his or her delinquent propensities. The medical, adjustment, and reintegration models are variants of this model because they are all committed to changing the offender.

reinforcement theory A perspective that holds that behavior is governed by its consequences, especially rewards and punishments that follow from it.

rejection by parents The disapproval, repudiation, or other uncaring behavior directed by parents toward children.

reliability The extent to which a questionnaire or interview yields the same answers from the same juveniles when they are questioned two or more times.

remote location monitoring (RLM) The use of electronic equipment to verify that an offender is at home or in a community correctional center during specified hours or to track his or her whereabouts; also called *electronic monitoring*.

residential program A program conducted for the rehabilitation of youthful offenders within community-based and institutional settings.

residential social system The social hierarchy that is established by residents in an institution.

resiliency The capacity to gain personal power and develop a strong sense of self in the face of poverty, severe family hardship, and community devastation.

respondent The defense attorney in the juvenile court system.

restitution The court-ordered repayment to the victim; often used together with community service as a condition of juvenile probation.

reverse waiver A provision that permits a juvenile who is being prosecuted as an adult in criminal court to petition to have the case transferred to juvenile court for adjudication or disposition.

revocation of aftercare The cancellation of parole and return of the offender to an institution. It takes effect if a juvenile on aftercare commits another offense or violates the conditions of parole.

right to treatment The entitlement of a juvenile who has been committed to a training school to receive any needed services (for example, therapy, education).

routine-activities approach The contention that crime-rate trends and cycles are related to the nature of everyday patterns of social interaction that characterize the society in which they occur.

running away The act of leaving the custody and home of parents or guardians without permission and failing to return within a reasonable length of time; a status offense.

school search The process of searching students and their lockers to determine whether drugs, weapons, or other contraband is present.

search and seizure The police procedure used in the investigation of crimes for the purpose of gathering evidence.

secondary deviation According to labeling theory, deviance that is a consequence of societal reaction to an initial delinquent act.

secondary prevention The intervention in the lives of juveniles or groups identified as being in circumstances that dispose them toward delinquency.

sedative A drug that is taken orally and affects the user by depressing the nervous system, causing drowsiness.

self-report study A study of juvenile crime based on surveys in which youths report on their own delinquent acts.

sex-role socialization The process by which boys and girls internalize their culture's norms, sanctions, and expectations for members of their gender.

sexual abuse The intentional and wrongful physical contact with a person, with or without his or her consent, that entails a sexual purpose or component.

shelter care A facility that is used primarily to provide short-term care for status offenders and for dependent or neglected youths.

social capital The norms, networks, and supportive relationships that people need if they are to realize their potential.

social contract An unstated or explicit agreement between people and their government as to the rights and obligations of each.

social control theory A perspective that delinquent acts result when a juvenile's bond to society is weak or broken.

social development model A perspective based on the integration of social control theory and cultural learning theory that holds that the development of attachments to parents will lead to attachments to school and a commitment to education, as well as a belief in and commitment to conventional behavior and the law.

social disorganization theory An approach that posits that juvenile delinquency results when social control among the traditional primary groups, such as the family and the neighborhood, breaks down because of social disarray within the community.

social history report A written report of a juvenile's social background that probation officers prepare for a juvenile judge to assist the court in making a disposition of a youth who has been ruled delinquent.

social injustice According to conflict-oriented criminologists, social injustice takes the form of unfairness in the juvenile justice system. It arises from poor youths being disproportionately represented, from female status offenders being subjected to sexist treatment, and from racial minorities being dealt with more harshly than whites.

social interactionist theory A theoretical perspective that derives its explanatory power from the give-and-take that continuously occurs between social groups and between individuals and society.

social process theories A theoretical approach to delinquency that examines the interactions between individuals and their environments, especially those that might influence them to become involved in delinquent behavior.

social structure The relatively stable formal and informal arrangements that characterize a society, including its economic arrangements, social institutions, and values and norms.

socialization The process by which individuals come to internalize their culture; through this process, an individual learns the norms, sanctions, and expectations of being a member of a particular society.

sociobiology An expression of biological positivism that stresses the interaction between biological factors within an individual and the influence of the person's particular environment; also the systematic study of the biological basis of all social behavior.

soft determinism The view that delinquents are neither wholly free nor wholly constrained in their choice of action.

specific deterrence A goal of criminal sentencing that seeks to prevent a particular offender from engaging in repeat criminality.

station adjustment One of several disposition options available to a police officer whereby a juvenile is taken to the police station following a complaint, the contact is recorded, and the juvenile is given an official reprimand and then released to his or her parents or guardians.

status frustration The stress that individuals experience when they cannot attain their goals because of their socioeconomic class.

status offender A juvenile who commits a minor act that is considered illegal only because he or she is underage.

status offense A nondelinquent/noncriminal offense; an offense that is illegal for underage persons but not for adults. Status offenses include curfew violations, incorrigibility, running away, truancy, and underage drinking.

strain theory A theory that proposes that the pressure the social structure exerts on youths who cannot attain cultural success goals will push them to engage in nonconforming behavior.

supervision and discipline The parental monitoring, guidance, and control of children's activities and behavior.

surveillance The observation of probationers by probation officers, intended to ensure that probationers comply with the conditions of probation and that they do not break the law.

symbolic interactionist theory A perspective in social psychology that analyzes the process of interaction among human beings at the symbolic level and that has influenced the development of several social process theories of delinquent behavior.

taking into custody The process of arresting a juvenile for socially unacceptable or unlawful behavior.

tertiary prevention A program directed at the prevention of recidivism among youthful offenders.

theory of differential oppression The view that in the United States, authority is unjustly used against children, who must adapt to adults' ideas of what constitutes "good children."

training school A correctional facility for long-term placement of juvenile delinquents; may be public (run by a state department of corrections or youth commission) or private.

trait-based personality model A theory that attributes delinquent behavior to an individual's basic inborn characteristics.

transfer The process of certifying a youth over to adult criminal court. It takes place by judicial waiver and legislative waiver.

Uniform Crime Reporting (UCR) Program The Federal Bureau of Investigation's program for compiling annual data about crimes committed in the United States.

utilitarianism A doctrine that holds that the useful is the good and that the aim of social or political action should be the greatest good for the greatest number.

validity The extent to which a research instrument measures what it says it measures.

vandalism The act of destroying or damaging, or attempting to destroy or damage, the property of another without the owner's consent or destroying or damaging public property (except by burning).

violence A forceful physical assault with or without weapons. It includes many kinds of fighting, rape, other attacks, gang warfare, and so on.

volunteer program The use of unpaid adult community members to assist probation officers in a variety of ways.

References

Chapter 1, Adolescence and Delinquency

1. J. D. Salinger, *The Catcher in the Rye* (New York: Little Brown, 1951).
2. Wray Herbert, "The Teenage Brain: How Do We Measure Maturity?" March 29, 2013, Huffington Post Science Blog, http://www.huffingtonpost.com/wray-herbert/the-teenage-brain-how-do_b_2980112.html (accessed April 2, 2014).
3. *Graham* v. *Florida*, 560 U.S. 48 (2010).
4. *Miller* v. *Alabama*, U.S. Supreme Court, No. 10-9646 (decided June 25, 2012).
5. D. Finkelhor, H. Turner, R. Ormrod, S. Hamby, and K. Kracke, *Children's Exposure to Violence: A Comprehensive National Survey*, Bulletin (Washington, D.C.: Office of Juvenile Justice and Delinquency Prevention, 2009). More information is available at http://www.ncjrs.gov/pdffiles1/ojjdp/227744.
6. U.S. Department of Justice, *FY 2011 Congressional Budget Submission*, http://www.justice.gov/jmd/2011justification.
7. Richard J. Bonnie, Betty M. Chemers, and Julie Schuck, Editors; Committee on Assessing Juvenile Justice Reform; Committee on Law and Justice; Division of Behavioral and Social Sciences and Education; National Research Council, *Reforming Juvenile Justice: A Developmental Approach* (Washington, D.C.: National Academies Press, 2014), p. 18.
8. Ibid.
9. For an examination of the crises and strategies of adolescence, see David A. Wolfe, Peter G. Jaffe, and Claire V. Crooks, *Adolescence Risk Behaviors: Why Teens Experiment and Strategies to Keep Them Safe* (New Haven: Yale University Press, 2006).
10. The concept of childhood is usually identified as beginning in the early decades of the twentieth century. For a good discussion of the social construction of adolescence, see Barry C. Feld, *Bad Kids: Race and the Transformation of the Juvenile Court* (New York: Oxford University Press, 1999), pp. 19–31.
11. Lloyd de Mause, ed., *The History of Childhood* (New York: Psycho-History Press, 1974), p. 1.
12. One of the exciting new areas of research is in relating adolescence to the life-course cycle or theory. See Silvia Bonimo, Elena Cattelino, and Silvia Ciairano, *Adolescents and Risk, Behavior, Functions, and Protective Factors* (New York: Springer-Verlag Italia, 1999), pp. 1–33.
13. Erik H. Erikson and Huey P. Newton, *In Search of Common Ground* (New York: W. W. Norton, 1973), p. 52.
14. Christopher R. Edginton, Christophere L. Kowalski, and Steven W. Randall, *Youth Work: Emerging Perspectives in Youth Development* (Champaign: Sagamore Publishing, 2005).
15. See David Kupelian, "Why Today's Youth Culture Has Gone Insane," *WorldNew Daily Exclusive Commentary*, January 16, 2004.
16. Pew Research Center, "Millennials: Confident. Connected. Open to Change." February 24, 2010, http://www.pewsocialtrends.org/2010/02/24/millennials-confident-connected-open-to-change (accessed August 24, 2014).
17. Pew Research Center, "Millennials in Adulthood," March 7, 2014, http://www.pewsocialtrends.org/2014/03/07/millennials-in-adulthood (accessed August 15, 2014).
18. William A. Draves and Julie Coates, *Nine Shift: Work, Life and Education in the 21st Century* (Learning Resources Network, 2007).
19. U.S. Census Bureau, *U.S. Census 2008* (Washington, D.C.: Government Printing Office, 2009).
20. Ibid.
21. Howard N. Snyder and Melissa Sickmund, *Juvenile Offenders and Victims: 2006 National Report* (Washington, DC: National Center for Juvenile Justice and Office of Justice Programs).
22. Federal Interagency Forum on Child and Family Statistics, ChildStats.gov, *America's Children: Key National Indicators of Well-Being, 2013*, http://www.childstats.gov/americaschildren/demo.asp (accessed July 4, 2014).
23. Ibid.
24. The Children's Defense Fund, *The State of America's Children 2014*, http://www.childrensdefense.org/child-research-data-publications/data/2014-soac.pdf?utm_source=2014-SOAC-PDF&utm_medium=link&utm_campaign=2014-SOAC, p. 2 (accessed April 2, 2014).
25. Ibid.
26. Ibid.
27. Danice K. Eaton et al., "Youth Risk Behavior Surveillance: United States, 2007," *MMWR Surveillance Summaries* 57 (2008), pp. 1–131.
28. Michael A. Gusseri, Teena Willoughby, and Heather Chalmers, "A Rationale and Method for Examining Reasons for Linkages Among Adolescent Risk Behaviors," *Youth Adolescence* 36 (2007), pp. 279–289.
29. Ibid.
30. Eaton et al., "Youth Risk Behavior Surveillance."
31. David Huizinga, Rolf Loeber, Terence P. Thornberry, and Lynn Cothern, *Co-Occurrence of Delinquency and Other Problem Behaviors* (Washington, D.C.: Office of Juvenile Justice and Delinquency Prevention, 2000), p. 1. For an examination of the prevalence and patterns of co-occurring mental health problem symptoms, substance use, and

31. delinquent conduct in a sample of multiple-problem and detained youths, see Cathryn C. Potter and Jeffrey M. Jenson, "Cluster Profiles of Multiple Problem Youth: Mental Health Problem Symptoms, Substance Use, and Delinquent Conduct," *Criminal Justice and Behavior* 30 (April 2003), pp. 230–250.

32. Carl McCurley and Howard N. Snyder, *Co-Occurrence of Substance Use Behaviors in Youth* (Washington, D.C.: U.S. Department of Justice, 2008).

33. Timothy Brezina, Erdal Tekin, and Volan Topalli, "'Might Not Be a Tomorrow': A Multimethods Approach to Anticipated Early Death and Youth Crime," *Criminology* 47 (November, 2010), pp. 1091–1129.

34. Children's Defense Fund, *The State of America's Children 2014* (Washington, D.C.: Children's Defense Fund, 2014).

35. Federal Bureau of Investigation, *Crime in the United States 2012*. Web posted at http://www.fbi.gov/about-us/cjis/ucr/crime-in-the-u s/2012/crime-in-the-u.s.-2012/tables/36tabledatadecoverviewpdf.

36. *In re Poff*, 135 F. Supp. 224 (C.C.C. 1955).

37. Barry Krisberg and James Austin, *The Children of Ishmael: Critical Perspectives on Juvenile Justice* (Palo Alto: Mayfield Publishing, 1978), p. 60.

38. Carol J. DeFrances, *Juveniles Prosecuted in State Criminal Courts* (Washington, D.C.: Office of Juvenile Justice and Delinquency Prevention, U.S. Department of Justice, 1997).

39. These interviews were conducted in two phases: as part of the juvenile victimization study in the 1970s and the follow-up of this study in 1989. In addition, Linda Dippold Bartollas interviewed parents, probation officers, juvenile court judges, and public school teachers in Illinois, Iowa, and Minnesota during the late 1980s and 1990s.

40. Meda Chesney-Lind and Lisa J. Pasko, *The Female Offender: Girls, Women, and Crime*, 2nd ed. (Thousand Oaks, Calif.: Sage, 2004).

41. Ibid.

42. U.S. Congress, Senate Committee on the Judiciary, Subcommittee to Investigate Juvenile Delinquency, 1973, The Juvenile Justice and Delinquency Prevention Act. S.3148 and s.821 92d Cong 2d sess, 93d Cong., 1st sess.

43. National Council on Juvenile Justice, *National Juvenile Court Case Records 1975–1992* (Pittsburgh: National Center for Juvenile Justice, 1994)

44. Federal Advisory Committee on Juvenile Justice, *Annual Report 2008* (Washington, D.C.: Office of Juvenile Justice and Delinquency Prevention, 2008), p. 1. See also The Coalition for Juvenile Justice, *National Standards for the Care of Youth Charged with Status Offenses* (Washington, D.C.: U.S. Government Office, 2013). This report, created as part of the coalition's SOS Project, provides policy.

45. Ibid., p. 2.

46. Charles W. Thomas, "Are Status Offenders Really So Different?" *Crime and Delinquency* 22 (1976) pp. 440–442.

47. Martin Rouse, "The Diversion of Status Offenders, Criminalization, and the New York Family Court," paper presented at the annual meeting of the American Society of Criminology, Reno, Nevada (November 1989), 1, 2, 10–11.

48. Thomas, "Are Status Offenders Really So Different?" pp. 438–455.

49. New York State Office of Children and Family Services, *PINS Reform Legislation,* http://www.ocfs.state.ny.us/main/legal/legislation/pins (accessed May 3, 2012).

50. Ibid.

51. Ibid (accessed June 12, 2012).

52. Federal Advisory Committee on Juvenile Justice, *Federal Advisory Committee on Juvenile Justice*: *Annual Report 2010* (Washington, D.C.: U.S. Department of Justice, 2010), p. 3. Also, the Center on Youth Justice at the Vera Institute of Justice has launched the online Status Offense Reform Center. This Web site is supported by funding from the MacArthur Foundation's Models for Change Resource Center Partnership, 2013.

53. T. R. Thornberry, "Co-Occurrence of Problem Behavior Among Adolescents," paper presented at Multi-System Approaches in Child Welfare and Juvenile Justice Wingspread Conference, Milwaukee, WI, May 7–9, 2008.

54. National Resource Center for Family Centered Practice, *Minority Youth and Facilities Initiative (MYFI)* (Baltimore: Anne E. Casey Foundation, 2005).

55. Federal Advisory Committee on Juvenile Justice, *Annual Report 2010,* p. 5.

56. Barry Krisberg, Ira M. Schwartz, Paul Litsky, and James Austin, "The Watershed of Juvenile Justice Reform," *Crime and Delinquency*, January 1986), Vol. 32, No. 1, pp. 5-38; Barry C. Feld, "Legislative Policies Toward the Serious Juvenile Offender," *Crime and Delinquency* 27 (October 1981), pp. 497–521.

57. Edward Cimler and Lee Roy Bearch, "Factors Involved in Juvenile Decisions About Crime," *Criminal Justice and Behavior* 8 (September 1981), pp. 275–286.

58. For the development of these trends, see the interview with Alfred Blumstein in *Law Enforcement News* 21 (April 30, 1995), pp. 1–2 and 11–12.

59. National Criminal Justice Association, *Juvenile Justice Reform Initiatives in the States: 1994–1996* (Washington, D.C.: Office of Juvenile Justice and Delinquency Prevention, 1997).

60. Toney Bissett Ford, *A Glance Backwards: An Analysis of Youth Resiliency Through Autoethniological and Life History Lenses,* Ed.D. dissertation, 2010.

61. J. Maselko, L. Kubzansky, L. Lipsitt, and S. L. Buka, "Mother's Affection at 8 Months Predicts Emotional Distress in Adulthood," *Journal of Epidemiology and Community Health* (July 2010), doi:10.1136/jech.2009.097873 (accessed June 24, 2012).

62. M. Rutter, "Psychopathological Development Across Adolescence," *Journal of Youth and Adolescence* 36 (January 2007), pp. 101–110.

63. B. Rodman, "Reclaiming Youth: What Restorative Practices Add to the Thinking: Reclaiming Children and Youth,"

Journal of Strength-Based Interventions 16 (Summer 2007), pp. 48–51, 59.

64. Ibid.
65. Glen H. Elder Jr., Monica Kirkpatrick Johnson, and Robert Crosnoe, "The Emergence and Development of Life Course Theory," in *Handbook of the Life Course*, edited by Jeylan T. Mortimer and Michael J. Shanahan (New York: Kluwer Academic/Plenum Publishers, 2003), pp. 3–19.
66. David P. Farrington, "Introduction to Integrated Developmental and Life-Course Theories of Offending," in *Integrated Developmental and Life-Course Theories of Offending*, edited by David P. Farrington (New Brunswick and London: Transaction Publishers, 2005), pp. 1–14.
67. John H. Laub, "Edwin H. Sutherland and the Michael-Adler Report: Searching for the Soul of Criminology: Seventy Years Later," *Criminology*, 44 (May 2006), pp. 235–258.
68. Children's Defense Fund, *The State of America's Children 2011*.
69. Office of Juvenile Justice and Delinquency Prevention, *OJJDP Model Programs Guide*, http://www.ojjdp.gov/mpg (accessed June 12, 2012).
70. Mark W. Lipsey, James C. Howell, Marion R. Kelly, Gabrielle Chapman, and Darin Carver, *Improving the Effectiveness of Juvenile Justice Programs: A New Perpsectrive on Evidence-Based Practice, 2010* and Clemens Bartollas and Stuart J. Miller, *Juvenile Justice in America*, 6th ed. (Upper Saddle River: Prentice-Hall, 2010), p. 58.

Chapter 2, The Measurement and Nature of Delinquency

1. Philip Caulfield, "Texas Rich Kid Who Killed 4 in Drunken Car Crash Spared Jail," *New York Daily News*, December 11, 2013; "Texas Teen Gets Probation for DUI Crash That Killed Four," *Toronto Sun*, December 11, 2013.
2. Donald J. Shoemaker, *Theories of Delinquency: An Examination of Explanations of Delinquent Behavior*, 6th ed. (New York: Oxford University Press, 2013).
3. Federal Bureau of Investigation, *Crime in the United States 2012*, http://www.fbi.gov/about-us/cjis/ucr/crime-in-the-u.s/2012/crime-in-the-u.s.-2012.
4. Charles Puzzanchera and Sarah Hockenberry, *Juvenile Court Statistics 2010* (Pittsburgh: National Center for Juvenile Justice, 2013).
5. Charles Puzzanchera and Crystal Robinson, *Delinquency Cases in Juvenile Court, 2010* (Washington, D.C.: OJJDP, 2014).
6. Puzzanchera and Hockenberry, *Juvenile Court Statistics 2010*.
7. Stephen A. Cernkovich, Peggy C. Giordano, and Meredith D. Pugh, "Chronic Offenders: The Missing Cases in Self-Report Delinquency," *Journal of Criminal Law and Criminology* 76 (1985), pp. 705–732.
8. Michael J. Hindelang, Travis Hirschi, and Joseph G. Weis, *Measuring Delinquency* (Beverly Hills: Sage, 1981), p. 22.
9. Ibid.
10. Hindelang et al., *Measuring Delinquency*.
11. Ibid., p. 126. For the reliability of self-report studies, see also David H. Huizinga and Delbert S. Elliot, *A Longitudinal Study of Drug Use and Delinquency in a National Sample of Youth: An Assessment of Causal Order*, A Report of the National Youth Survey (Boulder: Behavioral Research Institute, 1981); and Beatrice A. Rouse, Nicholas J. Kozel, and Louise G. Richards, eds., *Self-Report Methods of Estimating Drug Use: Meeting Current Challenges to Validity*, NIDA Research Monograph 57 (Rockville: National Institute on Drug Abuse, 1985).
12. Franklyn W. Dunford and Delbert S. Elliott, "Identifying Career Offenders Using Self-Reported Data," *Journal of Research in Crime and Delinquency* 21 (February 1984), pp. 57–82.
13. Ibid.
14. David H. Huizinga, Rolf Loeber, and Terence P. Thornberry, *Urban Delinquency and Substance Abuse: Initial Findings* (Washington, D.C.: U.S. Department of Justice, Office of Juvenile Justice and Delinquency Prevention, 1994).
15. Ibid. See also, *Guide for Implementing the Comprehensive Strategy for Serious, Violent, and Chronic Juvenile Offenders* (Washington, D.C.: Office of Juvenile Justice and Delinquency Prevention, 1995).
16. David S. Kirk, "Examining the Divergence Across Self-Report and Official Data Sources on Inferences About the Adolescent Life-Course of Crime," *Journal of Quantitative Criminology* 22 (2006), pp. 107–129.
17. Jerald G. Bachman and Patrick M. O'Malley, *A Continuing Study of American Youth (12th-Grade Survey, 1996)* (Ann Arbor: Institute for Social Research, 1998).
18. Jennifer Truman, Lynn Langton, and Michael Planty, *Criminal Victimization, 2012* (Washington, D.C.: BJS, 2013).
19. Ibid.
20. Ibid.
21. Ibid.
22. David Farmington, Darrick Joliffe, David Hawkins, Donald J. Catalano, Karl G. Hill, and Rick Kosterman, "Why Are Boys More Likely To Bee Refereed to Juvenile Court? Gender Differences in Official and Self-Reported Data," *Victims and Offenders* 5 (2010), pp. 25–44.
23. David P. Farrington, Rolf Loeber, Magda Stouthamer-Loeber, Welmoet B. Van Kammen, and Laura Schmidt, "Self-Reported Delinquency and a Combined Delinquency Seriousness Scale Based on Boys, Mothers, and Teachers: Concurrent and Predict Validity for African Americans and Caucasians," *Criminology* 34 (November 1996), pp. 493–517.
24. Thomas L. McNulty and Paul E. Bellair, "Explaining Racial and Ethnic Differences in Serious Adolescent Violent Behavior," *Criminology* 41 (August 2003), pp. 709–746.
25. Alex R. Piquero and Robert W. Brame, "Assessing the Race-Crime and Ethnicity-Crime Relationship in a Sample

of Serious Adolescent Delinquents," *Crime and Delinquency* 20 (2008), pp. 1–33.

26. Richard B. Felson, Glenn Deane, and David P. Armstrong, "Do Theories of Crime or Violence Explain Race Differences in Delinquency?" *Social Science Research* 37 (2008), pp. 623–641.

27. Joanne M. Kaufman, "Explaining the Race/Ethnicity-Violence Relationship: Neighborhood Context and Psychological Processes," *Justice Quarterly* 22 (June 2005), pp. 224–251.

28. Michael Rocques and Raymond Paternoster, "Understanding the Antecedents of the 'School-to-Jail' Link: The Relationship Between Race and School Discipline," *Journal of Criminal Law and Criminology* 10 (2011), pp. 633–655.

29. Michael O'Hear, Life Sentences Blog, http//www.life.sentencesblog com.? p=4043 (accessed June 14, 2011).

30. Ruth D. Peterson, "The Central Place of Race in Crime and Justice—The American Society of Criminology's 2011 Sutherland Address," *Criminology* 50 (2012), pp. 303–327.

31. Charles Tittle, Wayne Villemez, and Douglas Smith, "The Myth of Social Class and Criminalty: An Empirical Assessment of the Empirical Evidence," *American Sociological Review* 43 (1978), pp. 643–656.

32. Suzanne S. Ageton and Delbert S. Elliott, *The Incidence of Delinquent Behavior in a National Probability Sample of Adolescents* (Boulder: Behavioral Research Institute, 1978).

33. Delbert Elliott and David Huizinga, "Social Class and Delinquent Behavior in a National Youth Panel," *Criminology* 21 (May 1983), pp. 149–177. For a discussion about whether different definitions of class are likely to produce different results on social class and delinquency, see Margaret Farnworth, Terence P. Thornberry, Alan J. Lizotte, and Marvin D. Krohn, *Social Background and the Early Onset of Delinquency: Exploring the Utility of Various Indicators of Social Class Background* (Albany: Rochester Youth Development Study, June 1990).

34. For a listing of some of this longitudinal research, see David P. Farrington, *Integrated Developmental Life-Course Theories of Offending: Advances in Criminological Theory* (New Brunswick and London: Transaction Publishers, 2005), pp. 3–4.

35. Lila Kazemian and David P. Farrington, "Comparing the Validity of Prospective, Retrospective, and Official Onset for Different Offending Categories," *Journal of Quantitative Criminology* 21 (June 2005), pp. 224–251.

36. Alfred Blumstein, David P. Farrington, and Soumyo Moitra, "Delinquency Careers, Innocents, Desisters, and Persisters," in Michael Tonry and Norval Morris, eds., *Crime and Justice: An Annual Review*, 6th ed. (Chicago: University of Chicago Press, 1985), pp. 187–220.

37. David P. Farrington, "Offending from 10 to 25 Years of Age," in K. T. Van Dusen and S. A. Mednick, eds., *Prospective Studies of Crime and Delinquency* (Boston: Kluwer-Nijhoff, 1983), pp. 17–37.

38. David P. Farrington, Darrick Jolliffe, J. David Hawkins, Richard F. Catalano, Karl G. Hill, and Rick Kosterman, "Comparing Delinquency Careers in Court Records and Self-Reports," *Criminology* 41 (2003), pp. 933–942.

39. Kevin W. Alltucker, Michael Bullis, Daniel Close, and Paul Yovanoff, "Different Pathways to Juvenile Delinquency: Characteristics of Early and Late Starters in a Sample of Previously Incarcerated Youth," *Journal of Child and Family Studies* 15 (August 2006), pp. 479–492.

40. Rolf Loeber, Magda Stouthamer-Loeber, Welmoet Van Kammen, and David P. Farrington, "Initiation, Escalation and Desistance in Juvenile Offending and Their Correlates," *Journal of Criminal Law and Criminology* 82 (1991), pp. 36–82.

41. Rolf Loeber, Phen Wung, Kate Keenan, Bruce Giroux, Magda Stouthamer-Loeber, and Welmoet B. Van Kammen, "Developmental Pathways in Disruptive Child Behavior," *Development and Psychopathology* 5 (Winter–Spring, 1993), pp. 103–133.

42. See Barbara Tatem Kelley, Rolf Loeber, Kate Keenan, and Mary DeLamatre, *Developmental Pathways in Boys' Disruptive and Delinquent Behavior* (Washington, D.C.: Office of Juvenile Justice and Delinquency Prevention, 1997).

43. T. E. Moffitt, "Adolescent-Limited and Life-Course Persistent Antisocial Behavior: A Developmental Taxonomy," *Psychological Review* 100 (1993), pp. 674–701. For one of the studies that is highly supportive of Moffitt's taxonomy of offending behavior, see Paul Mazerolle, Robert Brame, Ray Paternoster, Alex Piquero, and Charles Dean, "Onset Age, Persistence, and Offending Versatility: Comparisons across Gender," *Criminology* 38 (November 2000), pp. 1143–1172.

44. Alex R. Piquero, Leah E. Daigle, Chris Gibson, Nicole Leeper Piquero, and Stephen G. Tibbetts, "Are Life-Course-Persistent Offenders at Risk for Adverse Health Outcomes?" *Journal of Research in Crime and Delinquency* 44 (May 2007), pp. 186–207.

45. Mazerolle et al., "Onset Age, Persistence, and Offending Versatility."

46. Glenn Deanne, David P. Armstrong, and Richard B. Felson, "An Examination of Offense Specialization Using Marginal Logit Models," *Criminology* 43 (November 2005), pp. 955–988.

47. D. Wayne Osgood and Christopher J. Schreck, "A New Method of Studying the Extent, Stability, and Predictors of Individual Specialization in Violence," *Criminology* 45 (2007), pp. 273–312.

48. For an investigation of gang involvement in crack cocaine sales, see Malcolm W. Klein, Cheryl L. Maxson, and Lea C. Cunningham, "'Crack,' Street Gangs, and Violence," *Criminology* 29 (1991), pp. 623–650.

49. Blumstein et al., "Delinquency Careers."

50. David P. Farrington and J. David Hawkins, "Predicting Participation, Early Onset and Later Persistence in Officially Recorded Offending," *Criminal Behaviour and Mental Health* 1 (1991), p. 1.

51. Lila Kazemian and David P. Farrington, "Exploring Residual Career Length and Residual Number of Offenses

for Two Generations of Repeat Offenders," *Journal of Research in Crime and Delinquency* 47 (February 2006), pp. 89–113.

52 Nadine Lanctot, Stephen A. Cernkovich, and Peggy C. Giordano, "Delinquent Behavior, Official Delinquency, and Gender: Consequences for Adulthood Functioning and Well-Being," *Criminology* 45 (2007), pp. 191–222. See also Michael Massoglia, "Desistance or Displacement? The Changing Patterns of Offending from Adolescence to Young Adulthood," *Journal of Quantitative Criminology* 22 (2006), pp. 215–229.

53 Michael Gottfredson and Travis Hirschi, *A General Theory of Crime* (Palo Alto.: Stanford University Press, 1990), p. 107.

54 James Q. Wilson and Richard Herrnstein, *Crime and Human Nature* (New York: Simon and Schuster, 1985), p. 209.

55 Daniel S. Nagin and Raymond Pasternoster, "On the Relationship of the Past to Future Delinquency," *Criminology* 29 (May 1991), p. 165.

56 Ibid., p. 163.

57 Ibid.

58 Robert J. Sampson and John H. Laub, *Crime in the Making: Pathways and Turning Points Through Life* (Cambridge: Harvard University Press, 1993). For further support of life-course theory, see Ronald L. Simons, Christine Johnson, Rand D. Conger, and Glen Elder, Jr., "A Test of Latent Trait Versus Life-Course Perspectives on the Stability of Adolescent Antisocial Behavior," *Criminology* 36 (May 1998), pp. 217–243.

59 John H. Laub and Robert J. Sampson, "Turning Points in the Life Course: Why Change Matters to the Study of Crime," *Criminology* 31 (August 1993), pp. 301–320.

60 For more discussion on these issues, see David P. Farrington, "Introduction to Integrated Developmental and Life-Course Theories of Offending," in *Integrated Developmental Life-Course Theories of Offending*, pp. 1–14.

61 Alan J. Lizotte, Marvin D. Krohn, James C. Howell, Kimberly Tobin, and Gregory J. Howard, "Factors Influencing Gun Carrying Among Young Urban Males over the Adolescent–Young Adult Life Course," *Criminology* 38 (2000), pp. 811–834; Philip J. Cook and Jens Ludwig, "Does Gun Prevalence Affect Teen Gun Carrying After All?" *Criminology* 42 (2004), pp. 27–54; and Anthony A. Braga, "Serious Youth Gun Offenders and the Epidemic of Youth Violence in Boston," *Journal of Quantitative Criminology* 19 (March 2003), pp. 33–54.

62 David M. Kennedy, Anthony A. Braga, and Anne M. Piehl, *Reducing Gun Violence: The Boston Gun Project's Operation Ceasefire* (Washington, D.C.: National Institute of Justice, 2001).

Chapter 3, Individual Causes of Delinquency

1 David E. Kalist and Daniel Y. Lee, "First Names and Crime: Does Unpopularity Spell Trouble?" *Social Science Quarterly* 90, No. 1 (2009), pp. 39–49.

2 Ibid, p. 40.

3 Ronald V. Clarke and Derek B. Cornish, "Modeling Offenders' Decisions: A Framework for Research and Policy," in Michael Tonry and Norval Morris, eds., *Crime and Justice*, 6th ed. (Chicago: University of Chicago Press, 1985), pp. 147–185

4 C. L. Montesquieu, *On the Spirit of the Laws*, translated by Thomas Nugent, edited by David W. Carithers (Berkeley: University of California Press, 1977), originally published as *L'Esprit des Lois* (1747); Cesare Bonesana Beccaria, *On Crimes and Punishments*, translated by H. Paolucci (1764; reprint ed., Indianapolis: Bobbs-Merrill, 1963); Jeremy Bentham, *An Introduction to the Principles of Morals and Legislation* (1823; reprint ed., New York: Hafner Publishing, 1948).

5 Montesquieu, *On the Spirit of the Laws,*

6 Ibid.

7 Beccaria, *On Crimes and Punishments*, p. 179.

8 Bentham, *An Introduction to the Principles of Morals and Translation.*

9 Edward Cimler and Lee Roy Bearch, "Factors Involved in Juvenile Decisions about Crime," *Criminal Justice and Behavior* 8 (September 1981), pp. 275–286.

10 A. Teseloni, R. Wittebrood, and G. Farell, "Burglary Victimization in England and Wales," *British Journal of Criminology* 44 (2004), pp. 66–91.

11 Clarke and Cornish, "Modeling Offenders' Decisions."

12 Derek B. Colrish and Ronald V. Clarke, eds., *The Reasoning Criminal: Rational Choice Perspectives on Offending* (New York: Springer, 1986); Melsus Felsoln, *Crime and Everyday Life: Insight and Inspiration for Society* (Thousand Oaks: Pine Forge Press, 1994.

13 Jeffrey Fagan and R. Piquero, "Rational Choice and Developmental Influence on Recidivism among Adolescent Felony Offenders," *Law and Society Review* 4 (2007), pp. 715–748.

14 Ronald L. Akers, "Rational Choice, Deterrence, and Social Learning Theory in Criminology: The Path Not Taken," *Journal of Criminal Law and Criminology* 81 (Fall 1990), pp. 653–676.

15 Raymond Paternoster, "Four Types of Common Delinquency: Deterrence and the Rational Choice Perspective," *Law and Society Review* 23 (1989), pp. 7–40.

16 Shamena Aniwar and Thomas Loughran, "Testing a Bayesian Learning Theory of Deterrence among Serious Juvenile Offenders," *Criminology* 49 (2011), pp. 667–698.

17 Fagan and Piquero, "Rational Choice and Developmental Influence."

18 Lawrence E. Cohen and Marcus Felson, "Social Change and Crime Rate Trends: A Routine Activity Approach," *American Sociological Review* (August 1979), pp. 588–609. For more recent expressions of the routine-activities approach, see Felson, *Crime and Everyday Life*.

19 Wayne Osgood and Amy Anderson, "Unstructured Socialization and Rates of Delinquency," *Criminology* 42 (2004), pp. 519–549.

20. Katherine Novak and Lizabeth Crawford, "Routine Activities as Determinants of Gender Differences in Delinquency," *Journal of Criminal Justice* 38 (2010), pp. 912–930.
21. Timothy Brezina, "Delinquent Problem-Solving: An Interpretive Framework," *Journal of Research in Crime and Delinquency* (2000), pp. 3–30.
22. See the desistance section at the end of this chapter.
23. Marvin E. Wolfgang, Terence P. Thornberry, and Robert M. Figlio, *From Boy to Man: From Delinquency to Crime* (Chicago: University of Chicago Press, 1987). See also James F. Short, Jr., and Fred L. Strodtbeck, *Group Process and Gang Delinquency* (Chicago: University of Chicago Press, 1965), pp. 248–265; and Charles W. Thomas and Donna M. Bishop, "The Effect of Formal and Informal Sanctions on Delinquency: A Longitudinal Comparison of Labeling and Deterrence Theories," *Journal of Criminal Law and Criminology* 75 (1984), p. 1244.
24. David Matza, *Delinquency and Drift* (New York: Wiley, 1964), p. 27. See also Silvan S. Tomkins, *Affect, Imagery, Consciousness: The Positive Affects* (New York: Springer, 1962), pp. 108–109.
25. Robert Agnew, "Determinism, Indeterminism, and Crime: An Empirical Exploration," *Criminology* 3 (1995), pp. 83–109.
26. See Matthew R. Durose, Alexia D. Cooper, and Howard N. Snyder, *Recidivism of Prisoners Released in 30 States in 2005: Patterns from 2005 to 2010* (Washington, D.C.: Bureau of Justice Statistics, 2014); and Roos Koolhof, Rolf Loeber, Evelyn Wei, Dustin Pardini, and Annematt Collot d'Escury, "Induction Deficits of Serious Delinquent Boys of Low Intelligence," *Criminal Behavior and Mental Health* 17 (2007), pp. 274–292. The discussion of recent studies of twins is based on John Paul Wright and Kevin M. Beaver, "Do Parents Matter in Creating Self-Control in Their Children?: A Genetically Based Test of Godttfredson and Hirschi Theory of Self-Esteem," *Criminology* (November 2006), pp. 1160–1202.
27. This section on the Progressive Era and the influence of positivism is based on David J. Rothman, *Conscience and Convenience: The Asylum and Its Alternatives in Progressive America* (Boston: Little, Brown, 1980), p. 32.
28. Ibid., See pp. 43–60.
29. Matza, *Delinquency and Drift*.
30. James Q. Wilson and Edward J. Herrstein, *The New Criminology: For a Social Theory of Delinquency* (New York: Simon and Schuster, 1973).
31. Ian Taylor, Paul Walton, and Jock Young, *The New Criminology: For a Social Theory of Deviance* (New York: Harper and Row, 1973).
32. Ibid.
33. John Slawson, *The Delinquent Boys* (Boston: Budget Press, 1926).
34. Edwin Sutherland, "Mental Deficiency and Crime," in Kimball Young, ed., *Social Attitudes*, (New York: Henry Hold, 1931), pp. 357–375.
35. Ibid.
36. William Sheldon, *Varieties of Delinquent Youth* (New York: Harper and Row, 1949).
37. Ibid.; Sheldon Glueck and Eleanor Glueck, *Physique and Delinquency* (New York: Harper and Row, 1956), p. 9; Juan B. Cortes with Florence M. Gatti, *Delinquency and Crime: A Biopsychosocial Approach: Empirical, Theoretical, and Practical Aspects of Criminal Behavior* (New York: Seminar Press, 1972); Saleem A. Shahn and Loren H. Roth, "Biological and Psychophysiological Factors in Criminality," in Daniel Glaser, ed., *Handbook of Criminology* (Chicago: Rand McNally, 1974), pp. 101–173.
38. Shahn and Roth, "Biological and Psychophysiological Factors in Criminality."
39. Karl O. Christiansen, "A Preliminary Study of Criminality Among Twins," in S. A. Mednick and K. O. Christiansen, eds., *Biosocial Bases of Criminal Behavior* (New York: Gardner, 1977), pp. 89–108; D. R. Cloninger et al., "Predisposition to Petty Criminality: II. Cross-Fostering Analysis of Gene-Environment Interaction," *Archives of General Psychiatry* 39 (November 1982), pp. 1242–1247; R. Crowe, "An Adoptive Study of Psychopathy: Preliminary Results from Arrest Records and Psychiatric Hospital Records," in R. Fieve et al., eds., *Genetic Research in Psychiatry* (Baltimore: Johns Hopkins University Press, 1975); William F. Gabrielli and Sarnoff A. Mednick, "Urban Environment, Genetics, and Crime," *Criminology* 22 (November 1984), pp. 645–652; S. Sigvardsson et al., "Predisposition to Petty Criminality in Swedish Adoptees: III. Sex Differences and Validation of Male Typology," *Archives of General Psychiatry* 39 (November 1982), pp. 1248–1253.
40. Donald J. Shoemaker, *Theories of Delinquency: An Examination of Explanations of Delinquent Behavior*, 6th ed. (New York: Oxford University Press, 2013).
41. Christiansen, "A Preliminary Study of Criminality Among Twins."
42. Thomas Bouchard, Jr., "Genes, Environment, and Personality," *Science* 264 (1994), pp. 1700–1701.
43. The discussion of recent study of twins is based on Wright and Beaver, "Do Parents Matter in Creating Self-Control in Their Children?"
44. Minnesota Twin Family Study, http://www.psych.umn.edu/_psylabs/mtfs/specialhtm (accessed April 16, 2009).
45. Christiansen, "A Preliminary Study of Criminality Among Twins."
46. Edwin H. Sutherland and Donald R. Cressey, *Criminology*, 10th ed. (New York: Lippincott, 1978).
47. Robert A. Gordon, "Prevalence: The Rare Datum in Delinquency Measurement and Its Implications for the Theory of Delinquency," in Malcolm Klein, ed., *The Juvenile Justice System* (Beverly Hills: Sage, 1976), pp. 184–201.
48. Robert A. Gordon, "IQ Commensurability of Black-White Differences in Crime and Delinquency," paper presented at the annual meeting of the American Psychological Association, Washington, D.C., August 1986, p. 1.

49. Travis Hirschi and Michael Hindelang, "Intelligence and Delinquency: A Revisionist Review," *American Sociological Review* 42 (1977), pp. 471–486.
50. Tom Kennedy, Kent Burnett, and William Edmonds, "Intellectual, Behavioral, and Personality Correlates of Violent Versus Nonviolent Juvenile Offenders," *Aggressive Behavior* 57 (2001), pp. 315–325.
51. Ross Koolhof, Ross Loeber, Evelyn Wei, Dustin Pardini, and Annematti Collot dEscury, "Intellectual, Behavioral, Behavioral, and Personality Correlates of Violent vs. Non-violent Juvenile Offenders," *Criminal Behavior and Mental Health* 17 (2007), pp. 274–292.
52. Hans Eysenck, "The Technology of Consent," *New Scientist* 26 (June 1969), p. 689. For two papers that tested Eysenck's contributions, see Coleta van Dam, Eric E. J. De Bruyn, and Jan M. A. Janssens, "Personality, Delinquency, and Criminal Recidivism," *Adolescence* 42 (Winter 2007), pp. 763–776; and Penelope A. Hasking, "Reinforcement, Sensitivity, Coping, and Delinquent Behaviour in Adolescents," *Journal of Adolescence* 30 (2007), pp. 739–749.
53. Ronald Simons, Kit Man Lei, Eric Stewart, Steve Beach, R. Gene, H. Brody, Robert Philbert, and Frederick Gibbons, "Social Adversity, Genetic Variation, Street Code, and Aggression: A Genetically Informed Model of Violent Behavior," *Youth Violence and Juvenile Justice* 10 (2012), pp. 3–24.
54. Patricia Stoddard Dare, Christopher Mallet, and Chris Botelm, "Associations Between Mental Health Disorders and Juveniles' Detention for a Personal Crime," *Crime and Adolescent Mental Health* (2011), pp. 378–392.
55. For additional information on reading disability in delinquent youths, see John Shelley-Tremblay, Natalie O'Brien, and Jennifer Langhinrichsen-Rohling, "Reading Disability in Adjudicated Youth: Prevalence Rates, Current Models, Traditional and Innovative Treatments," *Aggression and Violent Behavior* 12 (2007), pp. 376–392.
56. Attention deficit disorder (ADD) Web site, http://www.add.org (accessed July 15, 2011).
57. MTA Cooperative Group, "A 14-Month Randomized Clinical Trial of Treatment Strategies for Attention Deficit Hyperactivity Disorder," *Archives of General Psychiatry* 56 (1999), pp. 1088–1096.
58. Karen Stern, "A Treatment Study of Children with Attention Deficit Hyperactivity Disorder," *OJJDP Fact Sheet #20* (May 2001).
59. Sharyn Neuwirth, *Learning Disabilities* (Washington, D.C.: National Institute of Mental Health, 1993), p. 3.
60. Ibid.
61. Shoemaker, *Theories of Delinquency*, 6th ed.
62. Shahn and Roth, "Biological and Psychophysiological Factors of Delinquency."
63. Karen Matta Oshima, Jin Huang, Melissa Jonson-Reid, and Brett Drake, "Children with Disabilities in Poor Households: Association with Juvenile and Adult Offending," *Social Work Research* 34 (2010), pp. 102–113.
64. Ibid.
65. See Jianghong Lau, "Early Health Risk Factors for Violence, Conceptualization Evidence and Implications," *Aggression and Violent Behavior*, 16 (2011), pp. 63–73.
66. Ibid.
67. Adrian Raine et al., "Prefrontal Glucose Deficits in Murderers Lacking Psychosocial Deprivation," *Neuropsychiatry, Neuropsychology, and Behavioral Neurology* 11, No. 1 (1998), pp. 1–7.
68. Maggie Lee, "Lawmakers Study Neurology Along with New Juvenile Justice Policy Ideas," Juvenile Justice Information Exchange, August 14, 2013, https://jjie.org/lawmakers-study-neurology-along-with-new-juvenile-justice-policyideas/105157 (accessed November 5, 2014).
69. Sigmund Freud, *An Outline of Psychoanalysis*, translated by James Strachey (1940; reprint ed., New York: W. W. Norton, 1963).
70. Ibid.
71. Ibid.
72. William Healy, *Twenty-Five Years of Child Guidance: Studies from the Institute of Juvenile Research*, Series C, No. 256 (Chicago: Illinois Department of Public Welfare, 1934).
73. August Aichhorn, *Wayward Youth* (New York: Viking Press, 1963).
74. Kate Friedlander, *The Psychoanalytic Approach to Juvenile Delinquency* (London: Routledge and Kegan Paul, 1947).
75. Marvin Zuckerman, *Sensation Seeking Beyond the Optimal Level of Arousal* (Hillsdale: Lawrence Erlbaum, 1979), p. 10.
76. Ibid.
77. Frederick Thrasher, *The Gang* (Chicago: University of Chicago Press, 1936); Henry D. McKay, "The Neighborhood and Child Conduct," *Annals of the American Academy of Political and Social Science* 261 (1949), pp. 32–41; P. Tappan, *Juvenile Delinquency* (New York: McGraw-Hill, 1949); A. Cohen, "The Delinquent Subculture," in M. Wolfgang, L. Savitz, and N. Johnston, eds., *The Sociology of Crime and Delinquency*, 2nd ed. (New York: Wiley, 1970), pp. 127–140; J. J. Tobias, "The Affluent Suburban Male Delinquent," *Crime and Delinquency* 16 (1970), pp. 273–279; M. J. Hindelang, "The Relationship of Self-Reported Delinquency to Scales of the CPI and MMPI," *Journal of Criminal Law, Criminology and Police Science* 63 (1972), pp. 75–81.
78. R. N. Robbins, "Relationships Between Future Orientations, Impulsive Sensation Seeking and Risk Behavior Among Adjudicated Adolescents," *Journal of Adolescent Research* 19 (2004), pp. 428–455.
79. M. D. Slater, K. L. Henry, and R. C. Swaim, "Vulnerable Teens, Vulnerable Times: How Sensation Seeking, Alienation, and Victimization Moderate the Violent Media Content–Aggressiveness Relation," *Communication Research* 3 (2004), pp. 642-68.
80. Jack Katz, *Seductions of Crime: Moral and Sensual Attractions in Doing Evil* (New York: Basic Books, 1988).

81 Katz, *Seductions of Crime*. See also, Bill McCarthy, "Not Just 'For the Thrill of It': An Instrumentalist Elaboration of Katz's Explanation of Sneaky Thrill Property Crimes," *Criminology* 33 (November 1995). For other studies that have identified the importance of sensual experiences, see S. Lyng, "Edgework: A Social Psychological Analysis of Voluntary Risk Taking," *American Journal of Sociology* 95 (1990), pp. 851–856; and William J. Miller, "Edgework: A Model for Understanding Juvenile Delinquency," paper presented at the annual meeting of the Academy of Criminal Justice Sciences, Albuquerque, NM, March 1998.

82 Wilson and Herrnstein, *Crime and Human Nature*.

83 Ibid.

84 Jennifer Stevens, David May, Nancy Rice, and Roger Jarjoura, "Nonsocial Versus Social Reinforcers: Contrasting Theoretical Perspectives on Repetitive Serious Delinquency and Drug Use," *Youth Violence & Juvenile Justice* 9 (2011), pp. 295–312.

85 Avshalom Caspi, Terrie E. Moffitt, Phil A. Silva, Magda Stouthamer-Loeber, Robert F. Krueger, and Pamela S. Schmutte, "Are Some People Crime-Prone? Replications of the Personality-Crime Relationships Across Countries, Genders, Races, and Methods," *Criminology* 32 (1994), pp. 175–182. See also Douglas T. Kenrick and David C. Funder, "Profiting from Controversy: Lessons from the Person-Situation Debate," *American Psychologist* 43 (1988), pp. 23–34.

86 Caspi et al., "Are Some People Crime-Prone?"

87 Sheldon Glueck and Eleanor Glueck, *Unraveling Juvenile Delinquency* (Cambridge: Harvard University Press for the Commonwealth Fund, 1950).

88 Joshua D. Miller and Donald Lynam, "Structural Models of Personality and Their Relation to Antisocial Behavior: A Meta-Analytic Review," *Criminology* 39 (2001), pp. 765–798.

89 Rolf Loeber and Jeffrey Burke, "Developmental Pathways in Juvenile Externalizing and Internalizing Problems," *Journal of Research on Adolescence* 21 (2011), pp. 34–46.

90 See Harvey Cleckley, *The Mask of Sanity*, 3rd ed, (St. Louis: Mosby, 1955), pp. 382–417.

91 See R. Hare, "Psychopathy: Critical Construct Whose Time Has Come," *Criminal Justice and Behavior* (1996), pp. 25–54.

92 Linda Mealey, "The Sociobiology of Sociopathy: An Integrated Evolutionary Model," *Behavioral and Brain Sciences* 18 (1995), pp. 523–540.

93 Daniel C. Murrie, Dewey G. Comdell, Sebasitian Kepan, David McConville, and Andrea Levy-Eltoln, "Psychopathy Scores and Violence Among Juvenile Offenders: A Multi-Measure Study," *Behavioral Sciences and the Law* 22 (2004), pp. 49–67.

94 Raymond Corrado, Gina M. Vincent, Stephen D. Hart, and Irwin M. Cohen, "Predictive Validity of the Psychopathy Checklist: Youth Version for General and Violent Recidivism," *Behavioral Sciences and the Law* 22 (2004), pp. 5–22.

95 Jason Neland and Michel Miner, "Psychopathy Traits and Parental Dysfunction in Sexual Offending and General Delinquent Adolescent Males," *Journal of Sexual Aggression* 18 (2012), pp. 4–22.

96 Jean Piaget, *The Mechanisms of Perception* (New York: Basic Books, 1969).

97 Catherine Walsh, "Reconstructing Larry: Assessing the Legacy of Lawrence Kohlberg," *Elk Magazine,* October 1, 2000, p. 2, http:///www.gse.harvard.edu/news/features/larry10012000_page2.html.

98 See Thomas O'Connor, "Moral Development and Theories of Crime," http:/www.drtomoconnor.com/1060lect04.thm (accessed October 19, 2012).

99 Ibid.

100 Aaron T. Beck, *Prisoners of Hate: The Cognitive Basis of Anger, Hostility, and Violence* (New York: HarperCollins Publishers, 1999).

101 Stacy Tzoumakis, Patrick Lussier, and Raymond Corrado, "Female Juvenile Delinquency, Motherhood, and the Intergenerational Transmission of Aggression and Antisocial Behavior," *Behavioral Science & the Law* (2012), pp. 211–237.

102 Terrie E. Moffitt, Donald R. Lynam, and Phil A. Silva, "Neuropsychological Tests Predicting Persistent Male Delinquency," *Criminology* 32 (May 1994), p. 277.

103 Terrie E. Moffitt, "Adolescent-Limited and Life-Course-Persistent Antisocial Behavior: A Developmental Taxonomy," *Psychological Review* 100 (1993), pp. 674–701.

104 Terrie E. Moffitt, "The Neuropsychology of Conduct Disorder," *Development and Psychopathology* 5 (1993), pp. 135–151; and Terrie E. Moffitt, Avshalom Caspi, N. Dickson, Phil A. Silva, and W. Stanton, "Childhood-Onset Versus Adolescent-Onset Antisocial Conduct Problems in Males: Natural History from Ages 3 to 18," *Development and Psychopathology* 8 (1996), pp. 399–424.

105 Richard D. Tremblay, Frank Vtar, and David Nagin, et al., "The Montreal Longitudinal and Experimental Study Rediscovering the Power of Description," *Taking Stock of Delinquency: In Overview of Findings from Contemporary Longitudinal Studies*, edited by Terrence P. Thornberry and Marvin D. Krolhn (New York: Khwer Academic Publishers, 2003), pp. 205–254.

106 David P. Farrington, "Key Results from the First Forty Years of the Cambridge Study in Delinquent Development," in *Taking Stock of Delinquency*, edited by Terence P. Thornberry and Marvin D. Krohn (New York: Kluwer Academic/Plenum Publishers), pp. 137–183.

107 Ibid.

108 Ibid.

109 Richard Dembo, Jennifer Wareham, Norman Poythress, Kathleen Meyers, and James Schmeider, "Psychosocial Functioning Problems over Time among High-Risk Youths: A Latent Class Transition Analysis," *Crime and Delinquency* 54 (2008), pp. 664–670.

110 Ibid.

111. Farrington, "Age and Crime." This chapter's section on desistance and crime is adapted in part from Robert J. Sampson and John H. Laub, "Understanding Desistance from Crime," in Michael Tonry, ed., *Crime and Justice*, Vol. 28 (Chicago: University of Chicago Press, 2001), pp. 1–69.
112. Robert J. Sampson and John H. Laub, "A General Age-Graded Theory of Crime: Lessons Learned and the Future of Life-Course Criminology," in David P. Farrington, ed., *Integrated Developmental and Life Course Theories of Offending: Advances in Criminological Theory* (New Brunswick, 2005), pp. 165–181.

Chapter 4, Social Structural and Social Process Theories of Delinquency

1. "Young Girl Arrested: Accused of Selling Street Drugs," *WAR*, August 20, 2010.
2. Robert J. Sampson and W. B. Groves, "Community Structure and Crime: Testing Social-Disorganization Theory," *American Journal of Sociology* 94 (1989), pp. 774–802.
3. Robert J. Sampson and William Julius Wilson, "Toward a Theory of Race, Crime, and Urban Equality," in John Hagan and Ruth D. Peterson, eds., *Crime and Inequality* (Stanford: Stanford University Press, 1995), pp. 37–54.
4. See Emile Durkheim, *Suicide*, translated by John A. Spaulding and George Simpson (New York: Free Press of Glencoe, 1893).
5. There is a cultural deviance component to Shaw and McKay's perspective, but Ruth Rosner Kornhauser claims it is an unnecessary aspect of their social disorganization theory. See Ruth Rosner Kornhauser, *Social Sources of Delinquency: An Appraisal of Analytic Models* (Chicago: University of Chicago Press, 1978), p. 79.
6. Albert J. Reiss, Jr., "Settling the Frontiers of a Pioneer in American Criminology: Henry McKay," in James F. Short, Jr., ed., *Delinquency, Crime and Society* (Chicago: University of Chicago Press, 1976), pp. 64–86.
7. Harold Finestone, *Victims of Change: Juvenile Delinquents in American Society* (Westport: Greenwood Press, 1976).
8. George B. Vold and Thomas J. Bernard, *Theoretical Criminology*, 3rd ed. (New York: Oxford University Press, 1986).
9. Clifford R. Shaw, *Delinquency Areas* (Chicago: University of Chicago Press, 1929).
10. Clifford R. Shaw and Henry D. McKay, *Juvenile Delinquency and Urban Areas* (Chicago: University of Chicago Press, 1941).
11. Ysabel Rennie, *The Search for Criminal Man* (Lexington: Lexington Books, 1978).
12. Finestone, *Victims of Change*.
13. Ibid.
14. Ibid.
15. Shaw and McKay, *Juvenile Delinquency and Urban Areas*.
16. Rodney Stark, "Deviant Places: A Theory of the Ecology of Crime," *Criminology*, Vol. 25, No. 4, (November 1987), pp. 893-910.
17. Robert J. Bursik, Jr., "Ecological Stability and the Dynamics of Delinquency," in Reiss and Tonry, eds., *Communities and Crime*, p. 36.
18. Kornhauser, *Social Sources of Delinquency*, p. 25. For a review of the decline of cultural deviance theory, see J. Mitchell Miller, Albert K. Cohen, and Kevin M. Bryant, "On the Demise and Morrow of Subculture Theories of Crime and Delinquency," *Journal of Crime and Justice* 20 (1997), pp. 167–178.
19. Walter B. Miller, "Lower-Class Culture as a Generation Milieu of Gang Delinquency," *Journal of Social Issues* 14 (1958), pp. 9–10.
20. Ibid.
21. Marvin E. Wolfgang and Franco Ferracuti, *The Subculture of Violence* (London: Tavistock, 1957). For a study that challenges the black subculture of violence thesis, see Liqun Cao, Anthony Adams, and Vickie J. Jensen, "A Test of the Black Subculture of Violence Thesis: A Research Note," *Criminology* 35 (May 1997), pp. 367–379.
22. Richard A. Cloward and Lloyd E. Ohlin, *Delinquency and Opportunity: A Theory of Delinquent Boys: The Culture of the Gang* (Glencoe: Free Press, 1955).
23. This section's analysis of social structure and anomie is based on Robert K. Merton, *Social Theory and Social Structure*, 2nd ed. (New York: Free Press, 1957), pp. 131–132.
24. *Ibid.*, p. 131.
25. Ibid.
26. Morton Deutsch and Robert M. Krauss, *Theories in Social Psychology* (New York: Basic Books, 1965), p. 198.
27. Merton, *Social Theory and Social Structure*.
28. Ibid., p. 151.
29. Ibid., p. 155.
30. Ibid.
31. For Merton's recent thoughts about the emergence and present status of strain theory, see Robert K. Merton, "Opportunity Structure: The Emergence, Diffusion, and Differentiation of a Sociological Concept, 1930s–1950s," in Freda Adler and William S. Laufer, eds., *The Legacy of Anomie Theory: Advances in Criminological Theory*, Vol. 6 (New Brunswick: Transaction Publishers, 1995), pp. 3–78.
32. Velmer S. Burton, Jr., and Francis T. Cullen, "The Empirical Status of Strain Theory," *Journal of Crime and Justice* 15 (1992), pp. 1–30.
33. [Text to come]
34. Jukka Savolainen, "Inequality, Welfare State, and Homicide: Further Support for the Institutional Anomie Theory," *Criminology* 38 (November 2000), pp. 617–663.
35. Velmer S. Burton, Jr., and Francis T. Cullen, "The Empirical Status of Strain Theory," *Journal of Crime and Justice* 15 (1992), p. 5.

36. Marshall B. Clinard, "The Theoretical Implications of Anomie and Deviant Behavior," in Marshall B. Clinard, ed., *Anomie and Deviant Behavior* (New York: Free Press, 1964), p. 10.
37. Cloward and Ohlin, *Delinquency and Opportunity*; and Albert K. Cohen, *Delinquent Boys: The Culture of the Gang* (Glencoe: Free Press, 1955).
38. Burton and Cullen, "The Empirical Status of Strain Theory," pp. 2–3.
39. Travis Hirschi, *Causes of Crime* (Berkeley: University of California Press, 1969); and Kornhauser, *Social Sources of Delinquency*.
40. Robert Agnew, "Foundations for a General Strain Theory of Crime and Delinquency," *Criminology* 30 (February 1992), pp. 47–87.
41. Thomas J. Bernard, "Control Criticisms of Strain Theory: An Assessment of Theoretical and Empirical Adequacy," *Journal of Research in Crime and Delinquency* 21 (1984), pp. 353–372; Thomas J. Bernard, "Testing Structural Strain Theories," *Journal of Research in Crime and Delinquency* 24 (1987), pp. 262–280.
42. Robert Agnew, "A Revised Strain Theory of Delinquency," *Social Forces* 64 (1985), pp. 151–167.
43. Ibid., p. 151.
44. Terence P. Thornberry, *Developmental Theories of Crime and Delinquency* (New Brunswick: Transaction Publishers, 2004), p. 32.
45. Robert Agnew, "The Contribution of 'Mainstream' Theories of the Explanation of Female Delinquency," in Margaret A. Zahn, ed., *The Delinquent Girl* (Philadelphia: Temple University Press, 2009), p. 8.
46. Ibid., pp. 7–29.
47. Agnew, "Foundations for a General Theory of Crime and Delinquency." See also Robert Agnew, "Building on the Foundation for a General Strain Theory," paper presented at the Annual Meeting of the American Society of Criminology in Washington, D.C., November 1998; and John P. Hoffman and Alan S. Miller, "A Latent Variable Analysis of General Strain Theory," *Journal of Quantitative Criminology* 14 (1998), pp. 83–110.
48. John Rodriquez and Scott Belshaw, "General Strain Theory: A Comparative Analysis of Latino and White Youths," *Southwest Journal of Criminal Justice* 7 (2010), pp. 138–158.
49. Agnew, "Foundations for a General Theory of Crime and Delinquency." See also Agnew, "Building on the Foundation for a General Strain Theory," and Hoffman and Miller, "A Latent Variable Analysis of General Strain Theory"; Stephen W. Baron, "Street Youth, Unemployment, and Crime: Is It That Simple? Using General Strain Theory to Untangle the Relationship," *Canadian Journal of Criminology and Criminal Justice* 50 (2008), pp. 399–434; Deanna M. Penez, Wesley G. Jennings, and Angela R. Gover, "Specifying General Strain Theory: An Ethnically Relevant Approach," *Deviant Behavior* 29 (2008), pp. 544–578; and Byongoof Moon, David Blurton, and John D. McCluskey, "General Strain Theory and Delinquency: Focusing on the Influences of Key Strain Characteristics on Delinquency," *Crime and Delinquency* 54 (2008), pp. 582–613; Ekkaterina V. Botchkovah, Charles R. Tittle, and Olena Antonaccio, "General Strain Theory: Additional evidence Using Cross-Cultural Data," *Criminology* 47 (2009), pp. 131–173.
50. Cohen, *Delinquent Boys*.
51. Ibid.
52. Ibid., pp. 113–114.
53. Ibid.
54. Ibid.
55. Ibid.
56. Ibid.
57. Ibid.
58. Albert K. Cohen, "The Sociology of the Deviant Act: Anomie Theory and Beyond," *American Sociological Review* 30 (1965), pp. 5–14.
59. Vold and Bernard, *Theoretical Criminology*, p. 197.
60. Cloward and Ohlin, *Delinquency and Opportunity*, p. 97.
61. Ibid.
62. Ibid.
63. Ibid.
64. Ibid., p. 25.
65. Ibid.
66. Delbert S. Elliott and Harwin L. Voss, *Delinquency and Dropout* (Lexington: Lexington Books, 1974).
67. Gwynn Nettler, *Explaining Crime*, 3rd ed. (New York: McGraw-Hill, 1984).
68. For this symbolic interactionist perspective, see Charles H. Cooley, *Human Nature and the Social Order* (1902; reprint ed., New York: Schocken Books, 1964); George H. Mead, *Mind, Self and Society* (Chicago: University of Chicago Press, 1934).
69. Edwin H. Sutherland, "A Statement of the Theory," in Albert Cohen, Alfred Lindesmith, and Karl Schuessler, eds., *The Sutherland Papers* (Bloomington: Indiana University Press, 1956), pp. 7–29.
70. Ross L. Matsueda, "The Current State of Differential Association Theory," *Crime and Delinquency* 34 (July 1988), pp. 277–306.
71. Harold Finestone, *Victims of Change: Juvenile Delinquents in American Society* (Westport: Greenwood Press, 1976).
72. Matsueda, "The Current State of Differential Association Theory."
73. Donald J. Shoemaker, *Theories of Delinquency: An Examination of Explanations of Delinquent Behavior*, 5th ed. (New York: Oxford University Press, 2005).
74. Albert J. Reiss, Jr., "Delinquency as the Failure of Personal and Social Controls," *American Sociological Review* 16 (1951), pp. 196–207.
75. F. Ivan Nye, *Family Relationships and Delinquent Behavior* (New York: John Wiley, 1958).

76 The principles of containment theory draw on Walter C. Reckless, "A New Theory of Delinquency and Crime," *Federal Probation* 24 (December 1961), pp. 42–46.

77 Hirschi, *Causes of Delinquency*, p. 16.

78 Ibid., p. 31.

79 Ibid., p. 34.

80 Ibid.

81 Ibid.

82 Ibid.

83 Ibid., p. 86.

84 Ibid.

85 Ibid., p. 22.

86 Ibid.

87 Ibid., p. 200.

88 Barbara J. Costello and Paul R. Vowell, "Testing Control Theory and Differential Association: A Reanalysis of the Richmond Youth Project Data," *Criminology* 37 (November 1999), pp. 479–514; and Charles R. Tittle, *Control Balance: Toward a General Theory of Deviance* (Boulder: Westview, 1995). For a recent attempt to test Tittle's control balance theory, see Alex R. Piquero and Matthew Hickman, "An Empirical Test of Tittle's Control Balance Theory," *Criminology* 37 (May 1999), pp. 319–341. See also Steven A. Cernkovich, "Evaluating Two Models of Delinquency Causation: Structural Theory and Control Theory," *Criminology* 25 (1987), pp. 335–352; Raymond A. Eve, "A Study of the Efficacy and Interactions of Several Theories for Explaining Rebelliousness Among High School Students," *Journal of Criminal Law and Criminology* 69 (1978), pp. 115–125; Marvin D. Krohn and James L. Massey, "Social Control and Delinquent Behavior: An Examination of the Elements of the Social Bond," *Sociological Quarterly* 21 (August 1980), p. 542; Elliott et al., *Explaining Delinquency and Drug Use*; Joseph H. Rankin, "Investigating the Interrelations among Social Control Variables and Conformity," *Journal of Criminal Law and Criminology* 67 (1977), pp. 470–480; Robert Agnew, "Social Control Theory and Delinquency: A Longitudinal Test," *Criminology* 23 (1985), pp. 47–61; Randy L. LaGrange and Helene Raskin White, "Age Differences in Delinquency: A Test of Theory," *Criminology* 23 (1985), pp. 19–45; Kimberly Kempf Leonard and Scott H. Decker, "Theory of Social Control: Does It Apply to the Very Young?" *Journal of Criminal Justice* 22 (1994), pp. 89–105; Robert L. Gardner and Donald J. Shoemaker, "Social Bonding and Delinquency: A Comparative Analysis," *Sociological Quarterly* 39 (1989), pp. 481–500; and Eric A. Stewart, "School Social Bonds, Social Climate, and School Misbehavior: A Multilevel Analysis," *Justice Quarterly* 20 (September 2003), pp. 575–604.

89 Among the growing number of works citing the advantages of integrated theory are Richard Johnson, *Juvenile Delinquency and Its Origins: An Integrated Theoretical Approach* (New York: Cambridge University Press, 1979); Elliott et al., *Explaining Delinquency and Drug Use*; Steven Messner, Marvin Krohn, and Allen Liska, eds., *Theoretical Integration in the Study of Deviance and Crime: Problems and Prospects* (Albany: State University of New York at Albany Press, 1989); and John Hagan and Bill McCarthy, *Mean Streets: Youth Crime and Homelessness* (New York: Cambridge University Press, 1997).

90 For other integrated theories, see James Q. Wilson and Richard J. Herrnstein, *Crime and Human Nature* (New York: Simon and Schuster, 1985), which is discussed in Chapter 3; Robert J. Sampson and John H. Laub, *Crime in the Making: Pathways and Turning Points Through Life* (Cambridge: Harvard University Press, 1993), which is discussed in Chapter 2; Colvin and Pauly, "A Critique of Criminology," pp. 513–551, which is discussed in Chapter 5; John Hagan, A. R. Gillis, and John Simpson, "The Class Structure of Gender and Delinquency: Toward a Power-Control Theory of Common Delinquent Behavior," *American Journal of Sociology* 90 (1985), pp. 1151–1178.

91 Michael R. Gottfredson and Travis Hirschi, *A General Theory of Crime* (Palo Alto: Stanford University Press, 1990); Elliott et al., *Explaining Delinquency and Drug Use*; Delbert S. Elliott, Suzanne S. Ageton, and Rachelle J. Canter, "An Integrated Theoretical Perspective on Delinquent Behavior," *Journal of Research in Crime and Delinquency* 16 (1979), pp. 3–27; Terence P. Thornberry, "Toward an Interactional Theory of Delinquency," *Criminology* 25 (1987), pp. 862–891; Terence P. Thornberry, Alan J. Lizotte, Marvin D. Krohn, Margaret Farnworth, and Sung Joon Jang, "Testing Interactional Theory: An Examination of Reciprocal Causal Relationships among Family, School, and Delinquency," *Journal of Criminal Law and Criminology* 82 (1991), pp. 3–35; and J. David Hawkins and Joseph G. Weis, "The Social Development Model: An Integrated Approach to Delinquency Prevention," *Journal of Primary Prevention* 6 (Winter 1985), pp. 73–97.

92 Gottfredson and Hirschi, *A General Theory of Crime*.

93 Ibid., p. 87.

94 Ibid.

95 For a review of these studies, see T. David Evans, Francis T. Cullen, Velmer S. Burton, Jr., R. Gregory Dunaway, and Michael L. Benson, "The Social Consequences of Self-Control: Testing the General Theory of Crime," *Criminology* 35 (1997), pp. 476–477. See also Ryan Charles Meldrum, "Beyond Parenting: An Examination of the Etiology of Self-Control," *Journal of Criminal Justice* 36 (2008), pp. 244–251; Alexander T. Vazsonyi and Rudi Klanjsek, "A Test of Self-Control Theory Across Different Socioeconomic Strata," *Justice Quarterly* 25 (March 2008), pp. 101–131; and Stacey Nofziger, "The 'Cause' of Low Self-Control: The Influence of Maternal Self-Control," *Journal of Research in Crime and Delinquency* 45 (2008), pp. 191–224.

96 Shoemaker, *Theories of Delinquency*.

97 Delbert S. Elliott, Suzanne S. Ageton, and Rachelle J. Canter, "An Integrated Theoretical Perspective on Delinquent Behavior," *Journal of Research in Crime and Delinquency* 16 (1979), pp. 3–27.

98 Ibid.

99 Cynthia Chien, "Testing the Effect of the Key Theoretical Variable of Theories of Strain, Social Control and Social

Learning on Types of Delinquency," paper presented at the Annual Meeting of the American Society of Criminology, Baltimore, November 1990.
100. Thornberry, "Toward an Interactional Theory of Delinquency."
101. Ibid.
102. Ibid.
103. Ibid.
104. Hirschi, *Causes of Delinquency*.
105. For articles that examine children's poverty, see Greg J. Duncan, "Has Children's Poverty Become More Persistent?" *American Sociological Review* 56 (August 1991), pp. 538–550; and David J. Eggebeen and Daniel T. Lichter, "Race, Family Structure, and Changing Poverty among American Children," *American Sociological Review* 56 (December 1991), pp. 801–817.
106. G. Roger Jarjoura, Ruth A. Triplett, and Gregory P. Brinker, "Growing Up Poor: Examining the Link Between Persistent Poverty and Delinquency," *Journal of Quantitative Criminology* 18 (June 2002), pp. 159–187.
107. Marvin D. Krohn, Terence P. Thornberry, Craig Rivera, and Marc Le Blanc, "Later Delinquency Careers," in Rolf Loeber and David P. Farrington, eds., *Child Development* (Thousand Oaks: Sage, 2001), pp. 67–93.
108. John H. Laub and Robert J. Sampson, *Shared Beginnings, Divergent Lives: Delinquent Boys to Age 70* (Cambridge: Harvard University Press, 2003). See also Robert J. Sampson and John H. Laub, "A Life-Course Theory of Cumulative Disadvantage and the Stability of Delinquency," in Terence P. Thornberry, ed., *Developmental Theories of Crime and Delinquency* (New Brunswick: Transaction Publishers, 1997), pp. 133–161.
109. Inter-university Consortium for Political and Social Science, "Project on Human Development in Chicago Neighborhoods," http://www.icpsr.umich.edu/icpsrweb/PHDCN/about.jsp (accessed June 24, 2012).
110. Akiva Liberman, *Adolescents, Neighborhoods and Violence: Recent Findings from the Project on Human Development in Chicago Neighborhoods* (Washington, D.C.: National Institute of Justice, 2007), pp. 4–5, from which some of the wording in this section is taken.
111. From http://www.icpsr.umich.edu/PHDCN. For more information on collective efficacy, see Robert J. Sampson, "The Embeddedness of Child and Adolescent Development: A Community-Level Perspective on Urban Violence," in Joan McCord, ed., *Childhood Violence in the Inner City,* (New York: Cambridge, 1997), pp. 31–77; Robert J. Sampson, Jeffrey Morenoff, and Felton Earls, "Beyond Social Capital: Spatial Dynamics of Collective Efficacy for Children," *American Sociological Review* 64 (1999); and Robert J. Sampson, Stephen W. Raudenbush, and Felton Earls, "Neighborhoods and Violent Crime: A Multilevel Study of Collective Efficacy," *Science* 277 (1997) pp. 918–924.
112. http://www.icpsr.umich.edu/PHDCN.
113. Sampson et al., "Beyond Social Capital"; and Robert J. Sampson et al., "Neighborhoods and Violent Crime."
114. Ibid.
115. Adapted from Robert J. Sampson, "Chicago Project (PHDCN)," http://scholar.harvard.edu/sampson/content/chicago-project-phdcn-0 (accessed June 24, 2012).
116. Robert J. Sampson, *Great American City: Chicago and the Enduring Neighborhood Effect* (Chicago: University of Chicago Press, 2012).
117. RAND Corporation, "L.A. FANS: The Los Angeles Family and Neighborhood Survey," http://lasurvey.rand.org (accessed June 24, 2012).
118. Reanne Frank and Eileen Bjornstrom, "A Tale of Two Cities: Residential Context and Risky Behavior Among Adolescents in Los Angeles and Chicago," *Health and Place* 17, no. 1 (January 2011), pp. 67–77.

Chapter 5, Social Interactionist Theories of Delinquency

1. Mike Schneider and Jennifer Kay, "Rebecca Ann Sedwick Suicide: Two Girls Arrested for 'Terrorizing' Bullied Victim," *Huffington Post Miami,* October 10, 2013.
2. Martin Griffith and Scott Sonner, "Jose Reyes Nevada School Shooter Was Typical Kid, Not Loner," *Huffington Post Crime,* October 25, 2013.
3. Mike Pearce and Melanie Mason, "Anti-Bullying Video Questioned After Two Students' Suicides," *Los Angeles Times*, October 28, 2013.
4. Lening Zhang and Steven F. Messner, "The Severity of Official Punishment for Delinquency and Change in Interpersonal Relations in Chinese Society," *Journal of Research in Crime and Delinquency* 31 (November 1994), pp. 416–433.
5. Frank Tannenbaum, *Crime and the Community* (New York: Columbia University Press, 1938), pp. 19–20.
6. Ibid.
7. Edwin M. Lemert, *Social Pathology* (New York: McGraw-Hill, 1951).
8. Harold Finestone, *Victims of Change: Juvenile Delinquents in American Society* (Westport: Greenwood Press, 1976).
9. Finestone, *Victims of Change*.
10. Howard S. Becker, *Outsiders* (New York: Free Press, 1963), pp. 8–9.
11. Ibid.
12. Finestone, *Victims of Change*.
13. Edwin Schur, *Radical Nonintervention* (Englewood Cliffs: Prentice-Hall, 1973), p. 155.
14. Zhang and Messner, "The Severity of Official Punishment for Delinquency and Change in Interpersonal Relations in Chinese Society," p. 418.
15. Francis Polymeria, Francis T. Cullen, and Joanne C. Gersten, "The Effects of Police and Mental Health Intervention on Juvenile Delinquency: Specifying Contingencies

in the Impact of Formal Reaction," *Journal of Health and Social Behavior* 27 (1986), pp. 90–105.

16 Anthony Matarazzo, Peter J. Carrington, and Robert D. Hiscott, "The Effect of Prior Youth Court Dispositions on Current Disposition: An Application of Societal-Reaction Theory," *Theory of Quantitative Criminology* 17 (2001), pp. 169–200.

17 Jack P. Gibbs, "Conceptions of Deviant Behavior: The Old and the New," *Pacific Sociological Review* 9 (1966), pp. 9–14; Walter R. Gove, "Labeling and Mental Illness: A Critique," in Walter R. Gove, ed., *The Labeling of Deviance: Evaluating a Perspective*, 2nd ed. (Beverly Hills: Sage, 1980), pp. 53–59; John Hagan, "Extra-Legal Attitudes and Criminal Sanctioning: An Assessment and a Sociological Viewpoint," *Law and Society Review* 8 (1974), pp. 357–383; Travis Hirschi, "Labeling Theory and Juvenile Delinquency: An Assessment of the Evidence," in Walter R. Gove, ed., *The Labeling of Deviance: Evaluating a Perspective*, 2nd ed. (Beverly Hills: Sage, 1980), pp. 271–293; Charles R. Tittle, "Deterrence of Labeling?" *Social Forces* 53 (1975), pp. 399–410; Charles F. Wellford, "Labeling Theory and Criminology: An Assessment," *Social Problems* 22 (1975), pp. 332–345.

18 Zhang and Messner, "The Severity of Official Punishment for Delinquency and Change in Interpersonal Relations in Chinese Society," p. 419. See also Tittle, "Deterrence of Labeling?" and Gove, "Labeling and Mental Illness."

19 Raymond Paternoster and Leeann Iovanni, "The Labeling Perspective and Delinquency: An Elaboration of the Theory and an Assessment of the Evidence," *Justice Quarterly* 6 (1989), p. 359.

20 Zhang and Messner, "The Severity of Official Punishment for Delinquency and Change in Interpersonal Relations in Chinese Society."

21 Ruth A. Triplett and G. Roger Jarjoura, "Theoretical and Empirical Specification of a Model of Informal Labeling," *Journal of Quantitative Criminology* 10 (1994), p. 243.

22 Raymond Paternoster and Ruth A. Triplett, "Disaggregating Self-Reported Delinquency and Its Implications for Theory," *Criminology* 26 (1988), p. 6. See also Lening Zhang, "Informal Reactions and Delinquency," *Criminal Justice and Behavior* 24 (March 1997), pp. 129–150.

23 John Braithwaite, *Crime, Shame and Reintegration* (Cambridge: Cambridge University Press, 1989). See also Toni Makkai and John Braithwaite, "Reintegrative Shaming and Compliance with Regulatory Standards," *Criminology* 32 (August 1994), pp. 361–385.

24 Triplett and Jarjoura, "Theoretical and Empirical Specification of a Model of Informal Labeling."

25 Ruth Ann Triplett, "Labeling and Differential Association: The Effects on Delinquent Behavior," Ph.D. dissertation, University of Maryland, 1990. For a model of informal labeling, see Triplett and Jarjoura, "Theoretical and Empirical Specification of a Model of Informal Labeling," pp. 241–276.

26 Robert J. Sampson and John H. Laub, "A Life Course Theory of Cumulative Disadvantage and the Stability of Delinquency," in Terence P. Thornberry, ed., *Developmental Theories of Crime and Delinquency* (New Brunswick: Transaction Publishers, 1997), pp. 133–161.

27 John Gunnar Bernberg and Marvin D. Krohn, "Labeling Life Chances and Adult Crime: The Direct and Indirect Effect of Official Intervention in Adolescence on Crime in Early Adulthood," *Criminology* 41 (November 2003), pp. 1282–1313.

28 G. Nettler, *Explaining Crime*, 3rd ed. (New York: McGraw-Hill, 1984).

29 Donald J. Shoemaker, *Theories of Delinquency: An Examination of Explanations of Delinquency Behavior*, 5th ed. (New York: Oxford University Press, 2005).

30 Ross L. Matsueda, "Reflected Appraisals, Parental Labeling, and Delinquency: Specifying a Symbolic Interactional Theory," *American Journal of Sociology* 97 (1992), pp. 1577–1611; Karen Heimer and Ross L. Matsueda, "Role-Taking, Role Commitment, and Delinquency: A Theory of Differential Social Control," *American Sociological Review* 59 (1994), pp. 365–390; Karen Heimer, "Gender, Race, and the Pathways to Delinquency," in John Hagan and Ruth D. Peterson, eds., *Crime and Inequality* (Stanford: Stanford University Press, 1995), pp. 140–173; Karen Heimer and Ross L. Matsueda, "A Symbolic Interactionist Theory of Motivation and Deviance: Interpreting Psychological Research," in D. Wayne Osgood, ed., *Motivation and Delinquency*, Vol. 44 of the Nebraska Symposium on Motivation (Lincoln and London: University of Nebraska Press, 1997), pp. 223–276; and Ross L. Matsueda and Karen Heimer, "A Symbolic Interactionist Theory of Role-Transitions, Role Commitments, and Delinquency," in T. P. Thornberry, ed., *Advances in Criminological Theory* (New Brunswick: Transaction Publishers, 1997), pp. 163–213.

31 Matsueda, "Reflected Appraisals, Parental Labeling, and Delinquency."

32 Ibid.

33 Ibid.

34 Heimer, "Gender, Race, and Delinquency," p. 141.

35 Ibid.

36 Ibid.

37 The following discussion is based on ibid., pp. 1580–1581.

38 George H. Mead, *Mind, Self and Society* (Chicago: University of Chicago Press, 1934).

39 Matsueda, "Reflected Appraisals, Parental Labeling, and Delinquency," p. 1580. See also Mead, *Mind, Self and Society*, and Herbert Blumer, *Symbolic Interactionism: Perspective and Method* (Englewood Cliffs: Prentice-Hall, 1969).

40 Matsueda, "Reflected Appraisals, Parental Labeling, and Delinquency," p. 1581.

41 Matsueda, "Reflected Appraisals, Parental Labeling, and Delinquency."

42 Charles H. Cooley, *Human Nature and the Social Order*, rev. ed. (New York: Scribners, 1922).

43. Mead, *Mind, Self, and Society*.
44. Matsueda, "Reflected Appraisals, Parental Labeling, and Delinquency."
45. Ibid.
46. Ibid., p. 1602.
47. Ibid.
48. Ibid.
49. Heimer, "Gender, Race, and Delinquency," p. 145.
50. Ibid.
51. Ibid., p. 146.
52. Heimer and Matsueda, "Role-Taking, Role Commitment, and Delinquency."
53. Bartusch and Matsueda, "Gender, Reflected Appraisals, and Labeling"; Heimer, "Gender, Interaction, and Delinquency"; Heimer, "Gender, Race, and the Pathways to Delinquency"; and Stacy De Coster and Karen Heimer, "The Relationship Between Law Violation and Depression: An Interactionist Analysis," *Criminology* 39 (November 2001), pp. 799–836.
54. David Shichor, "The New Criminology: Some Critical Issues," *British Journal of Criminology* 20 (1980), pp. 29–48.
55. Viktor Afanasyer, *Marxist Philosophy* (Moscow: Foreign Language Publishing House, n.d.).
56. Jonathan H. Turner, *The Structure of Sociological Theory* (Homewood: Dorsey Press, 1978), p. 124.
57. Karl Marx and Frederick Engels, *The Communist Manifesto* (1848; reprint ed., New York: International Publishers, 1979).
58. Ibid., p. 9.
59. Ibid.
60. Ibid.
61. Mark Colvin and John Pauly, "A Critique of Criminology: Toward an Integrated Structural–Marxist Theory of Delinquency Production," *American Journal of Sociology* 89 (November 1983), pp. 513–551.
62. Herman Schwendinger and Julia S. Schwendinger, "Marginal Youth and Social Policy," *Social Problems* 24 (December 1976), pp. 84–91.
63. Herman Schwendinger and Julia Siegel Schwendinger, *Adolescent Subcultures and Delinquency* (New York: Praeger, 1985), p. 3.
64. Schwendinger and Schwendinger, "Marginal Youth and Social Policy," pp. 84–91.
65. Ibid.
66. David O. Friedrichs, "Victimology: A Consideration of the Radical Critique," *Crime and Delinquency* 29 (1983), pp. 283–294.
67. This interview took place in February 1984, and the information is used with permission.
68. Max Weber, "Class, Status, Party," in Richard Bendix and S. M. Lipset, eds., *Class, Status and Power* (New York: Macmillan, 1953), pp. 63–75.
69. Ralf Dahrendorf, *Class and Class Conflict in Industrial Society* (Palo Alto: Stanford University Press, 1959).
70. A. T. Turk, "Class, Conflict, and Criminalization," *Sociological Focus* 10 (August 1977), pp. 209–220.
71. Ian Taylor, Paul Walton, and Jock Young, *The New Criminology: For a Social Theory of Deviance* (Boston: Routledge and Kegan Paul, 1973).
72. John Hagan, A. R. Gillis, and John Simpson, "The Class Structure of Gender and Delinquency: Toward a Power-Control Theory of Common Delinquent Behavior," *American Journal of Sociology* 90 (1985) pp. 1151–1178; John Hagan, John Simpson, and A. R. Gillis, "The Sexual Stratification of Social Control: A Gender-Based Perspective on Crime and Delinquency," *British Journal of Sociology* 30 (1979), pp. 25–38; John Hagan, John Simpson, and A. R. Gillis, "Class in the Household: A Power-Control Theory of Gender and Delinquency," *American Journal of Sociology* 92 (January 1987), pp. 788–816; John Hagan, A. R. Gillis, and John Simpson, "Clarifying and Extending Power-Control Theory," *American Journal of Sociology* 95 (1990), pp. 1024–1037; and John Hagan, *Structural Criminology* (New Brunswick: Rutgers University Press, 1989).
73. Robert M. Regoli and John D. Hewitt, *Delinquency in Society*, 5th ed. (New York: McGraw-Hill, 2003).
74. Regoli and Hewitt, *Delinquency in Society*.
75. In *Social Sources of Delinquency*, Ruth Rosner Kornhauser includes the discussion of Sellin under cultural deviance theory.
76. Thorsten Sellin, *Culture, Conflict, and Crime* (New York: Social Science Research Council, 1938).
77. Ibid.
78. Ibid.
79. Ibid.
80. Ibid.
81. Ibid.
82. David O. Friedrichs, "Radical Criminology in the United States: An Interpretive Understanding," in James A. Inciardi, ed., *Radical Criminology: The Coming Crisis* (Beverly Hills: Sage, 1980), pp. 35-60.
83. For a review of radical humanism, see Kevin Anderson, "Humanism and Anti-Humanism in Radical Criminological Theory," in *Perspectives on Social Problems* 3 (1991), pp. 19–38; and Kevin Anderson, "Radical Criminology and the Overcoming of Alienation: Perspectives from Marxian and Gandhian Humanism," in Harold E. Pepinsky and Richard Quinney, eds., *Criminology as Peacemaking* (Bloomington: Indiana University Press, 1991), pp. 14–29.
84. Ibid.
85. Kay Pranis, "Empathy Development in Youth through Restorative Practices," *Public Service Psychology* 25 (Spring 2000), pp. 17–21.
86. Ibid.
87. Ibid.

88 S. Stuart, "Restorative Processes: Mediation, Conferencing, and Circles," http://www.restorativejustice.org.

89 Ibid. See also P. McCold, "Overview of Mediation, Conferencing and Circles," paper presented at the 10th United Nations Congress on Crime Prevention and Treatment of Offenders, International Institute for Restorative Practices, Vienna, Austria, April 10–17, 1998.

90 Nancy Rodriguez, "Restorative Justice at Work: Examining the Impact of Restorative Justice Resolutions on Juvenile Recidivism," *Crime and Delinquency* 53 (2007), pp. 355–378.

91 Kathleen J. Bergseth and Jeffrey A Bouffard, "The Long-Term Impact of Restorative Justice Programming for Juvenile Offenders," *Journal of Criminal Justice* 35 (2007), pp. 433–451.

92 Gwen Robinson and Joanna Shapland, "Reducing Recidivism: A Task for Restorative Justice," *British Journal of Criminology* 48 (2008), pp. 337–358.

93 Some groups perceive greater injustice than others. See Kevin Buckler and James D. Unnever, "Racial and Ethnic Perceptions of Injustice: Testing the Core Hypotheses of Comparative Conflict Theory," *Journal of Criminal Justice* 36 (2008), pp. 270–278.

Chapter 6, Gender and Delinquency

1 Michael Winter, "FBI: 79 Prostitutes Rescued, 104 Alleged Pimps Arrested," *USA Today*, June 25, 2012, http://content.usatoday.com/communities/ondeadline/post/2012/06/fbi-rescues-79-teen-prostitutes-arrests-104-allegedpimps/1?csp=hf#.T-nxRXB8zOU (accessed June 26, 2012).

2 Meda Chesney-Lind, "Girls, Crime and Women's Place," *Crime and Delinquency* 35 (1988), pp. 5–29. See also Kathleen Daly and Meda Chesney-Lind, "Feminism and Criminology," *Justice Quarterly* 5 (1988), pp. 497–538.

3 See Margaret A. Zahn, et al. *Girls Study Group: Understanding and Responding to Girl's Delinquency* (Washington, D.C.: OJJDP, 2010).

4 Office of Juvenile Justice and Delinquency Prevention, "Addressing Female Development in Treatment," in *Juvenile Female Offenders: A Status of the States Report* (Washington, DC: U.S. Department of Justice, 1998).

5 Ibid.

6 Karen Heimer, "Gender, Race, and the Pathways to Delinquency: An Interactionist Perspective," in J. Hagan and R. Peterson, eds., *Crime and Inequality* (Stanford: Stanford University Press, 1994), pp. 140–173.

7 Jody Miller, *One of the Guys* (New York: Oxford University Press, 2001).

8 Kathleen Daly, "Looking Back, Looking Forward: The Promise of Feminist Transformation," in *The Criminal Justice System and Women*, pp. 443–457.

9 Josephina Figueira-McDonough and Elaine Selo, "A Reformulation of the 'Equal Opportunity' Explanation of Female Delinquency," *Crime and Delinquency* 26 (1980), pp. 333–343; John Hagan, A. R. Gillis, and John Simpson, "The Class Structure of Gender and Delinquency: Toward a Power-Control Theory of Common Delinquent Behavior," *American Journal of Sociology* 90 (1985), pp. 1151–1178; and Douglas A. Smith and Raymond Paternoster, "The Gender Gap in Theories of Deviance: Issues and Evidence," *Journal of Research in Crime and Delinquency* 24 (1987), pp. 140–172.

10 Eileen Leonard, "Theoretical Criminology and Gender," in *The Criminal Justice System and Women*, pp. 55–70.

11 Chesney-Lind, "Girls, Crime and Women's Place." For an update of this article, see Meda Chesney-Lind, "Girls, Delinquency, and Juvenile Justice: Toward a Feminist Theory of Young Women's Crime," in *The Criminal Justice System and Women*, pp. 71–88.

12 Leonard, "Theoretical Criminology and Gender."

13 Elizabeth V. Spelman, *Inessential Woman: Problems of Exclusion in Feminist Thought* (Boston: Beacon Press, 1989).

14 Meda Chesney-Lind, *The Female Offender: Girls, Women, and Crime* (Thousand Oaks: Sage, 1974), p. 4.

15 Darrell Steffensmeier and Emilie Allen, "Gender and Crime: Toward a Gendered Theory of Female Delinquency," *Annual Review of Sociology* 22 (1996), pp. 459–487.

16 Kathleen Daly, "Gender, Crime, and Criminology," in Michael Tonry, ed., *The Handbook of Crime and Punishment* (New York: Oxford University Press, 1998), p. 100.

17 P. C. Giordano, J. A. Deines, and S. A. Cernkovich, "In and Out of Crime: A Life Course Perspective on Girls' Delinquency," in Karen Heimer and Candace Kruttschnitt, eds., *Gender and Crime: Patterns in Victimization and Offending* (New York: New York University Press, 2006), p. 18.

18 Ibid.

19 Ibid.

20 Daly and Chesney-Lind, "Feminism and Criminology."

21 Jody Miller and Christopher W. Mullins, "Taking Stock of the Status of Feminist Theories in Criminology," in F. Cullen, J. P. Wright, eds., with K. Blevins, F. Adler, and W. Laufer (series eds.), *The Status of Criminological Theory: Advances in Criminological Theory*, 15 (New Brunswick: Transaction, 2006), pp. 206–230.

22 D. Steffensmeier and J. Schwartz, "Trends in Female Criminality: Is Crime Still a Man's World?" in B. R. Price and N. J. Sokoloff, eds., *The Criminal Justice System and Women: Offenders, Prisoners, Victims and Workers*, 3rd ed. (New York: McGraw-Hill, 2004), pp. 95–111.

23 Miller and Mullins, "Taking Stock of the Status of Feminist Theories in Criminology."

24 Karen Heimer, Stazcy Wittrock, and Unal Haline, "The Crimes of Poverty: Economic Marginalization and the Gender Gap in Crime," in *Gender and Crime: Patterns in Victimization and Offending*, p. 115.

25 Ibid, p. 121.

26 Ibid.

27 Daly, "Gender, Crime, and Criminology."

28 Barrie Thorne, *Gender Play: Girls and Boys in School* (New Brunswick: Rutgers University Press, 1993), p. 2.

29 American Association of University Women (AAUW), *How Schools Are Shortchanging Girls* (Washington, D.C.: AAUW Educational Foundation, 1992).

30 P. Orenstein, *Schoolgirls* (New York: Doubleday, 1994).

31 Marcia Morgan and Pam Patton, *Oregon's Guidelines for Effective Gender Specific Programs for Girls*, 2012, http://www.ncjs.gov/App/publications/Abstract.aapx.id=19781

32 Barrie Thorne, *Gender Play: Girls and Boys in School* (New Brunswick: Rutgers University Press, 1994).

33 Marty Beyer, "Delinquent Girls: A Developmental Perspective," *Kentucky Children's Rights Journal* 9 (Spring 2001), p. 17.

34 Ibid.

35 C. S. Lederman, G. A. Dakof, M. A. Larreal, and L. Hua, "Characteristics of Adolescent Females in Juvenile Detention," *International Journal of Law and Psychiatry* 27 (2004), pp. 321–327; and M. Zahn, "The Causes of Girls' Delinquency and Their Program Implications," *Family Court Review* 45 (2007), pp. 456–465.

36 Lederman et al., "Characteristics of Adolescent Females in Juvenile Detention."

37 B. Bloom and S. Covington, "Effective Gender-Responsive Interventions in Juvenile Justice: Addressing the Lives of Delinquent Girls," paper presented at the Annual Meeting of the American Society of Criminology, Atlanta, Georgia, 2001.

38 Joanne Belknap and Karen Holsinger, "An Overview of Delinquent Girls: How Theory and Practice Failed and the Need for Innovative Changes," in R. T. Zaplin, ed., *Female Offenders: Critical Perspectives and Effective Interventions* (Gaithersburg: Aspen Publishers, 1998), p. 1.

39 Ibid.

40 Leslie Acoca, "Investing in Girls: A 21st Century Strategy," *Juvenile Justice* (October 1999), pp. 3–13.

41 Ibid.

42 W. R. Downs, T. Capshew, and B. Rindels, "Relationships Between Adult Men's Alcohol Problems and Their Childhood Experiences of Parental Violence and Psychological Aggression," *Journal of Studies on Alcohol* (2004), pp. 336–345; National Center on Addiction and Substance Abuse at Columbia University (CASA), "Reducing Teen Smoking Can Cut Marijuana Use Significantly," http://www.casacolumbia.org/newsletter1457 (accessed November 2011).

43 Paul Mazerolle, "Gender, General Strain, and Delinquency: An Empirical Examination," pp. 65–91.

44 Ibid.

45 Ibid.

46 These key factors from Konopka's *The Adolescent Girl in Conflict* are listed in Peter C. Kratcoski and John E. Kratcoski, "Changing Patterns in the Delinquent Activities of Boys and Girls: A Self-Reported Delinquency Analysis," *Adolescence* 18 (Spring 1975), pp. 83–91.

47 Gisela Konopka, *The Adolescent Girl in Conflict* (Englewood Cliffs: Prentice-Hall, 1966).

48 These key factors from Konopka's *The Adolescent Girl in Conflict* are listed in Peter C. Kratcoski and John E. Kratcoski, "Changing Patterns in the Delinquent Activities of Boys and Girls: A Self-Reported Delinquency Analysis," *Adolescence* 18 (Spring 1975), pp. 83–91.

49 O. Miazad, *Human Rights Brief 10*, Washington College of Law, http://www.wel.american.edu/hrbrief/10-gender.cfm (accessed October 2011).

50 Ibid.

51 Talcott Parsons, "Age and Sex in the Social Structure of the United States," *American Sociological Review* 7 (October 1942), pp. 614–616; James S. Coleman, *The Adolescent Society* (New York: Free Press, 1961); and Ruth Rittenhouse, "A Theory and Comparison of Male and Female Delinquency," Ph.D. dissertation, University of Michigan, Ann Arbor, 1963.

52 Susan K. Datesman, Frank R. Scarpitti, and Richard M. Stephenson, "Female Delinquency: An Application of Self and Opportunity Theories," *Journal of Research in Crime and Delinquency* 12 (1975), pp. 107–123; Jeffery O. Segrave and Douglas N. Hastad, "Evaluating Three Models of Delinquency Causation for Males and Females: Strain Theory, Subculture Theory, and Control Theory," *Sociological Focus* 18 (January 1985), pp. 1–17; and Stephen A. Cernkovich and Peggy C. Giordano, "Delinquency, Opportunity, and Gender," *Journal of Criminal Law and Criminology* 70 (1979), pp. 145–151.

53 Agnew, "The Contribution of 'Mainstream' Theories to the Explanation of Female Delinquency."

54 Travis Hirschi, *Causes of Delinquency* (Berkeley: University of California Press, 1969).

55 Agnew, "The Contribution of 'Mainstream' Theories to the Explanation of Female Delinquency," in Margaret A. Zahn, *The Delinquent Girl* (Philadelphia: Temple University Press, 2009).

56 Karen Heimer and Stacy De Coster, "The Gendering of Violent Behavior," *Criminology* 37 (1999), pp. 277–318.

57 Freda Adler, *Sisters in Crime* (New York: McGraw-Hill, 1975).

58 F. T. Cullen, K. M. Golden, and J. B. Cullen, "Sex and Delinquency: A Partial Test of the Masculinity Hypothesis," *Criminology* 15 (1977), pp. 87–104.

59 William E. Thornton and Jennifer James, "Masculinity and Delinquency Revisited," *British Journal of Criminology* 19 (July 1979), pp. 225–241.

60 John Hagan, John Simpson, and A. R. Gillis, "Class in the Household: A Power-Control Theory of Gender and Delinquency," *American Journal of Sociology* 92 (January 1987), pp. 788–816; and Hagan, Gillis, and Simpson, "The Class Structure of Gender and Delinquency."

61 Hagan, Simpson and Gillis, "Class in the Household."

62 Ibid, p. 793.

63 Ibid.

64 Agnew, "The Contribution of 'Mainstream' Theories to the Explanation of Female Delinquency."

65. Karen Heimer, "Gender, Interaction, and Delinquency: Testing a Theory of Differential Social Control," *Social Psychology Quarterly* 59 (1996), p. 57.
66. Agnew, "The Contribution of 'Mainstream' Theories to the Explanation of Female Delinquency"; and J. Hagan and B. McCarthy, *Mean Streets and Homelessness* (Cambridge: Cambridge University Press, 1997).
67. Ibid.
68. P. Giordano and S. Cernkovich, "Changing Patterns of Female Delinquency," unpublished paper presented at the annual meeting of the Society for the Study of Social Problems (New York, August 30, 1976).
69. Meda Chesney-Lind, "Girl's Crime and Woman's Place: Toward a Feminist Model of Female Delinquency," *Crime and Delinquency*, Vol. 35, No. 1 (January 1989), pp. 5-29.
70. Ibid.
71. Mimi Silbert and Ayala M. Pines, "Entrance into Prostitution," *Youth and Society* 13 (1982), pp. 471–500.
72. Cited in Chesney-Lind, "Girl's Crime and Woman's Place."
73. Spelman, *Inessential Woman*.
74. Ibid.
75. Etta A. Anderson, "The 'Chivalrous' Treatment of the Female Offender in the Arms of the Criminal Justice System: A Review of the Literature," *Social Problems* 23 (1976), pp. 350–357. See also Meda Chesney-Lind, "Judicial Enforcement of the Female Sex Role: The Family Court and Female Delinquency," *Issues in Criminology* 8 (1973), pp. 57–59; Kristine Olson Rogers, "For Her Own Protection: Conditions of Incarceration for Female Juvenile Offenders in the State of Connecticut," *Law and Society Review* 7 (1973), pp. 223–246; and John M. MacDonald and Meda Chesney-Lind, "Gender Bias and the Juvenile Justice Revisited: a Multiyear Analysis," *Crime and Delinquency* 47 (2001), pp. 173–198.
76. Marvin D. Krohn, James P. Curry, and Shirley Nelson-Kilger, "Is Chivalry Dead?" *Criminology* 21 (1983), pp. 417–439.
77. Christy A. Visher, "Gender, Police Arrest Decisions, and Notions of Chivalry," *Criminology* 21 (1983), pp. 5–28; and Chesney-Lind, "Judicial Enforcement of the Female Sex Role."
78. Jean Strauss, "To Be Minor and Female: The Legal Rights of Women Under Twenty-One," *Ms.* 1 (1972), pp. 70–75; Yona Cohn, "Criteria for Probation Officers' Recommendations to Juvenile Court," *Crime and Delinquency* 1 (1963), pp. 272–275; Rogers, "For Her Own Protection"; Chesney-Lind, "Judicial Enforcement of the Female Sex Role"; and Laurie Schaffner, "Female Juvenile Delinquency: Sexual Solutions and Gender Bias in Juvenile Justice," paper presented at the Annual Meeting of the American Society of Criminology in Washington, D.C., November 1998.
79. Rosemary C. Sarri, "Juvenile Law: How It Penalizes Females," in Laura Crites, ed., *The Female Offender* (Lexington: D. C. Heath and Co., 1977), pp. 67–85.
80. Ibid, p. 76.
81. Randall G. Shelden and John Horvath, "Processing Offenders in a Juvenile Court: A Comparison of Males and Females," paper presented at the Annual Meeting of the Western Society of Criminology, Newport Beach, California, February–March, 1986, cited in Coramae Richey Mann, *Female Crime and Delinquency* (Tuscaloosa: University of Alabama Press, 1984); Meda Chesney-Lind, "Girls and Status Offenses: Is Juvenile Justice Still Sexist?" *Criminal Justice Abstracts* 20 (March 1988), pp. 144–165.; Randall R. Beger and Harry Hoffman, "The Role of Gender in Detention Dispositioning of Juvenile Probation Violaters," *Journal of Crime and Justice* 21 (1998), pp. 173–186; Robert Terry, "Discrimination in the Police Handling of Juvenile Offenders by Social Control Agencies," *Journal of Research in Crime and Delinquency* 14 (1967), pp. 218–230; Rogers, "For Her Own Protection"; and Clemens Bartollas and Christopher M. Sieverdes, "Games Juveniles Play: How They Get Their Way," unpublished report, 1985.
82. Anne Rankin Mahoney and Carol Fenster, "Family Delinquents in a Suburban Court," in Nicole Hahn and Elizabeth Anne Stanko, eds., *Judge, Lawyer, Victim, Thief: Woman, Gender Roles and Criminal Justice* (Boston: Northeastern University Press, 1982), pp. 22–54.
83. Donna M. Bishop and Charles E. Frazier, "Gender Bias in Juvenile Justice Processing: Implications of the JJDP Act," *Journal of Criminal Law and Criminology* 82 (1992), pp. 1132–1152; and Carla P. Davis, "At Risk Girls and Delinquency Career Pathway," *Crime and Delinquency* 53 (July 2007), pp. 408–435.
84. Ibid.
85. Liz Watson and Peter Edelman, *Improving the Juvenile Justice System* (Washington, D.C.: Georgetown Center on Poverty, 2013), p. 11.
86. Media Chesney-Lind and Nikki Jones, *Fighting for Girls* (Albany: SUNY Press, 2010).
87. Ibid.
88. Chesney-Lind, *The Female Offender*.
89. Ibid.
90. Lee Bowker and Malcolm Klein, "The Etiology of Female Juvenile Delinquency and Gang Membership: A Test of Psychological and Social Structural Explanations," *Adolescence* 13 (1983), pp. 750–751.
91. For many of these findings, see Joy G. Dryfoos, *Adolescents at Risk: Prevalence and Prevention* (New York: Oxford University Press, 1990).
92. Michele R. Decker, Anita Raj, and Jay G. Silverman, "Sexual Violence against Girls: Influences of Immigration and Acculturation," *Violence Against Women* (May 2007), pp. 498–513.
93. Lori D. Moore and Irene Padavic, "Racial and Ethnic Dispositions in Girls' Sentencing to the Juvenile Justice System," *Feminist Criminology* 5 (2010), pp. 263-85.
94. Chesney-Lind, *The Female Offender*.

95. Finn-Aage Esbensen and L. Thomas Winfree, "Race and Gender Differences between Gang and Nongang Youths: Results from a Multisite Survey," *Justice Quarterly* 15 (September 1998), pp. 505–526.
96. H. C. Covey, Scott Menard, and R. Franzese, *Juvenile Gangs*, 2nd ed. (Springfield, Ill.: Charles C. Thomas, 1997), p. 240.
97. Chesney-Lind, *The Female Offender*, p. 23.
98. Spelman, *Inessential Woman*.
99. Diane K. Lewis, "A Response to Inequality: Black Women, Racism, and Sexism," *Signs: Journal of Women in Culture and Society* 3 (1977), p. 339. For this discussion on African-American women, I am indebted to Kathleen Daly, "Class–Race–Gender: Sloganeering in Search of Meaning," *Social Justice* 20 (1993), p. 58.
100. Lewis, "A Response to Inequality," p. 339.
101. Daly, "Class–Race–Gender," p. 58.
102. Spelman, *Inessential Woman*, p. 123.
103. Ibid.
104. Girls, Inc., https://www.girlsinc-online.org (accessed May 16, 2014).
105. Jean Bottcher, "Social Practices of Gender: How Gender Relates to Delinquency in the Everyday Lives of High-Risk Youths," *Criminology* 39 (2001), pp. 905–925.
106. Ibid.
107. Amy V. D'Unger, Kenneth C. Land, and Patricia L. McCall, "Sex Differences in Age Patterns of Delinquent/Criminal Careers: Results from Poisson Latent Class Analyses of the Philadelphia Cohort Study," *Journal of Quantitative Criminology* 18 (December 2002), pp. 349–375.
108. Rebecca S. Katz, "Explaining Girls' and Women's Crime and Desistance in the Context of Their Victimization Experiences," *Violence Against Women* 6 (June 2000), pp. 633–660.
109. Alex R. Piquero, Robert Brame, and Terrie E. Moffitt, "Extending the Study of Continuity and Change: Gender Differences in the Linkage Between Adolescent and Adult Offending," *Journal of Quantitative Criminology* 21 (June 2005), pp. 219–243.
110. I. Sommers, D. R. Baskin, and J. Fagan, "Getting Out of the Life: Crime Desistance by Female Street Offenders," *Deviant Behavior* 15 (1994), pp. 125–149.
111. I. Sommers and D. R. Baskin, "Situational or Generalized Violence in Drug Dealing Networks," *Journal of Drug Issues* 27 (1997), pp. 833–849.
112. Peggy C. Giordano, Stephen A. Cernkovich, and Jennifer L. Rudolph, "Gender, Crime, and Desistance: Toward a Theory of Cognitive Transformation," *American Journal of Sociology* 107 (January 2002), p. 1038.
113. B. Bloom, B. Owen, and S. Covington, "Women Offenders and the Gendered Effects of Public Policy," *Review of Policy Research* 21 (2004), pp. 31–48.
114. Ibid.
115. Ibid.

Chapter 7, Families and Delinquency

1. YouTube, "Smoking Baby Two Year Old Smoker and Drinker Too Latest Unseen Visuals with Alcohol," http://www.youtube.com/watch?v=duwS2sIG9lE (accessed April 8, 2011).
2. YouTube, "3 Year Old Chinese Toddler Drinks Liquer & Smokes Cigarettes," http://www.youtube.com/watch?v=CMxdFamwWVU&feature=related (accessed April 7, 2011).
3. Marvin D. Krohn, Susan B. Stern, Terence P. Thornberry, and Sung Joon Jang, "The Measurement of Family Process Variables: The Effect of Adolescent and Parent Perceptions of Family Life on Delinquent Behavior," *Journal of Quantitative Criminology* 8 (1992), p. 287. For these theories of delinquency, see Travis Hirschi, *Causes of Delinquency* (Berkeley: University of California Press, 1969); Marvin Krohn, "The Web of Conformity: A Network Approach to the Explanation of Delinquent Behavior," *Social Problems* 33 (1986), pp. 81–93; Gerald Patterson, *Coercive Family Process* (Eugene: Castilia Press, 1982); and Terence Thornberry, "Toward an Interactional Theory of Delinquency," *Criminology* 25 (1987), pp. 863–892.
4. Kristin Y. Mack, Michael J. Lieber, Richard A. Featherstone, and Maria A. Monserud, "Reassessing the Family-Delinquency Association: Do Family Types, Family Processes, and Economic Factors Make a Difference?" *Journal of Criminal Justice* 35 (2007), pp. 51–67.
5. Krohn et al., "The Measurement of Family Process Variables." For studies supporting the proposition that family relationships and parenting skills are related to delinquency, see D. Elliott, D. Huizinga, and S. Ageton, *Explaining Delinquency and Drug Use* (Beverly Hills: Sage, 1985); Walter R. Gove and R. Crutchfield, "The Family and Juvenile Delinquency," *Sociological Quarterly* 23 (1982), pp. 301–319; M. Krohn and J. Massey, "Social Control and Delinquent Behavior: An Examination of the Elements of the Social Bond," *Sociological Quarterly* 21 (1980), pp. 337–349; J. Laub and R. Sampson, "Unraveling Families and Delinquency: A Reanalysis of the Gluecks' Data," *Criminology* 26 (1988), pp. 355–380; R. Loeber and M. Stouthamer-Loeber, "Family Factors as Correlates and Predictors of Juvenile Conduct Problems and Delinquency," in M. Tonry and N. Morris, eds., *Crime and Justice: An Annual Review of Research* (Chicago: University of Chicago Press, 1986), pp. 29–149; W. J. McCord, J. McCord, and Irving Zola, *The Origins of Crime* (New York: Columbia University Press, 1959); F. I. Nye, *Family Relationships and Delinquency Behavior* (New York: John Wiley, 1958); G. R. Patterson and T. J. Dishion, "Contributions of Families and Peers to Delinquency," *Criminology* 23 (1985), pp. 63–79; and M. D. Wiatrowski, D. B. Griswold, and M. K. Roberts, "Social Control and Delinquency," *American Sociological Review* 46 (1981), pp. 524–541.
6. Lawrence Rosen, "Family and Delinquency: Structure or Function," *Criminology* 23 (1985), pp. 553–573.
7. Judith R. Harris, "Where Is the Child's Environment? A Group Socialization Theory of Development,"

Psychological Review 102 (1995), pp. 458–489; Judith R. Harris, *The Nurture Assumption: Why Children Turn Out the Way They Do* (New York: Free Press, 1998); and Judith R. Harris, *No Two Alike: Human Nature and Human Individuality* (New York: Norton, 2006).

8. Kevin M. Beaver and John Paul Wright, "A Child Effects Explanation for the Association between Family Risk and Involvement in an Antisocial Lifestyle," *Journal of Adolescent Research* 22 (2007), pp. 640–664.

9. Ibid.

10. W. D. Morrison, *Juvenile Offenders* (London: T. Fisher Unwin, 1896); Sophonisba P. Breckenridge and Edith Abbott, *The Delinquent Child and the Home* (New York: Russell Sage Foundation, 1912); William Healy, *The Individual Delinquent* (Boston: Little, Brown, 1915); William Healy and Augusta Bronner, *Delinquents and Criminals: Their Making and Unmaking* (New York: Macmillan, 1926); and Ernest H. Shideler, "Family Disintegration and the Delinquent Boy in the United States," *Journal of Criminal Law and Criminology* 8 (January 1918), pp. 709–732.

11. F. I. Nye, *Family Relationships and Delinquent Behavior* (New York: John Wiley, 1958); and R. A. Dentler and L. J. Monroe, "Social Correlates of Early Adolescent Theft," *American Sociological Review* 28 (1961), pp. 733–743.

12. Richard S. Sterne, *Delinquent Conduct and Broken Homes* (New Haven: College and University Press, 1964); J. Toby, "The Differential Impact of Family Disorganization," *American Sociological Review* 22 (1957), pp. 505–512; T. P. Monahan, "Family Status and the Delinquent Child: A Reappraisal and Some New Findings," *Social Forces* 35 (1957), pp. 250–258; and T. P. Monahan, "Broken Homes by Age of Delinquent Children," *Journal of Social Psychology* 51 (1960), pp. 387–397.

13. Ross L. Matsueda and Karen Heimer, "Race, Family Structure, and Delinquency: A Test of Differential Association and Social Control Theories," *American Sociological Review* 52 (1987), pp. 826–840.

14. Marvin D. Free, Jr., "Clarifying the Relationship between the Broken Home and Juvenile Delinquency: A Critique of the Current Literature," *Deviant Behavior* 12 (1991), pp. 109–167.

15. Sheldon Glueck and Eleanor Glueck, *Unraveling Juvenile Delinquency* (Cambridge: Harvard University Press for the Commonwealth Fund, 1950); Nye, *Family Relationships and Delinquent Behavior*; and W. J. McCord, J. McCord, and Irving Zola, *The Origins of Crime* (New York: Columbia University Press, 1959).

16. R. Loeber and M. Stouthamer-Loeber, "Family Factors as Correlates and Predictors of Juvenile Conduct Problems and Delinquency," in M. Tonry and N. Morris, eds., *Crime and Justice: An Annual Review of Research* (Chicago: University of Chicago Press, 1986), pp. 29–149.

17. Joan McCord, "Crime in Moral and Social Contexts," American Society of Criminology 1989 Presidential Address, *Criminology* 28 (1990), pp. 1–26; David P. Farrington and Barry J. Knight, "Stealing from a 'Lost' Letter: Effects of Victim Characteristics," *Criminal Justice and Behavior* 7 (1980), pp. 423–436; and Jenet L. Lauritsen, "Sibling Resemblance in Juvenile Delinquency: Findings from the National Youth Survey," *Criminology* 31 (August 1993), pp. 387–410.

18. Nye, *Family Relationships and Delinquent Behavior*; Glueck and Glueck, *Unraveling Juvenile Delinquency*; McCord, McCord, and Zola, *The Origins of Crime*; R. C. Audry, *Delinquency and Parental Pathology* (London: Methuen, 1960); Randy L. Lagrange and Helen R. White, "Age Differences in Delinquency: A Test of Theory," *Criminology* 23 (1985), pp. 19–45; Paul Howes and Howard J. Markman, "Marital Quality and Child Functioning: A Longitudinal Investigation," *Child Development* 60 (1989), pp. 1044–1051; and Joan McCord, "Family Relationships, Juvenile Delinquency, and Adult Criminality," *Criminology* 29 (August 1991), pp. 11–23.

19. Loeber and Stouthamer-Loeber, "Family Factors as Correlates and Predictors of Juvenile Conduct Problems and Delinquency."

20. John Paul Wright and Francis T. Cullen, "Parental Efficacy and Delinquent Behavior: Do Control and Support Matter?" *Criminology* 39 (2001), pp. 677–705.

21. Ronald L. Simons, Leslie Gordon Simons, Callie Harbin Burt, Gene H. Brody, and Carolyn Cutrona, "Collective Efficacy, Authoritative Parenting and Delinquency: A Longitudinal Test of a Model Integrating Community- and Family-Level Processes," *Criminology* (November 2005), pp. 989–1029. See also, Ronald L. Simons, Leslie Gordon Simons, Callie Harbin Burt, Gene H. Brody, and Carolyn Cutrona, "Collective Efficacy, Authoritative Parenting and Delinquency: A Longitudinal Test of a Model Integrating Community- and Family-Level Processes," *Criminology* (November 2005), pp. 989–1029.

22. Glueck and Glueck, *Unraveling Juvenile Delinquency*. See also, David Farrington's "Families and Crime," in J. Wilson and J. Petersilia, eds., *Crime: Public Policy for Crime Control*, 3rd ed. (New York: Oxford University Press, in press). This study *identified six family factors that predicted delinquent behavior*. See also J. Laub and R. Sampson, "Unraveling Families and Delinquency: A Reanalysis of the Gluecks' Data," *Criminology* 26 (1988), pp. 355–380; Robert J. Sampson and John H. Laub, *Crime in the Making: Pathways and Turning Points through Life* (Cambridge: Harvard University Press, 1993); and Loeber and Stouthamer-Loeber, "Family Factors as Correlates and Predictors of Juvenile Conduct Problems and Delinquency."

23. See Glueck and Glueck, *Unraveling Juvenile Delinquency*, pp. 91–92.

24. *America's Children: Key National Indicators of Well-Being, 2013* (Washington, D.C.: Federal Intragency Forum on Child and Family Statistics, 2014).

25. Terence P. Thornberry, Carolyn A. Smith, Craig Rivera, David Huizinga, and Magda Stouthamer-Loeber, "Family Disruption and Delinquency," *Juvenile Justice Bulletin* (September 1999).

26 *American's Children in Brief: National Indicators of Well-Being, 2010* (Washington, D.C.: Federal Interagency Forum on Child and Family Statistics, 2010), p. 3.

27 Ibid.

28 Ibid.

29 National Coalition for the Homeless, *Homeless Youth: NCH Fact Sheet #13* (Washington, DC: National Coalition for the Homeless, 2006).

30 Labor Force Statistics from the Current Population Survey, http://www.bls.gov/web/empsit/cpseea36.htm.

31 Ibid.

32 Federal Bureau of Investigation, *Crime in the United States 2007* (Washington, D.C.: U.S. Department of Justice, 2008).

33 Michael Hershorn and Alan Rosenbaum, "Children of Marital Violence: A Closer Look at the Unintended Victims," *American Journal of Orthopsychiatry* 55 (April 1985), pp. 169–184. See also R. L. McNeely and Gloria Robinson-Simpson, "The Truth About Domestic Violence: A Falsely Framed Issue," *Social Work* 32 (November-December 1997), pp. 485–490.

34 Karen Heimer, "Socioeconomic Status: Subcultural Definitions and Violent Delinquency," *Social Forces* 75 (1997), pp. 799–833.

35 Child Welfare Information Gateway, *Foster Care Statistics 2010* (Washington, D.C.: Children Bureau, May 2012,) p. 3.

36 Ibid.

37 Joseph Drake, "Child Protection and Child Outcomes: Measuring the Effects of Foster Care," *American Economy Review*, 2008, http://www.mit.edu/-jjdoyle/doyle_fosterIt_march07_aer.pdf (accessed June 18, 2012).

38 American Academy of Child & Adolescent Psychiatry, *Facts for Families*, March 2011, http://ascap.org/page.ww?name=The+Adopted+Child&section+Facts+for+families (accessed June 18, 2012).

39 Ibid.

40 Ibid.

41 American Academy of Child & Adolescent Psychiatry, *Fact for Families: Children with Lesbian, Gay, Bisexual and Transgender Parents*, August 2011, http://www.aacap.org/cs/root/facts_for_families_withlesbian_gay_bisexual_and_transgender_parents (accessed June 18, 2012).

42 Ibid.

43 Ibid.

44 Jennifer Ludden, *Study: Are Cohabiting Parents Bad for Kids?*, August 16, 2011, http://www.npr.org/2011/08/16/139651977study-are-cohabiting-parents-bad-far-kids (accessed June 18, 2012).

45 John Gottman has spent over 35 years investigating this subject. See http://www.gottman.com/49853/Research-FAQs.html.

46 Ibid.

47 Rlyan D. Schroeder, Aurea K. Osgood, and Michael J. Oghia,, "Family Transitions and Juvenile Delinquency" *Sociological Inquiry* 80 (November 2010), pp. 579–604.

48 For recommendations on reducing violence in those children exposed to violence, see Report of the Attorney's General National Task Force, *Children Exposed to Violence* (Washington, D.C.: U.S. Department of Justice; Office of Juvenile Justice and Delinquency Prevention, 2010).

49 Comments made by Mike Carlie in the *Into the Abyss: A Personal Journey into the World of Street Gangs*, Chapter 12. See http://www.faculty.missouristate.edu/M/MichaelCarlie/what_I_learned_about/media.htm.

50 This is the general consensus of the vast amount of research done on this topic.

51 See Walter B. Miller, *The Growth of Youth Gang Problems in the United States: 1970–98* (Washington, D.C.: U.S. Department of Justice, Office of Juvenile Justice and Delinquency Prevention, 2001).

52 Gregory Zimmerman and Greg Pogarsky, "The Consequences of Parents' Underestimation and Overestimation of Youth Exposure to Violence," *Journal of Marriage and Family* 73 (2011), pp. 194–208.

53 "Experts Debate Effects of Violent Video Games," September 26, 2005, http://homepage.mac.com/iajukes/blogwavestudio/LH20050626175144/LHA2005092622.

54 Ibid.

55 Ibid.

56 Ibid.

57 C. L. Olson and D. W. Warner, "The Role of Violent Video Game Content in Adolescent Development: Boys' Perspectives," *Journal of Adolescent Research* 23 (2008), pp. 55–75.

58 CATTA, *Protecting Our Children Against Internet Perpetrators* (Sonoma: Sonoma State University, California Institute of Human Services, 2006).

59 Becky Blanchard, "The Social Significance of Rap and Hip-Hop Culture," *Edge: Ethics of Development in a Global Environment*, http://www.stanford.edu/class/e29c/poverty_prejudice/mediarace/socialsignificance.htm (accessed January 8, 2013).

60 Ibid.

61 Ibid.

62 Tricia Rose, *Hip-Hop Wars: What We Talk About When We Talk About Hip-Hop and Why It Matters* (Jackson, Tenn.: Basic Civitas Books, 2008).

63 Matthew T. Zingraff and Michael J. Belyea, "Child Abuse and Violent Crime," in Kenneth C. Haas and Geoffrey P. Alpert, eds., *The Dilemmas of Punishment* (Prospect Heights: Waveland Press, 1986), pp. 49–53.

64 See a new report on child abuse and neglect: Committee on Child Maltreatment, Research, Policy, and Practice for the New Decade; Phase II; Board on Children, Youth, and Families, Institute of Medicine, National Research Council, *New Directions in Child Abuse and Neglect Research* (Washington, D.C.: The National Academy of Sciences, 2013).

65 Cathy Spatz Widom, "Child Abuse, Neglect, and Violent Criminal Behavior," *Criminology* 27 (1989), pp. 251–271. See also Cathy Spatz Widom, *The Cycle of Violence* (Washington, D.C.: National Institute of Justice, 1992), p. 3.

66. Cathy S. Widom and Michael G. Maxfield, "An Update on the 'Cycle of Violence,'" *Research in Brief* (Washington, D.C.: National Institute of Justice, 2001).
67. Ibid. For other support for the relationship between abuse and neglect and later violent behavior, see Carlos E. Climent and Frank R. Erwin, "Historical Data on the Evaluation of Violent Subjects: A Hypothesis-Generating Study," *American Journal of Psychiatry* 27 (1972), pp. 621–624; Dorothy O. Lewis, Shelly S. Shanok, Jonathan H. Pincus, and Gilbert H. Glaser, "Violent Juvenile Delinquents: Psychiatric, Neurological, Psychological and Abuse Factors," *Journal of the American Academy of Child Psychiatry* 18 (1979), pp. 307–319; and Mark Monane, "Physical Abuse in Psychiatrically Hospitalized Children and Adolescents," *Journal of the American Academy of Child Psychiatry* 23 (1984), pp. 653–658.
68. Children's Bureau, *Child Maltreatment 2012* (Washington, D.C.: U.S. Department of Health and Human Services, 2013), p. 40.
69. Ibid.
70. Ibid.
71. Ibid.
72. Ibid.
73. *In the Interest of Children: A Century of Progress* (Denver: American Humane Association, Children's Division, 1966).
74. Murray A. Straus, "Discipline and Deviance: Physical Punishment of Children and Violence and Other Crime in Adulthood," *Social Problems* 38 (May 1991), pp. 103–123.
75. James Garbarino and Gwen Gilliam, *Understanding Abusive Families* (Lexington, Mass.: D.C. Heath, 1980).
76. Interviewed in May 1981.
77. Stephanie Amedeo and John Gartrell, "An Empirical Examination of Five Theories of Physical Child Abuse," paper presented at the Annual Meeting of the American Society of Criminology, Reno, Nevada, November 1989.
78. The National Incidence Study, *Third National Study of Child Abuse and Neglect* (Washington, D.C.: Child Welfare Information Gateway, 1996), pp. 1–10.
79. David G. Gil, *Violence Against Children: Physical Abuse in the United States* (Cambridge: Harvard University Press, 1970).
80. Leontine Young, *Wednesday's Children: A Study of Child Neglect and Abuse* (New York: McGraw-Hill, 1964).
81. Blair Justice and Rita Justice, *The Broken Taboo: Sex in the Family* (New York: Human Sciences Press, 1979).
82. Ibid., p. 27.
83. For a more extensive discussion of the four types of incest possible within a family unit, see C. Corsson-Tower, *Understanding Child Abuse and Neglect*, 6th ed. (Boston: Allyn & Bacon, 2005), pp. 155-162.
84. Angela Browne and David Finkelhor, "Impact of Child Abuse: A Review of the Research," *Psychological Bulletin* 99 (1986), pp. 66–77.
85. K. C. Meiselman, *Incest: A Psychological Study of Causes and Effects with Treatment Recommendations* (San Francisco: Jossey-Bass, 1978); and Christine A. Curtois, *Adult Survivors of Child Sexual Abuse* (Milwaukee: Families International, 1993).
86. Interviewed as part of a court case with which one of the authors was involved.
87. Justice and Justice, *The Broken Taboo*.
88. A. Nicholas Groth, "Patterns of Sexual Assault against Children and Adolescents," in Ann Wolbert Burgess, A. Nicholas Groth, Lynda Lytle Holmstrom, and Suzanne M. Sgroi, eds., *Sexual Assault of Children and Adolescents* (Lexington: D.C. Heath, 1978).
89. Justice and Justice, *The Broken Taboo*.
90. Ibid.
91. The National Center for Victims of Crime, *Child Abuse Statistics* (Washington, D.C.: U.S. Government Printing Office, 2014).
92. Timothy O. Ireland, Carolyn A. Smith, and Terence P. Thornberry, "Developmental Issues in the Impact of Child Maltreatment on Later Delinquency and Drug Use," *Criminology* 40 (May 2002), pp. 359–401.
93. Peggy C. Giordano, Stephen A. Cernkovich, and Jennifer L. Rudolph, "Gender, Crime, and Delinquency: Toward a Theory of Cognitive Transformation," *American Journal of Sociology* 107 (January 2002), pp. 1000–1003.
94. The first part of the following section is modified from Howard N. Snyder and Melissa Sickmund, *Juvenile Offenders and Victims: 1999 National Report* (Washington, D.C.: Office of Juvenile Justice and Delinquency Prevention, 1999), pp. 43–44. See also David Finkelhor, Theodore P. Cross, and Elise N. Cantor, "How the Justice System Responds to Juvenile Victims: A Comprehensive Model, *Juvenile Justice Bulletin* (December 2005).
95. Finkelhor, Cross, and Cantor, "How the Justice System Responds to Juvenile Victims."
96. Timothy O. Ireland, Carolyn A. Smith, and Terence P. Thornberry, "Developmental Issues in the Impact of Child Maltreatment on Later Delinquency and Drug Use," *Criminology* 40 (May 2002), pp. 360–363. See also Robert J. Sampson and John H. Laub, "Crime and Deviance in the Life Course," in Alex Piquero and Paul Mazerolle, eds., *Life-Course Criminology* (Belmont: Wadsworth/Thompson Learning, 2001), pp. 21–42.
97. Cathy Spatz Widom, "Child Victims: Searching for Opportunities to Break the Cycle of Violence," *Applied & Preventive Psychology* 7, no. 4 (Winter 1998), pp. 225–234.
98. Brandon C. Welch and Alex Piquero, "Investing Where It Counts: Preventing Delinquency and Crime with Early Family-Based Programs," in *Contemporary Issues in Criminological Theory and Research*, eds., Richard Rosenfeld, Kenea Quniet, and Crystal Garcia (Australia: Griffith University, 2012), p. 14.
99. Cited in Ibid., p. 18. A. Piquero, D. Farrington, B. Welch, R. Tremblay, and W. Jennings, "Effects of Early Family/Parent Training Programs on Antisocial Behavior and Delinquency," *Journal of Experimental Criminology* 5 (2009), pp. 83–120.

Chapter 8, Schools and Delinquency

1. Gary D. Gottfredson, Denise C. Gottfredson, and Ellen R. Czeh, *National Study of Delinquency Prevention in Schools* (Ellicott City: Gottfredson Associates, Inc., 2000).
2. John F. Feldhusen, John R. Thurston, and James J. Benning, "A Longitudinal Study of Delinquency and Other Aspects of Children's Behavior," *International Journal of Criminology and Penology* 1 (1973), pp. 341–351.
3. Delbert S. Elliott and Harwin Voss, *Delinquency and Dropout* (Lexington: Lexington Books, 1974).
4. Arthur L. Stinchcombe, *Rebellion in a High School* (Chicago: Quadrangle Press, 1964).
5. Eugene Maguin and Rolf Loeber, "Academic Performance and Delinquency," in Michael Tonry, ed., *Crime and Justice: A Review of Research* (Chicago and London: University of Chicago Press, 1996), p. 145.
6. Joel H. Spring, *Education and the Rise of the Corporate State* (Boston: Beacon Press, 1972), p. 62.
7. Joan Newman and Graeme Newman, "Crime and Punishment in the Schooling Process: A Historical Analysis," in Keith Baker and Robert J. Rubel, eds., *Violence and Crime in the Schools* (Lexington: Lexington Books, 1980), pp. 729–768.
8. Horace Mann and the Reverend M. H. Smith, *Sequel to the So-Called Correspondence Between the Rev. M. H. Smith and Horace Mann* (Boston: W. B. Fowle, 1847).
9. John Dewey, "My Pedagogic Creed" (1897), reprinted in K. Gezi and J. Meyers, eds., *Teaching in American Culture* (New York: Holt, Rinehart, and Winston, 1968), pp. 408–411.
10. *Brown v. Board of Education of Topeka, Kansas* (1954), 347 U.S. 483.
11. John Goodlad, *A Place Called School* (New York: McGraw-Hill, 1984), p. 1.
12. Kathryn A. Buckner, "School Drug Tests: A Fourth Amendment Perspective," *University of Illinois Law Review* 5 (1987), pp. 275–310.
13. Ron Banks, "Bullying in Schools," ERIC Digest, http://www.ericddigests.org/1997-4bullying/bullying.htm.
14. "Bullying Statistics 2010," http//www.bullyingstatistics-2010.htm (accessed April 15, 2014).
15. Ibid.
16. Norman A. White and Rolf Loeber, "Bullying and Special Education as Predictors of Serious Delinquency," *Journal of Research in Crime and Delinquency* 45 (2008), pp. 380–397.
17. Gianluca Gini and Tiziana Pozzoli, "Association Between Bullying and Psychosomatic Problems: A Meta-Analysis," *Pediatrics* 123 (2009), pp. 1059–1065.
18. David B. Estell, Thomas W. Farmjer, Matthew J. Irvin, Amity Crowther, Patrick Akos, and Daniel Boudah, "Students with Exceptionalities and the Peer Group Context of Bullying and Victimization in Late Elementary School," *Journal of Child Family Studies* 18 (2009), pp. 136–150.
19. Anne L. Sawyer, Catherine P. Bradshaw, and Lindsey M. O'Brennan, "Examining Ethnic, Gender, and Developmental Differences in the Way Children Report Being a Victim of 'Bullying' on Self-Report Measures," *Journal of Adolescent Health* 43 (2008), pp. 106–114.
20. "Bullying Statistics, 2010."
21. LaMar T. Empey and S. G. Lubeck, *Explaining Delinquency* (Lexington, Mass.: Lexington Books, 1971); M. Gold, *Status Forces in Delinquent Boys* (Ann Arbor: Institute for Social Research, University of Michigan, 1963); Martin Gold and D. W. Mann, "Delinquency as Defense," *American Journal of Orthopsychiatry* 42 (1972), pp. 463–479; T. Hirschi, *Causes of Delinquency* (Berkeley: University of California Press, 1969); H. B. Kaplan, "Sequel of Self-Derogation: Predicting from a General Theory of Deviant Behavior," *Youth and Society* 7 (1975), pp. 171–197; and A. L. Rhodes and A. J. Reiss, Jr., "Apathy, Truancy, and Delinquency as Adaptations to School Failure," *Social Forces* 48 (1969), pp. 12–22.
22. Hirschi, *Causes of Delinquency*.
23. M. L. Erickson, M. L. Scott, and L. T. Empey, *School Experience and Delinquency* (Provo, Utah: Brigham Young University, 1964); R. J. Havighurst et al., *Growing Up in River City* (New York: John Wiley and Sons, 1962); W. Healy and A. F. Bronner, *New Light on Delinquency and Its Treatment* (New Haven: Yale University Press, 1963); and W. C. Kvaraceus, *Juvenile Delinquency and the School* (New York: World Book Company, 1945).
24. J. David Hawkins and Denise M. Lishner, "Schooling and Delinquency," in *Handbook on Crime and Delinquency Prevention* (Westport: Greenwood Press, 1987), pp. 23–54.
25. Albert K. Cohen, *Delinquent Boys: The Culture of the Gang* (Glencoe: Free Press, 1955).
26. John C. Phillips, "The Creation of Deviant Behavior in American High Schools," in Keith Baker and Robert J. Rubal, eds., *Violence and Crime in the Schools* (Lexington: Lexington Books, 1980), pp. 115–127.
27. Kenneth Polk and F. Lynn Richmond, "Those Who Fail," in *Schools and Delinquency* (Englewood Cliffs: Prentice-Hall, 1972), pp. 59–69.
28. For this discussion, see LaMar T. Empey, Mark C. Stafford, and Carter H. Hay, *American Delinquency: Its Meaning and Construction* (Belmont: Wadsworth, 1999), p. 195.
29. Cohen, *Delinquent Boys*.
30. Walter B. Miller, "Lower-Class Culture as a Generating Milieu of Gang Delinquency," *Journal of Social Issues* 14 (1958), pp. 5–19.
31. Hirschi, *Causes of Delinquency*. See Kevin M. Beaver, John Paul Wright, and Michael O. Maumem, "The Effects of School Classroom Characteristics on Low Self-Control: A Multilevel Analysis," *Journal of Criminal Justice* 36 (2008), pp. 174–181.
32. Edwin M. Lemert, *Social Pathology* (New York: McGraw-Hall, 1951).

33. Mark Colvin and John Pauly, "A Critique of Criminology: Toward an Integrated Structural-Marxist Theory of Delinquency Production," *American Journal of Sociology* 89 (November 1983), pp. 513–551.
34. Michael R. Gottfredson and Travis Hirschi, *A General Theory of Crime* (Palo Alto: Stanford University Press, 1990).
35. Terence P. Thornberry, "Toward an Interactional Theory of Delinquency," *Criminology* 25 (1987), pp. 862–891.
36. Wayne N. Welsh, Jack R. Greene, and Patricia H. Jenkins, "School Disorder: The Influence of Individual, Institutional, and Community Factors," *Criminology* 37 (February 1999), pp. 73–116.
37. Stephen Goldstein, "The Scope and Sources of School Board Authority to Regulate Student Conduct and Status: A Nonconstitutional Analysis," 117 U. Pa. L. Rev. 373, 1969.
38. E. Edmund Reutter, Jr., *Legal Aspects of Control of Student Activities by Public School Authorities* (Topeka: National Organization on Legal Problems of Education, 1970).
39. *Hanson v. Broothby*, 318 F. Supp. 1183 (D. Mass., 1970).
40. This section on the rights of students is derived in part from Robert J. Rubel and Arthur H. Goldsmith, "Reflections on the Rights of Students and the Rise of School Violence," in in Keith Baker and Robert J. Rubel, eds., *Violence and Crime in the Schools* (Lexington: Lexington Books, 1980), pp. 73–77.
41. *Dixon v. Alabama State Board of Education*, 294 F.2d 150, 158 (5th Cir. 1961; cert. denied, 368 U.S. 930).
42. *Tinker v. Des Moines Independent School District*, 383 U.S. 503 (1969).
43. *Bethel School District No. 403 v. Fraser*, 478 U.S. 675, 106 S.Ct. 3159, 92 L.Ed.2d 549 (1986).
44. *Hazelwood School District v. Kuhlmeier*, 488 U.S. 260, 108 S.Ct. 562, 98 L.Ed.2d 592 (1988).
45. *Goss v. Lopez*, 419 U.S. 565 (1975).
46. *Wood v. Strickland*, 420 U.S. 308 (1975).
47. *Baker v. Owen*, 423 U.S. 907, affirming 395 F. Supp. 294 (1975); and *Ingraham v. Wright*, 430 U.S. 651 (1975).
48. 423 U.S. 907, affirming 395 F. Supp. 294 (1975).
49. *West Virginia State Board of Education v. Barnette*, 319 U.S. 624 (1943).
50. *Tinker v. Des Moines Independent School District*.
51. *Yoo v. Moynihan*, 20 Conn. Supp. 375 (1969).
52. *Richards v. Thurston*, 424 F.2d 1281 (1st Cir. 1970).
53. *Crossen v. Fatsi*, 309 F. Supp. 114 (1970).
54. *Scott v. Board of Education*, Union Free School District #17, Hicksville, 305 N.Y.S.2d 601 (1969).
55. *Bannister v. Paradix*, 316 F. Supp. 185 (1970).
56. *Richards v. Thurston*.
57. Ronald D. Stephens, "School-Based Interventions: Safety and Security," in Arnold P. Goldstein and C. Ronald Huff, eds., *The Gang Intervention Handbook* (Champaign: Research Press, 1993), pp. 257–300.
58. *New Jersey v. T.L.O.*, 469 U.S. (1985).
59. Ibid.
60. Ibid.
61. For an extensive discussion of the relevant issues and court decisions related to the police in the schools, see Samuel M. Davis, *Rights of Juveniles: The Juvenile Justice System* (St. Paul: Thompson Publishing, 2003), Sections 3–19 to 3-34.3.
62. J. M. Sanchez, "Expelling the Fourth Amendment from American Schools: Students' Rights Six Years After T.L.O.," *Law and Education Journal* 21 (1992), pp. 381–413.
63. *Vernonia School District 47J v. Acton*, 115 S.Ct. 2394 (1995).
64. *Board of Education of Independent School District No. 92 of Pottawatomie County et al. v. Earls*, 536 U.S. 822 (2002).
65. Rubel and Goldsmith, "Reflections on the Rights of Students."
66. *Bounds v. Smith*, 430 U.S. 817 (1977)..
67. Committee on School Health, "Out of School Suspension and Expulsion," *Pediatrics* 112 (2003), pp. 1206–1209.
68. Kay Muphy,"Recent Spotlights Out-of-School Suspensions in California," *Oakland Tribune*, April 10, 2012.
69. *Texas' School-to-Prison Pipeline: School; Expulsion* (Austin, Texas: Texas Appleseed, 2010).
70. Daniel Princiotta and Ryan Reyna, *Achieving Graduation for All: A Governor's Guide to Dropout Prevention and Recovery* (Washington, D.C.: National Governors Association Center for Best practices, 2009), p. 3.
71. Ibid., p. 4.
72. Zeng-yin Chen and Howard B. Kaplan, "School Failure in Early Adolescence and Status Attainment in Middle Adulthood: A Longitudinal Study," *Sociology of Education* 76 (April 2003), pp. 110–127.
73. Wendy Schwartz, *After-School and Community Technology Programs for Low-Income Families* (Washington, D.C.: Educational Resource Information Center [ERIC] Clearinghouse on Urban Education, 2003).
74. Robert Sampson and John Laub, *Crime in the Making: Pathways and Turning Points through Life* (Cambridge: Harvard University Press, 1993).
75. Richard Arum and Irenee R. Beattie, "High School Experience and the Risk of Adult Incarceration," *Criminology* 37 (August 1999), pp. 515–539.
76. Ibid.
77. "Mentoring in America 2005: A Snapshot of the Current State of Mentoring," 2005, http://www.mentoring.org/program_staff/evaluation/2005_national_poll.php.
78. National Mentoring Center, "School-Based Mentoring," http://www.nerel.org/mentoring/topic_school.html.
79. "Public Alternative Schools for At-Risk Students," *Indicators* 27 (2003), http://165.224.221.98/programs/coe/2003/section4/indicator27.asp.
80. Ibid.
81. Jacqueline R. Scherer, "School-Community Relations Network Strategies," in Keith Baker and Robert J. Rubel, eds.,

Violence and Crime in the Schools (Lexington: Lexington Books, 1980), pp. 61–70.

82. Princiotta and Reyna, *Achieving Graduation for All*.
83. Allison Ann Payne and Kelly Welch, "Modeling the Effects of Racial Threat on Punitive and Restorative School Discipline Practices," *Criminology* 48 (2010), pp. 1019–1062.
84. Ibid. See also Kelly Welch, "The Influence of Racial Threat in Schools: Recent Research Findings," in Richard Rosenfeld, Kenna Quinet, and Crystal Garcia, eds., *Contemporary Issues in Criminological Theory and Research: The Role of Social Institutions* (Belmont: Wadsworth, 2012) pp. 51–68.

Chapter 9, Gangs and Delinquency

1. Caroline Miller, "Gangs Riot in Times Square," *Newser*, April 5, 2011.
2. Rob Quinn, "Philly Cracks Down on Teen Flash Mobs," *Newser*, March 25, 2010.
3. Robert Walker, "Mara Salvatrucha MS-13," *Gangs OR Us*, http://www.gangsorus.com/marasalvatrucha13.html (accessed September 10, 2011); and Gregg W. Etter, Sr., "Mara Salvatrucha 13: A Transnational Threat," *Journal of Gang Research* 17 (Winter 2010), pp. 2–17.
4. Ibid. For a perception of gang members, see Alejardro Del Carmen, John J. Rodriguez, Rhonda Dobbs, Richard Smith, Randall R. Butler, and Robert Sarver III, "In Their Own Words: A Study of Gang Members Through Their Own Perspective," *Journal of Gang Research* (Winter 2009), pp. 67–76.
5. Arlen Egley, Jr., and James C. Howell, *Highlights of the 2011 National Youth Gang Survey* (Washington, D.C.: Office of Juvenile Justice and Delinquency Prevention, 2013).
6. Frederick Thrasher, *The Gang: A Study of 1,313 Gangs in Chicago* (Chicago: University of Chicago Press, 1927) p. 57.
7. National Gang Center, Highlights of Gang-Related Legislation (Tallahassee: Institute for Intergovernmental Research, Spring, 2010).
8. For the role behavior of juveniles in gangs, see Mike Carlie, Into t*he Abyss: A Personal Journal into the World of Street Gangs*, http://people.-missouristate.edu/MichaelCarlie/.
9. James C. Howell, *Youth Gangs: An Overview* (Washington, D.C.: Office of Justice Programs; Office of Juvenile Justice and Delinquency Programs, 1999). See also Scott H. Decker and B. Van Winkle, *Life in the Gang: Family, Friends, and Violence* (New York: Cambridge University Press, 1996).
10. Ira Reiner, *Gangs, Crime and Violence in Los Angeles: Findings and Proposals from the District Attorney's Office* (Arlington: National Youth Gang Information Center, 1992).
11. Interview in 1982 at the Iowa State Penitentiary at Fort Madison, Iowa.
12. George W. Knox, David Laske, and Edward Tromanhauser, "Chicago Schools Revisited," *Bulletin of the Illinois Public Education Association* 16 (Spring 1992). For the relationship between gangs and weapons, see also Edward Tromanhauser, "The Relationship Between Street Gang Membership and the Possession and Use of Firearms," paper presented at the Annual Meeting of the American Society of Criminology, Boston, Massachusetts, November 1994.
13. Joseph F. Sheley and James D. Wright, "Gun Acquisition and Possession in Selected Juvenile Samples," *Research in Brief* (Washington, D.C.: National Institute of Justice, 1993).
14. Charles M. Callahan and Ira Rivara, "Urban High School Youth and Handguns: A School-Based Survey," *Journal of the American Medical Association* (June 1992), pp. 3038–3042.
15. Comment made in 1995 to one of the authors.
16. For more information on drive-by shootings, see William B. Sanders, *Gangbangs and Drive-Bys: Grounded Culture and Juvenile Gang Violence* (New York: Aldine de Gruyter, 1994).
17. See "Dope Fiend Teaches Algebra at Austin High," *Austin Voice* 9 (March 1 and March 8, 1994).
18. Patricia Wen, "Boston Gangs: A Hard World," *Boston Globe*, Tuesday, May 10, 1988. For a description of the various roles within gang drug trafficking, see Felix M. Padilla, *The Gang as an American Enterprise* (New Brunswick: Rutgers University Press, 1992).
19. Elaine S. Knapp, *Embattled Youth, Kids, and Drugs* (Chicago: Council of State Government, 1988), p. 13.
20. Interview with gang leader in 1995.
21. Carlie, *Into the Abyss*.
22. Jeffrey Fagan, "Social Processes of Delinquency and Drug Use among Urban Gangs," in *Gangs in America*, 2nd ed. (Thousand Oaks: Sage, 1996), pp. 182–219. See also Jeffrey Fagan, "The Social Organization of Drug Use and Drug Dealing among Urban Gangs." Criminology, 27 (November 1989), pp. 633–670.
23. Robert L. Listenbee, *OJJDP Fact Sheet: Highlights of the 2011 National Youth Gang Survey* (Washington, D.C.: Office of Juvenile Justice and Delinquency Prevention, 2013), p. 2.
24. *2011 National Gang Threat Assessment* (Washington, D.C.: Bureau of Justice Statistics, 2011).
25. Ibid.
26. Ibid.
27. Terence P. Thornberry, "Membership in Youth Gangs and Involvement in Serious and Violent Offending," in R. Loeber and D. P. Farrington, eds., *Serious and Violent Juvenile Offenders: Risk Factors and Successful Interventions* (Thousand Oaks: Sage, 1998), pp. 147–166.
28. Ronald C. Huff, *Criminal Behavior of Gang Members and At-Risk Youths* (Washington, D.C.: Office of Justice Programs; national Institute of Justice, 1998).
29. Scott H. Decker, Tim Bynum, and Deborah Weisel, "A Tale of Two Cities: Gangs as Organized Crime Groups," *Justice Quarterly* 15 (September 1998), pp. 395–425.
30. Thrasher, *The Gang*.
31. G. David Curry et al., *National Assessment of Law Enforcement Anti-Gang Information Resources* (Washington, D.C.: National Institute of Justice, 1992).

32. This seven-stage development scheme was developed from conversations with a variety of individuals, ranging from gang leaders and gang members to police administrators, school officials, and newspaper reporters, across the nation.
33. Gang youths were very reluctant to talk about the percentage.
34. Interview with youth in August 1990.
35. Interview with adolescent in February 1991.
36. Interview with gang member in October 1989.
37. Comment made by a teacher to the author following a gang seminar he presented in March 1990.
38. 2011 National Gang Assessment (Washington, D.C.: Bureau of Justice Statistics, 2011).
39. For an examination of Chicano gangs, see James Diego Vigil, *Barrio Gangs: Street Life and Identity in Southern California* (Austin: University of Texas Press, 1988); and Joan Moore, *Home Boys: Gangs, Drugs, and Prison in the Barrios of Los Angeles* (Philadelphia: Temple University Press, 1978).
40. See Ko-Lin Chin, "Chinese Gangs and Extortion," in *Gangs in America*, pp. 129–145.
41. James Diego Vigil and Steve Chong Yun, "Vietnamese Youth Gangs in Southern California," in *Gangs in America*, pp. 146–162.
42. Reiner, *Gangs, Crime and Violence in Los Angeles*.
43. Howell, *Youth Gangs*.
44. Finn-Aage Esbensen and D. W. Osgood, *National Evaluation of G.R.E.A.T.: Research in Brief* (Washington, D.C.: Office of Justice Programs, National Institute of Justice, 1997).
45. For an examination of the seriousness of the problem of Satanism among American youths, see Philip Jenkins and Daniel Maier-Katkin, "Satanism: Myth and Reality in a Contemporary Moral Panic," revised paper presented at the American Society of Criminology, Baltimore, Maryland, November 1990.
46. See Pete Simi, Lowell Smith, and Ann M. S. Reiser, "From Punk Kids to Public Enemy Number One," *Deviant Behavior* 29 (2009), pp. 753–774.
47. See Eric Henderson, Stephen J. Kunitz, and Jerrold E. Levy, "The Origins of Navajo Youth Gangs," *American Indian Culture and Research Journal* 23 (1999), pp. 243–264.
48. Ibid.
49. See Freda Adler, *Sisters in Crime: The Rise of the New Female Criminal* (New York: McGraw-Hill, 1975); W. B. Miller, "The Molls," *Society* 11 (1973), pp. 32–35; E. Ackley and B. Fliegel, "A Social Work Approach to Street Corner Girls," *Social Work* 5 (1960), pp. 29–31; and Peggy C. Giordano, "Girls, Guys and Gangs: The Changing Social Context of Female Delinquency," *Journal of Criminal Law and Criminology* 69 (1978), p. 130.
50. Lee Bowker and M. W. Klein, "Female Participation in Delinquent Gang Motivation," *Adolescence* 15 (1980), pp. 508–519; and J. C. Quicker, *Home Girls: Characterizing Chicano Gangs* (San Pedro: International University Press, 1983).
51. Quicker, *Home Girls*.
52. Finn-Aage Esbensen, Elizabeth Piper Deschenes, and L. Thomas Winfree, Jr., "Differences Between Gang Girls and Gang Boys: Results from a Multisite Survey," *Youth Society* 31 (1999), pp. 27–53.
53. Carl S. Taylor, *Girls, Gangs, Women and Drugs* (East Lansing: Michigan State University Press, 1993).
54. Beth Bjerregaard and Carolyn Smith, "Gender Differences in Gang Participation, Delinquency, and Substance Abuse," *Journal of Quantitative Criminology* 9 (1993), pp. 329–355.
55. Joan Moore and John Hagedorn, "Female Gangs: A Focus on Research," *Juvenile Justice Bulletin* (Washington, D.C.: Office of Juvenile Justice and Delinquency Prevention, 2001).
56. Esbensen, Deschenes, and Winfree, "Differences Between Gang Girls and Gang Boys."
57. Jody Miller and Rod K. Brunson, "Gender Dynamics in Youth Gangs: Comparison of Female Accounts, *Justice Quarterly* 16 (September 2000), pp. 420-447.
58. Karen Joe and Meda Chesney-Lind, "Just Every Mother's Angel: An Analysis of Gender and Ethnic Variations in Youth Gang Membership," paper presented at the Annual Meeting of the American Society of Criminology, Phoenix, Arizona, November 1993.
59. Ibid.
60. H. A. Bloch and A. Niederhoffer, *The Gang: A Study in Adolescent Behavior* (New York: Philosophical Library, 1958).
61. Richard A. Cloward and Lloyd E. Ohlin, *Delinquency and Opportunity: A Theory of Delinquent Gangs* (New York: Free Press, 1990)..
62. Albert K. Cohen, Delinquent Boys: The Culture of the Gang (Glencoe: Free Press, 1955).
63. Walter B. Miller, "Lower-Class Culture as a Generating Milieu of Gang Delinquency," *Journal of Social Issues* 14 (1958), pp. 5–19.
64. Lewis Yablonsky, *The Violent Gang* (New York: Macmillan, 1962).
65. Bjerregaard and Smith, "Gender Differences in Gang Participation, Delinquency, and Substance Use."
66. See Patrick G. Jackson, "Theories and Findings About Youth Gangs," *Criminal Justice Abstracts* (June 1989), pp. 322–323.
67. See Gerald D. Suttles, *The Social Order of the Slum: Ethnicity and Territory in the Inner City* (Chicago: University of Chicago Press, 1968); and Thrasher, *The Gang*.
68. Martin Jankowski, *Islands in the Street* (Oakland: University of California Press, 1991).
69. See William Julius Wilson, *The Truly Disadvantaged: The Inner City, the Underclass, and Public Policy* (Chicago: University of Chicago Press, 1987).
70. G. David Curry and Irving A. Spergel, "Gang Homicide, Delinquency, and Community," *Criminology* (1988), pp. 381–405.
71. J. E. Fagan, "Gangs, Drugs, and Neighborhood Change," in *Gangs in America*, pp. 39–74.

72. Chris Melde and Finn-Aage Esbhensen, "Gang Membership as a Turning Point in the Life Course," *Criminology*, 49 (May 2011), pp. 513–547.
73. Decker and Van Winkle, *Life in the Gang*.
74. Terence P. Thornberry, Marvin D. Krohn, Alan J. Lizotte, and Carolyn A. Smith, *Gangs and Delinquency in Developmental Perspective* (Cambridge, England: Cambridge Press, 2003).
75. Ibid.
76. I. A. Spergel, G. D. Curry, R. A. Ross, and R. Chance, *Survey of Youth Gang Problems and Programs in 45 Cities and 6 Sites*, Tech. Report No. 2, National Youth Gang Suppression and Intervention Project (Chicago: University of Chicago, School of Social Service Administration, 1989).
77. Ibid.
78. Ibid.
79. Ibid., p. 218.
80. Ibid.
81. Howell, *Youth Gangs*.
82. Ibid.
83. Terence P. Thornberry and James H. Burch II, "Gang Members and Delinquent Behavior," *Juvenile Justice Bulletin* (Washington, D.C.: Office of Justice Programs, Office of Juvenile Justice and Delinquency Prevention, 1997).

Chapter 10, Drugs and Delinquency

1. Jeff Slowikowski, "Highlights from Pathways to Desistance: A Longitudinal Study of Serious Adolescent Behavior," Office of Juvenile Justice and Delinquency Prevention, March 2011.
2. *Results from the 2012 National Survey on Drug Use and Health: National Findings* (Rockville: Substance Abuse and Mental Health Services Administration, September 2013). Web posted at http://oas.samhsa.gov/nsduh/2k8nsduh/2k8Results.cfm (accessed April 18, 2014).
3. Matthew G. Muters and Christina Bethke were extremely helpful in doing the literature review and in drafting materials for this chapter.
4. Rand Drug Policy Research Center, *Newsletter* (June 1995).
5. Howard Abadinsky, *Drug Use and Abuse: A Comprehensive Introduction*, 6th ed. (Belmont: Thompson Learning, 2008).
6. *Juveniles and Drugs* (Washington, D.C.: Office of National Drug Control Policy, 2004).
7. L. D. Johnston, P. M. O'Malley, R. A. O'Malley, J. G. Bachman, and J. E. Schulenberg, *Monitoring the Future: National Results on Adolescent Drug Use: Overview of Key Findings 2013* (Bethesda: National Institute on Drug Abuse, 2014).
8. Office of National Drug Control Policy, *2012 National Survey on Drug Use and Health* (Washington, D.C.: Office of National Drug Control Policy, 2013). p. 13
9. Ibid., p. 22.
10. Ibid., p. 24.
11. Ibid.
12. James A. Inciardi, *The War on Drugs, II* (Mountain View: Mayfield, 1992), p. 62.
13. Johnston, O'Malley, Bachman, and Schulenberg, *Monitoring the Future National Results on Adolescent Drug Use*.
14. *Results from the 2012 National Survey on Drug Use and Health: National Findings*, p. 46.
15. For many other names, see Inciardi, *The War on Drugs II*.
16. Inciardi, *The War on Drugs II*.
17. T. M. McSherry, "Program Experiences with the Solvent Abuser in Philadelphia," in R. A. Crider and B. A. Rouse, eds., *Epidemiology of Inhalant Abuse: An Update* (Washington, D.C.: National Institute on Drug Abuse Research Monograph 85, 1989), pp. 106–120.
18. Abadinsky, *Drugs*.
19. Bureau of Justice Statistics, *Drug Enforcement Report* (Washington, D.C.: U.S. Department of Justice, January 3, 1990).
20. Office of National Drug Control Policy, *2012 National Survey on Drug Use and Health* (Washington, D.C.: Office of National Drug Control Policy, 2013).
21. University of Michigan News and Information Services, January 24, 1991.
22. Ibid.
23. Inciardi, *The War on Drugs II*.
24. For an overview of medical complications associated with heroin addiction, see Jerome J. Platt, *Heroin Addiction: Theory, Research, and Treatment* (Malabar: Robert E. Krieger, 1986), pp. 80–102.
25. David M. Altschuler and Paul J. Brounstein, "Patterns of Drug Use, Drug Trafficking, and Other Delinquency Among Inner-City Adolescent Males in Washington, D.C.," *Criminology* 29 (1991), p. 590.
26. Lloyd D. Johnson et al., "Drugs and Delinquency: A Search for Causal Connections," in Denise B. Kandel, Ronald C. Kessler, and Rebecca Z. Margulies, eds., *Longitudinal Research on Drug Use: Empirical Finds and Methodological Issues* (Washington, D.C.: Hemisphere, 1978), pp. 137–156; J. C. Friedman and A. S. Friedman, "Drug Use and Delinquency Among Lower Class, Court Adjudicated Adolescent Boys," in *Drug Use in America 1* (Washington, D.C.: National Commission on Marijuana and Drug Abuse: Government Printing Office, 1973); J. A. Inciardi, "Heroin Use and Street Crime," *Crime and Delinquency* 25 (1979), pp. 335–346; and L. N. Robins and G. E. Murphy, "Drug Use in a Normal Population of Young Negro Men," *American Journal of Public Health* 57 (1967), pp. 1580–1596.
27. Altschuler and Brounstein, "Patterns of Drug Use, Drug Trafficking, and Other Delinquency Among Inner-City Adolescent Males in Washington, D.C."; Richard Jessor and Shirley L. Jessor, *Problem Behavior and Psychosocial Development: A Longitudinal Study of Youth* (New York: Academic Press, 1977); R. L. Akers, "Delinquent Behavior, Drugs and Alcohol: What Is the Relationship?" *Today's Delinquent* 3 (1984), pp. 19–47; D. S. Elliott and D. Huizinga,

The Relationship Between Delinquent Behavior and ADM Problems (Boulder: Behavior Research Institute, 1985); and Delbert S. Elliott, David Huizinga, and Scott Menard, *Multiple Problem Youth: Delinquency, Substance Use, and Mental Health Problems* (New York: Springer-Verlag, 1989). See also Richard Felson, Jukka Savolainer, Mikko Aaltonen, and Heta Moustgaard, "Is the Association Between Alcohol Use and Delinquency — Causal or Spurious?" *Criminology* 46 (2008), pp. 786–808.

28 See Marc Le Blanc and Nathalie Kaspy, "Trajectories of Delinquency and Problem Behavior: Comparison of Social and Personal Control Characteristics of Adjudicated Boys on Synchronous and Nonsynchronous Paths," *Journal of Quantitative Criminology* 14 (1998), pp. 181–214; and Helene Raskin White, "Marijuana Use and Delinquency: A Test of the 'Independent Cause' Hypothesis," *Journal of Drug Issues* (1991), pp. 231–256.

29 Bureau of Justice Statistics, *Drugs, Crime, and the Justice System* (Washington, D.C.: Government Printing Office, 1993).

30 Kandel, Kessler, and Margulies, *Longitudinal Research on Drug Use*.

31 J. David Hawkins, Richard F. Catalano, and Devon D. Brewer, "Preventing Serious, Violent, and Chronic Juvenile Offending," in James C. Howell, Barry Krisberg, J. David Hawkins, and John J. Wilson, eds., *A Sourcebook: Serious, Violent and Chronic Juvenile Offenders* (Thousand Oaks: Sage, 1995).

32 Delbert S. Elliott, David Huizinga, and Suzanne S. Ageton, *Explaining Delinquency and Drug Use* (Beverly Hills: Sage, 1985).

33 D. S. Elliott and D. Huizinga, "The Relationship Between Delinquent Behavior and ADM Problem Behaviors," paper prepared for the ADAMHA/OJJDP State of the Art Research Conference on Juvenile Offenders with Serious Drug/Alcohol and Mental Health Problems, Bethesda, Maryland, April 17–18, 1984.

34 J. Fagan, J. Weis, and Y. Cheng, "Delinquency and Substance Use Among Inner-City Students," *The Journal of Drug Abuse* (1990), pp. 351–402.

35 R. L. Simons, R. D. Conger, and L. B. Whitbeck, "A Multistage Social Learning Model of the Influence of Family and Peers upon Adolescent Substance Abuse," *Journal of Drug Issues* 18 (1988), p. 293.

36 John Petraitis, Brian R. Flay, and Todd Q. Miller, "Reviewing Theories of Adolescent Substance Use: Organizing Pieces in the Puzzle," *Psychological Bulletin* 117 (1995), pp. 67–86. See also W. Alex Mason, Julia E. Hitchings, Robert J. McMahon, and Richard L. Spoth, "A Test of Three Alternative Hypotheses Regarding the Effects of Early Delinquency on Adolescent Psychosocial Functioning and Substance Involvement," *Journal of Abnormal Child Psychology* 35 (2007), pp. 831–843; and David B. Henry and Kimberly Kobus, "Early Adolescent Social Networks and Substance Use," *Journal of Early Adolescence* 27 (2007), pp. 346–362.

37 Ibid.

38 I. Ajken and M. Fishbein, *Understanding Attitudes and Predicting Social Behavior* (Englewood Cliffs: Prentice-Hall, 1980).

39 Petraitis, Flay, and Miller, "Reviewing Theories of Adolescent Substance Use." See also Joan L. Neff and Dennis E. Waite, "Male Versus Female Substance Abuse Patterns Among Incarcerated Juvenile Offenders: Comparing Strain and Social Learning Variables," *Justice Quarterly* 24 (March 2007), pp. 106–132.

40 Travis Hirschi, *Causes of Delinquency* (Berkeley: University of California Press, 1969); J. D. Hawkins and J. G. Weis, "The Social Development Model: An Integrated Approach to Delinquency Prevention," *Journal of Primary Prevention* 6 (1985), pp. 73–97; Jayne A. Fulkerson, Keryn E. Pasch, Cheryl L. Perry, and Kelli Konro, "Relationships Between Alcohol-Related Informal Social Control, Parental Monitoring and Adolescent Problem Behaviors Among Racially Diverse Urban Youth," *Journal of Community Health* 33 (2008), pp. 425–433.

41 Hirschi, *Causes of Delinquency*.

42 J. D. Hawkins, R. F. Catalano, and J. Y. Miller, "Risk and Protective Factors for Alcohol and Other Drug Problems in Adolescence and Early Adulthood," *Psychological Bulletin* 112 (1992), pp. 64–105.

43 Radical theorists have made this a theme of their research on poor adolescents, especially minority ones. See Chapter 6.

44 Elliott, Huizinga, and Ageton, *Explaining Delinquency and Drug Use*.

45 D. S. Elliott, D. Huizinga, and S. Menard, *Multiple Problem Youth: Delinquency, Substance Abuse Mental Health Problems* (New York: Springer-Verlag, 1989).

46 Ibid.

47 Marcia Chaiken and Bruce Johnson, *Characteristics of Different Types of Drug-Involved Youth* (Washington, D.C.: National Institute of Justice, 1988).

48 Marvin S. Krohn, Alan J. Lizotte, and Cynthia M. Perez, "The Interrelationships Between Substance Use and Precocious Transitions to Adult Status," *Journal of Health and Social Behavior* 38 (March 1997), pp. 87–101.

49 Ibid.

50 Glen H. Elder, Jr., "Time, Human Agency, and Social Change: Perspectives on the Life Course," *Social Psychology Quarterly* 57 (1994), pp. 4–15.

51 Krohn, Lizotte, and Perez, "The Interrelationships Between Substance Use and Precocious Transitions to Adult Status."

52 Gary M. McClelland, Linda A. Teplin, and Karen M. Abram, *Detention and Prevalence of Substance Use Among Juvenile Detainees* (Washington, D.C.: Office of Juvenile Justice and Delinquency Prevention, 2004); see the report for the citations supporting each generalization.

53 See D. B. Kandel and J. A. Logan, "Patterns of Drug Use from Adolescence to Young Adulthood: Periods of Risk for Initiation, Continued Use, and Discontinuation," *American Public Health* 74 (1984), pp. 660–666.

54 L. A. Goodman and W. H. Kruskal, *Measures of Association for Cross Classification* (New York: Springer-Verlag, 1979).

55 L. Thomas Winfree, Jr., Christine S. Sellers, and Dennis L. Clason, "Social Learning and Adolescent Deviance Abstention: Toward Understanding the Reasons for Initiating, Quitting, and Avoiding Drugs," *Journal of Quantitative Criminology* 9 (1993), pp. 101–125.

56 Ryan D. Schroeder, Peggy C. Giordano, and Stephen A. Cernkovich, "Drug Use and Desistance Processes," *Criminology* 45 (2007), pp. 192–222.

57 Sharon Mihalic, Katherine Irwin, Abigail Fagan, Diane Ballard, and Delbert Elliott, *Blueprint for Violence Prevention* (Washington, D.C.: Office of Juvenile Justice and Delinquency Prevention, 2004).

58 G. Botvin, S. Mihalic, and J. K. Grotpeter, "Life Skills Training," in D. S. Elliott, ed., *Blueprint for Violence Prevention: Book 5* (Boulder: University of Colorado, Institute of Behavioral Sciences, Center for the Study and Prevention of Violence, 1998).

59 Mihalic, Irwin, Fagan, Ballard, and Elliott, *Blueprint for Violence Prevention*.

60 Ibid.

61 Ibid.

62 National Institute of Justice, *The D.A.R.E. Program: A Review of Prevalence, User Satisfaction, and Effectiveness* (Washington, D.C.: U.S. Department of Justice, 1994).

63 William DeJong, *Arresting the Demand for Drugs: Police and School Partnership to Prevent Drug Abuse* (Washington, D.C.: National Institute of Justice, 1987).

64 Phyllis Ellickson, Robert Bell, and K. McGuigan, "Preventing Adolescent Drug Use: Long-Term Results of a Junior High Program," *American Journal of Public Health* 83 (1993), pp. 856–861.

65 Deanna Atkinson, an administrator in the Élan program, suggested this list of noteworthy programs in a September 1995 telephone conversation.

66 *Drug Courts: The Second Decade* (Washington, D.C.: National Institute of Justice, 2006).

67 Gordon Bazemore and Lode Walgrave, "Restorative Juvenile Justice: In Search of Fundamentals and an Outline for Systemic Reform," in Gordon Bazemore and Lode Walgrave, eds., *Restorative Juvenile Justice: Repairing the Harm of Youth Crime* (Monsey: Criminal Justice Press, 1999), pp. 45–74

68 Ibid.

69 Thomas J. Dishion, Deborah Capaldi, Kathleen M. Spracklen, and L. Fuzhong, "Peer Ecology of Male Adolescent Drug Use," *Development and Psychopathology* 7 (1995), pp. 803–824.

Chapter 11, An Overview of Juvenile Justice in America

1 Jennifer Fratello, Annie Salsich, and Sara Moqulescu, *Juvenile Detention Reform in New York City: Measuring Risk Through Research* (New York: Vera Institute of Justice, 2011).

2 Elizabeth S. Scott and Thomas Grisso, "The Evolution of Adolescence: A Developmental Perspective on Juvenile Justice Reform," *Journal of Criminal Law & Criminology* 88 (1997), pp. 137–189.

3 David J. Rothman, *The Discovery of the Asylum* (Boston: Little, Brown, 1971).

4 Ibid.

5 Bradford Kinney Piece, *A Half Century with Juvenile Delinquents* (Montclair: Patterson Smith, 1969) [1869], p. 41.

6 Ibid. For interpretations similar to Platt's, see also Sanford J. Fox, "Juvenile Justice Reform: An Historic Perspective," *Stanford Law Review* 22 (1970), p. 1187; and Douglas Rendleman, "*Parens Patriae:* From Chancery to the Juvenile Court," *South Carolina Law Review* 28 (1971), p. 205.

7 John Augustus, *First Probation Officer* (Montclair: Patterson-Smith Company, 1972).

8 For development of these levels of prevention, see Steven P. Lab, *Crime Prevention: Approaches, Practices and Evaluations* (Cincinnati: Anderson, 2000), pp. 19–22.

9 Sharon Mihalic, Katherine Irwin, Abigail Fagan, Diane Ballard, and Delbert Elliott, *Successful Implementation: Lessons from Blueprints* (Washington, D.C.: Office of Juvenile Justice and Delinquency Prevention, 2004), p. 1.

10 D. E. McGill, S. Mihalic, and J. K. Grotpeter, "Big Brothers Big Sisters of America," in D. S. Elliott, ed., *Blueprints for Violence Prevention: Book 2* (Boulder: University of Colorado, Institute of Behavioral Science, Center for the Study and Prevention of Violence, 1997).

11 Mihalic et al., *Successful Implementation: Lessons from Blueprints*, pp. 30–31.

12 M. A. Pentz, S. Mihalic, and J. K. Grotpeter, "The Midwestern Prevention Project," in D. S. Elliott, ed., *Blueprints for Violence Prevention: Book 1* (Boulder: University of Colorado, Institute of Behavioral Science, Center for the Study and Prevention of Violence, 1997).

13 Mihalic et al., *Successful Implementation: Lessons from Blueprints*, pp. 26–27.

14 J. F. Alexander et al., "Functional Family Therapy," in D. S. Elliott, ed., *Blueprints for Violence Prevention: Book 3* (Boulder: University of Colorado, Institute of Behavioral Science, Center for the Study and Prevention of Violence, 2000).

15 Mihalic et al., *Successful Implementation: Lessons from Blueprints*, pp. 22–23.

16 C. Webster-Stratton et al., "The Incredible Years: Parent, Teacher and Child Training Series," in D. S. Elliott, ed., *Blueprints for Violence Prevention: Book 11* (Boulder: University of Colorado, Institute of Behavioral Science, Center for the Study and Prevention of Violence, 2001).

17 Mihalic et al., *Successful Implementation: Lessons from Blueprints*, p. 47.

18 G. Botvin, S. Mihalic, and J. K. Grotpeter, "Life Skills Training," in D. S. Elliott, ed., *Blueprints for Violence*

Prevention: Book 5 (Boulder: University of Colorado, Institute of Behavioral Science, Center for the Study and Prevention of Violence, 1998).

19. Mihalic et al., *Successful Implementation: Lessons from Blueprints*, pp. 31–33.

20. Pentz et al., "The Midwestern Prevention Project."

21. Mihalic et al., *Successful Implementation: Lessons from Blueprints*, pp. 56–58.

22. P. Chamberlain and S. Mihalic, "Multidimensional Treatment Foster Care," in D. S. Elliott, ed., *Blueprints for Violence Prevention: Book 8* (Boulder: University of Colorado, Institute of Behavioral Science, Center for the Study and Prevention of Violence, 1998).

23. Mihalic et al., *Successful Implementation: Lessons from Blueprints*, pp. 27–28.

24. S. W. Henggeler et al., "Multisystemic Therapy," in D. S. Elliott, ed., *Blueprints for Violence Prevention: Book 6* (Boulder: University of Colorado, Institute of Behavioral Science, Center for the Study and Prevention of Violence, 2001).

25. Mihalic D.C., *Successful Implementation: Lessons from Blueprints*, pp. 18–20.

26. D. Olds et al., "Prenatal and Infancy Home Visitation by Nurses," in D. S. Elliott, ed., *Blueprints for Violence Prevention: Book 7* (Boulder: University of Colorado, Institute of Behavioral Science, Center for the Study and Prevention of Violence, 1998).

27. Mihalic et al., *Successful Implementation: Lessons from Blueprints*, pp. 47–48.

28. Ibid., p. 48.

29. Ibid., p. 46.

30. M. Greenberg, M. Kusche, and S. Mihalic, "Promoting Alternative Thinking Strategies," in D. S. Elliott, ed., *Blueprints for Violence Prevention: Book 2* (Boulder: University of Colorado, Institute of Behavioral Science, Center for the Study and Prevention of Violence, 1998).

31. Scott B. Peterson and Jill Beres, *Report to the Nation 1993 to 2008: The Global Youth Justice Movement—15-Year Update on Youth Courts and Teen Courts* (Global Issues Resource Center Cuyahoga Community College, 2008).

32. National Association of Youth Courts, "Facts and Stats," http://www.youthcourt.net/?page_id=24 (accessed May 2, 2014).

33. Op. cit., *Report to the Nation 1993 to 2008: The Global Youth Justice Movement—15-Year Update on Youth Courts and Teen Courts*.

34. T. M. Godwin, *Peer Justice and Youth Empowerment: An Implementation Guide for Teen Court Programs* (Lexington: American Probation and Parole Association, 1998).

35. Marilyn Roberts, Jennifer Brophy, and Caroline Cooper, *The Juvenile Drug Court Movement* (Washington, D.C.: Office of the Juvenile Justice and Delinquency Prevention, 1997).

36. Ibid.

37. Ibid.

38. Andrew Rutherford and Robert McDermott, *National Evaluation Program Phase Report: Juvenile Diversion* (Washington, D.C.: U.S. Government Printing Office, 1976).

39. Ibid.

40. For specific numbers of staff in juvenile corrections, see Kathleen Maguire, ed., *Sourcebook of Criminal Justice Statistics* (Bureau of Justice Statistics), www.albany.edu/sourcebook (accessed November 28, 2011).

41. Ibid.

42. Andrew von Hirsch, *Doing Justice: The Choice of Punishments* (New York: Hill & Wang, 1976).

43. David Fogel, *"We Are the Living Proof": The Justice Model for Corrections* (Cincinnati: Anderson, 1975); von Hirsch, *Doing Justice*; and Twentieth Century Fund Task Force on Sentencing Policy Toward Young Offenders, *Confronting Youth Crime* (New York: Holmes and Meier, 1978).

44. Fogel, *"We Are the Living Proof."*

45. Daniel W. Van. Ness, "Justice That Restores: From Impersonal to Personal Justice," in Burt Galaway and Joe Hudson, eds., *Criminal Justice: Retribution vs. Restoration* (Binghamton, N.Y.: Hayworth Press, 2004), pp. 93–109; H. Zehr, *Retributive Justice, Restorative Justice* (Akron: Mennonite Central Committee, 1985); and H. Zehr, *Changing Lenses* (Scottsdale: Herald Press, 1990).

46. Ibid.

47. See James Q. Wilson, *Thinking About Crime*, rev. ed. (New York: Basic Books, 1983); and Ernest van den Haag, *Punishing Criminals: Concerning a Very Old and Painful Question* (New York: Hill and Wang, 1976).

48. Snyder and Sickmund, *Juvenile Offenders and Victims*.

49. Ibid., p. 89.

50. Ibid.

51. Gerald G. Gaes, Timothy J. Flanagan, Lawrence L. Motiuk, and Lynn Steward, "Adult Correctional Treatment," in Michael Tonry and Joan Petersilia, eds., *Crime and Justice, 26th Edition: Prisons* (Chicago: University of Chicago Press, 1999), pp. 374–375.

52. Harvey Milkman and Kenneth Wanberg, *Cognitive-Behavioral Treatment: A Review and Discussion for Correctional Professionals* (Washington, D.C.: National Institute of Corrections, 2007), p. 5.

53. Patricia van Voohis, Lis M. Spruance, P. Neal Richey, Shelley Johnson Listwan, and Renita Seebrook, "The Georgia Cognitive Skills Experiment: A Replication of Reasoning and Rehabilitation," *Criminal Justice and Behavior* 31 (2004), pp. 282–305.

54. Ibid.

55. Ibid.

56. Ibid.

57. Frank S. Pearson, Douglas S. Lipton, Charles M. Cleland, and Dorline S. Yee, "The Effects of Behavioral/Cognitive-Behavioral Programs on Recidivism," *Crime and Delinquency* 48 (2002), pp. 476–496.

58 Milkman and Wanberg, *Cognitive-Behavioral Treatment*, p. xix.
59 Ibid.
60 Pearson, Lipton, Cleland, and Yee, "The Effects of Behavioral/Cognitive-Behavioral Programs on Recidivism."
61 Interview with Harry Vorrath quoted in Oliver J. Keller, Jr., and Benedict S. Alper, *Halfway Houses: Community Centered Correction and Treatment* (Lexington: D.C. Heath, 1970), p. 55.
62 Ibid.
63 The following materials are adapted from Harry H. Vorrath and Larry K. Brendtro, *Positive Peer Culture* (Chicago: Aldine, 1974).
64 Ibid.
65 Ibid.
66 Interviewed in 1986 in a midwestern training school.
67 See the Federal Bureau of Prisons, "Substance Abuse Treatment," http://www.bop.gov/inmate_PROGRAMS_SUBSTACE.JSP (accessed May 18, 2012).
68 Lee Sechrest, Susan O. White, and Elizabeth D. Brown, eds., *The Rehabilitation of Criminal Offenders* (Washington, D.C., National Academy of Sciences, 1979); and Susan Martin, Lee Sechrest, and Robin Redner, eds., *Rehabilitation of Criminal Offenders: Directions for Research* (Washington, D.C.: National Academy of Sciences, 1981).
69 For an examination of the meta-analyses, see Ted Palmer, *The Re-Emergence of Intervention* (Beverly Hills: Sage 1999), pp. 48–76.
70 Palmer, *The Re-Emergence of Intervention*, p. 48.
71 Mark L. Lipsey, "Interventions for Juvenile Offenders: A Serendipitous Journey," *Criminology & Public Policy*, Vol. 13 (February 2014), pp. 1–14.
72 James. Howell, "Mark Lipsey's Contributions to Evidence-Based Services for Juveniles Offenders: What Works Across Juvenile Justice Systems," *Criminology & Public Policy*, Vol. 13 (February 2014), pp. 15–19.
73 Sechrest, White, and Brown, *The Rehabilitation of Criminal Offenders*, pp. 35–37.
74 Barry Krisberg, et.al., *Guide for Implementing the Comprehensive Strategy for Serious, Violent, and Chronic Juvenile offenders* (Washington, D.C.: Office of Juvenile Justice and Delinquency Prevention, 1995), p. 133.
75 Donna M. Bishop, "The Role of Race and Ethnicity in Juvenile Justice Processing," in Darnell F. Hawkins and Kimberly Kempf-Leonard, eds., *Our Children, Their Children: Confronting Racial and Ethnic Differences in American Juvenile Justice* (Chicago: University of Chicago Press, 2005), p. 24.
76 Ibid.
77 Janet L. Lauritsen, "Racial and Ethnic Difference in Judicial Offending," in *Our Children, Their Children*, pp. 91–95.
78 Ibid.
79 Bishop, "The Role of Race and Ethnicity in Juvenile Justice Processing."
80 Carl E. Pope and William Feyerherm, *Minorities and the Juvenile Justice System* (Washington, D.C.: Office of Juvenile Justice and Delinquency Prevention, 1995), pp. 2–3.
81 Ibid. See also Donna M. Bishop and Charles E. Frazier, *A Study of Race and Juvenile Processing in Florida, Report Submitted to the Florida Supreme Court Racial and Ethnic Bias Study Commission, 1990*; and Carl E. Pope, Rick Ovell, and Heidi M. Hsia, *Disproportionate Minority Confinement: A Review of the Research Literature from 1989 Through 2001* (Washington, D.C.: Office of Juvenile Justice and Delinquency Prevention, 2002).
82 Harold M. Snyder and Melissa Sickmund, *Juvenile Offenders and Victims: 2006 National Report* (Washington, D.C.: National Center for Juvenile Justice, 2006).
83 James C. Howell, ed., *Guide for Implementing the Comprehensive Strategy for Serious Violent, and Chronic Juvenile Offenders* (Washington, D.C.: Office of Juvenile Justice and Delinquency Prevention, 1995).
84 Ibid.
85 Ibid.
86 Ibid.
87 Ibid.
88 Ibid.
89 Kathleen Coolbaugh and Cynthia J. Hansel, "The Comprehensive Strategy: Lessons Learned from the Pilot Sites," *Juvenile Justice Bulletin* (2000).
90 Ibid.
91 M. Coates, R. Coates, and B. Vos, "The Impact of Victim–Offender Mediation—Two Decades of Research," *Federal Probation* 65 (2001), pp. 29–36.
92 Katherine van Wormer and Clemens Bartollas, *Women and the Criminal Justice System* (Boston: Allyn and Bacon, 2007).
93 Lawrence W. Sherman, David P. Farrington, and Brandon Welsh, *Understanding and Implementing Correctional Options That Work* (Harrisburg: Pennsylvania Department of Corrections, 2003).
94 Ibid.

Chapter 12, Police and the Juvenile

1 "Police Forced to Pepper Spray Unruly Second-Grader; Mother Claims Excessive Force," *The Daily Mail*, April 6, 2011. Web posted at Police Link, http://policelink.monster.com/news/articles/152776-police-forced-to-pepper-spray-unruly-second-grader-mother-claims-excessive-force?utm_source=nlet&utm_content=pl_c1_20110407_pepperspray_mem (accessed April 7, 2011).
2 L. Thomas Winfree Jr. and Curt T. Griffiths, "Adolescents' Attitudes Toward the Police: A Survey of High School Students," in *Juvenile Delinquency: Little Brother Grows Up* (Beverly Hills: Sage, 1977), pp. 79–99.
3 William T. Rusinko, W. Johnson Knowlton, and Carlton A. Hornung, "The Importance of Police Contact in the Formulation of Youths' Attitudes Toward Police," *Journal of Criminal Justice* 6 (1978), pp. 53–76; J. P. Clark and

E. P. Wenninger, "The Attitudes of Juveniles Toward the Legal Institution," *Journal of Criminal Law, Criminology, and Police Science* 55 (1964), pp. 482–489; D. C. Gibbons, *Delinquent Behavior* (Englewood Cliffs: Prentice-Hall, 1976); and V. I. Cizanckas and C. W. Purviance, "Changing Attitudes of Black Youths," *Police Chief* 40 (1973), pp. 42–45.

4. Scott H. Decker, "Citizen Attitudes Toward the Police: A Review of Past Findings and Suggestions for Future Policy," *Journal of Police Science and Administration* 9 (1981), pp. 80–87.

5. Komanduri S. Murty, Julian B. Roebuck, and Joann D. Smith, "The Image of Police in Black Atlanta Communities," *Journal of Police Science and Administration* 17 (1990), pp. 250–257.

6. Michael J. Leiber, Mahesh K. Nalla, and Margaret Farnworth, "Explaining Juveniles' Attitudes Toward the Police," *Justice Quarterly* 15 (March 1998), pp. 151–174.

7. Susan Guarino-Ghezzi and Bryan Carr, "Juvenile Offenders v. the Police: A Community Dilemma," *Caribbean Journal of Criminology and Social Psychology* 1 (July 1996), pp. 24–43.

8. Yolander G. Hurst, "Juvenile Attitudes Toward the Police," *Criminal Justice Review* 32 (2007), pp. 121–141.

9. Terry Nihart et al., "Kids, Cops, Parents and Teachers: Exploring Juvenile Attitudes Toward Authority Figures," *Western Criminology Review* 6 (2005), pp. 79–88.

10. Yolander G. Hurst, "Juvenile Attitudes Toward the Police: An Examination of Rural Youth, *Criminal Justice Review*, Vol. 32, No. 2 (June 2007), pp. 121–141.

11. Elena T. Broddus et al., "Building Connections Between Officers and Baltimore City Youth: Key Components of a Police-Youth Teambuilding Programs," *OJJDP Journal of Juvenile Justice*, 3 (Fall 2013), pp. 48–63, from which some of the wording in this section is adapted.

12. James Q. Wilson, "Dilemmas of Police Administration," *Police Administration Review* 28 (September–October 1968), pp. 407–417.

13. Stephanie M. Myers, *Police Encounters with Juvenile Suspects: Explaining the Use of Authority and Provision of Support* (Washington, D.C.: National Institute of Justice, 2004).

14. Donald J. Black and Albert J. Reiss, Jr., "Police Control of Juveniles," *American Sociological Review* 35 (February 1979), pp. 63–77.

15. Robert M. Terry, "Discrimination in the Handling of Juvenile Offenders by Social Control Agencies," *Journal of Research in Crime and Delinquency* 4 (July 1967), pp. 218–230; Nathan Goldman, *The Differential Selection of Juvenile Offenders for Court Appearance* (New York: National Council on Crime and Delinquency 1963); Black and Reiss, "Police Control of Juveniles"; and Irving Piliavin and Scott Briar, "Police Encounters with Juveniles," *American Journal of Sociology* 70 (September 1964), pp. 206–214.

16. Terry et al., "Discrimination in the Handling of Juvenile Offenders"; Black and Weiss, "Police Control of Juveniles"; and Robert M. Emerson, *Judging Delinquents: Context and Process in Juvenile Court* (Chicago: Aldine, 1969).

17. Gail Armstrong, "Females Under the Law—Protected but Unequal," *Crime and Delinquency* 23 (April 1977), pp. 109–120; Meda Chesney-Lind, "Judicial Paternalism and the Female Status Offender," *Crime and Delinquency* 23 (April 1977), pp. 121–130; and Meda Chesney-Lind, "Girls and Status Offenses: Is Juvenile Justice Still Sexist?" *Criminal Justice Abstracts* (March 1988), pp. 144–165.

18. Meda Chesney-Lind, "Juvenile Delinquency: The Sexualization of Female Crime," *Psychology Today* 8 (July 1974), pp. 43–46; and I. Richard Perleman, "Antisocial Behavior of the Minor in the United States," in Harwin L. Voss, ed., *Society, Delinquency, and Delinquent Behavior* (Boston: Little, Brown, 1970), pp. 35–43.

19. Theodore N. Ferdinand and Elmer C. Luchterhand, "Inner-City Youths, the Police, the Juvenile Court, and Justice," *Social Problems* 17 (Spring 1970), pp. 510–527; Goldman, *The Differential Selection of Juvenile Offenders for Court Appearance*; and Irving Piliavin and Scott Briar, "Police Encounters with Juveniles," *American Journal of Sociology* 70 (September 1964), pp. 206–214.

20. Philip W. Harris, "Race and Juvenile Justice: Examining the Impact of Structural and Policy Changes on Racial Disproportionality," paper presented at the 39th Annual Meeting of the American Society of Criminology, Montreal, Quebec, Canada, November 13, 1987.

21. James T. Carey et al., *The Handling of Juveniles from Offense to Disposition* (Washington, D.C.: U.S. Government Printing Office, 1976); A. W. McEachern and Riva Bauzer, "Factors Related to Disposition in Juvenile–Police Contacts," in Malcolm W. Klein, ed., *Juvenile Gangs in Context* (Englewood Cliffs: Prentice-Hall, 1967), pp. 148–160; Thorsten Sellin and Marvin E. Wolfgang, *The Measurement of Delinquency* (New York: John Wiley & Sons, 1964); and Ferdinand and Luchterhand, "Inner-City Youths."

22. Merry Morash, "Establishment of Juvenile Police Record," *Criminology* 22 (February 1984), pp. 97–111.

23. Piliavin and Briar, "Police Encounters with Juveniles," pp. 206–214; Carl Werthman and Irving Piliavin, "Gang Members and Police," in David Jo. Bordua, ed., *The Police* (New York: Wiley, 1967), pp. 56–98; and Richard J. Lundman, Richard E. Sykes, and John P. Clark, "Police Control of Juveniles: A Replication," *Journal of Research in Crime and Delinquency* 15 (January 1978), pp. 74–91.

24. Robert E. Worden and Robin L. Shepard, "Demeanor, Crime, and Police Behavior: A Reexamination of the Police Services Study Data," *Criminology* 34 (1996), pp. 83–105.

25. Goldman, *The Differential Selection of Juvenile Offenders for Court Appearance*.

26. Wilson, "Dilemmas of Police Administration."

27. Ibid.

28. The following section is based on H. Ted Rubin, *Juvenile Justice: Police Practice and Law* (Santa Monica: Goodyear, 1979), pp. 75–82.

29 *Mapp* v. *Ohio*, 367 U.S. 643 (1961).

30 *State* v. *Lowry*, 230 A. 2d 907 (1967).

31 *In re Two Brothers and a Case of Liquor*, Juvenile Court of the District of Columbia, 1966, reported in *Washington Law Reporter* 95 (1967), p. 113.

32 *Ciullo* v. *State*, 434 S.W. ed 948 (Tex. Civ App. 1968).

33 Ibid.

34 *Haley* v. *Ohio*, 332 U.S. 596 (1948).

35 Ibid.

36 *Brown* v. *Mississippi*, 399 F.2d 467 (5th Cir. 1968).

37 Samuel M. Davis, *Rights of Juveniles: The Juvenile Justice System*, 2nd ed. (New York: Thompson, 2005), Sections 3–45.

38 *Miranda* v. *Arizona*, 384 U.S. 436 (1966).

39 *In re Gault*, 387 U.S. (1967).

40 *Fare* v. *Michael C.*, 442 U.S. 23, 99 S.Ct. 2560 (1979).

41 T. Grisso, *Juveniles' Waiver of Rights: Legal and Psychological Competence* (New York: Plenum Press, 1981).

42 *People* v. *Lara*, 62 Cal. Rptr. 586 (1967); cert. denied, 392 U.S. 945 (1968).

43 *In re Mellot*, 217 S.E. 2d 745 (C.A.N. Ca. 1975).

44 *In re Dennis P. Fletcher*, 248 A.2d. 364 (Md. 1968); cert. denied, 396 U.S. 852 (1969).

45 *Commonwealth* v. *Guyton*, 405 Mass. 497 (1989).

46 *Commonwealth* v. *McNeil*, 399 Mass. 71 (1987).

47 Gisli H. Gudjonsson, Jon Fridrik Sigurdsson, Inga Dora Sigfusdottir, and Bryndis Bjork Asgeirsdottir, "False Confession and Individual Differences: The Importance of Victimization Among Youth," *Personality and Individual Differences* 45 (2008), pp. 801–805.

48 *J.D.B.* v. *North Carolina*, 564 U.S. _____ (2011).

49 Elyce Z. Ferster and Thomas F. Courtless, "The Beginning of Juvenile Justice, Police Practices, and the Juvenile Offender," *Vanderbilt Law Review* 22 (April 1969), pp. 598–601.

50 Howard N. Snyder and Melissa Sickmund, *Juvenile Offenders and Victims*, 2006 National Report (Washington D.C.: National Center for Juvenile Justice, Office of Juvenile Justice and Delinquency Prevention, 2006).

51 *United States* v. *Wade* 388 U.S. 218, 87 S.Ct. 1926 (1967).

52 *Kirby* v. *Illinois*, 406, U.S. 682 (1972).

53 In re Holley, 107 R.I. 615, 268 A.2d 723 (1970).

54 Howard N. Snyder and Melissa Sickmund, *Juvenile Offenders and Victims 2006 National Report* (Washington, D.C.: National Center for Juvenile Justice; Office of Juvenile Justice and Delinquency Prevention).

55 *In re Carl T.*, 81 Rpt 655 (2d A, 1969).

56 Office of Justice Programs, "America's Missing: Broadcast Emergency Response: Frequently Asked Questions on AMBER Alert," http://www.amberalert.gov/faqs.htm (accessed August 3, 2014).

57 Snyder and Sickmund, *Juvenile Offenders and Victims: 1999*.

58 Howard N. Snyder and Melissa Sickmund, *Juvenile Offenders and Victims: 2006 National Report* (Washington, D.C.: National Center for Juvenile Justice, Office of Juvenile Justice and Delinquency Prevention, 2006).

59 See Mark S. Hamm, *American Skinheads: The Criminology and Control of Hate Crime* (Westport: Praeger, 1993).

60 Snyder and Sickmund, *Juvenile Offenders and Victims: 2006 National Report*.

61 G.R.E.A.T., "A History of the G.R.E.A.T. Program," 2012, http://www.great.ca-org/Organization/History.Aspx (accessed on June 12, 2012).

62 F. A. Esbensen and D. W. Osgood, "Gang Resistance Education and Training (G.R.E.A.T.): Results from the National Evaluation," *Journal of Research in Crime and Delinquency* 36 (1999), pp. 194–225; F. A. Esbensen, D. W. T. J. Taylor, D. Peterson, and A. Frenger, "How Great Is G.R.E.A.T.: Results from a Longitudinal Quasi-Experimental Design," *Criminology and Public Policy* 1 (2001), pp. 87–118; and J. Achcroft, D. J. Daniels, and S. V. Hart, *Evaluating G.R.E.A.T.: A School-Based Gang Prevention Program* (Washington, D.C.: US. Department of Justice, 2004).

63 Norman D. Wright, "From Risk to Resiliency: The Role of Law-Related Education," Institute on Law and Civil Education pamphlet (Des Moines, Iowa, June 20–21, 1995).

64 Judith Warrent Little and Frances Haley, *Implementing Effective LRE Programs* (Boulder: Social Science Education Consortium, 1982).

65 William DeJong, *Arresting the Demand for Drugs: Police and School Partnership to Prevent Drug Abuse* (Washington, D.C.: National Institute of Justice, 1987).

66 *COPS in Schools: The COPS Commitment to School Safety* (Washington, D.C.: Office of Community-Oriented Policing Services, n.d.). For how police resource officers spend their time, see Richard Lawrence, "The Role of Police–School Liaison Officers in School Crime Prevention," paper presented at the Annual Meeting of the Academy of Criminal Justice Sciences, Albuquerque, New Mexico, March 11, 1998.

67 Ronald D. Stephens, "School-Based Interventions: Safety and Security," in Arnold P. Goldstein and Ronald C. Huff, *The Gang Intervention Handbook* (Champaign: Research Press, 1999), pp. 219–256.

68 Jerome A. Needle and William Vaughn Stapelton, "Police Handling of Youth Gangs," in *Reports of the National Juvenile Justice Assessment Centers* (Washington, D.C.: U.S. Department of Justice, 1983).

69 Ibid.

70 National Institute of Justice, *The D.A.R.E. Program: A Review of Prevalence, User Satisfaction, and Effectiveness* (Washington, D.C.: U.S. Department of Justice, 1994).

71 Dennis P. Rosenbaum, "Just Say No to D.A.R.E.," *Crime and Public Policy* 6 (2007), pp. 815–824.

72 Ibid.

73 Ibid.

Chapter 13, Juvenile Court

1. Details for this story come from Michael Rubinkam, "Pa. Judge Guilty of Racketeering in Kickback Case," AOL News, February 18, 2011, http://www.aolnews.com/2011/02/18/former-pa-judge-mark-ciavarella-guilty-of-racketeering-in-kick (accessed April 10, 2011).
2. See, Gustav L. Schramm, "Philosophy of the Juvenile Court," *Annals of the American Academy of Political and Social Science*, Vol. 261, *Juvenile Delinquency* (Jan. 1949), p. 101.
3. Barry Krisberg, *The Juvenile Court: Reclaiming the Vision* (San Francisco: National Council on Crime and Delinquency, 1988); Arnold Binder, "The Juvenile Court: The U.S. Constitution, and When the Twain Shall Meet," *Journal of Criminal Justice* 12 (1982), pp. 355–366; and Charles E. Springer, *Justice for Children* (Washington, D.C.: U.S. Department of Justice, 1986).
4. Lisa Aversa Richette, *The Throwaway Children* (New York: Lippincott, 1969); Patrick Murphy, *Our Kindly Parent—The State* (New York: Viking Press, 1974); Howard James, *Children in Trouble: A National Scandal* (New York: Pocket Books, 1971); and William Ayers, *A Kind and Just Parent* (Boston: Beacon Press, 1997).
5. Dean J. Champion, "Teenage Felons and Waiver Hearings: Some Recent Trends, 1980–1988," *Crime and Delinquency* 35 (October 1985), pp. 439–479.
6. Barry C. Feld, *Bad Kids: Race and the Transformation of Juvenile Court* (New York: Oxford University Press, 1999).
7. Ibid.
8. Frederic L. Faust and Paul J. Brantingham, eds., *Juvenile Justice Philosophy* (St. Paul: West, 1974).
9. *In re Gault*, 387 U.S. 1, 18 L.Ed.2d 527, 87 S.Ct. 1428 (1967).
10. *In re Winship*, 397 U.S. 358, 90 S.Ct. 1968, 25 L.Ed.2d 368 (1970).
11. *McKeiver* v. *Pennsylvania*, 403 U.S. 528, 535 (1971); *In re Barbara Burrus*, 275 N.C. 517, 169 S.E.2d 879 (1969); and *In re Terry*, 438 Pa., 339, 265A.2d 350 (1970).
12. *McKeiver* v. *Pennsylvania*.
13. Barry Feld, "Violent Youth and Public Policy: Minnesota Juvenile Justice Task Force and 1994 Legislative Reform," paper presented at the Annual Meeting of the American Society of Criminology, Miami, Florida, 1994.
14. *Breed* v. *Jones*, 421 U.S. 519, 95 S.Ct. 1779 (1975).
15. H. Ted Rubin, *Juvenile Justice: Policy, Practice, and Law* (Santa Monica: Goodyear Publishing, 1979).
16. See Charles Thomas and Ineke Marshall, "The Effect of Legal Representation on Juvenile Court Disposition," paper presented at the Southern Sociological Society in Louisville, April 8–11, 1981. Also see S. H. Clarke and G. G. Koch, "Juvenile Court: Therapy or Crime Control and Do Lawyers Make a Difference?" *Law and Society Review* 14 (1980), pp. 263–308.
17. Charles Puzzanchera and Crystal Robson, *Juvenile Court Statistics 2010* (Washington, D.C.: OJJDP, 2014).
18. Brenda R. McCarthy, "An Analysis of Detention," *Juvenile and Family Court Journal* 36 (1985), pp. 43–59. For other discussions of detention, see Lydia Rosner, "Juvenile Secure Detention," *Journal of Offender Counseling, Services, and Rehabilitation* 12 (1988), pp. 77–93; and Charles E. Frazier and Donna M. Bishop, "The Pretrial Detention of Juveniles and Its Impact on Case Disposition," *Journal of Criminal Law and Criminology* 76 (1985), pp. 1132–1152.
19. *Creek* v. *Stone*, 379 F.2d 106 (D.C. Cir. 1967).
20. *Schall* v. *Martin*, 467 U.S. 253 (1984).
21. Ibid.
22. Duran Bell, Jr., and Kevin Lang, "The Intake Dispositions of Juvenile Offenders," *Journal of Research on Crime and Delinquency* 22 (1985), pp. 309–328. See also Randall G. Sheldon and John A. Horvath, "Intake Processing in a Juvenile Court: A Comparison of Legal and Nonlegal Variables," *Juvenile and Family Court Journal* 38 (1987), pp. 13–19.
23. Puzzanchera and Robson, *Juvenile Court Statistics 2010*, from which the data in this paragraph are taken.
24. Bell and Lang, "The Intake Dispositions of Juvenile Offenders."
25. Charles Puzzanchera, Benjamin Adams, and Sarah Hochenberry, l., *Juvenile Court Statistics 2009*. Pittsburgh: National Center for Juvenile Justice, 2012.
26. Megan C. Kurlychek and Brian D. Johnson, "Juvenility and Punishment: Sentencing Juveniles in Adult Criminal Court," *Criminology* 48 (2010), pp. 725–757. See also Brian D. Johnson and Megan Kurlychek, "Transferred Juveniles in the Era of Sentencing Guidelines: Examining Judicial Departures for Juvenile Offenders in Adult Criminal Court," *Criminology*, 50 (May 2012), pp. 525–564.
27. Emily Gaarder and Joanne Belknap, "Tenuous Borders: Girls Transferred to Adult Court," *Criminology* (August 2002), pp. 481–517.
28. Charles W. Thomas and Shay Bilchik, "Prosecuting Juveniles in Criminal Courts: A Legal and Empirical Analysis," *Journal of Criminal Law and Criminology* 76 (Summer 1985), pp. 439–479.
29. Barry C. Feld, "The Juvenile Court Meets the Principle of the Offense: Legislative Changes in Juvenile Waiver Statutes," *Journal of Criminal Law and Criminology* 78 (1987), pp. 471–503.
30. Barry C. Feld, "Legislative Policies Toward the Serious Juvenile Offender," *Crime and Delinquency* 27 (October 1981), pp. 497–521.
31. Samuel M. Davis, *Rights of Juveniles: The Juvenile Justice System*, 2nd ed. (New York: Clark Boardman Company, 1986), Section 4-2. See also Melissa Sickmund, *How Juveniles Get to Juvenile Court* (Washington, D.C.: Juvenile Justice Bulletin, 1994).
32. Davis, *Rights of Juveniles*.
33. Marcy R. Podkopacz and Barry C. Feld, "The End of the Line: An Empirical Study of Judicial Waiver," *Journal of Criminal Law and Criminology* 86 (1996), pp. 449–492.

34 Lee Ann Osburn and Peter A Rose, "Prosecuting Juveniles as Adults: The Question for 'Objective' Decisions," *Criminology* 22 (1984), pp. 187–202.

35 Megan C. Kurlychek and Brian D. Johnson, "Juvenility and Punishment: Sentencing Juveniles in Adult Criminal Court," *Criminclogy* 48 (August 2010), pp. 725–758.

36 Puzzanchera and Robson, *Juvenile Court Statistics 2010*.

37 For example, in the laws of Pennsylvania, Act No. 333 (Section 18a) requires a hearing date within 10 days after the filing of a petition.

38 Rubin, *Juvenile Justice*.

39 Davis, *Rights of Juveniles*.

40 Ibid.

41 Feld, *Bad Kids*.

42 Barry Feld, "Violent Youth and Public Policy."

43 Richard E. Redding, "Juvenile Transfer Laws: An Effective Deterrent to Delinquency?" OJJDP Juvenile Justice Bulletin (August 2008), pp. 5-6.

44 "Death in Prison Sentences for 13- and 14-Year-Olds," http://www.cji.org/eji/childrenprison/deathinprison.

45 Associated Press, "High Court Looks at Life in Prison for Juveniles," http://www.msnbc.msn.com/id/33789880/ns/politics-more_politics/?gt1=43001 (accessed January 2, 2011).

46 National Council of Juvenile and Family Court Judges, *Juvenile Delinquency Guidelines: Improving Court Practice in Juvenile Delinquency Cases* (Reno: National Council of Juvenile and Family Court Judges, 2005).

Chapter 14, Juvenile Corrections

1 Christopher Murray, Chris Baird, Ned Loughran, Fred Mills, and John Platt, *Safety and Welfare Plan: Implementing Reform in California* (Sacramento: California Department of Corrections and Rehabilitation, Division of Juvenile Justice, 2006).

2 David W. Springer, *Transforming Juvenile Justice in Texas: A Framework for Action* (Austin: Blue Ribbon Task Force Report, 2007).

3 "Juvenile School Would Grow," *Hartford Courant*, February 10, 2008; Alison Leigh Cowan, "New Connecticut Law May Save a Troubled Prison for Juveniles," *New York Times*, July 30, 2007; Christine Smart, "Juvenile Injustice," *CT News Junkie*, July 19, 2006; and Nan Shnitzler, "Connecticut Juvenile Training School to Close," *New England Psychologist*, October 2005, http://www.mnasspsy.com/leading/0510_ne_CT.html (accessed November 12, 2011).

4 Holbrook Mohr, "18 Cruelty and Death in Juvenile Detention Centers," *Associated Press*, March 2, 2008.

5 Ibid.

6 Patrick Griffin and Patricia Torbet, eds., *Desktop Guide to Good Juvenile Probation Practice* Washington, D.C.: National Center for Juvenile Justice, 2002), p. 2.

7 Ibid.

8 Ibid.

9 Ibid.

10 OJJDP Model Program Guide, *Restitution/Community Service*, http://www.dsgonline.com/mpg_non_flash/restitution?community?service.htm.

11 Ibid.

12 See James Byrne, Arthur Lurigio, and Joan Petersilia, "Smart Sentencing: The Emergence of Intermediate Sanctions," *Federal Probation* 50 (1986), pp. 166–181; and Emily Walker, "The Community Intensive Treatment for Youth Program: A Specialized Community-Based Program for High-Risk Youth in Alabama," *Law and Psychology Review* 13 (1989), pp. 175–199.

13 Barry Krisberg et al., *Juvenile Intensive Planning Guide* (Washington, D.C.: Office of Juvenile Justice and Delinquency Prevention, 1994).

14 TDCJ-Community Justice Assistance Division, *Electronic Monitoring: Agency Brief* (Austin: Texas Department of Criminal Justice, 1997).

15 Joseph B. Vaughn, "A Survey of Juvenile Electronic Monitoring and Home Confinement Program," *Juvenile and Family Court Journal* 40 (1989), pp. 1–36.

16 Ibid.

17 Oliver J. Keller, Jr., and Benedict S. Alper, *Halfway Houses: Community-Centered Correction and Treatment* (Lexington: D.C. Heath, 1970).

18 Refer to Joshua L. Miner and Joe Boldt, *Outward Bound USA: Learning Through Experience* (New York: William Morrow, 1981). For other examinations of Outward Bound–type programs, see Steven Flagg Scott, "Outward Bound: An Adjunct to the Treatment of Juvenile Delinquents: Florida's STEP Program," *New England Journal on Criminal and Civil Confinement* 11 (1985), pp. 420–436; and Thomas C. Castellano and Irina R. Soderstrom, "Wilderness Challenges and Recidivism: A Program Evaluation," paper presented at the Annual Meeting of the American Society of Criminology, Baltimore, Maryland, November 1990.

19 Outward Bound USA, http://www.outwardbound.org.

20 Howard N. Snyder and Melissa Sickmund, *Juvenile Offenders and Victims: 2006 National Report* (Washington, D.C.: National Center for Juvenile Justice, Office of Justice Programs, 2006).

21 Data in this paragraph come from Sarah Hockenberry, *Juveniles in Residential Placement, 2010* (Washington, D.C.: OJJDP, 2013).

22 Murray et al., *Safety and Welfare Plan: Implementing Reform in California*.

23 Bryan Robinson, "Boy's Death Revives Boot Camp Debate," *ABC News*, July 12, 2009, http://abcnews.go.com/US?story?id=92908&page=1 (accessed October 8, 2011).

24 Alexandra Marks, "States Fall Out of (Tough) Love with Boot Camps." Christian Science Monitor, December 27, 1999, p. 1.

25. For the diverse forms of state juvenile institutionalization, see Kelly Dedel, "National Profile of the Organization of Juvenile Correctional Systems," *Crime and Delinquency* 44 (1998), pp. 507–525.
26. Bradford Smith, "Children in Custody: 20-Year Trends in Juvenile Detention, Correctional, and Shelter Facilities," *Crime and Delinquency* 44 (October 1998), pp. 526–543.
27. Randall G. Sheldon and Sharon Tracey, "Violent Female Juvenile Offenders: An Ignored Minority with the Juvenile Justice System," *Juvenile and Family Court Journal* 43 (1992), pp. 33–40.
28. See, for example, Gordon E. Barker and W. Thomas Adams, "The Social Structure of a Correctional Institution," *Journal of Criminal Law, Criminology and Police Science* 49 (1959), pp. 417–499; Howard Polsky, *Cottage Six: The Social System of Delinquent Boys in Residential Treatment* (New York: Russell Sage Foundation, 1963), pp. 69–88; Clemens Bartollas, Stuart J. Miller, and Simon Dinitz, *Juvenile Victimization: The Institutional Paradox* (New York: Halsted Press, 1976), pp. 131–150; and M. Forst, J. Fagan, and T. S. Vivona, "Youth in Prisons and Training Schools: Perceptions and Consequences of the Treatment-Custody Dichotomy," *Juvenile and Family Court Journal* 40 (1989), pp. 1–14.
29. See, for example, Richard Tewksbury, "What We Know About Sexual Violence in Juvenile Corrections," paper presented at the 2007 Winter Conference, Grapevine, Texas; A. Sedlack, "Sexual Assault of Youth in Residential Placement," presentation at Bureau of Justice Statistics Workshop, Washington, D.C., January 18, 2005; and A. J. Beck and T. A. Hugher, *Sexual Violence Reported by Correctional Authorities 2004* (Washington, D.C.: Bureau of Justice Statistics, 2005).
30. Tewksbury, "What We Know About Sexual Violence in Juvenile Corrections."
31. Christopher M. Sieverdes and Clemens Bartollas, "Institutional Adjustment Among Female Delinquents," in Alvin W. Cohn and Ben Ward, eds., *Administrative Issues in Criminal Justice* (Beverly Hills: Sage, 1981), pp. 91–103.
32. Ibid.
33. Clemens Bartollas and Christopher M. Sieverdes, "The Victimized White in a Juvenile Correctional System," *Crime and Delinquency* 34 (October 1981), pp. 534–543.
34. Patricia Puritz and Mary Ann Scali, *Beyond the Walls: Improving Conditions of Confinement for Youth in Custody: Report* (Washington, D.C.: Office of Juvenile Justice and Delinquency Prevention, 1998).
35. Patricia McFall Torbet, *Organization and Administration of Juvenile Services: Probation, Aftercare, and State Delinquent Institutions* (Pittsburgh: National Center for Juvenile Justice, 1988).
36. D. M. Altschuler and T. L. Armstrong, *Intensive Aftercare for High-Risk Juveniles: A Community Care Model* (Washington, D.C.: Office of Juvenile Justice and Delinquency Prevention, 1994).
37. Ted Palmer, *The Re-Emergence of Correctional Intervention* (Newbury Park: Sage, 1992), p. 82.
38. Altschuler and Armstrong, *Intensive Aftercare for High-Risk Juveniles: Policies and Procedures*.
39. For more extensive examination of these intensive aftercare programs, see Betsie McNulty, Richard Wiebush, and Thao Le, "Intensive Aftercare Programs for Serious Juvenile Offenders: Preliminary Results of Process and Outcome Evaluation," paper presented at the Annual Meeting of the American Society of Criminology, Washington, D.C., November 1998.
40. For an example of a house detention component of an aftercare program, see W. H. Barton and Jeffrey A. Butts, "Visible Options: Intensive Supervision Program for Juvenile Delinquents," *Crime and Delinquency* (1990), pp. 238–256.
41. Melissa Sickmund, *Juveniles in Corrections: National Report Series Bulletin* (Washington, D.C.: Office of Juvenile Justice and Delinquency Prevention, 2004).
42. Donna Hamparian et al., "Youth in Adult Court: Between Two Worlds," *Major Issues in Juvenile Justice Information and Training* (Columbus: Academy for Contemporary Problems, 1981).
43. Snyder and Sickmund, *Juvenile Offenders and Victims*.
44. Dedel, "National Profile of the Organization of State Juvenile Corrections Systems."
45. See *Criminal Justice Newsletter* (Letter Publications, 2008).
46. Joseph Heinz, Theresa Wise, and Clemens Bartollas, *Successful Management of Juvenile Residential Facilities: A Performance-Based Approach* (Washington, D.C.: American Correctional Association, 2010), pp. 43–44.

Name Index

A

Abram, Karen M., 168
Adler, Freda, 98
Agnew, Robert, 40, 63–64
Aichhorn, August, 46
Allen, Emilie, 93
Amedeo, Stephanie, 118
Anderson, Craig A., 114
Anderson, Elijah, 58
Aniwar, Shamena, 39
Arum, Richard, 139
Augustus, John, 177

B

Bartollas, Clemens, 236
Baskin, D. R., 103
Beattie, Irenee R., 139
Beck, Aaron T., 48
Becker, Howard, 78, 79
Belknap, Joanne, 95
Bell, Duran, Jr., 217
Belshaw, Scott, 64
Benning, J., 129
Bentham, Jeremy, 37, 38
Bernard, Thomas J., 63
Beyer, Marty, 95
Bjerregaard, Beth, 153
Bloch, Herbert A., 154
Bonesana, Cesare (Marquis of Beccaria), 37
Bouchard, Thomas, Jr., 42
Boyle, Greg, 156
Braithwaite, John, 80
Brame, Robert, 103
Brewer, Devon D., 166
Brinker, Gregory P., 71
Brockway, Zebulon, 177
Burke, Jeffrey, 47
Burnett, Kent, 43
Bynum, Tim, 150

C

Callahan, Charles M., 147
Carlie, Mike, 147
Carr, Bryan, 198
Casey, Annie E., 10
Catalano, Richard F., 166
Catherine T., 71, 72
Cauffman, Elizabeth, 45
Caulfield, Holden, 2
Cernkovich, Stephen A., 120, 168
Chambliss, William J., 84
Chen, Zeng-yin, 139
Chesney-Lind, Meda, 9, 92, 93, 99
Children Defense Fund (CDF), 5, 7
Christiansen, Karl O., 42
Clason, Dennis L., 168
Cleckley, Hervey, 47
Cloward, Richard A., 61, 65–66, 154
Coates, Julie, 5
Cohen, Albert K., 61, 64–65, 134, 154
Cohen, Lawrence E., 39
Colvin, Mark, 83
Cooley, Charles H., 82
Corrado, Raymond R., 47
Cortes, Juan B., 42
Couch, Ethan, 19
Covey, H. C., 102
Crawford, Lizabeth, 39
Cullen, Francis T., 98, 110

D

Dahrendorf, Ralf, 84
De Coster, Stacy, 98
Decker, Scott H., 150, 155, 197
Deschenes, Elizabeth Piper, 153
D'Escury, Annematt Collot, 43
Dewey, John, 2, 130
Draves, William A., 5
Dunford, Franklin W., 23

D'Unger, Amy C., 103
Durkheim, Emile, 58

E

Earls, Felton, 72
Edelman, Peter, 101
Edmonds, William, 43
Elliott, Delbert S., 23, 68–69, 129, 167
Erikson, Erik H., 3
Esbensen, Finn-Aage, 146, 153
Eysenck, Hans, 43

F

Fabiano, Elizabeth, 187
Fagan, Jeffrey, 39, 103, 166
Farnworth, Margaret, 197
Farrington, David P., 31, 49
Feld, Barry, 212
Feldhusen, J., 129
Felson, Marcus, 39
Fenster, Carol, 100
Ferracuti, Franco, 61
Feyerherm, William H., 190
Fogel, David, 184
Freud, Sigmund, 46
Friedlander, Kate, 46

G

Gartrell, John, 118
Gatti, Florence M., 42
Giordano, Peggy C., 93, 103, 120, 168
Glueck, Eleanor, 42, 47
Glueck, Sheldon, 42, 47
Goddard, Henry, 42
Goodman, L. A., 168
Gordon, Robert A., 43
Gottfredson, Michael R., 31, 68
Gottman, John, 113
Greene, Jack R., 135
Grisso, Thomas, 202
Guarino-Ghezzi, Susan, 198

H

Hagan, John, 84, 98
Hagedorn, John, 153

Hare, Robert D., 47
Harris, Judith Rick, 109
Hawkins, J. David, 31, 68, 70, 166, 167
Healy, William, 46
Heimer, Karen, 81, 93, 98
Herrnstein, Richard, 31, 46–47
Hewitt, John D., 84
Hindelang, Michael, 43
Hirschi, Travis, 31, 43, 67, 68, 133, 167
Holder, Eric H. Jr., 2
Holsinger, Kristi, 95
Hurst, Yolander G., 198

J

James, Jennifer, 98
Jarjoura, G. Roger, 71, 80
Jenkins, Patricia H., 135
John D., 71, 72
Johnson, Brian D., 217
Johnson, Kelly Dedel, 239
Johnson, Lyndon, 5
Jones, Nikki, 101

K

Kandel, Denise B., 165
Kaplan, Howard B., 139
Katz, Jack, 46
Katz, Rebecca S., 103
Kazemian, Lila, 31
Kennedy, Tom, 43
Kieffer, Keven M., 114
Kirk, David S., 23
Knox, George W., 147
Kohlberg, Lawrence, 48
Konopka, Gisela, 97
Koolhof, Roos, 43
Kretscher, Ernst, 42
Krohn, Marvin D., 168
Kruskal, W. H., 168
Kurlychek, Megan C., 217

L

Lang, Kevin, 217
LaRosa, John, 51
Laske, David, 147

Laub, John A., 13, 80, 139
Lauritsen, Janet L., 190
Leiber, Michael J., 197
Lemert, Edwin M., 78, 79
Leonard, Eileen, 93
Lewis, Diane, 102
Lipsey, Mark W., 189
Lizotte, Alan J., 168
Lloyd, Willie, 147
Loeber, Rolf, 29, 43, 47, 129
Lombroso, Cesare, 41
Loughran, Thomas, 39
Lynam, Donald R., 47, 49

M

Maguin, Eugene, 129
Mahoney, Anne R., 100
Mann, Horace, 130
Marx, Karl, 83
Maselko, Joanna, 12
Matsueda, Ross L., 81–82
Mause, Lloyd de, 2
Maxfield, Michael G., 115
McClelland, Gary M., 168
McKay, Henry D., 58
Mealey, Linda, 47
Mednick, S. A., 42
Merton, Robert K., 61, 62, 63
Messner, Steven, 63
Michaelowski, Raymond, 84
Miller, Jody, 154
Miller, Joshua D., 47
Miller, Walter B., 60–61, 154
Miner, Michael, 47
Moffitt, Terrie E., 30, 49, 103
Moore, Joan, 153
Moore, Lori D., 102
Morgan, M., 94
Mulvey, Edward, 51
Murrie, Daniel C., 47
Murty, Komanduri S., 197
Myers, Stephanie M., 198

N

Nagin, Daniel S., 31
Nalla, Mahesh K., 197
Neland, Jason, 47
Newkirk, Rahiem, 57
Niederhoffer, Arthur, 154
Nihart, Terry, 198
Novak, Katherine, 39
Nye, F. Ivan, 67

O

Ohlin, Lloyd E., 61, 65–66, 154
Olson, C. L., 114
Osgood, D. Wayne, 31, 39
Oshima, Karen Matta, 44

P

Padavic, Irene, 102
Pardini, Dustin, 43
Pasko, Lisa J., 9
Paternoster, Raymond, 31
Patton, P., 94
Pauly, John, 83
Perez, Cynthia M., 168
Perkins, Kevin, 92
Phelps, R. J., 100
Phillips, John C., 134
Piaget, Jean, 47
Pines, Ayala M., 100
Piquero, Alex R., 30, 39, 103
Platt, Anthony, 176
Pogarsky, Greg, 114
Pope, Carl E., 190
Pranis, Kay, 85

R

Raine, Adrian, 45
Raudenbush, Stephen, 72
Reckless, Walter C., 67
Redding, Richard E., 223
Regoli, Robert M., 84
Reiss, Albert J., 67
Reutter, E. Edmund, Jr., 136
Reyer, Jose, 78
Rietveld, M. J. H., 42
Rivara, Ira, 147
Robbins, R. N., 46
Robinson, Gwen, 86

Rodriguez, John, 64
Rodriguez, Nancy, 86
Roebuck, Julian B., 197
Rose, Tricia, 115
Rosenbaum, Dennis, 206–207
Rosenfeld, Richard, 63
Ross, Robert, 187
Rudolph, Jennifer L., 120

S

Salinger, J. D., 2
Salsich, Annie, 175
Sampson, John, 139
Sampson, Robert J., 31, 72, 80, 110
Sarri, Rosemary C., 100
Schreck, Christopher J., 31
Schroeder, Ryan D. 168
Schur, Edwin, 80
Schwartz, Wendy, 139
Schwendinger, Herman, 83
Schwendinger, Julia Siegel, 83
Secondat, Charles de
    (Baron de Montesquieu), 37
Sedwick, Rebecca Ann, 78
Sellers, Christine S., 168
Sellin, Thorsten, 84–85
Shapland, Joanna, 86
Shaw, Clifford R., 58–60
Sheldon, William, 42
Sheley, Joseph F., 147
Sieverdes, Christopher M., 236
Silbert, Mimi, 100
Silva, Phil A., 49
Simons, Ronald L., 43, 110
Slater, M. D., 46
Smith, Carolyn, 153
Smith, Joann D., 197
Sommers, I., 103
Spelman, Elizabeth V., 93, 102
Spergel, Irving, 155–156
Spring, Joel H., 129
Steffensmeier, Darrell, 93
Stevens, Jennifer, 47
Stinchcombe, Arthur L., 129
Stoddard-Dare, Patricia, 43

Straus, Murray A., 118
Sutherland, Edwin H., 65, 66, 79

T

Tannenbaum, Frank, 78, 79
Taylor, Carl S., 153
Teplin, Linda A., 168
Thornberry, Terence P., 68, 69, 71, 135, 155
Thorne, Barrie, 94
Thornton, William E., 98
Thurston, J., 129
Travis, Jeremy, 72
Tremblay, Richard E., 49
Triplett, Ruth Ann, 71, 80
Tromanhauser, Edward, 147
Turk, Austin T., 84

V

Vold, George B., 84, 85
Vorrath, Harry, 188
Voss, Harwin L., 129

W

Warner, D. W., 114
Watson, Liz, 101
Weber, Max, 84
Wei, Evelyn, 43
Weis, Joseph G., 43, 68, 70
Weisel, Deborah, 150
Welsh, Wayne N., 135
Widom, Cathy Spatz, 115
Wilson, James Q., 31, 46–47, 200
Winfree, L. Thomas, Jr., 153, 168
Winkle, Van, 155
Wolfgang, Marvin E., 43, 61
Wright, James D., 147
Wright, John Paul, 110

Y

Yablonsky, Lewis, 154

Z

Zimmerman, Gregory, 114

Subject Index

Note: Page numbers followed by *f* and t indicate figures and tables, respectively. Page numbers in **bold** indicate pages on which definitions appear.

A

abuse. *See* child abuse; sexual abuse
academic performance, **133**–134, 134*f*
Achievement Place, 232
Achieving Graduation for All (National Governors Association), 140
adaptation to anomie, types of, 62
addictive personality theory, 166
ADHD (attention deficit hyperactivity disorder), 43, 44, 44*f*
adjudication, **218**
adjudicatory hearings, 121, 182, **218**–219, 219*f*, 221*f*
adolescence, **3**
    bullying of, 78
    changing treatment of, 3–5
    culture of, 4–5
    defined, 3
    and delinquency, 1–14
    drug use in, 160–162
    high-risk behaviors of, 6–7
    at risk, 5–7
    as status offenders, 8–10
    treatment of, 4t
adolescent-limited (AL) offenders, **49**
adopted child, 113
adoption studies, 42–43
adult court. *See also* transfer procedure
    defined, **217**
    integration of juvenile court with, 212
adult facilities, 220
adulthood, youth crimes and criminality in, 31–32
adult justice system, 183–184, 184t
adult prisons, juveniles in, 239, 239*f*
African-American females
    desistance process among, 103
    discrimination against, 102
African-American gangs, 152

African-American males
    behavioral aggression, 43
    variants of genes, 43
aftercare
    administration and operation of, 237–239
    defined, **177**, 236
    juvenile, 236–239
    objectives of, 237*f*
    overview of, 236–237
    revocation of, 238
age groups
    child abuse and, 118
    crime by, 20–22
    sexual assault victimization rates by, 25*f*
age of onset
    defined, **29**
    specialization of offenses and, 30–31
aggressive behavior and violent video games, 114
alcohol, **162**
alternative schools, **140**
alternatives, judicial, 220, 221*f*
AMBER Alert system, 204
amphetamines, **163**–164
anabolic steroids, **164**, 165t
anomie, theory of, **62**, 62t
antisocial personality with conduct disorder, 47
aphasia, 44
appeal, **220**
appellate review, **221**
arrests
    defined, **201**
    by gender, 28*f*
    of juveniles, 20, 20*f*, 21, 21*f*
    by race, 28*f*
Asian gangs, 152–153
assessment of child abuse, 121
atavistic criminal theory, 41–42
attachment to conventional others, 67
attention deficit hyperactivity disorder (ADHD), **43**, 44, 44*f*

attention homes, **215**
attraction of gangs, 147, 148t
authoritarian conflict pathway to delinquent career, 29–30, 30f
autonomic nervous system, **43**

B

bail, **216**
Baker v. Owen, 136
balanced and restorative justice model, 169, 184–185, 185f
behavioral modification, **187**
behavioral therapy, 187
beliefs and social bond, 68
"best interest of the child" standard, 212
Bethel School District No. 403 v. Fraser, 136, 138t
beyond a reasonable doubt, **214**
bifurcated hearings, **219**
Big Brothers Big Sisters of America, 178
binding over, **218**
binge drinking, 162
biochemical factors, 44–45
biological explanations for female delinquency, 97
biological positivism, 41–42
biological theories, overview of, 48t
biosocial criminology, **45**
birth order, **110**
blended sentencing, **218**, 222f
blocked opportunity, **63**
blocked opportunity theory, 97, 134
Blueprints for Violence Prevention, 168–169, 178
Board of Education of Independent School District No. 92 of Pottawatomie County v. Earls, 137, 138t
body-type theory, 42
boot camps, **233–234**
born criminals, **41–42**
Boston Gun Project, 32
brain functioning and temperament, 43–44
Breed v. Jones, 214f, **215**, 218
broken homes, **109**
brother-sister incest, **119**
Brown v. Mississippi, 202
bullying
    defined, **131**
    in schools, 131–133
Bully Prevention Program, 178–179

C

Cambridge study, 49–50
capitalism, **83**
case closure, 121
case planning for child abuse, 121
cases referred by law enforcement, 201t
Caucasian gangs, 153
Causes of Delinquency (Hirschi), 67
certifications, 218
cessation of drug use, reasons for, 168
child abuse
    by age and sex, 116f
    defined, **115**
    definitions and severity ratings, 116t
    delinquency and, 119–120
    explanations for, 118–119
    extent and nature of problem, 117
    female delinquents and, 95–96, 99–100
    juvenile justice system and, 120–121, 122f
    nature of, 118–119
    neglect and, 115–120
    perpetrators of, 117
    prevention of, 121–123
    types of, 118
Child Abuse Prevention and Treatment Act, 117
childhood, concept of, 3
child labor laws, 6
child prostitution, 92
child protective services, 120
children's rights movement, 4
The Child Savers (Platt), 176
child savers, **176–177**
chivalry factor, **101**
chronic offending, 31
chronic violent offenders, 23
chronic youthful offenders, **31**
cigarette smoking, 162, 162f, 170
citations, **201**
citizen complaints, 199
Civil Rights of Institutionalized Persons Act (CRIPA), 236
class. *See* socioeconomic status
classical school of criminology, 37–38
classroom, self-esteem of girls in, 94
club drugs, 163, **164**
cocaine, **162**. *See also* crack cocaine
Code of the Streets (Anderson), 58

coeducational institutions, 236
coercive type of gang recruitment, 149f
cognitive-affective theories of drug use, 166
cognitive-behavioral therapy (CBT), **187**
cognitive theory, **47**–48
cognitive thinking skills program (CTSP), **187**
cohabitating parents, 113
cohort, **19**
cohort studies
    defined, **19**
    gender and delinquency, 27t
collective efficacy, 110
colonial period, 175–176
commitment
    to correctional facilities, **183**
    to gangs, 147
    to social bond, **68**, 68f
Commonwealth v. *Guyton*, 202
Communist Manifesto (Marx), 83
communities
    concentric zone hypothesis of urban growth, 58–59
    risk factors for delinquency and drug use in, 166
    small, gangs in, 150–152
    social disorganization of, 58–59
community-based corrections
    aftercare, 236–237, 237f
    defined, **229**
    emergence of, 177–178
    forms of, 229
    probation, 229–232
    residential and day treatment, 232–233
community-based interventions, 204, 233f
community-based residential programs, 220
community conferencing, 86
community-school relationships, 140
community volunteers, **232**
complaints, 199, **216**
Comprehensive Community-Wide Approach to Gang Prevention, Intervention, and Suppression Program, 156
concentric zone hypothesis of urban growth, 59, 59f
conduct disorder, antisocial personality with, 47
conduct norms, **84**–85
conflict subculture, 65
conflict theory
    defined, **83**
    dimensions of, 83–85

    evaluation of, 85
    perspectives on, 85t
    social policy, 86–87, 87f
conformity, 62
Connecticut Juvenile Training School, 229
consent decrees, **216**
constitutional explanations for female delinquency, 97
constitutionalists, **213**
containment theory, 67, 67t
contempt of court, 100
control
    of emotions and actions, 40
    of gangs, 155–156
control theory, **67**, 135
conviction experience and gender, 103
COPS in Schools program, 205
corporal punishment, 118, 137
correctional methods, 184–186, 185t
corrections system, 182
cottage systems, **178**
covert pathway to delinquent career, 29–30, 30f
crack, **145**
crack cocaine, 57
    epidemic of, 11
    street gangs and, 145
crime. *See also* violent crimes
    by age groups, 20–21, 20–22
    gangs and, 145, 149–150
    gendered, 94
    general theory of, 68, 69f, 135
    hate crimes, 12
    Internet-initiated, 114, 150
    maturing out of, 40, 50
    against property, 7, 21
    reporting of, 24–25
    trends in, 22, 24
    uniform reports of, 19–20
    victimization studies, 24–26
    and youth, 31–32
Crime and Human Nature (Wilson and Herrnstein), 46–47
Crime and the American Dream (Messner and Rosenfeld), 63
Crime and the Community (Tannenbaum), 79
crime-control model
    description of, **185**
    in schools, 140

Crime in the United States 2009 (FBI), 7
Crime in the United States 2010 (FBI), 19, 20–22, 27t
crime reduction
    aftercare and, 237–239
    probation and, 230–232
criminal subculture, 65
Crossen v. Fatsi, 135
crossover youth
    cross-system cases, 10
    dual jurisdiction cases, 10
    dully adjudicated youth, 10
cross-system cases, 10
cruel and unusual punishment, 223, **236**
cultural deviance theory, **60**–61, 61*f*, 62t
cultural learning theory, 70
culturally defined goals, **62**
cultural transmission theory, **59**–60
culture conflict theory, **84**, 85
cumulative disadvantage, 71
cyberbullying, **131**
cycling (steroid use pattern), 164

D

D.A.R.E. (Drug Abuse Resistance Education), 169, 205, 206–207
data sources
    Juvenile Court Statistics, 22
    major, 21t
    self-report studies, 22–24
    Uniform Crime Reporting Program, 19–21
    validity and reliability of, 20
    victimization studies, 24–26
day-treatment programs, 220, **232**
deaths at schools, 132t
decision making, moral development in, 48
Defending Childhood initiative, 2
deference and disposition of offenders, 199
deinstitutionalization of status offenders (DSO), **9**
delinquency. *See also* female delinquency; juvenile delinquency; life-course delinquency; social context of delinquency
    and adolescence, 1–14
    behaviors of, 9
    classical school of, 37–38
    comprehensive, 190–191
    contemporary treatment of, 10–11
    control of, 32–33, 50–51
    definition of, 7–8
    developmental theories of, 50–51
    dimensions of, 32t
    families and, 108–123
    as female, 95–99
    gender roles and, 26, 91–104
    individual causes of, 36–51
    across life course, 12–13, 70–71, 103, 121, 139, 155, 167–168, 206, 222–223, 239–240
    major data sources in, 19–26
    measurement and nature of, 18–35
    positivism and, 40–48
    prevention of, 12, 32–33, 40, 50–51, 102–103, 121–123, 190–191
    race and, 26–28, 82
    rationality and, 38–40
    related social factors of, 26–29
    role taking and, 81–82
    social class and, 28–29
    social context of, 85–86, 94–95, 109–113
    and social policy, 13–14, 71–72, 86–87, 104, 121–123, 139–140, 155–156, 168–170, 206–207, 223, 240
    themes of, 12–14
    transitions and, 110–112
delinquency prevention, 32–33, **178**–179, 190–191
Delinquent Boys (Cohen), 64, 65
delinquent sibling, **110**
delinquent subculture theory, 64–65, 65*f*
delinquent youth, 7–**8**
demeanor and disposition of offenders, 199
departmental policy and disposition of offenders, 200
desistance
    defined, **50**
    among women, 103
detention, **201**
detention centers, **215**
detention hearings, **215**–216, 215*f*
determinate sentencing, **221**
determinism, 37, **41**
deterrence/rational choice model, 39, 98
developmental life-course (DLC) theory. *See also* life-course delinquency
    criminal career features, 29
    desistance and, 50–51
    overview of, **12**–14, 15
developmental studies, 49–50, 50t

deviant careers, 79
dialectics, 83
diet and delinquency, 44–45
differential association theory
    of delinquency, **66**–67, 66f
    of female delinquency, 98
differential opportunity structure, **59**
differential oppression theory, **84**
discipline
    in home, 110
    in school, 137–139
discrimination
    against female status offenders, 100–101
    against minorities, 189–190
dismissal of complaints, 216, 220
disposal of cases, 216–217
disposition hearings, 183, **219**–**220**, 221f
dispositions
    factors influencing, 198–200, 199t
    informal and formal, 200–201
disproportionate minority confinement (DMC), **190**
disruptive behavior, **140**
diversion from juvenile justice system, 179–181, 180f
diversion programs, **179**
diversity of juvenile population, 5
Dixon v. *Alabama State Board of Education*, 136, 138t
dopamine receptor gene (DRD4), 43
double jeopardy, **215**
double standard, sexual, 100
dramatization of evil process, 79
dress codes in schools, 136
drive-by shootings, 149
dropouts, **139**
dropping out of school, 139
Drug Abuse Resistance Education (D.A.R.E.), 169, 205, 206–207
drug addiction, **162**
drug arrests, 21–22
drug courts, 169
drug-free zones, 136–137
drugs and gangs
    in schools, 149
    sell of, 57
    in small communities, 150–152
drug use and abuse
    among adolescents, 160–162
    definition of, 160

    delinquency and, 165–166
    explanations for onset of, 166–167
    by frequency, 165t
    in high school, 161t
    across life course, 167–168
    social policy to control, 168–170, 170t
    types of drugs, 162–165
dual jurisdiction cases, 10
due process rights, **136**
dully adjudicated youth, 10
dyslexia, 44

E

early death, anticipation of, 6
economic analysis of criminal behavior, 38
economic marginalization thesis, 93–94
Ecstasy (MDMA), **164**
Eddings v. *Oklahoma*, 214f
educational maltreatment, 116t
emerging gangs, **150**, 154t
emotional abuse, **118**
emotionality, 43
emotionality escalation of offenses, **29**
emotional maltreatment, 116t
employment bias due to names, 37
Equal Justice Initiative, 223
Equal Protection Clause of Fourteenth Amendment, 100
escalation of offenses, **29**
ethnic background
    chronic offending, 31
    delinquency and, 26–27
    gangs and, 152–153, 152f, 154t
    illicit drug use and, 161
    impact of broken homes and, 109
    institutional placement and, 233
evaluation of family progress, 121
evidence-based practice principles and approaches, 191
external pressures and disposition of offenders, 200

F

family. *See also* child abuse
    impact of, 109–110, 111f
    as primary agent for socialization, 109
    risk factors for delinquency related to, 121
    structures, 111f
    transitions in, 110–112

family courts, 121
family size, **110**
family therapy, **179**
Fare v. *Michael C.*, 202
fatalities from maltreatment, 117
father-daughter incest, **119**
father-son incest, **119**
Federal Bureau of Investigation (FBI)
   Crime in the United States 2009, 7
   Crime in the United States 2010, 19, 20–22
felicific calculus, **38**
female delinquency
   biological and constitutional explanations of, 97
   characteristics of, 95–96, 95*f*
   class and, 101–102
   evaluation of explanations of, 98–99
   explanations of, 99t
   gangs, 153–154, 154t
   gender bias, processing, and, 100–103, 101*f*
   psychological explanations of, 97
   sociological explanations of, 97–98
   theories of, 99–100
feminist perspective, 92
feminist theory of delinquency, **99**–100, 100*f*
fingerprinting, **203**
5 serotonin transporter gene (5-HTT), 43
flash mobs, 145
focal concerns of lower class, **60**, 134
forestry camps, **233**
foster care, **232**
Foster Care Statistics 2010, 113
foster home placement, 220
Fourth Amendment in schools, 137
fraternal twins, 42
fraternity type of gang recruitment, 149*f*
freebase cocaine, 162
freedom of religion in schools, 136
freedom of speech in schools, 136
free will, **38**
Functional Family Therapy, 179
functional perspective on family, 109

G

Gang Resistance Education and Training, 205
gangs
   age of membership, 146
   attraction of, 147, 148t
   commitment to, 147
   crime and, 149–150
   cultural deviance theory and, 61
   definitions of, **146**
   drug-trafficking, 11
   ethnicity and membership in, 102
   female, 153–154
   hand signs, 153*f*
   initiation rites, 149
   in juvenile correctional facilities, 236
   life-course delinquency and, 155
   nature and extent of activity of, 145, 146*f*
   organized crime and, 145
   prevention and control of, 155–156, 205–206
   racial and ethnic, 152–153, 152*f*
   recruitment by, 148, 149
   in schools, 147–149, 148*f*
   size of, 147
   in small communities, 150–153
   stages of development of, 151–152, 151*f*
   theories of formation of, 154–155, 155t
   trends in participation in, 7
   types of, 154t
gangsta rap, 114–115
gang units, **206**
Gang Violence Reduction Program, 156
Gender, **94**. *See also* female delinquency
   arrest trends by, 28*f*
   bias and processing of female delinquents, 100–103, 101*f*
   delinquency and, 24, 26, 27t, 91–104
   disposition of offenders and, 199
   impact of broken homes and, 109
   institutional placement and, 233
   life-course delinquency and, 103
   offending ratio of, 92–94
   overview of, 92–94
   of perpetrators of maltreatment, 117
   ratio in offending, 92–94
   -responsive policy approach, 104
   roles, 94–95, 95t
   roles of, delinquency, 94–95
   sexual assault victimization rates by, 25*f*
   specialization of offenses and, 30–31
   of status offenders, 9
   training schools and, 235
Gender Play (Thorne), 94
general deterrence, **40**

generalizability approach, 92
general strain theory, 64
general theory of crime, **135**
A General Theory of Crime (Gottfredson and Hirschi), 31, 68, 69f
genetic influences
    biological positivism and, 41–42
    twin and adoption studies and, 42–43
"get tough" attitudes toward delinquency, 10, 12
Girls' Study Group (GSG), 92
Girls' Study Group, 95
Goss v. *Lopez*, 136
group homes, **232**
guided group interaction (GGI), **188**
guided group interaction, 232
Gun-Free School Zones Act, 136
guns
    availability and use of, 11–12, 32, 33f
    in gangsta rap, 114–115
    violence with, strategies to reduce, 33f

H

hair codes in schools, 136
Haley v. *Ohio*, 201, 202
halfway houses, **237**
hallucinogens, **164**
harm reduction, 170
hate crimes, 12
Hazelwood School District v. *Kuhlmeier*, 136
heroin, **164–165**
hidden delinquency, **22**, 24
Highfields Project, 177
high-risk behaviors, 6–7
Hispanic/Latino gangs, 145, 152
home detention, **215**
homelessness, 112
homicide death rates, 32
house arrest, 231–232
houses of refuge, 176
hyperactivity, 43
hyperkinesis, 44

I

id, 46
identical twins, 42

identification of child abuse, 120
illicit drugs, 161. *See also* drug use and abuse
impulsivity, 43
inattention, 43
incapacitation, **40**
incest, **118**
incidence of delinquency
    defined, **19**
    social class and, 29
Incredible Years program, 179
indeterminate sentencing, **221**
Indicators of School Crime and Safety: 2008 (National Center for Education Statistics), 131
Indicators of School Crime and Safety: 2010 (National Center for Education Statistics), 132t
individual adaptation to anomie, types of, 62
individual characteristics and disposition of offenders, 199
informal adjustments, **216**
informal probation, **216**
Ingraham v. *Wright*, 136
inhalants, **163**
initiation rites of gangs, 149
in Loco parentis concept, **136**
innovation, 62
In Re Gault decision, 182, 202, **213**–214, 214f
In re Poff decision, 7
In re Winship decision, **214**, 214f
insight-based therapy, **187**
institutional anomie theory, 63
institutionalization
    in adult prisons, 239, 239f
    conditions of, 229
    impact of, 239–240
    in mental hospitals, 220
    sexual victimization during, 239
    types of, 233–235, 236t
institutionalized means, **62**
institutions for juveniles, development of, 178
intake
    defined, **216**
    investigation of child abuse and, 120
    for probation, 230
intake officers, 182
intake process, 215f
integrated social control model of intensive supervision, 231, 231f
integrated social process theory, 68–69, 69f

integrated theories
    of delinquency, 68–70, 69t
    of drug use, 167
intelligence and delinquency, 42, 43
intensity of juvenile offending, 29–32, 32t
intensive aftercare programs, 238, 238f
intensive supervision programs (ISPs), 231, 238
interactional theory of delinquency, 69–70, 70f
interactionist theory of delinquency, 98, 135
Internet-initiated crime, 114, 150
interrogation practices, 201–203
interstate compacts, **237**
interventions. *See also* prevention; treatment interventions
    for bullying, 133
    community-based, 204
    for gangs, 155–156, 205–206
    for schools, 139–140, 205–206
An Introduction to the Principles of Morals and Legislation (Bentham), 38
investigations by probation officers, 230
involvement, 68

J

jail, **215**
judicial waivers, **218**
jury trial, **219**
just deserts, **184**
justice as fairness, **184**
justice model
    description of, **184**
    juvenile court and, 212
juvenile, **5**
juvenile corrections, 228–240
    aftercare, **236**–239
    better facilities for, 240
    confined rights, 236
    institutionalization, 239–240
    probation, 229–232
    residential and day treatment, 232–233
    training schools, 235–236
    types of institutional placement, 233–235
juvenile court, 211–223
    adjudicated cases in, 219f
    approaches to delinquency control, 11f
    changes in legal norms, 213–215
    codes for, 7–8
    crossover youth, 10
    delinquency cases in, 22f, 23f
    excellence in, 223, 223f
    history of, 212–213
    ideals of, 212, 213f
    jurisdiction over status offenders, 9–10
    juvenile transfer impact, 222–223
    mischievous behavior and, 11
    origins of, 176–177
    parens patriae doctrine of, 11
    pretrial procedures, 215–218
    sentencing structures, 221–222
    serious crimes and, 11
    statistics of, 22–23
    trial proceedings, 218–221, 221f
    upper age limit for, 8, 8f
    U.S. Supreme Court decisions related to, 213–215, 214f, 216
juvenile court officers, **184**
juvenile court statistics, **19**, 21t
Juvenile Court Statistics (Office of Juvenile Justice and Delinquency Prevention), 22
juvenile delinquency. *See also* delinquency
    defined, **3**
    societal response to, 10–12, 11f
Juvenile Delinquency and Urban Areas (Shaw and McKay), 58–59
juvenile drug courts, 180–181
Juvenile Justice and Delinquency Prevention Act, **9**, 100, 101, 235
juvenile justice process
    labeling and, 80
    stages in, 182–184, 183f
juvenile justice system, 174–191. *See also* institutionalization; juvenile court; pretrial procedures
    adult justice system compared to, 183–184, 184t
    basic correctional models, 184–186
    child abuse and, 120–121, 122f
    development of, 175–178
    diversion from, 179–181
    future trends, 191
    graduated sanctions in, 189
    philosophical goals of, 186t
    police discretion and, 198
    prevention programs for, 178–179
    purpose of, 181
    race and, 189–190

stages in, 182–184
structure and functions, 181–182
subsystems of, 182f
treatment and, 186–189
juvenile offenses
as chronic, 31
escalation of, 29–30
length and intensity of, 29–32
specialization of, 30–31
juvenile officers, **200**
juvenile trial proceedings
adjudicatory hearings, 218–219
alternatives available, 220
disposition hearings, 219–220

K

Kent v. *United States*, **213**, 214f, 218
kindergarten, disruptive and aggressive behavior in, 49

L

labeling theory
applications of, 80
assumptions of, 79f
defined, **78**
developments in, 80
deviant careers, 79
evaluation of, 80–81, 81t
female delinquency and, 98
juvenile justice process, 80
primary and secondary deviation, 79f
schools and, 134–135
Law-Related Education, 205
learning disability (LD), **44**
legal protections for juveniles, 4
legal rights. *See* rights
legislative waivers, **218**
length of juvenile offending, 29–32, 32t
lesbian, gay, bisexual, and transgender parents (LGBT), 113
licit drugs, 162
life-course delinquency
desistance and, 51
dropping out of school, 139
drug use and, 168–169
family-related risk factors, 121
gangs and, 155

gender and, 103
impact of institutionalization, 239–240
police discretion and, 206
principles of, 13f
structural and social process theories, 70–71
transfer of juveniles, 222–223
life-course-persistent offenders, **49**
Life Skills Training, 169, 179
life without parole, sentences of, 223
lineups, 203
lives, gendered, 94
longitudinal studies, 49–50, 50t
looking-glass self, 82

M

male-oriented approach, 93
maltreatment. *See* child abuse; neglect
mandatory reporting requirements, 117, 120
mandatory sentencing, **221**
manhood, concept of, in street culture, 58
Mapp v. *Ohio*, 201
Mara Salvatrucha (MS-13), 145
marijuana, 57, **162**
masculinity hypothesis, **98**
mass media, 114–115, 115f
maturing out of crime, 40, 50
McKeiver v. *Pennsylvania*, **214**–215, 214f
MDMA (Ecstasy), **164**
mentoring relationships, 139–140
methamphetamine, 162,**163**, 163f
Midwestern Prevention Project, 169, 179
Miranda v. *Arizona*, **202**
mischievous behavior, 11
monoamine oxidase gene (MAOA), 43
Montreal Longitudinal Experimental Study, **49**
moral development in decision making, 48
moral-legal maltreatment, 116t
moral neglect, 116t
mother-son incest, **119**
movies, violence in, 114
MS-13 (*Mara Salvatrucha*), 145
Multidimensional Treatment Foster Care, 179
multiple marginality, 93, 101
Multisystemic Therapy, 179
murder rates, 12, 21

N

names, unpopular, 37
National Association of Youth Courts, 181f
National Council of Juvenile and Family Court Judges, 223, 223f
National Crime Victimization Survey (NCVS), 21t, 24, 26
National Institute of Juvenile Justice and Delinquency Prevention, 22
National Restitution Training Program, 231
Native American/Navajo gangs, 153
needle exchange programs, 170
neglect
    defined, **115**, **117**
    delinquency and, 119–120, 120t
    extent and nature of problem, 117
    perpetrators of, 117
    prevention of, 121–123
    and severity ratings, 116t
neuropsychological factors, 43–44
New Jersey v. *T.L.O.*, 137, 138t
Nurse-Family Partnership, 179

O

obligation type of gang recruitment, 149f
offenders. *See also* status offenders
    adolescent-limited, **49**
    chronic violent, 23
    chronic youthful, **31**
    demeanor and disposition of, 199
    life-course-persistent, **49**
offenses, 29, 199. *See also* status offenses
Office of Community Oriented Policing Services (COPS), 205
Office of Juvenile Justice and Delinquency Prevention (OJDP), **9**
    Blueprints for Violence Prevention, 178
    grants, 92
    intensive aftercare program, 238
    Juvenile Court Statistics, 22
    Partnership to Reduce Juvenile Gun Violence Program, 32–33
    Pathways to Desistance Study, 160
    restitution initiative, 231
Office on Child Abuse and Neglect, 117
Ohio Serious Offender Study, 93
Oklahoma Publishing Co. v. *District Court*, 214f
On Crimes and Punishments (Beccaria), 37

open classroom movement, 130
opportunity structure, 59
opportunity theory, **65**–66, 66t
oppression
    of African-American women, 102
    of children, 84
optimal arousal theory, 46
organized crime and street gangs, 145
orthomolecular imbalance, **44**
outpatient psychiatric therapy, 220
Outward Bound, **232**
overt pathway to delinquent career, 29–30, 30f

P

Parens patriae philosophy
    "best interest of child" standard and, 212
    defined, **7**
    history of, 176
    state juvenile codes and, 7
parental efficacy, 110
parental rejection, 110
parental rights, termination of, 121
parole, 236–237
paternalism and adolescent females, 101
pathways to delinquent career
    for females, 95–96
    gendered, 94
    for males, 29, 30f
    overview of, 94f
Pathways to Desistance Study, 160
PCP (phencyclidine), 164
peers
    communication technology and connections to, 4–5
    delinquency and, 26
personality traits
    criminal behavior and, 47
    heritability of, 42
    of police officers, and disposition of offenders, 200
petitioned cases, 22
petitioners, **184**
petitions, **184**
phencyclidine (PCP), 164
photographing of juveniles, 203
physical abuse, 116t. *See also* child abuse
physiognomy, 41

planning delinquent behavior, 40
police
   attitudes toward, 197–198, 198t
   D.A.R.E. Project, 206–207
   discretion effects, 206
   and juvenile, 196–207
   legal rights of juveniles, 201–203
   prevention of juvenile offenses and, 204–206, 206f
   processing of juvenile offenders, 198–201
   in schools, 205–206
police discretion, **198**–200, 206
police interrogation, **201**
policing children, 197
positive peer culture (PPC), **188**
positivism
   biological, 41–42
   defined, 37, **40**–41
   psychological, 45–48
poverty rates, 112, 112f
power and authority relationships, 84
power-control theory, **84**, 98
pretrial identification practices, **203**
pretrial procedures
   detention hearings, 215–216
   intake process, 216–218
   overview of, 215f
   transfer procedure, 217–218
prevalence of delinquency, **19**, 22
prevention
   of child maltreatment, 121–123
   community-based interventions, 204
   of delinquency, 32–33, **178**–179, 190–191
   of drug use, 168–169
   gang-based interventions, 205–206
   of gangs, 155–156
   school-based interventions, 205
   theme of, 12
primary culture conflict, 85
primary deviation, **79**
primary prevention, **178**
primary sociopath, 47
Prison Rape Elimination Act, 235, 239
private training schools, 234–235
probation, 229–232
   functions of, 230f
   goals of, 229
   history of, **177**–178
   informal, **216**
   as judicial alternative, 220
   operation of, 230–232
probation officers, **230**, 231
problem-solving behavior, delinquency as, 39
procedural due process, 136
processing of juvenile offenders, 198–201
process of becoming deviant, **79**
Program of Research on the Causes and Correlates of Delinquency, 6, 23
Progressive education movement, 130
Progressive Era, **41**
Project Alert, 169
Project on Human Development in Chicago Neighborhoods (PHDCN), 71–72
Project Toward No Drug Abuse, 169, 179
Promoting Alternative Thinking Strategies, 179
property crimes, 7, 21
prosecution of parents for child abuse, 121
prosecutorial discretion, states permitting, 217t
prosecutors, **215**
protectionist sanctions for females, 100
psychoanalytic theory, **46**
psychological explanations for female delinquency, 97
psychological positivism, 45–48, 48t
psychopaths, **47**
public schooling. *See also* schools
   commitment to, 129
   compulsory, 3
   homeless children enrolled in, 6f
   racial segregation and, 130
public training schools, 234–235
punishment
   classical school of criminology and, 37–38
   corporal, 118, 136
   cruel and unusual, 223, 236
pyramiding (steroid use pattern), 164

Q

quality of home life, 110
quality-of-life view, 109

R

race
   abuse and neglect and, 115
   arrest rates by, 28f
   delinquency and, 24, 26–27

race (*continued*)
    disposition of offenders and, 199
    gangs and, 152–153, 152*f*, 154t
    illicit drug use and, 161
    institutional placement and, 233
    intelligence and, 43
    juvenile justice system and, 189–190
    victimization and, 25
racial discrimination against females, 102
racial segregation in public schools, 130
radical criminology, **83**–**84**, 134
radical nonintervention, **80**
ranches, **233**
rational choice theory
    desistance and, 51
    female delinquency and, 98
    overview of, 39, 39t
rationality in delinquent behavior, 39–40
rational therapy, 234
reaction formation, **64**
rebellion, 62
reception and diagnostic centers, **233**
recidivism, 239
recruitment by gangs, 149
referral to diversion agencies, 200–201
rehabilitation model, **184**
reinforcement theory, 46–**47**
rejection by parents, **110**
reliability
    of data sources, 20
    defined, **20**
    of National Crime Victimization Survey data, 26
    of self-report studies, 22–23
remand, 218
remote location monitoring (RLM), **231**–**232**
reporting
    of child abuse, 117, 120
    of crimes, 24–25
repression of childhood, 4
research, theory, and social policy, 13*f*
residential programs, **177**–178, 220, 232–233
residential social system, **235**
resiliency, **12**
respect in street culture, 58
respondents, **184**
restitution, 220, **231**

Restitution Education, Specialized Training, and Technical Assistance Project (RESTTA), 231
restorative justice, 85–86, 86t, 191
restorative justice conferencing, 169
retreatism, 62
retreatist subculture, 65–66
reverse waivers, **218**
revocation of aftercare, **238**
Richards v. *Thurston*, 136
rights
    to appeal, 220–221, 221*f*
    children's rights movement, 4
    of confined juveniles, 236
    parental, termination of, 121
    of students, 136–138, 138t
    to treatment, **236**
rights of juveniles
    fingerprinting, 203
    interrogation practices, 201–203
    overview of, 203t
    pretrial identification practices, 203
    search and seizure, 201
risk assessment instrument, New York City, 175
risk control
    aftercare and, 237–239
    probation and, 230–232
risk factors
    for delinquency and drug use, 165–166
    related to family, 121
risk-taking behavior, 6–7
ritualism, 62
role taking, 81–82
Roper v. *Simmons*, 214*f*
routine activities approach
    female delinquency and, 98
    overview of, **39**, 39t
runaways, female, 99
running away, **119**

S

safety of students in schools, 137, 139
Schall v. *Martin*, 214*f*, 216
school climate theory, 135
school failure, 133–134, 134*f*
School Program to Educate and Control Drug Abuse (SPECDA), 169, 205

schools. *See also* training schools
- alternative, 140
- bullying in, 131–133
- community-school relationships, 140
- dress codes in, 136
- dropping out of, 139
- gangs in, 147–149, 148f
- history of American education, 129–130
- interventions for, 139–140, 205–206
- labeling theory and, 134–135
- no-drug zones around, 170
- police in, 205–206
- problem behavior in, 129
- racial segregation in, 130
- rights of students in, 136–138, 138t
- safety of students in, 137, 139
- theories on delinquency and, 134–135, 135t
- vandalism and violence in, 131, 132t
- victimization at, 132t
- weapons in, 129

school searches, 136–**137**
search and seizure, **201**
Seattle Social Development Project, 29
secondary culture conflict, 85
secondary deviation, **79**
secondary prevention, **178**
secondary sociopaths, 47
sedatives, **163**
Seductions of Crime (Katz), 46
self-esteem of girls in classrooms, 94
self-report studies, 22–24, 27t
self-report surveys
- as data sources, 21t
- defined, **22**
- example of, 24f

sensation seeking, 46
sentences
- gender bias in, 100
- life without parole, 223

sentencing circles, 86
sentencing structures, 221–222
sex-role socialization, **98**
sexual abuse
- cases of, 119f
- defined, **118**
- definitions and severity of, 116t

sexual activity of adolescent females, 100
sexual assault victimization
- during institutionalization, 239
- rates of, 25f

shelter care, **215**
siblings, delinquent, 110
single-parent families, 110
Smith v. *Daily Mail Publishing Co.*, 214f
social bond, elements of, 67–68, 68f
social capital, **71**
social context of delinquency
- foster family, 113
- gender roles, 94–95
- impact of families, 109–110
- mass media, 114–115
- police and prevention of juvenile offenses, 204–206
- restorative justice and peacemaking, 85–86
- theme of, 12–14
- training school life, 235–236
- transitions, 110–112

social contract, **37**
social control theory
- of delinquency, **67**–68, 68f
- of drug use, 167
- of female delinquency, 98
- schools and, 134
- social development theory compared to, 70

social development model
- of delinquency, **70**, 71f
- of drug use, 167

social disorganization theory
- of delinquency, **58**–59, 60f
- of drug use, 167
- of gang formation, 154
- schools and, 135

social factors in delinquency
- class, 28–29
- gender, 24, 26, 27t
- peers, 26
- race, 24, 26–27, 28f

social history reports, **230**
social injustice, **87**
social interactionist theory, **78**. *See also* conflict theory; labeling theory; symbolic interactionist theory
socialization, **109**

social learning theory
    of drug use, 167
    of female delinquency, 97–98
social policy
    conflict perspective and, 86–87
    for controlling drug use, 168–170
    D.A.R.E. program, 206–207
    excellence in juvenile courts, 223
    gender-responsive, 104
    interventions for schools, 139–140
    Project on Human Development in Chicago Neighborhoods, 71–72
    research, theory, and, 13f
    sexual victimization during institutionalization, 240
social process theories, **57**
social reaction theory. *See* labeling theory
social roles, learning, 109
social status and school achievement, 134
social stratification theory, 84
social structure, **57**
Social Theory and Social Structure (Merton), 62
sociobiology, **42**, 43, 48t
socioeconomic status
    cultural deviance theory and, 60–61
    delinquency and, 24, 28–29
    disposition of offenders and, 199
    females and, 101
    poverty, 112, 112f
    radical criminology and, 83–84
sociological explanations of female delinquency, 97–98
sociopaths, 47
soft determinism, **40**
specialization of offenses, 30–31
special units targeting juveniles, 204t
specific deterrence, **40**
speedballing, 163
stages of development of gangs, 151–152, 151f
Stanford v. Kentucky, 214f
state dependence, 31
The State of America's Children (Children's Defense Fund), 5, 7
states permitting prosecutorial discretion, 217t
station adjustment, **200**
status frustration, **64**
status offenders
    behaviors of, 9, 10t
    contempt of court and, 100
    defined, **9**
    juvenile court jurisdiction over, 9–10
    terminology for, 8–10
status offenses, **7**, 9
steroids, anabolic, **164**, 165t
stoners, 153
strain theory
    of delinquency, **63**–64, 63f, 63t
    of female delinquency, 97
    of gang formation, 154
    schools and, 134
street culture, 58
street gangs. *See* gangs
stress relief theory of drug use, 166
strict enforcement of drug laws, 169–170
structural perspective on family, 109
subcultural affiliation theory, 154
substance-related behavior. *See also* drug use and abuse
    in families, 112
    female delinquents and, 96
    overlap with other high-risk behavior, 6
    Pathways to Desistance Study, 160
supervision
    in home, **110**, 116t
    of probation, 231
surveillance, **230**
symbolic interactionist theory, 81–83, 83t

T

taking into custody, **184**
technocorrections, 191
technology use by gangs, 150
temperament and brain functioning, 43–44
termination of parental rights, 121
tertiary prevention, **178**
Texas Youth Commission, 229
themes
    delinquency across life course, 12–13
    prevention and social policy, 12, 13f
    social context of delinquency, 12–14
theories
    of classical school of criminology, 38
    importance of, 50–51
    of onset of drug abuse, 166–167

research, social policy, and, 13f
theories of delinquency. *See also specific theories*
    conflict, 83–85
    control and behavior, 67–68
    cultural deviance, 60–61
    differential association, 66–67
    feminist, 99–100
    gang formation, 154, 155t
    integrated, 68–70
    labeling, 78–81
    school and, 134–135, 135t
    social disorganization, 57–60
    social interactionist, 77–87
    strain and opportunity, 61–62
    structural and social process, 56–72, 70–71
    summary of, 48t
    symbolic interactionist, 81–83
theory of differential oppression, **84**
Thompson v. Oklahoma, 214f
Tinker v. Des Moines Independent School District, 136, 138t
tobacco use, 162, 162f, 170
training schools
    for boys, 235–236
    coeducational, 236
    description of, **178**, 234
    for girls, 236
    as judicial alternative, 220
    programs and services, 234–235
trait-based personality model, **47**
transfer procedure, 213, **215**, 215f, 222–223
transitions, off-time and out-of-order, 168
treatment interventions. *See also* interventions; prevention
    for bullying, 133
    comparison of effectiveness of, 235t
    for drug abuse, 169
    restorative justice and, 86t
treatment planning for child abuse cases, 120
trial proceedings, 221, 221f
TV, violence on, 114
twin studies, 42

U

unconventionality and high-risk behavior, 7
underclass theory, 154
Uniform Crime Reporting (UCR) Program, **19**–21, 21t, 27t
Unraveling Juvenile Delinquency (Glueck and Glueck), 47
urban gangs, 154t
urban growth, concentric zone hypothesis of, 59
U.S. Supreme Court decisions, 213–215, 214f. *See also specific cases*
utilitarianism, **38**

V

validity
    of data sources, 20, 22
    defined, **20**
    of National Crime Victimization Survey data, 26
    of self-report studies, 22–23
vandalism in schools, **131**
Vera Institute of Justice, 175
Vernonia School District 47J v. Acton, 137, 138t
victimization. *See also* sexual assault victimization
    of girls, 94, 95–96, 99–100
    by maltreatment type, 117
    rates of, 117
    at schools, 132t
    studies of, 24–26, 27t
video games, violent, 114
violence
    defined, **130**
    effects of exposure to, 2
    gangs and, 150
    in home, 112
    in schools, 130–131
    of TV and movies, 114
    of video games, 114
Violent Crime Control and Law Enforcement Act, 180
violent crimes
    chronic offenders, 232
    by juveniles, 7
    rates of, 25f
    victims of, 24–26
volunteer programs, **232**

W

waivers of jurisdiction, 218
wannabes, 151
warning and release, 200
"war on drugs", 169–170

weapons in schools, 129
West Virginia State Board of Education v. *Barnette*, 136, 138t
wilderness programs, 233
Wood v. *Strickland*, 136

Y

Yoo v. *Moynihan*, 136, 138t
youth courts, 180, 180*f*, 181*f*

youth culture, 4–5
youthful offender facilities, 220
youths at risk
    delinquency and, 6*f*
    high-risk behaviors, 6–7
    populations of, 5
Youth Service Program, 206